Lecture Notes in Computer Science 13309

More information about this series at https://link.springer.com/bookseries/558

Margherita Antona ·
Constantine Stephanidis (Eds.)

Universal Access in Human-Computer Interaction

User and Context Diversity

16th International Conference, UAHCI 2022
Held as Part of the 24th HCI International Conference, HCII 2022
Virtual Event, June 26 – July 1, 2022
Proceedings, Part II

 Springer

Editors
Margherita Antona
Foundation for Research and Technology -
Hellas (FORTH)
Heraklion, Crete, Greece

Constantine Stephanidis
University of Crete and Foundation for
Research and Technology - Hellas (FORTH)
Heraklion, Crete, Greece

ISSN 0302-9743   ISSN 1611-3349   (electronic)
Lecture Notes in Computer Science
ISBN 978-3-031-05038-1   ISBN 978-3-031-05039-8   (eBook)
https://doi.org/10.1007/978-3-031-05039-8

This Springer imprint is published by the registered company Springer Nature Switzerland AG
The registered company address is: Gewerbestrasse 11, 6330 Cham, Switzerland

Foreword

Human-computer interaction (HCI) is acquiring an ever-increasing scientific and industrial importance, as well as having more impact on people's everyday life, as an ever-growing number of human activities are progressively moving from the physical to the digital world. This process, which has been ongoing for some time now, has been dramatically accelerated by the COVID-19 pandemic. The HCI International (HCII) conference series, held yearly, aims to respond to the compelling need to advance the exchange of knowledge and research and development efforts on the human aspects of design and use of computing systems.

The 24th International Conference on Human-Computer Interaction, HCI International 2022 (HCII 2022), was planned to be held at the Gothia Towers Hotel and Swedish Exhibition & Congress Centre, Göteborg, Sweden, during June 26 to July 1, 2022. Due to the COVID-19 pandemic and with everyone's health and safety in mind, HCII 2022 was organized and run as a virtual conference. It incorporated the 21 thematic areas and affiliated conferences listed on the following page.

A total of 5583 individuals from academia, research institutes, industry, and governmental agencies from 88 countries submitted contributions, and 1276 papers and 275 posters were included in the proceedings to appear just before the start of the conference. The contributions thoroughly cover the entire field of human-computer interaction, addressing major advances in knowledge and effective use of computers in a variety of application areas. These papers provide academics, researchers, engineers, scientists, practitioners, and students with state-of-the-art information on the most recent advances in HCI. The volumes constituting the set of proceedings to appear before the start of the conference are listed in the following pages.

The HCI International (HCII) conference also offers the option of 'Late Breaking Work' which applies both for papers and posters, and the corresponding volume(s) of the proceedings will appear after the conference. Full papers will be included in the 'HCII 2022 - Late Breaking Papers' volumes of the proceedings to be published in the Springer LNCS series, while 'Poster Extended Abstracts' will be included as short research papers in the 'HCII 2022 - Late Breaking Posters' volumes to be published in the Springer CCIS series.

I would like to thank the Program Board Chairs and the members of the Program Boards of all thematic areas and affiliated conferences for their contribution and support towards the highest scientific quality and overall success of the HCI International 2022 conference; they have helped in so many ways, including session organization, paper reviewing (single-blind review process, with a minimum of two reviews per submission) and, more generally, acting as goodwill ambassadors for the HCII conference.

This conference would not have been possible without the continuous and unwavering support and advice of Gavriel Salvendy, founder, General Chair Emeritus, and Scientific Advisor. For his outstanding efforts, I would like to express my appreciation to Abbas Moallem, Communications Chair and Editor of HCI International News.

June 2022   Constantine Stephanidis

HCI International 2022 Thematic Areas and Affiliated Conferences

Thematic Areas

- HCI: Human-Computer Interaction
- HIMI: Human Interface and the Management of Information

Affiliated Conferences

- EPCE: 19th International Conference on Engineering Psychology and Cognitive Ergonomics
- AC: 16th International Conference on Augmented Cognition
- UAHCI: 16th International Conference on Universal Access in Human-Computer Interaction
- CCD: 14th International Conference on Cross-Cultural Design
- SCSM: 14th International Conference on Social Computing and Social Media
- VAMR: 14th International Conference on Virtual, Augmented and Mixed Reality
- DHM: 13th International Conference on Digital Human Modeling and Applications in Health, Safety, Ergonomics and Risk Management
- DUXU: 11th International Conference on Design, User Experience and Usability
- C&C: 10th International Conference on Culture and Computing
- DAPI: 10th International Conference on Distributed, Ambient and Pervasive Interactions
- HCIBGO: 9th International Conference on HCI in Business, Government and Organizations
- LCT: 9th International Conference on Learning and Collaboration Technologies
- ITAP: 8th International Conference on Human Aspects of IT for the Aged Population
- AIS: 4th International Conference on Adaptive Instructional Systems
- HCI-CPT: 4th International Conference on HCI for Cybersecurity, Privacy and Trust
- HCI-Games: 4th International Conference on HCI in Games
- MobiTAS: 4th International Conference on HCI in Mobility, Transport and Automotive Systems
- AI-HCI: 3rd International Conference on Artificial Intelligence in HCI
- MOBILE: 3rd International Conference on Design, Operation and Evaluation of Mobile Communications

List of Conference Proceedings Volumes Appearing
Before the Conference

39. CCIS 1582, HCI International 2022 Posters - Part III, edited by Constantine Stephanidis, Margherita Antona and Stavroula Ntoa
40. CCIS 1583, HCI International 2022 Posters - Part IV, edited by Constantine Stephanidis, Margherita Antona and Stavroula Ntoa

http://2022.hci.international/proceedings

Preface

The 16th International Conference on Universal Access in Human-Computer Interaction (UAHCI 2022), an affiliated conference of the HCI International (HCII) conference, provided an established international forum for the exchange and dissemination of scientific information on theoretical, methodological, and empirical research that addresses all issues related to the attainment of universal access in the development of interactive software. It comprehensively addressed accessibility and quality of interaction in the user interface development life-cycle from a multidisciplinary perspective, taking into account dimensions of diversity, such as functional limitations, age, culture, background knowledge, etc., in the target user population, as well various dimensions of diversity which affect the context of use and the technological platform and arise from the emergence of mobile, wearable, ubiquitous, and intelligent devices and technologies.

UAHCI 2022 aimed to help, promote, and encourage research by providing a forum for interaction and exchanges among researchers, academics, and practitioners in the field. The conference welcomed papers on the design, development, evaluation, use, and impact of user interfaces, as well as standardization, policy, and other non-technological issues that facilitate and promote universal access.

Universal access is not a new topic in the field of human-computer interaction and information technology. Yet, in the new interaction environment shaped by current technological advancements, it becomes of prominent importance to ensure that individuals have access to interactive products and services that span a wide variety of everyday life domains and are used in fundamental human activities. The papers accepted to this year's UAHCI conference present research, methods, and practices addressing universal access issues related to user experience and interaction, and approaches targeted to provide appropriate interaction means to individuals with specific disabilities, but also issues related to extended reality – a prominent technological medium presenting novel accessibility challenges, as well as advancements in learning and education, a domain which was considerably challenged in the context of the ongoing pandemic.

Two volumes of the HCII 2022 proceedings are dedicated to this year's edition of the UAHCI conference, entitled Universal Access in Human-Computer Interaction: Novel Design Approaches and Technologies (Part I) and Universal Access in Human-Computer Interaction: User and Context Diversity (Part II). The first focuses on topics related to novel approaches to accessibility, user experience, and technology acceptance in universal access, and multimodal and psychophysiological interaction, while the second focuses on topics related to universal access to learning and education, extended reality in universal access, design for cognitive and learning disabilities, and design for visual disabilities.

Papers of these volumes are included for publication after a minimum of two single-blind reviews from the members of the UAHCI Program Board or, in some cases, from members of the Program Boards of other affiliated conferences. We would like to thank all of them for their invaluable contribution, support and efforts.

June 2022   Margherita Antona
                                                               Constantine Stephanidis

16th International Conference on Universal Access in Human-Computer Interaction (UAHCI 2022)

Program Board Chairs: Margherita Antona, Foundation for Research and Technology – Hellas (FORTH), Greece, and Constantine Stephanidis, University of Crete and Foundation for Research and Technology – Hellas (FORTH), Greece

- João Barroso, INESC TEC and UTAD, Portugal
- Ingo Bosse, Interkantonale Hochschule für Heilpädagogik, Switzerland
- Laura Burzagli, IFAC-CNR, Italy
- Pedro J. S. Cardoso, University of Algarve, Portugal
- Silvia Ceccacci, Università Politecnica delle Marche, Italy
- Carlos Duarte, Universidade de Lisboa, Portugal
- Pier Luigi Emiliani, National Research Council of Italy, Italy
- Andrina Granic, University of Split, Croatia
- Gian Maria Greco, University of Warsaw, Poland, and POIESIS, Italy
- Simeon Keates, University of Chichester, UK
- Georgios Kouroupetroglou, National and Kapodistrian University of Athens, Greece
- Barbara Leporini, ISTI-CNR, Italy
- Jun-Li Lu, University of Tsukuba, Japan
- John Magee, Clark University, USA
- Daniela Marghitu, Auburn University, USA
- Jorge Martín-Gutiérrez, Universidad de La Laguna, Spain
- Troy McDaniel, Arizona State University, USA
- Maura Mengoni, Università Politecnica delle Marche, Italy
- Silvia Mirri, University of Bologna, Italy
- Federica Pallavicini, Università degli Studi di Milano-Bicocca, Italy
- Hugo Paredes, INESC TEC and UTAD, Portugal
- Enrico Pontelli, New Mexico State University, USA
- João M. F. Rodrigues, University of the Algarve, Portugal
- Frode Eika Sandnes, Oslo Metropolitan University, Norway
- J. Andrés Sandoval-Bringas, Universidad Autónoma de Baja California Sur, Mexico
- Volker Sorge, University of Birmingham, UK
- Hiroki Takada, University of Fukui, Japan
- Philippe Truillet, Université de Toulouse, France
- Kevin Tseng, National Taipei University of Technology, Taiwan
- Gerhard Weber, Technische Universität Dresden, Germany

The full list with the Program Board Chairs and the members of the Program Boards of all thematic areas and affiliated conferences is available online at

http://www.hci.international/board-members-2022.php

HCI International 2023

The 25th International Conference on Human-Computer Interaction, HCI International 2023, will be held jointly with the affiliated conferences at the AC Bella Sky Hotel and Bella Center, Copenhagen, Denmark, 23–28 July 2023. It will cover a broad spectrum of themes related to human-computer interaction, including theoretical issues, methods, tools, processes, and case studies in HCI design, as well as novel interaction techniques, interfaces, and applications. The proceedings will be published by Springer. More information will be available on the conference website: http://2023.hci.international/.

General Chair
Constantine Stephanidis
University of Crete and ICS-FORTH
Heraklion, Crete, Greece
Email: general_chair@hcii2023.org

http://2023.hci.international/

Contents – Part II

Extended Reality in Universal Access

Design for Visual Disabilities

Contents – Part I

User Experience and Technology Acceptance in Universal Access

Universal Access to Learning and Education

Analysing Visual Representations of Adult Online Learning Across Formats

Nina Bergdahl[1,2](✉) ⓘ and Lisbeth Gyllander Torkildsen[1,2] ⓘ

[1] Halmstad University, Akademin för lärande, humaniora och samhälle, Box 823, S - 301 18 Halmstad, Sweden
nina.bergdahl@hh.se
[2] Malmo University, Nordenskiöldsgatan 1, 211 19 Malmö, Sweden

Abstract. The past years have triggered the established blended learning format to develop into other kinds of online teaching formats, with, for example, combinations of a/synchronous learning with more flexible (co-)location requirements for teachers and students. This has led to a renewed exploration of ways to ensure accessible and life-long learning through developed educational practices. Comparing online education formats can be challenging but is necessary. Building on case study methodology, the objective of this study was to explore online learning situations (n = 21): Asynchronous Distance Education (ADE) (n = 15) and (synchronous) Emergency Remote Teaching (ERT) (n = 6), to develop a method to systematically analyse and evaluate different formats of online education using engagement theory. To do so, a schema was developed through which visual representations of learning situations were analysed. Results show that visual representations of learning situations enable nuanced comparisons across different formats of online education. Analysis reveals that the format of education affects the conditions under which the teacher more readily facilitates student engagement and that asynchronous and synchronous formats supported different nuances of engagement.

Keywords: Visual representation · Visual display · Method · Engagement · Learning design

1 Introduction

1.1 Broad-Scale Qualitative Data to Visualise Learning Designs

Researchers are increasingly interested in broader-scale analysis of observational data [1]. However, teaching is complex and often builds on a step-by-step approach, meaning that the teacher designs learning activities (LA) that together scaffold students' learning progress. As such, observations of single LA cannot exhaust all variations on how enactment of lesson designs are linked together. Yet, observations are empirically grounded, and may reflect both form and content of a LA [2]. In the wake of the COVID-19 pandemic, a plethora of online educational formats is emerging [3–5]. Researchers have suggested that the pandemic-related shift into distance education, should be addressed

M. Antona and C. Stephanidis (Eds.): HCII 2022, LNCS 13309, pp. 3–14, 2022.
https://doi.org/10.1007/978-3-031-05039-8_1

as something other than distance education: and suggested the term emergency-remote education (ERT). This, as ERT should not be considered equivalent to "regular" or "traditional" (often asynchronous) distance education (ADE) as teachers (and students) did not choose ERT, had little time to prepare for ERT and had not received formal training to deliver distance education [4]. Currently, it is unexplored how ERT and ADE differ in practice; for example, how they enhance interaction and inclusion through stimulating and facilitating social engagement. How different formats facilitate student engagement is important as emerging formats may grow into new standardised formats of educational delivery. In that respect, teachers must design and deliver engaging LAs regardless of the format of online education, even though it may be challenging [6]. It is well-established that student engagement is critical for learning as it correlates significantly with school success, grades, attendance and students' overall well-being [7–9]. On the other hand, engagement may be perceived and supported differently in an online setting [10, 11]. This study employs a nuanced conceptualisation of engagement. Engagement is viewed as a multi-dimensional construct [12] with four dimensions: a behavioural, an emotional, a cognitive and a social (ibid.). Varied learning designs should facilitate for all dimensions of engagement as students' engagement profiles differ [13, 14] and as the design and implementation of learning scenarios has a greater influence on engagement than students' individual engagement disposition [15, 16]. Thus, engagement should be a core element in both learning designs and their enactment. To design engaging LAs that also are cognitively challenging has been observed to be challenging [2] and even more so when learning includes synchronous and asynchronous elements across multiple platforms [17, 18]. Thus, designing for engagement online requires different strategies than in a face-to-face classroom, and remains critical [19, 20]. For example: online learning can trigger disconnectedness and a sense of isolation [21]. As perceived social presence online stimulates learning, teachers may want to design to ensure that students' social needs are met [22, 23]. Linking design to performance, Teoetenel and Rientes analysed 157 learning designs (undertaken by 60.000 university students) to explore significance in relation to outcome. They found that a high proportion of activities that primarily stimulated cognitive engagement, (i.e., reading, watching videos and listening) were found to correlate negatively with student grades [24]. Importantly, however, it is not the design per se, but the execution of a LA in an online setting that will lead to positive results [25–28].

2 Method

Building on case study methodology [29] this study used observations of online learning situations (lessons and estimated learning time) in second language learning (Swedish and English) by observing ADE (n = 15) and ERT (n = 6) learning situations (see Table 1) to develop a method to collect and systematically analyse different formats of online education from the perspective of engagement. While ERT consisted of scheduled lessons, ADE (mainly) consisted of online LA, not regulated by a schedule. Thus, to refer to both of the occurrences of learning, we use the term learning situation when referring to lessons and learning in ADE. The study was conducted in a school for adult education in one of the larger cities in Sweden. The school offered BYOD Internet access,

Google workspace for Education and laptops to all teachers and students. After receiving the principal's approval, purposive sampling (Bryman, 2016) was employed, meaning that principals selected groups of adult education teachers who taught second language classes online. The teachers were then invited to participate. This selection was made to enable comparison of patterns across second language education in synchronous and asynchronous formats [30]. The Subjects were: English as a second language (ESL) or Swedish as a second language (SSL) levels 1–4, offered in the (synchronous) emergency remote teaching (ERT) format or the (asynchronous) distance education (ADE) format (see Table 1).

Table 1 Respondent demographic data

Gender	Format	Subject	Level	Observations
Female	ERT	ESL	Course 4	1
Female	ERT	ESL	Course 4	1
Female	ERT	ESL	Course 3	1
Female	ERT	ESL	Course 2	1
Female	ADE	ESL	Course 3	3
Male	ERT	ESL	Course 1	1
Female	ERT	ESL	Course 3	1
Female	ADE	SSL	Course 1	2
Female	ADE	SSL	Course 4	2
Female	ADE	SSL	Course 4	2
Female	ADE	SSL	Course 3	2
Female	ADE	SSL	Course 1	2
Female	ADE	SSL	Course 3	2

2.1 Data Analysis

Observations were conducted using an observation schema that covered A) the background data (form, subject, duration, teacher years in occupation) and B) the design elements; here: LA, [31]. LA were captured using a minute-by-minute momentaneous coding of LAs in situ. Thus, collection and coding were conducted in parallel. The ADE teachers were asked to take on a student role and imagine their learning situation using a think-aloud technique. When think-aloud is used, teachers may approach their LD from a student perspective, in which the arrangement functions as a stimulated recall [32]. Teachers were asked to estimate the duration of each LA. Duration has been recognised as a "major factor in the teaching and learning environment" [34: p 684] as it influences teacher decisions and considerations in LD. The (produced) data was analysed at a meta-level adjacent to the observation. These were the stages to prepare data for analysis:

1. Transcription of recorded and live teacher interaction and instruction using a minute-by-minute approach to LAs in MS Excel 16.54
2. Colour and written text used to code transcription.
3. Each code was linked to a specific colour using MS Excel 16.54, (see Table 2), in which a visual basic macro was set up to automate production of visual displays, displaying respondent ID, time, format, and engagement (see Fig. 1).
4. The visual representations, sequence overview and pie charts were used to compare content and form.

2.2 The Engagement Dimensions in Learning Activities (EDLA) Schema

A schema connecting 24 (inductively identified) LAs to the four engagement dimensions was developed (see Table 2). While several facets of engagement may be active during one LA (student may for example read and feel bored at the same time), one was regarded to be in the forefront.

Table 2 Engagement dimensions and learning activities (EDLA) schema

Cognitive		L	Listen, look (silent reading)
		SRL/O	Orientation
		SRL/P	Planning
		SRL/C	Checking and submitting work
Social		D	Discussion
		C	Collaboration
		I(S)	Student led interaction
		I(T)	Teacher led interaction
		I(Tech)	IT-led interaction
		SSRL	Socially Shared Regulation
		AI	Asynchronous interaction
Behavioural		P	Practice
		P(a/s)	Practice a/synchronous
		P(a/i)	Asynchronous interaction
		P(a)	Practice asynchronous (no int)
Emotional		DO	Produce
		IA	Individual Assessment (i.e., checklist)
		A	Test and assessment
Break		TeB	Technology breakdown
		B	Paus (intentional)
		DRL	Digital relocation
		ID	Paus (unintentional)
Course-administration		CI	Course information
		Adm	Administration (i.e., create accounts)

Table 2 reflects the cognitive, social, behavioural, and emotional engagement dimensions. The EDLA schema was used to colour code LAs to enable visual representations. Blue colours reflect; red reflect the social dimension. Green nuances were used to reflect facilitation of behaviour, and yellow nuances were used to reflect facilitation of emotional engagement.

3 Results

Figure 1 is a visual representation of all observations that reflects the dimension of facilitated engagement (building on the EDLA schema), explored using a minute- by-minute approach. The visualisation covers the first 120 min of the learning situation (five learning situations were longer- than 120 min but displayed no additional patterns).

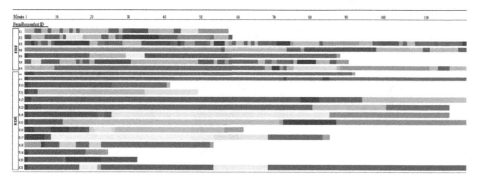

Fig. 1. Visual representation of facilitated dimensions of engagement in learning activities (Colour figure online)

Figure 1 shows, that the learning sequences differed between ADE and ERT. The cognitive orientation (blue) was longer for the ADE teachers. ERT teachers would rely more synchronous decisions in relation to the pace and let the progression of activities unfold as results of negotiation with students.).

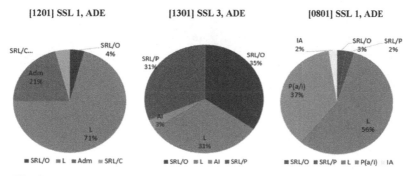

Fig. 2. Facilitated engagement in asynchronous formats (1201, 1301 and 0801)

A collated overview on how ERT and ADE teachers would support student engagement provides additional information on the differences. Most commonly, a learning situation lasted between 61–90 min. Learning situations that were shorter 30 min (see 1201 and 1301 in Fig. 2), focused on facilitating one, or two, engagement dimensions. Learning situations that lasted 41 min could include facilitation of three nuances of engagement (see 0801 in Fig. 2).

Results indicate that it is possible to facilitate more nuances in shorter learning situations: that duration not necessarily is a hindering factor.

3.1 The Subjects

Exploring patterns of facilitation of engagement within each subject (ESL/SSL) we also identified that it was the format, more than the subject taught, that influenced the enactment of the design.

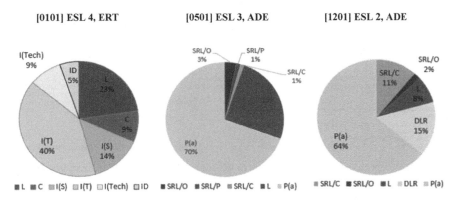

Fig. 3. Facilitated engagement in synchronous (0101) and asynchronous (0501, 1201) lessons

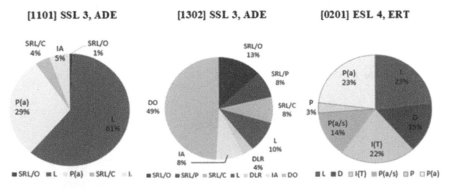

Fig. 4. Facilitated engagement in SSL (1101, 1302) and ESL (0201)

3.2   The Formats

While a learning situation in ERT is the duration of the scheduled lesson, in ADE it is the teacher's idea of the duration a student spends learning whilst being connected to the LMS (from logging in to logging out). ERT and ADE have different characteristics, where the former is mainly and the latter mainly asynchronous.

3.3   The Engagement Dimensions

Behaviour. All ADE teachers facilitated for one type of behavioural engagement (asynchronous production see Fig. 1), where 4/6 ERT teacher facilitated for 1–3 nuances (see example 0101 in Fig. 3, and 0201 in Fig. 4).

Cognition. Cognitive engagement can be assimilative, where students listen, look and read. Assimilative LA is characterised by a lack of interaction and active learning. Results show that more than 50% of the ADE designs only supported cognitive engagement. However, wow to facilitate cognitive nuances also differed between ERT and ADE teachers, with ERT teachers displaying no nuances (see example 0101 in Fig. 3), and ADE teachers displaying 2–4 nuances of cognitive facilitation (see Fig. 1, and examples 1101 and 1302 in Fig. 4). Thus, even cognitive facilitation can be nuanced.

Social. In ADE, fewer than half (5/12) of the designs stimulated the social dimension, and when they did, they displayed one (the same) type of social interaction (see examples in Figs. 1, 2 and 3). The opposite was found in ERT designs, where the social dimension was dominant. All ERT teachers included social engagement with 2–5 nuances (see 0501 in Fig. 3, and 0201 in Fig. 4), and typically arranged their learning situations (here: lessons) around the social dimension.

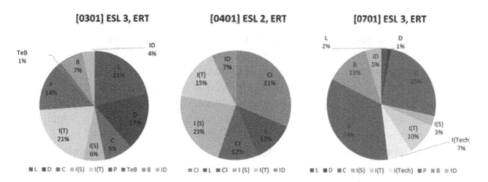

Fig. 5. Facilitated engagement in ESL lesson (0301, 0401, 0701) (synchronous formats)

Emotion. In this study, facilitation of emotional engagement was considered to be online assessments (i.e., tests and exams) and hypothetically digital and online creation. (The latter was not observed). ERT teachers did not include any facilitation for emotional engagement (see for example Fig. 2, Fig. 3, Fig. 4 and Fig. 5). 10/15 ADE teachers

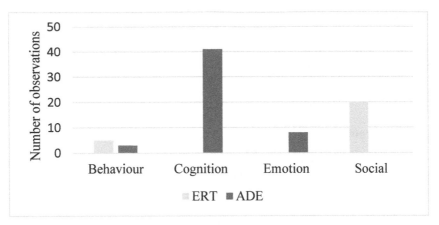

Fig. 6. Nuances facilitated for within engagement dimensions

designed for emotional engagement with 1–2 nuances (see examples 1101 and 1302 in Fig. 4).

Figure 6 shows how enacted designs in ERT and ADE and ERT supported student engagement. Both ERT and ADE teachers used LAs that support behavioural engagement to stimulate students to become active in their learning. Where ERT teachers generally started with establishing a social arena for learning and could vary the nuances of social engagement, ADE displayed similar skills in facilitating for nuanced within cognition. Both formats lacked reflecting one of the engagement dimensions: social engagement for ADE, and emotional engagement for ERT.

4   Discussion

The visual representations were used to analyse learning sequences, facilitation of engagement dimensions and nuances of engagement. A comparison of the two online formats of education reveals that teachers in ERT can rely on their management of learning sequences in situ, in which they control the duration ad hoc. ADE, on the other hand, has longer and fewer learning LAs. Asynchronous learning design requires making aware design decisions in advance. All ERT designs rely on social engagement, to which cognitive elements and behavioural elements were added. ERT teachers would, in the above observations, not facilitate emotional engagement. ADE designs build mainly on cognitive engagement, readily support emotional engagement, and elements of behavioural engagement. More seldom, ADE would facilitate social engagement. Even though a comparison of patterns reveals that ERT and ADE formats of online education more readily facilitate different engagement dimensions, data also reveals that they often facilitate different nuances within the dimensions. For example, ERT teachers facilitated a range of nuances of social engagement, while few ADE teachers did that, and when they did; it was asynchronous social interaction. On the other hand, ADE teachers would not only support cognitive and emotional engagement but would also demonstrate skills to facilitate three nuances within those dimensions. Only one teacher (who in this case was an ADE teacher) facilitated for all four engagement dimensions. Results reveal that the EDLA schema provides nuanced insights in how ERT and ADE formats facilitate student engagement in learning. In line with previous research [34, 35] this study proposed that instead of connecting LD to outcomes (which can be a static tick off list), teachers may want to connect their LD to student engagement, as engagement reflects a process, is malleable and doesn't signal school failure like addressing results or outcomes only. Such insights could also support teachers in developing their tacit knowledge on how to adjust their designs to better stimulate learner engagement. The EDLA schema could have included novel and innovative LA. For example, immersive learning experiences and digital creation that could have stimulated emotional engagement. Such LA were not identified in ERT nor ADE, indicating that there is a possibility to develop LA in this direction. The visual representation can be used to analyse learning sequences and how LAs support student engagement. It remains important (expanding on the works of [36]) to establish that designing for synchronous and asynchronous learning differs. This paper contributes with highlighting some of these differences. For example, the absences of pace, place and time in asynchronous LDs affects the design significantly; instead of frequent shifts in learning sequences, separate sections of learning skills and LAs were planned for. Moreover, online teaching prevents insight and control that the teachers in the on-site school are used to (but that regular distance teachers regularly plan for and manage). These findings expand and nuance previous research (e.g., [37, 38]). Teachers need knowledge of which designs for learning that better stimulate knowledge construction, progression, active learning, creation, equal participation collaboration [2], and how to support development of self-regulation and a sense of online community where wellbeing is nurtured.

- The visualisations are representations of learning situations - these enable comparisons across qualitative observations, something that is hard to achieve in qualitative observations, and can be challenging [1], especially when comparing different formats of learning delivery (online, face-to-face).
- The visualisation provides a caption of the abstract phenomenon at focus, and thus makes the situation tangible
- A larger number of representations of learning situations are now possible to manage. This enables qualitative analysis, as well as quantifying qualitative observation-data and thus enables analysis of both form and content.

4.1 Limitation and Future Research

While the results cannot and do not claim to capture all practises, when several learning situations show similar patterns, these indicate that there may be certain conditions linked to an educational format that promotes or hinders specific types of facilitation of engagement. For example, assimilative practises have previously been linked to lower results, and interaction, social inclusion, and co-presence to increased graduation; the results offer suggestions on how to develop particular educational formats, where certain facilitations of engagement are under-represented. One-sided facilitation of engagement suggests monotonous LA, that may cause boredom, lack of connection and separateness. On the other hand, teachers cannot merely focus on designing for any general type of engagement but must focus on engagement *in learning*. As engagement is strongly linked to performance, it is hard to imagine any learning passing from the content to the learner without being mediated by engagement [39]. While previous research (i.e., [24]), has concluded that designs that stimulate engagement are related to student progress, future research could explore if and how teachers' digital competence relates to how they design to support engagement in online learning, and if all the nuances of engagement are equally important for wellbeing and school success.

4.2 Conclusion

Comparing manifested LDs in different modes of delivery may be challenging. This study provides a theory-informed inductive schema that allows for systematic exploration of content and patterns across online formats of education. Results show that there is an essential difference between ERT and ADE: the synchronous and asynchronous blend, where ERT is mainly synchronous, and ADE is mainly asynchronous. There were situations when the teacher displayed a/synchronous (the opposite) elements and facilitated for all engagement dimensions, but these were rare. The implication is that teachers can benefit from becoming aware of the challenges of a particular form and try to overcome these with professional development. While ERT and ADE teachers may inspire each other, teachers' may not own the tacit knowledge of how to enact LDs that stimulate engagement in varied ways, taking the conditions of their specific form of online education into account.

Funding.   The Research is a Part of the Malmo IT in Education Research Project (MITis) and is Funded by the City of Malmo.

Declaration of Interest.   The authors declare that they have no competing interests.

References

1. Cao, H., Bowers, S., Schildhauer, M.P.: Approaches for semantically annotating and discovering scientific observational data. In: Hameurlain, A., Liddle, S.W., Schewe, K.-D., Zhou, X. (eds.) DEXA 2011. LNCS, vol. 6860, pp. 526–541. Springer, Heidelberg (2011). https://doi.org/10.1007/978-3-642-23088-2_39
2. Ainley, J., Pratt, D., Hansen, A.: Connecting engagement and focus in pedagogic task design. Br. Educ. Res. J. **32**(1), 23–38 (2006). https://doi.org/10.1080/01411920500401971
3. Abdelmalak, M.M.M., Parra, J.L.: Expanding learning opportunities for graduate students with HyFlex course design. Int. J. Online Pedagog. Course Des. **6**, 19–37 (2016). https://doi.org/10.4018/IJOPCD.2016100102
4. Hodges, C., Moore, S., Lockee, B., Trust, T., Bond, A.: The difference between emergency remote teaching and online learning (2020). https://er.educause.edu/articles/2020/3/the-difference-between-emergency-remote-teaching-and-online-learning
5. Nørgård, R.T.: Theorising hybrid lifelong learning. Br. J. Educ. Technol. **52**(4), 1709–1723 (2021). https://doi.org/10.1111/bjet.13121
6. Zydney, J.M., McKimmy, P., Lindberg, R., Schmidt, M.: Here or there instruction: lessons learned in implementing innovative approaches to blended synchronous learning. TechTrends **63**(2), 123–132 (2018). https://doi.org/10.1007/s11528-018-0344-z

7. Alrashidi, O., Phan, H.P., Ngu, B.H.: Academic engagement: an overview of its definitions, dimensions, and major conceptualisations. Int. Educ. Stud. **9**(12), 41–52 (2016). https://doi.org/10.5539/ies.v9n12p41

8. Fredricks, J.A., Blumenfeld, P.C., Paris, A.: School engagement: potential of the concept, state of the evidence. Rev. Educ. Res. **74**(1), 59–109 (2004). https://doi.org/10.3102/00346543074001059

9. Wang, M.-T., Hofkens, T.L.: Beyond classroom academics: a school-wide and multi-contextual perspective on student engagement in school. Adolesc. Res. Rev. **5**(4), 419–433 (2019). https://doi.org/10.1007/s40894-019-00115-z

10. Alispahic, S., Alispahic, B.: How can teachers engage students in online learning? A conceptual framework. Tech. Soc. Sci. J. **17**(June), 235–243 (2021)

11. Bergdahl, N.: Lärares förståelse av elevers engagemang online. Pedagog. Forsk. i Sverige (2022)

12. Te Wang, M.-T., Fredricks, J., Ye, F., Hofkens, T., Linn, J.S.: Conceptualization and assessment of adolescents' engagement and disengagement in school. Eur. J. Psychol. Assess. **35**(4), 592–606 (2017). https://doi.org/10.1027/1015-5759/a000431

13. Salmela-Aro, K., Muotka, J., Hakkarainen, K., Alho, K., Lonka, K.: School burnout and engagement profiles among digital natives in Finland: a person-oriented approach. Eur. J. Dev. Psychol. **13**(6), 704–718 (2016). https://doi.org/10.1080/17405629.2015.1107542

14. Salmela-Aro, K., Read, S.: Study engagement and burnout profiles among Finnish higher education students. Burn. Res. **7**, 21–28 (2017). https://doi.org/10.1016/j.burn.2017.11.001

15. de Brito Lima, F., Lautert, S.L., Gomes, A.S.: Contrasting levels of student engagement in blended and non-blended learning scenarios. Comput. Educ. **172**, 104241 (2021). https://doi.org/10.1016/j.compedu.2021.104241

16. Manwaring, K.C., Larsen, R., Graham, C.R., Henrie, C.R., Halverson, L.R.: Investigating student engagement in blended learning settings using experience sampling and structural equation modeling. Internet High. Educ. **35**, 21–33 (2017). https://doi.org/10.1016/j.iheduc.2017.06.002

17. Bowers, S., et al.: Reflective design in action: a collaborative autoethnography of faculty learning design. TechTrends **66**, 17–28 (2021). https://doi.org/10.1007/s11528-021-00679-5

18. Bower, M., Dalgarno, B., Kennedy, G.E., Lee, M.J., Kenney, J.: Blended synchronous learning: a handbook for educators. Canberra: office for learning and teaching, Australian Department of Education (2014)

19. Kennedy, G.: What is student engagement in online learning … and how do i know when it is there? Melbourne CSHE Discussion Paper, Melb. CSHE Discuss. Pap., pp. 1–6 (2020)

20. Khan, A., Egbue, O., Palkie, B., Madden, J.: Active learning: engaging students to maximize learning in an online course. Electron. J. E-Learning **15**(2), 107–115 (2017)

21. Hoi, V.N., Le Hang, H.: The structure of student engagement in online learning: a bi-factor exploratory structural equation modelling approach. J. Comput. Assist. Learn. **37**(4), 1141–1153 (2021). https://doi.org/10.1111/jcal.12551

22. Bayham, J., Fenichel, E.P.: The impact of school closure for COVID-19 on the US healthcare workforce and the net mortality effects. medRxiv, p. 2020.03.09.20033415 (March 2020). https://doi.org/10.1101/2020.03.09.20033415

23. Akyol, Z., Randy Garrison, D., Yasar Ozden, M.: Online and blended communities of inquiry: exploring the developmental and perceptional differences. Int. Rev. Res. Open Distance Learn. **10**(6), 65–83 (2009). https://doi.org/10.19173/irrodl.v10i6.765

24. Toetenel, L., Rienties, B.: Analysing 157 learning designs using learning analytic approaches as a means to evaluate the impact of pedagogical decision making. Br. J. Educ. Technol. **47**(5), 981–992 (2016). https://doi.org/10.1111/bjet.12423

25. Awuor, O., Weng, N.C., Piedad, E., Militar, R.: Teamwork competency and satisfaction in online group project-based engineering course: the cross-level moderating effect of collective efficacy and flipped instruction. Comput. Educ. **176**, 104357 (2021). https://doi.org/10.1016/j.compedu.2021.104357

26. Missildine, K., Fountain, R., Summers, L., Gosselin, K.: Flipping the classroom to improve student performance and satisfaction. J. Nurs. Educ. **52**(10), 597–599 (2013). https://doi.org/10.3928/01484834-20130919-03

27. Pettersson, F.: Understanding digitalization and educational change in school by means of activity theory and the levels of learning concept. Educ. Inf. Technol. **26**(1), 187–204 (2020). https://doi.org/10.1007/s10639-020-10239-8

28. Teng, M.F.: Flipping the classroom and tertiary level EFL students' academic performance and satisfaction. J. Asia TEFL **14**(4), 605 (2017). https://doi.org/10.18823/asiatefl.2017.14.4.2.605

29. Yin, R.K.: Case Study Research: Design and Methods, 3rd edn. Sage Publications, USA (2003)

30. Olofsson, A.D., Fransson, G., Lindberg, J.O.: A study of the use of digital technology and its conditions with a view to understanding what "adequate digital competence" may mean in a national policy initiative. Educ. Stud. **46**(6), 727–743 (2020). https://doi.org/10.1080/03055698.2019.1651694

31. Cazden, C., Cope, B., Fairclough, N., Gee, J., Kalantis, M., Kress, G.: A pedagogy of multi-literacies: designing social futures. Harv. Educ. Rev. **66**(1), 60–92 (1996). https://doi.org/10.17763/haer.66.1.17370n67v22j160u

32. Li, J.: The Interactions between Emotion, Cognition, and Action in the Activity of Assessing Undergraduates' Written Work', in Activity Theory in Education, pp. 105–119. Brill Sense (2016)

33. Kyndt, E., Berghmans, I., Dochy, F., Bulckens, L.: "Time is not enough." Workload in higher education: a student perspective. High. Educ. Res. Dev. **33**(4), 684–698 (2014). https://doi.org/10.1080/07294360.2013.863839

34. Cochran-Smith, M., Barnatt, J., Friedman, A., Pine, G.: Inquiry on inquiry: practitioner research and student learning. Action Teach. Educ. **31**(2), 17–32 (2009). https://doi.org/10.1080/01626620.2009.10463515

35. Kress, G., Selander, S.: Multimodal design, learning and cultures of recognition. Internet High. Educ. **15**, 265–268 (2012). https://doi.org/10.1016/j.iheduc.2011.12.003

36. Suliani, M., Juniati, D., Ulfah, F.: Learning mathematics in Madrasah Aliyah Muhammadiyah 2 Banjarmasin during the covid-19 pandemic era. In: Journal of Physics: Conference Series, vol. 1747, no. 1, p. 12018 (February 2021). https://doi.org/10.1088/1742-6596/1747/1/012018

37. Rap, S., et al.: An applied research-based approach to support chemistry teachers during the COVID-19 pandemic. J. Chem. Educ. **97**(9), 3278–3284 (2020). https://doi.org/10.1021/acs.jchemed.0c00687

38. Bergdahl, N.: Adaptive professional development during the pandemic. Des. Learn. **10**(2022), 1–14 (2022). https://doi.org/10.16993/dfl.172

39. Reeve, J.: A self-determination theory perspective on student engagement. In: Christenson, S., Reschly, A., Wylie, C. (eds.) Handbook of Research on Student Engagement. Springer, Boston (2012). https://doi.org/10.1007/978-1-4614-2018-7_7

Educational Robots and Their Control Interfaces: How Can We Make Them More Accessible for Special Education?

Maria Jose Galvez Trigo[1,2]([✉]) [iD], Penelope Jane Standen[2] [iD],
and Sue Valerie Gray Cobb[2] [iD]

[1] University of Lincoln, Brayford Way, Brayford Pool, Lincoln LN6 7TS, UK
mgalveztrigo@lincoln.ac.uk
[2] University of Nottingham, University Park, Nottingham NG7 2RD, UK
{p.standen,sue.cobb}@nottingham.ac.uk

Abstract. Existing design standards and guidelines provide guidance on what factors to consider to produce interactive systems that are not only usable, but also accessible. However, these standards are usually general, and when it comes to designing an interactive system for children with Learning Difficulties or Disabilities (LD) and/or Autism Spectrum Conditions (ASC) they are often not specific enough, leading to systems that are not fit for that purpose. If we dive into the area of educational robotics, we face even more issues, in part due to the relative novelty of these technologies. In this paper, we present an analysis of 26 existing educational robots and the interfaces used to control them. Furthermore, we present the results of running focus groups and a questionnaire with 32 educators with expertise in Special Education and parents at four different institutions, to explore potential accessibility issues of existing systems and to identify desirable characteristics. We conclude introducing an initial set of design recommendations, to complement existing design standards and guidelines, that would help with producing future more accessible control interfaces for educational robots, with an especial focus on helping pupils with LDs and/or ASC.

Keywords: Access to education and learning · Assistive robots · Design for all best practice · Design for children with and without disabilities · ASC · Learning difficulties · Learning disabilities · Educational robots

1 Introduction

Current standards applying to the design and development of interactive systems, such as those created by the International Organization for Standardization (ISO) [18], provide requirements and guidelines to help designers and developers produce systems that are fit for their purpose. In terms of the creation of usable and accessible new technologies, there is an increasing number of ISO publications that provide guidance on the ergonomics of human-system

M. Antona and C. Stephanidis (Eds.): HCII 2022, LNCS 13309, pp. 15–34, 2022.
https://doi.org/10.1007/978-3-031-05039-8_2

interaction [7–12, 25, 26]. These standards are usually complemented with others related to software ergonomics for interfaces [18] and the accessibility of user interface components [13]. However, these standards are very general, and this is because they address all systems that involve human-system interaction and user interfaces. They clearly indicate that the needs of the end-user have to be taken into account, and that depending on the user the requirements of each system will be different. Nonetheless, they also require that all systems make a provision for allowing the use to those people with accessibility needs. This again is not very strict, because they also specify that when the nature or main objective of the system is lost or altered when making adaptations to ensure its accessibility, then, it is not required to make such adaptations.

The design of interactive systems may also be informed by more specific principles or guidelines, like Nielsen's ten "heuristics" for user interface (UI) design [23], as well as by advice given by organisations or institutions representing different user groups.

In terms of guidelines specific to accessibility, the Web Content Accessibility Guidelines (WCAG) 2.1 [20] and the more recent working draft [1] are normally the ones against which web accessibility is measured. However, these standards, principles, guidelines, and pieces of advice are usually general, covering a very wide range of uses for the system to be designed and developed. Whilst the WCGA guidelines [1, 20] address matters related specifically to accessibility, and their use could be extended to other interactive systems and not only web content, they do not look into the accessibility of more complex systems, such as those necessary for the control of robots, since these systems may involve not only a graphical user interface (GUI), but also the physical robots and any buttons or sensors that these might have. Furthermore, and although it is normally considered good practice to follow those guidelines, in many cases certain accessibility features are disregarded by designers and/or developers.

A possible reason behind paying less attention to the integration of accessibility features in control interfaces for educational robots, is that these interfaces are usually designed and developed for them to be used by programmers, by people learning how to code, or simply as games. The complexity of those interfaces targeted at programmers is usually high, which makes integrating certain accessibility features more complex. A similar issue occurs with interfaces aimed at people learning how to code. For those interfaces designed as games, and for games in general, the results of a recently published survey targeting professional game developers [16], reveals that only 39% of games developers have implemented accessibility measures (for those with sensory impairment, motor impairment, or other impairments) into their games. The report highlights that *"Unfortunately there is still a lot of pushback in implementing accessibility features"*, and most of the accessibility measures taken focus on hearing or visual impairments.

More recently, Qbilat and Iglesias have proposed accessibility guidelines specific to tactile displays in Human-Robot Interaction (HRI) [27], however, these focus on service robots, and whilst many of them can be applied to educational robots, the nature of the use of these devices varies.

As a field, Educational Robotics (ER) has been recently defined as *"a field of study that aims to improve learning experience of people through the creation, implementation, improvement and validation of pedagogical activities, tools (e.g. guidelines and templates) and technologies, where robots play an active role and pedagogical methods inform each decision."* [3], and therefore, the robots used with those aims can be considered educational robots.

Educational robots have been used from the 1980's as tools to assist with the teaching of subjects in the area of Science, Technology, Engineering and Mathematics (STEM) [24], and from the late 1990's as rehabilitation and education tools for children with ASC [22]. Nowadays, educational robots are mainly used to help with the teaching of STEM subjects, with an emphasis on programming and the logic behind it [4,19,21], but there is also an increasing number of studies and initiatives successfully introducing their use to help children with LD and ASC, focusing more on the later group [2,5,29,30]. However, despite the advantages that educational robots offer to children with LD and/or ASC, recent studies have highlighted the lack of uptake for this technology in schools for children with Special Educational Needs (SEN), such as LD an/or ASC, mentioning, among other issues, the non-commercial availability and inadequate design of the interactive systems used to control them [14,15,17].

This paper presents an exploratory study where we aimed to answer the following research questions:

1. What are the main accessibility issues present in existing educational robots and their control interfaces?
2. How can future systems be made more accessible?

2   Methods

This paper presents the results of the analysis of existing interactive systems along with the results of focus groups with experts and an online questionnaire. The methods for each of them are presented.

2.1   Analysis of Existing Interactive Systems

Design. Analysis of existing systems looking at: capabilities of the control interface, main purpose and hardware needed to operate the robot.

Eligibility Criteria. For the educational robot system to be considered within this study, we applied the following eligibility criteria:

1. The system should be commercially available;
2. The system should have educational capabilities;
3. The system should include a robot and offer a clear way of interacting with it, such as an app that can be used from a mobile device or a computer, a remote, or buttons on the robot (i.e., not simply a turn-on, turn-off button or an autonomous robot);

4. A throughout description of the control interface should be available (i.e., from the manufacturer website, a manual, or a third-party review) or, for those where the control interface is an app and a detailed description is not available, the control interface should be freely available for us to download and check.

Procedure. An initial selection of systems was drawn from a previous study [15], in which the five main reasons for low uptake of robots in Special Education were highlighted along with a table with information about different studies that used robots for interventions with children with Special Educational Needs (SEN). From that table we identified the three systems that met the eligibility criteria.

Since we did not want to limit the analysis to robots previously reported as used in research studies, we carried out a search in various online retailers of educational robots for other systems that met the eligibility criteria, even if these did not target children with SEN.

From both sources, a total of 26 systems were identified.

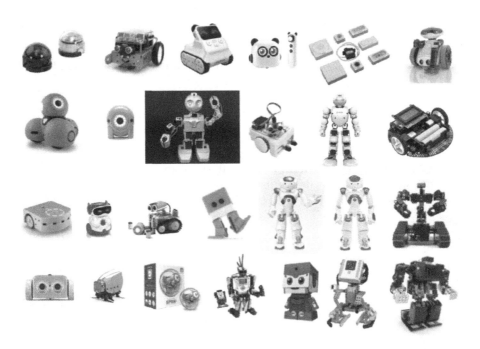

Fig. 1. Robots of the 26 systems analysed. Their names can be found in the first column of Table 1 and the order to follow in the image is row by row, from left to right and from top to bottom.

Analysis. A member of the research team searched for information about each of the systems on the manufacturer's website as well as on retailers' websites. The information looked at included: the advertised main purpose of the robot, the control interface/s and the capabilities that it offered in terms of different activity types or ways of interacting with the robot, and the hardware needed to be able to interact with it. The characteristics of the systems as analysed can be seen in Table 1, and a picture of the relevant robots can be seen in Fig. 1.

When a manual was available this was checked to gain a better understanding of the system being analysed.

In those cases in which an app was available for controlling the robot this was downloaded and explored to gain a better understanding of its capabilities, as well as of the potential accessibility issues that could be present in them. It is important to note that several apps were available to be downloaded and explored even if the relevant physical robot was not available to the researchers.

We took into account during the analysis the five main reasons of low uptake of robots in Special Education that were found during a previous study [15] to see if there was a clear evidence of any of them being present in the analysed systems. These five issues are: price, lack of user-friendly interface, lack of appropriate alternative ways of interaction for Special Education pupils, contents not being appropriate for Special Education students, and not being able to use different robots with the same control interface. When further expertise was necessary to determine if any of the issues was present with a specific system (i.e., expertise educating or living with children with SEN) this was sought during the focus groups with experts and parents described in the next subsection.

2.2   Focus Groups with Experts and Parents, and Questionnaire

Design. Focus groups followed by an online questionnaire.

Participants. Participants had to meet the following eligibility criteria to be able to participate in the study:

1. Be 18 years old or older;
2. Be an educator or expert in Special Education, through work-experience or training, or the parent or a close family member of a child with SEN;
3. Be fluent in either English or Spanish, as these were the languages in which the content and the focus groups would be presented.

A total of 32 participants were recruited across Spain and the United Kingdom (26 from Spain, 6 from the UK). Three of the participants were parents or close family members of a child with SEN at two different institutions, with one of them being the official Parents' Representative for the institution that the child attended. The total sample belonged to four institutions: a state-funded school for children with SEN in Toledo, Spain (6 participants); a partially state-funded school for children with SEN in Toledo, Spain (5 participants); the faculty

Table 1. Description of the educational robots analysed, the systems/interfaces used to control them, their main purpose, and the hardware needed to control them.

Robot	Control interface and capabilities	Main purpose	Hardware needed
Ozobot Evo and Bit	App: block programming, remote control, draw, drag & drop, coding cards	Teaching coding/programming	Computer or mobile device
Makeblock mBot series	App: block programming, remote control, piano game, draw, drag & drop	Teaching coding/programming	Computer or mobile device
MakeBlock Codey Rocky	App: block programming, remote control, remote programmer on robot	Teaching coding/programming	Computer or mobile device and physical buttons on robot
MakeBlock mTiny	Remote programmer with tap-to-code interaction, coding cards	Teaching skills through coding concepts	Remote similar to Nintendo Wii's controller
MakeBlock Neuron	App: block programming	Teaching coding/programming	Computer or mobile device
Mio The Robot 2.0	Remote programmer on robot	Teaching coding/programming	Physical buttons on robot
Wonder Workshop Dash	App: block programming, remote control	Teaching coding/programming	Computer or mobile device
Wonder Workshop Dot	App: block programming, remote control	Teaching coding/programming	Computer or mobile device
EZ-Robot (various models)	App: block programming, remote control, drag & drop to create interface, traditional coding/programming	Teaching coding/programming	Computer or mobile device
ArcBotics Sparki	App: block programming, traditional coding/programming	Teaching coding/programming	Computer or mobile device
UBTECH Alpha 1 Pro	App: block programming, traditional coding/programming	Teaching coding/programming, dancing, yoga	Computer or mobile device
Pololu 3pi	Traditional coding/programming	Teaching coding/programming	Computer
Thymio	App: block programming, traditional coding/programming, 6 pre-programmed buttons	Teaching coding/programming	Computer

(*continued*)

Table 1. (*continued*)

Robot	Control interface and capabilities	Main purpose	Hardware needed
Doc Interactive Talking Robot	Remote programmer on robot	Teaching coding/programming	Physical buttons on robot
Tinkerbots My First Robot Educational Kit	App: simplified block programming	Teaching coding/programming	Mobile device
Zowi	App: block programming and remote control	Teaching coding/programming	Mobile device
NAO Robot	App: drag & drop to create complex behaviours, traditional coding/programming	Teaching coding/programming	Computer
ZoraBots NAO	App: remote control, text-to-speech, predefined drag & drop activities	Healthcare companion	Mobile device
Lynxmotion Johnny 5	App: servo controller interface	Teaching robotics	Computer
Botley The Coding Robot	Remote programmer, coding cards	Teaching coding/programming	Physical buttons on a remote
Mattel Kamigami Programmable Robot Kit	App: simplified block programming, remote control	Teaching coding/programming	Mobile device
Sphero robots	Apps: remote control block programming, traditional coding/programming	Teaching coding/programming	Mobile device
LEGO Mindstorms	Apps: remote control, simplified block programming, traditional programming	Teaching coding/programming	Computer and mobile device
MU SpaceBot	App: block programming	Teaching coding/programming	Mobile device
Abilix Krypton Modular Construction Robot Kits	Apps: remote control, simplified block programming, block programming	Teaching coding/programming	Mobile device
RQ-HUNO Robotic Humanoid Kit	Apps: servo controller interface, action sequencing interface, traditional coding/programming	Teaching coding/programming	Computer

of education of the University of Castilla-la Mancha in Toledo, Spain (15 participants); and a state-funded school for children with SEN in Nottingham, United Kingdom (6 participants).

Procedure. Before the research activities commenced, ethics approval was obtained from the Faculty of Engineering Ethics Committee of the University of Nottingham.

To proceed with the recruitment of participants, four institutions from which recruitment for a previous study had taken place were contacted. Information about the current phase was given to the main point of contact, and they put us in touch with those that were interested in participating and met the eligibility criteria.

One in-person focus group lasting for approximately two hours was held at each of four institutions, three of them with 5–6 participants and one with 15.

During the focus group sessions, and after receiving informed consent from the participants, an initial presentation of the study was followed by an introduction to the results of the analysis of the 26 systems that can be seen in Table 1. Pictures and videos of the relevant systems were also shown to them, and a live demo of three representative systems that were available to the research team and their control interfaces. These systems were NAO Robot[1] (only for the focus group held in the UK), EZ-Robot JD[2], Wonder Workshop Dash[3], and a Sphero[4]. Participants were given the chance to ask questions about the systems presented to them and to try and interact with the ones that were available during the live demo. They were encouraged to share their thoughts whilst interacting with the systems. During the focus groups we asked them questions about the appropriateness of the systems for their use in Special Education. Among other questions we asked them how easy they found using the systems, if they would change anything and how, and if they would use them during a learning session with pupils with SEN or if they found any particular issues with them. We obtained permission to record the audio of two of the focus groups, during the other two, detailed notes were taken to ensure that relevant themes and opinions could be identified during the analysis. The focus groups were organised close in time and were run by the same researcher, which allowed to maintain consistency and facilitated the note-taking process.

At the end of the focus groups, an online questionnaire was sent to participants to help us identify more specific requirements for the design of interactive systems used to control educational robots, paying especial attention to usability and accessibility aspects of the design.

Analysis. The analysis was performed in three stages.

---

[1] https://www.softbankrobotics.com/emea/en/nao.
[2] https://www.ez-robot.com/learn-robotics-getting-started-humanoid-robot-kit.html.
[3] https://uk.makewonder.com/dash/.
[4] https://sphero.com/collections/all/products/sphero-sprk-plus.

First, a researcher transcribed and analysed the audio recordings of the two focus groups that were recorded, along with the notes taken during the other two focus groups. Initial codes were assigned to then lead to the main themes that could, as described by Braun and Clarke [6], capture important information about the data in relation to the research question and represent meaning within the data set. A set of themes was defined, as well as extracts from the transcripts or the notes that represented each theme.

Further to the thematic analysis of the focus groups, the answers provided to the questionnaires were analysed. Some of the questions allowed for free-text answers. In this cases we explored if these fitted within the themes identified in the previous stage or if new themes arose.

A final exercise of consolidation of the results of the two prior stages was done to ensure that a final list of design recommendations could be produced.

3   Results

3.1   Analysis of Existing Systems

Main Purpose of the System. We observed that most systems (23 of the 26 analysed) focused on teaching coding/programming skills and the logic behind it. Of the remaining 3, 1 was aimed at teaching robotics focusing more on the hardware side of the discipline, and 2 had a focus to act as healthcare companions or to teach other activities.

Interactive System Used to Control the Robot. The main control method offered by 14 of the 26 systems analysed was an app with a block programming interface (see Table 2), which is the representation of coding concepts as interlocking blocks similar to puzzle pieces that are combined to create larger, more complicated sequences of actions. 17 systems offered various control systems using an app for a mobile device such as a smartphone o tablet. However, upon downloading and trying the apps, these could not be successfully controlled using embedded accessibility features provided by the device's operating system (usually called Switch Control or Switch Access) and therefore required the user to be able to interact with the screen of the device via drag & drop gestures.

5 systems could only be used from a computer, with limited control or functionalities when using assistive technologies, and 4 systems had to be used with a physical remote programmer.

For those systems that used a control interfaced based on block programming, these were nearly identical, however, despite this fact, in all cases, each app or control interface could only be used with the robots from the same manufacturer.

3.2   Focus Groups with Experts and Parents and Questionnaire

Four main themes that relate to our question on how to make educational robots and their control interfaces more accessible were identified after the consolidation

Table 2. Number of interactive systems offering each type of control system

Type of control system	No. of systems (total = 26)
Block-programming	14
Drag & drop of pre-existing activities	4
Coding cards	4
Remote programmer not on robot	3
Remote programmer on robot	4
Remote control through app	11

of the results from the focus groups and the free-text questions in the online questionnaire. These are:

1. Assistive technologies;
2. Layout of User Interface (UI);
3. Purpose/activities offered;
4. Physical aspects of the robot.

Further to this, the results of the questionnaire answers to more specific questions related to the requirements for a desirable system are presented.

Theme 1: Assistive Technologies. Participants believed that some of their pupils could successfully interact with a mobile device using drag & drop gestures without the need for assistive technologies, but that this was limited to those that had better fine motor skills. Some indicated that being able to control the robot could serve as an incentive for some pupils to work on improving them, but that limiting those interaction to drag & drop was not the best approach, as it would exclude many children. Regarding this, and after discussing the case of children with limited mobility that need to attend physiotherapy sessions for cervical rehabilitation, one participant said:

"For many children it is more interesting to work on some things through play, rather than for instance working on them with the physiotherapist, it is different".

When we asked specifically about whether or not they considered that existing interfaces were accessible enough, they highlighted that they are not accessible enough for a Special School.

The three schools taking part in the study had several pupils that could only move their eyes, and therefore thought that more should be done to make the interfaces more accessible. Participants highlighted that they were already using assistive technologies such as micro-switches, eye-trackers or devices that kept a screen on if the child maintained their head up (for those following cervical rehabilitation), and that it would be great it those devices could be used with a robot.

"In our classrooms we do have micro-switches, then, that's it, depending on the characteristics of the child, if they can use a bigger or smaller switch, or

even if they can use it only with one finger or with the whole hand, then... it would be really motivating".

Participants mentioned as well that, whilst some of the interfaces could be used by the educators to trigger certain actions on the robot even if the child could not operate it, this was not ideal:

"It is not that much that teachers used the robots to teach the children, but that the children could use the robots themselves, that they could learn with them themselves".

Theme 2: Layout of User Interface (UI). When it came to control interfaces for the robots, participants found more interesting the use of apps than the use of buttons on the robot or on a remote, and some did not feel that it was safe for the robot to be handled/touched by some of their pupils:

"Our pupils... that, some of them interact with things with slaps and, imagine! rraass! to the floor, and the materials they are made of are so rigid...".

Participants indicated that, in most cases, items on the screen were very small and that, even those pupils that could successfully interact with the interface without assistive technologies would likely find it too difficult.

"I don't know you, but I find those buttons too small even for me, look at all that empty space on the screen".

They also highlighted that the icons used to depict the action that a button would trigger were in some instances confusing. Whilst testing some of the apps themselves, one participant was very vocal in that regard, asking other participants if they knew what some of the icons meant, because they didn't.

When talking more specifically about block programming, participants in general found very interesting that you could program your own activities using the interface. However, they believed that without proper training or enough time to get familiar with the interface, it could be confusing, and that it requires to dedicate time and effort to create any activities that they could later use with they pupils:

"It's not just creating the activity in the app, I'd have to, I don't know, learn how to create anything with it first, then think of an activity that I could make, and then make it, and what if after having designed the activity I see that I cannot create it with the blockly?".

An issue highlighted relating to the layout of the UI was that participants considered that most apps had too many unnecessary distractions on screen, which could lead to attention problems for pupils.

Theme 3: Purpose/Activities Offered. In general, participants felt that, whilst some pupils could benefit from learning how to code or the logic behind it, for their pupils this was not appropriate at a cognitive level:

"We have pupils with a very low cognitive level, then there are children that, precisely, you can expect a really light response from them, and so it's what it is, basic responses, but these things (of the robots) catch their attention".

They also indicated that these technologies could be used to teach them how to anticipate things that would happen during the day, and that it was not a matter of being able to create complicated activities, that sometimes simple ones can be used to teach many concepts:

"Many times, with showing them, I don't know, a plate, a child can learn that after that we are going to see the menu because it's nearly lunch time or things like that, activities as simple as that, you can adapt it a bit to the different activities that the school does".

Participants felt as well that the ideal would be to be able to load pre-made activities onto the app and the robot:

"Having a bank of activities that you could load and use would be very useful, and that you could get and use those activities without needing to code. That would save on work or at least make that work easier... it would be quicker."

Theme 4: Physical Aspects of the Robot. Participants did not limit themselves to commenting on the control interfaces for the robots. Some physical aspects of these were also considered an issue.

During the demo of one of the robots, participants observed the use of flickering lights by one of the default behaviours of a robot, and they emphasised the importance of either adding a warning or disabling any flickering light by default, as this could negatively affect people with epilepsy.

In one of the focus groups it was also mentioned that robots that use ultra-sounds to communicate with a control device should likely be avoided in Special Schools:

"It's supposedly designed for a school environment. It can interfere mainly with hearing aids. Sometimes my child says: dad, that sound is very loud; and I tell him: what a hearing sense you have! I can't hear anything! With young children that must be... don't use it, that really caught my attention".

Participants also raised privacy concerns regarding the existence of cameras in some of the robots, and one participant suggested he would tell others to *"put a piece of tape"* on the camera before using it in a school. Another participant suggested the avoidance of Internet connection from the robot and to use Bluetooth connectivity to communicate with its control interface instead.

Another aspect that was already mentioned within Theme 2 is that the robots seem to be made of very rigid materials and thus are not very robust for them to trust that a child would be able to interact with it via touching its sensors or buttons without damaging it.

Other Questionnaire Responses. From the responses to the questionnaires that participants filled in after the interviews, we observed the following:

- 27 of the 32 participants recommend the colour combination of black and yellow for a Graphical User Interface (GUI). The other 5 participants each recommended a different colour combination different from black and yellow (see Fig. 2).

- 22 participants recommended to use round-shaped buttons in the interface instead of those with other shapes.
- There was no consensus on whether the font type to use should be upper or lower case, and normal or bold face.
- The two font faces identified as the best to use were Comic Sans and Arial (see Fig. 3).
- There is a general consensus on the need to include characteristics such as: 1) showing circular buttons on screen; 2) allowing the user the configuration of the number of buttons to have; 3) showing pictograms, although again, there is no agreement on the type of pictograms to use; 4) offering alternative ways of interaction; 5) not requiring Internet to work; 6) being able to create user profiles for pupils; 7) Allow access to pupil's profiles to their teachers and parents; 8) being able to use the same system to control different robots; 9) offering rewards to the pupils; and 10) not requiring any coding/programming knowledge to be able to use the system effectively.
- In Table 3 we can see the assistive technologies that participants recommended to integrate as compatible with these systems, and how many participants recommended each of them.
- In Table 4 we can see how many participants recommended each feature to have in the pupil's profile.
- In Table 5 the activities that participants recommended it would be desirable to have in the interactive system can be seen.
- As last factors to be taken into account, we can see in Table 6 the types of rewards that participants recommended the robots should produce when a pupil performed well enough in an activity.

Table 3. Number of participants that recommended compatibility with each assistive technology

Assistive technology	No. participants (total − 32)
Eye-tracking	26
Movement-tracking	23
Switches	21
Speech	21
Sound	17
Sip'n puff	16

3.3   Design Recommendations

Do Not Focus on Solely One Way of Interaction. It is important to create a system that can gather for different ways of interaction such as control through eye-tracking or movement tracking. This is because a great number of children with SEN also have accessibility needs that make their use of tablet screens, for instance, more difficult or even impossible.

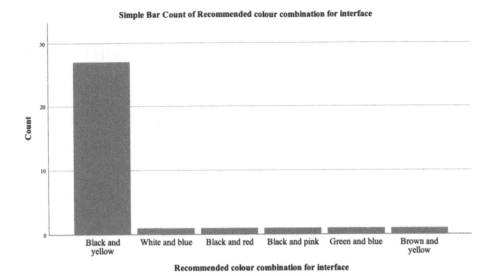

Fig. 2. Black and yellow is the colour combination recommended by most participants (Color figure online)

Table 4. Features recommended by participants to have in the pupil's profile

Features	No. participants (total = 32)
Favourites activities	24
Characteristics and preferences	23
Buttons preferences	22
Font type preferences	14
Score	14
Notes and comments	12

Check the Compatibility of the System with Accessibility Features Embedded into the Operating System of the Device Being Used, or Separately with Assistive Technologies. There are numerous assistive technologies that are already compatible with the most widespread operating systems. Very often it is only necessary to check that the system or app being developed complies with the accessibility guidance given by the developer of the operating system.

For a Graphical User Interface (GUI) Use Preferably Black Text over Yellow/cream Background. This colour combination has been suggested as the one that works best for children with SEN. It is important to pay attention to the contrast as well.

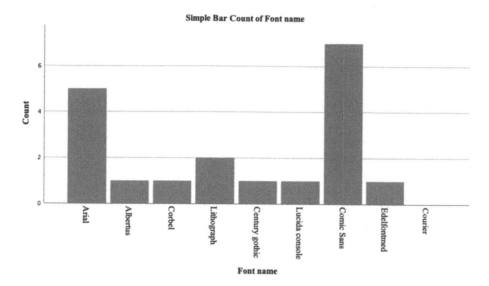

Fig. 3. Questions such as the font face to use didn't receive a consensus in responses even after comparing between institutions

Avoid the Use of Flickering Lights. In Special Education settings it is very possible to find children with epilepsy. It is better to incorporate this feature as an option that can be enabled if the user of the system knows that it is not going to cause any harm to them.

For a GUI, Use Circular Buttons that Fill Well the Screen. A circular shape has been recommended for buttons, as it is a shape that children can more easily associate with the action of a button (it resembles a physical button). It is also recommended to avoid big empty gaps in the screen unless this is required for a particular reason.

Complement the Text on Screen with Pictograms that Convey a Clear Meaning. Not all children can read, and not all can see a screen correctly. Therefore, it is very important to complement information given in the form of text with pictograms that convey the same meaning in a clear manner. This will enable an easier interaction with the system and will help children learn what the text that accompanies each pictogram means.

Avoid Reliance on an Internet Connection. Many schools do not have a reliable Internet connection, and many families do not feel safe leaving their children using a device connected to the Internet.

Table 5. Types of activities recommended by participants

Types of activities	No. participants (total = 32)
Social interaction	29
Daily life	26
Q&A customised by teacher or parent	26
Imitation	25
Directions and navigation	24
Numbers and mathematics	23
Colours	19
Language	16

Table 6. Types of rewards recommended by participants

Types of reward	No. participants (total = 32)
Cheering sentences	22
Dances	19
Custom sentences	19
Custom sounds	17
Sounds	16
Cheering movements	16
Custom songs	15
Lights	15
Predefined songs	11

Provide Personalisation Options and User Profiles for Different Users. It is very important to take into account that each user is different, and that although these recommendations are meant to make the development of systems easier for their use by children with SEN, personalisation options should be provided whenever possible.

Make Systems Compatible with More Than One Robot. This will allow schools and families to use in an easier way a wider range of educational robots without the pressure to acquire and learn how to use different control interfaces for nearly the same purpose.

Implement Different Rewards for the Pupils. Rewards, delivered as dances, sounds, songs, or encouraging sentences, among others, should be included in every system that is going to be used by children with SEN. Many children with SEN need this kind of stimulus to be keen to continue with a learning session.

Do Not Require Users to Have to Code or to Understand the Logic Behind Programming. Many teachers and parents do not feel comfortable using educational robots because it is usually a requirement to at least understand the basis of programming, even if this is done through block programming. Whenever possible this should be avoided, and users should be provided with alternative ways of using their robots.

4 Discussion

Whilst this study was limited by not being able to physically access and thoroughly evaluate all of the analysed robotic systems, it has allowed us to gain a better understanding of the main accessibility issues that educators and parents of children with SEN see as barriers for the uptake and use of educational robotics in Special Schools as well as their potential.

The results match the findings of a previous study [15] that highlighted that the lack of contents appropriate for Special Education pupils, with most systems focusing on teaching coding, was one of the five main reason of low uptake of this technology by Special Schools, and where the lack of compatibility with assistive technologies to provide alternative ways of interaction for those with Severe Learning Difficulties (SLD) or Profound and Multiple Learning Difficulties (PMLD) was considered as an important barrier for uptake. Furthermore, during that same study, something that our participants observed was also highlighted: needing a different control interface for each robot was "confusing" and also a factor affecting negatively the uptake of robots in Special Education.

The opinions of the participants given during the focus groups and in the questionnaires resonate with recently proposed HRI accessibility guidelines by Qbilat et al. [28]. These guidelines were evaluated with HRI designers and/or developers instead of with potential users of the systems and were focused on socially assistive robotics. However, and although we present some more detailed recommendations specific to the use of educational robots in Special Education, the fact that there is an overlap between them seems to indicate that similar accessibility issues have to be tackled in both cases.

Some robots can be considered expensive, but participants indicated that the value-for-money that these offer is more important than their price alone, and that, although currently it is difficult to justify the purchase of some of the robots based on some of the issues highlighted, if future control interfaces take into consideration the recommendations given in this paper, the value that these robots offer to Special Schools may increase, as more pupils and educators would be able to benefit from using them.

This study has allowed us to identify the main accessibility issues present in existing educational robots and their control interfaces from the perspective of Special Education, as well as to gather a set of recommendations that the designers of future systems could follow as an initial guide, along with existing guidelines and standards, to ensure that their systems are fit for purpose when it comes to using them with children with SEN. We believe that it is important to recognise the role of educators and parents when a new technology is to be introduced in the classroom, and consequently, their opinions and recommendations should be considered.

Future directions could take us to explore the same issues from the perspective of a designer or developer, as well as to a formal evaluation of an interface designed following the recommendations given.

References

1. Adams, C., Campbell, A., Montgomery, R., Cooper, M., Kirkpatrick, A.: Web Content Accessibility Guidelines (WCAG) 2.2, W3C Working Draft (May 2021). https://www.w3.org/TR/WCAG22/. Accessed 10 Feb 2022
2. Andruseac, G.G., Adochiei, R.I., Păsărică, A., Adochiei, F., Corciovă, C., Costin, H.: Training program for dyslexic children using educational robotics. In: 2015 E-Health and Bioengineering Conference (EHB), pp. 1–4 (November 2015). https://doi.org/10.1109/EHB.2015.7391547
3. Angel-Fernandez, J.M., Vincze, M.: Towards a formal definition of educational robotics. In: Proceedings of the Austrian Robotics Workshop 2018, pp. 37–42. Innsbruck University Press (July 2018). https://doi.org/10.15203/3187-22-1-08
4. Armesto, L., Fuentes-Durá, P., Perry, D.: Low-cost printable robots in education. J. Intell. Robot. Syst. **81**(1), 5–24 (2015). https://doi.org/10.1007/s10846-015-0199-x
5. Barakova, E.I., Bajracharya, P., Willemsen, M., Lourens, T., Huskens, B.: Long-term LEGO therapy with humanoid robot for children with ASD. Expert Syst. **32**(6), 698–709 (2015)
6. Braun, V., Clarke, V.: Using thematic analysis in psychology. Qual. Res. Psychol. **3**(2), 77–101 (2006). https://doi.org/10.1191/1478088706qp063oa
7. Ergonomics of human-system interaction - part 112: Principles for the presentation of information (iso 9241-112:2017). Standard, International Organization for Standardization
8. Ergonomics of human-system interaction - part 161: Guidance on visual user-interface elements (iso 9241-161:2016). Standard, International Organization for Standardization
9. Ergonomics of human- system interaction - part 171: Guidance on software accessibility (iso 9241-171:2008). Standard, International Organization for Standardization
10. Ergonomics of human-system interaction - part 210: Human-centred design for interactive systems (iso 9241-210:2010). Standard, International Organization for Standardization
11. Ergonomics of human-system interaction - part 420: Selection of physical input devices (iso 9241-420:2011). Standard, International Organization for Standardization
12. Ergonomics of human-system interaction part 920: Guidance on tactile and haptic interactions (iso 9241-920:2009). Standard, International Organization for Standardization

13. Information technology - user interface component accessibility - part 23: Visual presentation of audio information (including captions and subtitles) (iso/iec 20071-23:2018). Standard, International Organization for Standardization

14. Cruz, A.M., Rincon, A.M.R., Duenas, W.R.R., Torres, D.A.Q., Bohorquez-Heredia, A.F.: What does the literature say about using robots on children with disabilities? Disabil. Rehabil.: Assist. Technol. **12**(5), 429–440 (2017). https://doi.org/10.1080/17483107.2017.131830. pMID: 28440095

15. Galvez Trigo, M.J., Standen, P.J., Cobb, S.V.G.: Robots in special education: reasons for low uptake. J. Enabling Technol. **13**(2), 59–69 (2019). https://doi.org/10.1108/JET-12-2018-0070

16. Game Developers Conference: State of the Game Industry 2022 (January 2022). https://reg.gdconf.com/LP=3493. Accessed 10 Feb 2022

17. van den Heuvel, R.J.F., Lexis, M.A.S., Gelderblom, G.J., Jansens, R.M.L., de Witte, L.P.: Robots and ICT to support play in children with severe physical disabilities: a systematic review. Disabil. Rehabil.: Assist. Technol. **11**(2), 103–116 (2016)

18. Software ergonomics for multimedia user interfaces - part 2: Multimedia navigation and control (iso 14915-2:2003). Standard, International Organization for Standardization

19. Kay, J.S., Moss, J.G.: Using robots to teach programming to k-12 teachers. In: 2012 Frontiers in Education Conference Proceedings, pp. 1–6 (October 2012). https://doi.org/10.1109/FIE.2012.6462375

20. Kirkpatrick, A., Connor, J.O., Campbell, A., Cooper, M.: Web Content Accessibility Guidelines (WCAG) 2.1, W3C Recommendation (June 2018). https://www.w3.org/TR/WCAG21/. Accessed 10 Feb 2022

21. Knight, V.F., Wright, J., Wilson, K., Hooper, A.: Teaching digital, block-based coding of robots to high school students with autism spectrum disorder and challenging behavior. J. Autism Dev. Disord. **49**(8), 3113–3126 (2019). https://doi.org/10.1007/s10803-019-04033-w

22. Lees, D., Lepage, P.: Robots in education: the current state of the art. J. Educ. Technol. Syst. **24**(4), 299–320 (1996). https://doi.org/10.2190/39YJ-CHWF-NBL8-3WA4

23. Nielsen, J., Mack, R.L. (eds.): Usability Inspection Methods. Wiley, New York (1994)

24. Papert, S.: Mindstorms: Children, Computers, and Powerful Ideas. Basic Books Inc., New York (1980)

25. Ergonomics of human-system interaction - part 100: Introduction to standards related to software ergonomics (iso/tr 9241-100:2011). Standard, International Organization for Standardization

26. Ergonomics of human-system interaction - part 411: Evaluation methods for the design of physical input devices (iso/ts 9241-411:2014). Standard, International Organization for Standardization

27. Qbilat, M., Iglesias, A.: Accessibility guidelines for tactile displays in human-robot interaction. A comparative study and proposal. In: Miesenberger, K., Kouroupetroglou, G. (eds.) ICCHP 2018, Part II. LNCS, vol. 10897, pp. 217–220. Springer, Cham (2018). https://doi.org/10.1007/978-3-319-94274-2_29

28. Qbilat, M., Iglesias, A., Belpaeme, T.: A proposal of accessibility guidelines for human-robot interaction. Electronics **10**(5), 561 (2021). https://doi.org/10.3390/electronics10050561

29. Roscoe, J., et al.: Engaging students with profound and multiple disabilities using humanoid robots. In: Stephanidis, C., Antona, M. (eds.) UAHCI 2014, Part II. LNCS, vol. 8514, pp. 419–430. Springer, Cham (2014). https://doi.org/10.1007/978-3-319-07440-5_39
30. Wood, L.J., Robins, B., Lakatos, G., Syrdal, D.S., Zaraki, A., Dautenhahn, K.: Developing a protocol and experimental setup for using a humanoid robot to assist children with autism to develop visual perspective taking skills. Paladyn, J. Behav. Robot. 10(1), 167–179 (2019). https://doi.org/10.1515/pjbr-2019-0013

Emotion Analysis Platform to Investigate Student-Teacher Interaction

Andrea Generosi[1], Silvia Ceccacci[1 (✉)], Ilaria D'Angelo[2], Noemi Del Bianco[2], Gianluca Cimini[3], Maura Mengoni[1], and Catia Giaconi[2]

[1] Department of Industrial Engineering and Mathematical Sciences, Università Politecnica delle Marche, Ancona, Italy
{a.generosi,s.ceccacci,m.mengoni}@univpm.it
[2] Department of Education, Cultural Heritage and Tourism, University of Macerata, Macerata, Italy
{i.dangelo,n.delbianco,catia.giaconi}@unimc.it
[3] Emoj Srl, Ancona, Italy
g.cimini@emojlab.com

Abstract. This paper introduces a system that enable the collection of relevant data related to the emotional behavior and attention of both student and professor during exams. It exploits facial coding techniques to enable the collection of a large amount of data from the automatic analysis of students and professors faces using video analysis, advanced techniques for gaze tracking based on deep Learning, and technologies and the principles related to the Affective Computing branch derived from the research of Paul Ekman. It provides tools that facilitates the interpretation of the collected data by means of a dashboard. A preliminary experiment has been carried out to investigate whether such a system may help in assessing the evaluation setting and support reflection on the evaluation processes in the light of the different situations, so as to improve the adoption of inclusive approaches. Results suggest that information provided by the proposed system can be helpful in assessing the setting and the evaluation process.

Keywords: E-leaning · Affective computing · Emotion recognition · Gaze tracking · Deep learning

1 Introduction

In recent years, the demand for inclusive approaches to support the design of training and teaching strategies able to respond in an increasingly effective and efficient way to the requirement of diversification according to individual students' needs, emerges more and more [1–3]. The growing number of students with disabilities and Learning Disorders attending Universities, documented all over the world [4–6], should lead to redesigning teaching materials and methods, to meet their needs. In particular, a reorganization of assessment practices is considered necessary also through the design of specific technologies capable of supporting the process of formulating a fair judgment for all students and, in particular, for those with disabilities or Specific Learning Disorders (SpLDs) [7]. This requires new solutions to support the analysis and understanding of difficulties experienced by students during their academic careers.

Achieving educational success for all students requires that the moment of final evaluation has to be taken into consideration. This, in fact, is an event full of expectations and anxieties, and the construction of a welcoming context becomes essential to provide the conditions for success, especially for students with SpLDs or disabilities [7].

In the last few years, evidence emerged that suggests how emotions significantly contribute to student engagement [8], and positive academic outcomes [9]. As observed in [10] and based on studies on emotional development [11], the "emotional availability" of teachers along with their "mood background" provide a good "shape" to the student's emotional, mental states during the final exam of a discipline. This should be considered as a capacitating feature, and not as a critical feature, of a particular learning context in which not only disciplinary knowledge should be assessed, but above all, the ability to act in front of a given task of the fragile student [12] and therefore his resilience in an inclusive perspective [13]. Therefore, emotional feedback in the teacher-student interaction during the final tests can be helpful in assessing the setting and the evaluation process [14]. Another important factor is represented by the students' engagement, or interest, to accomplish the learning task [15]. Measuring the user level of engagement in e-learning can be useful in detecting states such as fatigue, lack of interest and difficulty in understanding the content [16].

In this context, this paper introduces a system, which exploits facial coding techniques to enable the collection of relevant data related to the emotional behavior of both student and teacher, and the level of student's attention, in order to help in assessing the evaluation setting and support reflection on the evaluation processes in the light of the different situations and the specificity of the interaction contexts that arise in the final assessment.

2   Research Background

In the last years, emerging evidence suggested how emotion influence the cognitive processes in humans [17], including attention [18], learning and memory [19], reasoning [20], and problem solving [21]. So that, emotional influences should be carefully considered in educational courses design to maximize learner engagement. New emotion recognition technologies and tools for assessing student engagement represent a useful method to better support teachers in considering student emotions in order to positively influence student motivation and performance by modulating mutual interaction.

Today several methods and technologies allow the recognition of human emotions, which differ in level of intrusiveness. Most of such techniques, methods and tools refer to three research areas: facial expression analysis, speech recognition analysis and biofeedback emotion analysis. In the last years, much progress has been made in the field of facial expression recognition systems, which have allowed the development of more accurate and less invasive systems, so they represent the technology of choice to automatically perform emotion recognition in a learning context [22]. Facial expression analysis aims to recognize patterns from facial expressions and to connect them to emotions, based on a certain theoretical model. Most of such systems implements Deep Learning algorithms, based on Convolutional Neural Networks (CNNs) [23], based on the theoretical model known as "Facial Action Coding System" (FACS) [24]. They allow the identification of the "big six" Ekman's emotions (i.e., joy, surprise, sadness, anger, fear and disgust) by tracking the movements of the face muscles. The accuracy of such a system strongly depends on the characteristics of the dataset used to train the CNNs. In general, models trained using datasets built in controlled environments achieve the best accuracy scores, but are less reliable in real context of use, while those trained with data obtained by crawlers on the web are less accurate but more suitable to be used in real contexts. Consequently, to ensure good accuracy in the recognition of human emotions in different contexts of use, the system introduced in this paper implements the tool described in [25], which exploits a CNN, based on Keras and Tensorflow frameworks, which has been trained merging three different public datasets.

Automatic engagement prediction can be based on various kinds of data modalities, which include student response [26, 27], LMSs logs [28], physiological and neurological measures (e.g., electroencephalogram, heart rate, and skin response) through specialized sensors [29, 30], or features extracted on the basis of facial movements, head postures and eye gaze [31, 32]. Among the various methods the last ones are the least invasive, and probably the most suitable to be used in a learning context. Gaze tracking techniques can be globally divided into two main categories [33]: feature-based and appearance-based. Feature-based approaches strongly rely on high quality images for determining precise small scale eye features, such as corneal infrared reflections [34], pupil center [35], and iris contour [36]. These systems are characterized by high accuracy, but they require the use of special equipment (e.g., special glasses/IR cameras) and need for system calibration. In general, appearance-based approaches are less accurate [37]. However, in recent years research has aimed to achieve increasingly accurate results, using less and less invasive and off-the-shelf systems (especially webcams). They use deep learning approaches mainly based on CNN. The gaze-tracking solution implemented in the system described in this paper adopts an architecture similar to the one proposed in [38], which represents one of the more solid CNN actually proposed for gaze tracking. It is based on the AlexNet model [39].

3   The Proposed System

Hereafter, an architectural and technological solution is described that enable collection and analysis, in an automated way, of data about behaviors and emotional mood of students and professors during university exams.

This system has a twofold purpose:

- to collect a large amount of data from the automatic analysis of students and professors faces using video analysis, Deep Learning technologies and the principles related to the Affective Computing branch derived from the research of Paul Ekman,
- to provide tools that facilitates the interpretation of the collected data by means of a dashboard, which with charts and insights, show and suggest to the professor which are the emotional trends that best represent the course of the exam.

For each of these objectives a tool was developed: a desktop client application developed in C++ to analyze the face of students and professors during the exam, and a data visualization dashboard developed using Python and JavaScript to display the data collected by the client application.

3.1 System Architecture

The server-side application is written in Python taking advantage of the Flask micro-framework.

The analysis of the face of the person captured by the camera, on the other hand, is provided by the client-side application by means of Deep Learning models trained using the Python version of the Tensorflow framework and converted to be used in C++ ò These models perform the tasks of face detection, age and gender estimation [40], facial expression recognition [41], attention level assessment [22, 25] and facial recognition [22].

The aim is to provide, from every video frame, the following indicators:

- Number of people in the video frame
- Attention metrics about the user (face rotation degree with respect to the camera and gaze direction with respect to the PC monitor)
- Identification of the user
- Emotional Mood of the user
- Age
- Gender

The use of Deep Learning algorithms can be problematic on general purpose PCs and it is for this reason that leaving the video stream processing to the client hardware (i.e. the professor's laptop) could seem a risky choice. However, at the same time offering the possibility of carrying out a server-side analysis in real-time would require a stable and high-speed internet connection, that often it is not guaranteed.

In order to provide a highly flexible solution to user requirements, this research proposes an architectural solution capable of responding to different exams registration needs:

- A solution for real-time analysis directly from a webcam video stream
- A solution for real-time analysis from the PC desktop (e.g. in case of exams taking place remotely using tools such as MS Teams or Google Meet), where the professor's face can appear with the student's on the same frame
- A solution for post-exam analysis of a recorded video (from a webcam or desktop). This solution can be particularly useful if the client software runs on a PC with poor hardware resources.

A cloud native architecture was deployed to host the application allowing for both vertical and horizontal automatic scaling. It was designed on the AWS cloud infrastructure and the architecture scheme is presented in Fig. 1.

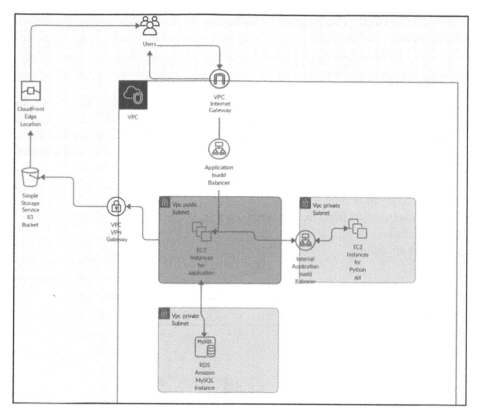

Fig. 1. Cloud architecture

A load balancer sits in front of the application automatically balances the traffic through a target group which contains several ec2 instances containing the code for the web dashboard application.

The number of ec2 instances inside such a target group is elastically scaled based on the average CPU consumption of the instances.

A second target group is deployed with other ec2 instances which serve the python APIs for the data storing and retrieval: when the client elaborates a video frame, the data results are sent to the remote server and received by these APIs that must store every string in a database and send a response to the client asynchronously. The database instance is a RDS MySQL instance with both master and read instances.

As far as the client-side hardware is concerned, the system simply requires the use of at least one webcam and one PC connected to the internet.

To ensure a rapid exchange of data between client and server and considering the absence of particular criticalities related to the privacy of the exchanged data (which are just numerical values related to mood and attention parameters obtained by the system), it was decided to use the MQTT communication protocol rather than HTTPS, which is more secure but less performing in terms of communication speed. To this end, the APIs in Python were developed using the Mosquitto broker and with a subscriber that handles the calls received by the client and forwards them to the service that handles the storage to the Database.

3.2 Client Application

The client application is a C++ software developed using the Ultralight framework for the GUI implementation, which processes frame by frame a video stream that can be acquired in real-time or processed a posteriori from a pre-recorded video. In particular, a configuration form allows the user to choose between the previously defined acquisition modes (Fig. 2):

- real-time acquisition from webcam,
- real-time acquisition from the desktop (analysis of everything is displayed on the desktop), and
- Video file uploading.

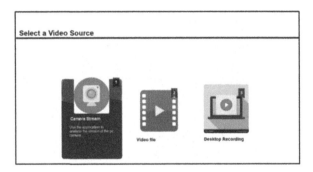

Fig. 2. Video source selection in the client C++ application

Once the source has been selected, the software allows the user to analyze different characteristics of the subject's face (usually synchronizing the analysis of the student's face and the professor's face), which can be configured as required. As previously mentioned, the client makes use of models trained by specific Convolutional Neural Networks to acquire the subject's age and gender, the subject's level of attention to the monitor, the gaze direction, and the subject's main emotion among the Ekman's "big six" (i.e., happiness, surprise, sadness, anger, disgust, and fear) plus a Neutral value, and the corresponding emotional valence and engagement.

Valence allows differentiating between pleasant and unpleasant emotions. Therefore, it provides a trend on a scale from -100 to 100 of the positivity or negativity of the emotion experienced in real-time, considering happiness and surprise as positive emotions and anger, sadness, disgust and fear as negative emotions. On this scale, neutrality is 0. Similarly, Engagement provides a simple scale given by the intensity of the felt emotion regardless of whether it may be negative or positive, providing a value from 0 (total absence of emotions) to 100 (maximum level).

In order to discriminate the student's face from the professor's in cases where both appear simultaneously on the screen (e.g. when the source is a video recorded from the desktop during an exam session carried out remotely using teleconferencing tools), a Face Recognition model capable of recognising only the professor's face is applied to every frame, assuming that the other face appearing in the screen belongs to the student, following the method set out in [22].

In terms of design, the main objective was to keep the client software light and less resource-demanding as possible. To do this, it was decided to use a compiled language over an interpreted one (i.e. the C++ language) and to convert the Deep Learning models into a lighter version using the Tf-lite framework.

The application's strengths lie in its great configurability to allow different types of face analysis and different modes of real-time or retrospective video acquisition. All the face analysis modules are optional as required, in accordance with the modular nature of the system architecture. The possibility to process different video input formats also allows the system to operate with different architectures and e-learning web platforms: using desktop recordings indeed, it is potentially possible to analyze any video stream, including those coming from teleconferencing applications for remote examinations, still very popular given the particular historical period.

3.3 Dashboard

The data managed by the MYSQL DBMS are analyzed and visualized through specific charts within a dashboard developed in Python and Flask (Fig. 3).

Through this dashboard it is possible to filter data on the exam session or date, surname, name or matriculation number for students and/or professors, eventual students disability category. The interface offers tools that allow you to visualize the relationships between the emotional and attention data of a student and his professor during a particular exam, i.e. the correlations on the time axis (the duration of the exam) between the Valence and Engagement values or the direction of gaze, to understand if a particular emotional state of the student may have been triggered by a particular behavior of the professor. More in detail, it is possible to check:

- the age and gender distribution through tow dedicated pie charts, which respectively represent the percentage of times in which the system detects the user focused on the monitor (Attention pie chart), and the aggregated percentage of each of Ekman's emotions (Emotions pie chart),
- the trend over time of Valence, Engagement, Ekman's emotions and gaze direction showing the moving average for each time unit, with the possibility of selecting the level of aggregation over time by choosing between 1 s, 30 s, 1 min, 5 min and 10 min.

The Dashboard also provides the possibility of downloading a report with a pdf printout of all the generated charts and a CSV log with the data collected from the database filtered through the relative widgets.

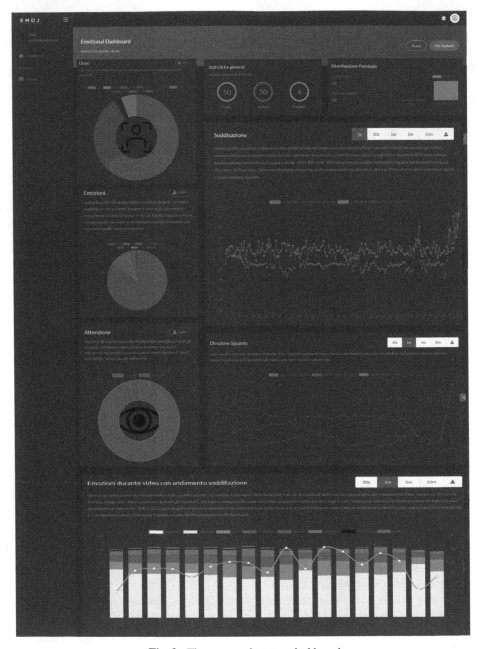

Fig. 3. The proposed system dashboard

4 Preliminary Experimentation

A preliminary experimentation was conducted with the aim of observing if the information provided by the proposed system can be useful to analyze and understand the dynamics of the relationship between the student and the professor, at an emotional level, during the final exam, and more specifically:

- can be useful to ensure inclusive university teaching and to guarantee opportunities for social inclusion and equity of treatment,
- may support the evaluation of the exam setting followed by the professors during the assessment process.

To this end, a pilot study was carried out at the Department of Education, Cultural Heritage and Tourism of the University of Macerata in the academic year 2020–2021 and was coordinated by a multidisciplinary team composed of experts in pedagogy and special education, developmental psychology and experts in human factors and human-computer interaction.

A total of 50 students, including 5 students with a certification for SpLDs and disabilities, enrolled in the fourth year of Primary Education, have been involved. They were randomly assigned to 4 professors and took the online oral assessment test in Pedagogy and Special Education through Microsoft Teams. After collecting the informed consent to participate in the research from each student, the study included an examination registration phase, during which an external observer filled in an Excel table with personal data, the presence of any disability certifications, the year of the course, the frequency of the course delivered online, participation in part of the teaching, and the final grade. Video recording was carried out over the entire duration of the examination, using the tools provided by the MS Teams platform. The videos were collected with specific caution related to recording sitting. Each recording captures audio and video, of both student and professor, and screen sharing activity. Video files have been processed frame by frame through the system described above (see paragraph 3).

5 Results and Discussion

The analysis of the data collected during the experiment allowed to evaluate the usefulness of the various tools offered by the proposed system. The Attention and the Emotion pie charts provide an initial overview and allow to compare the students' behavior with different professors.

For example, emotion pie charts related to students respectively promoted by the four considered professors, with a grade equal or higher than 27/30, are reported in Fig. 4 and Fig. 5.

As can be seen, students who took the exam with Professors 1 and 2 exhibited a slightly higher level of attention (98%) than those who took the exam with Professors 3 (94%) and 4 (96%). Students who took the exam with professor 2 expressed more positive emotions (i.e., joy = 16%, surprise = 13%) than the others. While students who interacted with Professor 1 showed a higher level of negative emotions (i.e., sadness = 12%, disgust = 2%) than the others.

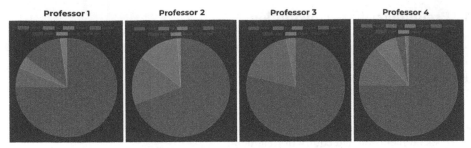

Fig. 4. Emotion pie charts related to students respectively promoted by the four considered professors, with a grade equal or higher than 27/30 (red = neutral, green = sadness, blue = joy, yellow = surprice, orange = disgust) (Color figure online)

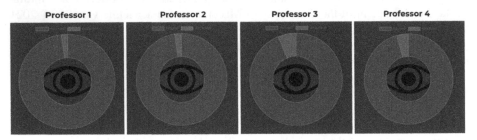

Fig. 5. Attention pie charts related to students respectively promoted by the four considered professors, with a grade equal or higher than 27/30 (red = attention, blue = inattention) (Color figure online)

The other widgets the system displays allow for a better understanding of the differences between professors' individual styles and attitudes toward accommodating students based on their needs and functioning profiles.

In particular, the analysis of the emotional curves allowed to highlight the singularities that characterize the various students during the assessment process.

For example, in Fig. 6 the valence moving average trendlines (computed considering a period equal to 30 s) of three students are reported, who took the exam with Professor 1. They are related to:

- a student who failed the exam,
- a student who achieved the high marks,
- a promoted student with dyslexia, who took the exam using compensatory tools.

Surprisingly, it is possible to observed that the emotional curve tends more toward high positive values in the case of the student who failed the exam than in the case of the students who passed. This occurs mainly in the final phase of the examination.

By analyzing the emotional outcomes of the two promoted students, we can also observe that the curve related to the student with dyslexia is a less regular than the other. In fact, while the first has several peaks of positive valance, the second is almost flat.

Fig. 6. Valance moving average trendlines (30 s) related to: a failed student (on the left), a student promoted with high marks (on the right), a student with dyslexia, promoted with high marks, who took the exam using compensatory tools (in the middle).

The reason for these differences can be investigated by looking more closely at the dynamics of the relationship between students and teacher during the exam. This can be seen by analyzing the relationships between the emotional and attention data of a student and his/her professor during a particular exam (Fig. 7).

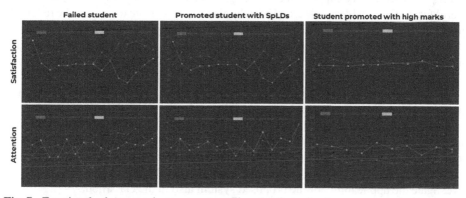

Fig. 7. Emotional valance moving average trendlines (on the top) and engagement moving average trendlines (on the bottom) registered from a failed student, a promoted student with SpLDs and a promoted student with high marks (in orange) and from the professor (in green). (Color figure online)

It is possible to observe that the professor showed a higher level of attention with the failed student and the student with dyslexia than in the case of the student promoted with high marks. Moreover, the first two cases are characterized by a stronger emotional student-teacher interaction: as confirmed through a manual video analysis of the exams, the teacher intentionally attempts to activate feedback to support the student's exposition, support the student with SpLDs to recover from specific difficulties of people with dyslexia, and take care of the communication of not passing the exam. In this way, the failed student managed from the interaction with the teacher to face the rejection as an opportunity to improve his/her preparation and not as a failure, consequently the emotional curve presents high values of valance also at the end of the evaluation process. On the other hand, where the student does not need support, the emotional involvement of the teacher is low.

These results suggest how the system can enhance the assessment process that, while necessarily having to comply with the standards, must be appropriately customized according to the peculiarities of each student, to ensure a path that can best support the process of self-evaluation and learning.

6 Conclusion

This paper introduces a system for the collection of relevant data related to the emotional behavior and attention of both student and teacher during the examinations.

The novelties introduced by the proposed system in the context, in terms of the opportunity to obtain insight useful to train university teachers in the principles and practices of inclusive assessment is discussed.

Considering the need to support assessment procedures capable of supporting reflection on learning, allowing students to arrive at adequate forms of self-assessment [42], results of a preliminary experimentation suggest that the application of the platform is useful for more equitable construction of judgments and therefore to support the redefinition of the evaluation context in a more inclusive way. The system allows the acquisition of important information in the structuring of inclusive processes, highlighting the alignment (or not) between the different functioning profiles of the students, the discipline, the attitude and the style of the teacher [2, 42, 43].

Providing emotional feedback related to the student-professor interaction can be therefore helpful in assessing the setting and the evaluation process.

Future developments should aim at providing real time information about emotional feedback, to provide a better support professor in preparing interventions aimed at improving the climate and context of the examination, and the identification of procedures for a more accurate assessment. Future studies should be also conducted to investigate the applicability of the proposed system also in the classroom.

References

1. D'Angelo, I., Del Bianco, N. (eds.): Inclusion at the University. Studies and Practices. Milano: FrancoAngeli (2019)
2. Giaconi, C.: Qualità della Vita e adulti con disabilità. Percorsi di ricerca e prospettive inclusive. FrancoAngeli, Milano (2015)
3. Perla, L.: Formare il docente alla didattica universitaria: il cantiere dell'innovazione. Riflessioni sull'innovazione didattica universitaria. Interventi alla tavola rotonda GEO (30 giugno 2017), 79–88 (2018)
4. Giaconi, C., Capellini, S.A., Del Bianco, N., Taddei, A., D'Angelo, I.: Study empowerment for inclusion. Educ. Sci. Soc.-Open Access 9(2), 166–183 (2019)
5. Pino, M., Mortari, L.: The inclusion of students with dyslexia in higher education: a systematic review using narrative synthesis. Dyslexia 20, 46–369 (2014)
6. Rivera, C.J., Wood, C.L., James, M., Williams, S.: Improving study outcomes for college students with executive functioning challenges. Career Dev. Transition Exceptional Individuals, 42(3), 139–147 (2019)
7. Mengoni, M., et al.: Emotional Feedback in evaluation processes: case studies in the University context (in press)

8. Pentaraki, A., Burkholder, G.J.: Emerging evidence regarding the roles of emotional, behavioural, and cognitive aspects of student engagement in the online classroom. Eur. J. Open Distance E-learning **20**(1), 1–21 (2017)
9. D'Errico, F., Paciello, M., Cerniglia, L.: When emotions enhance students' engagement in e-learning processes. J. e-Learning Knowl. Soc. **12**(4), 9–23 (2016)
10. Romeo, F.P.: Investimento affettivo nei processi di insegnamento-apprendimento. Tre criteri per la didattica a distanza nelle emergenze. Open Journal of IUL University **2**(1), 267–279 (2021)
11. Sroufe, L.A.: Lo sviluppo delle emozioni. I primi anni di vita. Milano, Raffaello Cortina (2000)
12. Le Boterf, G.: Costruire le competenze individuali e collettive. Guida, Napoli (2000)
13. Romeo, F.P.: Sollecitare la resilienza. Emergenze educative e strategie didattiche. Trento, Erickson (2020)
14. Mengoni, M., et al.: Evaluation strategies at University for students with Dyslexia: a pilot study supported by face emotion recognition. In: 2021 International Conference on Computational Science and Computational Intelligence (CSCI)
15. Nicholls, M.E.R., Loveless, K.M., Thomas, N.A., Loetscher, T., Churches, O.: Some participants may be better than others: sustained attention and motivation are higher early in semester. Quarterly J. Exp. Psychol. **68**(1), 10–18 (2015)
16. J. Whitehill, Z. Serpell, Y. Lin, A. Foster and J. R. Movellan, The faces of engagement: automatic recognition of student engagement from facial expressions. In: IEEE Transactions on Affective Computing, vol. 5, no. 1, pp. 86–98, 1 January-March 2014. https://doi.org/10.1109/TAFFC.2014.2316163
17. Tyng, C.M., Amin, H.U., Saad, M.N., Malik, A.S.: The influences of emotion on learning and memory. Front. Psychol. **8**, 1454 (2017)
18. Vuilleumier, P.: How brains beware: neural mechanisms of emotional attention. Trends Cogn. Sci. **9**, 585–594 (2005). https://doi.org/10.1016/j.tics.2005.10.011
19. Um, E., Plass, J.L., Hayward, E.O., Homer, B.D.: Emo-tional design in multimedia learning. J. Educ. Psychol. **104**, 485–498 (2012). https://doi.org/10.1037/a0026609
20. Jung, N., Wranke, C., Hamburger, K., Knauff, M.: How emotions affect logical reasoning: evidence from experiments with mood-manipulated participants, spider phobics, and people with exam anxie-ty. Front. Psychol. **5**, 570 (2014). https://doi.org/10.3389/fpsyg.2014.00570
21. Isen, A.M., Daubman, K.A., Nowicki, G.P.: Positive affect facilitates creative problem solving. J. Pers. Soc. Psychol. **52**, 1122–1131 (1987). https://doi.org/10.1037/0022-3514.52.6.1122
22. Ceccacci, S., Generosi, A., Cimini, G., Faggiano, S., Giraldi, L., Mengoni, M.: Facial coding as a mean to enable continuous monitoring of student's behavior in e-Learning. In: CEUR Workshop Proceedings, vol. 2817 (2021)
23. Generosi, A., Ceccacci, S., Mengoni, M.: A deep learning-based system to track and analyze customer behavior in retail store, in 2018 IEEE 8th International Conference on Consumer Electronics-Berlin (ICCE-Berlin) (2018). https://doi.org/10.1109/ICCE-Berlin.2018.8576169
24. Ekman, P., Wallace, V.F.: Manual for the facial action coding system. Consulting Psychologists Press (1978)
25. Generosi, A., Ceccacci, S., Faggiano, S., Giraldi, L., Mengoni, M.: A toolkit for the automatic analysis of human behavior in HCI applications in the wild. Adv. Sci. Technol. Eng. Syst. **5**(6), 185–192 (2020)
26. Beck, J.: Engagement tracing: using response times to model student disengagement. In: Proceedings of International Conference on Artificial Intelligence and Education, pp. 88–95 (2005)
27. Johns, J., Woolf, B.: A dynamic mixture model to detect student motivation and proficiency. In: Proceedings of 21st Nat. Conf. Artif. Intell., pp. 2–8 (2006)

28. Hussain, M., Zhu, W., Zhang, W., Abidi, S.M.R.: Student engagement predictions in an e-learning system and their impact on student course assessment scores. Comput. Intell. Neurosci. (2018). https://doi.org/10.1155/2018/6347186

29. Goldberg, B.S., Sottilare, R.A., Brawner, K.W., Holden, H.K.: Predicting learner engagement during well-defined and Ill-defined computer-based intercultural interactions. In: D'Mello, S., Graesser, A., Schuller, B., Martin, J.-C. (eds.) ACII 2011. LNCS, vol. 6974, pp. 538–547. Springer, Heidelberg (2011). https://doi.org/10.1007/978-3-642-24600-5_57

30. Xiao, X., Wang, J.: Understanding and detecting divided attention in mobile MOOC learning. In: Proceedings of the 2017 CHI Conference on Human Factors in Computing Systems. ACM, pp. 2411–2415 (2017)

31. Kaur, A., Mustafa, A., Mehta, L., Dhall, A.: Prediction and localization of student engagement in the wild. In: 2018 Digital Image Computing: Techniques and Applications (DICTA), Canberra, Australia, pp. 1–8 (2018). https://doi.org/10.1109/DICTA.2018.8615851

32. Whitehill, J., Serpell, Z., Lin, Y., Foster, A., Movellan, J.R.: The faces of engagement: automatic recognition of student engagement from facial expressions. IEEE Trans. Affect. Comput. **5**(1), 86–98 (2014). https://doi.org/10.1109/TAFFC.2014.2316163

33. Hansen, D.W., Ji, Q.: In the eye of the beholder: a survey of models for eyes and gaze. IEEE Trans. Pattern Anal. Mach. Intell. **32**(3), 478–500 (2010). https://doi.org/10.1109/TPAMI.2009.30

34. Sigut, J., Sidha, S.A.: Iris center corneal reflection method for gaze tracking using visible light. IEEE Trans. Biomed. Eng. **58**(2), 411–419 (2010). https://doi.org/10.1109/TBME.2010.2087330

35. Valenti, R., Gevers, T.: Accurate eye center location and tracking using isophote curvature. In: 2008 IEEE Conference on Computer Vision and Pattern Recognition (2008). https://doi.org/10.1109/CVPR.2008.4587529

36. Wu, H., Kitagawa, Y., Wada, T., Kato, T., Chen, Q.: Tracking Iris contour with a 3D eye-model for gaze estimation. In: Yagi, Y., Kang, S.B., Kweon, I.S., Zha, H. (eds.) ACCV 2007. LNCS, vol. 4843, pp. 688–697. Springer, Heidelberg (2007). https://doi.org/10.1007/978-3-540-76386-4_65

37. Zhang, X., Sugano, Y., Fritz, M., Bulling, A.: Appearance-based gaze estimation in the wild. In: Proceedings of the IEEE Conference on Computer Vision and Pattern Recognition (2019)-. https://doi.org/10.1109/CVPR.2015.7299081

38. Krafka, K., et al.: Eye tracking for everyone. In: Proceedings of the IEEE Conference on Computer Vision and Pattern Recognition (2016). https://doi.org/10.1109/CVPR.2016.239

39. Krizhevsky, A., Sutskever, I., Hinton, G.E.: Imagenet classification with deep convolutional neural networks. In: Advances in Neural Information Processing Systems (2012). https://doi.org/10.1145/3065386

40. Ceccacci, S., Generosi, A., Giraldi, L., Mengoni, M.: An emotion recognition system for monitoring shopping experience. In: Proceedings of the 11th PErvasive Technologies Related to Assistive Environments Conference, pp. 102–103, June 2018

41. Talipu, A., Generosi, A., Mengoni, M., Giraldi, L.: Evaluation of deep convolutional neural network architectures for emotion recognition in the wild. In: 2019 IEEE 23rd International Symposium on Consumer Technologies (ISCT), pp. 25–27. IEEE, June 2019

42. Rossi, P.G., Pentucci, M., Fedeli, L., Giannandrea, L., Pennazio, V.: From the informative feedback to the generative feedback. Educ. Sci. Soc.-Open Access **9**(2), 83–107 (2018)

43. Rossi, P.G.: Didattica enattiva. Complessità, teorie dell'azione, professionalità docente: Complessità, teorie dell'azione, professionalità docente. Milano, FrancoAngeli (2011)

A Systematic Mapping
of MathML-Enabled Editors for Users
with Visual Impairment

Luis Naranjo-Zeledón[ID] and Mario Chacón-Rivas[✉][ID]

Instituto Tecnológico de Costa Rica, Cartago, Costa Rica
{lnaranjo,machacon}@itcr.ac.cr

Abstract. The teaching and learning processes in science, technology, engineering and mathematics (STEM) pose challenges that are particularly hard to overcome when some part involved is visually impaired. Despite the fact that these areas tend to be generators of many jobs, people with this disability often prefer to study other careers, in which they do not require intensive use of STEM. This paper presents a systematic mapping of the technologies that have been proposed to solve this problem, usually in the form of editors that allow the inclusion of mathematical symbology. In addition, we introduce EULER (Editor of Universal Learning Resources), a software tool which allows for accessible editing and sharing of learning resources for mathematics in compliance with the standard MathML format, in order to easily exchange information between sighted and visually impaired people. EULER has been designed to allow it for adapting to areas other than mathematics, such as chemistry or physics. The results of this study show that most of the identified proposals have limitations, either regarding the lack of use of the MathML standard or they are not designed to grow towards other areas of STEM aside from mathematics.

Keywords: STEM editor · Mathematics software · Math education for visually impaired people · Math software accessible

1 Introduction

The study, understanding and mastery of mathematics is a necessity and advantage to carry out STEM studies. But also, it is well known that mathematics and related subjects have been seen as difficult and complex, which makes some people prefer to avoid STEM studies.

At the labor level, STEM-based professions have been among the most valued, with higher growth projections, job stability and high income ranges.

However, for some populations the use and mastery of mathematics is related to barriers that go beyond cognitive and intellectual aspects. A clear example of these populations are people with visual disabilities, who in order to carry out

M. Antona and C. Stephanidis (Eds.): HCII 2022, LNCS 13309, pp. 49–61, 2022.
https://doi.org/10.1007/978-3-031-05039-8_4

studies or work based on mathematical tools must solve various difficulties by graphically representing them.

The foregoing has led research groups and academics, interested in the subject of inclusive technologies as well as inclusive education, to work on the study of some conditions and the design of technological proposals that support the elimination or mitigation of some barriers.

In the activities of these groups, an urgent and recurrent task is to know the state of the art of technological developments at an academic level and at an industry level. For this reason, systematic mapping is a highly valuable research support tool.

In this particular work, the results of a systematic mapping study carried out on the subject of mathematical editors for people with visual disabilities are presented. The objective is to provide researchers, developers of inclusive technologies or those interested in the subject with a quantitative overview of the projects or research of inclusive mathematical publishers and specifically aimed at the visually impaired population.

The work presents in Sect. 2 the work methodology summarizing the principles of systematic mapping (Sect. 2.1), the scope of the study and the research questions addressed in the search processes (Sect. 2.2). Then Sect. 2.3 presents a summary of the data obtained from the searches. Section 2.4 summarizes the classification of the results. Section 3 presents the main results of the study. Section 4 summarizes some important findings and the final Sect. 5 presents the conclusions reached by the authors.

2   Methodology

Empirical studies are used more and more frequently due to the possibility of validating the evidence as well as the sources of information, these are based on data collected through observation or systematic searches that allow them to be validated.

These studies also become a valuable tool for decision makers, investors, and researchers, as they allow *quantitative* or *qualitative* results to be seen, depending on the methods used, as well as providing high-value summary information to gain insight into the context of a topic of interest. These studies require less time than the previous ones and are recommended where there is a lack of relevant primary studies of very high quality [2].

In the case of systematic mapping, they are quantitative studies, with a limited scope, based on a systematic or ordered and documented process, which seeks synthesized and integrated results that demonstrate professional practice, mainly in terms of publication frequencies [9].

2.1 Systematic Mapping

A systematic mapping seeks to achieve a summarized vision from a qualitative approach of the publications made on a specific topic, in a range of time and scope. The process is based on the activities enumerated in Fig. 1.

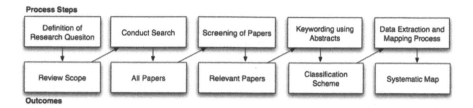

Fig. 1. Systematic mapping process. Source [9]

The systematic mapping activities are composed of (1) definition of the research question(s), (2) conduct of the search, (3) Filtering of papers, (4) analysis of the papers from abstracts and keywords, (5) data extraction and results mapping process. These activities and outcomes are enumerated in the Table 1.

Table 1. Activities and products in systematic mapping.

Activity	Description	Product	Description
Research question	Plan and execute the searchs	All papers	List of source of publication. List of papers returned from the search activity
Conduct research	Define at least one research question	Review Scope, list of filtered papers	Enumerate some characteristics of search scope and results. Sometimes defines some restrictions
Screening of papers	This activity filters some papers	Relevant papers	List of relevant papers that complaint the restrictions in the previous activity
Keywording using abstracts	Review abstracts and classify papers using some keywords defined to the research	Classification scheme	Obtain a classification scheme of papers
Data extraction and mapping process	Extract information about research's interest that will be fundamental for the graphics and summaries	Systematic mapping	All the information returned and classified that will be later graphics

The results are sought to be classified by various criteria, among the most common are authorship, geographic regions of publication, publication sources, publication periods, among others. In the particular case of this study, emphasis is placed on time and geography, authorship and publication sources.

In addition, something unusual academically, is that it is expanded with a section of non-academic findings (Sect. 3.4) in order to locate what products, applications or components for mathematical editing, available either freely or commercially, can be made available on public (not necessarily free) access to the visually impaired population.

2.2   Scope and Detailed Research Questions

The objective of the systematic mapping is to know the amount of research and publications carried out on the subject of mathematical editing tools that support people with visual disabilities.

From the above, the initial research questions were built:

– What research papers on mathematical editors for visually impaired people have been published in the last 15 years?

These questions were addressed by using these search strings:

1. +MathML+editor
2. MathML AND editor AND accessible
3. editor +math AND (blind OR ("visually impaired"))
4. +MathML AND editor AND math AND (blind OR ("visually impaired"))

Concerning source of publications, in the first instance, the ACM, IEEE and Web of Science repositories were identified, which were submitted for consultation to those in charge of the project, who suggested looking for the categories "informatics" or "computing" in the subscribed databases of the TEC, such as part of the electronic resources of its online Library System. Due to this, the decision was made to include EBSCO, ScienceDirect and SpringerLink as repositories to complete the study. In addition, the researcher in charge suggested verifying if any relevant pre-publication was found in Cornell University's arXiv.

Inclusion Criteria. Regarding inclusion criteria, the title and abstract of each article that refers to mathematical editors for people with visual disabilities will be reviewed. This allows us to see in the first instance how the words are related and why the article has been preselected. Additionally, a sample was followed using the snowball technique, in order to identify some primary or complementary publications.

Exclusion Criteria. As exclusion criteria, the information collected in the reading and analysis of the abstract and the conclusions will be used, deepening in the cases that are deemed necessary and a more detailed reading of other parts of the document is needed. With this criterion, it is possible to appreciate with a greater level of detail what each document deals with, to relate it to the objectives sought and decide if it is relevant for this review, moving on to the group of primary studies. All redundant papers were excluded, also papers focused on educational issues of math learning for visually impaired students, but they did not include any technological edition math tools were excluded. Finally, non English or Spanish articles were excluded.

Definition of the Types of Study. The type of studies selected were those closely related to proposals from accessible mathematical editors, whether the development techniques used are made explicit or just the results of the exposed tools are exposed, with their scope and limitations. Also, special interest was placed on those publications that referenced available end products.

2.3 Data Collection

After the application of search strings in the repositories, the results obtained are summarized in the Table 2.

The ongoing process of filtering search strings is evident, as well as the impact, on the results obtained. The table shows the changes in the results obtained according to the search string, it is important for systematic mapping studies that various search strings are analyzed and that changes in the results achieved are also identified.

Table 2. Results obtained by repository.

Repository	Search string	Number of hits
ACM Digital Library	1	7
ACM Digital Library	3	117
ACM Digital Library	4	2
IEEE Xplore Digital Library	2	62
IEEE Xplore Digital Library	4	6
Web of Science	1–4	0
EBSCOhost Web	2	7
EBSCOhost Web	3	1
EBSCOhost Web	4	19
Elsevier ScienceDirect	1	84
Elsevier ScienceDirect	2	64
Elsevier ScienceDirect	3	11
SpringerLink	1	21
SpringerLink	4	3
CoRR de Cornell University	1	2
CoRR de Cornell University	2	3

In most cases larger or more complex search strings tend to filter more information and return fewer strings, but are expected to be more accurate for search purposes.

In addition to these results, searches in Spanish were applied, which returned 2 links to short articles that did not give the study greater relevance.

Then, as a result of the expert criteria of the professors consulted, a refinement of the search strings was carried out using the following:

- intitle: "editor" intitle: "mathematical" +(blind OR ("visually impaired") or disabilities)
- intitle: "editor" "mathematical content" "accessible formats"

This returned the reference to two projects very much aimed at mathematical editing for people with visual disabilities. One of the articles was published in the year 2002 and there are no more appearances of the project. While the second is published in the year 2020 and does present a product in validation stages.

Based on the results achieved (146 articles), the inclusion and exclusion criteria are expanded. Primary sources are reviewed and the need to include some publications was determined due to their relevance to the topic. This process resulted in 90 relevant publications and the inclusion of some publication or reference sources.

2.4   Classification

The process of classifying the results was based primarily on identifying the most relevant publication repositories. The publication repositories in which the most publications were found were ACM Communications and IEEE. In both cases, the articles were not subclassified by societies or chapters, because in both publication sources there are many subclassifications.

Another criterion for classifying the results achieved in the searches was to classify the papers according to their *year of publication*. Presenting a clear concentration of a greater number of publications between the years 2008 to 2014. However, between the years 2016 to 2018, 5 publications are located in each year, as seen in Fig. 2. This is a reflection of a need that cannot be satisfied with the results of previous years.

Finally, the relevance classification criterion is the *country of publication*. This criterion is based on identifying the country of the university that is specified in the affiliation of the authors. In the case of papers with multiple authors and from various countries, the paper is assigned to the identified countries. This criterion shows a publication trend mostly in the USA with 24 papers, France with 7 papers, as well as Canada. Japan places 5 papers, Italy with 4 papers and Germany with 3 papers.

3   Results

The primary study selection procedure involved executing the query in each selected repository, thus obtaining a set of "studies" to which the inclusion criteria were subsequently applied to obtain the "relevant" studies. Finally, the

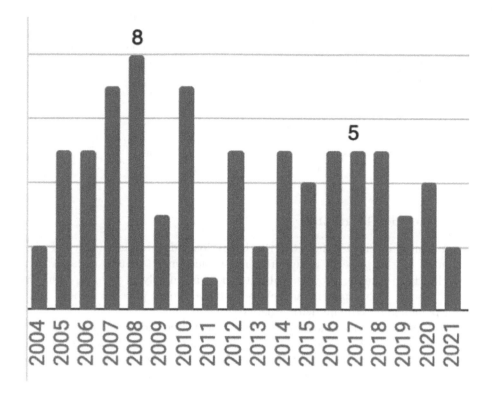

Fig. 2. Publications by year.

exclusion criteria were applied to the relevant studies and thus the "primary" studies were obtained. A refinement stage was carried out on the primary studies in which important studies related to the topic can be identified and, given their importance, were added as primary studies after refinement. In this systematic review, 417 studies have been detected, of which 55 were considered relevant and 19 primary studies have persisted after refinement (Table 3).

In Fig. 3 the topics of published literature classifications are summarized by year. This information is useful to find the years and topics with more publications based on the classifications schemes defined. So, for instance, it is evident that *Education* along with *Editor* predominate throughout the years. These topics show, respectively, a particular research interest during periods 2006–2009 and 2012–2017.

On the other hand, Fig. 4 summarizes the top 7 authors with 3 or more publications related to the main topic of this research. It is very important to mention that there are many authors with 1 or 2 publications, but for simplicity and easily reading of the graphic, they were not included. It is clear that authors Ali Awde and Dominique Archambault, working separately, have dominated the scene from 2005 to 2018.

Table 3. Summary of results obtained by repository.

Repository	Number of hits	Relevant	Primary	Primary after refinement
ACM Digital Library	129	30	11	+1
IEEE Xplore Digital Library	68	11	4	0
Web of Science	0	0	0	0
EBSCOhost Web	35	3	0	0
Elsevier ScienceDirect	159	5	0	0
SpringerLink	24	5	2	0
CoRR de Cornell University	2	1	1	0
Total	417	54	18	1

3.1   Time and Geography

As commented in the classification criteria section, knowing the country of publication or of the projects is relevant in the academy to build collaboration networks. This criterion shows a publication trend mostly in the USA with 24 papers, France with 7 papers, as well as Canada. Japan places 5 papers, Italy with 4 papers and Germany with 3 papers.

Regarding the time periods, defined in years, a considerable publication is presented between 2005 and 2020. The importance of this finding is that it reflects a degree of attention paid in the academy to the development of inclusive technologies for support. teaching mathematics to people with visual disabilities.

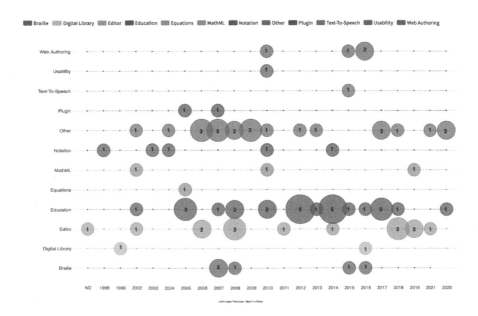

Fig. 3. Topics classification.

Fig. 4. Top 7 authors with 3 or more publications.

3.2   Authorship, Papers and Citations

The trends of the authors are a reflection of lines of research that are carried out from research centers or from postgraduate programs, generally in regions or countries in which research is supported more. Figure 4 shows a trend of authors and is classified by years. The authors that were most located in the search are A Awde with 6 publications, B Stöger with 5 publications and D. Archambault with 6 publications (Fig. 5).

In the classification of the works consulted, based on the type of publication, 49 works published in conferences, 28 journal articles, 7 works published as book chapters and 1 published in a workshop were found.

3.3   Publication Sources

The publication repositories in which the most publications were found were ACM Communications and IEEE. In both cases, the articles were not subclassified by societies or chapters, because in both publication sources there are many subclassifications.

Further detailing the publication sources shows that 31 publications were located in the ACM Digital Library. In IEEE library 17 publications were located. Seven publications were included that were located in ResearchGate as a result of the inclusion and exclusion processes, or also the snowball process. Then in Springer 7 publications were located and in Elsevier 6 papers were located.

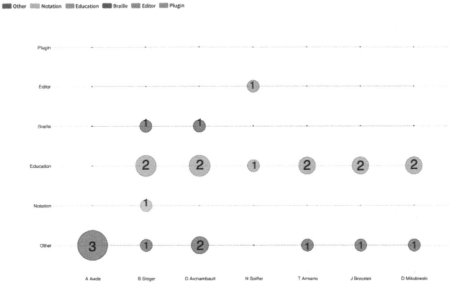

Fig. 5. Top 7 authors and topics.

3.4 Non Academic Applications

In the context of this study, the interest is not only focused on academic publications, else in current available math editor tools.

Aware that many of the investigations and publications are the product of academic projects, that once the researcher manages to finish his doctoral or master's studies, the projects are not implemented for final use by the population, is that in addition to the research and publications, an extension is made to locate what tools are currently available. Although this search cannot generally be carried out in the same publication sources as those used for the investigations.

EDICO is an accessible and inclusive scientific editor, designed to work with the JAWS [3] and braille screen reader, available for the licensed Windows operating system. This editor allows you to write linear expressions and display them in standard format and braille font. It incorporates six default user profiles. It is possible to create custom profiles from the "teacher" profile, hiding symbols or groups of symbols. Its interface is available in Spanish, Catalan, Basque, Galician and English.

Mathtype is a semantic formula editor, formerly known as WIRIS [8]. It has a desktop version for the Windows operating system and can be integrated into Microsoft Word and Google Documents under license. This tool incorporates the use of predefined profiles, based on the PARCC (Partnership for Assessment of Readiness for College and Careers) symbology. It allows you to customize the toolbar to keep the equations and symbols used frequently, it is compatible with MathML presentation and LateX and also incorporates functionalities accessible from the web. The functionalities accessible from the web that are integrated correspond to a "text associated with a formula in the ALT attribute that most closely resembles natural language". It makes no reference to browsing or editing mathematical content in an accessible way. Its interface is available in English, German, French, Chinese and Japanese.

Lambda is a scientific-mathematical editor, available in its desktop version for the Windows operating system and JAWS screen reader under license. It includes the appropriate mathematical symbols for students with a bachelor's degree and for those who are studying for the first years in the university [4]. Lambda allows to write linear expressions, oriented to the input and output of braille. It also allows browsing, contracting or expanding expressions in an accessible way, and incorporates a scientific calculator that allows numerical calculations. It makes no reference to the use of profiles.

InftyEditor was designed to create scientific documents from scanned material; It also allows the editing of mathematical texts using the QWERTY keyboard using LateX commands. In addition, it has a WYSIWYG environment. It allows exporting resources in LateX, MathML and HTML format. It also has an English and Japanese version [13].

MathPlayer is a complement to Microsoft Internet Explorer (IE), visually renders MathML and interprets it. In addition, it has features that allow users to maintain the origin, size and color of their environment with custom settings [10].

MathJax consists of a library for the web that allows viewing mathematical content written in TeX and MathML formats in SVG (Scalable Vector Graphics) format. MathJaX works together with programs such as MathPlayer to convert mathematical expressions into that format for accessible reading with screen readers [5].

MathShare is an accessible math editor that allows high school students to navigate or cancel subexpressions and take notes on the steps he or she is taking. It allows teachers to evaluate student reasoning [10].

Accessible Equation Editor is a mathematical editor that allows the editing and navigation of mathematical text through braille using MathML as an internal format [6]. However, "the expression of mathematics is your biggest problem and we still haven't been able to solve it. Therefore, most of the time what NVDA says is not going to be very helpful. This is because NVDA tries to read MathJax's output and is confused" [1].

EULER consists of an accessible scientific-mathematical tool for people with visual disabilities, of any educational level [7]. It facilitates the reading, exploration, edition, import and export to different formats of mathematical educational resources, through the use of a computer. It supports the teaching-learning process of mathematics in people with visual disabilities, as well as their communication with other people. The tool allows to use user profiles based on the level of mathematical knowledge (primary education, basic secondary education, advanced secondary education and university education). These levels correspond to the symbology used in the PISA tests according to the OECD.

4   Discussion

The systematic mapping study showed that it is common to find research studies on inclusive technologies, but that these come to be applied in daily use is somewhat complex. The products of academic research tend to remain in publications and prototypes, in some cases following a publication culture known as "publish or perish" [11].

For its part, also bringing these prototypes to an end user requires significant efforts in time and resources, as well as platforms and support that goes beyond the scope of academic research. As discussed in [12], the industry is now focused on short-term research, while academia is focused on publishing or focused in many roles: *"teaching, supervising students, seeking research funding, publishing, and more. They are typically conducting research only on a part-time basis. Moreover, their research will depend on the quality of students they attract. And even so, many of today's Ph.D. students who plan to work in industry are not focused on long-term research but on product development and even marketing."*

In the Latin American context, it is less common to see investment in inclusive projects with a focus on continuity, due to budget limitations and few collaborative work networks. This shows a clear opportunity for improvement for the academy and research centers.

5   Conclusions

Systematic mapping studies return quantitative information that is highly supportive of research. They are studies that are used to locate the state of the art of a specific topic or technology. However, one of the attentions that must be taken is in the construction of the search strings and, in addition, it must have the flexibility that may be necessary to refine the search processes.

Another important element in this type of study is to identify and document the information classification criteria. These criteria are the shortcuts for readers or researchers who are interested in this type of study. In our case, it was very important to locate information on the publication sources, years and main authors, since this will allow us to monitor projects.

In the case of the particular interest of the authors, our study extends to locating editing tools that are in use by the target population. This also allows you to see features and functionality beyond the research results. In our case, it is important to locate similarities and differences in the available technologies, to also identify possible improvements.

Acknowledgements. The authors thank the Inclutec team, from the Technological Institute of Costa Rica for the support in the research and development of the projects. Special thanks to Ing. Verónica Mora Lezcano, Mr. Tribet Rivas for the development support of the EULER editor.

References

1. http://accessibility.pearson.com/aee/faq.html
2. Brereton, P., Kitchenham, B., Budgen, D., Turner, M., Khalil, M.: Lessons from applying the systematic literature review process within the software engineering domain. J. Syst. Softw. **80**, 571–583 (2007). www.sciencedirect.com
3. Carenas, J.M., Cabra, A.B., García, M.G.M., Gea, P.C., Hernández, D.H.: Edico. Integración: Revista sobre ceguera y deficiencia visual (72), 100–108 (2018)
4. Carenas, J.M., del Campo, J.E.F.: El editor lambda para matemáticas. Integración: Revista sobre ceguera y deficiencia visual (59), 5 (2011)
5. Cervone, D.: Mathjax: a platform for mathematics on the web. Notices AMS **59**(2), 312–316 (2012)
6. Dooley, S.S., Park, S.H.: Generating nemeth braille output sequences from content mathml markup (2016)
7. Estrella, P., Bruno, L., Perassi, M.L., Garda, M.P., Mora-Lezcano, V., Chacon-Rivas, M.: Software localization: The case of the euler editor. In: 2019 XIV Latin American Conference on Learning Technologies (LACLO), pp. 1–7. IEEE, October 2019. https://doi.org/10.1109/LACLO49268.2019.00011, https://ieeexplore.ieee.org/document/8994990/
8. Marquès, D., Eixarch, R., Casanellas, G., Martínez, B., Smith, T.J.: Wiris om tools: a semantic formula editor (2006)
9. Petersen, K., Feldt, R., Mujtaba, S., Mattsson, M.: Systematic mapping studies in software engineering, June 2008. https://doi.org/10.14236/ewic/EASE2008.8. https://scienceopen.com/document?vid=6d552894-2cc3-4e2b-a483-41fa48a37ef8
10. Soiffer, N.: Mathplayer: web-based math accessibility. In: ACM SIGACCESS Conference on Assistive Technologies: Proceedings of the 7th International ACM SIGACCESS Conference on Computers and Accessibility, vol. 9, pp. 204–205 (2005)
11. Toh, C.: The culture of 'publish or perish' is hurting research - ieee - the institute, March 2018. http://theinstitute.ieee.org/ieee-roundup/blogs/blog/the-culture-of-publish-or-perish-is-hurting-research
12. Toh, C.: The state of research: Where are we headed? - ieee - the institute, February 2018. http://theinstitute.ieee.org/ieee-roundup/blogs/blog/the-state-of-research-where-are-we-headed
13. Yamaguchi, K., Komada, T., Kawane, F., Suzuki, M.: New features in math accessibility with infty software. In: Miesenberger, K., Klaus, J., Zagler, W., Karshmer, A. (eds.) ICCHP 2008. LNCS, vol. 5105, pp. 892–899. Springer, Heidelberg (2008). https://doi.org/10.1007/978-3-540-70540-6_134

Helping Students with Motor Impairments Program via Voice-Enabled Block-Based Programming

Obianuju Okafor$^{(\boxtimes)}$ (ID) and Stephanie Ludi (ID)

University of North Texas, Denton, TX 76205, USA
{obianujuokafor,stephanie.ludi}@unt.edu

Abstract. Existing programming environments pose a challenge for students with upper-body motor impairments. This is because these environments require a level of dexterity that these students do not possess. For example, text-based programming environments require a lot of typing using a keyboard, while block-based programming environments require the use of a pointing device to drag and drop blocks of code. In our research, we aim to make the block-based programming environment Blockly, accessible to students with upper-body motor impairment, by adding speech as an alternative form of input. This voice-enabled version of Blockly will reduce the need for the use of a mouse or keyboard, hence making it more accessible. Our system consists of the original Blockly application, a speech recognition API, predefined voice commands, and a custom function. A preliminary study has been conducted. The results are encouraging, but they also revealed the need to broaden the target population, which was originally people with cerebral palsy, to people with any type of upper-body motor disability. Additionally, the study showed the need to redesign some voice commands. A prototype of the system has been implemented. As a next step, two additional studies will be conducted using this prototype, a usability study, and an A/B test.

Keywords: Accessibility · Block-based programming · CS education · Speech recognition

1 Introduction

Students with upper body motor impairments (UBMI) such as cerebral palsy, muscular dystrophy, multiple sclerosis, etc., often suffer from paralysis, muscle weakness, and poor coordination [19]. This makes performing actions like typing on a keyboard, or dragging and dropping objects using a mouse, quite hard [29]. These challenges are more apparent in environments such as schools, particularly in hands-on classes, where such actions are frequently performed. An example of such classes is the introductory programming classes, which are

M. Antona and C. Stephanidis (Eds.): HCII 2022, LNCS 13309, pp. 62–77, 2022.
https://doi.org/10.1007/978-3-031-05039-8_5

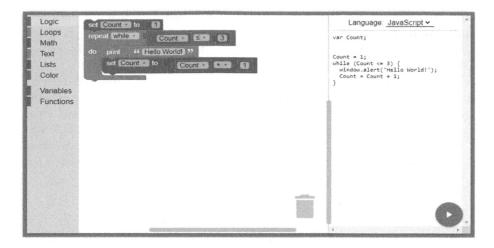

Fig. 1. User interface of the BBPE blockly

being incorporated into the curriculum across the United States as part of the **"Computer Science for All"** initiative [4,10,26]. In these classes, students are taught programming concepts and computational thinking using different programming tools [2,3,5]. Sadly, a lot of these programming tools are inaccessible to students having UBMI as they rely heavily on the use of a mouse or keyboard.

A particular set of programming tools that pose a challenge are block-based programming environments (BBPE) such as MIT's Scratch[1] or Google's Blockly[2]. In BBPEs, programs are created by dragging and dropping code blocks using a mouse or keyboard (see Fig. 1). Due to their highly engaging nature and simplicity, BBPEs are often used in curricula to teach children how to program [2,13,24,25]. However, their reliance on the physical controlling of a pointing device poses a barrier for students with UBMI. This limitation excludes a significant portion of students from participating in activities in classrooms that may allow them to explore career paths in computing.

This research addresses the obstacles that students with UBMI face in the BBPE Blockly, and seeks to come up with an effective solution. In our approach, we explore speech as an alternative input modality to increase Blockly's accessibility to students with UBMI. With the rise in the use of conversational agents, like Amazon's Alexa[3] and Apple's Siri[4], speech is rapidly becoming a popular way of interacting with computers or digital devices, even for people with motor disabilities [6,11,12,16]. This could be attributed to its convenience and speed in sending and receiving information. For these reasons,

---

[1] https://scratch.mit.edu/.
[2] https://developers.google.com/blockly/.
[3] https://developer.amazon.com/en-US/alexa.
[4] https://www.apple.com/siri/.

we see speech as a possible method to alleviate the challenges that students with UBMI face in BBPEs. The goal here is not to replace the mouse or keyboard as a form of input in Blockly, but to provide an alternative for those who cannot use the mouse or keyboard.

In our system, we incorporate a speech recognition API into the Blockly application. To confirm the feasibility of the voice-based system, we conducted a preliminary study. The study yielded promising results, it also exposed areas for growth. We go into details about this preliminary study in Sect. 4. Based on the feedback from the preliminary study, we have created a prototype of the proposed system, which we present in this paper. We aim to evaluate the prototype through 2 additional studies.

The main contributions of this paper are:

1. The system design of the novel voice-enabled Blockly system
2. A guide on how to incorporate speech recognition into an existing application
3. Design considerations for future voice-based systems based on analyses of user feedback.

The rest of the document is structured as follows. In Sect. 2, we talk about the works that relate to our research. In the 3rd section, we give an overview of our system. In Sect. 4, we present the experimental setup and findings of the preliminary study we conducted. In the last section, we conclude and discuss the next steps.

2   Related Work

We found several research studies relating to how speech can be used to assist people with motor challenges when interacting with computer applications and devices, and when programming.

A popular use of speech for people with motor impairments is for mouse cursor control. A lot of people with UBMI face difficulty when moving a mouse cursor or performing a variety of other continuous control tasks. Speech was considered as a possible workaround to circumvent these challenges. Dai et al. [6,18] present a speech-controlled grid-based cursor control mechanism. This mechanism was created to address the inadequacy of existing cursor control solutions, as they were found to be both slow and error prone. They evaluated two 3×3 grid-based variations of their system. One provided a single cursor in the middle of the grid, the other allows users to select a target using any of the nine cursors. They found out that the nine-cursor solution outperformed the one-cursor solution in terms of speed. Overall, both grid-based solutions performed better than other speech-based cursor control solutions.

Similarly in [11], to combat the challenges people with motor impairment face when moving a mouse cursor or performing other continuous control tasks, the authors present a system called the Vocal Joystick. This system allows users to continuously control the mouse cursor using verbal and nonverbal vocalizations, along with varying vocal characteristics such as vowel quality, loudness, and pitch. The results of the two studies they conducted showed that Vocal Joystick performed as optimally as conventional hand-operated joysticks. The findings also showed that it can be used by people without extensive training, and that it could be an alternative to existing speech-based cursor control methods.

Speech is not only useful for cursor control, but also for text entry. In [20] Vertanen et Mckay presented a speech-based text entry system called Speech Dasher. In this system, first, users speak what they want to write and then through zooming, they navigate through the space of recognition hypotheses to correct any errors. Speech Dasher's model uses a combination of information from a speech recognizer, the user, and a letter-based language model. The formative user study that was conducted with Speech Dasher revealed that expert users were able to write 40 words per minute (wpm), and they were able to do this in spite of a recognition word error rate of 22%. This confirmed that Speech Dasher successfully utilizes information from speech recognition to greatly improve users' writing efficiency.

The use of speech for cursor control and text entry makes it particularly useful in programming environments. The authors in [17] synthesized the results of a Wizard of Oz based design process to develop VocalIDE. VocalIDE is a voice-based programming environment prototype that allows people with limited dexterity to write and edit code using a set of vocal commands. They evaluated the usefulness of VocalIDE with 8 participants who have upper limb motor impairments. Their results showed that VocalIDE improved the participants' ability to make navigational edits and select text while programming.

Desilets et al. [8], created several voice-based programming tools, one of which is VoiceCode. VoiceCode was proposed as a solution for people suffering from Repetitive Strain Injury (RSI). This tool allows developers to use naturally spoken syntax to write, navigate, and modify code. The naturally spoken commands get converted to actual code in real-time. The system was found to be useful, but it could not be effectively used to teach programming to novices or students with visual impairment. VoiceGrip is the other tool created by Désilets et al. [7]. Akin to VoiceCode, VoiceGrip enables programmers to dictate code using an easy-to-utter pseudocode, which is automatically translated to native code in the appropriate programming language. Voicegrip was created to address some of the usability problems associated with programming by voice.

The research most similar to ours is the one by Wagner et al. [21–23]. In their work, they address the challenges people with UBMI face in the BBPE Scratch. They created a voice-driven Java tool called Myna, that enables programming by voice within Scratch. This tool processes voice commands from users, interprets those commands according to a preset grammar, and simulates the synonymous actions of a mouse and keyboard within Scratch. In contrast, in our project, the block-based platform we added speech input to is Blockly, not Scratch. Also, we added speech as one of Blockly's input modalities and not as a stand-alone tool as in the case of Myna. The rationale behind this is that this will make the user experience more seamless, and will leave room for collaboration among children with and without dexterity skills. Additionally, Myna was not evaluated by enough users, we plan to conduct 2 user studies on the voice-enabled Blockly prototype using a larger number of participants.

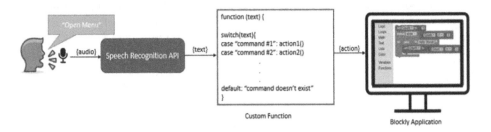

Fig. 2. System overview

3   System Overview

Our system is a voice-enabled version of the Blockly application. Originally, in Blockly, the primary form of input is a mouse or keyboard. We added speech as an additional input modality for people with UBMI. An overview of the system can be seen in Fig. 2.

The system comprises four major components; the Blockly application, speech recognition API (SRAPI), voice commands, and a custom function. These components will interact in the following way: The speech recognition API receives speech input through the device's microphone. The audio input is processed and converted to text. The generated text is sent to the custom function. The custom function checks through all switch statement cases to see if there is a voice command that matches the text. If there is a match, the action associated with that voice command is executed, which triggers a change to Blockly's user interface. We go into more details about each component in the subsections below.

3.1   Blockly Application

Blockly is a browser-based block-based programming environment (see Fig. 1). In Blockly, programs are created by dragging and dropping blocks of code using a mouse or keyboard, onto a workspace. These code blocks represent programming constructs, e.g., loops, conditional statements, variables, etc. The constructed program can be translated into code text by the Blockly application. The programming languages supported include Javascript, Python, PHP, Dart, Lua.

Blockly's source code was made available online via GitHub[5], hence the code used in this research project was downloaded from Blockly's GitHub repository.

---

[5] https://github.com/google/blockly.

Most of the functions in the original code were executed based on mouse clicks or keyboard presses. The code was modified so that the same set of functions can be executed using speech.

```
 1  window.SpeechRecognition = window.webkitSpeechRecognition
 2                             || window.SpeechRecognition;
 3  let recognition = new window.SpeechRecognition();
 4  recognition.lang = "en-US";
 5
 6
 7  recognition.onresult = function (event) {
 8  const transcript = event.results[event.results.length - 1][0]
 9                            .transcript
10                            .toLowerCase()
11                            .trim();
12
13      custom_function(transcript);
14  };
15
16  recognition.start();
```

Fig. 3. Code showing how the speech recognition API was integrated with Blockly

3.2   Speech Recognition API

Speech recognition API (SRAPI) is a robust prebuilt library that records speech in real-time, converts it to text, and returns the text. There are several state-of-the-art SRAPIs that exist, such as CMU Sphinx[6], Google Cloud Speech API[7], and Dragon Speech[8]. The SRAPI we chose was Web speech API[9], reasons being that it is JavaScript-based like Blockly, open-sourced, and compatible with most web browsers. This API was also used in several researches [14,17].

Web Speech API was integrated with the Blockly application by adding a few lines of code to Blockly's source code. Figure 3 is a code excerpt showing how Web speech API is integrated into the Blockly application. Lines 1–4 show how it is initialized. Lines 7–14 show the function that processes speech input, converts it to text, and sends the text to the custom function. Line 15 shows how speech recognition is started.

---

[6] https://cmusphinx.github.io/.
[7] https://cloud.google.com/speech-to-text.
[8] https://www.nuance.com/dragon/for-developers/dragon-software-developer-kit.html.
[9] https://developer.mozilla.org/en-US/docs/Web/API/Web_Speech_API.

3.3 Voice Commands

The voice commands in our system are limited and predefined. This helps prevent any ambiguity associated with more verbose speech recognition systems. Each voice command has an action that they trigger. These actions, when triggered, simulate different keyboard or mouse actions, e.g., selecting, dropping, etc. Table 1 shows all the commands in this system and their function in different modes.

These voice commands can be broken down into 5 categories:

1. Navigation Commands: These are the commands used to move through menus, drop-down menus, and in between a stack of blocks on the workspace. Using these commands, a user is able to control and move the cursor from one point to another. This set of commands are similar to the WASD keyboard shortcuts. Some examples include: *"up"*, *"down"*, *"in"*, *"out"*.
2. Placement Commands: These commands are used to select blocks on the menu and place them on the workspace. They can also be used to remove blocks from the workspace. These commands are synonymous with dragging and dropping blocks using a mouse or keyboard. Some examples include: *"select"*, *"delete"*.
3. Control Commands: These set of commands are responsible for controlling elements in the interface, such as opening and closing menus. Some examples include: *"menu"*, *"close"*.
4. Edit Commands: These commands are used to edit a block's comment or their text value. It can also be used to change the option selected from the dropdown menu. Some examples include: *"edit field"*, *"save"*.
5. Mode Commands: These commands are used to switch between the 3 modes in our system. The modes are navigation mode, connect mode, and edit mode. The default mode is **navigation mode**. In this mode, the user can move the cursor around using the navigation commands. In the **connection mode**, a user can connect blocks together on the workspace. To make edits using the edit commands, the user will enter **edit mode**. They include: *"connect"*, *"edit"*, *"escape"*.

3.4 Custom Function

Originally in Blockly, actions are performed using a mouse or keyboard. To perform actions in Blockly using speech, we created a function that maps voice commands to actions. This function entails a switch statement [28]. In the switch statement, each case is a voice command. Each voice command is paired with a corresponding action function to be executed. For instance, the voice command *'delete'* is paired with the block deletion function.

This custom function takes as input the text generated by the speech recognition API (see Fig 3). This text is compared to all cases in the switch statement to determine what action to perform. If there is a match, the action associated with that command is executed. If there is no match, no action is performed, also, the message "command doesn't exist" is displayed to the user in the console.

Table 1. Voice commands and their function in the different modes

Command	Navigation mode	Connection mode	Edit mode
Menu	Go to first item on menu	–	–
Up	Move up to the previous item on the menu or to the previous block on the workspace	Move to the previous connection point	–
Down	Move down to the next item on the menu or to the next block on the workspace	Move to the next connection point	–
In	Move into the inner menu or move from an outer block (parent) to an inner block (child)	Move to the next connection point	–
Out	Come out of the inner menu or move from an inner block (child) to an outter block (parent)	Move to the previous connection point	–
Inline	Move to a block on the same line as the block you are currently on	-	–
Select	Select a block on the menu	Select a connection point	Select an option in a drop down menu
Connect	Switch to connection mode where you can connect blocks together	–	–
Edit	Switch to edit mode where you can make changes to text fields or dropdown menus	–	–
Edit field	–	–	Edit selected text field or dropdown menu
Escape	–	Switch back to navigation mode	Switch back to navigation mode
Add comment	Create a comment for selected block	–	–
Save	–	–	Save new text field input or new comment text
Delete	Delete selected block from the workspace	–	–
Undo	Undo last action	–	–
1–9	Quick jump to menu category according to their position	–	–
First	Jump to first block in the workspace	–	–
Last	Jump to last block in the workspace	–	–

Table 2. Participant information

Participant ID	Age	Gender	Assistive technology used
P1	40	Male	ECO2 augmentative communication device
P2	68	Female	None
P3	68	Female	None
P4	34	Male	None
P5	66	Female	None

4 Preliminary Study

Before implementing the system, we conducted a preliminary study. The study aimed to confirm the feasibility of the use of voice as an input modality, particularly for people with cerebral palsy who were our target audience at the time, as they are known to sometimes have speech impediments [9,15]. The study also helped us to test the appropriateness of our voice commands. To achieve our research goals, we recruited participants with cerebral palsy to read out commands to the selected speech recognition API, Web Speech API.

4.1 Participants

6 people with cerebral palsy agreed to participate in the study, however, on the day of the study, only 5 of them participated. The participants comprised of 3 females and 2 males. The average age was 55.2 years (SD = 14.99). We got in contact with them through a nonprofit organization called Ability Connection [1], which they were members of. This organization caters to people with intellectual or developmental disabilities. Table 2 shows information about the participants.

4.2 Experimental Procedure

The study was conducted in person in a vacant room at the Ability Connection facility. In the experiment, the participants voiced 10 commands to the demo interface of the speech recognition API, Web Speech API. They interacted with this system via a demo interface[10] which was made available online by Google. Figure 4 shows a screenshot of this interface. Each participant was met individually. Each session lasted about 30–45 min. At the end of the study session, each participant was given a $20 Amazon gift card.

At the start of each session, introductions were made and the participant was asked to choose an alias they would like to be addressed as. The participants were all excited about this and often chose the name of a character from their favorite movie or show. Next, the task to be performed during the study was

---

[10] https://www.google.com/intl/en/chrome/demos/speech.html.

described. It was also made known to each participant that they can pause or stop at any time if the task becomes too cumbersome for them. Most of the participants did not own a laptop, so we used one of our laptops for the study.

To start the experiment, the participant was handed a list of 10 commands (see the first column of Table 4) and then asked to read each one out to the speech recognition interface which was opened up in a browser on the laptop. For each command, they had 3 attempts. The participants were observed as they read each command. For each command, the participants were given a score according to how well the system is able to recognize the command.

Fig. 4. Demo interface of web speech API

At the end of the study, the participant was given a survey. The survey had a total of 10 questions. Some of the questions include; age, assistive technology (if any), their overall experience while using this speech recognition system, the difficulty of pronouncing each command, what commands they liked, what commands they disliked, what they would like to change, etc. As most of them could not type or write, they were asked each question and their responses were written down. Table 4 shows a summary of some of the survey responses.

4.3 Result

In this section, we present the results of the study. We break the results down into two sections, the performance of the speech recognition system and the responses from the survey.

Speech Recognition System Performance. Word error rate (WER) and word accuracy (WAcc) are common metrics used to rate the performance of a speech recognition system [27]. In this study, we would be using WAcc. The

WAcc score represents how well the system is able to recognize each command the participant vocalized. Table 3 shows the WAcc per command for each participant. The WAcc for each command is added to form a total WAcc. There were 10 commands in the task, each command weighed 1 point, therefore, the maximum total WAcc a participant could have was 10. The higher the WAcc score, the better the performance.

We calculated the WAcc as follows: for each command, the system was able to recognize completely, 1 point was awarded, else points were deducted accordingly. For each attempt failed, extra points were deducted. You can see the formula for WAcc below:

$$WAcc = 1 - WER$$
$$WER = \frac{U + I}{N} + F(0.1)$$

where:

N: number of words in a command
U: number of undetected words in a command
I: number of incorrect words in the command
F: number of failed attempts

Table 3. Participant WAcc score per command

PID	Command #										
	1	2	3	4	5	6	7	8	9	10	Total WAcc
P1	1	1	0.8	0.9	1	1	0.9	0.9	1	1	9.5
P2	1	1	1	1	1	1	1	0.9	1	1	9.9
P3	1	0.6	1	1	0.9	0.6	0.8	0.7	0.6	0.3	7.5
P4	0	0	0.7	0	0	0	0.6	0	0	0	1.3
P5	0.9	0.8	0.3	0.7	0.9	0.9	0.6	0	0.3	0	5.4

The mean score for WAcc was 6.66 (SD = 3.5). The maximum total WAcc score of 9.9 was by P2, who had no speech impediment at all, so the speech recognition system could understand her perfectly. She also took the least time to complete tasks. The second highest total WAcc score was by P1. He scored a 9.5. He could not speak, but he used an ECO2 Augmentative Communication device to vocalize the 10 commands. His session took the longest as he had to type each command. Due to his limited dexterity, he sometimes hit the wrong key and had to erase the entire text and type it again. However, out of all participants, he was the only one who had some programming experience.

Occasionally, the system failed to detect speech and this affected the WAcc of P3 and P5 who had a total WAcc of 7.7 and 5.4, respectively. They both spoke coherently, however, they had a peculiar accent which sometimes made it hard for the speech recognition system to detect their speech. A lot of times they had to repeat a command multiple times. Additionally, P5 spoke in a low voice. For the system to detect her voice, she was told to speak more loudly, however, there was a limit to how loud she could speak. This further exacerbated her score, giving her the second to the lowest total WAcc score.

Additionally, the system performed poorly when the user's speech was slurred, due to this, P4 had the lowest cumulative WAcc of 1.3. The system was only able to partially recognize 2 out of the 10 commands he pronounced. Although the system was not able to detect his speech, he was still comprehensible. He gave a great suggestion which we will discuss in the next section.

Table 4. Total number of likes, dislikes, and average difficulty rating of each command

Command	No. of likes	No. of dislikes	Average difficulty rating (1–5)
1. Move Up	3	1	1.5
2. Move Down	2	0	2
3. Move In	1	1	1.75
4. Move Out	0	0	1.25
5. Open Menu	2	0	2
6. Close Menu	0	2	2.25
7. Select Block	1	1	2
8. Select First Block	1	3	3
9. Delete Block	0	1	2.75
10. Edit Mode	2	2	2

Survey Responses. We present a summary of some of the survey responses. Table 4 shows the total number of likes and dislikes each command received, as well as its average difficulty rating.

According to the survey responses, 60% rated their experience using the speech recognition system as positive. The rest of the participants rated their experience as average. Some reported that they enjoyed interacting with the speech recognition system and even stated they would like to do it again.

When asked what command they liked, over half of the participants stated that they liked the first command *"move up"*. This could be because it was the first command on the list. The second most liked command were these three commands; *"move down"*, *"open menu"* and *"edit mode"*. In particular, P3 said she liked the sound of *"edit mode"*, and she giggled whenever she said it. In contrast, the most disliked command was the command *"select first block"*. It was also rated as the most difficult to pronounce. Based on observation, this was also the command that most participants struggled to pronounce. Perhaps this could be attributed to the fact that it was the lengthiest. The second most difficult command to pronounce according to the ratings was *"delete block"*.

When asked to give comments or suggestions on how to improve, P4 gave a great suggestion. He suggested that some of the commands should be shortened to enable people with speech impediments to pronounce them more easily. For instance, *"move up"* could be changed to *"up"*, *"select block"* to *"select"*, and *"select first block"* to *"select first"* or *"first"*. This suggestion was insightful, as based on observation, the longer the command, the harder it was for the participants to pronounce, and the harder it was for the system to recognize what the participant was saying. P2 also gave the same suggestion as P4.

4.4   Discussion

The results are promising, 80% of participants had an above-average performance (mean WAcc = 6.66), of which one of the participants used an assistive device to vocalize code. Some of the participants would have had a higher score, if not for glitches on the part of the speech recognition system. The participants who performed well above average without any assistance had little to no speech impairment. Their ability to voice commands implies that potentially they could use voice to write programs in the block-based programming environment Blockly. The participants' positive reaction to using the speech recognition system also reinforces this notion.

Although the results are encouraging, it revealed that not all people with cerebral palsy can use a speech recognition system. In particular, people with speech impediments struggled when enunciating commands to the system. They struggled even more when the command was lengthy or the words in the command were polysyllabic. For instance, the command *"select first block"* which was the longest command in the experiment, proved difficult for all participants except one. When a command is difficult to pronounce, it ends up being mispronounced or slurred, which makes it harder for the system to decipher what is being said. Additionally, the system also had problems detecting speech in low voices and atypical accents.

Some workarounds have to be implemented to overcome some of these barriers to adoption posed by the speech recognition system. An adjustment could be the use of a noise-canceling headset with a microphone when interacting with the system. This will help to reduce noise and increase the volume of the user's voice, which could improve the system's accuracy when capturing speech. Another hack would be having each user train the speech recognition system with their voice before they start using it. That way, the system is accustomed to the way the user will pronounce different words. Windows and IOS devices do something similar, where they have a user repeat several phrases when setting up speech recognition on their device. A more general solution would be training the system on different types of accents; that way it is robust enough to handle the different ways people pronounce different words.

Based on the findings, we decided to make some changes to our research project. The biggest modification to be made lies in the expansion of the target population of this tool. The new population is no longer limited to students with cerebral palsy, but it is open to any student with a UBMI. This is because there is a significant portion of people with cerebral palsy who cannot speak and cannot benefit from this application. Therefore, there is a need to broaden the target population to enable more people to benefit from this application. The qualifying condition for any user of the system will be that they have a UBMI and they do not have a heavy speech impediment.

Another change we made based on the feedback received, was to reform some of the voice commands. We reduced the number of words in the commands to one or at most two. This will make it easier for people with speech impairments to pronounce, it will also reduce the time spent when performing tasks. We also made sure that each command was distinct enough to enable the speech recognition system to recognize it easily. Some examples of commands that were changed include:

- Move Up → Up
- Move Out → Out
- Select Block → Select
- Delete Block → Delete

5   Conclusion

In this paper, we present our research problem which entails the challenges that students with UBMI face in block-based programming environments such as Blocky. As a solution, we propose the use of speech as an alternative form of input in the Blockly platform. In our approach, we integrated a speech recognition API into the Blockly environment.

To confirm the feasibility of a voice-based system, we have conducted a preliminary study. Although the findings from the study are auspicious, they revealed areas of improvement such as the expansion of our intended users and the modification of some voice commands. These issues when addressed, could significantly enhance the overall outcome of this research project. We took the findings from the preliminary study into account as we implemented the prototype of the system.

As a future work, this prototype will be tested on our target population through a usability study. Based on the findings from the usability study, we will make the necessary updates and finalize the implementation of the end system. Finally, this system will be evaluated alongside the original Blockly system in an A/B test.

References

1. Ability connection. https://abilityconnection.org/. Accessed 13 Jan 2022
2. Hour of Code: Hour of code activities. https://hourofcode.com/us/learn
3. Code.org: Projects. https://studio.code.org/projects/public
4. CSforALL: About csforall—csforall. https://www.csforall.org/about/. Accessed 13 Jan 2022
5. CSforALL: Curriculum directory. https://www.csforall.org/projects_and_programs/curriculum_directory/. Accessed 13 Jan 2022
6. Dai, L., Goldman, R., Sears, A., Lozier, J.: Speech-based cursor control: a study of grid-based solutions, pp. 94–101, January 2004. https://doi.org/10.1145/1028630.1028648
7. Desilets, A.: Voicegrip: a tool for programming-by-voice. Int. J. Speech Technol. **4**, June 2001. https://doi.org/10.1023/A:1011323308477
8. Desilets, A., Fox, D., Norton, S.: Voicecode: an innovative speech interface for programming-by-voice, pp. 239–242, April 2006. https://doi.org/10.1145/1125451.1125502
9. Centers for Disease Control, Prevention: What is cerebral palsy? https://www.cdc.gov/ncbddd/cp/facts.html. Accessed 13 Jan 2022
10. The New York City Department of Education: Computer science for all. https://sites.google.com/strongschools.nyc/cs4all/
11. Harada, S., Landay, J.A., Malkin, J., Li, X., Bilmes, J.A.: The vocal joystick: evaluation of voice-based cursor control techniques. In: Proceedings of the 8th International ACM SIGACCESS Conference on Computers and Accessibility, Assets 2006, pp. 197–204. Association for Computing Machinery, New York (2006). https://doi.org/10.1145/1168987.1169021
12. Harada, S., Wobbrock, J., Landay, J.: Voicedraw: a hands-free voice-driven drawing application for people with motor impairments, pp. 27–34, January 2007. https://doi.org/10.1145/1296843.1296850
13. Humble, N.: Developing computational thinking skills in k-12 education through block programming tools. In: ICERI2019 Proceedings, pp. 4865–4873. 12th annual International Conference of Education, Research and Innovation, IATED, 11–13 November, 2019. https://doi.org/10.21125/iceri.2019.1190
14. Lin, P., Van Brummelen, J., Lukin, G., Williams, R., Breazeal, C.: Zhorai: designing a conversational agent for children to explore machine learning concepts. Proceedings of the AAAI Conference on Artificial Intelligence 34, pp. 13381–13388, April 2020. https://doi.org/10.1609/aaai.v34i09.7061
15. National Institute of Neurological Disorders, Stroke: Cerebral palsy: Hope through research. https://www.ninds.nih.gov/Disorders/Patient-Caregiver-Education/Hope-Through-Research/Cerebral-Palsy-Hope-Through-Research. Accessed 13 Jan 2022
16. Oviatt, S.: Multimodal interactive maps: designing for human performance. Hum.-Comput. Interact. **12**(1), 93–129 (1997). https://doi.org/10.1207/s15327051hci1201
17. Rosenblatt, L., Carrington, P., Hara, K., Bigham, J.: Vocal programming for people with upper-body motor impairments, pp. 1–10, April 2018. https://doi.org/10.1145/3192714.3192821
18. Sears, A., Lin, M., Karimullah, A.S.: Speech-based cursor control: understanding the effects of target size, cursor speed, and command selection 2, pp. 30–43 (2002). https://doi.org/10.1007/s10209-002-0034-6

19. Society, I.N.: Motor impairment, April 2012. https://www.neuromodulation.com/motor-impairment. Accessed 12 Jan 2022
20. Vertanen, K., MacKay, D.: Speech dasher: fast writing using speech and gaze. In: CHI (2010)
21. Wagner, A., Gray, J.: An empirical evaluation of a vocal user interface for programming by voice. Int. J. Inf. Technol. Syst. Approach **8**, 47–63 (2015). https://doi.org/10.4018/IJITSA.2015070104
22. Wagner, A., Gray, J.: An Empirical Evaluation of a Vocal User Interface for Programming by Voice, January 2017. https://doi.org/10.4018/978-1-5225-1759-7.ch012
23. Wagner, A., Rudraraju, R., Datla, S., Banerjee, A., Sudame, M., Gray, J.: Programming by voice: a hands-free approach for motorically challenged children, May 2012. https://doi.org/10.1145/2212776.2223757
24. Weintrop, D.: Block-based programming in computer science education. Commun. ACM **62**(8), 22–25 (2019)
25. Weintrop, D., Wilensky, U.: To block or not to block, that is the question: Students' perceptions of blocks-based programming. In: Proceedings of the 14th International Conference on Interaction Design and Children, IDC 2015, pp. 199–208. Association for Computing Machinery, New York (2015). https://doi.org/10.1145/2771839.2771860
26. Whitehouse.gov: Computer science for all. https://obamawhitehouse.archives.gov/blog/2016/01/30/computer-science-all
27. Wikipedia Contributors: Word error rate - Wikipedia, the free encyclopedia (2020). https://en.wikipedia.org/wiki/Word_error_rate. Accessed 10 Feb 2022
28. Wikipedia contributors: Switch statement – Wikipedia, the free encyclopedia (2021). https://en.wikipedia.org/w/index.php?title=Switch_statement&oldid=1062689945. Accessed 14 Feb 2022)
29. Williamson, J.: What i've learned about motor impairment, June 2017. http://simpleprimate.com/blog/motor. Accessed 12 Jan 2022

The Impact of Accessing Mechanisms for Group Collaboration for Students in Higher Education

Eric Owusu[1](✉) and Brittani S. Washington[2]

[1] Department of Computing Sciences, SUNY Brockport, 350 New Campus Drive, Brockport, NY 14420, USA
eowusu@brockport.edu
[2] Department of Business Information Systems and Operations Management, University of North Carolina at Charlotte, 9201 University City Blvd, Charlotte, NC 28223, USA
bwashington@uncc.edu

Abstract. The COVID-19 pandemic has impacted the use of technology in classroom experience with group collaborative projects. Group collaboration and the skills absorbed at the time of collaboration is an essential part of a student's higher educational journey, because it prepares students for workplace collaboration post-graduation [1]. Prior to graduating, an undergraduate student will encounter at least one group project that is classified as a required deliverable in at least one of their course curriculums. In all technology related curriculums, computer-mediated communication (CMC) is an essential part of an instructor's course material deliverable process, the way instructors communicate with their students, and the way students communicate with their peers. The need for a shift in the way humans communicate with one another has increased tremendously within the past two years [2]. We evaluated how effective CMC tools can enhance student outcomes for group projects specifically in the Covid-19 era and how students adopt to creative ways to engage and apply technology for effective communication. We also analyzed human factors confronting the use of CMC tools in the context of social distance policies and collaborative projects. We concluded by examining implications of group collaboration projects mandated in institutions for student success in the pandemic era.

Keywords: Collaborative · Computer-mediated communication · Human factors · Measure of effectiveness · Usability

1 Introduction

The impact of the COVID-19 pandemic in higher education in recent years as it relates to student group collaboration has become a critical issue that needs to be addressed. The Centers for Disease Control and Prevention (CDC) has developed a set of recommended guidelines for Institutions of Higher Education (IHEs) that can be used to prevent the spread of COVID-19 among students, faculty, and staff [3]. Some of those prevention measures include offering and promoting vaccination, consistent and the correct use of facemasks, physical distancing, handwashing, respiratory etiquette, testing, contact

© The Author(s), under exclusive license to Springer Nature Switzerland AG 2022
M. Antona and C. Stephanidis (Eds.): HCII 2022, LNCS 13309, pp. 78–93, 2022.
https://doi.org/10.1007/978-3-031-05039-8_6

tracing and maintaining clean and healthy environments [3]. Since these prevention measures do not 100% guarantee that humans will not contract the virus, entities are forced to get creative in the way they collaborate.

Group collaboration and the skills absorbed at the time of collaboration is an essential part of a student's higher educational journey, because it prepares students for workplace collaboration post-graduation [1]. Prior to graduating, an undergraduate student will encounter at least one group project that is classified as a required deliverable in at least one of their course curriculums. In all technology related curriculums, computer-mediated communication (CMC) is an essential part of an instructor's course material deliverable process, the way instructors communicate with their students, and the way students communicate with their peers. CMC is defined as a term that involves many different forms of human communication through network computers either in a synchronous or asynchronous way. Forms of CMC tools used includes instant messages, peer-to-peer networks, e-mails, and online chat rooms which are accessible through commercially available application such as Blackboard and Canvas [4–6].

The purpose of this study is to investigate the impact on mechanism for group collaboration for students in higher education. By having effective collaborative tools students can communicate and produce high-quality project delivery which could result in higher rate of knowledge exchange/sharing, increase the speed to turn around projects deliverables, group performance, higher engagement, and the ability to receive real-time feedback from groupmates through features such as chat and live video.

2 Background of the Study

In higher education, courses require group collaboration in the form of group projects to support the notion that diverse teams produce better outputs faster than individuals working on their own [7]. These group collaborative efforts are used to test and demonstrate enrolled students knowledge of course core competencies at higher education institutions [6]. Each of these institutions fall into one of these three categories as it relates to the strategy of instructional delivery: 100% online teaching, partially online, or 100% in person. In each of these categories, a student's ability to interact with their instructor or peers has a higher rate of failure because of the COVID-19 pandemic. Students and instructors can be described in different ways:

1. In-person student - One who is required to join a class session on campus inside of a physical classroom.
2. Online Student - One whose classes are 100% online in the form as synchronous or asynchronous.
3. Hybrid Student - One who has class sessions in-person and online.
4. In-person instructor - One who is required to teach a class session on campus inside of a physical classroom. They mainly utilize the technology tools needed to instruct the class. The class is designed to have many in-class assignments. The instructor has a limited a virtual experience.
5. Online instructor - One who is required to teach a class session online as synchronous or asynchronous. They mainly utilize the technology tools needed to instruct the class. The instructor has an advanced virtual experience level.

6. Hybrid – One who instructs classes in-person and online. The instructor has a moderate virtual experience level.

In each of these ways, the course objectives are expected to be accomplished and applied. It is common for students to utilize an external collaborative technology mechanism, rather than the platform the instructor uses to administer the course. There is also not enough time allocated for students to completely work on their group projects in-class, and for the instructor to teach all the required course materials to accomplish the course objectives. As a result, students must use applications such as Zoom, Teams, GroupMe, G Suite, Office 365, etc. to work efficiently. To obtain an understanding of applicable collaborative applications, instructors must provide recommended resources to guide students. In this study, we identified three problems that impacts group collaboration for students in higher education. To examine these problems, a survey was conducted to answer three research questions:

- R1: Does having a recommended mechanism influence a student's project deliverable?
- R2: Does the COVID-19 pandemic influence how students use collaborative tools?
- R3: Is there enough time allocated to students to work on their group projects be it inside or outside of the classroom setting?

The study focused on the human computer interaction factors that assist in assessing the measure of effectiveness (MOE) of CMC tools.

2.1 Human Factors and Group Collaboration

In measuring the effectiveness of computer mediated communication tools during group projects, it is critical to understand the perspectives of end-users who interact with these tools. Research reveals that, user centered design approach significantly impacts the use of technology in our everyday life [8]. To produce usable and functional systems, the system should be designed to match student requirements [9]. Task factors complexity, easy of interaction, Productivity factors such as increased output, errors reduction and increase innovation are among the factors to be considered and measured (Fig. 1).

- Workload efficiency – How is the work allocated and what are the determining factors?
- Communication – How often does the team interact with one another?
- Collaboration – What were the tools used to execute a deliverable and what was the determining factor?
- Time-allocation – What is the amount of time it takes for each team member to complete their assigned deliverable?
- Task Dependencies – Is a student's task dependent on another student's completion?
- External factors – Can external circumstances influence your successful rate of completion?

2.2 Higher Education and Computer-Mediated Communication tools

One of the Accreditation Board for Engineering and Technology (ABET) computing accreditation requirements for student outcomes includes the ability for a student to

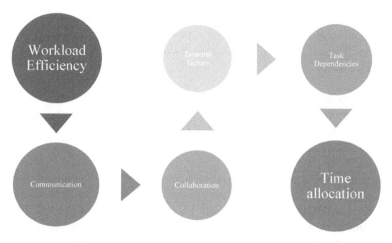

Fig. 1. Measure of Effectiveness (MOE) indicator

"function effectively as a member or leader of a team engaged in activities appropriate to the program's discipline" [10]. This criterion for student outcomes therefore demands an effective communication tool for team members to provide feedback and share information. ABET requirements for assessment for student outcome, is required to support the conception that diverse teams produce better outputs faster than individuals working on their own [11]. In an exploratory experimental study conducted by Szewkis et al [12], an application software was developed to measure the ease of use for a computer-supported collaborative mechanism for classroom learning. Their findings indicated that silent collaboration tools are effective mechanisms to promote learning in large groups in the classroom [12]. However, with the current policies surrounding COVID-19 in higher education institutions, there is the need for more effective CMC tools to assess group collaboration. Research indicates that CMC enhances communication among teachers and students, specifically from the perspective of pedagogy [13]. To realize effective CMC integration, Smith and Clark define measure of effectiveness (MOE) as the ability of a system to meet a specified need from a particular viewpoint [14].

With the disruption caused by the COVID-19 pandemic, the impact of accessing mechanisms for group collaboration tools such as CMC needs to critically examine human factors relating to students preferences to better understand the effectiveness of these required mechanisms. A critical analysis of human factors that affect project success will highlight essential techniques to promote success in collaborative project [15]. This will prevent redundant tools or systems which potentially decrease collaborative efforts for student success.

3 Methodology

The study was carried out over a 6-month period. For the purposes of this study, a qualitative and quantitative questionnaire was developed with Likert scale questions and distributed to active enrolled undergraduate students at higher education institutions for participation in this study. Participants were recruited through Department Chairs in charge of departments with students 18 years or older who are enrolled in technology-related majors. To qualify as an active enrolled undergraduate student the prospective participant must have:

- Completed at least one semester at the institution.
- Be enrolled in the minimum amount course credit requirements to be considered at least part-time, working toward a bachelor's degree, and
- Be classified as a Freshman, Sophomore, Junior, or Senior.

The research study was explained to them as a study that will investigate the impact of accessing mechanisms for group collaboration for students in higher education. This questionnaire was developed using Qualtrics to capture the data needed. This study focused on the human computer factors that assists in measuring the effectiveness of students prior knowledge and experience of CMC tools, and how this affects their collaborative efforts and project deliverables.

The goal of the study was to obtain at least 200 participant responses. The estimated time of completion was 15 min from start to finish. After cleaning the data, the number entries was reduced from 156 to 127 accepted entries. The students who did not meet the technology-related degree, age requirements, and did not answer any of the questions were removed from the data set.

3.1 Questionnaire Design

The factor effectiveness questionnaire (FEQ) opened with 5 demographic questions to use as independent variables later in the study. This was further grouped into 3 dimensions to measure and assess the overall factors of human computer interaction (HCI) and the measure of effectiveness [16]. The dimensions assessed by the FEQ are Human Computer Factors (HCF), Supporting Factors (SF), and Measure of Effectiveness (MOE). The questionnaire contained 35 questions grouped as indicated in Table 1.

Table 1. Description of factors and indicators.

Dimension	Factor/Indicator	Description
HCF	Environmental Factors (EF)	Noise, Heating, Lighting, Ventilation. Health and Safety Factors
	The User (U)	Cognitive processes and capabilities. Motivation, Enjoyment, Satisfaction, Personality, Experience
	Comfort Factors (CF)	Seating, Equipment, Layout
	User Interface (UI)	Input devices, Output devices, Dialogue structures, Use of color, Icons, Commands, Navigation, Graphics, Natural language, User support, Multimedia

(continued)

Table 1. (*continued*)

Dimension	Factor/Indicator	Description
	System Functionality (SF)	Hardware, Software, Application
	Productivity Factors (PF)	Increase output, Increase quality, Decrease costs, Decrease errors, Increase innovation
SF	Constraint (C)	Cost, Timescales, Budgets, Staff, Equipment, Buildings
	Platforms (P)	Platforms for course instruction
	Tools (T)	Tools that were used and how they were used
MOE	Workload Efficiency (WE)	How the work is allocated and what are the determining factors?
	Communication (COM)	How often does the team interact with one another?
	Collaboration (COL)	What were the tools used to execute a deliverable and what was the determining factor?
	Time-Allocation (TA)	What is the amount of time it takes for each team member to complete their assigned deliverable?
	Task Dependencies (TD)	Is a student's task dependent on another student's completion?
	External factors (EF)	Can external circumstances influence your successful rate of completion?

Each FEQ question response that was part of the HCF and MOE dimensions was given a numeric value of the assessments on a scale of $1 - 5$ for each of the questions within those two dimensions for each participant. The SF dimension (11 questions) results were used as underlying influences or impact on each participant's overall effectiveness score. To calculate the overall effectiveness score for each participant, the FEQ questions were designed on a Likert scale that reveals the levels of satisfaction, agreeance, and effectiveness each question has on the research questions. We calculated the total of each of the dimensions for each participant., There were 24 questions overall between the two dimensions HCF (12 questions) and MOE (12 questions). The equation was structured as following:

$$ES = \sum \left(\left(\sum HCF/6 \right) : \left(\sum MOE/6 \right) \right)$$

After the total scores were calculated, they were then divided by 6 to calculate the average of each of the two dimensions HCF and MOE. The sum of average of each of the two dimensions equals the overall effectiveness score (ES) per participant (Fig. 2).

The effective scores were analyzed further to determine if age, gender, class year, and enrollment status suggests any significance. Those roles were used as an independent variable, while the overall effectiveness score of each participant was used as the dependent variable. The ages ranged from the age 18 to 62 years or more in order to factor in those that may be defined as nontraditional students. The National Center for Education

	HCF		MOE
	——		——
	——		——
	——		——
Total =	——		——
Average =	——		——
Divide total by 6			
Total of the HCF & MOE average scores =			**= Effectiveness Score**

Fig. 2. Calculation of each participant's overall effectiveness score

Statistics (NCES) defines a nontraditional student as a student who delays enrolling in postsecondary education [17]. The gender identifiers used were Male, Female, Non-binary/third gender, and those the preferred not to identify. The class year identifiers used were Freshman, Sophomore, Junior, and Senior. The enrollment status identifiers were Part-Time and Full-Time.

4   Results

As shown in Fig. 3, the effectiveness scores ranged from 4.17 to 19.17, with a mean of 13.95, median of 14.00, and a mode of 14.33. The mean is less than the mode which implies that the overall effectiveness score is negatively skewed. This means that more participants have experienced a higher level of impact of accessing mechanisms for group collaboration. The mean, median, and mode are fairly close together, which imp-lies the responses from the students have a symmetrical distribution.

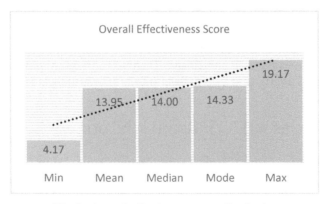

Fig. 3. Overall effectiveness score distribution

4.1 Mechanisms for Group Collaboration Impact on Project Deliverables

As indicated in Table 3, majority of the participants agreed that if they were given a recommended list of tools to use for group collaboration it would positively impact their collaborative efforts with their peers, N = 55, M = 14.23, SD = 2.03. ANOVA tests with the effectiveness score as the dependent variable and the agreeance of having a list of recommended tools as the independent variable suggests that there is significant difference between the effectiveness scores and the agreeance of having a list of recommended tools, $F(4,122) = 5.66, p < .001$. Post-hoc Tukey test suggests that there is significance between the effectiveness score and those participants that were neutral and either agreed or strongly agreed (Table 2).

Table 2. Multiple comparisons for having a list of recommended tools.

Comparison test	P-value (SIG.)	Significant?
Strongly disagree vs. disagree	.880	No
Strongly disagree vs. neutral	.983	No
Strongly disagree vs. agree	.508	No
Strongly disagree vs. strongly agree	.260	No
Disagree vs. neutral	.932	No
Disagree vs. agree	.969	No
Disagree vs. strongly agree	.723	No
Neutral vs. agree	.009	Yes
Neutral vs. strongly agree	<.001	Yes
Agree vs. strongly agree	.552	No

The means of the 5 levels of agreeance the two comparisons which displayed a significant outcome, Neutral levels displayed effectiveness scores significantly lower than Agree, and somewhat lower than Strongly Agree.

As indicated in Table 3, there is a significant difference between the effectiveness scores and independent variable, "if a student agreed that they were aware or knew how to use the tools that are applicable for collaborative use, they would produce a high quality project deliverable that will increase their degree of success," $F(4,122) = 7.20$, $p < .001$. Majority of the participants agree, N = 55, M = 14.23, SD = 1.66.

There is not a significant difference between the effectiveness scores and independent variable, that a student would feel uneasy if they were given a school project where they had to use only CMC tools that were designated by the institution, $F(4,122) = 2.38, p < .055$. Majority of the participants were neutral, N = 55, M = 14.16, SD = 1.77.

There is not a significant difference between the effectiveness scores and independent variable, that a student would feel that may not be able to collaborate effectively if they do not use CMC tools, $F(4,122) = 1.35, p < .253$. Majority of the participants were neutral, N = 58, M = 13.78, SD = 2.03.

Table 3. Mean comparison for having a recommended list.

	N	Mean (M)	Std. deviation (SD)
Strongly disagree	2	11.6650	.23335
Disagree	4	13.5000	1.11173
Neutral	32	12.5513	1.86419
Agree	55	14.2389	2.03536
Strongly agree	34	14.9856	2.93019
Total	127	13.9498	2.41268

N = Number of Participants.

This means that students believe that if instructors provide a recommended tool for collaboration, it will positively influence a student's project deliverable.

4.2 Global Pandemic Impacts on the Use of Collaborative Tools

As it relates to the COVID-19 Pandemic, majority of the participants stated that they were moderately impacted by the pandemic, $N = 37$, $M = 13.77$, $SD = 2.31$. ANOVA tests with the effectiveness score as the dependent variable and the impact of COVID-19 on the participants group project as the independent variable suggests that there is significant difference in the effectiveness scores between the responses, $F(4, 106) = .36$, $p = .833$.

Majority of the participants are satisfied with feeling safe using collaborative tools during the COVID-19 pandemic, $N = 58$, $M = 13.51$, $SD = 1.94$. ANOVA tests with the effectiveness score as the dependent variable and the satisfaction of feeling safe during the pandemic as the independent variable suggests that there is significant difference with the effectiveness scores and the level of satisfaction, $F(3,123) = 12.61$, $p < .001$. Post-hoc Tukey test suggests that there is significance between the effectiveness score and those participants that were unsatisfied vs. very satisfied, neutral vs. very satisfied, and satisfied vs. very satisfied.

As shown in Table 4, the means of the 5 levels of satisfaction of the three comparisons which displayed a significant outcome of Unsatisfied and Neutral levels displayed effectiveness scores significantly lower than Very Satisfied. However, the Satisfied level displayed effectiveness scores significantly higher than Very Satisfied (Table 5).

Table 4. Multiple comparisons for level of satisfaction with feeling safe during the COVID-19 pandemic.

Comparison test	p-value (sig.)	Significant?
Unsatisfied vs. neutral	.452	No
Unsatisfied vs. satisfied	.123	No
Unsatisfied vs. very satisfied	<.001	Yes
Neutral vs. satisified	.606	No
Neutral vs. very satisified	<.001	Yes
Satisfied vs0. very satisifed	<.001	Yes

Table 5. Mean comparison for COVID-19 levels of satisfaction as it relates to the use of collaborative tools.

	N	Mean (M)
Unsatisfied	5	11.3000
Neutral	23	12.8613
Satisfied	58	13.5110
Very satisfied	41	15.5041
Total	127	13.9498

This means that the COVID-19 pandemic did not negatively influence how students use collaborative tools.

4.3   Time-Allocations Impact on the Setting

Majority of the participants agreed that there was enough time allocated that allowed students to work on their group projects inside, $N = 51$, $M = 13.94$, $SD = 1.4,7$ and outside of the classroom, $N = 59$, $M = 14.00$, $SD = 1.51$ but more students identified that group projects were mostly worked on outside of the classroom. ANOVA tests with the effectiveness score as the dependent variable and time allocated that allowed students to work on their group projects inside as the independent variable suggests that there is significant difference with the effectiveness scores and the time allocated inside of the classroom, $F(4,117) = 17.14$, $p < .001$ (Fig. 4).

With the effectiveness score as the dependent variable and time allocated that allowed students to work on their group projects outside as the independent variable suggests that there is significant difference with the effectiveness scores and the time allocated outside of the classroom, $F(4,118) = 15.01$, $p < .001$ (Fig. 5).

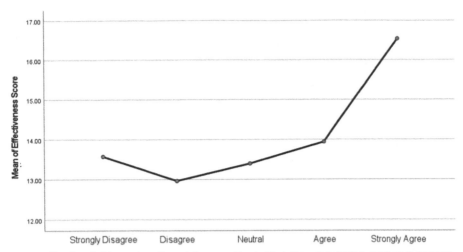

Fig. 4. Time allocated (inside classroom)

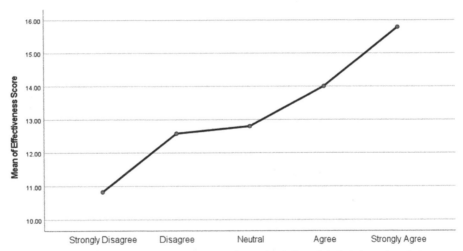

Fig. 5. Time allocated (outside classroom).

When comparing the means for the two variables students identified that is more difficult to work on group projects outside of the classroom rather than inside of the classroom even though there is more time allowed (Fig. 6).

Most participants revealed that their teams interacted with one another at least one time per week. However, the number of students that fall in the categories of reporting neutral, disagree, and strongly disagree is alarming. This outcome suggests that even though students have more time to work on group projects, they prefer to take advantage

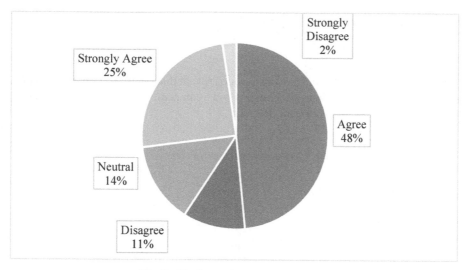

Fig. 6. % of team interaction per week.

of meeting during the designated class period since that is the only guaranteed time that they all with meet in the same place at the same time. The assumption is if instructors allocate more time to work on group projects during the class period, it will positively impact the project groups.

4.4 Impacts of Demographics

One-Way Analysis of Variance (ANOVA) was further used to analyze the impact of age, gender, class year, and enrollment status on the overall Effectiveness Scores.

Class Year. Participants that identify as Junior were the highest population group, N = 38, M = 13.62, SD = 2.09. The representation from each classification year was almost symmetrically identical. ANOVA tests with the effectiveness score as the dependent variable and the classification year of the participant as the independent variable suggests that there is significant difference with the effectiveness scores and the classification

Table 6. Multiple comparisons for class years.

Comparison test	p-value (sig.)	Significant?
Freshman vs. sophomore	.006	Yes
Freshman vs. junior	.202	No
Freshman vs. senior	<.001	Yes
Sophomore vs. junior	.346	No
Sophomore vs. senior	.977	No
Junior vs. senior	.127	No

years, $F(3,123) = 6.07, p < .001$. Post-hoc Tukey test suggests that there is significance with the effectiveness score and the Freshman vs. Sophomore and Freshman vs. Senior classification years (Table 6).

The means of the 4 classification year groups reveal that the two comparisons which displayed a significant outcome, Sophomores and Seniors displayed effectiveness scores significantly higher than Freshman (Table 7).

Table 7. Mean comparison for class years

Classification years	N	Mean (N)
Freshman	24	12.4508
Sophomore	29	14.5631
Junior	38	13.6266
Senior	36	14.7961
Total	127	13.9498

Enrollment Status. Participants that identify as Full-time were the highest population group, $N = 122$, $M = 13.92$, $SD = 2.43$. ANOVA tests with the effectiveness score as the dependent variable and the enrollment status of the participant as the independent variable suggests that there is no significant difference with the effectiveness scores between the enrollment status, $F(1,125) = .41, p = .521$.

5   Discussion

The Course curriculum structure in higher education varies based on many different settings, such as the institution, the college within that institution, and each major within that college. For many institutions, the traditional design of a course curriculum is comprised of the following components, Lecture Presentations, Individual Course Assignments, and Exams/Quizzes. Based on the assessments of the majors, instructors may include discussion topics that are used to get students to think practically, and group projects that are designed to ensure that the skills taught within the classroom are reinforced, relevant, and applied [18]. Group projects require the use of different tools to carry out different functions to manage the overall project as well as the deliverables within the project. All the components involved contribute to the success of receiving a passing grade on the project.

Findings from this study indicates students believe that if they had the prior knowledge of the tools that are available to use and instruction on how to use them, they would have a better outcome on the project deliverables. A major component that contributes to the success of group projects is the collaborative tools that are used. However, groups are made up of different people with different backgrounds and preferences. Effective communication and collaborative teamwork are essential for academic and non-academic careers, but the complexity of it all can be overpowering if not managed properly [19]. Students also stated that if they were only allowed to use the tools that they were given, it would negatively impact their degree of success because of the mental shift that has to be made in the short amount of time. Therefore, a hybrid approach is revealed as the preferred method.

The dataset included responses from full-time and part-time students, which indicates that students who are enrolled full-time are taking courses with students who are enrolled part-time with both groups following under same major. Part-time students fall within the non-traditional student category. A person chooses a non-traditional setting or path because external factors affect their ability to navigate the degree path in the same manner a full-time student would [17]. This implies that time plays an important role in the success of group projects. Even though students agreed that there was time allocated to work on their projects inside and outside of the classroom, most students worked on their projects outside of the classroom even though it is more difficult to do so. The benefit of being able to work on projects inside of the classroom is because that is the location where all students are required to be at a particular date and time. Working on projects outside of the classroom requires each group member to review their schedules and find a day and time that works for the majority.

When an instructor is setting up their courses for the semester, they must find the time to incorporate all the components needed to achieve the course objectives. Work-integrated learning can be more time consuming and resource intensive with building and delivering a curriculum [20]. This suggests that time factor affects both student and instructors In addition to time being a factor, the impact of the COVID-19 pandemic has played a role in instruction delivery and the students ability to execute curricula deliverables. From the onset of the pandemic, many students agree that they have an increase in knowledge of how-to use collaborative tools because they were required to work in a virtual environment where space, distance, and time played a major role.

The results also implies that the student classification year played a role in how they responded to certain questions. Freshman displayed in their responses that they were neutral, not impacted, or somewhat impacted due to the lack of experience within the higher education setting, whereas Seniors displayed that they were strongly impacted since majority of their courses were in-person.

6 Conclusion

Due to the COVID-19 pandemic there is increased emphasis on promoting collaborative projects using CMC tools. CMC tools have the potential to enhance group collaboration and promote student success in higher education institution. Findings from this study indicates that the COVID -19 pandemic did not have a negative effect on how students use collaboration tools. To promote the use of these tools for student success, instructors can be encouraged to recommend collaborative tools for student use. Enough time must be allocated to students inside classroom settings to enable them work efficiently. It is also necessary to create a balance for Freshmen by implementing a system where students have prior knowledge and experience of CMC tools to promote project success.

Establishing effective collaborative tools will increase students' communication and produce high-quality project deliverables. This will impact the rate of knowledge exchange and enhance group performance and higher engagement. Future research patterns should include expanding this study to encompass other key components such as measure of performance, optimizing CMC tools, and analyzing open-source CMC tools for higher education institutions.

References

1. de-J. Lozoya-Santos, J., et al.: Transdisciplinary learning community: a model to enhance collaboration between higher education institutions and society. In: 2019 IEEE Global Engineering Education Conference (EDUCON), pp. 622–627 (2019). https://doi.org/10.1109/EDUCON.2019.8725108
2. Nguyen, M.H., Gruber, J., Fuchs, J., Marler, W., Hunsaker, A., Hargittai, E.: Changes in digital communication during the COVID-19 global pandemic: implications for digital inequality and future research. Social Media+ Society, 6(3), 2056305120948255 (2020)
3. Cardona, M., Harris-Aikens, D.: ED COVID-19 Handbook Volume 3: Strategies for Safe Operation and Addressing the Impact of COVID-19 on Higher Education Students, Faculty, and Staff (2021). https://www2.ed.gov/documents/coronavirus/reopening-3.pdf
4. Lee, E., Oh, S.Y.: Computer-mediated communication. Communication (2015). https://doi.org/10.1093/obo/9780199756841-0160
5. Treem, J.W., Leonardi, P.M., van den Hooff, B.: Computer-mediated communication in the age of communication visibility. J. Comput.-Mediat. Commun. 25(1), 44–59 (2020)
6. Lo, H.C.: Utilizing computer-mediated communication tools for problem-based learning. J. Educ. Technol. Soc. 12(1), 205–213 (2009)
7. Argote, L., Lee, S., Park, J.: Organizational learning processes and outcomes: major findings and future research directions. Manage. Sci. 67(9), 5399–5429 (2021)
8. Owusu, E., Chakraborty, J.: User requirements gathering in mHealth: Perspective from Ghanaian end users. In International Conference on Human-Computer Interaction, pp. 386–396, July 2019
9. Goodwin, N.C.: Functionality and usability. Commun. ACM 30(3), 229–233 (1987)
10. ABET.   https://www.abet.org/wp-content/uploads/2018/02/C001-18-19-CAC-Criteria-Version-2.0-updated-02-12-18.pdf
11. Engineering Accreditation Commission. (2000). Accreditation Board for Engineering and Technology (ABET)
12. Szewkis, E., Nussbaum, M., Rosen, T., et al.: Collaboration within large groups in the classroom. Comput. Supp. Learn. 6, 561–575 (2011). https://doi.org/10.1007/s11412-011-9123-y
13. McComb, M.: Benefits of computer-mediated communication in college courses. Commun. Educ. 43(2), 159–170 (1994)
14. Smith, N., Clark, T.: An exploration of C2 effectiveness–A holistic approach. In: 2004 Command and Control Research and Technology Symposium, September 2004
15. Bond-Barnard, T.J., Fletcher, L., Steyn, H.: Linking trust and collaboration in project teams to project management success. Int. J. Manag. Proj. Bus. 11(2), 432–457 (2018). https://doi.org/10.1108/IJMPB-06-2017-0068
16. Brathwaite, C., Vernon, J., Ventura, C.: Analyzing the group effectiveness and dynamics of a heterogeneous international research group in Cartagena (Colombia): a case study. In: 2019 ASEE Annual Conference & Exposition Proceedings (2019). https://doi.org/10.18260/1-2--32093

17. Horn, L.J., Carroll, C.D.: Nontraditional Undergraduates: Trends in Enrollment from 1986 to 1992 and Persistence and Attainment Among 1989–90 Beginning Postsecondary Students. Nontraditional undergraduates/definitions and Data, November 1996. https://nces.ed. gov/pubs/web/97578e.asp

18. Bajada, C., Kandlbinder, P., Trayler, R.: A general framework for cultivating innovations in Higher Education curriculum. High. Educ. Res. Dev. **38**(3), 465–478 (2019). https://doi.org/ 10.1080/07294360.2019.1572715

19. Borowczak, M.: Communication in STEM education: a non-intrusive method for assessment & K20 educator feedback. Problems Educ. 21st Century **65**, 18–27 (2015)

20. Clark, L., Rowe, A., Cantori, A., Bilgin, A., Mukuria, V.: The power dynamics and politics of survey design: measuring workload associated with teaching, administering and supporting work-integrated learning courses. Stud. High. Educ. **41**(6), 1055–1073 (2014). https://doi. org/10.1080/03075079.2014.966071

Drawing and Understanding Diagrams: An Accessible Approach Dedicated to Blind People

Frederic Serin[1] and Katerine Romeo[2](✉)

[1] LITIS, University of Le Havre Normandy, Le Havre, France
`frederic.serin@univ-lehavre.fr`
[2] LITIS, University of Rouen Normandy, Saint Etienne du Rouvray, France
`katerine.romeo@univ-rouen.fr`

Abstract. Our research activity focuses on accessibility for document design and consultation, especially in the field of computer science. In this article, we focus on the design and reading of class diagrams according to the UML standard. Our goal is to enable collaboration between blind and sighted people, which means inclusion and accessibility. We will present the user-centered approach, regardless of the user's profile. For the blind, we have chosen to use a screen reader, with speech synthesis. For a designer, especially for a visually impaired person, it is essential to perceive the structure of a model, to understand it in all its dimensions. In the case of a UML class diagram, we propose a pattern combining visibility and readability, which we call intelligibility. Our model aims at presenting a simple, complete and fast way to understand an object model.

Keywords: UML · Class diagram · Accessibility · Visually impaired persons · Blindness · Object-oriented design · Screen reader · SVG · WCAG · ARIA

1 Introduction

We present how to create a UML class diagram [1, 2] and then how the result of this realization can appear in the most useful, intelligible and accessible way.

Many solutions are already proposed, we wish to add to this offer our approach that we have been testing for three years with our students, an audience of non-blind computer scientists. Our goal is to make any document accessible without problem, with the widest possible appropriation. Also, it seems fundamental to us that the users, in their diversity, take over our solution, use it even with a public prevented from reading.

Our software is called Latitude meaning Light and Accessible Tags Into plain Text using Universal DEsign [3–5]. It allows, from a plain text enriched with light and non-intrusive tags, to automatically generate documents in HTML format and, especially for graphics and diagrams, in SVG format. These two XML-structured formats are particularly accessible to screen readers [6–8]. They are, moreover, light in size and it is easy to add information tags according to the ARIA model [9–12]. This project started several years ago and is gradually being enriched [4, 5, 13].

M. Antona and C. Stephanidis (Eds.): HCII 2022, LNCS 13309, pp. 94–109, 2022.
https://doi.org/10.1007/978-3-031-05039-8_7

The technical choices will be exposed in Sect. 2. They are motivated by the educational approach and the wish to obtain the appropriation from all. That is why we follow a universal design approach [14–17]. The choice to present the realization of class diagrams comes from the fact that this diagram is featured among all those proposed by UML. With Latitude, we already propose three other diagrams, object, sequence and activity. The project is enriched progressively as an iterative approach that gradually enriches the offer, taking advantage of the enhancements, additions and modeling. We also listen to our students' suggestions in order to respond to their wishes. The goal is to make the product as inclusive as possible without being an obligation.

Of the four parts that structure this presentation, this article will therefore specify our motivation in Sect. 2. We will discuss the audiences considered, the constraints imposed and the orientations chosen.

In Sect. 3, we present the way to create a class diagram, from a textual approach. We want it to be accessible, i.e. audible and understandable. We will justify some specific choices and, to facilitate appropriation, we will indicate borrowings from existing languages, especially the syntax proposed by PlantUML, one of the most used free software by model designers.

The Sect. 4 presents the visual result. It is automatically computed by our software. The ergonomic choices will be justified, some of them will be put in relation with other options and in particular with those proposed by PlantUML [18].

Before concluding this article with perspectives of improvements and enhancements of our product, the Sect. 5 will present a supplementary element. This is a complementary document describing the realized diagram.

To end this introduction, please note that we are testing our software with our 80 undergraduate students. They are in their 2nd year of studies, in the Department of Computer Science of IUT of Le Havre, France. They have a free access to the open code which respects the specifications of object programming in Java, with more than 13000 lines and 8500 lines of comments.

2 Motivation

In this part, we expose the constraints considered and the specific choices. We want an inclusive product, that is to say accessible to the visually impaired people (VIP). Initially, this profile motivates this work. But we cannot ignore the fact that inclusion requires the acceptance of the use of this solution by a non-blind public, people who will be qualified for lack of a precise term as ordinary public [19–22].

In a project, with a prevalence of 0.5%, visually impaired people are likely to be alone among ordinary developers, for whom accessibility does not pose the same constraints. A VIP has a 98% probability of being the only one in his situation in a group of 5 people, and 95.6% in a group of 10. These proportions are similar to the fact that a working group that doesn't encounter a VIP, and it seems important to us that the tools should already be accepted. This is why we want to propose an interest, a universal design, which invites to appropriation a product which, finally, will bring its inclusive dimension quite naturally, without having to change habits already anchored in a community [23, 24].

We do not claim that our software is the solution. We hope, however, that our presentation will convince those who develop solutions to adopt our propositions, or at least our orientations.

At the exclusion of a human assistance, there are three ways of assisting blind people to make a digital document accessible: haptic tablets, Braille displays and TTS (text-to-speech) screen readers. The first two tools are the subject of multiple researches and publications [17, 20, 22, 25, 26] and we chose to focus on speech synthesis. The two main reasons are first of all the availability of any type of hardware and the zero-space requirement since this support is integrated and software. Obviously, the price of the materials is also an important parameter as well as the fact that their use also induces a visibility of the handicap situation.

Screen readers allow you to have the same tools as everyone else. And, also, everyone can test the rendering of the Latitude software. VoiceOver is available on all Apple OS and NVDA is free and can be installed on any Windows system. The only situation with difficulties we encountered was voice feedback with ORCA on Linux.

We talk about universal design and consider the inclusion in the scope of screen readers and vocalization because the majority of blind people are not fluent with Braille reading or writing.

We therefore wish to achieve a double objective:

1. Permit to a blind to produce a document, attractive and conforming to graphic standards for sighted people.
2. To provide sighted people with an equivalent, effective and easy-to-understand creation of the diagram.

According to the designer's needs, VIP or non-blind, the document must be perfectly accessible and understandable via a screen reader. The creation must be free of any complexities on the part of the creator and the reader [27, 28]. To obtain a good result, we test our software with VoiceOver for Mac OS and NVDA for Windows. To facilitate a collaborative context, we propose an inclusive approach, both for the creation of diagrams, but also for their comprehensibility without requiring different support for different audiences.

It is a debate among the VIP, but we have chosen to generate a well-draining diagram, considering importance of visual message. It is one of our choice: in diagrams, the visual presentation does not have to be aesthetically pleasing in order to offer a diagram that is eye-pleasing. Nevertheless, this aesthetic also conveys meaning, invites understandability of the model and facilitates its mind appropriation [2, 22, 26, 29].

Also, among our goals, the separation of substance from form by the textual presentation of the model allows to present in a factual way the various elements that participate in a model, their presence and their interactions. The formal description is important, it reinforces the model. Nevertheless, when we see a diagram, the form has its importance for the ease of understanding, and ignoring it would be a mistake.

This is the reason why we propose a hybrid version in which the designer can introduce information on the position of the elements which, far from being aesthetic, is a message carrying meaning on the salient points that participate in the presentation of our approach, facilitates the mental integration of the elements we wish to explain.

It is not the least objective, we need to which we will return throughout this article is the need to make the information we place in a graph accessible, following an inclusive objective. Also, this accessibility which will follow the three properties stated previously will impose choices in the syntax elaborated.

3 Creating the Document

The template proposed by Latitude (or Lttd) uses the design pattern Factory. From the raw document, the software generates an HTML document that will automatically include the graphics in SVG format. We will see in the 4th part that descriptive documents are also generated to be linked to give information and advices to the designers, and in particular the VIPs.

The raw document, a plain text enriched with tags, is sent to the main factory, Latitude factory. The factory generates the html accessible document (Fig. 1).

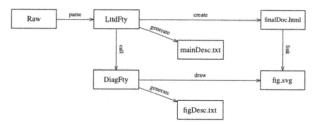

Fig. 1. Creation process.

Note that all the txt documents are in Latitude format, i.e. they can also translate into a HTML document, after generation by Lttd factory. They can include SVG graphics.

The description, (the writing) of the diagrams is done in a textual way. The syntax, inspired by the one used by PlantUML, has been arranged so that the symbols used are clearly vocalized and their visual appearance is reminiscent of the graphic nature that will be generated.

The proposed tags must be light, non-intrusive, so that their vocalization does not hide essential information such as the elements of the diagram: names of classes, multiplicities, properties, etc. The use by our students tends to validate the ability to be used by any public, VIP or non-blind [30].

Through few examples, directed by a simple case study, we will present the syntax of Latitude and compare it to PlantUML.

Here is a first-class diagram description, written with the Latitude syntax. It contains 3 classes and 2 associations.

Sensor
Controller
Trigger
Sensor * ---- > 1..* Controller
Controller 1 ----- > * Trigger

Sensors send information to a controller. Then this one sends instructions to triggers. This example comes from our exercises on modeling problems in home automation. The rendering of this code is given in the following figure.

Fig. 2. Rendering of the encoding (Lttd).

With PlantUML tool, the syntax is relatively simpler.

Sensor "1..*" - > "1..*" Controller
Controller "1" - > "*" Trigger

A first remark: with the screen reader, it is easier to hear a series of dashes rather than a single one. In addition, with PlantUML, syntax: one or two dashes causes the presentation to change from a horizontal to a vertical presentation. For a visually impaired person, this detail is unnoticed, and can produce an undesired result.

Another difference is that with Latitude, it is necessary to specify all the classes in the first part of the description, whereas PlantUML will automatically enter the identified classes when they appear. This cumbersomeness nevertheless allows to avoid some errors such as a spelling mistake that would not be noticed by ear. One can think in particular of forgetting an upper case which would have as a consequence with PlantUML to create a second class in the model.

One default that we can consider of some available tools is the automatic positioning, thanks to sophisticated algorithms. This service, which may seem very beneficial, has a major drawback, depending on our needs: it hides the interest of placing the elements of a diagram in such a way as to give a visual indication of the salient points that we want to highlight.

The diagrams description allows several approaches: by grid or by precise coordinates, in relative or absolute positions. We have chosen absolute coordinates because of the difficulty to maintain the meaning of the diagrams by following the other options. At present, the coordinates are those, in pixels, with some indications, of the choices made after some tests. The dimensions of a class are fixed at 80×60 and the distance between two classes will be at least 70 horizontally and 50 vertically. These values have been chosen to allow a good readability in the most frequent cases. If the name of a class or the distance between associated elements is too small, an indication will be given in the description document (see Sect. 5). This is undoubtedly one of the points on which we will have to work to propose a simpler syntax. At the moment, we have not succeeded in proposing a scale that satisfies all our constraints, and in particular that of being able to manage the location of classes in the diagram as freely as possible. We have simply opted for values that are multiples of ten in order not to overload the calculation requirements. With the first example, we can see that by not specifying coordinates, these were automatically fixed by moving the classes to the right as they were declared.

For aggregations and compositions, we did not choose the PlantUML syntax but a representation visually reminding the diamonds drawn in the class diagram. Chevrons are closer to the shape of a diamond compared to stars.

Another interest that we will address in part 2 by representing this figure, is the choice left to the designer in the order of appearance of the classes. Thus, the speech description can also be modified to give more importance to one element rather than another.

```
__classdiag   The controller commands the Device
Controller (0,150)
Sensor (0,0)
Trigger (0,300)
Sensor * ----<> 1..* Controller
Controller 1 <<>>----- 1..* Trigger
__end
```

the equivalent PlantUML code will be the following:

```
@startuml
scale 1.5
Sensor "*" --o "1..*" Controller
Controller "1" *-- "1..*" Trigger
@enduml
```

For a last example, we propose a representation of inheritance with both Latitude and PlantUML.

```
__diagclasse Home automation management
*Controller(0,110)
<Room
*Device(200,0)
<Radiator
<lamp
Controller 1 <<>>----- * Radiator
Room 1 <<>>----- * lamp
__fin
```
The code for this inheritance with PlantUML will be as follows:
```
Device <|-- Radiator
Device <|-- lamp
Controller "1" *- "*" Radiator
Controller <|-- Room
lamp "*" --* "1" Room
```

The representation of inheritance is well discernible with PlantUML, but the use of the chevron can be confused with the dependency arrow seen in the first example.

Moreover, the inheritances are placed on various lines with repetition of the mother class, this can also induce a cognitive overload. Finally, but this will be seen in the next section, inheritances do not necessarily allow the control of the placement in the space.

Our students have expressed the wish to be able to represent the heritage in a different way than vertically from top to bottom. At the moment, we have not granted this wish, since we consider that the representation must visually recall this tree structure very clearly. Nevertheless, we are thinking about allowing, at least, a left-to-right inheritance.

Inheritance, by gathering classes together, allows a clearer understanding. Here is a last example with two levels of subclasses and the inscription of properties in a class.

```
*Device {-state:boolean}
<Radiator
<lamp
<Opening {-open:boolean;+open()}
<<Window
<<Door
```

In this example, we introduce the syntax used for properties (fields, constructors, methods). We have been inspired directly by the PlantUML syntax for this element.

In conclusion, the plain text uses a syntax that allows you to remember the meaning of the symbols when you see the code. Signs such as braces, chevrons and dashes are used both for this recall and because they are clearly audible when read by a TTS. We wanted to avoid the use of the same symbol, such as the star, to avoid polysemy.

4 Drawing a Diagram

A UML diagram is not a simple picture. It is a highly structured representation, carrying meaning and requiring knowledge of a syntax initially thought of as visual. For screen readers, HTML is adapted to the structuring and rendering of textual content. SVG, for graphics, has the same advantages because it is also derived from XML. To improve group descriptions, useful for accessibility, we need to include the ARIA-*describedby* attribute to introduce semantic information in the figure [31, 32].

Accessibility is taken care of automatically by our software. For our students as well as for people who wish to have a more complete description of a diagram, a document in HTML format is linked to the graph and gives details such as coordinates, links between elements. This appendix also gives warnings if errors or overlaps are detected. This supplement helps designers to write a textual explanation. Particularly useful for the blind, this supplement has an educational purpose.

An example of automatic drawing by Latitude gives the following diagram showing an aggregation between two classes.

When we place the cursor of the screen reader into the figure, we can hear the following description, group after group:

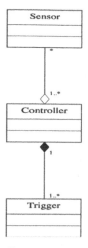

Fig. 3. The controller commands the Trigger (Lttd).

Class Controller (0,150)
Class Sensor (0,0)
Each instance of Controller may aggregate any number of instances of Sensor.
Each instance of Sensor is aggregated from 1 to many instances of Controller.

Class Trigger (0,300)

Each instance of Controller is composed from 1 to many instances of Trigger. Each instance of Trigger is component of Controller.

We go through the diagram with the VoiceOver cursor. Step by step, the screen reader details each element. These elements are classes, properties (optional) and associations. We move forward with the right arrow, we can of course go back. At each step, the description tag, present in the group of the element is reading.

The reading order is that of the writing of the groups in the SVG document. It is our program that schedule, before generating the code, the groups so that the description of an association is done only after reading the two linked classes.

For the diagram made with PlantUML, we obtain:

Fig. 4. The controller commands the Trigger (PlantUML).

This time, the screen reader vocalizes the following information:

Sensor
Controller

Trigger
*
1..*
1
1..*

The cursor only reads the textual elements present in the diagram. Because there is not the desc tag into the code. So, consequently, we cannot know on which side of the association a multiplicity is located. The composition is not vocalized because it is just a graphical element. We see the difference of PlantUML vs Latitude where the simple text indicating a class is just vocalized by the name, when we create an augmented text precising the category.

The benefit of augmented description proposed by Latitude for associations is even more obvious.

We have structured our speech description in such a way that both classes must be presented before the association that links them is described.

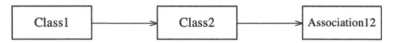

Fig. 5. Association narration after the class descriptions.

Obviously, it is possible that other classes are presented before the second associated class appears, which can create an immediate memory problem for the understanding of the diagram (memory load). In the same way that a scene can be visually complex, it will probably also be complex, or even more so, by the linear description that oralisation requires.

Another approach would be relational: to recreate a description of the link between two objects by placing the linked relations of these two objects, or even the possible interactions between their respective neighborhoods. We have not opted for this version, as it creates too much verbosity and ultimately weighs down the understanding of the diagram. On the other hand, this detailed information will be described in the description file which we discuss in the following Sect. 5. We therefore speak of the main description, integrated directly into the described scene, and of secondary descriptions participating in a variation of points of view.

The figures below show the representation of the inheritance. As for the associations, we have chosen with Latitude to draw the lines either horizontally or vertically. Sometimes, because it cannot be avoided, lines with right angles are used. It is recognized that this usage allows a better understanding of the represented links. We see the difference with PlantUML which draws oblique or even, sometimes, curved lines. From a text-to-speech perspective, this is inaudible, of course. But Latitude wants to be a tool with reverse accessibility, so that ordinary people can easily understand a class diagram.

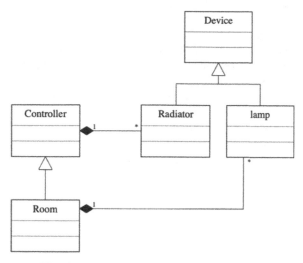

Fig. 6. Home automation management (Lttd).

The class diagram realized by PlantUML is somewhat different. But what allows visually to understand the model disappears totally with the use of the screen reader.

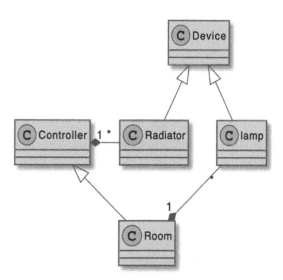

Fig. 7. Home automation management (PlantUML).

Our software generates SVG figures from a plain text source, enriched with a dedicated syntax including tags. The description from the screen reader only from the shapes of the graphics is not enough to create an understandable diagram. Indeed, without adding any information, a UML class will be for example a rectangle, an association, a line… The semantics of a diagram must be included so that the rectangle is clearly identified as a class, the line as an association. This is where our modeling and implementation differs from software such as PlantUML.

Thus, each semantic element of a diagram is placed in an SVG group. This block is enriched with an ad hoc description, generated in natural language. The decomposition into blocks is the most strategic choice. We made it after different tests following UML descriptions and learning approaches with our students. The following section starts with an example of the SVG code that illustrates our way of coding the <g> blocks.

Remember the example, situated at the end of the previous section. It presents both inheritance and properties, we end these examples to specify that the software tries to balance the inheritance tree as well as possible so that it is sufficiently compact to clearly indicate the dependencies between overclasses and subclasses.

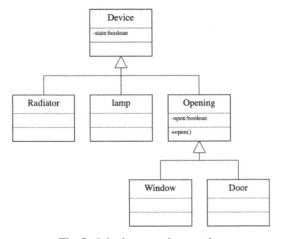

Fig. 8. Inheritance and properties.

In order for a user to be able to quickly switch to the properties during the description, we have placed the properties in a different block <g> but immediately adjacent to the one describing the class. Like associations, whose multiplicities are translated by sentences giving meaning to the symbols, properties, written according to the UML syntax, allow an easier understanding.

Surclass root Device (100, 0).

One private Attribute state of type boolean.

The 3 subclasses Radiator, lamp, and Opening inherit from Device

Subclass Radiator (0, 110) inherits from Device
Subclass lamp (100, 110) inherits from Device
Surclass Opening (200, 110) inherits from Device

One private Attribute open of type boolean. Public method open returns nothing without arguments.

The 2 subclasses Window, and Door inherit from Opening

Subclass Window (150, 220) inherits from Opening

Subclass Door (250, 220) inherits from Opening

The redundancy in the inheritance reminders both when passing from an overclass to its subclasses and then when reading a subclass has been added, noting that this lightened the mental load, especially in the case of multi-level trees. It is also according to this principle that the number of attributes and then operations registered in a class is specified.

5   Added Value - Doc Description

We have presented the descriptive assistance that the screen reader can return when navigating the image made in SVG. We also consider the accessibility of the raw SVG code. Here is for example (extracted from Fig. 3) the SVG code generated by Latitude for the Trigger class and the association between Trigger and Controller.

```
<!-- Class Trigger (0,300) -->
<g aria-labelledby="Classe4">
<use xlink:href="#classe" x="0" y="300" />
<text x="40" y="310" text-anchor="middle" font-size="12" fill="black" dominant-
baseline="central">
Trigger</text>
<desc id="Classe4">
Classe Trigger (0,300)</desc>
</g>
<!-- Association between Controller and Trigger -->
<g aria-labelledby="5">
<polyline points="40,300 40,210 " style="fill:none; stroke: black; stroke-width:
0.6;markerend:
url(#composition); " />
<text x="45" y="227" text-anchor="start" font-size="8" fill="black" dominant-
baseline="central">
1</text>
<text x="45" y="295" text-anchor="start" font-size="8" fill="black" dominant-
baseline="central">
1..*</text>
<desc id="5">
```

Each instance of Controller is composed from 1 to many instances of Trigger. Each instance of Trigger is component of Controller.</desc>
</g>

For comparison, here is the code generated by PlantUML for the same Trigger class:

```
<!--MD5=[f8158362d3f9eaf6b261520465ba7069]
class Trigger-->
<rect fill="#FEFECE" filter="url(#f1uuzf6k1th9i8)" height="72" id="Trigger"
style="stroke:#A80036;strokewidth:
2.25;" width="114" x="365.25" y="10.5"/>
<ellipse cx="387.75" cy="34.5" fill="#ADD1B2" rx="16.5" ry="16.5"
style="stroke:#A80036;stroke-width:1.5;"/>
<path d="M391.266,28.008 C389.859,27.352 etc.
L391.2656,28.0078 Z " fill="#000000"/>
<text fill="#000000" font-family="sans-serif" font-size="18" lengthAdjust="spacing"
textLength="66" x="408.75" y="40.7314">
Trigger</text>
<line style="stroke:#A80036;stroke-width:2.25;" x1="366.75" x2="477.75"
y1="58.5" y2="58.5"/>
<line style="stroke:#A80036;stroke-width:2.25;" x1="366.75" x2="477.75"
y1="70.5" y2="70.5"/>
```

We think that this example does not need any comment. Thus, with Latitude, computer scientists can check the relevance of the code, and even, for those who would like to do so, modify it quite easily. The used format also has a pedagogical objective allowing our students to understand the syntax of this language. Let us specify that a drawing in SVG format is of course much lighter than an image in PNG format... beyond the accessibility defended in this article. We have between 6 kB and 8 kB for the drawings, an SVG file weighing around 30 kB.

A description also appears in the generated SVG files, in the form of comment lines that allow to recall the positioning, the role of the objects described in the following group.

In addition to the information specified in the SVG code with the use of the attribute *aria-labelledby* which allows to indicate to the screen reader to read the content of the desc tag, a plain text document with light Latitude tags is generated for each figure. The Lttd factory then generates the HTML file which is accessible via a hyperlink on the figure's legend.

These description files offer various information that allow access to a more detailed description of the diagram. For example, for Fig. 2, the document will contain:

- a title remembering the caption of the figure;
- this diagram has 3 classes and 2 associations. This diagram is linear.
- the list of all the classes;
- the list of all the associations;
- the list of associations linked to a class;
- a reminder of the linear description by the screen reader.

In addition to this information, there will also be a description of inheritances if there is any tree. Finally, an optional last section indicates if elements of the diagram overlap: detection of conflicts between classes and associations, crossings for example.

As for the textual documents, we would like to be able to present a complexity score of the diagram informing about understandability. For texts, we use the Flesch score [33]. For diagrams, we are looking for a way to indicate if it is complex, difficult to read. We have already worked on the description of an inheritance, presenting for example if the tree is well balanced, we would like to be able to evaluate the difficulty to read and understand such a structure.

6 Conclusion and Perspectives

The software has been quite successful with our students. A majority of them indicated that they would use it later. They have also requested that other teachers in the department use the same tool, which they find convenient. They also appreciate the description file which allows them to clearly establish the meaning given to classes and associations. They therefore have a better understanding of the value of class diagrams. Incidentally, the description also allows them to realize some design errors, such as indicating the meaning of multiplicities.

As a blind teacher, one of the authors has been able to gain autonomy and can thus present live diagrams to the students to illustrate a problem or answer a question. Thus, the inclusion is proven and appreciable.

We use HTML and SVG as content supports. Thus, a set of files like the one representing this article weighs 116 kB while a PDF file will be 130 kB with less accessibility. And if we have to transform the diagrams into PNG images, we will exceed 300 kB with a further loss in accessibility.

We aim to make a tool that allows communication and can be useful by both blind and ordinary people, whether for design or reading.

To continue, we must test our tool among young blinds, especially learning computer science. We apply this approach of oral description, dedicated to UML diagrams as activity, sequence, object diagrams. We hope to develop use case diagrams, but also bar and pie charts. The ultimate, for some years, is to assume a curve description, helping blind writers to do an appropriate pattern to explain their numeric information.

Incremental development leads us to carry over to other diagrams structures tested on class diagrams. This is the case for the structure of <g> blocks in SVG, as well as for tree modeling. The latter is already introduced to represent the dependencies present in UML sequence and activity diagrams.

Among the medium-term perspectives, besides the addition of new types of diagrams, we should be able, after the end of the pandemic, to test this software on a public of young blind students in computer science.

Finally, this article has been translated to English for the publication of this paper, but the integrated descriptions or annexes of our diagrams are, actually, automatically generated in French...

Acknowledgment. We thank Quentin Savean, for the realization of the PlantUML diagrams, and all the students of the Computer Science Department of IUT du Havre, for testing the software Latitude.

References

1. OMG: Unified Modeling Language (UML) – Version 2.5. http://www.omg.org/spec/UML/2. 5/PDF. March 2015
2. Seifermann, S., Groenda, H.: Survey on textual notations for the unified modeling language. In: MODELSWARD 2016, pp. 20–31. SciTePress (2016)
3. Romeo, K., Pissaloux, E., Serin, F.: Accessibilité des sites web pour les personnes présentant une incapacité visuelle. In: CNRIUT 2018, Aix-en-Provence, pp. 163–165, 7–8 June 2018
4. Romeo, K., Pissaloux, E., Serin, F.: Tableaux accessibles dans les documents numériques. In: CNRIUT 2019, Toulon, pp. 138–140, 6–7 June 2019
5. Romeo, K., Pissaloux, E., Serin, F.: Accessibilité aux informations textuelles et visuelles sur les sites web pour les personnes avec une déficience visuelle. In: HANDICAP 2018, 13–15 June 2018, Paris
6. Mazanec, M., Macek, O.: On General-purpose Textual Modeling Languages. In: DATESO 2012, pp. 1–12 (2012)
7. W3C: Accessibility Principles - How People with Disabilities Use the Web, August 2012. https://www.w3.org/WAI/intro/people-use-web/principles. Accessed 28 Jan 2016
8. Sutton, J.: A Guide to Making Documents Accessible to People Who Are Blind or Visually Impaired. Published by the American Council of the Blind, Washington, DC (2002)
9. https://webaim.org/techniques/screenreader/ consulted on 04 Dec 2019
10. Leuthold, S., Bargas-Avila, J.A., Opwis, K.: Beyond web content accessibility guidelines: design of enhanced text user interfaces for blind internet users. Int. J. Human-Comput. Stud. **66**, 257–270 (2008)
11. https://www.w3.org/TR/wai-aria-1.1/. Accessed 18 Mar 2019
12. Web Content Accessibility Guidelines (WCAG) 2.0. https://www.w3.org/TR/2008/REC-WCAG20-20081211/. Accessed 10 May 2020
13. Serin, F., Romeo, K.: Towards accessible complete plain text to general public reader. Conférence internationale ICCHP, 9–11 September 2020, Lecco, Italy, pp. 34–42 (2020)
14. Grönninger, H., Krahn, H., Rumpe, B., Schindler, M., Vo Ïkel, S.: Textbased Modeling. In: ATEM 2007 (2007)
15. Patil, B., Maetzel, K., Neuhold, E.J.: Universal usability issues of textual information structures, commands, and languages of native visually challenged users: an inclusive design framework. In: Miesenberger, K., Klaus, J., Zagler, W. (eds.) ICCHP 2002. LNCS, vol. 2398, pp. 403–405. Springer, Heidelberg (2002). https://doi.org/10.1007/3-540-45491-8_79
16. Paige, R.F., Ostroff, J.S., Brooke, P.J.: Principles for modeling language design. Inf. Software Technol. **42**(10), 665–675 (2000)
17. Vanderheiden, G.: Fundamental principles and priority setting for universal usability. ACM Conference on Universal Usability, Arlington, Virginia, USA, pp. 32–38 (2000)
18. https://plantuml.com/en/. Accessed 01 Feb 2020
19. Doherty, B., Cheng, B.H.C.: UML modeling for visually-impaired persons. In: HuFaMo 2015, pp. 4–10 (2015)
20. Luque, L., de Oliveira Brandao, L., Tori, R., Brandao, A.A.F.: On the inclusion of blind people in UML e-learning activities. In: RBIE 2015, vol. 23, no. 02, p. 18 (2015)

21. Müller, K.: How to make unified modeling language diagrams accessible for blind students. In: Miesenberger, K., Karshmer, A., Penaz, P., Zagler, W. (eds.) ICCHP 2012. LNCS, vol. 7382, pp. 186–190. Springer, Heidelberg (2012). https://doi.org/10.1007/978-3-642-31522-0_27
22. Luque, L., de Oliveira Brandão, L., Tori, R., Brandão, A.A.F.: On the inclusion of blind people in UML e-learning activities. Brazilian J. Comput. Educ. **23**(02). 2015
23. Bourne, R., et al.: Magnitude, temporal trends, and projections of the global prevalence of blindness and distance and near vision impairment: a systematic review and meta-analysis. Published 1 September 2017. Medicine, The Lancet (2017)
24. Department of Health Statistics and Information Systems, World Health Organization (WHO), Geneva, Switzerland
25. Loitsch, C., Weber, G.: Viable haptic UML for blind people. In: Miesenberger, K., Karshmer, A., Penaz, P., Zagler, W. (eds.) ICCHP 2012. LNCS, vol. 7383, pp. 509–516. Springer, Heidelberg (2012). https://doi.org/10.1007/978-3-642-31534-3_75
26. Murphy, S.: Accessibility of graphics in technical documentation for the cognitive and visually impaired. SIGDOC 2005. In: Proceedings of the 23rd Annual International Conference on Design of Communication: Documenting & Designing for Pervasive Information, (12–17) September 2005
27. Porras, G.C.: Analyse, à l'aide d'oculomètres, de techniques de visualisation UML de patrons de conception pour la compréhension de programmes. Université de Montréal. Département d'informatique et de recherche opérationnelle. Mémoire MSc. en informatique. Aout (2008)
28. Ciampa, K.: The effects of an online reading program on grade 1 students' engagement and comprehension strategy use. J. Res. Technol. Educ. **45**(1), 27–59 (2012)
29. Karsai, G., Krahn, H., Pinkernell, C., Rumpe, B., Schindler, M., Voïkel, S.: Design guidelines for domain specific languages. In: DSM 2009 (2014)
30. Beech, M.: Assisting Students with Disabilities. Bureau of Exceptional Education and Student Services (BEESS), Florida. 3rd edn. (2010)
31. Altmanninger, K., Wöß, W.: Dynamically generated scalable vector graphics (SVG) for barrier-free web-applications. In: Miesenberger, K., Klaus, J., Zagler, W.L., Karshmer, A.I. (eds.) ICCHP 2006. LNCS, vol. 4061, pp. 128–135. Springer, Heidelberg (2006). https://doi.org/10.1007/11788713_20
32. van der Marcel: A guide for scientific writing. Utrecht University, April 2015
33. Flesch, R.: How to Test Readability. Harper and Row, New York (1949)

Improving Accessibility and Personalisation for HE Students with Disabilities in Two Countries in the Indian Subcontinent - Initial Findings

Nicholas Shopland[1]([✉]) [iD], David J. Brown[1] [iD], Linda Daniela[2] [iD],
Arta Rūdolfa[2] [iD], Astra Rūdolfa[2] [iD], Muhammad Arifur Rahman[1] [iD],
Andrew Burton[1] [iD], Mufti Mahmud[1] [iD], and Karel van Isacker[3] [iD]

[1] Interactive Systems Research Group, Computer Science and Informatics,
Nottingham Trent University, Nottingham, UK
{nicholas.shopland,david.brown}@ntu.ac.uk
[2] Faculty of Education, Psychology and Art, University of Latvia, Riga, Latvia
[3] PhoenixKM, Amersveldestraat 189, 8610 Kortemark, Belgium
https://www.ntu.ac.uk/research/groups-and-centres/groups/interactive-
systems-research-group/
https://phoenixkm.eu/
https://www.pzi.lu.lv/

Abstract. National reports indicate access to HE for students with disabilities is limited in India and Bangladesh. These reports highlight the issue of exclusion of people with disabilities, women and economically disadvantaged students. The Supreme Court of India directed all higher education institutions to reserve 5% of places for people with disabilities and make the institutions accessible, as mandated by the Rights of Persons with Disabilities (RPWD) Act, 2016. It was observed that even premier educational institutions have failed so far to implement the provisions of the RPWD Act.

Surveys have been conducted to assess the provision available, the knowledge of and opinions about this provision amongst staff and students at Indian and Bangladeshi Universities. This paper examines the initial findings of these surveys and reviews the state of the art for technical ameliorations which might be implemented, in the context of DiversAsia, a three-year capacity building project. Specifically, the aim is to develop accessible HE OERs and MOOCs, and personalisation using AI, that will enable better provision of open distance learning for those that experience architectural barriers. These accessibility solutions are a clear response to the challenges and barriers identified in the staff and student surveys.

The accessibility approaches to be adopted will address the challenges faced by students with disabilities (including socio-economic and gender issues) entering higher education in Asia and will focus upon: a handbook suggesting strategies to overcome the issues of inclusion, diversity and cultural differences; a toolkit with guidelines, checklists, good/best practices to implement universal design of learning; and an assessment and validation strategy for OERs and MOOCs to review and assess their level of accessibility.

Here we discuss the survey findings and review the state of the art, to describe what specific and concrete actions can be considered within the context of the project.

Keywords: Accessibility · Artificial intelligence · Capacity building · Disability · Higher education · Inclusion · Massive open online courses · Open educational resources

1   Introduction

DIVERSASIA's overall aim is to ensure students with sensorial and cognitive disabilities in India and Bangladesh can enjoy the same access to Higher Education as their peers without disabilities, and have access to digital training materials - open educational resources (OERs) and massive open online courses (MOOCs), this is especially relevant to students who cannot physically access the Higher Educational Institution (HEI) due to existing architectural barriers. These barriers to accessing Higher Education can manifest in various ways, and different approaches will be required to address the specific challenges.

1.1   Access to HE for Marginalised Groups

National reports for both India [1,3] and Bangladesh [15,17] highlight the exclusion of economically disadvantaged and differently-abled students [1,10], females [9,16] and people from remote areas. Such students are disadvantaged by their gender, impoverished or remote backgrounds. Hardly any reference to learning difference in HEIs are made in the national reports we have referenced.

1.2   Non-compliance of Access to Higher Education for Students with Disabilities

In Disability Rights Group vs. UOI [5] and Rajive Raturi vs. UOI [6], the Supreme Court of India directed that all HEIs must reserve 5% of their seats for people with disabilities and make the institutions accessible, as mandated by the RPWD Act. It was noted that even foremost educational institutions had failed to implement the provisions of the RPWD Act. Pressure has been put on educational institutions to make improvements to accessibility, especially once India signed the United Nations Convention on Rights of Persons with Disabilities (UNCRPD). Although there is much legislation in India promoting education for students with disabilities, it is clear that little has been done to promote disability in higher education in India. Bangladesh is similarly culpable - its 'Persons with Disabilities Rights and Protection Act' stipulates that institutions cannot deny admission to any student with special needs under any circumstances; inclusive and equal opportunities education must be provided all students with disabilities, at all levels of education in Bangladesh.

1.3 Access to Online Resources for Students with Disabilities in HE

Research shows that a limited number of university web sites meet even basic accessibility standards [7,11]. Open access and open educational resources will be highly beneficial in enabling students with disabilities in HE.

1.4 The Fourth Industrial Revolution

The Fourth Industrial Revolution is a real and coming fact and the need for 21st Century skills (collaboration, communication, creativity, critical thinking, information and communication technology (ICT) skills and problem solving) over rote learning will be key. "By introducing a new curriculum, teaching and learning methodologies and technologies, universities (in Bangladesh) are striving hard to responding to the challenges of the 21st century." [8]

1.5 Open and Distance Learning (ODL)

ODL (OERs and MOOCs) need to be re-imagined to ensure that they are best-in-class programmes. Such programmes will extend the reach and scope of higher education, thus improving access. Both India [14] and Bangladesh [4] call for expansion of ODL systems in order to respond to the increasing demand for education in all age groups.

1.6 Emergence of Disruptive Tech in HE

National reports in India [1,3] and Bangladesh [15,17] confirm it is getting easier to collect and process data, and tools which can perform sophisticated data analysis are becoming easier to use (AI). Also noted is the accelerating rate of emergence and development of disruptive technologies. For example, India has the National Strategy for Artificial Intelligence: #AIForAll". Software which can create individualised learning trajectories, and their combination with serious games, simulations, augmented and virtual reality (AR/VR) are called for. The addition of AI for personalisation (an aim of DIVERSASIA) and creating guidelines for accessible OERs aligns with this. By developing, testing and adapting such tools, the opportunity to better exploit the potential of ICT, strengthen the internationalisation of HEIs and their capacity to network effectively in technological innovation, and upgrade facilities necessary for the implementation of innovative practices will expand.

1.7 AI for Personalisation to Enhance Technological Innovation

Capacity building in AI for personalised learning can address constraints of the Indian and Bangladeshi HE systems and provide personalised support to students fitting to their needs. Adaptive learning platforms [2] provide the opportunity to retain the benefits of learning with a class cohort (social bonds and skills, motivation, learning from the experiences of others, and many more) and those of personalised instruction (the benefits of one-to-one tuition are well documented). Inconsistency of education provision and lack of social mobility can also be addressed by applying AI and ML to materials and their delivery.

The quality of education provision varies widely, and thus limits the ability of HE to promote social mobility. AI-based solutions offer opportunities to share best practice - at scale, improve the quality of teaching and enable increased access to quality learning materials for all.

1.8   Free/Libre and Open-Source Software for Education (FOSSEE)

The use of open-source software in education is another area that requires considerable support, and FOSSEE [13] needs to become much more widespread. Educational content should be made available under open and permissive licenses, particularly, Creative Commons Licensing.

1.9   Teacher Training (Promoted in DIVERSASIA)

Pedagogical strategies for utilising e-content are required in India (including classes in flipped learning and making good and proper use of MOOCs), and making use of appropriate tools to enhance the learning and teaching processes (e.g., tools to assist students with special needs). Even where there is good provision of facilities, digital literacy remains low, among both teachers and students in Bangladesh [12], leading to more limited uptake of digital materials and techniques in teaching and learning.

1.10   Call for Partnering with High Quality Foreign Universities

Developing partnerships with well respected foreign universities [17] through twinning or joint programs is an effective method of raising teaching and learning quality in Indian and Bangladeshi universities, which DIVERSASIA directly addresses.

2   Methodology

At the beginning of the DIVERSASIA project a suite of information gathering activities were conducted. These consisted of surveys of the HEI staff and students in India and Bangladesh, and desk based research into the best practices known to the consortium from around the world, that will inform and feed into the later toolkit and platform development.

Surveys were prepared for online completion by staff and students at two HEIs in India and two in Bangladesh. There were two distinct surveys administered, one targeted at academic staff, university administrators and policy makers and other gatekeepers, the other aimed at students, potential students and other potential beneficiaries of DIVERSASIA. The surveys were delivered as online questionnaires using Google Forms, with additional support given to students who may have difficulty accessing the forms online. They were designed in English and also translated into Bangla. As this paper goes to press, there are yet more survey results to be gathered in, so this report can only be a very preliminary overview of the staff survey results, the student survey results is still being captured. The staff survey has been promoted widely, and has sought and received responses from many more than the two universities directly involved in this project.

3   Survey Results

These survey results are presented in raw tabulated form, and there has been little opportunity to perform any kind of analysis on them. Responses were received from 177 respondents from India and 25 from Bangladesh; 125 of them are from Universities. 104 female and 98 male. The tabulated data and a brief discussion of them follows.

4   Discussion

Overall, most respondents believed that educational institutions do not tend to exclude students with disabilities. But 11 of them observed that it happens and 34 of them agree that in some cases it is true. Most of the respondents believed that in their institutions 5–10% of students have some kind of disability.

The majority of respondents felt that there were policies and programmes in place to support people with disabilities, although around 10% felt that accessibility issues were not addressed, and surprisingly, twice that number were unaware of their institutions policies and guidelines (Table 1). Similarly a large majority of respondents reported that assistive technology was provided at HEIs, although 31 reported that "no support is provided" and 76 responded that resources are not or only minimally provided, with students having to purchase assistive technology from their own budget (Table 2).

Many respondents reported multiple ways in which their institution promotes inclusion in the curriculum, although again, more than 10% said that their institution had no approaches to promote an inclusive curriculum (Table 3), and a similar broad application of approaches was reported with respect to learner centred teaching practices, with this time less than 10% reporting that their institution had no such practicem (Table 4). A large majority observed that financial help was available to encourage inclusion, with a smaller number also listing more proactive approaches such as encouraging contact the development of relationships between students of different background and targeted enrollment (Table 5).

Provision of an inclusive environment is not so widely or fully available, with 20–25% disagreeing that their institution provides an inclusive environment (Table 6). The physical environment fares better with half to three quarters observing the positive state of various accessible and inclusive ameliorations

Table 1. To what extent do the following statements apply to your institution

	Fully addressed	Partially addressed	Not addressed	Unaware
There are inclusive policy guidelines in my institution	118	45	8	31
There are yearly audits of inclusive policies and practices at my institution	119	36	13	34
There are checklists for evaluating inclusivity of university facilities and services at my institution	125	38	10	29
There is compulsory training on inclusion for faculty in my institution	114	32	26	31
There is compulsory training on inclusion for administrators in my institution	101	42	25	34
Collaboration and networking is promoted in my institution	138	39	8	17
There is plan for inclusive education in HEIs in crisis situations	99	42	18	42
There is a plan for inclusive education in HEIs in a normal situation	104	40	14	44
There is an inclusion unit responsible for the support of students with disabilities during their enrollment at my institution	99	45	18	40
There is an inclusion unit responsible for the support of students with disabilities during their study at my institution	101	44	16	41
There is a specialized programme for peer support between non-disabled students and students with disabilities	88	48	21	45

Table 2. Which assistive technology and software are available in HE

Technological support (if necessary) is provided for all students (the educational institution has good and knowledgeable IT support staff)	123
Assistive technology and software are provided for students who need it	84
Assistive technology resources are provided minimally and insufficiently (the student has to individually reach the resource - they can be bought from a student's own budget)	49
Assistive technology resources are not provided at all (the student has to individually reach the resource - they can be bought from a student's own budget)	27
No support is provided	31

Table 3. Institution promotes an inclusive curriculum by applying the following

Learner-centered design approach with a focus on the student and learning instead of teaching	124
Collaborative learning	129
Flexible ways of assessment	99
Individual course guides and/or learning-paths	93
Flexibility in the choice of studies	108
Flexible examination and practical sessions	59
Diversity oriented curriculum	71
None	23

Table 4. Institution ensures that teaching and learning practices are learner-centred by encouraging the following

Flexible course design	136
Flexible instructional methods	116
Flexible course assessment	102
Flexible and accessible course content	99
Extra time for studies and/or exams to those students who need it	103
Non-discriminatory use of language	52
None	15

Table 5. Institution promotes and encourages inclusion by applying and encouraging the following

Waiving tuition fees for marginalized groups	103
Flexible admission language requirement	66
Scholarships	159
Study grants	109
Free education	75
Targeted enrolment, for instance by making information about university application easily accessible to minority students and their parents	48
Student orientation and guidance (such as tutoring/peer-to-peer tutoring, introductory tours by volunteer students etc.)	97
Contact between students with different backgrounds (for instance students with disabilities or minority backgrounds and other disadvantaged students and students without)	58
Inclusion of different gender and sexual diversity (GSD) students	43
Group work and interaction	84

Table 6. My institution promotes an inclusive environment by...

	Strongly agree	Agree	Neutral	Disagree	Strongly disagree
Ensuring the environment is physically accessible	56	74	41	6	30
The climate and culture are open, respectful, and inclusive	62	74	37	6	25
Providing educational materials (text books, PowerPoints, lectures) in alternative accessible formats.	80	61	34	6	25
Arranging all types of exams in a flexible manner adjusted to the needs of students with different disabilities.	59	54	66	7	25

Table 7. My institution ensures that the physical environment is accessible and inclusive by providing

Easy access to campus facilities (including indoor and outdoor paths, elevators, wheelchair ramps, automatic door openers, accessible/barrier-free toilets, accessible lighting, etc.)	148
Online campus maps that demonstrate accessible areas	130
Workstation with Access Ability sticker	87
University bus that is accessible for students with mobility disabilities	80
Parking space close to the entrance	119
Gender neutral facilities (toilets etc.)	103

Table 8. Self rate of knowledge in the field of Inclusion, Equality and Access for students with disabilities in HEIs

Sufficient and professional	36
Fairly good	49
Average	51
Could be better	37
Not sufficient	27

Table 9. Experience working with students with disabilities in HEIs

Extensive and professional	18
Fair	28
Average	51
Limited	60
None	43

Table 10. Which of the following Pedagogical inclusive methods of an online environment in HEIs do you know?

	Fully	Partly	Not at all
Perceptual methods	60	86	54
Logical methods	68	90	42
Gnostic methods	36	81	85
Methods for learning management	72	89	39

Table 11. Which of the following Pedagogical inclusive methods of an online environment in HEIs do you know?

	Fully	Partly	Not at all
Methods for stimulating interest in learning	75	97	28
Methods for stimulating the depth and the responsibility in the educational activity	82	80	38

Table 12. Which of the following Pedagogical inclusive methods of an online environment in HEIs do you know?

	Fully	Partly	Not at all
Methods for oral control	77	83	40
Methods for written control	67	94	39
Methods for laboratory-practical control	75	90	35
Methods for control over using technologies for learning and daily functioning	78	89	35

(Table 7). The majority of respondents felt that their knowledge of the field of inclusion was no more than average (Table 8), and more than half had limited or no experience of working with people with disabilities, and only 10% saying the their experience was "extensive and professional" (Table 9).

Table 13. Please rate your knowledge of these tools and features

	I am familiar with this tool and have worked with it practically	I've heard of this and got a sense of how it works, but I haven't tried it in practice	I don't know what it is and what it is for
Pencil grips	58	88	54
Magnifying glasses	83	84	33
Walking canes	40	99	61
Wheelchair ramps	74	93	33
Tablets	116	61	23
Switches	87	82	31
Hearing aids	61	111	28
Calculators	134	48	18
Alternative and augmentative communication - AAC	46	91	63
Powered wheelchairs	57	99	44
Eye recognition software	58	94	48
Voice output devices	69	99	32
Wheelchair lifts	56	101	43
Reading spectacles for color blindness	47	104	49
Human assistance	73	94	33
Browser extensions for color blindness	41	94	65
Tactile devices for motion detection	41	101	58
Screen readers for blind/visually impaired users	60	88	52
Word prediction	74	84	42
Touch screens	104	74	22
Voice control	81	95	24
Audio-recording	112	71	17
Audio-visual assistance	91	85	24
Voice amplification	85	78	37
Specific technical examples	70	91	39
Google Chromebooks audio-visual assistance	70	99	31
Microsoft's Surface Pro - assistive technology, including text-to-speech software, word prediction and settings that allow screens to be adjusted for students with epilepsy and colour blindness	60	107	33
Guide dogs for mobility and orientation	39	99	62

Table 14. Which assistive technologies for students in inclusive HEIs do you consider to be most useful?

	Very useful	Needs some development	Not useful	I don't know this technology/tool
Video/braille display or speech synthesizer-Assisted Learning in inclusive HE teaching	120	53	6	30
Block-chain technology in inclusive HE teaching	87	74	13	32
Learning Analytics in inclusive HE teaching	93	72	9	30
Gamification in inclusive HE teaching	87	69	10	37
STEAM in inclusive HE teaching	71	68	14	49
Social Media In inclusive HE teaching	88	75	19	22
Adaptive and assistive technologies for realization of the process of inclusive HE teaching	108	56	12	29
Mobile Apps for inclusive HE teaching	110	65	9	21
Big Data for inclusive HE teaching	95	71	9	27
Massive Open Online Courses (MOOCs) for inclusive HE teaching	122	55	12	20
Virtual Reality (VR) and Augmented Reality (AR) for inclusive HE teaching	123	57	8	19
Artificial intelligence, Machine learning for inclusive HE teaching.	128	49	9	18
Internet of Things (IoT) for inclusive HE teaching.	130	47	9	19
Real-time simulation for inclusive HE teaching	123	54	7	21

Table 15. The biggest challenges for students with disabilities (also for remote learning) in HEIs

Web accessibility	114
Lack of technological devices	122
Lack of support staff (student side)	105
Lack of support staff (on the teaching side)	81
Lack of universal design for buildings, environments, products	60
Level of technological development - Assistive Technologies	85
Lack of universal materials	69
Etiquette and behaviour of teachers from HEIs in an electronic environment	43
Etiquette and behaviour of other students from HEIs in an electronic environment	48
Lack of blended learning/teaching approaches	82
Lack of assistive technologies - for mobility use	71
Lack of assistive technologies - for communication use	68
Lack of assistive technologies - for learning use	67
Crisis situations in HEI	43

Knowledge of pedagogical methods of online environments can certainly be improved, with the majority of respondents reporting partial or no knowledge

Table 16. In your opinion, what support is needed for teaching and administrative staff to successfully work with students with disabilities, to help them in the study process and in accessing education

	Required	Preferably	Not important
Information promoting inclusive education	152	50	4
Guidelines for different tools	146	56	4
Training on pedagogical methods in inclusive education	147	51	6
Training on EdTech possibilities in inclusive education	138	62	5
Accessible Open Education Resources (OERs) and Massive Open Online Courses (MOOCs)	147	55	3
Accessible presentations, data sheets, documents	136	63	7
Remote access to specific assistive technologies (hardware or software)	144	56	6
Available solutions (.odt to Braille, etc.)	134	65	8
Electronic platforms and functionalities (E-teaching/E-learning) that support inclusive HE teaching	141	58	5

of the range of methods suggested (Tables 10, 11 and 12). A surprisingly large number of those surveyed reported that "I don't know what it is and what it is for" for, for a large range of accessibility tools (E.g. Walking canes, Alternative and augmentative communication and browser extensions for colour blindness), so this is definitely an area where some simple exposure/training can bring quick and worthwhile rewards (Table 13). The picture is somewhat better when it comes to assistive technologies, with only 10–15% not knowing about the various technologies, and only 5% saying that they are not useful (Table 14).

Web accessibility and lack of technological devices were reported to be the biggest challenges for students with disabilities (Table 15), and the vast majority of respondents understand the need for a variety of solutions when it comes to working with and supporting students with disabilities, in order to support them in their studies (Table 16).

5   Conclusion

This has been an early review of preliminary and unprocessed data, which will be extended before the final analysis. However, we can see the need for developing disability and inclusion practice in India and Bangladesh from our brief survey of the initial survey data. There is a desire to develop and extend the practice within the HEIs surveyed, and the opportunity to transfer and extend our systems is an exciting opportunity. Our focus goes beyond transferring knowledge developed

in Europe, to finding new ways to adapt and customise the learning experience
with AI and ML, to allow the broadest open access to HE possible.

References

1. Ahmad, W.: Higher education for persons with disabilities in India: challenges and concerns. JDMR **2**(1), 1–4 (2016). https://doi.org/10.29120/jdmr.2016.v2.i1.14
2. Baker, T., Smith, L., Anissa, N.: Educ-AI-tion rebooted? Exploring the future of artificial intelligence in schools and colleges. Technical report, NESTA, London, February 2019
3. Basant, R., Sen, G.D.: Access to higher education in India: an exploration of its antecedents. SSRN J. (2014). https://doi.org/10.2139/ssrn.2535644
4. Daniel, S.J., Kanwar, P.A.: Open and Distance Learning (ODL): An Imperative for Bangladesh, October 2009
5. indiankanoon.org: Disabled Right Group vs Union Of India on 15 December 2017. https://indiankanoon.org/doc/152494913/. Accessed Dec 2017
6. indiankanoon.org: Rajive Raturi vs Union Of India on 15 December 2017. https://indiankanoon.org/doc/149818296/. Accessed Dec 2017
7. Islam, A., Tsuji, K.: Evaluation of Usage of University Websites in Bangladesh. DJLIT **31**(6), 469–479 (2011). https://doi.org/10.14429/DJLIT.31.6.1322
8. Islam, M.S.: Future of higher education in Bangladesh, February 2016. https://www.thedailystar.net/supplements/25th-anniversary-special-part-3/future-higher-education-bangladesh-211417
9. Jadon, D.A., Shrivastava, S.: Women education in India: an analysis. Res. Humanit. Soc. Sci. **8**(13), 4 (2018)
10. Malak, S., Begum, H.A., Habib, A., Shaila, M., Moninoor, M.: Inclusive Education in Bangladesh: Policy and Practice, p. 15 (2013)
11. Martin, P.J.M., Kalbage, A.: Accessibility of higher educational institution's websites — a study. Indian J. Open Learn. **22**(2), 18 (2013). ISSN: 0971-2690
12. Monem, M., Baniamin, H.: Higher education in Bangladesh: status, issues and prospects. Pak. J. Soc. Sci. **30**, 293–305 (2011)
13. Moudgalya, K.M.: Free/Libre and Open Source Software (FLOSS) Resources for Online Courses, August 2020
14. Ramanujam, P.R.: Possibilities of utilising the potential of open distance learning (ODL) resources in the implementation of major schemes of government of India: notes towards evolving a practical frame work. Technical report, India Foundation, New Delhi, July 2018
15. Sarkar, S.H., Hossain, S.Z.: Higher education systems and institutions, Bangladesh. In: Teixeira, P., Shin, J. (eds.) Encyclopedia of International Higher Education Systems and Institutions, pp. 1–10. Springer, Dordrecht (2018). https://doi.org/10.1007/978-94-017-9553-1_499-1
16. Shilpi, M.M., Hasnayen, S., Ilahi, T., Parven, M., Sultana, K.: Education Scenario in Bangladesh: Gender Perspective, February 2017
17. World Bank: Bangladesh tertiary education sector review: skills and innovation for growth. Technical report AUS0000659, The World Bank, Dhaka, March 2019

Creativity, Learning and Technology in MOOC: The DoCENT Approach Between Teaching and Gaming

Luigia Simona Sica[1]([✉]), Michela Ponticorvo[1,2], and Raffaele Di Fuccio[2]

[1] NacLab, University of Naples Federico II, Naples, Italy
lusisica@unina.it
[2] University of Foggia, Foggia, Italy

Abstract. In this paper we describe an approach that combines MOOCs with games to stimulate creativity in teachers' design and production of learning scenarios. This approach is exemplified by DoCENT MOOC, the final product of the European DoCENT project, where innovative training stimulates the creative use of technology in the teaching/learning processes. DoCENT MOOC is built in strict connection with serious gaming, as they were both designed according to an innovative methodology called Situated Psychological Agents (SPA). SPA allows to design and implement educational products by representing the flows inside the educational product in terms of agents interacting with educational, psychological, and pedagogical features, implemented with AI methods. The study describes theoretical underpinnings, designing the approach of both MOOC and Game. A pilot study is reported to support the effectiveness of this approach discussing the implications of using AI tools embedded in agent-based models to support teaching/learning processes.

Keywords: Digital creativity · Learning · Situated psychological agents · Serious game

1 Introduction

The study of teaching/learning processes has been one of the pillars of developmental and educational psychology. It aims to understand the processes that allow the individual to learn effectively and satisfactorily and, on the other hand, to identify the most effective teaching strategies to stimulate and support learning.

However, although the research in this field can now be defined as "classic", nevertheless the updating on these issues is always constant and requires ever greater efforts to capture the changes in learning processes, according to new tools and stimuli that are used by both students and teachers. The technological revolution has introduced new stimulus-tools (computers, Internet, tablets, podcasts, etc.) that have activated the design of new teaching/learning models including the use of new technologies and according to cognitive changes in processes of knowledge creation. MOOCs have certainly been an example of this trend, and they have been used as the starting point of open educational paths. Actually, as such, the use of MOOCs paves the way for individual motivation (or good will or curiosity) to keep learning and deepening their study in a creative way. This motivation cannot always be defined as intrinsic, genuine, constant, although it certainly is a privileged way to learning.

Based on the consolidate psychology literature (on which we will focus later) identifying intrinsic motivation (as well as creativity) as an element to be strengthened to promote learning, the current study suggests that MOOCs design could benefit from being positioned within a framework according to scientific evidence for successful learning. In other words, we need a new psychology-based approach applied to technologies that considers the contextual dimension of the learning process.

In fact, it is already starting from teaching that creativity, learning and technology could be linked through the digital creativity-concept. In education, creativity can stimulate imaginative activity generating outcomes that are original and valuable in relation to the learner. Digital technology can be a medium to promote creativity under the guidance of teachers promoting creative expression through digital tools, teaching how to use digital tools in a creative way, designing, implementing and proposing to learners creative learning scenarios.

Thus, in this paper we propose an approach that combines MOOCs with games to stimulate creativity in teachers' design and production of learning scenarios. In doing so, we describe DoCENT MOOC as the final product of an experimentation path, within the European DoCENT project (Digital Creativity ENhanced in Teacher education, funded under ERASMUS + framework; https://docent-project.eu), of an innovative training approach to stimulate the creative use of technologies in the teaching/learning processes and enhance positive learning, that is to say: digital creativity. Online modules in MOOC focus on how to use the technologies suggested by the project and how to apply them in educational contexts to promote digital creativity. However, alongside the original contents of MOOC, the most important challenge is the innovative methodology of design, development and implementation of MOOC itself, based on a tight connection with serious game design.

Both MOOC and Game implementation are designed according to an innovative methodology based on Situated Psychological Agents (SPA; Ponticorvo et al. 2019; Dell'Aquila et al. 2017) that is fruitfully applied to design and implement educational games. SPA allows to design and implement educational products by representing the flows inside the educational product in terms of agents interacting with educational, psychological, and pedagogical features, which can be implemented with AI methods. The SPA approach has been applied to game design (Ponticorvo et al. 2019; Ponticorvo et al. 2017).

For the sake of simplicity, we can summarize the SPA approach as follows: agents with Artificial Intelligence which can be based on rules, neural networks, expert systems, etc., can be OSA (on-stage agents) or BSA (back-stage agents), with the former interacting directly with the learning ground, be it physical or digital, and the tools to modify the ground state directly. In a learning scenario the OSA is often the learner, whereas in educational games the OSA is often the player. The BSA do not interact directly with the learning ground, but they can affect the OSA who, in turn, can affect the environment. BSA are particularly important in DoCENT MOOC, as it is addressed to teachers in order to stimulate their creativity in teaching processes.

We have chosen this approach as it can be a fruitful way to introduce agents endowed with artificial intelligence to an audience which can be unfamiliar with technological issues. Indeed, the application of SPA to MOOC design was a new challenge in DoCENT MOOC as this approach presents various advantages, leading to adopt automatic control systems and software based on artificial intelligence systems to model educational practices. Thus, we may delegate both on-stage and backstage functionalities to intelligent and autonomous artificial agents, making it possible to run educational games with mixed teams composed of human and artificial agents.

This paper is structured as follows. Firstly, before outlining the study objectives, we review the literature pertaining to learning processes through the link between psychology and technology. Next, we describe the approach adopted in both designing and implementing MOOC, based on the theoretical framework of digital creativity in education (Sica et al. 2019). This is followed by the description of MOOC developed within the DoCENT project as an example for the creation of dynamic, open and creative training tools. Then, we report the results of a pilot study that investigated the effectiveness of this approach. Finally, we conclude the study and make recommendations for further research.

1.1 The Psychological Processes Underlying the Creation of Knowledge: The Positive Creative Learning

Both educational and general psychology disciplines have long investigated the learning processes and how they can be enhanced (for a review, see Sica et al. 2019). Recently, the fundamental role of intrinsic motivation within learning processes has been underlined (Karwowski 2018; Kashdan 2004). Being genuinely interested in a topic, flow and curiosity seem to be fundamental factors in stabilizing learning and, at the same time, promoting exploratory behaviors that lead to expand one's sources of knowledge. In other words, they stimulate to try again to find out more. Some psychologists define this dynamic as the stimulus of curiosity, others emphasize the importance of the emotional and self-evaluation dimension connected to it, referring to the sensation of flow (Karwowski 2018). Referring to curiosity, many scholars have hypothesized its key role in learning processes. It was conceptualized as a form of intrinsic motivation that has a crucial role in fostering both spontaneous exploration and active learning. Thus, curiosity-driven learning and intrinsic motivation have been pointed out as fundamental elements for efficient education (Freeman et al. 2014). On the other side, according to Berlyne's studies (1954), two types of curiosity can be detected: perceptual (the impulse activated by new stimuli) and epistemic (the desire for knowledge). These two types of curiosity could be also distinguished between specific (desire for particular information) and diverse (a more general search for stimulation). According to this approach, curiosity is defined as the predisposition to recognize and seek new knowledge and experiences (Kashdan et al. 2013).

From our point of view, intrinsic motivation, curiosity, flow and exploration constitute joint processes all leading to search for active knowledge, characterized by individual commitment, ability to independently manage new information and integrate it into a coherent and renewed *unicum*, as well as a constant need for novelty and ability to face the challenges resulting from coping with them. Most of these characteristics relate to the processes involved in creative thinking. Even without going into the extensive literature on creativity, it is worth remembering what was stated about the relationship between curiosity and creativity and creativity and risk taking (Williams 1980). Defining an affective dimension of creativity, Williams (1980) indicated four dimensions, including curiosity and risk taking:

- curiosity (as the capacity to investigate elements and ideas, finding new and not obvious connections between them);
- complexity (as the tendency to look for new alternatives and solutions to problems, with the aim to restore order);
- imagination (as the ability to visualize the mental images);
- and risk-taking (as the ability to act under unstructured conditions and to defend one's own ideas).

At this point it is possible to deduce that the learning process could represent a particular case of a creative process during which people combine their previous knowledge with new information in a way that is unique for them (Mumford et al. 2013). More specifically, it seems to us that intrinsic motivation-learning-exploration-curiosity-flow constitute elements that, taken together, constitute a positive model of "creative learning" (which from here on we will define as PCL: positive creative learning). In other words, all the processes described above can produce meaningful learning when they interact with each other, add up and integrate, offering different methods of approaches to knowledge, which can intercept differentiated individual methods. To help an individual develop pleasure in the creation of knowledge by following their own strategies, activating their curiosity towards the process of knowledge itself, the thirst for knowledge built in a manner congenial to them may, therefore, be appropriate to use the greatest number of means at our disposal, or a combination thereof. In fact, this combination would stimulate curiosity with both playful (games) and traditional (online lessons) tools, and activate creativity through the exemplification of the various paths for learning that can be used both separately and (even better) in an integrated manner. This is because not only choosing the content of one's learning can give a sense of self-efficacy and personal satisfaction, but also identifying and building the path that leads to integrative learning.

While PCL could be assumed as the ideal to be pursued, it becomes necessary to deepen how psychological research can provide indications or tools useful to the approach. Among the main answers, the use of new technologies based on exploratory behavior and on game is an ever-increasing range of application, with respect to which a fairly large amount of empirical evidence begins to be available (de Freitas and Oliver 2006). Summarizing, we can say that playing implies learning and this feature can be exploited to make games into useful vehicles to transfer knowledge.

On the other hand, also a more open and flexible form of teaching - based on times and methods more easily manipulated by students, without physical boundaries and based on an open model of knowledge use - such as in MOOCs case - represents a response to the goal of strengthening intrinsic motivation. As argued by Oudeyer et al. (2016), a line of research has considered how formal and computational models of curiosity and intrinsic motivation could be applied to intelligent tutoring systems and MOOCs (Liyanagunawardena et al. 2013), mainly to personalize teaching sequences using artificial intelligence techniques.

Previously we delved into the concept of curiosity, but at this point it is time to expand our discourse a little further about another concept that is relevant for learning; the elements allowing intrinsic motivation. Indeed, among the elements that favor the intrinsic motivation for learning, it seems interesting for our discussion to mention what reported by the *self-determination theory* (Deci and Ryan 2000).

This theory suggests that people are motivated to grow and change (and lo learn) by three innate and universal psychological needs: competence, autonomy, and connectedness. The need for autonomy denotes the desire to choose personal life direction on one's own with the psychological freedom to carry out one's actions.

The need for connectedness refers to the necessity to establish close relationships. Finally, the need for competence refers to the ambition to feel capable in activities and obtaining the desired goals. When these needs are satisfied, people will experience high levels of psychological wellbeing. In learning terms, self-determined people (with intrinsic motivation, curiosity and control on their learning process) are more likely to feel motivated to achieve learning goals (Kashdan 2004; Silvia 2005, 2006, 2008). Without forgetting, as Vygotskij already suggested - and in a more complex way Bruner - that the learning process is based on an interactive and dynamic relationship with the context: there is always a teaching/learning dynamic, whoever the interlocutors are. Human teachers and robot teachers are both agents of the educational relationship who use mediating stimuli and cultural artefacts (books, games, technologies) that convey the contents of knowledge.

"As educational technologies are now thriving, in particular with the wide spread of Massive Open Online Courses (MOOCs) and educational applications on tablets and smartphones, it has become natural to enquire how fundamental understanding of curiosity, intrinsic motivation, and learning could be leveraged and incorporated in these educational tools to increase their efficiency" (Oudeyer et al. 2016, 275). Our challenge is, therefore, to design and build tools meant to enhance precisely this specific type of intrinsic motivation which, in turn, can promote PCL (DPCL: *digital positive creative learning*). And to do this we must adopt an appropriate implementation approach, which we identify in the Situated Psychological Agents Model (SPA; Ponticorvo et al. 2019).

1.2 From Psychology to Technology: The Context of Learning and the Situated Psychological Agents (SPA) Model

In the context of education and educational technology it is extremely important to find the right methodology to combine the needs coming from psychology and pedagogy with the opportunities offered by technology. Moreover, psychological theories and pedagogical models can foster the active involvement of the learner in the learning process (Dell'Aquila et al. 2016; Dewey 1986), and this way it is possible to conceive and design educational technologies such as educational games and MOOC.

On the other side, the massive diffusion and relevant impact of information and communication technology in our everyday life has offered new and innovative solutions in education, enlarging the space where education can take place and the amount of accessible learning and educational resources (Prensky 2003; Kapp 2012). In other words, learners can take advantage of books, as usual, but also multimedia contents, simulations, virtual labs, games and social media following an educational pathway everywhere and in every moment: as a result, MOOCs are the potential technology to achieve this goal.

The notable impact of these new tools that have obtained a great success in the educational context has not been accompanied by an extensive reflection on the methodology to introduce them in a learning pathway, more in general, and as a learning resource, more in particular. A proposal of reflection has come by the introduction of the SPA (Situated Psychological Agents) methodology, described in detail elsewhere and summarized above, which permits to represent in formal terms the main elements of educational resources including connections and interactions (Hylén 2006).

The SPA methodology is inspired by the learning mechanics-game mechanics model (Arnab et al. 2005), which defines a set of pre-defined game mechanics and pedagogical elements connecting them to identify the main pedagogical and entertainment features of a game. It focuses on the design process which is crucial in determining the success of educational resources. If the goal we aim to achieve is to build an educational resource (ER), designers have to try to answer the following questions: "What is the learning goal of the ER? How can it be achieved by actively involving the player?" Bloom's contribution is useful to reply to these points: in his updated taxonomy (Anderson and Krathwohl 2001; Bloom 1956), learning goals are remembering, understanding, applying, analyzing, evaluating and creating.

After the learning objectives are defined, designers must define three fundamental and interconnected levels: the shell level, the core level and the educational level.

These levels have been described in detail in previous works (Dell'Aquila et al. 2016; Ponticorvo et al. 2019), but we can briefly say that these three interconnected levels define the ER; whereas the shell level and the core level can be found in every kind of ER, the educational one is characterizing educational resources. The shell level represents what is visible and immediately accessible for the player, including the game's narrative elements (who are the characters, what actions they can perform, what interactions are possible between them and the environment within which those actions take place; in other words, the plot, the scenario, the roles, the setting). The shell level embraces the hidden level with specific mechanisms and defined rules: the core. In the video-gaming jargon, this level is the game engine (Gregory 2017), which implements functionalities related to the game's dynamics including artificial intelligence. These levels interact as they strongly affect one another. In the ER, the shell level offers a significant context for the educational activities, whereas the core level is related to skills, abilities, competences to learn, together with learning objectives. The educational level covers evaluation and tutoring functions allowing learners to reach specific learning goals. This is another core aspect to focus on during the design process of the ER. The evaluation function deals with the players' performances relative to the specified training objectives; it provides the players and the trainer with important information and data about the learning process (i.e. learning analytics). The SPA approach, therefore, describes the ER elements as interacting agents (artificial and real) at each level. This description has the power to represent interactions between the various actors of the educational process in the ER, when the agent's conception and design is based on psychological and pedagogical models. Indeed, the various agents at the various levels of the SPA approach (at the shell level: users, players, learners; at the core level: interacting agents; at the educational level: trainers, facilitators, educators, tutors) can be represented as agents with specific features and functions.

Almost every educational pathway is characterized by interactions between the learner, at the center, and other people involved in the whole educational processes (Adomssent et al. 2007; Griffin 1994; Hodkinson et al. 2007). Moreover, it is possible to identify the following elements: the playground hosting the agents' actions and containing objects that can be manipulated; the learners acting in the playground, changing it directly as they are situated in the learning scenario and their actions modify the playground; the trainers, that is teachers or people who affect the playground in an indirect way with educational functions. As already hinted at in the introduction, learners and other agents present on the shell level belong to the narrative aspect of the ER and are called on-stage agents (OSA), as they directly interact and affect the core level; on the contrary, the BSA (back-stage agents) can interact indirectly through the OSA and are mainly present on the educational level. The description of the design process and the focus on interacting agents and playground is the strongest contribution of the SPA approach for building ER. We can say that SPA agents have the following features:

– they are situated: they are "immersed" in the educational pathway;
– they are psychological: they have cognitive and emotional functions.

If the agent is human, it automatically has psychological features. In the case of artificial agents with artificial intelligence, it is possible to derive from psychological theories how to model their psychological features and consequent behavior (Di Ferdinando et al. 2015). The SPA approach to develop ER allows to use software based on artificial intelligence systems to build the interactions between OSA and BSA. The tutor can be a human being but also a virtual entity endowed with artificial intelligence.

1.3 The Current Study

According to the literature described, the current study focuses on the hypothesis that, in order to promote PCL (*positive creative learning*), it is possible to use tools supporting the autonomous open management of teaching times and methods (MOOC) and stimulating self-evaluation and intrinsic motivation based on exploration and curiosity (Serious Game), within a psychological framework applied to new technologies that considers the contextual dimension of the learning process (SPA).

The aim is to pave the way to the adoption of automatic control systems and software based on artificial intelligence systems to model educational practices, according to a clear learning objective (in our case, to enhance digital creativity in teacher-educators).

Thus, the present study aims to illustrate how to design and implement a new kind of MOOC through the description of DoCENT-MOOC as *exemplar* for this approach.

In doing so, the current paper describes: the methodological path that led to the creation of MOOC; the technical and methodological aspects of designing and integrating a serious game within the MOOC training course; the final product of DoCENT MOOC.

Then, we report the results of a pilot study that explored the users' evaluation of this approach in terms of digital creativity and game evaluation.

2 Method

2.1 Procedure and Materials

DoCENT MOOC was developed as a core intellectual output of the DoCENT Project (Digital Creativity ENhanced in Teacher education, funded under ERASMUS + program)[1], based on another output, the psycho-pedagogical framework developed under the project. The main goal of the DoCENT project was to enhance digital creativity in ITE (Initial Teacher Education), through the development, the implementation, the validation and the dissemination of an innovative model to guide teacher-educators in applying digital creative teaching practices.

Figure 1 describes the overall structure of the project. The current study is specifically focused on both MOOC and the Game.

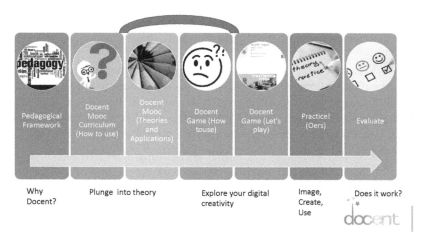

Fig. 1. The DoCENT project model

---

[1] More at https://docent-project.eu; Program: Erasmus +, Strategic Partnerships for higher education, 2017–2019.Project number: 2017-1- IT02-KA203- 036807. The DoCENT project involved seven partners in four EU countries, i.e., Italy (University of Naples Federico II – UNINA; SMARTED), Spain (University of Barcelona - UB; CreaTIC Nens - CREATIC), Greece (University of Athens - NKUA; FORTH), and Luxembourg (European University Foundation - EUF) to achieve the project goal to enhance digital creativity in Initial Teacher Education (ITE) context and to develop, implement, validate and disseminate an innovative model to guide teacher educators in applying digital creative teaching practices. In this context, the DoCENT has provided new models for promoting teachers' and learners' creativity.

MOOC Design: Co-creation Process

According to the educational contents of DoCENT MOOC, the goal was to provide teachers and teacher-educators with indications to make their lessons more digitally creative and creatively digital and to describe some of the tools that can be included in their teaching routines. In order to achieve this goal, the MOOC implementation (in terms of MOOC lessons' contents definition and open educational resources production - OERs) was a shared and co-creative process realized by the DoCENT team and 120 teacher-educators from three EU countries involved in the project (Italy, Spain and Greece). Each country organized two localized workshops based on face-to-face activities with the aim to introduce teacher-educators to digital creativity (first workshop) and to support them in the co-creation of MOOC's contents in terms of content lessons and scenarios for the game (second workshop).

Subsequently, an on-line module was focused on: the evaluation of game scenarios using a grid produced by the project consortium; the selection of the scenarios implementable in the game; they way to use the technologies suggested by the project and how to apply them in educational contexts.

Using the described procedure, we have followed the "training the trainer" approach, sketching an innovative training curriculum for teacher-educators. Specifically, the face-to-face modules focus on participants acquainted with the main concepts of digital creativity and the competence model developed as the first step of the DoCENT project (Sica et al. 2019). Furthermore, they included hands-on activities in which participants tried out different types of technologies and analyzed their educational affordances. Finally, they included brainstorming activities in which they reflected on the way to apply digital creativity to their teaching contexts, according to their teaching objectives. More in detail, the modules were arranged in the following steps: raising teachers' awareness on digital creative teaching strategies ("task identification"); developing their competences in terms of how to use and apply digital technologies for teaching creatively ("preparation"); guiding them in planning their own learning scenarios ("response generation"); accompanying them in the application of their scenarios with their students ("outcome") and validating their scenarios and practices ("response validation").

The Game Design

The design of the DoCENT Game (Di Fuccio et al. 2019) was based on the SPA model. The main aim of the game is to elicit dynamics regarding digital creativity in classroom situations. The user, in a role-playing situation, acts as a teacher who manages the problems involving the students in a typical classroom scenario. Users are able to learn in a safe environment, anticipating and preventing problems which may arise in the classroom promoting digital creativity and providing choices during their interaction with the students.

The DoCENT Game is delivered for PCs and mobile platforms, and it is available on Windows and Android[2] operating systems. In its design, the player is an OSA and it represents the only agent acting on the playground. The OSA is depicted as an avatar that in the DoCENT game is the class teacher. Externally, an artificial BSA assesses the play and provides support and assistance to the MOOC student, referring to the

---

[2] https://play.google.com/store/apps/details?id=it.smarted.docent_en.

DoCENT Competence Framework and in parallel with the MOOC contents. The BSA is represented by an artificial avatar assuming the shape of miss Gray. It is presented as an expert in education and it is this BSA that provides the feedback to the OSA (Figs. 2–3).

Fig. 2. Miss Gray, the artificial Avatar in the DoCENT Game

Fig. 3. A screenshot from the Game

When the OSA completes the scenario, the BSA provides feedbacks in a specific section of the APP, based on the interactions in the game. The BSA can access to a more detailed feedback where each decision is analyzed presenting the previous interactions, the competence area of the decisions and expert comments and additional tips in order to encourage digital creativity. At the end of this section, the avatar, namely dr. Grey, suggests a new scenario to play, starting from the scenarios with lowest scores. When the OSA plays all the scenarios, the BSA provides a general feedback, detailed for each of the six competence areas and accompanied by an extended description of them and references to the MOOC lessons covering those subjects. The DOCENT game has been conceived as a client-server application based on multiple technologies and programming languages. The client was developed as an APP using the c# language for scripting based on a property platform named STELT (Miglino et al. 2013).

2.2 The Pilot Study

In order to evaluate the effectiveness of the proposed model integrating MOOC and Game (based on the SPA model) to support PCL (focusing on digital creative competences and game contribution on learning processes) a pilot study was implemented[3]. To this aim, digital creativity and game evaluation were explored in the Italian group of participants to the co-creation process.

The participants were 36 Italian teachers (from two teaching areas: humanities and technology). A self-report tool was used, exploring both the components of the DoCENT MOOC Model: (a) the impact of the pilot implementation on the teacher-educators' confidence regarding the integration of educational technologies in their profession and (b) the impact of the game on teaching competences. (a) In order to investigate the teacher-educators' *digital creative teaching competences*, a self-report measure was created informed by the DoCENT competence framework on /for digital creativity (Kikis-Papadakis and Chaimala 2019). As for the framework, this part considers: educators' professional competences; educators' pedagogical competences; and learners' competences. The proposed competences and the descriptors aligned to them have been adopted and translated into indicators for evaluating the educators' competence performance. The measure consists of 23 items, one for each descriptor/indicator of the competence framework. Sample item: "I am capable of using technologies to evaluate students' creativity by applying criteria (e.g., fluency, flexibility, originality, elaboration) and tools (e.g. digital rubrics)". Participants responded to the items on a 5-point Likert scale ranging from 1 (strongly disagree) to 5 (strongly agree).

(b) To quantify the experience of playing digital games as the "player experience of need satisfaction", the PENS (Player Experience of Need Satisfaction; Johnson et al. 2018) was used. It is a heavily-researched framework theorizing that sustained player engagement (retention) can be measured by a game's ability to deliver on three central axes: autonomy, competence and relatedness. The questionnaire contains 18 items reviewing the experience in terms of 5 components, such as competence, autonomy, relatedness, immersion/presence and intuitive controls. All but one was measured using a 7-point Likert scale.

Participation in the study was voluntary and anonymity was guaranteed, and the respondents did not receive any payment for their participation. Completion time was between 20 and 40 min.

---

[3] The complete version of the evaluation phase of the DoCENT Project is available on the project website.

3 Results

3.1 DoCENT MOOC

As a result of the described procedure, DoCENT MOOC had the structure graphically described in Fig. 4. MOOC was made up of: a. theoretical contents to enhance digital creativity learning (eight lessons on digital creativity); b. serious game with three game scenarios to assess and train digital creativity competence. Lessons and game are integrated in the MOOC structure with a circular approach (described in the following sections).

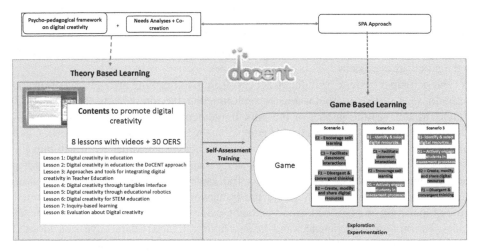

Fig. 4. The DoCENT MOOC structure

3.1.1 Lessons

According to the co-creation phase, MOOC was made up of eight lessons (enriched with links to additional materials; good practices, articles of interest; tutorials; additional resources) addressing the following contents: digital creativity in education, DoCENT approach to digital creativity, approaches and tools for integrating creativity in teachers' education, like game-based learning, digital creativity through tangible interfaces, creativity through educational robotics, digital creativity through STEM education, digital creativity through inquiry-based learning and evaluation of digital creativity. We included educational videos related to all these themes, produced by the partners of the consortium with the technical support of *Federicaweblearning*, as well as OERs produced by teacher-educators during the co-creation of the contents' MOOC phase[4].

---

[4] For a complete description of the contents see Sica, Ponticorvo and Miglino (Sica et al., 2019) and the MOOC at https://www.federica.eu/c/digital_creativity_in_teacher_education.

3.1.2 The DoCENT Serious Game

The game has three different scenarios based on different topics of digital creativity including digital skills and coding, application of Tangible User Interfaces (Ishii 2007) and gamification approach. When the user performs the three scenarios, the artificial tutor (BSA) provides a detailed feedback on the session and the adherence to the DoCENT Competence Framework (Sica et al. 2019).

The scenarios have the following sequential structure. At the beginning, there is an introduction describing the context of the scene and the situation involving the class. The description includes information about the technical features that the user meets in the simulation, including the descriptions of the tools used in the story (Fig. 5).

Fig. 5. The introduction window of the DoCENT Game

Next, the user plays the game and finds four different interacting moments. Each interaction (depicted in the figure as blocks) represents a piece of the story ending with a critical situation that requires a decision from the user, as shown in the next figure (Fig. 6).

At this stage the user can select among three different alternatives, each of those is related to a specific level of digital creativity (hidden for the player). Each alternative is a specific dialogue that the avatar representing the teacher will vocalize. The selection can be enhanced by some contextual information in parenthesis (Fig. 7). Each chosen answer can influence the course of events in the next part of the story.

The four different pieces of the story have a direct association with a different Competence Framework area. The game is designed to cover all the areas defined in the DoCENT framework and with the aim to experience it. If now we represent the DoCENT game in terms of the SPA framework, the player, the teacher whose creative use of technology is assessed, is the OSA, as it can select the option that determine the playground. The BSA is the artificial tutor that builds a profile of the player using its artificial intelligence in the form of a tutoring system: the teacher records the replies step by step and adapts

Fig. 6. Example of Game block

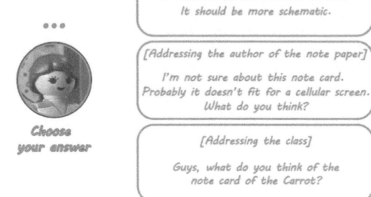

Fig. 7. Chosen process in the Game

the coming replies depending on the choices. Then, in accordance with the complete pathway, it builds a profile of the teacher and offers a feedback that is related to the actual level of creativity and the MOOC content.

The feedbacks provided by the BSA are strongly related to MOOC and refer to it, allowing the player to study or re-study some specific parts of the online course, or some defined lessons.

3.1.3 An Example of a Learning Scenario Developed by the Teacher According to SPA

As a result of the co-creation process (face-to-face workshops plus an on-line module for the evaluation and selection of the scenarios implementable in the game) a total of 30 scenarios were produced, available in the form of OERs on the project website. Indeed, along the DoCENT project, a very important step was represented by the creation of learning scenarios according to the SPA framework. To better explain how the SPA approach was used together with Artificial Intelligence methods to design learning scenarios, now we describe in detail an example of a scenario developed by teachers.

The title of the learning scenario is *Recicreating*; it has the goal to increase the awareness of pupils on the issue of environmental protection, educating them in a sustainable development thanks to a conscious and durable use of resources. Moreover, a related goal is to enhance pupils' creativity and manual skills in creating objects with waste materials.

The playground is a recycling workshop with various objects endowed with digital technology. The target population is represented by pupils of kindergarten and primary school. The laboratory is complemented by a game where the player learns to recycle waste materials in a creative way. The game has three layers:

- In the first one the player, the OSA in the kitchen that is the playground, is instructed to segregate different materials that can be recycled or must be trashed. The BSA is an artificial tutor registering the players' ability and proposing specific activities in order to learn how to distinguish materials.
- The second layer hosts a labyrinth which is the playground where players have to look for objects that can be recycled: in this case, the BSA is an artificial tutor assessing the players' competence, building a profile and suggesting multimedia contents to learn how to recycle more objects.
- In the third layer we have the player, who is an OSA, and an artificial OSA that modifies the playground to enhance the player's creativity. In fact, the player can build a product starting from waste materials and the OSA stimulates the player by suggesting solutions, proposing new materials etc.

It is important to underline that the application of the SPA approach can be very effective in helping professionals who have little expertise in computer science in designing learning materials which use artificial intelligence models and methods.

3.2 The Pilot Study: Results and Comments

The descriptive statistics for digital creativity showed that educators from the Humanities area tended to score highest (M = 4.11, SD = 0.45), followed by educators from the Technology area (M = 3.92, SD = 0.42). This result gives interesting indications regarding the potential use of the model especially with educators from humanistic areas, who are traditionally considered less competent in the use of technology. This is probably due to the SPA approach, close to a model that considers psychological relational modalities.

The descriptive statistics for the game evaluation showed that the highest mean values (with a low standard deviation) are related to the following items: The game controls are intuitive (M = 6.38, SD = 1.4); Learning the game controls was easy (M = 6.38, SD = 0.77). These data suggest that the game has a high level of interaction and it is intuitive. Other values relevant for their high scores are related to the question regarding the competence of the game (M = 5.85, SD = 0.90) and the interesting elements of the game (M = 5.92, SD = 0.95). Low scores were related to the degree of freedom (M = 3.77, SD = 0.73) and on effectivity (M = 4.15 = with a high variability (SD = 1.52). Finally, relevant feedback came from the emotional aspects of the measure. The participants gave a low-medium score to the negative question (I am not impacted emotionally by events in the game) with a mean of 3.00 but the question "The game was emotionally engaging" produced a result with a mean of 3.85. The questions related to the immersivity gained values up to 4. Summarizing, the game was well-accepted and seen as easy to play. It allowed to learn something but had a low degree of freedom and not a huge emotional impact; however, it had a good grade of immersivity and realism.

4 Discussion

4.1 Grasping the Exemplar: The Rational of DoCENT MOOC

The challenge of this paper was to describe an example of developing MOOC designed with the aim to enhance PCL (*positive creative learning*) defined as autonomous, open management of learning times and methods, based on self-evaluation and intrinsic motivation supported by exploration and curiosity, within a psychological framework applied to new technologies that considers the contextual dimension of the learning process (SPA). That beyond the contents of MOOC itself. The implementation of DoCENT MOOC, according the hypothesized approach, has given an exemplar development model for future MOOC design.

Given its nature of first application in this field, this study is not without limits of generalizability and verification of effectiveness in terms of learning. However, it shows interesting results in terms of adaptation between psycho-pedagogical purposes, MOOC's modeling and technologies integration that are worth underlining and deepening.

4.1.1 Positive Creative Learning Elements: Which Are Stimulated and How

Intrinsic motivation, self-evaluation, curiosity, exploration of contents, experimentation were the core processes to address the development of our MOOC. The implementation of DoCENT MOOC has tried to achieve these objectives through the integration of theory-based learning and game-based learning. Let's see how. Contents exploration and curiosity are stimulated by the nature of the lessons, based on scientifically constructed content, rich in examples and links to additional materials, supported by introductory videos. Self-evaluation, experimentation and intrinsic motivation were supported by the Serious Game, which, at the same time, provides scenarios that allow the user to have a self-assessment on the specific skills promoted by the content of MOOC (in our case digital creativity); through its dynamic, gaming allows a sort of virtual gym to train your skills and refers, in a circular way, to the contents (lessons) necessary for learning. Remarkably, the game provides the user with descriptive feedbacks on the user's skills, but these feedbacks are not expressed as judgments or scores as they stimulate the user to "study in-depth" in order to continue the game. This is possible thanks to the well-known emotional engagement produced by the game, to the pleasantness of the playful dynamics and therefore, indirectly, to the intrinsic motivation. Overall, the described MOOC leads to both a more traditional learning, albeit open, based on the acquisition of content, and a learning based on the game and experimentation. Together they can offer an experience that overall stimulates the user's intrinsic motivation and digital creativity. Indeed, in our view, the transition from theory to practice, mediated by the self-reflection stimulated by the assessment phase of the game, can allow the user to experience a training strongly based on the feeling of control and understanding of the training experience within their own capabilities, exactly in line with what is suggested by the self-determination theory.

4.1.2 The Advantages of the SPA: To Automate Without Forgetting the Educational Relationship

Looking at the technical implication of our study, the SPA approach to ER has various advantages. It paves the way to the adoption of automatic control systems and software based on artificial intelligence systems to model the OSA and BSA behavior. Thus, it becomes possible to assign both on-stage and backstage functions to intelligent and autonomous artificial agents, mixing human and artificial agents in ER. Moreover, SPA allows to reproduce, model and feed the dialogic interaction offering a formal representation of the people involved in the learning/teaching dynamic. SPA offers an effective methodology to build up games moving on the shell and core level as well as the educational one. Last but not least, it proposes a comprehensive framework that can be easily understood by specialists with different expertise.

The EG design and development involve education specialists, teachers and trainers as well as computer scientists, software engineers, etc. These specialists can share their knowledge through this framework in a very effective way.

4.2 Conclusion and Future Perspective

Both psychological and technological research is starting to propose hybrid models of tools' design to support teaching and learning processes. Psychological studies have indicated clear directions based, on a general level, on the self-determination theory and, on a more precise one, on those processes that this study defined as *positive creative learning*. However, in order to exploit their full potential, these processes must be stimulated with technologically advanced tools that consider the "relational" level, necessary to complete the educational relationship and, in turn, the satisfaction of the three basic needs. This is a complex challenge for psychologists and technological developers, but it is not an impossible one. In this study we have provided an exemplar development of MOOC that goes in this direction. It is a pilot study from which it will be possible to develop more complex systems where the suggested form of educational psychology can be integrated in game and MOOC designing, with the shared aim to favor positive creative learning with the most appropriate tools.

Funding. The DoCENT project has been funded with support from the European Commission with the program Erasmus +, Strategic Partnerships for higher education, 2017–2019 (Project number: 2017–1- IT02-KA203- 036807).

Declaration of Conflicting Interests. The authors declared no potential conflicts of interest with respect to the research, authorship, and/or publication of this article.

References

Adomssent, M., Godemann, J., Michelsen, G., Barth, M., Rieckmann, M., Stoltenberg, U.: Developing key competencies for sustainable development in higher education. Int. J. Sustain. High. Educ. **8**, 416–430 (2007)

Anderson, L.W., Krathwohl, D.R.A.: Taxonomy for Learning, Teaching and Assessing: A Revision of Bloom's Taxonomy. Longman Publishing, Harlow, UK (2001)

Arnab, S., et al.: Mapping learning and game mechanics for serious games analysis. Br. J. Educ. Technol. **46**, 391–411 (2015)

Berlyne, D.E.: A theory of human curiosity. Br. J. Psychol. Gen. Sect. **45**(3), 180–191 (1954)

Bloom, B.S. (1956) Taxonomy of Educational Objectives. Vol. 1: Cognitive Domain; Edwards Bros.: Ann Arbor, MI, USA; pp. 20–24

de Freitas, S., Oliver, M.: How can exploratory learning with games and simulations within the curriculum be most effectively evaluated? Comput. Educ. **46**(2006), 249–264 (2006)

Deci, E.L., Ryan, R.M.: The "what" and "why" of goal pursuits: human needs and the self-determination of behavior. Psychol. Inq. **11**(4), 227–268 (2000)

Dell'Aquila, E., Marocco, D., Ponticorvo, M., Di Ferdinando, A., Schembri, M., Miglino, O.: Educational Games for Soft-Skills Training in Digital Environments: New Perspectives. Springer, Berlin (2016). https://doi.org/10.1007/978-3-319-06311-9

Dewey, J.: Experience and education. Educ. Forum **50**, 241–252 (1986)

Di Ferdinando, A., Schembri, M., Ponticorvo, M., Miglino, O.: Agent based modelling to build serious games: the learn to lead game. In: FerrándezVicente, J.M., Álvarez-Sánchez, J.R., dela PazLópez, F., ToledoMoreo, F.J., Adeli, H. (eds.) IWINAC 2015. LNCS, vol. 9108, pp. 349–358. Springer, Cham (2015). https://doi.org/10.1007/978-3-319-18833-1_37

Di Fuccio, R., Ferrara, F., Di Ferdinando, A.: The DoCENT game: an immersive role-playing game for the enhancement of digital-creativity. In: Popescu, E., BelénGil, A., Lancia, L., SimonaSica, L., Mavroudi, A. (eds.) MIS4TEL 2019. AISC, vol. 1008, pp. 96–102. Springer, Cham (2020). https://doi.org/10.1007/978-3-030-23884-1_13

Freeman, S., et al.: Active learning increases student performance in science, engineering, and mathematics. PNAS **111**(23), 8410–8415 (2014)

Gregory, J.: Game Engine Architecture. CRC Press, Boca Raton (2017)

Griffin, J.: Learning to learn in informal science settings. Res. Sci. Educ **24**, 121–128 (1994)

Hodkinson, P., Biesta, G., James, D.: Understanding learning cultures. Educ. Rev. **59**, 415–427 (2007)

Hylén, J.: Open educational resources: opportunities and challenges. Proc. open Educ. 4963 (2006)

Ishii, H.: Tangible user interfaces. Hum.-Comput. Interact. Des. Issues, Solut. Appl. pp. 141–157 (2007)

Johnson, D., Gardner, M.J., Perry, R.: Validation of two game experience scales: the player experience of need satisfaction (PENS) and game experience questionnaire (GEQ). Int. J. Hum Comput Stud. **118**, 38–46 (2018)

Kapp, K.M.: The Gamification of Learning and Instruction. Wiley, Hoboken (2012)

Karwowski, M.: The flow of learning. Eur. J. Psychol. **14**(2), 291 (2018)

Kashdan, T.B.: Curiosity. In: Peterson, C., Seligman, M.E.P. (eds.) Character Strengths and Virtues: A Handbook and Classification, pp. 125–141. Oxford University Press, New York (2004)

Kashdan, T. B., Sherman, R. A., Yarbro, J., Funder, D.C.: How are curious people viewed and how do they behave in social situations? From the perspectives of self, friends, parents, and unacquainted observers. J. Person. **81**(2), 142–154 (2013)

Kikis-Papadakis, K., & Chaimala, F. (2019). Assessing competences for digital creativity. *PSYCHOBIT*

Kiili, K., De Freitas, S., Arnab, S., Lainema, T.: The design principles for flow experience in educational games. Procedia Comput. Sci. **15**, 78–91 (2012)

Liyanagunawardena, T.R., Adams, A.A., Williams, S.A.: MOOCs: a systematic study of the published literature. Int. Rev. Res. Open Distrib. Learn. **14**(3), 202–227 (2013)

Miglino, O., Di Ferdinando, A., Schembri, M., Caretti, M., Rega, A., Ricci, C.: STELT (smart technologies to enhance learning and teaching): a toolkit devoted to produce augmented reality applications for learning teaching and playing. Sistemi Intelligenti **25**(2), 397–404 (2013)

Mumford, M.D., Giorgini, V., Gibson, C., Mecca, J.: Creative thinking: processes, strategies and knowledge. In: Handbook of Research on Creativity. Edward Elgar Publishing (2013)

Oudeyer, P.Y., Gottlieb, J., Lopes, M.: Intrinsic motivation, curiosity, and learning: theory and applications in educational technologies. In: Progress in Brain Research, vol. 229, pp. 257–284. Elsevier (2016)

Ponticorvo, M., Dell'Aquila, E., Marocco, D., Miglino, O.: Situated psychological agents: a methodology for educational games. Appl. Sci. **9**(22), 4887 (2019)

Ponticorvo, M., Di Fuccio, R., Di Ferdinando, A., Miglino, O.: An agent-based modelling approach to build up educational digital games for kindergarten and primary schools. Expert Systems **34**(4), e12196 (2017)

Prensky, M.: Digital game-based learning. Comput. Entertain. **1**, 21 (2003)

Sica, L., Ponticorvo, M., Miglino, O.: Enhancing digital creativity in education: the docent project approach. In: Popescu, E., BelénGil, A., Lancia, L., SimonaSica, L., Mavroudi, A. (eds.) MIS4TEL 2019. AISC, vol. 1008, pp. 103–110. Springer, Cham (2020). https://doi.org/10.1007/978-3-030-23884-1_14

Silvia, P.J.: What is interesting? Exploring the appraisal structure of interest. Emotion **5**, 89–102 (2005)

Silvia, P.J.: Exploring the Psychology of Interest. Oxford University Press, New York (2006)

Silvia, P.J.: Interest - the curious emotion. Curr. Dir. Psychol. Sci. **17**, 57–60 (2008)

Williams, F.E.: Creativity Assessment Packet: Manual. DOK Publication, Buffalo, NY (1980)

JLoad: An Accessible Learning Object to Support Hearing Impaired in Learning Java Programming

Lidiane Castro[1], Marcos Nascimento[2(✉)], Francisco Oliveira[1],
Adriano Freitas[3], and Nelson Lima[1]

[1] Universidade Estadual do Ceará, Fortaleza, CE, Brazil
[2] Universidade de São Paulo, São Paulo, SP, Brazil
marcos.devaner@dellead.com
[3] Instituto Federal de Educação, Ciência e Tecnologia do Ceará,
Fortaleza, CE, Brazil

Abstract. According to the Brazilian Institute of Statistical Geography, the Brazilian population is made up of more than 10 million people with hearing impairment. These people often face various barriers to getting a proper education. In teaching and learning programming, the use of environments that are not adapted for people with hearing impairments can make it difficult to understand iconography signs, textual instructions, and the degree of abstraction necessary for programming logic. This work proposes the JLoad (Java Learning Object to Assist the Deaf), aiming to support the hearing impaired in practical Java programming activities. JLoad works as a virtual programming laboratory, allowing collaboration between students and a tutor, asynchronously and remotely. We performed a comparative analysis between JLoad and Eclipse, a traditional tool, to assess its impact on people with hearing impairments in terms of motivation, performance, and usability in the execution of learning tasks. In all criteria, JLoad presented better averages and most of them were ratified by the statistical tests presenting significant differences, indicating a better performance of JLoad.

Keywords: E-learning · Accessibility · Hearing Impaired · Java

1 Introduction

The World Health Organization [22] defines disability as activity limitations and participation restrictions that involve negative aspects of the interaction between an individual and the environment. For instance, a significant part of people with disabilities (PwD) faces difficulties accessing proper formal education. According to the Brazilian Institute of Statistical Geography [5], the Brazilian population is made up of more than 10 million people with hearing impairment (DHI). These people face a lack of methodologies and learning materials adapted for this audience [4].

M. Antona and C. Stephanidis (Eds.): HCII 2022, LNCS 13309, pp. 142–156, 2022.
https://doi.org/10.1007/978-3-031-05039-8_10

Regarding inclusive education, the resources of information and communication technology used in the teaching and learning process must also be accessible. In this case, they should include learning objects, defined as an entity, either digital or not, which can be used and reused or referenced during a process of technological support for teaching and learning. Information and communication technology has been a good ally for inclusive education. Nevertheless, technological resources used to support teaching and learning must conform with accessibility standards. In this context, the World Wide Web Consortium proposes a Web Content Accessibility Guidelines (WCAG)[1]. WCAG presents some accessibility guidelines to make web content widely accessible [7].

In the context of remotely teaching/learning a programming language, other barriers may be encountered besides the lack of accessibility. For example, in Java courses, students also have to download and install an Integrated Development Environment (IDE) such as Eclipse to perform some of the course-required activities. In several cases, they are at home with no one nearby to assist them. Furthermore, the DHI may present difficulties such as icon comprehension, text language, and abstract concepts [17].

The Virtual Learning Labs, used for technology-mediated hands-on workshops, have been a way to motivate students and improve learning effectiveness. The immersive learning approach such as the Virtual Programming Laboratory [3,20], has shown positive results for the engagement and motivation of students and, consequently, might reduce student dropout. In the DHI context, accessibility resources available in a Virtual Learning Lab might attenuate the difference of performance between deaf and listeners students, during programming activities [17].

In this work are proposed JLoad, an accessible learning object integrated a Learning Management System (LMS), aiming to support DHI in activities of Java programming. The JLoad's environment enables pupils to share code with tutors, highlighting problematic points in the code produced. Such sharing functionality allows, up to some point, direct communication between a DHI who does not speak the tutor's language and a tutor who cant understand sign language. Using JLoad students can participate in programming workshops (organized in a step-by-step fashion) as part of the programming courses; get remote situated asynchronous tutor assistance (who has access to source-code and markings over the code to sign where the doubts are); get interpreters' help to mediate communication between deaf student and a tutor who is not fluent in sign language.

To verify the efficiency of JLoad for deaf students, a comparative study between JLoad and Eclipse was carried out. A group of 15 (fifteen) deaf people participated in this study. Participants were invited to take a Java programming class and perform a programming task. Part of the group used JLoad and while others had Eclipse to perform the proposed task. The triangulation technique [1] was applied, comparing usability, motivation, and performance metrics pointed out by the participants. In all criteria, JLoad presented better

---

[1] https://www.w3.org/WAI/standards-guidelines/wcag/.

averages and most of them were ratified by the statistical tests presenting significant differences, indicating a better performance of JLoad.

This text is divided into sections. Section 2 presents the theoretical background that supports our research, especially challenges DHI faces to learn and along with theories and solutions that can support them in the learning process. In Sect. 3 (three) we present and discuss related work. In Sect. 4 (four) we introduce the JLoad. In Sect. 5 (five) presents the methods and evaluation carried out on the study. Finally, Sects. 6 and 7 (six and seven) are present the results and discussion.

2   Background

In this section we discuss some learning challenges faced by DHI people. We also discusses the influence of active learning and Virtual Programming Lab in JLoad's conception. Finally, we also present the accessible LMS that uses JLoad as a Learning Object for Java programming activities.

2.1   Learning Challenges Faced by DHI People

DHI people have difficulties in traditional education. They present lower academic performance when compared to their hearing counterparts [13,18,28]. However, the lack of hearing capabilities itself might not be the source of the problem. For example, time, type of education, and learning opportunities also influence low mathematical accomplishment [19].

Software and educational materials are normally produced for listeners, using textual language. Therefore, DHI people need extra effort to understand a subject or to adapt to the software. On the other hand, when we consider the DHI performance in programming activities, the use of accessible tools results in positive impacts [17], matching the performance of DHI and hearing people during a programming task. Furthermore, the use of an accessible tool may increase the degree of satisfaction of deaf users. In this context, we can improve the learning process, providing translated content into sign language and ways of exchange information between DHI and listeners.

2.2   Active Learning for Programming Learning

The Virtual Labs for Programming allows the applicability of active learning [14] since students are motivated, hands-on way, to solve real-world problems through the algorithms. For instance, JLoad is a tool that implements this concept through workshops, hands-on Java programming activities, it has been used as a tool to solve real-world problems algorithmically. Through accessible chat, the students can be supported by a tutor. Finally, using Jload the students can have learning experiences as a protagonist and develop their learning hands-on to build prototypes and software products.

Acquiring advanced knowledge usually results in a cognitive load. This load can increase even more when it comes to learning a programming language. For example, Java, in addition to adopting a language-specific syntax, also appropriates the textual signs of the English language. The DHI, who use sign language, should strive to learn the abstraction inherent in the programming language, the meaning of English words, and programming logic, further increasing your cognitive load. As an alternative for this problem, the collaboration and interaction between tutors and students may reduce part of this cognitive load [23]. In addition, JLoad is embedded into an accessible LMS [16] that provides resources for interaction and communication through sign language.

2.3   An Accessible LMS

The DELL Accessible Learning (DAL) is an accessible LMS that provides several features to help PwD to teach and learn. It is also in conformity with the WCAG 2.0. In the LMS, each disability has a specific profile with features for its needs. As shown in Fig. 1, the student perspective is divided into four areas: (1) accessibility bar with accessibility resources, language options, and profile selector; (2) a tool menu for students: courses, calendar, mail, grades, glossary, and settings; (3) enrolled courses of a student and links to access them; (4) panel with student's agenda and warnings posted by the tutor.

Fig. 1. Student interface.

On the LMS are available several professional training courses in various areas such as education, entrepreneurship and sales, foreign languages and Information Technology. The contents are available in Portuguese, English and in Brazilian Sign Language (LIBRAS) and also in American Sign Language (ASL). Access to the platform is made available exclusively to students enrolled in courses. Once registered, students can access all the contents of the classes through computers connected to the Internet. In general, courses are made available through partnerships with private, governmental and third sector institutions.

Several types of users are available in the LMS: student (DHI and listeners), tutor, system administrator, pedagogical coordination, and interpreter of sign language. Students access classes and performance reports. Tutors support students in doubts, forums, and programming activities. The pedagogical coordinator can generate reports and evaluate courses, and the system administrator has complete control over the LMS. An interpreter receives translation requests from tutors and students. All content is available in Portuguese and LIBRAS.

3   Related Work

This section presents the tools that implement the concept of virtual labs and active learning. The presented tools are Virtual Programming Lab plugin [3], ViPLab [25] and iVProg [10]. These tools aim to support the teaching and learning of programming.

3.1   Virtual Programming Lab Plugin

The Virtual Programming Lab plugin(VPL-plugin) is a plug-in for the Moodle LMS. It supports students in their first steps as programmers. The VPL-plugin architecture consists of three modules. The Moodle module has characteristics such as submission management, evaluation, and support of anti-plagiarism. The browser-based code editor allows students to edit, execute, and test programs without an installed compiler, and the last module allows student evaluation remotely.

A survey of satisfaction with the use of the tool, applied by Castro and Rocha (2018), shows that of 63 students only 17.5% of these disagreed with using the VPL-plugin to solve more exercises. The results of the user experience are promising, but the authors point out that the tool still needs some improvements to make its use even more efficient.

3.2   The ViPLab

The ViPLab [25] is a virtual online programming laboratory for the ILIAS learning management system. Its architecture has two different modes for code evaluation: manual and automatic. In manual mode, the teacher manually activates correction and evaluation phases through ILIAS. In automatic mode, the processing occurs without manual interference or interaction. ViPLab supports students and teachers in programming learning, but it is a demo version, and it is not available for use. Therefore it is not possible to evaluate its impact in the programming learning context.

3.3   The iVProg

The Interactive Visual Programming (iVProg) [10,20] aims to support the teaching and learning of introductory programming concepts. In its most current version, the tool applies the paradigms of visual programming, but it is also possible to create textual codes, in a language inspired by the Portugol Studio [20]. iVProg can be integrated with Moodle through an interactive activity module called iTarefa [21].

A usability study applied to iVProg [20] shows that, although the tool has a strong potential for teaching and learning programming, there are still usability barriers to be overcome. Study participants were asked how pleasurable it was to use iVProg. The results show that 46.8% responded neutral, pleasant or very pleasant, but 53.2% classified the use as unpleasant or very unpleasant. On the other hand, studies previously conducted [24] show that the use of iVProg increased class attendance by more than 3.3%, and there was also an increase in average grades by more than 0.53 points.

All these tools help teachers and students in teaching and learning programming. However, they do not have accessibility's resources to support deaf students. In next section, we present the JLoad, an programming lab that may support DHI during practical workshop development.

4   Introducing JLoad

The JLoad is a Learn Object available in the DAL (Dell Accessible Learning) presented in Sect. 2.3. It aims to reduce the cognitive effort of students. Thus they do not need to open, install, and configure other code-creating programs. Besides, it allows studying and accessing data from anywhere with Internet access. DHI students have accessible resources such as activities description in sign language, chat with record videos, and interpreter support.

JLoad proposes workshops to allow students to build up their programming knowledge in Java. A workshop consists of a list of programming activities. Each activity has its own set of instructions (displayed in Portuguese and Libras). Typically, a JLoad activity requires: (a) some coding, compilation and execution of a Java program; (b) submission of the code for evaluation; and (3) requesting and getting situated help - all done within JLoad. This all-in-one approach saves the student from having to install and learn to use an integrated development environment like Eclipse before running their first program. Supported by the theories presented above, JLoad programming workshops are divided into smaller, simpler subtasks with achievable goals, allowing for gradual and monitored progress. The simple interface lets you keep students focused on the subtask goals. Students can submit questions to tutors through JLoad itself. Such questions are accessed in the tutor's area. All information such as: Libras videos, workshop content and coding questions are stored in the JLoad repository. JLoad is also responsible for compiling and executing student-created code, all remotely.

The approach proposes that students should assume a more active role. They need to solve problems, develop projects, and create opportunities for the construction of their knowledge [29]. In this context, JLoad allows students to build their learning from activities focused on achievable goals, allowing gradual and monitored progress. Besides, JLoad also offers tutor support to guide and answer doubts.

We constantly need to rethink PwD teaching and learning methodologies. They have to consider access to information and explore PwD abilities in an adapted learning model [26]. JLoad offers challenges so that DHI can develop their programming skills. We combine active learning with accessible features to attenuate the barriers of interaction.

4.1 User Types

JLoad inherits resources and user types from the AccessLearning LMS. Thus, beyond resources for DHI, it has other accessibility resources such as auto-contrast, font resizing, shortcut keys, and labels. We have four user types: student, tutor, interpreter, and administrator.

Student. The student's workspace consists of a code editor, a console, and an inclusive chat. They access the workshop contents in text and sign language. Figure 2 shows the student's workspace. We indicate the resources using numbers from one to six.

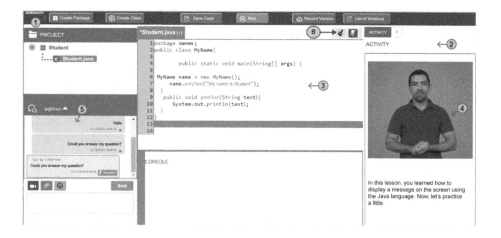

Fig. 2. Student's Workspace.

1. Menu and navigation: the students can access the main functions.
2. Workshop steps: the student can navigate through the workshop steps. We present the step details in sign language.

3. Development and feedback: It is a midi-IDE to write codes, compile, and run.
4. Workshop's content: The students can check the accessible content and instructions about the activity that they need to perform.
5. Tutor-student interaction: It is a chat for accessible communication between student and tutor. They can also highlight code lines and sending them to the tutor.
6. Highlighted code: Students can highlight parts of the code and send it to the tutor. It helps to find the doubt or problem.

JLoad is a web-based tool, and its users can access it using the Internet. We design it to be responsive, and, therefore, we can use it on different devices such as laptops, tablets, and other computers (Fig. 3).

Fig. 3. Tutor's workspace.

Tutor. The tutor's workspace is similar to the student's. Tutors have access to a list of students whose activities they are monitoring. This environment allows tutors to visualize, edit, and evaluate the student's workshops. Also, the tutor can interact with the student through the chat, observe the steps already completed and can rate a workshop and give a feedback about it (Fig. 4).

Interpreter. The interpreter's workspace has a panel on the left with a list of students and their respective translation requests. The requests can be from sign language to text or vice-versa. The interpreter environment does not have the development area that exists in the student and tutor workspace.

Fig. 4. Interpreter's workspace.

4.2   Technology and Architecture

JLoad is developed using the MVC architectural model [8]. This architecture facilitates the division and understanding of the code. To improve performance, JLoad uses asynchronous calls through client-side web technologies (AJAX) [12]. For example, we use AJAX features when JLoad loads project file directories, and messages in the chat.

The JLoad architecture is composed of a user-interface (client-side) and the core of the application with the main functionalities (server-side). The persistence component contains the data of the students, tutors, classes, projects, codes, and libraries in a MySql database. JLoad allows the distribution of these components on more than one server. Since JLoad must allow communication in LIBRAS using videos (workshops and chat), the tool communicates with the Real-Time Transport (RTP) protocol. We use the Red5[2] software for recording, transmission, and video playback.

JLoad and the AccessLearning LMS are integrated using SCORM (Shareable Content Object Reference Model) file. The SCORM standard defines communications between client-side content and the execution environment [2].

JLoad supports only the Java programming language. Since we project it to be an LO for e-learning, to use JLoad, we need to integrate it into an LMS. And so far, the server-side is adapted just with the AccessLearning LMS. Integration with other LMS needs adjustments in JLoad core.

5   Methods and Evaluation

To evaluate the applicability for DHI people, we carry out experiments to check usability, performance, and motivation using JLoad and the Eclipse IDE. Then,

---

[2] http://red5.org/.

we perform a comparative analysis of the results of the two tools. We select 15 participants, all DHI students from programming courses in e-learning modality. First, they answer a sociodemographic questionnaire and a free consent term. We summarize their profile in Table 1.

Table 1. Participants' profile

	Summarized result
Age	16 up to 29 years old
Gender	Male 73.3% and female 26.7%
Educational level	Elementary school: 6.7%; high school: 66.7%; higher education: 26.7%
Type of deafness	Congenital deafness: 73.3%; acquired deafness: 20%; don't know how to report: 6.7%
Level of deafness	Profound: 66.7%; moderate: 20%; severe: 6.7%; mild: 6.7%

The results indicate that 53.3% of the participants communicate predominantly through LIBRAS, and they do not speak other languages. On the other hand, 46.7% of them have good knowledge and understanding of Portuguese.

To assess JLoad, we use the triangulation method. It applies three technique of evaluation to have different perspectives about a problem [1].

The first is the usability test. To assess usability, participants answer a questionnaire adapted from Lewis (1995), the Post-Study System Usability Questionnaire (PSSUQ) [15]. With the collected data, we compare the usability of JLoad and Eclipse IDE. When we apply the PSSUQ, we can analyze for each tool: system utility (SysUse), information quality (InfoQual), and interface quality (IntQual).

The second technique is the analysis of the user performing the workshop [1]. For each tool, we analyze execution time, assistances about the tool, interpreter requests, and workshop grades. We assign one same tutor to evaluate all participants' workshops to obtain the grades.

Finally, we perform a motivation analysis. We apply the Situational Motivation Scale (SIMS) [11]. Thus, we evaluate the motivation levels for each activity in the two tools. We translate all questions from the SIMS to LIBRAS for a better understanding of the participants.

5.1   The Experiment Design

Before we apply the methods, the participants have a class about Java programming language. It was available through the *AccessLearning* LMS, aiming to lead participants to the same level of knowledge. For this, the participants have remote support of a tutor and an interpreter of LIBRAS.

Randomly, we divide the participants into two groups. Then, we expose the groups to the two conditions, as in a typical within-subject design [6]. In our case, both groups carry out a workshop using JLoad and Eclipse. To avoid the learning effect, group 1 starts using Eclipse and group 2 starts with JLoad. The experiments happen in two days. On the first day, both groups have the class. Group 1 uses Eclipse to perform the workshop, and group 2 uses JLoad. On the second day, group 1 uses JLoad, and group 2 uses Eclipse.

During the workshops, an observer takes note of the performance parameters. After the workshops, the participants respond to the usability and motivation questionnaire. We apply the collected data to statistical tests to verify differences in performance using Eclipse and JLoad.

6 Results

In this section, we verify for DHI the impacts of JLoad and Eclipse on performance, motivation, and usability. We submit the data to statistical analysis to assess significant differences between both tools. Thus, we aim to find a more accessible tool for DHI, supporting their learning in Java programming.

We use the Student's t-test for paired samples [9] in our analysis. A significant difference is explicit when we have a p-value less or equal to 0.05. We present the results in Tables 2, 3, and 4.

6.1 Usability Results

Through the PSSUQ, we have four usability metrics: SysUse, InfoQual, IntQual, and general average. For each DHI, we have four values for JLoad and four for Eclipse.

Table 2 shows the average value of each metric for each tool and its respective p-value.

Table 2. Usability results

Usability metric	Average score*		p-value
	JLoad	Eclipse	
SysUse	2.52	3.31	0.101548
InfoQual	1.91	3.11	0.030102
IntQual	1.71	3.09	0.015533
General average	2.14	3.16	0.032804

*Smaller values are better

The general average is 2.14 for JLoad and 3.16 for Eclipse. These results indicate participants' preference for using JLoad (t(14) = 2.36682, p = 0.032804). Besides the general average, we verify statistically significant differences in Info-Qual and IntQual metrics. These results suggest better usability for JLoad.

6.2 Performance Results

We use four metrics to assess performance: (a) time to complete the task; (b) the number of help requests about the tool; (c) the number of translation requests to interpreters; and (d) the grades (obtained by blind correction of programming workshops).

Table 3 summarizes data for performance metrics. We present the averages of the results for each tool and the p-values from the statistical tests.

Table 3. Performance results

Performance metric	Average score		p-value
	JLoad	Eclipse	
Time to complete the task	44 min 40 s	64 min 28 s	0.0336
Help requests about the tool	1	5.133	0.0005
Translation requests	2.2	3.8	0.1901
Grades	9.20	8.15	0.0208

The results indicate that the JLoad participants complete their activities faster (44 min 40 s), p-value 0.0336. It shows a significant difference in this metric.

JLoad participants present an average of tool help requests equal to one, while Eclipse participants show a value of 5.133. The statistical test shows a significant difference in this metric ($t(14) = 4.46678$, $p = 0.0005$).

During the experiment, the participants can request translations to the LIBRAS interpreter in case of doubts. The average number of translation requests is 2.2 for JLoad and 3.8 for Eclipse. The statistical result does not show a significant difference ($t(14) = 1.376818$, $p = 0.190188$).

To measure the learning process, a single evaluator performs a blind correction on the created codes. We omit the author and the tool used to create the code. The average of the grades using JLoad is 9.2, and 8.153 using Eclipse. The statistical test confirms a significant difference ($t(14) = -2.447275$, $p = 0.028191$).

6.3 Motivation Results

Table 4 shows the average of motivation scores obtained through the SIMS questionnaire. We analyze three metrics: general motivation, demotivation, and intrinsic motivation. Since data from general motivation does not conform to a normal distribution, we use Wilcox on Signed-Rank test [27] for this metric. We use the paired Student's t-test for the other two metrics.

The results are similar, with slightly better results for JLoad. However, the statistical tests did not find any significant difference.

Table 4. Motivation results

Motivation metric	Average score		Observation	Statistical value
	JLoad	Eclipse		
General motivation	5.58	5.07	Higher is better	w = 38
Demotivation	3.68	3.73	Smaller is better	p-value = 0.91
Intrinsic motivation	6.22	5.25	Higher is better	p-value = 0.09

7 Conclusion and Future Works

We design JLoad to reduce the evasion in the initial classes of online programming courses. The purpose of the research is creating a tool for deaf people in the Java programming area. In the design of JLoad, we carry out participatory design with the target audience, and we develop it under international accessibility criteria.

The usability and motivation results favor JLoad. The general usability average is 2.14 for JLoad and 3.16 for Eclipse (in this case, smaller values are better). JLoad also performs better on general motivation with 5.58 versus 5.07 for Eclipse.

JLoad provides better usability and greater motivation. On average, it allows its users to finish the workshops about 20 min faster, and the students also get better grades. The social presence of the tutor is higher, allowing the student's engagement to ask for help. JLoad students request about 70% more assistance than the ones using Eclipse.

As future work, the tool can evolve to meet other disabilities. We can develop a mobile version, and we can give learning support to other programming languages. JLoad can also become a collaborative workspace for different audiences, such as listeners and deaf.

Acknowledgment. This study was an initiative of Dell Computers and Universidade Estadual do Ceará. In addition, developed by Lead - Research, Development and Innovation Center Dell.

References

1. Barbosa, S., Silva, B.: Interação humano-computador. Elsevier Brasil (2010)
2. Bohl, O., Scheuhase, J., Sengler, R., Winand, U.: The sharable content object reference model (SCORM) - a critical review. In: International Conference on Computers in Education, Proceedings, pp. 950–951. IEEE (2002)
3. Cardoso, M., de Castro, A.V., Rocha, A.: Integration of virtual programming lab in a process of teaching programming EduScrum based. In: 2018 13th Iberian Conference on Information Systems and Technologies (CISTI), pp. 1–6. IEEE (2018)
4. de Carvalho, R.P.Q.: O surdo e o mercado de trabalho: conquistas e desafios. Caleidoscópio **1**(4), 105–111 (2014)
5. Censo, I.: Disponível em. http://www.censo2010.ibge.gov.br/. Acesso em 23 (2010)

6. Charness, G., Gneezy, U., Kuhn, M.A.: Experimental methods: between-subject and within-subject design. J. Econ. Behav. Org. **81**(1), 1–8 (2012)
7. WWW Consortium, et al.: Web content accessibility guidelines (WCAG) 2.0 (2008)
8. Curry, E., Grace, P.: Flexible self-management using the model-view-controller pattern. IEEE Softw. **25**(3), 84–90 (2008)
9. De Winter, J.C.: Using the student's t-test with extremely small sample sizes. Practical Assess. Res. Eval. **18**(10) (2013)
10. Felix, I., Souza, L., Brandão, L., Ferreira, B., Brandão, A.: ivprog: Programação interativa visual e textual na internet. In: Anais dos Workshops do Congresso Brasileiro de Informática na Educação, vol. 8, p. 1164 (2019)
11. Gamboa, V., Valadas, S.T., Paixão, O.: Validação da versão portuguesa da situational motivation scale (sims) em contextos académicos. In: Atas do XII Congresso Galego-Português de Psicopedagogia, 11–13 de setembro de 2013, pp. 4868–4882. Universidade do Minho (2013)
12. Garrett, J.J., et al.: Ajax: a new approach to web applications (2005)
13. Gregory, S.: Mathematics and deaf children. Issues in deaf education, pp. 119–126 (1998)
14. Johnson, R.T., Johnson, D.W.: Active learning: cooperation in the classroom. Annu. Rep. Educ. Psychol. Jpn. **47**, 29–30 (2008)
15. Lewis, J.R.: IBM computer usability satisfaction questionnaires: psychometric evaluation and instructions for use. Int. J. Hum.-Comput. Interact. **7**(1), 57–78 (1995)
16. Nascimento, M., et al.: Plataforma de aprendizado acessível da dell (dell accessible learning) uma plataforma de ensino a distância acessível para todos. In: Anais dos Workshops do Congresso Brasileiro de Informática na Educação, vol. 8, p. 1148 (2019)
17. do Nascimento, M.D., de MB Oliveira, F.C., Alves, S.S.A., de Freitas, A.T., Gomes, L.A.C., de Matos, A.S.: A comparative study of deaf and non-deaf students' performance when using a visual Java debugger. In: Frontiers in Education Conference (FIE), pp. 1–8. IEEE (2017)
18. Nogueira, C., Zanquetta, M.: Deafness, bilingualism and traditional teaching of mathematics. Zetetiké: Revista de Educação Matemática **16**(30), 219–237 (2009)
19. Nunes, T., Moreno, C.: Is hearing impairment a cause of difficulties in learning mathematics. Dev. Math. Skills **7**, 227–254 (1998)
20. de Oliveira Brandão, L., Bosse, Y., Gerosa, M.A.: Visual programming and automatic evaluation of exercises: an experience with a stem course. In: 2016 IEEE Frontiers in Education Conference (FIE), pp. 1–9. IEEE (2016)
21. de Oliveira Brandao, L., Félix, I.M., Pereira, P.A., Brandao, A.A.F.: Evolving technology to better support teaching introductory programming inside Moodle. In: 2018 XIII Latin American Conference on Learning Technologies (LACLO), pp. 436–443. IEEE (2018)
22. World Health Organization, et al.: World report on disability 2011 (2011)
23. Revans, R.: ABC of Action Learning. Routledge, Milton Park (2017)
24. Ribeiro, R.d.S.: Construção e uso de ambiente visual para o ensino de programação introdutória. Ph.D. thesis, Universidade de São Paulo (2015)
25. Richter, T., Boehringer, D.: Viplab-an online programming lab. In: 2016 13th International Conference on Remote Engineering and Virtual Instrumentation (REV), pp. 269–270. IEEE (2016)
26. Rose, D.: Universal design for learning. J. Spec. Educ. Technol. **15**(3), 45–49 (2000)
27. Royston, P.: Approximating the Shapiro-Wilk w-test for non-normality. Stat. Comput. **2**(3), 117–119 (1992)

28. Traxler, C.B.: The Stanford achievement test: national norming and performance standards for deaf and hard-of-hearing students. J. Deaf Stud. Deaf Educ. 5(4), 337–348 (2000)
29. Valente, J.A.: Aprendizagem ativa no ensino superior: a proposta da sala de aula invertida. Puc. São Paulo (2014)

Accessible Videos in Higher Education – Lost in Translation?!

Leevke Wilkens[(✉)] [iD] and Christian Bühler [iD]

Department of Rehabilitation Technology, TU Dortmund University, Dortmund, Germany
{leevke.wilkens,christian.buehler}@tu-dortmund.de

Abstract. The usage of videos is widespread across various disciplines and learning contexts (e.g., leisure time, school, and work) and is widely used in (higher) education. Learning videos are among the most important digital media in higher education [27]. However, if not designed accessible, videos pose new challenges [34, 41]. In line with the UN-CRPD and respective legislation, higher education has to be accessible for all students, including accessible learning materials such as videos. Accessible videos comprise an accessible video player, captions, and audio description) [29]. Because the accessibility features audio description and caption are both translations [22], it is worth analyzing what information is considered when implementing these accessibility features. As educational institutions are responsible for accessibility, we investigate in this study which information they provide about producing and providing accessible videos on their web pages. In total, 36 national and international higher education institutions are included in the analysis.

Keywords: Accessible videos · Higher education · Web page analysis

1 Introduction

The usage of videos is widespread across various disciplines and learning contexts (e.g., leisure time, school, and work) and is also popular in (higher) education. By now, learning videos are among the most important digital media in higher education [27]. Benefits such as the increased flexibility of learning regarding time, place, and speed or repetition and revisions are associated with the usage of videos [12]. Furthermore, videos can represent a complex and simultaneous situation, such as teaching in a classroom, and are utilized as a basis for reflection on teaching [16, 24]. Thus, videos provide various opportunities for learning and education.

Videos in learning contexts can be differentiated into two categories: explanatory videos, and demonstration videos [27]. Explanatory videos are produced to convey content, which is explicitly formulated in the video. In contrast, the primary objective of demonstration videos is not to explain but to demonstrate and show certain situations. Typical demonstration videos are, for example, videos of (school) lessons or videos of social interaction in different settings [27].

M. Antona and C. Stephanidis (Eds.): HCII 2022, LNCS 13309, pp. 157–171, 2022.
https://doi.org/10.1007/978-3-031-05039-8_11

Furthermore, the usage of videos can be differentiated on three levels which differ regarding the intended usage of videos. In line with the intended usage, the complexity of accessibility needs increases. On the first level, "only" the video and the video player must be accessible. On the second level, tools for commenting and highlighting specific video sequences and the respective presentation have to be accessible, too. Additionally, on the third level all used functionalities to edit the video and the newly created video need to be accessible. However, all levels have in common that the video must be accessible [41]. Despite the potential videos have, if not designed accessible, they pose new challenges [34] and can lead to exclusion.

Furthermore, in line with the UN-CRPD and respective legislation, accessibility for all students is mandatory for higher education. Therefore all learning materials need to be accessible, including modern media, such as videos. Accessible videos comprise an accessible video player, captions, and the translation of purely visual information (e.g., audio description) [29].

Accessible video players are crucial to access (accessible) videos. The difficulties and evaluation of different video players are addressed, for example, by Wild [39]. She stated that only Able Player and OzPlayer did not have any show-stoppers. Nevertheless, this article primarily addresses the implementation of captions and audio descriptions.

Educational institutions are responsible for the accessibility, but the actual adaption of the material is the responsibility of the person who is using or providing the material. So, they must have access to appropriate information [8] to learn about accessibility issues and ways to adapt the material. Therefore, we investigate in this study which information higher education institutions provide about producing and providing accessible videos.

2   Accessible Videos in Higher Education

The design of accessible videos is a complex task, which is mandatory for higher education institutions to fulfill their obligation to provide accessible learning materials (e.g., American Disability Act, BITV 2.0).

Non-accessible documents and other media are barriers to participation in education [15]. For example, if students are offered a video as an alternative to text, students with hearing impairments will be excluded if the video has no captions. Therefore, consistent care must be taken to ensure that every form of presentation is accessible [35]. In an assessment of the quality of learning materials, the accessibility of lecture recordings and learning videos was rated poor [25]. These low ratings reveal a need to address, in particular, the accessibility of videos. Nevertheless, there are organizational challenges such as the lack of needed resources (time, costs) for designing captions and audio descriptions or technical difficulties in making them available for students [29, 39].

However, captions and audio descriptions are also audiovisual translations [22], entailing content issues. Audiovisual translation are translations of media with visual and auditory elements. In audiovisual translation, the original material is changed; Parts of the material remain and are supplemented or combined with new parts [22]. In Translation Studies, the translation method is closely connected to the content of the text due to the underlying premise that the translation type or method is different depending on the particular nature of the text. For example, the distinction between literary or technical translations [31].

Therefore, it is essential to look at the type of translation needed to create captions and audio descriptions. If provided in the same language as the audio in the video, captions are intralingual translations: the audible information is translated into written text that is presented in addition to the original material. Standards for captions provide information regarding font, the position of the captions, the number of characters per line, etc. [22]. These standards are often published for broadcasters. Thus, some standards may differ in higher education [29].

Audio description is an intersemiotic translation, in which the sign system changed from pictorial representation into speech. Thus, the visual information of a video is translated into a verbal description and inserted into the gaps in the audio track [22]. However, audio description is also called partial translation because not everything seen can be described, will be described, or needs to be described [4].

There are different guidelines for producing audio descriptions. Having a closer look at audio description guidelines, two difficulties are to be named. First, there are guidelines providing information on how to design an audio description for different genres, which at some points differ widely. As Hughes, Orero, Rai [20] state: „It hardly seems feasible to merge these three [television, live AD and buildings/museums] into one set of guidelines." In this context, educational videos are not even considered. Another challenge is that because of the nature of audio description, the information provided via the audio description needs to be prioritized [30]. The prioritizing of the described information is often a task for the describer. But the decisions on what is how described are influenced by the knowledge and view of the describer [4]. Again, this may pose challenges for audio descriptions in educational contexts if the describer is not the lecturer or is familiar with the learning objectives because the audio description needs to be aligned with the given task [40]. While, in explanatory videos, the learning objective is explicitly formulated and the primary aim of this kind of video is to convey specific information. Demonstration videos pose two sets of difficulties for the implementation of accessibility. First, demonstration videos do not have an explicit learning objective by themselves, only combined with a given task [27]. Therefore, it is essential that the task and respective learning objective is known so that the important visual information can be translated. Because only if the audio description conveys the important visual information for the given task students with visual impairment can work on the task. Furthermore, because not all visual information can be translated, it might be necessary to create different audio descriptions for the same video if used for different tasks. Second, the amount of information included in the audio description depends on the length of the gaps in the audio track, where the description can be inserted. This might be especially difficult if the video has a high level of visual information, e.g., a video of a classroom situation. Thus, the translation process to design captions and audio descriptions for educational videos has to include didactical considerations to decide which content can be covered to what extent by the accessibility features [40]. So implementing accessibility features for videos has organizational, technical, and content-related challenges.

3   Method

Most common, the responsibility to provide accessible learning materials lies within the respective higher education institution. Web pages of higher education institutions are used for multiple purposes. For example, to recruit, to inform or as an "entrance to the university" [17]. Thus, examining what information higher education institutions provide about accessible videos is worthwhile.

A content analysis of different web pages of selected higher education institutions has been carried out to answer the following research questions:

Which standards/guidelines are used in higher education for the design of accessible videos, what aspects do they address, and how do higher education institutions address the content-related challenges of the translation process for captions and audio description?

To answer these questions, web pages of national and international higher education institutions were examined.

3.1   Sample

Different approaches were chosen to identify national and international higher education institutions, which most likely provide information about accessible videos on their web pages. First, the online library about accessible teaching on the web page of the German "Studying with Disabilities – Information and Advice center" (IBS) [32] was used. This library provides a list of German universities with information about accessible teaching. Higher education institutions located in the categories "accessible online-teaching as an overview" or "accessible videos" were included in the sample (n = 16).

Second, higher education institutions from the US were included in the sample. They are considered a model regarding the implementation of accessibility in higher education [26, 28]. In line with a study by Oberschelp [26], who focused accessibility in general of higher education institutions from the US and analyzed different web pages from different higher education institutions, the top ten universities and colleges from the rankings "America's Top 50 Colleges For Students With Disabilities: Disabled Students Thrive In These Colleges!" [18] and "50 Best Disability Friendly Colleges and Universities" [9] were added in the sample. These two rankings had two duplicates. Thus eighteen colleges and universities were added to the sample.

And last, higher education institutions with members in the Ed-ICT network were added to the sample (n = 5). The Ed-ICT network is an international network that explores the role of Information and Communication Technologies (ICT) for students with disabilities in post-compulsory education [13]. This network was chosen because its members are, on the one hand, known authors for accessibility issues in higher education. On the other hand, the membership in this network could be a sign that the respective universities consider accessibility hence accessible videos in their teaching. In total, the sample consists of 36 higher education institutions (Table 1).

Table 1. Sample

Source	Colleges/Universities
IBS	1. Hochschule für Wirtschaft und Recht Berlin (Germany) 2. Technische Universität Chemnitz (Germany) 3. Technische Universität Dresden (Germany) 4. Universität Hamburg (Germany) 5. Technische Hochschule Köln (Germany) 6. Philipps Universität Marburg (Germany) 7. Ludwig-Maximilians-Universität München (Germany) 8. Westfälische Wilhelms Universität Münster (Germany) 9. Universität Stuttgart (Germany) 10. Universität Rostock (Germany) 11. Hochschule Mittweida (Germany) 12. Technische Universität Dortmund (Germany) 13. Universität zu Köln (Germany)
Great Value Colleges 2021	14. Landmark College (USA) 15. University of Arizona (USA) 16. Beacon College (USA) 17. University of Connecticut (USA) 18. University of Iowa (USA) 19. American University (USA) 20. Ball State University (USA) 21. Lynn University (USA) 22. University of California, Berkeley (USA) 23. Marist College (USA)
CollegeChoice.net 2021	24. University of Michigan-Ann Arbor (USA) 25. University of Southern California (USA) 26. Northeastern University (USA) 27. Xavier University (USA) 28. The University of Texas at Austin (USA) 29. College of Charleston (USA) 30. Messiah College (USA) 31. University of the Ozarks (USA)
Ed-ICT	32. The Open University Israel (Israel) 33. University of Washington (USA) 34. The Open University UK (UK) 35. Dawson College (Canada) 36. FernUniversität Hagen (Germany)

3.2 Procedure

After identifying the higher education institutions, each publicly available web page was examined Starting from the home page, two strategies were used to locate the relevant information. First, the keywords "Accessible Videos, Captions and Audio description (in English and German) were separately searched for via the search engine provided on the home page. All listed websites were then scanned for information and recorded. Second, the Service Center for Students with Disabilities (or respective offices) was identified for each university/college, and their web presence was also scanned for information about accessible videos. The acquired information was then categorized.

Because of the explorative nature of this analysis, only a few categories were formed upfront: guidelines/standards and recommended tools for both captions and audio description. Then, derived from the material, more inductive categories were developed, such as definition, necessity, realization, other.

4   Results

Of the identified 36 web pages, six universities or colleges did not provide publicly available information about accessible videos. All other web pages provided some information about accessible videos. Hereafter, the results are presented using the developed categories as structure.

4.1   Captions

Most higher education institutions provide some definition: Captions translate the audio content (including sound effects, music description, and speaker identification) into written text. Captions are usually displayed at the bottom edge of the video screen. There are two types of captions: Closed Captions and Open Captions. Open Captions are permanently displayed, while the user can turn closed captions off and on. One university states that closed captions are the "technique to use" (HS 22).

Necessity. Nearly all universities/colleges state that videos have to be captioned. Many universities add that not just students with hearing impairment benefit from captions but also students with another native language or when listening to a video in a loud environment (e.g., HS 4; HS 2; HS 3; HS 4; HS 12; HS 17; HS 30; HS 28).

There are also statements that all publicly posted videos have to be captioned. One university even states that "streaming without captions could expose the university to serious risk, and will be perceived as a proceeding that is contrary to the inclusion ideals of American Universities" (HS 19). It becomes obvious that the necessity to provide captions in line with the ADA, BITV, etc. is communicated by the higher education institutions. Nevertheless, there is also information regarding the prioritization of the captioning effort. This mainly refers to the intern service of universities to caption videos. One example is the following hierarchy: Critical – Media used in courses, where captions are included in a current accommodation, and media which is publicly available; High – Media used in large courses, or will be used multiple times; Medium – Media from third-party vendors, and does not meet criteria named above; Upon request – Media which is not currently used, but is available in an archive; Helpful – Media is used for a limited time, for repetition purposes only, and it is verified, that there is no accommodation need (HS 18).

This prioritizing is a way to handle the growing number of video use and captions. However, it should be noted that there is no lower priority than helpful. Thus, it seems that if the capacities allow, all media should be captioned.

Guidelines/Standards. Regarding guidelines/standards, the information provided by the universities differs. Some refer to guidelines of other universities or known standards, such as BIK, Aktion Mensch (Germany), Captioning Key (America), or WCAG (both). The Guidelines by Aktion Mensch and WCAG do not specify the type of video addressed [1, 38]. The introduction to the Captioning Key [10] states that the guidelines are for both entertainment and educational media, while the BIK Guidelines are developed for usage in educational contexts (vocational training and higher education) [7]. Furthermore, the guidelines differ in the level of detail: The tips by Aktion Mensch propose SubtitleCreator as a free tool, and include that everything which is heard and has meaning needs to be captioned. Additionally, important noises and background music, and speaker identification have to be included in the captions. Regarding the appearance of captions, the length of the caption (two lines) with a minimum of reading time of two seconds is listed. Finally, they provide another link to a general guideline for broadcasters in German-speaking countries.

The guideline by BIK focuses on the captioning process and provides a list of Tools (e.g., Subtitle Edit, Aegisub, etc.), and also names YouTube as an editing tool. As a standard, they recommend the standards developed for German-speaking broadcasters.

The Captioning Key is the most detailed guideline. It covers topics such as "elements of quality captioning," what to caption, "language mechanics," "sound effects and music," "speaker identification," "numbers," and tools for captioning, including YouTube. In contrast to the other guidelines, the Captioning Key illustrates most information with examples.

Other universities provide comprehensive information on their web pages regarding color, font, size, location, format, length, reading time, and how to indicate turns. This information is similar across the web pages: high contrast, bottom edge, sans serif fonts, not longer than two lines, aligned with the audio (HS 12; HS 18). Sometimes these instructions are systemized along "Elements of Quality": Accuracy, Consistency, Clarity, Readability (HS 17) or Synchronized, Equivalent, Accessible (HS 18). These quality elements are introduced on the web pages to determine the quality of the captions, done by oneself or from videos already captioned.

Even though not all web pages refer to a specific guideline, and the level of detail differs, there seems to be a broad consensus on designing captions. While the basics are nearly the same, differences exist in what symbol to use to indicate music (e.g. ♪, #).

Recommended Tools. On the web pages, it is often stated that there are two approaches to caption videos: Do it yourself or outsource. In order to caption the video yourself, a variety of tools is named. Some of them are Open Source others are commercial. To name a few: Subtitle Edit, Gaupol, Aegisub, Camtasia, Amara, AnnotationEdit, Subtile Horse, Streamer, MovieCaptioner (Registered trademarks), and more (HS 2; HS 10; HS 12; HS 18; HS 28; HS 33).

Automatic Captioning. Next to the recommended tools, automatic captioning is addressed as an easy way to create captions for videos, often with the warning that automatic captioning might not be sufficient enough, because depending on the audio quality errors occur, which need to be corrected (e.g. HS 3; HS 12; HS 35; HS 33; HS 15; HS 17; HS 22; HS 28; HS 29). Nevertheless, YouTube's feature to create automatic captions for videos, including instructions, seems quite popular among the examined universities and colleges.

Outsource. To outsource captioning, the higher education institutions propose different approaches. Some universities have a contract with a third-party provider (e.g., 3Play Media from the US). Others have an intern provider who does the captioning for the university (HS 5). This service is often integrated into the Office for Students with Disabilities or Accessible Technology Service (HS 33; HS 17; HS 26; HS 28; HS 12; HS 35). Some of these intern services seem to be free. Others charge per hour or minute of video. Costs seem to depend on whether the captions are included in a granted accommodation for a student with disability or not, at least in the US. If the captions are part of an accommodation, the Office for Students with Disabilities often supports lecturers in providing captions (HS 33; HS 17; HS 28).

The way how captions can be outsourced differs between the universities. For example, some universities have online forms to request captions for specific videos. These videos are then provided for the student with the accommodation via the respective Learning Management System (LMS) or are available to download for the lecturer (HS 5; HS 24). Other universities indicate the address where to request captions or name the third-party vendor (HS 22; HS 26).

Other. Some universities also provide information on how to caption live Zoom-Conferences and provide workarounds using software for video recording and live streaming when the Zoom-Service is not sufficient (HS 13).

4.2 Audio Description

Audio description is an additional audio track that provides the description of visual information covered in the video. The descriptions are inserted into the gaps of the audio track. The additional audio track must be recorded and inserted manually.

This technique provides access to the visual content of a video for people with visual impairment.

Necessity. Like the information about captions, most universities state that audio description is essential. Videos conveying information that the audio track does not cover need an audio description. One university illustrates the effect of audio description with a video example: The university has a "Best of" Video with visual illustrations of activities and other things on campus. The video is just music, no spoken word. Thus, with no audio description, people who cannot see the video only can hear the music but still do not know what happens on campus (HS 33).

While many universities state that captions are helpful for various students, this is not so prominent for audio descriptions. Only one university demonstrates in two examples the benefits for all students (HS 22):

- Watching a video on a small screen, where students cannot see everything on the screen, especially diagrams with small numbers

- Watching a video while commuting by public transportation or by car on their mobile phones

However, the urgency to provide audio descriptions is not stated as clearly as for captions.

Guidelines/Standards. Once again, guidelines by "BIK für Alle" and "Aktion Mensch" are named by German universities. In addition, some universities refer to the "Description Key" by Described and Captioned Media Program [11], an equivalent to the Captioning Key. While this guideline specifically targets educational media, the intended audience is K-12-Students. Thus, the examples and some recommendations are for a younger audience than higher education students. Therefore, the question arises whether all recommendations are actually suitable for the intended use in higher education.

Not many higher education institutions posted standards or guidelines. However, a basic rule derived from the definition is that the audio description is inserted into the gaps of the audio track of the original video and that "important" visual information needs to be described. Furthermore, some universities state that everything seen in the video, which is essential to understand the video, must be described (HS 2; HS3; HS 4; HS 9; HS 11; HS 12; HS 15; HS 22; 33; HS 28). The question of defining "important" visual information and the problem of gaps in the audio track restricting the time for a description are not addressed.

Nevertheless, in line with a statement in the guideline of Aktion Mensch, some universities state that "audio description is an art" (HS 33; HS 28), which impacts the viewers' experience. Even though not designed for educational videos, some universities and BIK für alle refer to standards and guidelines by broadcasters. The University of Washington adds that no "officially sanctioned standard exists that assures quality and consistency across described videos" (HS 33).

Recommended Tools. As stated above, audio descriptions need to be recorded and inserted manually. Therefore, customarily used editing software is recommended. Additionally, one university refers to YouDescribe (HS 33). "YouDescribe is a free, web-based platform for adding audio description to YouTube content" [33]. It provides a range of already audio-described YouTube-Videos and offers the means to add audio description to any YouTube video.

Realization. Audio description itself may look different, depending on the video itself. A short description of the scenario is sufficient for lecture videos if the content is properly described (HS 5; HS 17; HS 22; HS 27; HS 34). As one university put it: "Hosts and Co-Hosts should act as their own alternative text for visual elements" (HS 28). A similar approach is recommended for explanatory videos. If possible, everything that is happening visually should be described in the original audio track (HS 3; HS 4).

The more is described in the video itself, the less needs to be described in the audio description. To teach lecturers to include a description of the visual content upfront in their video/talk is "the easiest and most cost-effective method" to provide a video where an audio description is not or nearly not needed anymore (HS 22).

One Problem is the access to the audio description. Most video players do not provide the possibility to turn on the audio description when needed. Instead, a second video with the inserted audio description needs to be available most of the time (e.g. HS 12). One exception is "Able Player", an Open Source Media Player developed by the University of Washington (HS 33). This player has a feature that can access a timed text file in which the visual information is provided. A screen reader can also access these timed text files if the player cannot include the file (HS 26).

As for captions, there are also two ways to produce audio descriptions: Do-it-yourself or outsource (HS 33). As stated in the chapter above, higher education institutions do not provide much information about tools that can be used to produce audio descriptions. Also, the information about who can produce audio descriptions, if not the lecturer, is not as prominent as for captions. Only a few universities state that audio descriptions can be ordered at specialized centers, such as the Student Accessibility Center or similar (HS 4; HS 13; HS 35, HS 12).

The University of Washington provides a list of vendors "that seems to be a good match for higher education institutions" to outsource audio descriptions. They also state that the American Council of the Blind has compiled a list of commercial services (HS 33). This list is displayed by categories: Full Service, Writing, Voicing, Audio Engineering, Training, Quality Control and Consulting, and Local AD Providers [2]. Vendors in Germany are listed by BIK für Alle [6].

Surprisingly, often audio descriptions are not listed as a provided accommodation for students with disabilities, as is the case for captions (e.g., HS 17; HS 20; HS 27).

4.3 Other

When designing accessible videos, some universities provide some general tips and information. In line with the recommendation to consider accessibility up front, this is also suggested for captions and audio descriptions. Scripts for videos make it easier to design the captions. Including as much description as possible or gaps in the audio track makes it easier to provide audio descriptions. It is also recommended to apply the two senses principle on videos (HS 11). Others provide a FAQ section for accessible videos, providing information such as who is responsible for providing accessible videos, who pays, accessible videos, how do I get accessible videos, and so on (HS 33; HS 22; HS 4). Some provide a checklist for accessible videos, which includes captioning, transcripts for audio files, audio description of visual-only content, and can the video be accessed by keyboard (HS 5; HS 27).

5 Discussion

The chosen approach has some limitations. First, higher education institutions that were not included in the chosen rankings or web pages are not analyzed. Thus, institutions with a great deal of information regarding accessible videos might have been missed. Second, only publicly available information was considered. Thus, there might be more information in the respective intranet. Moreover, only information provided in English or German is analyzed; thus, the information provided by the Open University Israel might be missed out because it is in Hebrew.

However, the amount of information provided by higher education institutions on their web pages about captions is high compared with the amount of information about audio descriptions. It is strongly recommended to provide captions on the web pages, especially in the US. If a student with a granted accommodation for captions participates in the lecture, the universities often take care of the captioning. Otherwise, the lecturer is responsible for deciding whether captions are necessary or not and providing them. In order to help lecturers to prioritize the effort for captioning, additional information is provided. This prioritization can be regarded as a way to handle the growing need for captions. However, the hierarchy seems to be influenced by the risk of lawsuits [26] if a higher education institution from the US makes a not-accessible video publicly available. While this approach is understandable, the benefits or potential exclusion risks should be more focused on in an inclusive learning environment.

However, considering that for adaptations for accessibility, working time seems to be "a narrow bottleneck" [8], the competence of lecturers to decide and provide captioned videos should be questioned.

Thus, in light of the growing need for captions, it is no surprise that tools like YouTube are recommended because they simplify the production of captions and save time. While problems like the occurring errors are addressed, privacy issues are not. If only the lecturer is seen and heard in the video, it might be the lecturer's own choice. However, the privacy issue becomes even more relevant when using a demonstration video, such as a classroom situation with children. Additionally, the audio quality is often not as high as it would be needed for YouTube to provide useful captions.

The need for audio description is not as urgently formulated as for captions, which is surprising because the need for a media alternative or audio description is on the same conformance level (A) as the need for captions unless the time-based media is a media alternative itself [37]. But, the fact that captions are more common than audio descriptions is not unique to higher education. Also, in television and movies, the availability of audio descriptions is below the availability of captions [14]. For example, only since 2015 has Netflix offered selected videos with audio descriptions [3]. Still, it seems that audio description is often the last feature of a movie that is considered [21]. Possible causes may be the relatively high effort to create audio descriptions [5] or the difficulties of making them available for the audience [29].

However, the benefits of audio description for videos in higher education for all students – that videos can be followed while commuting or when watched on a small screen – reflect observations of developments when watching Netflix or TV shows. Audio description can be used as a tool to turn a TV show into an audiobook, which can be listened to while doing other things [14]. This use of audio description might not be seen as beneficial for educational media, where the video aims is to teach the viewers something rather than to entertain. Nevertheless, there are also observations that the audio description is used as an additional source of information, which can help to follow complex videos [14]. Other approaches use audio description as a didactical tool to approve writing abilities, attention to detail, and to deepen an analysis of the video material [19, 23]. Even though these considerations are beyond the scope of this article, it is essential to note that the potential audio description offers is not yet fully utilized.

Furthermore, the instruction on producing an audio description is strongly abbreviated. It is often stated that it is necessary to describe what you see and what is important to understand the video for the audio description, but how to decide what is necessary and important to describe is often not addressed on the web pages, except for the universities which refer to different guidelines such as the Description Key [11]. In the Description key and other guidelines for audio description, it is recommended to describe visual elements which cover the questions where?; when?; who?; what? and how? Additionally, sound effects, which are difficult to identify and on-screen text, need to be included [36]. While this basic information might help when producing an audio description, the didactical dimension of audio description and the need to align the description to the learning objective and task are not mentioned on any web page. Thus, important visual information needed to reach the respective learning objective runs the risk of getting lost in the translation of the pictorial representation into speech.

Moreover, all information about accessible videos on the web pages seems to refer to certain kinds of videos: explanation videos and lecture recordings. In this kind of video, it is possible to integrate the (audio) description into the original audio track. This approach has two benefits: The need for post-editing and the creation of an audio description is minimized. And more importantly, this approach follows the principle of the Universal Design. More students than anticipated can benefit from this integrated description of visual information, for example, simply students looking away [34]. It seems that the description itself and the integration into the video is easier than for demonstration videos. It seems that on the web pages, it is neglected that different types of videos need different types of captions and audio descriptions [41] and that captions and audio descriptions are translations, which need careful considerations during the translation process [22]. When producing captions and audio descriptions for demonstration videos, difficulties were not explicitly addressed on any web page.

6   Conclusion

Regarding the research questions, we can conclude that, at least on public web pages, standards such as BIK für Alle, Aktion Mensch, Captioning Key respective Description Key, and WCAG are used to produce captions and audio descriptions. Nevertheless, the amount of information differs. Higher education institutions seem to provide more detailed information on the design of captions than on audio descriptions. This might be because captions are seemingly easier to produce, especially with the different captioning software or automatic tools, such as YouTube or speech-to-text-converters.

Also noticeable is that specific information for demonstration videos and how to include didactical dimension in the design process of audio description is missing. It seems that mere information and instruction are considered in the design process. However, when using (demonstration) videos with specific reflective tasks or specific learning objectives, the provided audio description must be produced with didactical considerations in mind. Even though both captions and audio descriptions are translations, this is particularly important for audio descriptions. Since when translating something from visual to verbal, it is nearly impossible to describe everything you see and without any interpretation. The didactical dimension of the design process can get lost in translation if

27. Persike, M.: Videos in der Lehre: Wirkungen und Nebenwirkungen. In: Niegemann, H.M., Weinberger, A. (eds.) Handbuch Bildungstechnologie. Konzeption und Einsatz digitaler Lernumgebungen, pp. 271–301. Springer; Ciando, Berlin, München (2020). https://doi.org/10.1007/978-3-662-54373-3_23-1
28. Peschke, S.: Chancengleichheit und Hochschule. Springer Fachmedien Wiesbaden, Wiesbaden (2019)
29. Puhl, S., Lerche, S.: Barrierefreie Videos in der Hochschullehre. Eine Initiative von BIK für Alle und der Justus-Liebig-Universität Gießen. In: Tolle, P., Plümmer, A., Horbach, A. (eds.) Hochschule als interdisziplinäres barrierefreies System. kassel university press c/o Universität Kassel - Universitätsbibliothek, Kassel, pp. 84–111 (2019)
30. Rai, S., Greening, J., Petré, L.: A Comparative Study of Audio Description Guidelines Prevalent in Differenz Countries (2010). Accessed 26 May 2020
31. Schäffner, C.: Systematische Übersetzungsdefinitionen. In: Kittel, H., Frank, A.P., Greiner, N., et al. (eds.) Übersetzung.Translation.Traduction. Ein internationales handbuch zur Übersetzungsforschung, 1. Teilband. De Gruyter, Berlin, pp. 101–117 (2004)
32. Studentenwerk (2021) Barrierefreie Lehre. https://www.studentenwerke.de/de/content/barrierefreie-lehre#videos. Accessed 05 Nov 2021
33. The Smith-Kettlewell Eye Research Institute (2019) YouDescribe. https://www.ski.org/project/youdescribe. Accessed 10 Feb 2022
34. Thompson, T.: Video for All. Accessibility of Video Content and Universal Design of a Media Player. In: Burgstahler, S.E. (ed.) Universal Design in Higher Education. From Principles to Practice, 2nd edn., pp. 259–273. Harvard Education Press, Cambridge (2015)
35. Thomson, R., Fichten, C.S., Havel, A., et al.: Blending universal design, e-learning, and information and communication technologies. In: Burgstahler, S.E. (ed.) Universal Design in higher education. From Principles to Practice, 2nd edn., pp. 275–284. Harvard Education Press, Cambridge (2015)
36. Vercauteren, G.: Towards a European guideline for audio description. In: Díaz Cintas, J., Orero, P., Remael, A. (eds.) Media for All. Subtitling for the Deaf, Audio Description, and Sign Language, pp. 139–149. BRILL, Leiden (2007)
37. W3C: Web Content Accessibility Guidelines (WCAG) 2.1. W3C Recommendation 05 June 2018 (2018). https://www.w3.org/TR/2018/REC-WCAG21-20180605/. Accessed 06 Dec 2021
38. W3C Web Accessibility Initiative (WAI) (2021) Making Audio and Video Media Accessible. https://www.w3.org/WAI/media/av/. Accessed 06 Dec 2021
39. Wild, G.: The inaccessibility of video players. In: Miesenberger, K., Kouroupetroglou, G. (eds.) ICCHP 2018. LNCS, vol. 10896, pp. 47–51. Springer, Cham (2018). https://doi.org/10.1007/978-3-319-94277-3_9
40. Wilkens, L., Bühler, C., Bosse, I.: Accessible learning management systems in higher education. In: Antona, M., Stephanidis, C. (eds.) Universal Access in Human-Computer Interaction. Applications and Practice, vol. 12189, pp. 315–328. Springer, Cham (2020). https://doi.org/10.1007/978-3-030-49108-6_23
41. Wilkens, L., Heitplatz, V.N., Bühler, C.: Designing accessible videos for people with disabilities. In: Antona, M., Stephanidis, C. (eds.) UAHCI 2021, HCII 2021, Part II, LNCS, vol. 12769, pp 328–344. Springer, Cham (2021). https://doi.org/10.1007/978-3-030-78095-1_24

Extended Reality in Universal Access

Integrating Machine Learning with Augmented Reality for Accessible Assistive Technologies

Basel Barakat[1]($\boxtimes$) (iD), Lynne Hall[1] (iD), and Simeon Keates[2] (iD)

[1] School of Computer Science, University of Sunderland,
Sir Tom Cowie Campus, St Peters Way, Sunderland SR6 0DD, UK
`basel.barakat@sunderland.ac.uk`
[2] University of Chichester, Chichester PO169 6PE, UK

Abstract. Augmented Reality (AR) is a technology which enhances physical environments by superimposing digital data on top of a real-world view. AR has multiple applications and use cases, bringing digital data into the physical world enabling experiences such as training staff on complicated machinery without the risks that come with such activities. Numerous other uses have been developed including for entertainment, with AR games and cultural experiences now emerging. Recently, AR has been used for developing assistive technologies, with applications across a range of disabilities. To achieve the high-quality interactions expected by users, there has been increasing integration of AR with Machine Learning (ML) algorithms. This integration offers additional functionality to increase the scope of AR applications. In this paper we present the potential of integrating AR with ML algorithms for developing assistive technologies, for the use case of locating objects in the home context.

Keywords: Machine learning · Computer vision · Speech recognition · Emotion detection · Assistive technologies

1 Introduction

Technology is seen as a significant driver to enable, empower and include the 15% of the world's population that have a disability [1]. Recent technological advances, from voice recognition to brain computer interfaces offer a wealth of solutions and opportunities. Identifying and applying technologies can considerably improve the quality of life for disabled users. One of the technologies that is currently pushing the limits of our interaction with computers is Augmented Reality (AR).

AR technology uses 3-D images and animations that can be displayed in the physical environment. Most of the currently developed applications for AR are for entertainment [2] and training [3]. However, the specialised hardware and software developed for AR has massive potential for developing assistive technologies. For example, the available cameras and microphones, see Fig. 1, can provide data from the user surroundings. The software developed for imposing 3D images can benefit users by pointing them to a specific area or object.

M. Antona and C. Stephanidis (Eds.): HCII 2022, LNCS 13309, pp. 175–186, 2022.
https://doi.org/10.1007/978-3-031-05039-8_12

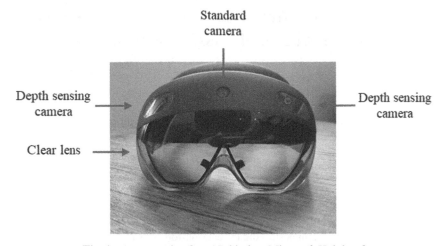

Fig. 1. An example of an AR kit, i.e., Microsoft Hololens2

The AR kits provide functionalities that can be extended, for example, using Machine Learning algorithms to improve understanding of contextual data, such as providing users with information about their surroundings that they might not have observed. These algorithms can be very useful as they can help the users with their unique requirements. The requirements this paper focuses on are provided by a visually impaired user in the home context aiming to locate objects. The goal is to is to show the potential of integrating computer vision and speech recognition algorithms with the AR to provide assistive technologies.

This paper investigates the exploratory research question: Can AR and ML be integrated to provide an assistive technology for the use case of locating objects in the home context? Sect. 2 briefly outlines recent assistive technologies for a range of sensory, physical and cognitive disabilities, impairments and neurodiversity. Section 3 focuses on visual impairment and the use of Augmented Reality as assistive technology. Section 4 considers empowering assistive technologies using Machine Learning algorithms. Section 5 presents a prototype system integrating computer vision and an AR headset. Section 6 outlines potential next steps and applications.

2   Assistive Technology

The World Health Organisation (WHO) defines assistive technologies as *"assistive products and related systems and services developed for people to maintain or improve functioning and thereby promote well-being"* [4]. The WHO estimated that over one billion people need some form of assistive technology with this figure expected to increase significantly in the coming decades. As the market for assistive technologies strengthens, grows and diversifies, commercialisation is increasing, with more assistive and inclusive technologies emerging.

Figure 1 highlights the wide range of impairments in the UK, many of which can be supported with assistive technologies. This growing requirement for assistive technology is emerging against the ongoing widening of participation in education, work, recreation and society, with a massive increase in the mainstreaming and inclusion of children, teenagers and adults with disabilities, impairments and neurodiversity. There is also an inevitable significant growth in the need for assistive technologies to enable independent living for an increasingly ageing population [4]. Such challenges, include, for example, visual impairment arising from age-related macular degeneration, cataracts or glaucoma; and cognitive impairment such as dementia and Alzheimer's. Supporting independent living is not only the most cost effective solution, but additionally improves quality of life allowing people to continue to live in their own homes.

Greater awareness of how assistive technologies can improve quality of life for those with disabilities, impairments and neurodiversity has also led to statutory regulation. The Convention on the Rights of Persons with Disabilities recognises access to assistive technology as a human right (Fig. 2).

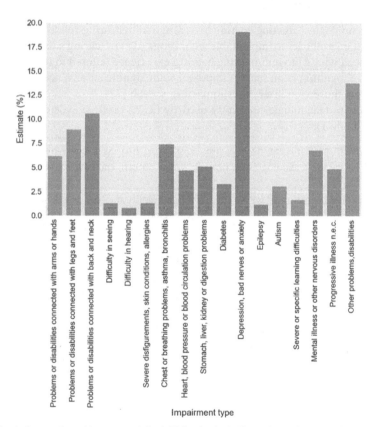

Fig. 2. Statistics on the wide range of disabilities in the UK, as shown by the Office for National Statistics - Annual Population Survey [5]

2.1 Visually Impaired

Assistive technologies for visual impairment include magnifying devices incorporated into wearables such as IrisVision, eSight or Oxsight smart glasses. These magnify, improve contrast, highlight edges and so on in real space. Additionally, some, such as eSight [6], can also be connected to digital experiences, such as games consoles and screens or Nu Eyes Pro glasses that incorporate voice and optical character recognition. There are also voice-only applications, such as Envision Glasses that enable the user to 'hear what they want to see' using AI to provide scene descriptions, facial recognition, to scan, remember and read text and make video calls [7].

In addition to wearables, there have been attempts to support the visually impaired with devices including for orientation and mobility training, such as augmented reality multi-sensory maps [8]; for navigation, including robot dogs [9]; and devices such as smart canes [10] for mobility support.

2.2 Hearing, Voice, Speech, or Language Disorders

Assistive technologies targeting hearing loss, range from hearing-related products being embedded in smartphones to implantable technologies [11]. Hearing aids will be increasingly enhanced with AI to optimise the hearing experience tailored to the user and context. Voice recognition continues to improve, with significant advances in processing language from those with disabilities impacting speech [12].

The assistive technologies currently used by health professionals can be classified as follows (Table 1):

Table 1. Assistive technologies for hearing, voice, speech, and language disorders [11]

Assistive listening devices (ALDs)	Help amplify the sounds you want to hear, especially where there's a lot of background noise. ALDs can be used with a hearing aid or cochlear implant to help a wearer hear certain sounds better
Augmentative and alternative communication (AAC) devices	Help people with communication disorders to express themselves. These devices can range from a simple picture board to a computer programme that synthesises speech from text
Alerting devices	Connect to a doorbell, telephone, or alarm that emits a loud sound or blinking light to let someone with hearing loss know that an event is taking place

2.3 Neurodiversity, Intellectual Disabilities and Cognitive Impairment

Assistive technologies have been developed to support neurodiverse and intellectually disabled populations, with mainstream as well as assistive technologies being effectively used. This includes aiming to provide neurodiverse and disabled users with the same experiences as their peers, using everyday devices, with EasyReading [13, 14], for example, providing an app that can make any webpage accessible across a wide range of disabilities. Text can be read-aloud, simplified, replaced by pictograms and so on, depending on the preference and needs of the user. Assistive technologies have been developed to support therapy for neurological conditions, such as Polipo [12] (Tam, Gelsomini & Garzotto, 2017) a multisensory interactive toy. Minecraft has been successfully used to support social skill development for children and teenagers with autism [15]. Similarly, virtual agents and social robots have been used to trigger pro-social behaviour [16], and to support social and emotional development.

3 Augmented Reality (AR)

Coughlin and Miele [17] categorise AR as an assistive technology into global applications that are used to augment the physical world to enable the user to navigate and interact more easily with it, and local applications, which augment physical objects that the user can touch, explore and use. Here, the focus is on the latter, creating a local application to assist a visually impaired user with locating objects in the home context.

AR has been used effectively to support users with visual impairments in a range of contexts and use cases, particularly in work, training [18] and educational contexts [19]. Through incorporating computer vision, the AR experience can enable visually impaired users to navigate and use spaces more effectively. For example, computer vision has been used to support navigation in indoor environments [20] with object recognition used to recognise doors and elevators enabling the visually impaired user to navigate an unfamiliar building [21] and to assist visually impaired users with sign reading using existing signage [22]. The Bright platform, an augmented reality assistive platform, provides contextual features enabled by vision processing, such as recognising contacts through facial recognition [23]. AR applications for visual impairment for users in the home include safety such as fall prevention applications [24].

4 Assistive Technologies Empowered by Machine Learning Algorithms

Machine learning is the field of study that gives computers the ability to learn without being explicitly programmed [25]. Unlike the traditional approach where we ought to explicitly define the problem and write the rules to solve it, in machine learning we provide the computers with a dataset and let them propose a method for solving it. This approach has several advantages as we do not always know the optimal method for setting the rules.

Machine learning algorithms form rules by observing the datasets. They can extract rules that we might not know or understand. This is particularly beneficial for developing assistive technologies, as the range of problems and possible solutions are substantial. In this paper, we discuss two fields of ML that has have great potential to support visually impaired users: Speech recognition and Computer Vision.

4.1 Speech Recognition

Recently, Speech Recognition systems have become part of everyday life especially with the wide spread of smartphone assistants (e.g., Siri, Cortana, Google Now) and voice assistants such as Amazon Echo, and Kinect Xbox One [26, 27]. These systems uses accurate machine learning algorithms for 'understanding' the human voice and speech. Speech recognition has been an active research area for a long time [28, 29], with major contributions having been made using Hidden Markov Chains [28, 29]; machine learning algorithms [30] [31]; and Deep learning [31].

In essence the speech recognition algorithms take the speech signal as an input and extract information from it [30], as outlined in Table 2.

Table 2. Extracted information from speech signals

Extracted information	Details & related reference
Speech content	Recognise the content of words and phrases [30]
Speaker identity	Recognise the speaker by utilising the information embedded in his/her speech signal [32]
Emotions	Recognise the speaker emotion such as happy, scared, sad, etc.[33]
Language	Recognise the spoken langue can be challenging for languages that share phrases [34]
Accent	Recognition of a speaker's regional accent, within a predetermined language [32]
Age and gender	Recognising the age and gender of the user [35]

Accruing this remarkable amount of information using speech has a great potential for developing assistive language. For instance, it can be used to help in developing assistive technologies for users who suffer from hearing loss and/langue difficulties. It can also be very helpful for the users that might have problems interacting with the peripherals.

4.2 Computer Vision

Computer vision is another very active research area in machine learning. Computer vision algorithms extract information from images and videos. The information we can extract can be very helpful in developing assistive technologies for the visually impaired. Figure 3 presents some of the capabilities of computer vision in developing assistive technologies.

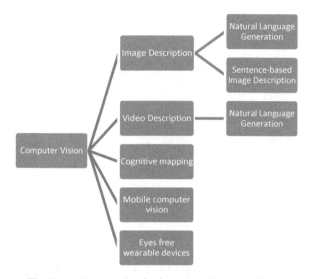

Fig. 3. Assistive technologies using Computer Vision

Recently major contributions in Computer vision have empowered the algorithms to detect multiple objects in an image in real time, as shown in Fig. 4. In particular, the algorithms that use deep learning have shown a huge potential for accurate and timely detection of objects. For instant You-Only-Look-Once (YOLO) algorithm has shown great performance and the potential scalability [32].

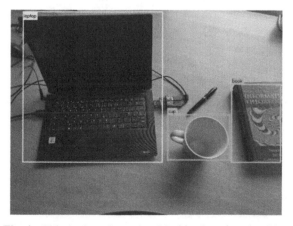

Fig. 4. Objects detection using Machine learning algorithm

An example of using object detection in assistive technologies had been developed in [33], where the presented framework (shown in Fig. 5) was developed to provide assistive technology to support a user in locating their items. The framework uses speech recognition, computer vision and optimises queue performance to locate items in real time. In this approach the user does need help from other people hence they can use it without worrying about invading their privacy. It also interacts with the user only using speech thus a visually impaired user can use it.

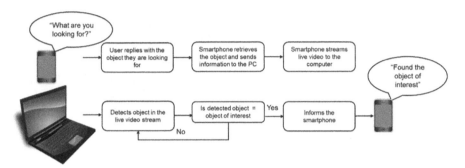

Fig. 5. Computer Vision assistive technology example [34]

5 Proposed Integration of AR with ML Algorithms

5.1 Overview

In this section, we present a potential assistive technology based on the framework outlined in Fig. 5, that integrates machine learning with augmented reality kits. The main idea is to utilise the AR capability of interacting with the physical word and integrate it with machine learning algorithms capabilities to make accurate and timely decisions. Generally, the proposed solution is for in-home assistance as shown in Fig. 6. However, it can be extended for outdoor applications.

Fig. 6. Potential solution for integrating computer vision and AR headsets

The user would interact with the AR through the microphone, then we can extract the content from the speech signal using a machine learning algorithm. For example, the user might ask to locate the keys. Then wearing the AR kit, they would walk around the home, in the meantime the AR would stream the live video to their personal computer where an object detection algorithm would analyze the frames and identify the object. If the item is in the sight of the AR, it would notify the user using an audio signal or even through imposing arrows to the location of the item, as shown in Fig. 7.

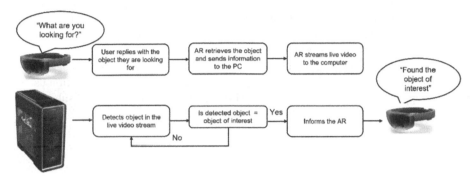

Fig. 7. Proposed framework for integrating AR with Machine learning

5.2 Practical Implantation Consideration and Challenges

Practical Implantation Consideration and Challenges. While implementing an integration between AR and ML, it is critical to the practical implications of these systems. One of the most challenging issues in complying ML algorithms is the required computational computer. As it has a massive effect on the processing duration and hence the usability of the assistive technologies. Hence, it is crucial to balance the ML algorithm accuracy with the processing duration.

ML algorithms can be complied on the AR kit or another device such as remote server. Having an ML algorithm compiled on the AR kit might sound like the more convenient method, however, it would generate several challenges such as compellability, RAM size and processor power. For example, if we consider the Microsoft HoloLens 2 it has 4GB RAM and a Qualcomm Snapdragon 850 processor. Which would make it very hard to develop onboard algorithms. On the other hand, if the algorithm was developed on an external server, then the computational power would not be as challenging. In this scenario it is critical to optimise the communication (between the AR kit and the server) performance.

In our implantation we took the second approach, as we had an external server running the ML algorithm. One of the problems we faced was the massive delay in transmitting the live video stream. To stream a video can be done by activating the developer mode on the kit and streaming the video using the 'Mixed Reality Capture' function on the device portal. This approach is quite easy to implant, and on the other hand, it has a significantly high streaming delay. To overcome this, we have used the Microsoft HoloLens app [35]. Further improvements can be made using the Microsoft Mixed reality Real-Time Communication for Web (Web-RTC) protocol [36].

6 Discussion

Integrating AR technologies with Machine Learning algorithms offers considerable potential for creating assistive technologies. The proof-of-concept in this paper demonstrates one such integration, that of enhancing AR with speech recognition and machine vision. This integration provides an improved assistive experience for a visually impaired user supporting them in locating objects.

Current work is focusing on testing the application in a lab with the goal of then moving to the home context of a visually impaired user to assess the application usability. This approach is also likely to have utility for users with cognitive disabilities or impairments related to age, enabling them to rapidly locate objects.

7 Conclusions

As technology advances the potential of using it to help people grows. Through integrating Augmented Reality with Machine Learning it becomes possible to create assistive technologies that can help users with a wide range of requirements. We presented a proof-of-concept example aimed at users with visual impairment integrating AR with machine learning algorithms for machine vision and speech recognition creating an interaction that helped users to locate their items.

References

1. World Report on Disability Summary. https://www.who.int/publications/i/item/WHO-NMH-VIP-11.01. Accessed 24 Feb 2022
2. Hung, S.-W., Chang, C.-W., Ma, Y.-C.: A new reality: exploring continuance intention to use mobile augmented reality for entertainment purposes. Technol. Soc. **67**, 101757 (2021). https://doi.org/10.1016/j.techsoc.2021.101757
3. Li, X., Yi, W., Chi, H.-L., Wang, X., Chan, A.P.C.: A critical review of virtual and augmented reality (VR/AR) applications in construction safety. Autom. Constr. **86**, 150–162 (2018). https://doi.org/10.1016/j.autcon.2017.11.003
4. "Assistive technology." https://www.who.int/news-room/fact-sheets/detail/assistive-technology. Accessed 24 Feb 2022
5. "Labour Force Survey - Office for National Statistics." https://www.ons.gov.uk/surveys/information/forhouseholdsandindividuals/householdandindividualsurveys/labourforcesurvey. Accessed 22 Feb 2022
6. "New Home gb - eSight." https://esighteyewear.com/gb. Accessed 24 Feb 2022
7. "Envision Glasses." https://www.letsenvision.com/envision-glasses. Accessed 24 Feb 2022
8. Laviole, J., Thevin, L., Albouys-Perrois, J., Brock, A.: Nectar. In: Proceedings of the Virtual Reality International Conference - Laval Virtual, April 2018, pp. 1–6 (2018). https://doi.org/10.1145/3234253.3234317

9. Chuang, T.-K., et al.: Deep trail-following robotic guide dog in pedestrian environments for people who are blind and visually impaired - learning from virtual and real worlds. In: 2018 IEEE International Conference on Robotics and Automation (ICRA), May 2018, pp. 5849–5855. https://doi.org/10.1109/ICRA.2018.8460994

10. Albouys-Perrois, J., Laviole, J., Briant, C., Brock, A.M.: Towards a multisensory augmented reality map for blind and low vision people. In: Proceedings of the 2018 CHI Conference on Human Factors in Computing Systems, April 2018, vol. 2018, pp. 1–14 (2018). https://doi.org/10.1145/3173574.3174203

11. Assistive Devices for People with Hearing or Speech Disorders | NIDCD. https://www.nidcd.nih.gov/health/assistive-devices-people-hearing-voice-speech-or-language-disorders. Accessed 22 Feb 2022

12. Tam, V., Gelsomini, M., Garzotto, F.: Polipo. In: Proceedings of the Eleventh International Conference on Tangible, Embedded, and Embodied Interaction, March 2017, pp. 11–20 (2017). https://doi.org/10.1145/3024969.3025006

13. Stone, B.G., Mills, K.A., Saggers, B.: Online multiplayer games for the social interactions of children with autism spectrum disorder: a resource for inclusive education. Int. J. Incl. Educ. **23**(2), 209–228 (2019). https://doi.org/10.1080/13603116.2018.1426051

14. EASY READING – Keeping the user at the digital original. https://www.easyreading.eu/. Accessed 24 Feb 2022

15. Pradhan, A., Mehta, K., Findlater, L.: Accessibility came by accident. In: Proceedings of the 2018 CHI Conference on Human Factors in Computing Systems, April 2018, vol. 2018-April, pp. 1–13 (2018). https://doi.org/10.1145/3173574.3174033

16. Oliveira, R., Arriaga, P., Santos, F.P., Mascarenhas, S., Paiva, A.: Towards pro-social design: a scoping review of the use of robots and virtual agents to trigger prosocial behaviour. Comput. Hum. Behav. **114**, 106547 (2021). https://doi.org/10.1016/j.chb.2020.106547

17. Coughlan, J.M., Miele, J.: AR4VI: AR as an accessibility tool for people with visual impairments. In: 2017 IEEE International Symposium on Mixed and Augmented Reality (ISMAR-Adjunct), October 2017, pp. 288–292 (2017). https://doi.org/10.1109/ISMAR-Adjunct.2017.89

18. Cavus, N., Al-Dosakee, K., Abdi, A., Sadiq, S.: The utilization of augmented reality technology for sustainable skill development for people with special needs: a systematic literature review. Sustainability **13**(19), 10532 (2021). https://doi.org/10.3390/su131910532

19. Quintero, J., Baldiris, S., Rubira, R., Cerón, J., Velez, G.: Augmented reality in educational inclusion. A systematic review on the last decade. Front. Psychol. **10**, 1835 (2019). https://doi.org/10.3389/FPSYG.2019.01835/BIBTEX

20. Yoon, C., et al.: Leveraging augmented reality to create apps for people with visual disabilities. In: The 21st International ACM SIGACCESS Conference on Computers and Accessibility, October 2019, pp. 210–221 (2019). https://doi.org/10.1145/3308561.3353788

21. Tian, Y., Yang, X., Yi, C., Arditi, A.: Toward a computer vision-based wayfinding aid for blind persons to access unfamiliar indoor environments. Mach. Vis. Appl. **24**(3), 521–535 (2013). https://doi.org/10.1007/s00138-012-0431-7

22. Huang, J., Kinateder, M., Dunn, M.J., Jarosz, W., Yang, X.-D., Cooper, E.A.: An augmented reality sign-reading assistant for users with reduced vision. PLoS ONE **14**(1), e0210630 (2019). https://doi.org/10.1371/journal.pone.0210630

23. Bakshi, A.M., Simson, J., de Castro, C., Yu, C.C., Dias, A.: Bright: an augmented reality assistive platform for visual impairment. In: 2019 IEEE Games, Entertainment, Media Conference (GEM), June 2019, pp. 1–4 (2019). https://doi.org/10.1109/GEM.2019.8811556

24. lo Bianco, M., Pedell, S., Renda, G.: Augmented reality and home modifications. In: Proceedings of the 28th Australian Conference on Computer-Human Interaction - OzCHI 2016, November 2016, pp. 499–507 (2016). https://doi.org/10.1145/3010915.3010929

25. Géron, A.: Hands-on machine learning with Scikit-Learn, Keras and TensorFlow: concepts, tools, and techniques to build intelligent systems (2019). https://www.oreilly.com/library/view/hands-on-machine-learning/9781492032632/. Accessed 22 Feb 2022
26. Dabran, I., Avny, T., Singher, E., ben Danan, H.: Augmented reality speech recognition for the hearing impaired. In: 2017 IEEE International Conference on Microwaves, Antennas, Communications and Electronic Systems (COMCAS), November 2017, vol. 2017-November, pp. 1–4 (2017). https://doi.org/10.1109/COMCAS.2017.8244731
27. Zhang, Z., Geiger, J., Pohjalainen, J., Mousa, A.E.-D., Jin, W., Schuller, B.: Deep learning for environmentally robust speech recognition. ACM Trans. Intell. Syst. Technol. 9(5), 1–28 (2018). https://doi.org/10.1145/3178115
28. Gales, M., Young, S.: The application of hidden markov models in speech recognition. Found. Trends® Sig. Process. 1(3), 195–304 (2007). https://doi.org/10.1561/2000000004
29. Rabiner, L., Juang, B.: An introduction to hidden Markov models. IEEE ASSP Mag. 3(1), 4–16 (1986). https://doi.org/10.1109/MASSP.1986.1165342
30. Abdel-Hamid, O., Mohamed, A.R., Jiang, H., Deng, L., Penn, G., Yu, D.: Convolutional neural networks for speech recognition. IEEE Trans. Audio Speech Lang. Process. 22(10), 1533–1545 (2014). https://doi.org/10.1109/TASLP.2014.2339736
31. Nassif, A.B., Shahin, I., Attili, I., Azzeh, M., Shaalan, K.: Speech recognition using deep neural networks: a systematic review. IEEE Access 7, 19143–19165 (2019). https://doi.org/10.1109/ACCESS.2019.2896880
32. Redmon, J., Farhadi, A.: YOLOv3: an incremental improvement, April 2018. http://arxiv.org/abs/1804.02767. Accessed 22 Feb 2022
33. Barakat, B., Steponenaite, A., Lall, G.S., Arshad, K., Wassell, I.J., Keates, S.: Assistive technology for the visually impaired: optimizing frame rate (freshness) to improve the performance of real-time objects detection application. In: Antona, M., Stephanidis, C. (eds.) HCII 2020. LNCS, vol. 12189, pp. 479–492. Springer, Cham (2020). https://doi.org/10.1007/978-3-030-49108-6_34
34. Barakat, B., et al.: 6G opportunities arising from internet of things use cases: a review paper. Future Internet 13(6), 159 (2021). https://doi.org/10.3390/fi13060159
35. Get Microsoft HoloLens - Microsoft Store en-GB. https://www.microsoft.com/en-gb/p/microsoft-hololens/9nblggh4qwnx?activetab=pivot:overviewtab. Accessed 25 Feb 2022
36. Microsoft. MixedReality-WebRTC Documentation. https://microsoft.github.io/MixedReality-WebRTC/. Accessed 25 Feb 2022

Automated Generation of Digital Twin in Virtual Reality for Interaction with Specific Nature Ecosystem

Arnis Cirulis [ID], Lauris Taube[✉], and Zintis Erics[✉]

Faculty of Engineering, Vidzeme University of Applied Sciences, Valmiera, Latvia
{arnis.cirulis,lauris.taube,zintis.erics}@va.lv

Abstract. This paper analyses the most suitable technological approaches to design a workflow and develop a virtual reality system - BogSim-VR, to run real time simulations for bog ecosystems (ecological systems) or peatlands in different countries and regions. Currently few technologies reflect data in an understandable way. There is also no suitable system that allows for different human actions and the visualization of consequences. Virtual reality technologies can address this problem. The BogSim-VR system is adaptable to any bog ecosystem thus creating a digital twin for experimenting with various interactions in a replicated environment.

Keywords: Virtual reality · Digital twin · 3D content generation · Bog ecosystem · Onsite simulation

1 Introduction

An already developed simulation model was the basis for the design and development of a digital bog ecosystem twin in virtual reality. Various implementations of system dynamics justify this technology [1–3]. The logic for a bog ecosystem simulation model was available in Stella Architect and Insight Maker [4–6], and is implemented in Python using calculations based on 35 criteria. The main outcome of this simulation model is generated charts, which depict the level of ground water for a specified period. This simulation model is verified and validated; it includes all components forming the hydrological system of the bog and mathematically reflects the relationships between them [4–6]. The hydrological system as an emphasis on depicting the bog ecosystem was chosen because the exact level of groundwater ensures the growth of sphagnum moss as a function of carbon storage while preventing rapid growth of forest stands, which would interfere with precipitation supplementing the water balance of the ecosystem [4–6]. Bog ecosystems have an important role in carbon sequestration and mitigation of global climate change. Bogs in the boreal and sub-arctic regions store around 15–30% of global soil carbon [7]. In the European Union, the move towards climate neutrality policy includes activities specifically aimed at the reduction of negative greenhouse gas emissions from bogs through nature conservation and renewal [8].

M. Antona and C. Stephanidis (Eds.): HCII 2022, LNCS 13309, pp. 187–202, 2022.
https://doi.org/10.1007/978-3-031-05039-8_13

Bogs are one of the most endangered types of natural habitats in Europe [9] and it was important to develop the BogSim-VR system to highlight the actuality and role of bogs. This system is adaptable to any bog ecosystem thus creating a digital twin for experimenting with various interactions in a replicated environment. In a bog such interactions include cutting down trees, tree planting, digging ditches, traces of tractor equipment, fire damage etc. The BogSim-VR digital twin was developed in the Unity engine. A three-dimensional world is generated based on GIS (geographic information system) data gathered for a specific area. For a more precise three-dimensional representation LIDAR data from a drone was also used. Python simulation logic is realized in C# and currently most influence in calculations is assigned to leaf area index (LAI) values, which change depending on actions carried out in the digital twin, for example, the LAI value decreases if trees are cut down, however the ground water level increases in future predictions. The virtual environment is accessed via an Oculus Quest2 headset. Navigation uses best practices to reduce cyber sickness, and is customizable. The participant can utilize various virtual tools, instruments, devices or machinery, for example, a virtual tablet to customize interaction settings for convenient UX (user experience) and to instantly depict simulation results. By choosing a virtual chainsaw, the participant can pretend to be a forest worker and cut down trees, changing the LAI value for the area. For LAI and groundwater calculations, it is crucial to have precise data about a specific date, for example, the amount of snow and rain, temperature, sun radiation, humidity, peat depth and many other (35 variables in total). Currently data is acquired from meteorological services for the closest station in the area, but to increase accuracy of calculations, an IoT network is developed directly in the bog to gather essential parameters all year. For that purpose, narrowband Internet of Things (NB-IoT) technology is used. This allows implementing a low-power solution.

The developed virtual environment could be also used for decision makers of sensitive ecosystems or to provide a training course in environmental sciences. Since BogSim-VR system is adaptable to various bogs, it can also be customized to ecological systems, mostly land systems, like forests, grasslands and deserts. The designed flowchart and practical implementation will be used to develop similar systems, and to improve accuracy for currently developed virtual reality simulation systems.

2 Algorithms and Methods to Develop a Digital Twin and Implement a Simulation

The BogSim-VR system uses compute shaders from the Unity game engine [10]. The package also supplies data structures and API for programmatic access and execution. Additionally, there is I/O functionality support for reading/writing simulation data from/to CSV/TIFF files. Note that all of this is done in a manner that should facilitate reuse and extension of included components. Main features and working principles of the package include core data structures and general working principles, I/O options and formats, bog simulation specific functionality and reuse. Generally, compute shaders are programs that run on the graphics card, outside of the normal rendering pipeline. They can be used for massively parallel GPGPU (General-purpose Computing on Graphics Processing Units) algorithms, or to accelerate parts of game rendering. To use them efficiently often an in-depth knowledge of GPU architectures and parallel algorithms is needed [10]. Various approaches are used to implement this technology in simulations, terrain visualizations, image processing [11, 12] and use its benefits, especially in applications that acquire real time pipelines. There are several techniques to accelerate physics simulations [13]. Compute shaders provide support for computing various mathematical operations needed as part of the usual graphics-generating pipeline. They can also act as powerful mathematical co-processors for applications outside of the graphics pipeline [14]. General data structures used for the BogSim-VR shader include Simulation class, Frame class and Layer class. Simulation class provides the necessary API to execute simulation, move data from/to CPU/GPU and acts as a list of Frame class instances. In the middle, instances of the Frame class represent states of the simulation at every time step. This class organizes and provides mapping of Layer class instances to Layer types. At the bottom, instances of the Layer class hold the actual data of the simulation. This class provides both generic and low-level access to the data. Layer types help to identify the data held within Layer class instances as variables corresponding to the current simulation.

On the CPU side, the aforementioned classes are directly represented in C#. The Simulation class has various methods for Frame instance manipulation, compute shader execution and data transfer, it also implements IList and IDisposable interfaces for easy data access and resource management respectively. The Frame class implements the IDictionary interface for the Layer class instance and type mapping. The Layer class holds data in a byte array and provides both direct untyped access and generic unmanaged indexers in both 1D and 2D forms. Layer types are implemented and accepted as a generic enum (see Fig. 1.).

On the GPU side all data is stored in two memory buffers and various additional parameters are used. The input buffer holds all data from layers the simulation reads and does not write. The input parameters hold input layer dimensions. The output buffer holds data from the layers the simulation writes. This is also where the intermediate states of stocks reside. The output parameters hold output layer dimensions and 1D size for convenience as there is very little available in ways of data structuring, and extensive use of abstraction and indirection may hinder the performance, especially considering any points of synchronization during parallel execution.

The use of the developed shader package is straightforward. First, create an instance of Simulation class and add loaded Frame instances. Second, execute the simulation using the Simulate method. This method transfers input layers of the current frame to the GPU and dispatches the simulation shader, optionally calling the initialization shader beforehand. Both shaders are provided to the Simulation instance during its creation. Use the LoadLastFrame method to fetch the resulting output layers from the GPU, if necessary. Repeat the last two steps in a loop until there are no more input frames. Write the resulting frames to CSV/TIFF files.

Depending on simulation and layer resolution, each frame may take up considerable memory. In this case it is anywhere from 138 to 202 MB depending on input layer resolution. While this may be acceptable for a few frames, it will reach unreasonable memory requirements for a 1000 frame simulation; therefore, two options should be considered. Providing a filter argument to the Simulation class during creation. This

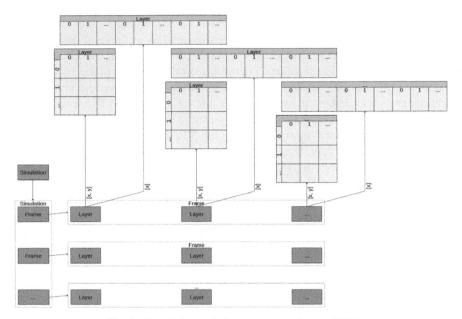

Fig. 1. Simulation and class representation on CPU.

will enable LoadLastFrame to fetch only the layers present in the filter, and not call LoadLastFrame for every frame simulated. The SetData method used by the Simulation class to transfer data to the GPU seems to cause a memory leak if used multiple times within a single Update call, therefore refrain from simulating too many frames per single Update call (see Fig. 2). The I/O facilities use a simple framework to move data in both directions. Sinks write the data to a location. Sources read the data from a location. Sinks/Sources have a limited capability to guess which specific implementation to use based on the data location identified by Uri. The simplest and least efficient supported format is CSV. Here Sinks/Sources come in three variations. As the name implies the Single variant reads/writes data from/to a single CSV file. This is also the default variant guessed when the framework is presented with a Uri pointing to a CSV file. The Grouped variant reads/writes a new CSV file for each frame of data. This variant expects a Uri pointing to a directory; therefore, it can't be guessed from Uri alone. Since the data needs to be split among multiple files, each file is named with the frame number. The Source expects data to be in this is format. The Distinct variant reads/writes a new CSV file for each layer within each frame. As with the Grouped variant, it expects a directory and cannot be guessed.

Again, the data is split among multiple files; therefore, each file is named and expected with the frame number and Layer type name. TIFF is the most efficient format in terms of file size and processing time. As with CSV, the Sinks/Sources come in three variations. The Single variant works with a single TIFF file and can be guessed from Uri. The Grouped variant splits data among files based on the frame and layer dimensions. This effectively places each potentially multi-spectral image in its own file because several TIFF viewers can handle multi-spectral images but cannot deal with multi-image

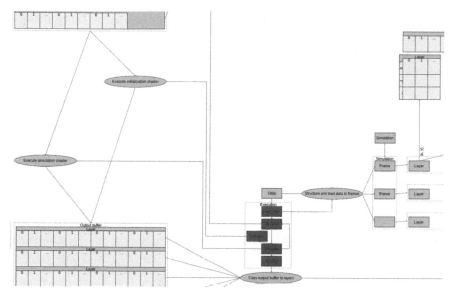

Fig. 2. Fragment of general topology for the developed shader.

TIFF files. The Distinct variant splits the data amongst files based on the frame and layer. This effectively places each channel in its own grayscale image. This is the most flexible format. Each file can hold multiple images and each image can have an arbitrary number of channels with an arbitrary sample width and format. As a result, this is the most efficient format but can cause some headache for viewers not prepared to handle its internal structure. This is most obvious when working with multi-image files, since most general-purpose image viewers cannot go past the first image. This format can also store georeferenced data, potentially with proper support for the time dimension. While the Sources have no problem reading such files, Sinks do not forward this information when writing as the data may come from any Source including some not storing such information.

Shader is not a traditional Source and certainly not a Sink of any kind. Instead, this Source uses an algorithm to generate data from a shader. Two algorithm variations are available: Perlin noise and Simplex noise. Both can be guessed and configured from Uri. The Scheme indicates which Source to use. The Host indicates whether to generate data in 'input', 'output' or 'all' layers. The Port indicates the divider to use to downscale the generated layer's resolution. This source is used to generate arbitrary data during development in cases where the real data is not available.

In addition to general use and data structures, there are some algorithms of note specifically for bog simulation. The terraform algorithm (see Fig. 3) uses data from an arbitrary layer to change and scale a height map of the Terrain. The algorithm employs some simple checks to ensure the layer dimensions are divisible by the implied resolution. The shortest side of the layer is the resolution baseline from which the next lowest base of two is calculated. As a result, the layer used should have the longest side be a multiple of the shortest one and the shortest side should be a multiple of two. The algorithm can handle non-square layers larger than the height map but those used by Unity are square exclusively. This is compensated by scaling the terrain and should not be a problem unless extremely elongated strips of data are used, in which case an obvious visual directionality may form depending on the height map data variation. The height maps in Unity are of an odd size, power of 2 plus 1; therefore, the algorithm uses extrapolation to calculate the potential values of this semi-border. This is done purely for aesthetic reasons and has no impact on the simulation. It must be noted that there seem to be limits to the size range a height map in Unity can take, at least from the editor UI. Currently the algorithm does not account for this and some problems have been observed when using height maps below minimal resolution. The potential implications of this are unclear, but caution is advised when working outside the editor's range.

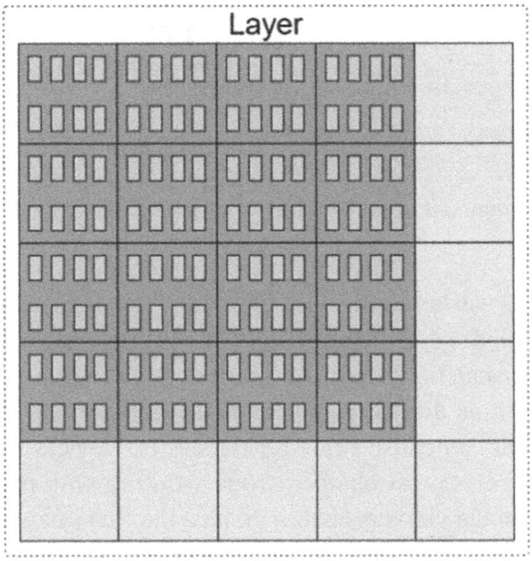

Fig. 3. Terraform algorithm to change and scale the height map of Terrain.

Plant algorithm (see Fig. 4) uses the data from an arbitrary layer to place various Plants. The placement of Plants is determined by their Species. These Species have several parameters directing the algorithm:

- The radius indicates the area the members of the Species affect.
- The falloff indicates how quickly, if at all, the effect of the Species wanes with distance.
- The value range indicates the limits of where the Species can spawn.
- The intensity range indicates the limits of the Species' effect on the surroundings; this is scaled from the value.
- The height range indicates the limits of the Species' physical size; this is scaled from the intensity.
- The type indicates the type of Plant the Species should spawn.

The algorithm operates as follows; it starts at the layer origin and then moves in a row-major order along the second interpretation of the data. At each stop, it checks

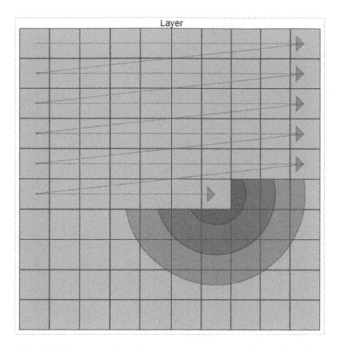

Fig. 4. Plant algorithm to generate various species on Terrain.

if any known Species can be spawned there. If a compatible Species is found, a Plant is spawned and the following surrounding area is affected. The algorithm is used to calculate potential tree positions based on the LAI (Leaf area index) layer. There is a pair of derived equations used for calculating the opposite effect on Near infrared and Red reflectance layers through the NDVI (normalized difference vegetation index) layer [5]. These change both reflectance layers when virtually planting or chopping trees. The algorithm is not based on scientific theory. It was deemed good enough at generating a canopy visually matching the distribution of the real one (see Fig. 5), and the derived equations, while mathematically sound and able to maintain correct NDVI, may go into negatives in the resulting Near infrared and Red reflectance. This is mitigated by only using them in the calculation of NDVI. Still, care is advised when using the resulting reflectance values. This algorithm is rather linear and is executed on the CPU side. This is in contrast to the Terraform algorithm, which runs mostly on the GPU side.

Since most of the code involved is abstract and generic, the reuse of this project is straightforward. Provide a different compute shader realizing the desired simulation. When providing a different Layer type enumeration matching the shader, the following needs to be considered. The enum should clearly label input and output types with 'Input' and 'Output' prefixes respectively; this determines buffer sizes. The inputs should come before the outputs; this is required since the code uses enum values as offsets in the buffers. The enum should clearly label stocks that require intermediate states with 'Stock' suffix, this is used to allocate extra memory in the output buffer. Optionally, a different value type for data interpretation should be provided.

```
# the original lai equation with embedded ndvi
lai = 3.187 * (nir - red) / (nir + red) + 0.792

# extract and invert constants
(lai - 0.792) / 3.187 = (nir - red) / (nir + red)
(0.3137747097583935 * lai) - 0.24850957012864766 = (nir - red) / (nir + red)

# assign to variables for simplicity
i = 0.3137747097583935
j = 0.24850957012864766

# add variables and move some terms
(i * lai) - j = (nir - red) / (nir + red)
((i * lai) - j) * (nir + red) = nir - red

# the original derived equations, these are recursive and kept here only as a reminder
nir = ((i * lai) - j) * (nir + red) + red
red = -(((i * lai) - j) * (nir + red) - nir)

# multiply and move some terms
i * lai * nir + i * lai * red - j * nir - j * red = nir - red
i * lai * red - j * red + red = nir + j * nir - i * lai * nir
i * lai * red + (1 - j) * red = (1 + j) * nir - i * lai * nir

# flip sides
(i * lai + 1 - j) * red = (-i * lai + 1 + j) * nir
(i * lai + 1 - j) / (-i * lai + 1 + j) = nir / red

# here's our derived equations
nir = i * lai + 1 - j
red = -i * lai + 1 + j

# those are only good for ndvi as such need to be scaled to fit reflectance ranges using reference values
k = (nirr / nir + redr / red) / 2
nir *= k
red *= k
```

Fig. 5. Source code and implementation of Plant algorithm.

3 Visualization of Simulation Data and Interaction Feedback Delivery

To achieve the main goal a virtual reality (VR) scene should be developed for visualizing simulation data. This is done by creating a 3D environment with realistic terrain where the user can move around, and trees to interact with. The terrain and trees are generated based on real-world data.

The user can see various types of data from the simulation in easy-to-understand ways – images and charts. The user can also interact with the trees – cut them down and see how that action has affected the simulation in real-time.

In the visualization stage the Unity project uses the Universal Render Pipeline (URP) for its graphical performance optimizations. Some custom shaders were needed for this project. For this purpose, the visual shader package 'Amplify Shader Editor' was used [15]. For VR integration 'BNG VR Interaction Framework' [16] provides movement and object and UI interactions for the user. Oculus headsets were used for development and testing, and in Unity the Oculus SDK was necessary. 'BNG Framework' provides integrations for other major VR SDKs (such as SteamVR), so other brand headsets can be used. The main logic is split into multiple scripts that perform their own specific tasks.

Simulation controller is one of the main scripts. It follows the singleton pattern and is easily accessible from any other script.

It loads data from a specific TIFF file and uses that to perform the simulation. After the simulation, its data is stored in a variable. Later this variable and its data is used in multiple other scripts. The stored simulation data includes positional data which corresponds to a position on the 3D terrain. To acquire and display various data based on position, this script also contains a method to get and return data based on that position for a specified data type.

The vegetation placer script performs the creation and placement of vegetation objects on the 3D terrain. The user can set and adjust some settings for this script in the Unity Editor. Terrain – specify which Terrain object to use. Position Offset – specify how much random positional offset to add to each tree. Vegetation Radius Multiplier – a value that adjusts how dense the forest can be (the higher the value, the less dense it is). Vegetation – a list of vegetation objects and their parameters (height, type and prefab to spawn).

For Terrain Tree Prototypes the project uses the built-in Unity terrain and tree systems. Therefore, creating and placing tree objects is not as straightforward as simply instantiating object prefabs. Before a tree object can be placed on the terrain, a specific 'TreePrototype' class object must be created. It has multiple properties, but for this use case only the 'prefab' property is changed. For each entry in the 'Vegetation' list, a tree prototype is created with the specified prefab. After that the created tree prototypes are set in terrain settings. That allows prefabs to be spawned on the terrain.

The simulation contains real terrain height data from which the 3D terrain is created. Terrain creation is done in this script, but potentially could be implemented in any other. This is done before creating and placing the tree objects. To create the terrain, the 'Terraform()' method is used from 'Simulation'. The terrain is created in the size specified in the Simulation (for example, if the Simulation is set to X = 1000 and Y = 500, then the terrain will be 1000 × 500 units in size on X and Z axis in Unity).

Placing the tree objects occurs as follows. Before instantiating the trees, specific 'Plant' class objects must be retrieved from the simulation. For this purpose, a 'Dictionary' is created based on values specified in the 'Vegetation' list. This is passed as a parameter to the 'Simulation.Plant()' which returns a list of 'Plant' class objects. The 'Plant' object contains information about the tree's height and position, among other parameters. Then for each of the 'Plant' objects a 'Tree instance' is created and placed on the terrain. A 'Tree instance' is Unity Terrain specific data and contains various parameters about the placed tree object. This data includes a prototype index to correspond to the necessary 'TreePrototype' entry created earlier, position according to the simulation data, random rotation on the vertical axis and random height based on specified height range in the 'Vegetation' list. Then the 'Tree instance' gets added to the terrain (see Fig. 6). Two more tasks are performed while creating the instances: 'Destroyable trees' and 'Overlay controller'.

Fig. 6. Generated tree on terrain.

Development of Destroyable trees (see Fig. 7). Unity terrain trees are not interactive by default. To be able to cut down trees, an extra object is created in the scene for each tree. When creating previously mentioned 'TreeInstance's, a method is called from the 'DestroyableTreeGenerator' script. It creates a capsule game object with a collider at the position of the tree and attaches a 'DestroyableTree' script component to it. The script component holds references and data of the terrain tree. The 'DestroyableTree' script allows the tree to be cut down. When the tree is cut down, the script removes the tree's terrain instance and, in its place, instantiates an object prefab with the same graphics, but with an added 'Rigidbody' physics component that allows the tree to fall. When a tree is cut, that event is sent back to the simulation. The simulation gets refreshed and outputs new data that represents the changes caused by cutting down a tree. To achieve Tree cutter specifics, the user must use a specific object to cut down the tree: a chainsaw. The object has various components attached to it, as well as a control script for tree cutting.

At the position of the chainsaw blade, there is a box trigger zone, which detects if a tree object is in it (see Fig. 8). If there is and the user has pressed the trigger button on the controller, the cutting logic executes. Each 'DestroyableTree' has 'life points', and, while the cutting logic is being executed, they are being reduced for the tree that is in the trigger zone. If the 'life points' decrease to 0, the tree is cut down. While the cutting logic is being executed, a particle system and audio is played to indicate activities performed.

Fig. 7. Destroyable tree object in 3D scene and components.

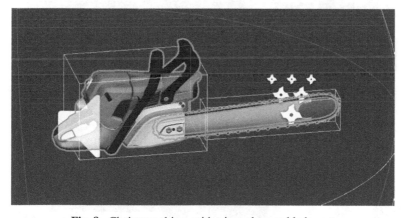

Fig. 8. Chainsaw object with trigger box on blade part.

4   Discussion on Interaction Capabilities

A user interface (UI) is needed to display data to the user. In virtual reality a traditional screen-space UI cannot be used, it needs to be a part of the environment. For this project a tablet computer object is used, and the data and information are displayed on its screen. This is done with the Unity UI system set to work in world-space. The user has the ability to view various data in image form. Those images are displayed on the tablet object (see Fig. 9). They are created and controlled by the 'OverlayController' script. These images and the data represent the 3D world and its form. It is vital for the user to know where they are in relation to the image. Therefore, a user icon is shown on top of these images to let the user know where they are. The user icon logic is described in the chapter "Overlay User Controller". When starting the application, each described image texture is created at runtime based on simulation resolution and its aspect ratio. Then they are assigned to UI references for displaying them to the user. If the image has data that corresponds to a world-space position on the 3D terrain, that position cannot be used directly to specify which pixels to affect. This position must be converted (normalized) to UV coordinates, which are in range of 0–1 on X and Y axis (2D space). The conversion is simple – the world-space position must be divided by the simulation resolution. This allows the image to be any resolution to adjust the performance and detail. This normalized value is essentially used as a positional percentage on the image – for example, a position of [0.1, 0.7] on an 1000 × 1000 pixel image would be at [100, 700]. Theoretically, if the image was the same resolution as the simulation, it could be possible to use the integer value of the world-space position directly to specify which pixel to affect. However, this approach could have a big impact on performance – larger images take longer to process.

When creating trees, their data is saved and sent to 'OverlayController'. That data contains tree position and its value. After all trees are generated, an image texture is created where each of the trees is shown as a colourful dot. The colour is determined from tree value. The position of this dot corresponds to the positions in 3D world-space.

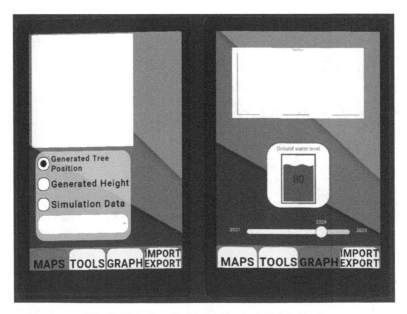

Fig. 9. User interface examples and tablet object.

The resulting image texture is created by going over the list of trees, using their position to determine where each dot must be. This position is in world-space and must be normalized as described above. Dot colour is determined by using the tree value (which is in range of 0–1) in a pre-made colour gradient. That colour is then assigned to pixels in the determined position (see Fig. 10). If the user cuts down a tree, the image is updated, and that trees' dot is removed (see Fig. 10).

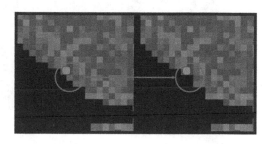

Fig. 10. Generated tree representation on tree map and changes in tree map after cutting down a tree.

While simulation data already includes elevation data, we create a separate height map based on the generated terrain. This is for comparing the simulation data with what is generated, and its precision.

The height map is created by sampling the height of the terrain in a grid-like pattern. The sampling step size is adjustable and controls how detailed the resulting image will be (a lower step size means a more detailed image). Also, it is important to mention that having a lower step size impacts the speed of image generation and setting it too low will take a long time. Unity terrain has a scripting method 'SampleHeight()' that returns the height of a position. The returned value is then normalized (to a range of 0–1) to be used in a colour gradient to determine pixel colour. (See Fig. 11).

The simulation has various layers with different data. To view this data in a more comprehensible way, it can be converted to images. This process is slightly different from previous image generation as layer data is in byte array form. To begin generating the image, simulation layer data needs to be converted to float values to create colour data. This is done by 'BitConverter.ToSingle()'. The returned float value is then used to create a grayscale colour using it for all three colour channels. This is done for all bytes in the array, and each created colour is added to a list for later use. Finally, the texture is created by setting pixel colours with the aforementioned colour list using 'Texture2D.SetPixels()' method.

For some image overlays it is important to know where they are in relation to the user. For this a user icon was created. It is always on top of the image overlays and follows the players' position. The logic for moving the user icon is as follows; get the user position in the 3D world and normalize it to a range of 0–1 based on simulation resolution so it can be used on any size overlay image – the normalized value is used as a positional percentage on the image. Then set the icons' position to a value that is calculated with this formula "overlay image size * normalized position".

Fig. 11. Generated height map and simulation data in image form.

In addition to image-based data output, simulation data can also be displayed as a chart. For the chart logic and visuals, a third-party asset was used - 'XCharts' [17]. This project uses bar charts. Data displayed is based on the users' position in 3D space and is updated in real-time as the user moves around. The logic for this is simple – each frame the game runs, the application checks if the player position has changed, and if it has, get data for the position from the simulation and send it to the chart to show that value. The 'XCharts' asset provides built-in easy updating of data– by specifying which chart an entry to update and new data values, the chart gets updated.

For this project various tree 3D models were needed. To make the creation process easier and simpler, a third-party asset was used to generate the tree models – 'MTree' [18]. It provides various useful features that Unity's built-in tree creator does not. Multiple pine tree models at different stages of growth were created with this tool. Since a large amount of tree models can cause performance issues when creating forest environments, some of the 'MTree' optimization features were used. Mainly adjusting the polygon count to be as low as possible while still maintaining a good overall look of the trees and using the automatic generation of LOD (Level of detail) objects for the model. LOD objects are copies of the original object, but with decreasing number of polygons. The LODs are useful at runtime when trying to maintain a good number of objects that the user sees while decreasing the performance as little as possible. Essentially, the tree objects that are closer to the user are shown as the higher detailed LOD objects, but the objects farther away from the user are shown as less detailed. Since it's generated at runtime, texturing by hand is not possible. For this reason, a special shader was created in 'Amplify' shader editor. This shader is based on terrain height, where at different heights a different texture is shown. The user needs to supply four textures to be used and adjust height settings. These textures must be tile-able and seamless, and to provide adequate detail, the textures need to be repeated multiple times across the terrain. By doing this, the repetition of the textures becomes very visible. To circumvent this, random noise-based colour variation was introduced – by mapping Perlin noise through a colour gradient, a seemingly random colour texture was created. This texture was then overlaid over the base textures. This broke up the repeating patterns and resulted in realistic ground texturing.

5 Conclusions

The BogSim-VR virtual reality system is functional and can be rated as TRL (technology readiness level) 3–4. The system was designed and developed to support the requirements and features of digital twin technology offering a 3D replica of a real bog ecosystem located in northern Latvia. The system prototype was tested and verified at Vidzeme University of Applied Sciences, Virtual Reality Technologies laboratory (ViA VR-Lab). The BogSim-VR system will be approbated in the next phase by performing statistical analysis and user tests. Prototype functionality improvements are also planned. Future activities involve actions to decrease the time of digital twin generation, integration of adjustment settings and improvement of UX (user experience) for convenient interaction and cybersickness reduction.

Acknowledgements. This work is research project funded by Latvian Council of Science, project number: lzp-2020/2-0396. Project name: Visualization of real-time bog hydrological regime and simulation data in virtual reality. Research activities took place at the Faculty of Engineering at Vidzeme University of Applied Sciences, and specifically, in the Virtual Reality Technologies laboratory (ViA VR-Lab). The laboratory was established in 2009 in cooperation with the Fraunhofer Institute Virtual Reality Training and Development Centre (Magdeburg, Germany) and the University of Agder (Kristiansand, Norway), pointing to its long history and years of experience. The activities of the ViA VR-Lab include industry training, urban planning, interactive study tools and equipment in medicine, visualization solutions in logistics, tourism and history, entertaining educational environments, marketing and product demonstration.

References

1. Wu, X., et al.: Impacts of lean construction on safety systems: a system dynamics approach. Int. J. Environ. Res. Publ. Health **16**(2), 221 (2019)
2. Muravev, D., et al.: The introduction to system dynamics approach to operational efficiency and sustainability of dry port's main parameters. Sustainability **11**(8), 2413 (2019)
3. Alefari, M., Barahona, A.M.F., Salonitis, K.: Modelling manufacturing employees' performance based on a system dynamics approach. Procedia CIRP **72**, 438–443 (2018)
4. Java, O.: The specification of hydrological model requirements for bog restoration. Baltic J. Mod. Comput. **8**(1), 164–173 (2020)

5. Java, O.: Restoration of a degraded bog hydrological regime using system dynamics modeling. In: CBU International Conference Proceedings, vol. 6. ISE Research Institute (2018)
6. Java, O., Kohv, M., Lõhmus, A.: Performance of a bog hydrological system dynamics simulation modeling an ecological restoration context: Soomaa case study, Estonia. Water **13**, 2217 (2021). https://doi.org/10.3390/w13162217
7. Limpens, J., et al.: Peatlands and the carbon cycle: from local processes to global implications – a synthesis. Biogeosciences **5**, 1475–1491 (2008). https://doi.org/10.5194/bg-5-1475-2008
8. IPBES (The Intergovernmental Science-Policy Platform on Biodiversity and Ecosystem Services): Kopsavilkumsricibpolitikas veidotajiem, [Summary for policy makers], vol. 4, lpp., A.4 (2019). (in Latvian)
9. Kiely, G., et al.: PeatGHG - Survey of GHG Emission and Sink Potential of Blanket Peatlands, pp. 1–35. EPA Research, Wexford (2018)
10. Compute Shaders: Copyright 2016 Unity Technologies. Publication 5.3-X. https://docs.unity3d.com/530/Documentation/Manual/ComputeShaders.html
11. Khoury, J., Dupuy, J., Riccio, C.: Adaptive GPU tessellation with compute shaders (2018)
12. Tornai, R., Fürjes-Benke, P.: Compute shader in image processing development (2021)
13. Mihai, C.-C., Lupu, C.: Using graphics processing units and compute shaders in real time multimodel adaptive robust control. Electronics **10**(20), 2462 (2021)
14. Vassilev, T.: Review of several techniques for accelerating physical simulations on the GPU 3 (2020)
15. Amplify Creations: Amplify Shader Editor. https://assetstore.unity.com/packages/tools/visual-scripting/amplify-shader-editor-68570. Accessed 12 Jan 2022
16. Bearded Ninja Games: VR Interaction Framework. https://assetstore.unity.com/packages/templates/systems/vr-interaction-framework-161066. Accessed 14 Oct 2021
17. XCharts 2.0: unity-ugui-XCharts. https://github.com/monitor1394/unity-ugui-Xcharts. Accessed 29 Dec 2021
18. Mx: Mtree - Tree Creation. https://assetstore.unity.com/packages/tools/modeling/mtree-tree-creation-132433. Accessed 6 July 2021

HMD Eye-Tracking Measurement of Miniature Eye Movement Toward VR Image Navigation

Seita Fujimoto[1], Masayuki Iwase[2], and Shu Matsuura[1(✉)]

[1] Faculty of Education, Tokyo Gakugei University, 4-1-1 Nukuikita, Koganei, Tokyo 184-8501,
Japan
shum00@u-gakugei.ac.jp
[2] United Graduate School of Education, Tokyo Gakugei University, 4-1-1 Nukuikita, Koganei,
Tokyo 184-8501, Japan

Abstract. We conducted preliminary eye and head mount display (HMD) movement measurements to collect primary data to create a spatio-temporal virtual
reality (VR) navigation system. Furthermore, we used the eye-tracking function
of the Vive Pro Eye HMD to perform eye and rotational movement measurements
of the HMD when gazing at a VR marker. We compared gazing at a fixed point
with randomly bouncing linear motion along with horizontal and vertical motion
by determining the Hurst exponent and the anisotropy of the gaze trajectories.

Trajectories of the fixed vision and the slow marker chasing showed the Hurst
exponent less than 1/2, indicating anti-persistency. In contrast, as the marker velocity increased, the displacements of gaze trajectories were stretched and showed
persistency to the marker motion direction. As the marker speed decreased, the
gaze trajectory expanded perpendicular to the marker motion, suggesting that the
antipersistent miniature motion enhanced the collection of visual information.
Users were found unconsciously superimposed a persistent motion of HMD on
the gaze motion in the horizontal direction. We inferred this tendency to help to
generate miniature gaze motion to collect visual information.

Keywords: HMD eye-tracking · Hurst exponent · VR navigation

1 Introduction

There are increasing attempts to use immersive virtual reality (VR) as a pedagogical
method using a Head Mounted Display (HMD) [1]. Immersive virtual environments may
facilitate students' proactive finding and learning in VR experiences, and multifaceted
studies are underway to introduce HMDs in K-12 education [2].

Various 3D interfaces have emerged for virtual and augmented reality experiences
[3]. In the case of video content, learners require easy-to-understand spatio-temporal
navigation, such as directing attention to images that appear at specific times and spatial
locations in the video.

In the VR space, eye-gazing is a typical navigation method [2–5]. The most popular
interface for navigation using visual cues is probably the use of visual markers such as

M. Antona and C. Stephanidis (Eds.): HCII 2022, LNCS 13309, pp. 203–216, 2022.
https://doi.org/10.1007/978-3-031-05039-8_14

pointers and circles, which display different shapes in the background image as visual markers and move them to the desired video location to direct the viewer's attention.

Fixational eye movements (FEMs) are fine, irregular, and involuntary and occur when gazing at a single fixed point, but the eyes are not entirely fixed [4, 6, 7]. FEMs prevent the loss of perception during gaze fixation [5] and are categorized into three types: tremors, drifts, and microsaccades (MSs). A tremor is an aperiodic motion with an amplitude of $0.02°$ and a frequency of about 90 Hz [4, 6], a drift is an irregular motion with a slow amplitude of about $0.5°/s$ and $0.02–0.1°$ [6]. Additionally, a microsaccade is a quick ballistic movement with an amplitude and duration of about $0.5°$ and 25 ms, respectively [4, 8, 9]. Miniature eye movements are believed to play a role in acquiring detailed spatial information [10–14].

A long-range positive (persistent) correlation in FEMs was found by measuring the Hurst exponent of motion trajectory fluctuations [15]. Mergenthaler et al. experimentally showed a transition from persistent to antipersistent correlation occurred in FEMs on short time scales and discussed the neurophysiological delay using a FEM model with time-delayed random walks [16]. Engbert et al. (2011) explained the transition from persistent to antipersistent FEMs with a model of a self-avoiding random walk in a self-generating potential [17]. Furthermore, Herrmann et al. (2017) reproduced the features leading to time-delayed feedback in the control of drifting motion on long time scales through a self-avoiding walk with neural delays [18].

On the other hand, HMDs with integrated eye-tracking functions have recently been developed and are commercially available. Conventionally, controller-based interaction has been implemented in VR immersive spaces [19]. Eye-tracking is expected to be applied to gaze-based interaction and detects the user's learning state and intention for assistance [20, 21]. The HTC Vive Pro Eye [22] has a spatial resolution of 1440×1600 pixels per eye, a refresh rate of 90 Hz, and a field of view of $110°$ [23]. It has also been reported that the HTC Vive Pro Eye can serve as an assessment tool for saccade eye movement [24].

Immersive VR spatio-temporal learning materials require navigation through time and space [25]. In VR, the gaze is essential for navigation in a visual-oriented space [26–29].

One of the authors composed a $180°$ video from time-lapse photos of the entire sky taken with a fisheye lens on the roof of an elementary school, and he used it as a teaching material [30]. The authors created a prototype of teaching material, as shown in Fig. 1, that allows users to switch between a panoramic image and a fisheye image on a flat surface and observe it with an HMD. In the panoramic image (Fig. 1b), we indicated the direction of observation through a rotating magnetic needle. In this teaching material, the user must pay attention to notable phenomena in a spatial region at a specific time.

In the fisheye image, as shown in Fig. 1a, the user can perceive the entire sky, but in the panoramic image in Fig. 1b, the user has to turn his head to comprehend the space. An arrow displayed in the front, as shown in Fig. 1b, signifies the direction of a selected phenomenon, and the user can navigate to the desired direction by moving his/her head. This navigation requires the user to move the viewpoint in the required direction and appropriately perceive the video's visual information. In addition, a bar representing the timeline is displayed at the bottom center of the screen to guide the viewer, making it easier to find the time when the phenomenon of interest occurs.

What design principles must be considered when designing such spatio-temporal navigation with the visual perception of visual elements, when using viewing devices such as HMDs, and when giving a presentation while indicating with a laser pointer? What are the principles of marker navigation? The fundamental purpose of this research is to focus on the nature of the gaze and clarify the characteristics required for navigation by analyzing the gaze at the navigation marker.

This study analyzes the characteristics of the miniature gaze movement when looking at a stationary marker and a marker in constant linear motion. This research is a preliminary study for constructing visual marker point navigation in VR video materials using HMD.

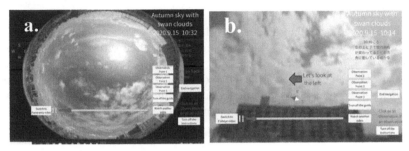

Fig. 1. **a**: Sky view through the fisheye lens, **b**: a panorama view with a navigation arrow and a timeline bar.

2 Method

Vive Pro Eye (HTC Corporation), an HMD with eye-tracking capability, was used for gaze measurement. For eye-tracking, we used the 3D game engine Unity 2019 (Unity Technologies) [31] with the VR platform SDK Steam VR (Valve Corporation) [32] to implement the Vive Pro Eye. We used the VIVE Sense Eye, and Facial Tracking SDK provided on the Vive website [33] for eye-tracking.

In this study, we use the values of the direction cosine $G_x(t)$, $G_y(t)$ in the unit direction vector $\hat{d}_g$ i.e.

$$\hat{d}_g = G_x(t)\mathbf{i} + G_y(t)\mathbf{j} + G_z(t)\mathbf{k}$$

to quantify the gaze motion. The participant faces in the direction of the z-axis. Similarly, let $R_x(t)$, $R_y(t)$, and $R_z(t)$ denote the rotation angles of the HMD with the x, y, and z-axes as the rotation axes, respectively. Moreover, let $h_x(t)$ and $h_y(t)$ denote the head motion in the x and y-axis directions, respectively.

In this paper, we measured the head motion utilizing $h_x(t) = R_y(t)$ and $h_y(t) = R_x(t)$. The participants mainly observe the object's motion in the horizontal and vertical directions on the screen. We analyze the time series of $G_x(t)$ and $G_y(t)$ for eye movements and $h_x(t)$ and $h_y(t)$ for HMD rotation.

$G_x(t)$, $G_y(t)$ was obtained by eye-tracking to represent the gaze fluctuations in the x and y-axis directions. The root-mean-square displacement (RMSD), $\sigma_x(\tau)$ and $\sigma_y(\tau)$ of $G_x(t)$ and $G_y(t)$, represents the fluctuation characteristics

$$\sigma_x(\tau) = \sqrt{\frac{1}{T-\tau} \sum_{i=\tau}^{T-\tau} (G_x(i-\tau) - G_x(i))^2}$$

where T is the measurement time and τ is the time lag.

Generally, for the random motion of $G_x(t)$, $\sigma_x(\tau)$ shows the following relation for time lag τ,

$$\sigma_x(\tau) \propto \tau^{H_x}$$

where H_x is called the Hurst exponent, and G_x is Brownian motion (non-correlated) when $H_x = 1/2$, G_x is a persistent fluctuation when $H_x > 1/2$, and G_x is an antipersistent fluctuation when $H_x < 1/2$ [33]. We eliminated the time series data during the eye blinking.

As shown in Table 1, we performed the following three types of gaze measurements: "fixed vision," "random bouncing motion vision," and "linear motion chasing" using a white circular planar image that was large enough to cover the entire view area of 1440 × 1600 pixels per eye.

Table 1. Eye-tracking tests.

Test	Field	Task	Marker motion
"*Fixed vision*"	Circular plane	Gaze at a fixed marker	Fixed
"*Random bouncing vision*"	Circular plane	Gaze at a randomly bouncing marker	Moderately highspeed linear motion in a randomly chosen direction. The direction changes randomly at a square boundary
"*Linear motion chasing*"	Circular plane	Gaze at a linearly moving marker	Slow speed: One round trip in 2 min Mid speed: One round trip in 1 min Fast speed: One round trip in 2 s Horizontal and vertical movement at each speed

1) Fixed vision: Participants fixated on a red circular marker point for about 30 s.

2) Random bouncing vision: Participants gazed and tracked a single circular marker that moved in a straight line in a square area in a circular field and changed direction randomly at the boundary. The marker always moves in a straight line and completes the test in 10 round trips, which is slightly slower than the fast linear motion described below since the elapsed time is about 40 s for 10 round trips.

3) Linear motion chasing: Participants gazed at a single marker moving horizontally and vertically back and forth on the screen (marker chasing). The motion speed was set to the three levels shown in the table: slow, mid, and fast.

These levels assume that the markers help users visually navigate the educational material. We did not fix the participants' HMD so that they could move their heads.

The participants were 11 university students aged 21–22. They wore the Vive Pro Eye HMD and performed the four types of trials listed in Table 1 in succession after calibrating their gaze in a seated posture.

3   Results and Discussions

Figure 2 shows an example of the gaze trajectory of fixed vision and random bouncing marker chasing. The fact that G_y is lower than the origin of the $G_x(t) - G_y(t)$ coordinate signifies that the observer held the HMD slightly upward and looked downward.

This fixed-vision trajectory consists of 1038 steps (0.011s/step), and the random bouncing vision trajectory comprises 4322 steps. The trajectory is confined itself within a narrow range in fixational vision, but microsaccades with relatively large step widths occurred frequently. In contrast, random bouncing vision exhibited a trajectory with a large step width, and it demonstrated drift induced by the marker movement. Overall the trajectory range was limited to the range of the entire marker motion.

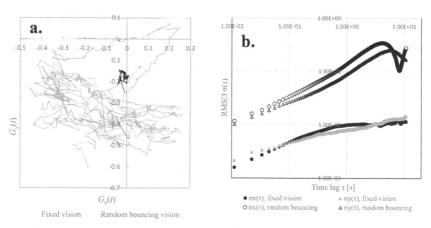

Fixed vision   Random bouncing vision

Fig. 2. a: Example of eye-tracking trajectory for a fixed vision and a random bouncing motion. **b**: RMSD of G_x and G_y vs. the time lag τ for the trajectories in **a**.

Figure 2**b** displays the RMSD, $\sigma_x(\tau)$ and $\sigma_y(\tau)$ of $G_x(t)$ and $G_y(t)$ for the two types of trajectories shown in Fig. 2**a** plotted against lag time τ. The fixed-vision fluctuations seemed saturated at longer time scales of 1 s. In contrast, random bouncing vision showed decay in RMSD over a long range, indicating the bouncing of the marker.

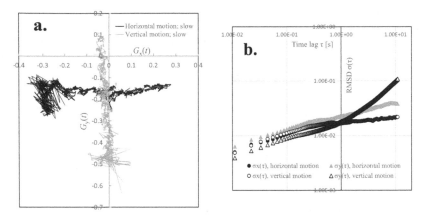

Fig. 3. a: Eye-tracking trajectory chasing slow marker moving horizontally and vertically. **b**: RMSD of G_x and G_y, plotted against τ.

Figure 3 presents the gaze trajectory and RMSD for a slow-speed marker that moves back and forth horizontally and vertically in 2 min. The horizontal motion trajectory consists of 11185 steps, and the vertical motion trajectory comprises 11058 steps. The values of σ are slightly larger compared to the fixed gaze case (in Fig. 2**b**). Neither horizontal nor vertical chasing motion demonstrates the horizontal-vertical disparity of RMSD for time scales of less than 1 s seen in the highspeed marker motion described below. There are fine irregular motions in both directions.

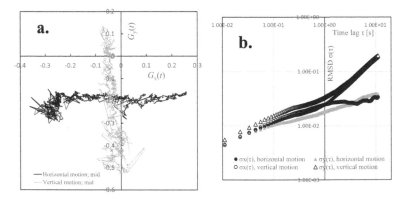

Fig. 4. a: Eye-tracking trajectory chasing mid-speed marker moving horizontally and vertically. **b**: RMSD of G_x and G_y, plotted against τ.

Figure 4 displays an example of one round trip (1 min) marker chasing, where the marker moves at mid-speed in the horizontal and vertical directions. The trajectory consists of 5612 steps in the horizontal direction and 5840 steps in the vertical direction. The $\sigma(\tau)$ of the mid-speed in Fig. **4b** is larger than the low-speed marker vision in Fig. **3b** for the same τ. As the marker speed increases, the gaze displacement tends to increase.

In addition, Fig. **4b** shows the disparity between horizontal and vertical eye movements on a time scale of 1 s. The gaze in the horizontal direction is stretched in the case of horizontal marker motion, and the vertical gaze is stretched under vertical marker motion. On the contrary, the increase of $\sigma(\tau)$ with respect to time τ in the case of horizontal marker motion is suppressed for the vertical (y-axis) gaze motion. Similarly, in the case of vertical marker motion, the motion in the horizontal (x-axis) direction of the gaze is suppressed.

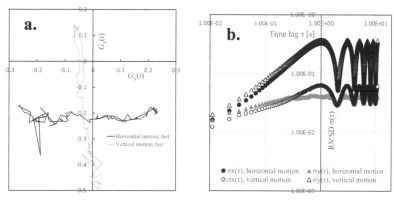

Fig. 5. a: Eye-tracking trajectory chasing highspeed marker moving horizontally and vertically. **b:** σ of G_x and G_y, plotted against τ.

Figure 5 presents an example of the chasing vision of the highspeed marker. Figure 5a shows trajectories for 2 s round-trip marker chasing, consisting of 183 and 183 steps for horizontal and vertical marker chasing views, respectively.

As shown in Fig. **5b**, σ clearly exhibits an anisotropy-based disparity in the direction of the marker motion on a time scale of 0.01 s. On time scales of 1 s or more, the oscillatory nature of the marker motion appears. The oscillations are also observed in the eye movement perpendicular to the marker motion. In the case of chasing vision, some couplings may occur in the directions of motion.

In order to compare the magnitude of the spatial extent of the gaze trajectory and the isotropic and anisotropic properties, we define the range of the x, y components G_x, G_y of the gaze direction vector as $\Delta G_x \equiv \max_{t \leq T} G_x(t) - \min_{t \leq T} G_x(t)$, $\Delta G_y \equiv \max_{t \leq T} G_y(t) - \min_{t \leq T} G_y(t)$, and the range of HMD motion h_x, h_y as $\Delta h_x \equiv \max_{t \leq T} h_x(t) - \min_{t \leq T} h_x(t)$, $\Delta h_y \equiv \max_{t \leq T} h_y(t) - \min_{t \leq T} h_y(t)$, respectively.

The spatial extent of the trajectories of fixed and chase vision for each participant is shown in Fig. 6 as a plot of the x and y components of the direction vector, ΔG_x and ΔG_y. Also, Table 2 shows the values of ΔG_x and ΔG_y averaged over the participants with their standard deviations as the error values. The mean square deviations from

210   S. Fujimoto et al.

$\Delta G_y = \Delta G_x$, which we calculated as an index of the degree of anisotropy between ΔG_x and ΔG_y, was shown in the table. In the cases of fixed vision and random bouncing vision, there found relatively small x-y anisotropy. Particularly, the trajectory of fixed vision is confined to a narrow range. The trajectory is almost isotropic and extends over the entire area where the marker moves for the chasing vision of the bouncing marker, which changes direction isotropically.

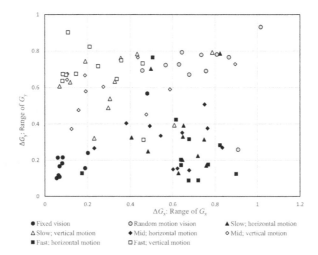

Fig. 6. The spatial range of the gaze trajectories of all participants.

The anisotropic nature of the gaze trajectory increases when chasing the high-speed marker, becoming more expansive in the direction of the marker's motion and narrower in the perpendicular direction. As the marker speed decreases, the trajectory becomes slightly broader in the direction perpendicular to the direction of the marker's motion, even though the marker moves in the same range.

Table 2. Range of trajectories in horizontal(x) and vertical(y) directions.

(Averages over $N = 11$ samples)	ΔG_x: range of G_x	ΔG_y: range of G_y	Anisotropy: mean square deviation from $\Delta G_x = \Delta G_y$ $\Sigma(\Delta G_x - \Delta G_y)^2/N$
Fixed vision	0.13 ± 0.13	0.20 ± 0.13	0.01
Random bouncing	0.73 ± 0.16	0.71 ± 0.17	0.05
Slow marker, horizontal	0.64 ± 0.13	0.35 ± 0.21	0.14
Slow marker, vertical	0.34 ± 0.21	0.61 ± 0.16	0.13

(*continued*)

Table 2. (*continued*)

(Averages over $N = 11$ samples)	ΔG_x: range of G_x	ΔG_y: range of G_y	Anisotropy: mean square deviation from $\Delta G_x = \Delta G_y$ $\Sigma(\Delta G_x - \Delta G_y)^2/N$
Mid-spd marker, horizontal	0.59 ± 0.18	0.30 ± 0.12	0.13
Mid-spd marker, vertical	0.32 ± 0.25	0.59 ± 0.12	0.13
Fast marker, horizontal	0.65 ± 0.19	0.25 ± 0.20	0.24
Fast marker, vertical	0.24 ± 0.15	0.68 ± 0.15	0.26

In the chasing vision of a moving marker, the faster the speed of motion, the more attention is focused on the marker, and the stronger the consciousness of tracking motion. Conversely, when the marker speed is low, there are active miniature eye movements instead, suggesting that the eye gaze collects visual information more acutely. In addition, since the anisotropy of the trajectory area is lower, the trajectory may acquire visual information more uniformly.

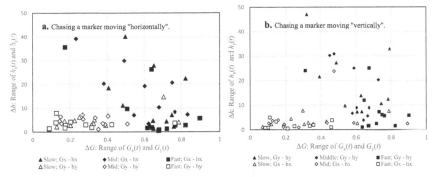

Fig. 7. Relationships between the spatial range of the gaze trajectories and the rotational motion of HMD during the linear movement of the target marker. **a**: Horizontal motion of the marker. **b**: Vertical motion of the marker. Marker shapes indicate the speed of the target marker and filled/blank designate the motion projected onto the x-axis (horizontal) and y-axis (vertical).

Now we examine the link between the participant's gaze and head shaking. Figures 7**a** and **b** show plots of the range of eye movement ΔG and the range of HMD rotation Δh for the horizontal and vertical marker motions. In the case of chasing the horizontal motion marker in Fig. 7**a**, the vertical motion range of the HMD (denoted by the blank mark) is narrow, but the value of ΔG is quite broad and varies significantly among individuals. Alternatively, the horizontal motion range (indicated by the filled-in markers) exhibits varied values of Δh. When Δh is large, ΔG is small, signifying that the participants maintain a small eye movement range ΔG by unconsciously shaking their heads.

This tendency is also observed for the vertical motion marker in Fig. 7**b**. The HMD motion is small in the horizontal direction but considerably varied in the vertical direction. Here, the vertical rotation of the HMD seems to be less than that in the horizontal direction. It might increase users' burden to look up vertically by swinging their heads in 180° images.

Figure 8 shows the plot of the Hurst exponents H_x and H_y for G_x and G_y for all participants. In this study, we measured the Hurst exponents in the time domain of 0.02 s to 0.2 s, corresponding to the most minute motion feature extraction that can be measured by eye-tracking in the Vive Pro Eye. Table 3 shows the list of Hurst exponents averaged over participants and the mean square deviations from $H_x = H_y$. Errors indicate the standard deviations.

As a whole, the values of the Hurst exponent averaged over the participants were lower than 0.5 and showed low deviations from the relationship of $H_x = H_y$ for fixed vision, random bouncing vision, and low or mid-speed marker chasing. In contrast, the Hurst exponent $H_{\parallel}$ in the moving direction of the tracking eye tends to be $H_{\parallel} > 0.5$ when the velocity of the marker is large. That is, the trajectory of the eye movement in the tracking direction is stretched, and its fluctuation shows persistent characteristics. However, the Hurst exponent $H_{\perp}$ of the eye movement perpendicular to the tracking direction is $H_{\perp} < 0.5$, signifying that the fluctuation is antipersistent. As the marker speed is raised, the effect of suppressing the development of fluctuations seems to work in the direction perpendicular to the chasing.

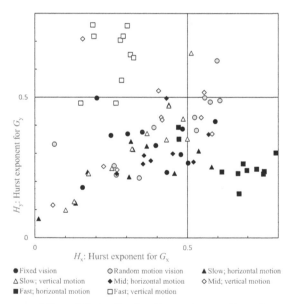

Fig. 8. Hurst exponents of G_x and G_y for fixed and isotropic as well as anisotropic chasing visions of all participants.

In the fixed-vision condition, $H_x, H_y \leq 0.5$, with a considerable variation among participants. In Fig. 6, the gaze trajectories in the fixation condition appeared to cluster in a narrower range than in the other conditions, but the Hurst exponent in Fig. 8 showed a wide range, suggesting that there may be unintended individual differences in the miniature gaze motion when gazing at a single point.

Table 3. Hurst exponents in horizontal(x) and vertical(y) directions averaged over participants.

	H_x for G_x	H_y for G_y	$\Sigma(H_x - H_y)^2/N$
Fixed vision	0.38 ± 0.14	0.34 ± 0.09	0.03
Random bouncing	0.43 ± 0.18	0.39 ± 0.13	0.01
Slow marker, horizontal	0.33 ± 0.17	0.26 ± 0.11	0.02
Slow marker, vertical	0.34 ± 0.15	0.33 ± 0.16	0.01
Mid-spd marker, horizontal	0.39 ± 0.10	0.40 ± 0.19	0.05
Mid-spd marker, vertical	0.36 ± 0.18	0.40 ± 0.17	0.04
Fast marker, horizontal	0.66 ± 0.11	0.26 ± 0.07	0.18
Fast marker, vertical	0.26 ± 0.06	0.65 ± 0.11	0.16

Random bouncing has a broader range of the Hurst exponent H. $H > 0.5$ found in some cases is consistent with the fact that persistent eye movements emerge during highspeed marker chasing since the marker speed of random bouncing is close to the highspeed linear motion chasing.

In the marker chasing, the values of $H_{\parallel}$, $H_{\perp}$ were mainly found smaller than 0.5 for slow or mid-speed markers. In other words, when viewing a slow-moving marker, we may say that there is a tendency to explore the visual information with anti-persistent miniature eye movements.

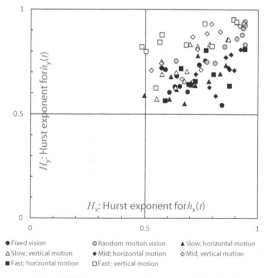

Fig. 9. Hurst exponents of the HMD movement during the fixed and marker-chasing visions.

A couple of participants chased the marker mainly by swinging their heads. In such cases, values of the Hurst exponent were found close to 0 as seen in Fig. 8. Trajectories of such cases exhibited compact and concentrated at around the origin of the frame.

The Hurst exponent of the HMD motion during chasing visions is presented in Fig. 9. Also, Table 4 shows the Hurst exponent, H_x and H_y, averaged over the participants and the mean square deviation from the relationship $H_x = H_y$. The Hurst exponents for fixed vision, random bouncing, and linear motion were above 0.5, representing persistent characteristics. Comparing fixed vision and random bouncing in Fig. 9, the Hurst exponent of fixed vision was closer to 0.5, while the Hurst exponent of random bouncing was relatively closer to 1, suggesting that the HMD motion in random bouncing was persistent and unconsciously tracking the marker. This higher persistence of the HMD motion is seen more strongly in the direction of marker motion when chasing the marker.

Table 4. Hurst exponents of HMD motion in horizontal(x) and vertical(y) directions.

	H_x for h_x	H_y for h_y	$\Sigma(H_x - H_y)^2/N$
Fixed vision	0.68 ± 0.08	0.66 ± 0.07	0.01
Random bouncing	0.87 ± 0.10	0.85 ± 0.08	0.003
Slow marker, horizontal	0.71 ± 0.11	0.67 ± 0.09	0.01
Slow marker, vertical	0.67 ± 0.10	0.73 ± 0.10	0.01
Mid-spd marker, horizontal	0.84 ± 0.07	0.72 ± 0.07	0.02
Mid-spd marker, vertical	0.73 ± 0.11	0.80 ± 0.10	0.01
Fast marker, horizontal	0.75 ± 0.11	0.68 ± 0.08	0.01
Fast marker, vertical	0.67 ± 0.19	0.84 ± 0.09	0.04

4   Conclusions

Using the eye-tracking function of the Vive Pro Eye, we made preliminary measurements of the gaze motion and the swinging motion of the HMD when gazing at the VR image observed with the HMD. In particular, by measuring the spatial extension and the Hurst exponent of the motion trajectories, we compared gazing at a fixed marker with gazing at a linear random bouncing marker and gazing at a horizontally moving marker with gazing at a vertically moving one.

FEMs showed antipersistent features confined to the vicinity of the fixed point of the marker. In contrast, the gaze trajectory for the linearly moving marker exhibited elongation and had persistency in the direction of pursuit. The trajectory spread in the direction perpendicular to the marker motion tended to decrease as the motion speed of the marker increased. Furthermore, the FEM of low-velocity chasing is more likely to capture visual information since the fine motion of the trajectory leads to the establishment of visual information. Conversely, high-velocity chasing is less likely to affect peripheral vision. We also observed that the participants unconsciously rotated the HMD to compensate for the tracking vision, which may be related to the ease of establishing vision near the marker.

In the VR space, the vision establishes and refines visual recognition through fine irregular movements, while moving navigation markers cause the gaze to fluctuate persistently and promote visual guidance rather than the collection of visual information. When necessary, the effective use of moving navigation markers, when necessary, may be expected to refresh the observer's perception and attract attention.

Acknowledgments. The authors would like to thank all the participants for their cooperation and helpful discussions. They would also like to thank Enago for English language review.

References

1. Hamilton, D., McKechnie, J., Edgerton, E., Wilson, C.: Immersive virtual reality as a pedagogical tool in education: a systematic literature review of quantitative learning outcomes and experimental design. J. Comput. Educ. **8**(1), 1–32 (2021)
2. Fransson, G., Holmberg, J., Westelius, C.: The challenges of using head mounted virtual reality in K-12 schools from a teacher perspective. Educ. Inf. Technol. **25**(4), 3383–3404 (2020)
3. LaViola Jr., J.J., Kruijff, E., McMahan, R.P., Bowman, D.A., Poupyrev, I.: 3D User Interfaces: Theory and Practice, 2nd edn. Addison-Wesley Professional, Boston (2017)
4. Hubel, D.H.: Eye, Brain, and Vision. Scientific American Library, New York (1988)
5. McCamy, M.B., Macknik, S.L., Martinez-Conde, S.: Different fixational eye movements mediate the prevention and the reversal of visual fading: fading prevention by fixational eye movements. J. Physiol. **592**(19), 4381–4394 (2014)
6. Leigh, R.J., Zee, D.S.: The Neurology of Eye Movement, 2nd edn. F. A. Davis, Philadelphia (1991)
7. Martinez-Conde, S., Macknik, S.L., Hubel, D.H.: The role of fixational eye movements in visual perception. Nat. Rev. Neurosci. **5**(3), 229–240 (2004)
8. Martinez-Conde, S., Macknik, S.L., Troncoso, X.G., Hubel, D.H.: Microsaccades: a neurophysiological analysis. Trends Neurosci. **32**(9), 463–475 (2009)
9. Martinez-Conde, S., Otero-Millan, J., Macknik, S.L.: The impact of microsaccades on vision: towards a unified theory of saccadic function. Nat. Rev. Neurosci. **14**(2), 83–96 (2013)
10. Rucci, M., Iovin, R., Poletti, M., Santini, F.: Miniature eye movements enhance fine spatial detail. Nature **447**(7146), 851–854 (2007)
11. Greschner, M., Bongard, M., Rujan, P., Ammermüller, J.: Retinal ganglion cell synchronization by fixational eye movements improves feature estimation. Nat. Neurosci. **5**(4), 341–347 (2002)
12. Ahiaar, E., Arieli, A.: Figuring space by time. Neuron **32**(2), 185–201 (2001)
13. Ahiaar, E., Arieli, A.: Seeing via miniature eye movements: a dynamic hypothesis for vision. Front. Comput. Neurosci. **6**, 1–27 (2012)
14. Ko, H.-K., Poletti, M., Rucci, M.: Microsaccades precisely relocate gaze in a high visual acuity task. Nat. Neurosci. **13**, 1549–1553 (2010)
15. Amor, T.A., Reis, S.D.S., Campos, D., Herrmann, H.J., Andrade Jr., J.S.: Persistence in eye movement during visual search. Sci. Rep. **6**, 20815 (2016)
16. Mergenthaler, K., Engbert, R.: Modeling the control of fixational eye movements with neurophysiological delays. Phys. Rev. Lett. **98**, 138104 (2007)
17. Engbert, R., Mergenthaler, K., Sinn, P., Pikovsky, A.: An integrated model of fixational eye movements and microsaccades. Proc. Natl. Acad. Sci. U.S.A. **108**(39), E765–E770 (2011)

18. Herrmann, C.J.J., Metzler, R., Engbert, R.: A self-avoiding walk with neural delays as a model of fixational eye movements. Sci. Rep. **7**, 12958 (2017)
19. Wagner, J., Stuerzlinger, W., Nedel, L.: Comparing and combining virtual hand and virtual ray pointer interactions for data manipulation in immersive analytics. IEEE Trans. Visual. Comput. Graph. **27**(5), 2513–2523 (2021)
20. Peukert, C., Lechner, J., Pfeiffer, J., Weinhardt, C.: Intelligent invocation: towards designing context-aware user assistance systems based on real-time eye tracking data analysis. In: Davis, F.D., Riedl, R., vomBrocke, J., Léger, P.-M., Randolph, A., Fischer, T. (eds.) NeuroIS Retreat 2019. LNISO, vol. 32, pp. 73–82. Springer, Cham (2020). https://doi.org/10.1007/978-3-030-28144-1_8
21. Matthews, S., et al.: Work-in-progress-a preliminary eye tracking and HMD orientation comparison to determine focus on a cardiac auscultation training environment. In: 7-th International Conference on the Immersive Learning Research Network (iLRN) (2021)
22. HTC Corporation: HTC Vive Pro Eye. https://www.vive.com/us/product/vive-pro-eye/specs/. Accessed 25 Jan 2022
23. Stein, N., et al.: A comparison of eye tracking latencies among several commercial head-mounted displays. i-Perception **12**(1), 1–16 (2021)
24. Imaoka, Y., Flury, A., de Bruin, E.D.: Assessing saccadic eye movements with head-mounted display virtual reality technology. Front. Psych. **11**, 922 (2020)
25. Wagner Filho, J., Stuerzlinger, W., Nedel, L.: Evaluating an immersive space-time cube geo-visualization for intuitive trajectory data exploration. IEEE Trans. Visual Comput. Graph. **26**(1), 514–524 (2020)
26. Berton, F., Hoyet, L., Oliver, A.-H., Bruneau, J., Le Meur, O., Pettre, J.: Eye-gaze activity in crowds: impact of virtual reality and density. In: 2020 IEEE Conference on Virtual Reality and 3D User Interfaces, pp. 322–331 (1991)
27. Yoshimura, A., Khokhar, A., Borst, C.W.: Eye-gaze-triggered visual cues to restore attention in educational VR. In: 2019 IEEE Conference on Virtual Reality and 3D User Interfaces, pp. 1255–1256 (2019)
28. Wang, P., et al.: Head pointer or eye gaze: which helps more in MR remote collaboration? In: 2019 IEEE Conference on Virtual Reality and 3D User Interfaces, pp. 1219–1220 (2019)
29. Khokhar, A, Yoshimura, A, Borst, C.W.: Pedagogical agent responsive to eye tracking in educational VR. In: 2019 IEEE Conference on Virtual Reality and 3D User Interfaces, pp. 1018–1019 (2019)
30. Iwase, M.: All Sky Planetarium. https://www.youtube.com/channel/UCDwhG6BRwd_m42 y6Wm8C4zw/featured. Accessed 31 Jan 2022
31. Unity, Unity Technologies. https://unity.com/. Accessed 30 Jan 2022
32. Steam, Valve Corporation: https://store.steampowered.com/about/. Accessed 30 Jan 2022. (VIVE Developers: Eye and Facial Tracking SDK. https://developer.vive.com/resources/vive-sense/eye-and-facial-tracking-sdk/. Accessed 30 Jan 2022)
33. Mandelbrot, B.B., Van Ness, J.W.: Fractional Brownian motions, fractional noises and applications. SIAM Rev. **10**(4), 422–437 (1968)

A Methodology for the Co-design of Shared VR Environments with People with Intellectual Disabilities: Insights from the Preparation Phase

Matthew C. Harris(✉), David J. Brown, Pratik Vyas, and James Lewis

Nottingham Trent University,
Clifton Campus, Clifton Lane, Nottingham NG11 8NS, UK
matthew.harris@ntu.ac.uk
http://www.ntu.ac.uk

Abstract. Research suggests that Virtual Reality (VR) has many applications for those with intellectual disabilities, and as the hardware needed to create such applications has become increasingly available and mature, it is now possible to further investigate these claims. We aim to use co-design methodology to identify, design, develop and validate a VR environment. Co-design treats the participants of research as "co-researchers". They are "experts by experience" in accessibility and disability issues and can provide valuable input.

Five preparation phase sessions were held with n = 13 intellectually disabled individuals (supported by 4 teaching assistants). Using the Oculus Quest 2, they were able to try a range of VR applications. After completing the activities, they were prompted in follow-up post immersion focus groups to suggest what future applications of VR might be appropriate or desirable for the group as a whole and provide their thoughts and experiences on using the system.

It was found that most experienced little difficulty in using the controllers, including performing the grip gesture to pick up and drop objects in the virtual environment. Even those that struggled with the controls engaged with the system and demonstrated interaction and engagement with the system that surpassed teaching assistants' expectations. Some indicated that they found aspects of the system relaxing and most were keen to try other VR applications.

It is hoped that these insights will be useful moving forward in developing a virtual environment with this group and for progressing to the next stages in the co-design methodology - fieldwork and ideation.

Keywords: Co-design · Intellectual disabilities · Accessible virtual environments · Accessible virtual and Augmented reality

1 Introduction

This paper discusses the preparation phase of our methodology for co-designing experiences with individuals with intellectual disabilities (ID) using current VR

M. Antona and C. Stephanidis (Eds.): HCII 2022, LNCS 13309, pp. 217–230, 2022.
https://doi.org/10.1007/978-3-031-05039-8_15

technology. Significant developments in VR systems (such as the Meta Quest 2), including "untethered" standalone devices and simplified setup make use of VR a realistic prospect for people with ID. The potential of headset based VR to make a meaningful contribution to solving the real-world problems of those with ID is now an opportunity worthy of serious consideration.

VR based rehabilitation has received a lot of attention in research literature, including in those with ID (Standen and Brown 2005; Brown et al. 2001; Lannen et al. 2002; Cunha et al. 2018). However, fewer studies have investigated the uses of immersive VR with those with ID, which current VR systems use. These systems might consist of a head mounted display with a small screen in front of the eyes, or could also be in the form of a specially created room with large screens (such as the CAVE system: "Virtual Reality CAVE Solutions—Antycip", n.d.) A systematic review found that of 28 studies reviewed on VR as a support tool for those with ID, only 3 studies used immersive VR (Cunha et al. 2018). While it may seem intuitively that this may be due to the level of cognitive and coordination skills required to use assistive technologies, it has been demonstrated that those with ID can use immersive VR technologies with varying degrees of assistance (Harris et al. 2020; Kongsilp and Komuro 2019).

To frame our approach to the research, we will describe how we strive to position participants with ID as co-designers. This means the research team act as facilitator, observer, note taker and organiser while the decisions are taken by the participants themselves. This stems from the empathic design method proposed by Lee in Lee (2014) as well as 'method stories' proposed by Hendriks et al. (2015) which help the researchers to understand their participant's experience, contextualising the use of technology, and explore the solution space 'with' rather than 'for' the participants with ID.

1.1   Co-design

Co-design treats the participants of research as "co-researchers". They are "experts by experience" (Sanders 2005) in accessibility and disability issues and can provide valuable input. Thus, a co-design methodology would treat the voices of those with ID as equally important, and therefore must ensure that any barriers to this participation are addressed. A good way to address barriers is to give each individual the opportunity to have their voice heard. This involves making the meaning of the questions relevant to the users through the incorporation of a skilled facilitator in the group. Another approach is to carefully consider the development of any questions used in co-design sessions, and have the questions reviewed by experts in the domain so that co-researchers with ID are able to easily understand them.

Our co-design methodology is based on an existing method (Spencer González et al. 2020) who use a double diamond design model and divided the methodology into 4 phases: preparation, fieldwork, ideation and validation. We will hold workshops within each of these phases with the participants (from here referred to as "co-researchers").

1.2   Preparation Phase

The preparation phase involves identifying the problem with help from the users. Aiding the user in identifying the context of the problem becomes a primary task. There are plenty of immersive VR applications, therefore our aims included showing the co-researchers how the VR systems worked, and what was possible with the technology. We also invited the co-researchers to propose potential uses for VR.

2   Materials and Equipment

2.1   Virtual Reality Systems

With the Facebook acquisition of Oculus the public perception of Virtual Reality changed drastically in 2016 ("Why Virtual Reality Is About to Change the World" 2015). These systems are able to simulate a virtual environment through use of a "6 degrees of freedom" (6DoF) head mounted display and controllers. 6DoF systems track the user's orientation and position in 3D space, allowing them to explore the virtual environment by walking around. They support much higher resolution display of realistic environments compared to their predecessors. Examples of systems released around this time include the original HTC Vive and Oculus Rift. However, these systems are required to be connected to a high-performance PC, which both increases the overall cost, and adds to setup complexity. They also require "base stations" which assist in tracking the headset and controllers' movement in space, further increasing setup complexity.

Mobile phone-based VR systems were introduced as a response to these issues and often involve the user inserting their phone into a headset, which they use to drive the VR experience. Google cardboard ("Google Cardboard – Google VR", n.d.) and Samsung Gear VR ("Samsung Gear VR with Controller", n.d.) are examples of this kind of technology. These work well for simple 360 experiences such as viewing 360 videos; however, these systems are only capable of tracking the orientation (not position) of the headset. This is known as 3DoF tracking and limits the user's immersion somewhat. A study exploring how geographically separated users could interact in social VR (Moustafa and Steed 2018), distributed Samsung Gear VR devices (and Samsung smartphones) to 17 participants. In the feedback collected from diaries after use for a few weeks, participants reported technological issues when using the equipment, including audio difficulties and issues with the wearability of the headset (heat/weight issues). It was reported that these issues are not prohibitive to the use of the headset but did affect the participants' immersion. The participants reported that the primary barrier to use of the equipment was the inability to move naturally. This highlights both the weaknesses of 3DoF tracking and the potential effectiveness of this technology.

The Oculus Quest was released in 2019 and marked the start of a new wave of VR devices. These new devices are completely "untethered", meaning they are capable of running standalone without the use of a high-performance PC and make use of "inside out", 6DoF tracking. They do not require external tracking hardware. Such a compact tool is, therefore, much more feasible to deploy in the home, as setup complexity is kept to a minimum. The methodology adopted will target the recently released Oculus Quest 2, which is relatively inexpensive at £299. This is far more accessible to most users compared with the £1,000+ cost of PC based VR (as of February 2022).

The Oculus Quest 2 has been chosen as the headset to use based on the reasons outlined above, however should the co-designers indicate that another system might be more suitable, our methodology is flexible enough to account for this.

3   Method

3.1   Co-researchers

Two groups took part in the study: Adults from the "NICER" group, and pupils from a community special school with a SEND (Special educational needs and disability) focus. "NICER" are a group of young adults with learning difficulties who have prior experience of participating in academic research.

From the NICER group, 4 took part. Of these, two have Williams syndrome, one has Down syndrome, and one had severe learning difficulties. From the School group 9 took part and included those with physical difficulties, severe learning disabilities and profound multiple learning difficulties aged 12–16 years. Participation in the study was voluntary, and the co-researchers received an introductory talk on the headset and the study aims. Ethical approval for the study was granted by Nottingham Trent University's Non-Invasive Ethics Committee.

3.2   Exploratory Immersive Sessions with Students with SEND

Due to time constraints the adult group were only able to take part in one session, though all of them have experienced VR before in a previous study (Harris et al. 2020). The school group attended 2 sessions (on different days) guided by the research team. For the sessions taking place at school a teacher was present. Each session was attended by 4 to 5 co-researchers, and while one was using the headset the rest had the opportunity to watch (through casting what can be seen through the headset to a laptop).

The co-researchers were invited to try 4 Oculus Quest applications. These four were chosen as they are gentle activities which showcase what's possible with the Oculus Quest in a fairly short space of time. These are described here:

VR Software to Demonstrate the Potential of the System. "First steps", is an introductory application that teaches the user how to use the controllers and how to interact with their virtual surroundings. The co-researchers were taught the function of each button through integrated prompts which signpost possible interactions. They were also taught how to perform specific gestures such as pointing and grabbing. Shortly following this they were presented with a range of virtual objects such as paper aeroplanes, a bat and ball and rockets with which to practice these gestures. When they had completed this, they could apply what they had learnt in completing a dancing minigame. This activity takes in total about 15 min and is linear in nature. Some of NICER group had tried this activity before in a previous study (Harris et al. 2020).

Fig. 1. Users' view of "First Steps" for the Oculus Quest

The second activity the users tried was "first contact". This is also designed to introduce the user to the Oculus touch controllers, but does so in a more sandbox, less constrained, explorable 3D space station environment, with no specific instructions given to the user. The users are handed cartridges for a 3D printer which spawns in objects they can interact with.

Fig. 2. Users' view of "First Contact" for the Oculus Quest

The next activity they completed was "Bogo". This is a virtual pet game where the user can interact with a virtual monster. They can feed/pet/play with the pet which causes the environment to "evolve".

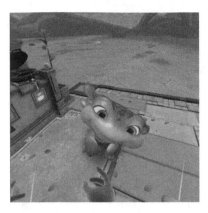

Fig. 3. Users' view of "Bogo" for the Oculus Quest

Finally, they tried "hand physics lab" which is effectively a puzzle game using the Oculus Quest's hand tracking capabilities. The user might be tasked with pushing buttons in the right order, or stacking blocks etc.

Fig. 4. Users' view of "Hand Physics Lab" for the Oculus Quest

Focus Group Discussion. The co-researchers were not permitted to spend longer than 15 min continuously using the headset to avoid the possibility of motion sickness. The sessions were 2 h long in total allowing the co-researchers to try 2 activities per session. Based on advice from the teaching assistants present, those with more severe learning difficulties and physical disabilities were instead shown a stationary "desert terrace" house environment. While there is less to interact with here and use of the controllers is not required, they are able to look around this 360° environment.

After completing the activities the co-researchers were asked about their current socialisation habits. These questions were asked by the research team then further explained or offered communicational support where necessary by the teachers present to ensure understanding. These sessions were audio recorded, then transcribed and anonymised. Observational notes were taken throughout the sessions.

The questions used as a basis for this discussion are as follows:

1. Where do you normally socialise/meet and talk with people?
2. What do you do if this isn't available?
3. What is your favourite activity to do with friends?
4. What hurdles (transport/availability etc.) prevent you from doing this?
5. What would you like to be able to go out and do with friends that you can't currently do?

3.3   Interviews with Experienced Facilitators/Researchers

Interviews with highly experienced teachers and researchers in the field of VR for students with SEND were also held: Penny Standen (Standen and Brown 2005; Standen et al. 2001b; Standen et al. 2001a) and David Stewart (Kirby and Stewart 2011; Hedgecock et al. 2014; Standen et al. 2014). Given the 25 years of experience these individuals have in working with those with ID concerning the use of VR to develop independent living and cognitive skills, their insights into co-design and further application of virtual environments will be highly valuable in the fieldwork and ideation phases.

Another aspect of co-design is investigating how best to work with those with ID. We will be working closely with teachers from the school and the chair of the NICER group, and are keen to have them help facilitate the sessions as they are the people most familiar with this group and skilled in communication. As mentioned previously, the teachers of the pupils will be present at each session, and in addition to assisting the research team in helping the co-researchers through the study, their ideas and observations will be recorded as well. Six teachers were present across the sessions held so far, of which five work with the pupils on a daily basis.

4   Results

The table below contains notes of each co-researchers's experience using the different VR applications described in 3.2. Co-researchers have been given an ID based on which group they were part of (NP for those that were part of the adult group, and SP for those that were part of the school group). The session each took part in has also been stated next to their comments (S1-5). Only co-researchers SP1-4 took part in multiple sessions.

4.1 Observations

Co-researcher ID	Disability	Observations
NP1	Down syndrome	Session 1: Initially didn't realise they were pressing the grip button, though after around 5 mins appeared to have developed good use of the controllers. Immersed for 15 mins. Mentioned they found it relaxing (referring to "Bogo")
NP2	Williams syndrome	Session 1: Remained stationary to begin with (Bogo starts in a darkened area) though became more engrossed after being shown the controls and progressing to a lighter environment
NP3	Williams syndrome	Session 1: Used a slightly abnormal grip on the controllers, though was still able to use them effectively
NP4	Severe learning disabilities	Session 1: Used left hand predominantly for control (Disability affects use of their right hand). Was able to use Bogo effectively. Mentioned they'd like to try a rollercoaster experience
SP1	Physical difficulties, severe learning disabilities and profound multiple learning difficulties aged 12–16 years.	Session 2: Picked up usage of the controllers very quickly. Mentioned previous experience with games consoles. Demonstrated lots of exploration and interaction from the beginning. Session 4: Was able to get the hang of hand tracking after a bit of practice
SP2		Session 2: Had a bit of trouble getting the headset's straps adjusted initially. Also seemed to have trouble understanding the operation of the controllers. Session 4: Said he didn't like HandPhysicsLab as much as the activities in the first session
SP3		Session 2: TAs recommended was best if they remained seated. Put their hand on the table in front of them to stabilise themselves. Started to verbalise when they saw something. Seemed happy to be immersed. Session 4: Also engaged well with the stationary environment this time. A similar response to the first session

Co-researcher ID	Disability	Observations
SP4		Session 2: Needed to take off their head protector to use the system, therefore must remain seated when using the headset. Found operating the controllers difficult, but eventually managed to interact with some of the objects. Session 4: Used HandPhysicsLab sitting down. Spent a long time on one puzzle, though was fully engaged throughout despite finding it difficult
SP5		Session 2: Needs head support to use the headset. Wasn't able to use the controllers. Screencasting wasn't working due to technical issues when this individual tried the headset, and they are non-verbal so it was difficult to know what they were seeing
SP6		Session 3: Used the headset sitting down on T4's knee. Swapped headset with T4 throughout, and was keen for others to see what they were seeing (casting wasn't working during this session). Pointed at the headset a lot
SP7		Session 3: Also happy to be immersed for over 5 min. Was able to use controllers to pick up virtual objects effectively. When asked what he could see, TA4 mentioned he wasn't really listening as he was so engrossed
SP8		Session 3: T4 mentioned they don't usually like trying new things, but they appeared happy to be immersed for well over 5 min. Dropped one of the controllers, T4 suggested this might have been because they were relaxed
SP9		Session 3: Picked up the use of one controller faster than T3 expected. T4 held the second controller close to their face which caused a strong reaction (and dropping the headset!)

4.2   Teaching Assistant Comments

Teaching assistant ID	Comments
T2	Session 2: Mentioned lots of students are motivated by food and cooking food
T3	Session 3: Suggested having them draw what they had seen to understand what they could see and what they liked
T4	Session 3: Suggested having a bag of symbols so they could describe what was in the virtual environment afterwards
T5	Session 4: Suggested kitchen environment as a potentially useful scenario. When things SP3 can watch/observe are best, bright colour visuals and symbols are best
T6	Session 5: Was surprised by the amount of time SP8 had spent engaged with Bogo

4.3   Usability Issues

Grip controls Most found it pretty straightforward to use the controls (especially in the adult group held at NTU Clifton Campus, UK). Almost all that were given "first contact" mastered the "grip" gesture to pick up and drop objects pretty quickly. Even those that struggled with the controls engaged with the system. For example, one of the two co-researchers present who were profoundly learning disabled started verbalising and the other indicated afterwards that he enjoyed it. It was observed that they moved around and interacted much more extensively than in the previous study using VR with the NICER group Harris et al. (2020). This might have been a combination of their previous experience and this being a more relaxed environment.

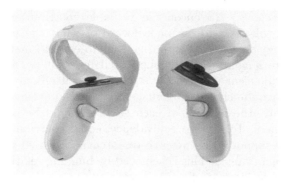

Fig. 5. Oculus Quest 2 controllers

Hand Tracking. Removing the abstraction of a controller didn't have the assumed outcome of making things simpler for the co-researchers. Most found the controllers much simpler to use. Reasons for this might be that making a fist gesture over a cube lacks the tactile feedback that picking up a real cube does. Also, a few of the co-researchers were already familiar with games console controllers, which have a lot in common with the Oculus touch controllers.

Cybersickness. While the exposure time was kept to 15 mins with all, there were no cases where the co-researchers experienced any symptoms of cybersickness.

4.4   Engagement

While the sample size for this study was quite low, there were two separate instances where the teaching assistant present was surprised at how long co-researchers remained engaged with the headset and associated virtual environments. This likely highlights a potential advantage immersive VR has over other mediums.

4.5   Suggestions from Interviews with Experts

It was pointed out that building trust and relationships with this group is important, and that they are more likely to be open about the system if they feel confident/relaxed with the research team. Sharing food at the sessions was suggested as a potential means to ensure individuals feel relaxed and able to share their thoughts.

Facilitating Discussion. Encouraging discussion is important to gather more detailed feedback from the co-researchers. Building relationships and having a familiarity with the group assists with this. This could be achieved through having prior experience in working with the group and collecting feedback over other activities. Co-researchers are more likely to be open with their thoughts on the system design if they feel confident and relaxed with the research team.

Aiming for Equivalence. To encourage valuable contributions from the co-researchers, they will need to be made aware of what the potential aims of using the technology are. To help with this, the project information sheet should use clear, concrete language and be supported by symbols, and the information should be made clear through the study design itself. Accessibility can be achieved through careful choice of language, and by taking time to explain what is meant. Therefore, the purpose of each session should be easily understood by the co-researchers. To aim for equivalence, equal contributions and collaboration should be supported between co-researchers. Each co-researcher should have their viewpoints valued. This is achieved by building relationships with the co-researchers and facilitating effective discussion.

Facilitators/Carers. It was also pointed out that those that care for individuals with ID have a good understanding of the special needs of such individuals. They can be considered the gatekeepers to the use of new technologies by intellectually disabled individuals, and including them in design increases the chance of uptake. It is important that the carers are included in the co-design process where possible.

5   Conclusion

This study builds on existing literature investigating the uses of VR with individuals with ID. This study will further show the potential VR has to improve the lives of individuals in this group, if approached in a sensitive and inclusive way.

The length of time many of the co-researchers spent engaged in the activities highlights a potential strength that contemporary VR systems hold for this group. Engagement in particular has been described as the single best indicator of learning, without which there is no deep learning (Hargreaves 2006; Iovannone et al. 2003) and has been used to assess inclusion in special education in previous studies (Hughes-Roberts et al. 2020) where it is defined as time focused on a task.

5.1   Moving to Fieldwork Phase

The insights gained from this paper can be taken forward to the fieldwork phase to further scaffold co-design of virtual environments with students with ID. Within this phase, the use of design probes and the exploration of appropriate contexts and applications of VR will be explored with co-researchers with ID, their teachers, parents and carers.

References

Brown, D.J., Standen, P.J., Proctor, T., Sterland, D.: Advanced design methodologies for the production of virtual learning environments for use by people with learning disabilities. Teleop. Virtual Environ. **10**(4), 401–415 (2001). https://doi.org/10.1162/1054746011470253

Cunha, R., Neiva, F., Silva, R.: Virtual reality as a support tool for the treatment of people with intellectual and multiple disabilities: a systematic literature review. Revista de Informática Teórica e Aplicada **25**, 67 (2018). https://doi.org/10.22456/2175-2745.77994

Google Cardboard - Google VR (n.d.). https://arvr.google.com/cardboard/. Accessed 6 May 2021

Hargreaves, D.H.: A new shape for schooling? Specialist Schools and Academies Trust London (2006)

Harris, M.C., Lewis, J., Brown, D.J., Vyas, P.: Assessing the usability of current generation virtual reality in adults with intellectual disabilities, vol. 9 (2020)

Hedgecock, J., Standen, P., Beer, C., Brown, D., S. Stewart, D.: Evaluating the role of a humanoid robot to support learning in children with profound and multiple disabilities. J. Assist. Technol. **8**(3), 111–123 (2014). https://doi.org/10.1108/JAT-02-2014-0006

Hendriks, N., Slegers, K., Duysburgh, P.: Codesign with people living with cognitive or sensory impairments: a case for method stories and uniqueness. CoDesign **11**(1), 70–82 (2015). https://doi.org/10.1080/15710882.2015.1020316

Hughes-Roberts, T., Brown, D., Boulton, H., Burton, A., Shopland, N., Martinovs, D.: Examining the potential impact of digital game making in curricula based teaching: initial observations. Comput. Educ. **158**, 103988 (2020). https://doi.org/10.1016/j.compedu.2020.103988

Iovannone, R., Dunlap, G., Huber, H., Kincaid, D.: Effective educational practices for students with autism spectrum disorders. Focus Autism Other Dev. Disabil. **18**(3), 150–165 (2003). https://doi.org/10.1177/10883576030180030301

Kirby, M., Stewart, D.: Creative approaches to promoting voice. In: Kirby, M., Stewart, D. (eds.) In Creative Learning for Inclusion. Oak Field Special School, Routledge, Nottingham (2011)

Kongsilp, S., Komuro, T.: An evaluation of head-mounted virtual reality for special education from the teachers' perspective. In: 25th ACM Symposium on Virtual Reality Software and Technology, pp. 1–2 (2019). https://doi.org/10.1145/3359996.3364721

Lannen, T., Brown, D.J., Standen, P.J.: Design of virtual environment input devices for people with moderate to severe learning difficulties - a user-centred approach. Virtual Real. **8** (2002)

Lee, J.-J.: The true benefits of designing design methods. Artifact **3**, 5.1–5.12 (2014). https://doi.org/10.14434/artifact.v3i2.3951

Moustafa, F., Steed, A.: A longitudinal study of small group interaction in social virtual reality. In: Proceedings of the 24th ACM Symposium on Virtual Reality Software and Technology, pp. 1–10 (2018). https://doi.org/10.1145/3281505.3281527

Samsung Gear VR with Controller (n.d.). The Official Samsung Galaxy Site. http://www.samsung.com/global/galaxy/gear-vr/. Accessed 6 May 2021

Sanders, E.B.: Information, inspiration and co-creation. In: Proceedings of the 6th International Conference of the European Academy of Design (2005)

Spencer González, H., Vega Córdova, V., Exss Cid, K., Jarpa Azagra, M., Álvarez-Aguado, I.: Including intellectual disability in participatory design processes: methodological adaptations and supports. In: Proceedings of the 16th Participatory Design Conference 2020 - Participation(s) Otherwise, vol. 1, pp. 55–63 (2020). https://doi.org/10.1145/3385010.3385023

Standen, P.J., Brown, D.J., Cromby, J.J.: The effective employment of virtual environments in the training and rehabilitation of people with intellectual disabilities. Br. J. Educ. Technol. **32**(3), 289–299 (2001a). https://irep.ntu.ac.uk/id/eprint/11354/. Accessed 2 April 2021

Standen, P.J., Brown, D.J., Cromby, J.J.: The effective use of virtual environments in the education and rehabilitation of students with intellectual disabilities. Br. J. Educ. Technol. **32**(3), 289–299 (2001b). https://doi.org/10.1111/1467-8535.00199

Standen, P., et al.: Engaging students with profound and multiple disabilities using humanoid robots. In: Stephanidis, C., Antona, M. (eds.) UAHCI 2014. LNCS, vol. 8514, pp. 419–430. Springer, Cham (2014). https://doi.org/10.1007/978-3-319-07440-5_39

Standen, P.J., Brown, D.J.: Virtual reality in the rehabilitation of people with intellectual disabilities: review. CyberPsychol. Behav. **8**(3), 272–282 (2005). https://doi.org/10.1089/cpb.2005.8.272

Virtual Reality CAVE Solutions - Antycip (n.d.). https://steantycip.com/vr-cave/. Accessed 4 Feb 2022

Why Virtual Reality is About to Change the World. Time (2015). https://time.com/3987022/why-virtual-realityis-about-to-change-the-world/. Accessed 3 Feb 2022

Leveraging Virtual Reality and Machine Learning as Mediated Learning Tools for Social Skill Development in Learners with Autism Spectrum Condition

Thomas Hughes-Roberts[1(✉)], Vanessa Cui[3], Mufti Mahmud[2], and David J. Brown[2]

[1] University of Debry, Markeaton Street Campus, Derby, UK
t.hughesroberts@derby.ac.uk
[2] Nottingham Trent University, Clifton Campus, Clifton, UK
[3] Birmingham City University, Birmingham, UK

Abstract. Learners with Autism Spectrum Condition (ASC) are often character-ized as having deficits in core social competencies affecting ability to communi-cate and interact with other people across multiple contexts. However, such deficit views of ASC lead to narrow interventions that cannot be generalized to wider learning contexts nor the real world. Taking a non-deficit view can offer a means of broadening understanding of ASC by taking a more holistic view of an individual. Thoughtfully designed VR solutions that take a non-deficit view can provide learn-ing tools allow learners to develop their self-determination awareness and skills such as decision-making, self-advocacy, reflective problem-solving. Furthermore, through the use of machine learning approaches such solutions have the potential to provide real-time monitoring of learners during interaction offering a holistic understanding of individuals with ASC. This position paper sets out the support case for utilizing VR through non-deficit models and examines the role machine learning can play in further understanding of learners with ASC. It is intended that this sets out a case for future research directions.

Keywords: Virtual Reality · Autism · Machine learning

1 Introduction

This position paper is to review the current "state-of-play" of Virtual Reality (VR) and its use in providing a platform for adolescent learners with Autism Spectrum Condition (ASC) with particular focus on social skill development. From this, we intend to outline gaps in the field and propose avenues for further research that utilize modern approaches to understanding learners with ASC.

Learners with ASC are often characterized as having deficits in core social compe-tencies affecting ability to communicate and interact with other people across multiple contexts (Bölte 2014). As such, Virtual Environments (VEs) such as those presented in VR systems can provide a vehicle for teaching and learning social skills (Mitchell

© The Author(s), under exclusive license to Springer Nature Switzerland AG 2022
M. Antona and C. Stephanidis (Eds.): HCII 2022, LNCS 13309, pp. 231–240, 2022.
https://doi.org/10.1007/978-3-031-05039-8_16

et al. 2007) by providing safe, realistic 3D scenarios that can represent everyday situated interactions (Parsons et al. 2006).

However, the view of modeling ASC in terms of deficits is open criticism as it overlooks the strengths or neutral differences that can also be associated with autism (Dinishak 2016; Robertson 2010). Consideration of ASC through this holistic lens provides new avenues of consideration for the design of VR solutions tailored towards social skill development. A need has been highlighted, for example, to shift the focus of research onto modeling real life challenges (Robertson 2010) and this requires a holistic understanding of individual learners and their needs. This is true both in the design of suitable solutions but also in the real-time monitoring of the impact of these solutions.

This paper, therefore, aims to review current research through this lens of a "non-deficit" model of ASC and provide suggestions for VR solution designs. We explore how we can gain a more holistic understanding of target users and feed this into real-time monitoring aiming to provide effective feedback of the users' state. To this end, machine learning can potentially provide a powerful means of monitoring the user in real-time to assess their affective state. However, such approaches must be considered carefully to avoid also feeding into a deficit view of the ASC learner, that there is a desired state they should be in.

This paper therefore has the following research questions:

1. How is VR currently utilized and to what extent is it influenced by a deficit view of ASC?
2. What role can VR solutions play in providing opportunities for social skill development when taking a non-deficit view of ASC?
3. What role can machine learning play in offering a meaningful and holistic understanding of ASC learners?

The remainder of this paper is structured as follows: first, a review of the current use of VEs and VR in ASC research with a view to defining what problems are being tackled and how, secondly, a summary of the field that highlights the potential gaps in work when viewed through a non-deficit view of ASC, thirdly, a review of the role machine learning can play in informing a holistic understanding of the user, finally, conclusions and recommendations are made from the point of view of the position taken in this paper.

2   Research on the Use of VR with ASC Learners

This section aims to outline why VR can play an important role in social skill development in learners with ASC and examine how the technology is currently utilized in cutting-edge research. We focus on the design of VR systems and seek to unify the language used in this field study in order to clarify the terms used.

2.1   Why VR?

As noted, virtual environments provide opportunity to engage with safe scenarios for experiencing and practicing social interaction. VR builds on this and can provide additional benefits because it can offer authentic real-world situations modelled in controlled environments (Parsons and Cobb 2011). The concepts of presence and embodiment promoted by authentic VR simulations make learning experiential and potentially more powerful (Slater 2017; Wallace et al. 2017). When discussing VR, the field does suffer from a lack of formalization with regard to terms used. Studies may use the term VR but refer to "desktop" VR (Ke et al. 2020), the use of CAVE systems (Yuan and Ip 2018) or the use of general VEs (Ghanouni et al. 2019). Although there may be some crossover in the design of such systems, VR where a Head Mounted Display (HMD) is used, will have its own unique challenges in relation to achieving that sense presence through immersion that makes is a powerful tool for experiential learning. As such, this paper refers to VR as that which requires an HMD to stereoscopically view the environment being experienced and recommends this as a formal definition in future work.

VR platforms utilize an array of tracking points that enable their functionality. Tracking points such as gaze direction, posture and postural stability, accelerometer data etc. where each of these provide some insight into the user and their state of interaction. Additional data points can also easily be added through non-invasive techniques; for example, measures of electro-dermal activity (EDA), heart rate or EEG data. When combined together in a multi-modal data fusion approach, there is the potential to gain a holistic view of a user's affective state using machine learning approaches. Affective computing has seen application within VR systems. For example, it is seen as an attractive prospect for those studying emotion due to VRs potential to provide controlled environments that have a high degree of presence (Marín-Morales et al. 2018).

As such, VR and affective computing solutions would seem ideally suited to tackling ASC by both aiding those with ASC and furthering understanding of the individual needs during learning. We therefore seek to examine what work has been done in this area and how is the issue of deficit dealt with in the design of VR and associated research studies?

2.2 Towards a Non-deficit Model

Latest developments in VR and ASC education calls for a user centered approach to the design and evaluation of applications in order to ensure the authenticity of VRs interventions in autism (Parsons 2016) and the empowerment of ASC learners (Parsons et al. 2020; Robertson 2010).

The non-deficit view of learning ability is underpinned by research on neurodiversity which challenges the myth of the ideal rational person. The concept of neurodiversity commonly refers to perceived variations seen in cognitive, affectual, and sensory functioning differing from the majority of the general population, usually known as the 'neurotypical' population (Rosqvist et al. 2020). While defining the scoping of neurodiversity is currently an ongoing empirical investigation among scholars in the field, this concept strongly challenges the view and practices that put learners with ASC as persons with defects/disorders. This deficit model of learning ability is underpinned by the idea of persons with disorders that impact on their social engagement and flourishment. Interventions which aim to fix their disorders thus use approaches that promote how to behave according to a social norm.

Rather than suggesting there is a 'normal' way to think and act in which learners with ASC need to meet, the non-deficit view considers persons with a wide range of cognitive, affective and sensory abilities and behaviors. Through this consideration, individuals should have choice and control over their own authentic lives. It acknowledges that there are areas that learners with ASC want to learn and develop in social engagement, but crucially it recognizes the strengths and neutral differences of ASC learners in social situations.

2.3 Current VR Research and ASC

VR then, can provide a means to explore interaction that is not based on deficits and can provide a holistic understanding of learners through the sandbox experiences that can be created. The creation of sandbox environments allow users to explore situations on their own terms and learn through a process of careful self-reflection. The following review aims to examine research through this lens and highlight areas for opportunity.

VR has been demonstrated to have positive outcomes when used to tackle developmental concerns in learners with ASC as shown in a systematic review of the field (Mesa-Gresa et al. 2018). From this review, social skill development was the most common topic of research being addressed as this is the "hallmark deficit" for learners with ASC. This concurs with a separate review that also demonstrates the effectiveness of VR for working within the field of ASC (Bozgeyikli et al. 2017). This work further summarized the field in terms of a set of design guidelines for creating VR systems. These guidelines, while useful, focus on accessibility of VR systems rather than how they can be designed to further understanding of individuals from a non-deficit perspective.

Didehbani et al. (2016) note that that work within the field of ASC and VR research tend to focus on designs that are of scripted interactions where participants communicate passively with the scenarios presented. Halabi et al. (2017) for example, outline a study in which scripted scenarios are used to develop communicated skills in learners with ASC. A scenario may require a learner to correctly greet their tutor within the virtual setting after having observed this interaction taking place. The use of speech recognition determines when a response has occurred and if it has taken place at the correct turn in the conversation. While this utilizes the technology well it also exemplifies the deficit-oriented approach to ASC and VR research; that there is a correct way of going about interactions that must be trained. This no doubt serves an important purpose, however, there is scope for the field to also provide approaches that move beyond such definitive outcomes based on "correct" behavior. Such studies do not allow generalization of learning to untrained situations or to real life (Parsons and Cobb 2011).

VR can be used to model very specific environments that offer a safe means of performing social interactions, such as a shop floor for practicing conversations for shopping (Stewart Rosenfield et al. 2019). This study also utilized speech recognition to detect several "hot" words such that the conversation transitioned at the correct time. Findings suggest that such applications provide a means of practicing communication that is free from negative consequences and learners can improve their social skill through repeated use. While this is perhaps not as scripted as previously discussed it does assume that there is a specific conversation to be followed and certain words need to be said for progression through the scenario. This may, in part, be a result of technological limitations; having a free-flowing interaction with an AI driven avatar may not be feasible but what of alternate designs?

Some flexibility can be added into scenarios through the addition of third party-controlled characters. Such designs can include a confederate whose role it is to coach the learner through more open and dynamic interactions that can be altered based on the needs of the participants (e.g., Didehbani et al. 2016). A similar approach was taken by Ke et al. (2020), where researchers controlled virtual characters through voice morphing software. Rather than requiring a specific outcome, general social skills were measured (e.g., initiation, negotiation etc.) demonstrating the flexibility offered through less prescriptive approaches to scenarios. However, this study utilized "desktop VR" which, as mentioned, holds different design challenges to those that may use an HMD. Full VR using an HMD was utilized in a similar study by Herrero and Lorenzo (2019) where a researcher controlled the interactable avatars by selecting from a series of pre-defined responses ranging from positive to negative. Such approaches are well utilized in VR research outside of ASC interventions. A "wizard of oz" approach where a virtual agent can be driven by an external confederate is common in work rooted in social psychology (Pan et al. 2015; Pan et al. 2016). Such VR designs avoid a potential model where specific responses are required in scripted scenarios thus avoiding a deficit view where there is a "right" way of going about social interaction. Furthermore, such designs open up the possibility for furthering work in learning and education as the VR tool can provide a mediated learning experience with educators playing a key role in the interaction. This provides opportunity for the confederate (e.g., a teacher) who controls virtual characters to also benefit from the interaction. As they are involved in the mediated learning process, they in turn can potentially learn more about their students through the mediated VR environment. Such applications of VR where a more holistic approach to teaching and learning is possible, appear underexplored. Few studies, if any, have explored the implications of such a tool in terms of the dynamics this would create between educators and learners nor attempted to define formal pedagogies for future work.

There is a need, then, for VR pedagogical frameworks that has the experiential learning and immersion offered by VR at its core (Fowler 2015) that enhance and improve learners' social interaction through a more holistic understanding of individual learners. This understanding can be conveyed to the educator through participation in the interactions such that together these learner-teacher dyads develop. It is important to consider how the pedagogy and learning tools allow learners to develop their self-determination, awareness and skills such as decision-making, self-advocacy, reflective problem-solving (Carter et al. 2009) while developing their social interaction competencies.

3 Opportunities

There is a need for a more thorough consideration of designs of VR based interventions where ASC is concerned. Designs tend to fall into one of two camps: scripted scenarios that expect certain responses, and more flexible scenarios made possible by the addition of external control by a suitable confederate. The former tends to derive designs from a deficit-model view of ASC. Where there is a correct response or behavior that should be exhibited by the participant and the aim of the scenario is to train this correct response. As ASC exists on a spectrum, scripted approaches may address only a narrow part of that spectrum. Such approaches have their place, and it is not the purpose of this paper to reject their importance. However, non-deficit based approaches should also be explored as these have the potential to empower ASC learners by not focusing on their apparent weaknesses. For example, rather than assuming a specific learning outcome, engagement with the VR system may demonstrate behaviors or strengths that were previously unknown to both the learner and teacher. Sandbox like systems with flexible designs that adapt to individual needs allow the learner to explore scenarios and outcomes for themselves and the manner of that exploration potentially informative for educators.

The latter design of VR solutions (illustrated in Fig. 1) has the potential to provide this while also offering flexible approaches that can cater to the needs of learners across the ASC spectrum. As scenarios are not necessarily scripted (it is up to the confederate), they can be more individually nuanced and tailored to the needs of the learner. Rather than being hamstrung by technology, the design may only be limited by the number of pre-recorded responses and animations that the confederate has to choose from. It would be a significant design challenge to decide on what pre-recorded responses are needed, how many, and how much variation should be catered for. Future work is needed that creates design frameworks to assist in this process. The addition of a suitable confederate can provide a VR mediated learning experience. The interactions of which can further understanding of individual learners by virtue of a teacher (for example) guiding the scenario where they can in turn learn about their charges through the mediated interactions.

Hence, VR as an intervention for learning social skills for those with ASC can offer more than social skills training with defined experience outcomes. It can also broaden understanding of individuals both for themselves and educators through the non-deficit view of thinking. While VR based interventions could also be designed that are intended to further the research field of ASC from medical, psychological and social standpoints.

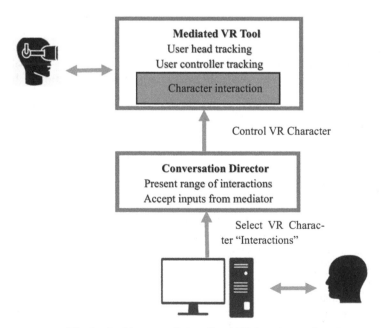

Fig. 1. Architecture of a mediated VR learning tool

Furthermore, through interaction with VR systems, a wide range of sensory input and modalities are utilized. These data points may be used to create a picture of the experience within VR and therefore raises the question of how these can be integrated into providing the holistic understanding of learners discussed in this paper. The following section reviews the ways in which such techniques could be implemented into VR based interventions for social skill development for ASC learners.

4 Leveraging Machine Learning

While AI could be utilized within scenarios themselves, for example driving interactions in the form of chatbots (Torous et al. 2021), there is significant potential in capturing information about the user and their affective state. The latest VR set-ups provide opportunity to capture a range of behavioral and performance data (Zhang et al. 2018). This can include gaze direction, posture, tracking data etc. Each of this in isolation may be of interest to an educator while observing interaction within a scenario. Gaze direction, for example, is often an important metric of social interaction particularly for learners with ASC and has been used in VR oriented studies in past work (Lahiri et al. 2012). While this may be from a deficit perspective, that there is not enough or the right amount of eye-contact, in combination with other data points a more complete picture of the user is possible. The use of affective computing in VR is not new and it has been used to modify the parameters of a scenario in real-time. For example, a VR driving simulator for those with ASC modified the difficulty based on the affective state of individuals during interaction (Bian et al. 2013).

Within the field of personalized education, outside of VR, affective computing has been utilized to assess learner "state". Techniques utilizing affective computing have been used within special education to determine levels of engagement with learning material (Standen et al. 2020). When deployed within a classroom setting, such multi-modal data fusion techniques provide an insight into the learning process of students (Taheri et al. 2020). Where students with individual needs are concerned, this affords educators an important opportunity to learn more about their students which can often be difficult to observe in those with ASC. Utilization of such approaches within the field of VR warrants further exploration, particularly given the range of data points on offer through VR hardware and additional non-invasive sensors such as, eye-gaze, posture analysis, electro-dermal activity, heart rate. This multimodal data fusion approach can utilize predictive AI to provide the mediator with information about their learner's affective state in real-time. What this information might be is an open question from this paper and further research is needed to determine how machine learning approaches can be used to further this understanding using the described non-deficit ways of viewing ASC.

Hence, when using VR through a non-deficit perspective as a mediated learning tool alongside real-time feedback on affective state, there is the potential to create new avenues of understanding ASC learners based on a holistic view of the individual.

5 Conclusions and Recommendations for Further Work

This position paper has outlined the case for considering methods of deploying VR based interventions utilizing a non-deficit based approach to design. From RQ1, it is noted that when taking a deficit based view of learners the focus of interventions is on training a "correct" behavior. While this has an important role to play it should also be augmented with approaches that empower learners on paths to self-discovery, highlighting their strengths and neutral differences. With regard to RQ2, such non-deficit approaches can offer this and by doing so further the understanding of learners for both themselves and their educators where said strengths and neutral difference may previously have been difficult to ascertain.

The example architecture illustrated in Fig. 1 provides an overarching view of a broader VR design. However, consideration should also be made to the design of the scenarios deployed. Studies cited in this paper focused on areas which are common to the learner, their school, a shop etc. As Parson (2016) noted, such scenarios should be authentic to the learner in order to be relatable. This poses further research questions when considering the spectrum on which ASC exists and how to capture that authenticity for learners across the spectrum while maintaining the flexibility of the systems proposed in this position paper. Furthermore, past work has done well to outline accessibility-based design requirements (Bozgeyikli et al. 2017), however, there remains VR specific research questions dealing with the impact of design on experiential learning. For example, what role does graphical fidelity play in the systems discussed in this paper? What of the design of characters? It is known, for example, that those with ASC engage more with non-anthropomorphic entities such as robots (Hughes-Roberts et al. 2019). Future work should also consider the design and fidelity of character driven experience and examine impact of different character designs. Ultimately, design methodologies, heuristics and broad guidelines are needed across the field of VR to aid in the creation of simulations that are impactful for their target users. In order to complete this holistic understanding of learners (RQ3), there is opportunity to leverage machine learning in order to provide real-time information of their affective state during interaction.

This paper has provided a review of some seminal work. However, further work should include a full systematic review that examines the use of VR and machine learning as interventions in ASC social skill development from the perspectives described here. This review is needed to formally define the terms the field utilizes, categorize VR designs in relation to ASC learning, determine designs based on the two perspectives and formalize design guidelines for non-deficit approaches to creating VR interventions. Outcomes from this will provide researchers and educators the ability to choose from a set of interventions that are suitable to the needs of their target user group.

This paper has set out the case for taking non-deficit based approaches to VR design that leverage machine learning. By doing so, applications can be created that provide opportunities for self-discovery that consider the strengths and neutral differences as well as potential areas for development learners with ASC may have. Furthermore, this process of self-discovery is informative for educators and researchers also who will be able to gain a more holistic understanding of their students/participants.

References

Bian, D., et al.: A novel virtual reality driving environment for autism intervention. In: Stephanidis, C., Antona, M. (eds.) UAHCI 2013. LNCS, vol. 8010, pp. 474–483. Springer, Heidelberg (2013). https://doi.org/10.1007/978-3-642-39191-0_52

Bölte, S.: Is autism curable? Dev. Med. Child Neurol. **56**(10), 927–931 (2014)

Bozgeyikli, L., Raij, A., Katkoori, S., Alqasemi, R.: A survey on virtual reality for individuals with autism spectrum disorder: design considerations. IEEE Trans. Learn. Technol. **11**(2), 133–151 (2017)

Carter, E.W., Owens, L., Trainor, A.A., Sun, Y., Swedeen, B.: Self-determination skills and opportunities of adolescents with severe intellectual and developmental disabilities. Am. J. Intellect. Dev. Disabil. **114**, 179–192 (2009). https://doi.org/10.1352/1944-7558-114.3.179

Didehbani, N., Allen, T., Kandalaft, M., Krawczyk, D., Chapman, S.: Virtual reality social cognition training for children with high functioning autism. Comput. Hum. Behav. **62**, 703–711 (2016)

Dinishak, J.: The deficit view and its critics. Disabil. Stud. Q. **36**(4) (2016). ISSN 2159-8371 (Online), 1041-5718 (Print)

Fowler, C.: Virtual reality and learning: where is the pedagogy? Br. J. Edu. Technol. **46**(2), 412–422 (2015)

Ghanouni, P., Jarus, T., Zwicker, J.G., Lucyshyn, J., Mow, K., Ledingham, A.: Social stories for children with autism spectrum disorder: validating the content of a virtual reality program. J. Autism Dev. Disord. **49**(2), 660–668 (2019)

Halabi, O., El-Seoud, S.A., Alja'am, J.M., Alpona, H., Al-Hemadi, M., Al-Hassan, D.: Design of immersive virtual reality system to improve communication skills in individuals with autism. Int. J. Emerg. Technol. Learn. **12**(5) (2017)

Herrero, J.F., Lorenzo, G.: An immersive virtual reality educational intervention on people with autism spectrum disorders (ASD) for the development of communication skills and problem solving. Educ. Inf. Technol. **25**(3), 1689–1722 (2019). https://doi.org/10.1007/s10639-019-100 50-0

Hughes-Roberts, T., et al.: Examining engagement and achievement in learners with individual needs through robotic-based teaching sessions. Br. J. Edu. Technol. **50**(5), 2736–2750 (2019)

Ke, F., Moon, J., Sokolikj, Z.: Virtual reality-based social skills training for children with autism spectrum disorder. J. Spec. Educ. Technol. (2020). https://doi.org/10.1177/0162643420945603

Lahiri, U., Bekele, E., Dohrmann, E., Warren, Z., Sarkar, N.: Design of a virtual reality based adaptive response technology for children with autism. IEEE Trans. Neural Syst. Rehabil. Eng. **21**(1), 55–64 (2012)

Marín-Morales, J., et al.: Affective computing in virtual reality: emotion recognition from brain and heartbeat dynamics using wearable sensors. Sci. Rep. **8**(1), 1–15 (2018)

Mesa-Gresa, P., Gil-Gómez, H., Lozano-Quilis, J.A., Gil-Gómez, J.A.: Effectiveness of virtual reality for children and adolescents with autism spectrum disorder: an evidence-based systematic review. Sensors **18**(8), 2486 (2018)

Mitchell, P., Parsons, S., Leonard, A.: Using virtual environments for teaching social understanding to 6 adolescents with autistic spectrum disorders. J. Autism Dev. Disord. **37**(3), 589–600 (2007)

Pan, X., Gillies, M., Slater, M.: Virtual character personality influences participant attitudes and behavior–an interview with a virtual human character about her social anxiety. Front. Robot. AI **2**, 1 (2015)

Pan, X., et al.: The responses of medical general practitioners to unreasonable patient demand for antibiotics-a study of medical ethics using immersive virtual reality. PloS ONE **11**(2) (2016)

Parsons, S.: Authenticity in virtual reality for assessment intervention in autism: a conceptual review. Educ. Res. Rev. **19**, 138–157 (2016)

Parsons, S., Cobb, S.: State-of-the-art of virtual reality technologies for children on the autism spectrum. Eur. J. Spec. Needs Educ. **26**(3), 355–366 (2011)

Parsons, S., Leonard, A., Mitchell, P.: Virtual environments for social skills training: comments from two adolescents with autistic spectrum disorder. Comput. Educ. **47**(2), 186–206 (2006)

Parsons, S., Yuill, N., Good, J., Brosnan, M.: "Whose agenda? Who knows best? Whose voices?": co-creating a technology research roadmap with autism stakeholders. Disabil. Soc. **35**(2), 201–234 (2020)

Rosqvist, H.B., Stenning, A., Chown, N.: Introduction. In: Stenning, A., Rosqvist, H. B., Chown, N. (eds.) Neurodiversity Studies. Taylor and Francis, Milton Park (2020)

Robertson, S.M.: Neurodiversity, quality of life, and autistic adults: shifting research and professional focuses onto real life challenges. Disabil. Stud. Q. **30**(1) (2010)

Standen, P.J., et al.: An evaluation of an adaptive learning system based on multimodal affect recognition for learners with intellectual disabilities. Br. J. Educ. Technol. (2020)

Stewart Rosenfield, N., Lamkin, K., Re, J., Day, K., Boyd, L., Linstead, E.: A virtual reality system for practicing conversation skills for children with autism. Multimodal Technol. Interact. **3**(2), 28 (2019)

Taheri, M.H., Brown, D.J., Sherkat, N.: Modeling engagement with multimodal multisensor data: the continuous performance test as an objective tool to track flow. Int. J. Comput. Inf. Eng. **14**(6), 197–208 (2020)

Torous, J., et al.: The growing field of digital psychiatry: current evidence and the future of apps, social media, chatbots, and virtual reality. World Psychiatry **20**(3), 318–335 (2021)

Yuan, S.N.V., Ip, H.H.S.: Using virtual reality to train emotional and social skills in children with autism spectrum disorder. Lond. J. Prim. Care **10**(4), 110–112 (2018)

Zhang, L., Warren, Z., Swanson, A., Weitlauf, A., Sarkar, N.: Understanding performance and verbal-communication of children with ASD in a collaborative virtual environment. J. Autism Dev. Disord. **48**(8), 2779–2789 (2018)

Designing AI-Support VR by Self-supervised and Initiative Selective Supports

Ritwika Mukherjee[1], Jun-Li Lu[1,2(✉)], and Yoichi Ochiai[1,2]

[1] Research and Development Center for Digital Nature, University of Tsukuba, Tsukuba, Japan
jllu@slis.tsukuba.ac.jp
[2] Faculty of Library, Information and Media Science, University of Tsukuba, Tsukuba, Japan

Abstract. To provide flexible support ways and intelligent support contents for users in VR contexts, compared with the existing support ways of either single or combination of sensing functions, e.g., support of gesture, head or body movement. In our proposal, to provide flexible support functions conditioned on VR contexts or user's feedbacks, we propose to use a semi-automatic selection of interactive supports. In modeling of semi-selection by user's feedbacks and VR contexts, we propose to evaluate the performance by consideration of both intelligent AI evaluation, based on data of users' performance in VR, and user's initiative feedbacks. Furthermore, to provide customizable or personalized estimation in the VR support, we propose to apply the machine learning of self-supervised learning. Therefore, we are able to train or retrain estimation models with efficiency of low-cost of data works, including reduction of data-labeling cost or reuse of existing models. We require to evaluate the timing of applying selection or modification of support ways, the balance of ratios of automatics or user-initiative due to user preference or experiences or smoothness of VR contexts, and even user awareness or understanding, etc. Further, we require to evaluate the scale, numbers, size, and limitation of data or training that are needed for stable, accurate, and useful estimations of VR support.

Keywords: AI support VR · Self-supervised selective supports · Multi-factor modeling

1 Introduction

In the contexts of VR with human factors on issues, proposals, modeling, studies, analysis or discussions for supports or related [1, 8, 13–15, 18, 20, 22, 23, 25, 26, 28–30], we study and design AI support systems that utilize multiple factors about human body, behaviors, and performance for considering the modeling of flexible and intelligent support in VR contexts. E.g., in VR shooting games, not only gazing or movement of head or hand are used to reflect the performance or concentration of user, but other factors such as voices or facial expressions can be used to determine the response of user.

To provide flexible and intelligent ways of supports in VR contexts, compared with the existing supports of either single or combination of sensing functions, we propose to apply semi-automatic selections of flexible supports. We consider each body or sensing parts to be supported and the support can be involved in one or more parts. E.g., a support can be involved in eye gazing and reaction time of hand movement, or a support can be composed of head movement and sensing by voice. Specifically, we propose to apply the combination of supports that can be selected and adjusted during VR contexts. For selection of the combination of supports, we propose to evaluate the performance of supports, by merging the auto-evaluation of trained AI and the user's evaluation or preference. Note that we customize the AI to fit user evaluation or preference during the VR contexts.

Furthermore, to provide customizable or personalized estimation in the VR support, we propose to apply the machine learning of self-supervised learning. Therefore, we are able to train or retrain estimation models with efficiency of low-cost of data works, including reduction of data-labeling cost or reuse of existing models. Since the training or retraining of models are flexible and depending on the input factors of users, we select the suitable self-supervised learnings based on the given one or multiple user factors. Note that we apply self-supervised learning due to the effective training or retraining models with efficiency of data works including data labeling or the preprocessing or refinement of data. After one or multiple models are trained, we need to combine models for making suitable estimation or prediction forms of results.

The analysis of design, expectation of system performance or user studies, limitations, and future works are discussed. We require to evaluate the timing of applying selection or modification of support ways, the balance of ratios of auto-matics or user-initiative due to user preference or experiences or smoothness of VR contexts, and even user awareness or understanding, etc. Further, we require to evaluate the scale, numbers, size, and limitation of data or training that are needed for stable, accurate, and useful estimations of VR support. Especially, the combination or correlation among multiple types of data and multiple training of self-supervised learnings may be important for implementation or applications. Note that due to multiple factors of users, VR-devices, and VR contexts, the workable or applicable data and training methods and their combinations are needed extensively evaluated.

2   Related Work: Estimate User Perception and Interaction with Body Factors

2.1   Eye or Gaze Modeling of Interaction or Prediction

Eye tracking has been playing a significant role in detecting user's intentions. Eye tracking has proven to be suitable for using in various IICI domain as an input modality [19]. Real time face detection combined with eye gaze tracking can provide a means of user input into a gaming environment, eye-gaze information in various ways to enhance UI design providing smarter modes of gameplay interaction and UI modalities that are sensitive to a user's behaviors and mood [5]. Web page interfaces introspected and both the browser interface and the interaction elements on Web pages can be adapted based on gaze input [21].

One of the major application areas is using the gaze information and trajectory to enter text [11]. The raw eye tracking data can be utilized to attach to the game elements in VR environment for a better individualized gaming [6]. Gaze based rendering to cope-up with the display limitations has proved to be promising in the past research finding. A solution improved the previous work on gaze-based rendering during the gaze saccadic movements [2]. It is evident that gaze information pays a key role in the immersive environment for understanding the user's intentions and choices while interacting with the environmental components.

2.2 Gesture, Body, or Non-verbal Modeling of Interaction or Prediction

The main goal of gesture recognition is to predict the user's intended action based on the current movement trajectory. This recognition relies on the user's hand gestures and body movements during performing an action. Previous research has explored template matching based simultaneous recognition of a working action and a cognitive long-term motion prediction [10]. Compared to classification models, regression outcomes better suites trajectory prediction without requiring a seed sequence [17]. This motion human motion prediction in VR can be a very useful technique to initiate rendering of visuals and game components or game cues for better user's performance and encouragement.

In VR the primary modalities to use for motions prediction is head motion, hand motions and gaze motion. In previous work gaze contingent rendering has been used for certain limitations on the device or game engine [2]. Long Short-Term Memory network has been used on users' reach trajectories to predict intended targets to reuse physical props by decoupling user's real and virtual hands [4]. There are various head motion prediction methods [3,9] which are useful in VR is beneficial as its very closely related to user's future gaze point and actions. In VR environments, hand is the primary mode of integration and selections. Hence tracking the hand motion over time and recognizing the actions as well as predicting the long-term trajectory becomes a key [10]. Clarance et al. has proposed deep learning models to predict intended targets for pre-rendering of haptics [4]. Another method extends a 2D kinematic template matching method to VR environment to predict the user's hand ray final position and angle [12]. Vu et al. explores possibilities using wrist worn devices to track hand movement and gestures for immersive environment tennis sport setup [27].

A recent study contributed an user and activity independent regression base hand movement prediction model in VR [7]. A combination of hand and head gesture along with the gaze ray informations can be well utilized to collectively

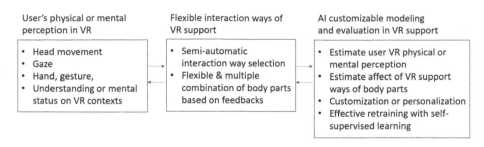

User's physical or mental perception in VR	Flexible interaction ways of VR support	AI customizable modeling and evaluation in VR support
• Head movement • Gaze • Hand, gesture, • Understanding or mental status on VR contexts	• Semi-automatic interaction way selection • Flexible & multiple combination of body parts based on feedbacks	• Estimate user VR physical or mental perception • Estimate affect of VR support ways of body parts • Customization or personalization • Effective retraining with self-supervised learning

Fig. 1. Designing AI-support VR with flexible interactions and intelligent evaluation.

understand the user's intention as well as future activity. This information can be applied to enhancing the user's individual experience as well as pre-rendering to do away with the device latencies and other limitations. Sound signals can act as a query and input signal to interact with various systems. There is also ongoing research in the field of non-verbal vocal interaction (NVVI), i.e., using other sounds than speech such as humming to control user interfaces [24]. Humming can as well be used for the retrieval of music information from database [16]. Humming has been used for marking the start and end of words in a gaze-based text entry solution [11]. Hence, it is evident that non-verbal form of communication can also find its way in interacting with the VR environments with all the other modalities kept side by side (Fig. 1).

3   Designing AI-Support VR with Flexible Interactions and Intelligent Evaluation

3.1   Semi-automatic Selection of Combined Supports and Advantages

To provide flexible support ways and intelligent support contents for users in VR contexts, compared with the existing support ways of either single or combination of sensing functions, e.g., support of gesture, head or body movement. In our proposal, to provide flexible support functions conditioned on VR contexts or user's feedbacks, we propose to use a semi-automatic selection of interactive supports. In modeling of semi-selection by user's feedbacks and VR contexts, we propose to evaluate the performance by consideration of both intelligent AI evaluation, based on data of users' performance in VR, and user's initiative feedbacks. As the advantages described above, the expected affect will be flexible semi-selective supports, efficient AI and personal evaluation, and customizable support conditioned on VR or user contexts.

3.2 Customizable AI-Support VR by Effective Retraining of Prediction Models with Low-Cost Data Works

Furthermore, to provide customizable or personalized estimation used in the VR support, we propose to apply the machine learning of self-supervised learning. Therefore, we are able to train or retrain estimation models with efficiency of low-cost of data works, including reduction of data-labeling cost or reuse of existing models. Further, we can build a more intelligent and up-to-date models by using the existing models (e.g., accurate prediction or tracking of gazing or head movement) and thus retraining novel models with less efforts and the merged estimation of more accurate or diverse results.

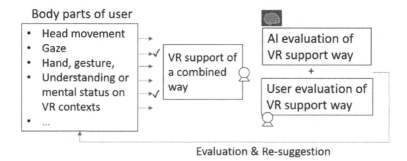

Fig. 2. System: Flexible combination of supports by semi-automatic selection.

4   Flexible Combination of Supports by Semi-automatic Selection

4.1   Design

In Fig. 2, we show the design of semi-selection support in VR contexts. In the support ways, we consider each body or sensing parts to be supported and the support way can be involved in one or more parts. For example, a support can be involved in eye gazing and reaction time of hand movement, or a support can be composed of head movement and sensing by voice. Specifically, we propose to apply the combination of supports that can be flexibly selected and adjusted during the process of VR context. For flexible selection of the combination of supports, we propose to evaluate the performance of the combination of supports, by merging the auto-evaluation of trained AI and the user evaluation. Note that the evaluation of AI can be customized to fit user selection or preference during the process of VR context.

5 Customizable AI-Support VR by Effective Retraining of Prediction Models with Low-Cost Data Works

5.1 Design

In Fig. 3, we show the concepts of effectively training the estimation models with low cost of data works, with the factors of multiple body parts or performance of users in VR contexts. Since the training or retraining of models are flexible and depending on the input factors of users, we select the suitable self-supervised learnings based on the given one or multiple user factors. Note that we apply self-supervised learning since it can be applied in effective training or retraining models with efficiency of data works including data labeling or the preprocessing or refinement of data. After one or multiple models are trained, we need to combine models for making suitable estimation or prediction forms of results.

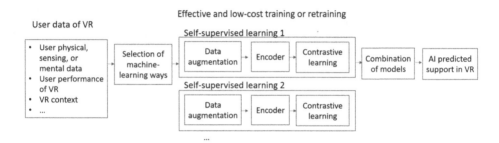

Fig. 3. System: Customizable AI-support VR by effective retraining of prediction models with low-cost data works.

6 Discussion, Analysis of Design, Expectation of System Performance, Implementation of User Studies, Limitations, and Future Works

We propose the framework of designing AI-support VR with interactions and intelligent evaluation. Since the design of AI-support VR are flexible with user's body or sensing parts, the design could be applied to most systems or VR devices of various types. Further, since the ways of supports can be involved in multiple user factors and performance of VR context, this flexibility of the design can be applied to various VR or user contexts. Further, the application of the design can be separated or independent with the devices of VR and the contexts in VR.

In design of semi-automatic selection of combined supports, the usability or accessibility of users in VR contexts are important. We require to evaluate and find the timing of applying selection or modification of support ways, the balance of ratios of automatics or user-initiative due to user preference or experiences or smoothness of VR contexts, and even user awareness or understanding, etc.

In customizing AI-support VR by effective retraining of prediction models with low-cost data works, the following are required. Although the estimation results could be flexible and improved with the flexible modeling of multiple factors, we require to evaluate the scale, numbers, size, and limitation of data or training that are needed for stable, accurate, and useful estimations of VR support. Especially, the combination or correlation among multiple types of data and multiple training of self-supervised learnings may be important for implementation or applications. Note that due to multiple factors of users, VR-devices, and VR contexts, the workable or applicable data and training methods and their combinations are needed extensively evaluated.

Although the proposed AI-support VR seemed flexible and intelligent, the limitations or concerns are still how the system are smoothly applied to real-world VR-devices and VR contexts. Through extensive or possible implementations or user studies, the system could be clear on real-world VR applications. In the future development, not just the mentioned issues or researches, we also expect the corresponding researches towards VR devices or hardwares or relatively systematic or functional levels, could be discussed or developed.

Acknowledgement. This work was supported by Japan Science and Technology Agency (JST CREST: JPMJCR19F2, Research Representative: Prof. Yoichi Ochiai, University of Tsukuba, Japan), and by University of Tsukuba (Basic Research Support Program Type A).

Demonstration

Demonstration of prediction of user support using gazing in VR game: We showed a simple demo of AI support VR by using gazing, body language, and voice. The user was expected to support the shooting by AI using the analyzed gazing behaviors or head or hand movement during the VR game (Fig. 4).

Fig. 4. User's gaze (pink line) and hand position (the position of gun) were shown in a shooting game of VR. (Color figure online)

Modeling of Self-supervised Learning

We also show a example of modeling self-supervised learning by using multi-factor data of users in VR contexts. In the model of Fig. 5, the given images

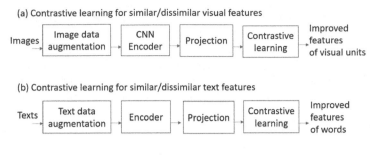

(a) Contrastive learning for similar/dissimilar visual features

Images → Image data augmentation → CNN Encoder → Projection → Contrastive learning → Improved features of visual units

(b) Contrastive learning for similar/dissimilar text features

Texts → Text data augmentation → Encoder → Projection → Contrastive learning → Improved features of words

(c) Contrastive learning for similar/dissimilar text-image pairs

Fig. 5. A modeling of self-supervised learning by using contrastive learning on images and related data of users.

from VR context can be trained to be suitable representation of features, thus the prediction of user supports can be updated or improved by a dataset of VR without additional data works on labeling or cleaning data.

References

1. Ahuja, K., Islam, R., Parashar, V., Dey, K., Harrison, C., Goel, M.: EyeSpyVR: interactive eye sensing using off-the-shelf, smartphone-based VR headsets. Proc. ACM Interact. Mob. Wearable Ubiquitous Technol. **2**(2), 57:1–57:10 (2018)
2. Arabadzhiyska, E., Tursun, O.T., Myszkowski, K., Seidel, H., Didyk, P.: Saccade landing position prediction for gaze-contingent rendering. ACM Trans. Graph. **36**(4), 50:1–50:12 (2017)
3. Azuma, R.T., Bishop, G.: A frequency-domain analysis of head-motion prediction. In: Mair, S.G., Cook, R. (eds.) Proceedings of the 22nd Annual Conference on Computer Graphics and Interactive Techniques, SIGGRAPH 1995, Los Angeles, CA, USA, 6–11 August 1995, pp. 401–408. ACM (1995)
4. Clarence, A., Knibbe, J., Cordeil, M., Wybrow, M.: Unscripted retargeting: reach prediction for haptic retargeting in virtual reality. In: IEEE Virtual Reality and 3D User Interfaces, VR 2021, Lisbon, Portugal, 27 March–1 April 2021, pp. 150–159. IEEE (2021)
5. Corcoran, P.M., Nanu, F., Petrescu, S., Bigioi, P.: Real-time eye gaze tracking for gaming design and consumer electronics systems. IEEE Trans. Consum. Electron. **58**(2), 347–355 (2012)
6. Dohan, M., Mu, M.: Understanding user attention in VR using gaze controlled games. In: Hook, J., Stenton, P., Ursu, M.F., Schofield, G., Vatavu, R. (eds.) Proceedings of the 2019 ACM International Conference on Interactive Experiences for TV and Online Video, TVX 2019, Salford (Manchester), UK, 5–7 June 2019, pp. 167–173. ACM (2019)
7. Gamage, N.M., Ishtaweera, D., Weigel, M., Withana, A.: So predictable! Continuous 3D hand trajectory prediction in virtual reality. In: Nichols, J., Kumar, R., Nebeling, M. (eds.) UIST 2021: The 34th Annual ACM Symposium on User Interface Software and Technology, Virtual Event, USA, 10–14 October 2021, pp. 332–343. ACM (2021)

8. Gao, C., Zhang, X., Banerjee, S.: Conductive inkjet printed passive 2D trackpad for VR interaction. In: Shorey, R., Murty, R., Chen, Y.J., Jamieson, K. (eds.) Proceedings of the 24th Annual International Conference on Mobile Computing and Networking, MobiCom 2018, New Delhi, India, 29 October–02 November 2018, pp. 83–98. ACM (2018)

9. Gül, S., et al.: Reproducibility companion paper: Kalman filter-based head motion prediction for cloud-based mixed reality. In: Shen, H.T., et al. (eds.) MM 2021: ACM Multimedia Conference, Virtual Event, China, 20–24 October 2021, pp. 3619–3621. ACM (2021)

10. Hahn, M., Krüger, L., Wöhler, C.: 3D action recognition and long-term prediction of human motion. In: Gasteratos, A., Vincze, M., Tsotsos, J.K. (eds.) ICVS 2008. LNCS, vol. 5008, pp. 23–32. Springer, Heidelberg (2008). https://doi.org/10.1007/978-3-540-79547-6_3

11. Hedeshy, R., Kumar, C., Menges, R., Staab, S.: Hummer: text entry by gaze and hum. In: Kitamura, Y., Quigley, A., Isbister, K., Igarashi, T., Bjørn, P., Drucker, S.M. (eds.) CHI 2021: CHI Conference on Human Factors in Computing Systems, Virtual Event/Yokohama, Japan, 8–13 May 2021, pp. 741:1–741:11. ACM (2021)

12. Henrikson, R., Grossman, T., Trowbridge, S., Wigdor, D., Benko, H.: Head-coupled kinematic template matching: a prediction model for ray pointing in VR. In: Bernhaupt, R., et al. (eds.) CHI 2020: CHI Conference on Human Factors in Computing Systems, Honolulu, HI, USA, 25–30 April 2020, pp. 1–14. ACM (2020)

13. Herman, L., Jurík, V., Stachon, Z., Vrbík, D., Russnák, J., Rezník, T.: Evaluation of user performance in interactive and static 3D maps. ISPRS Int. J. Geo Inf. **7**(11), 415 (2018)

14. Houser, S., Okafor, I., Raghav, V., Yoganathan, A.: Flow visualization of the non-parallel jet-vortex interaction. J. Vis. **21**(4), 533–542 (2018). https://doi.org/10.1007/s12650-018-0478-2

15. Humski, L., Pintar, D., Vranic, M.: Analysis of Facebook interaction as basis for synthetic expanded social graph generation. IEEE Access **7**, 6622–6636 (2019)

16. Jang, J.R., Hsu, C., Lee, H.: Continuous HMM and its enhancement for singing/humming query retrieval. In: ISMIR 2005, 6th International Conference on Music Information Retrieval, London, UK, 11–15 September 2005, Proceedings, pp. 546–551 (2005)

17. Lank, E., Cheng, Y.N., Ruiz, J.: Endpoint prediction using motion kinematics. In: Rosson, M.B., Gilmore, D.J. (eds.) Proceedings of the 2007 Conference on Human Factors in Computing Systems, CHI 2007, San Jose, California, USA, 28 April–3 May 2007, pp. 637–646. ACM (2007)

18. Laville, V., et al.: Deriving stratified effects from joint models investigating gene-environment interactions. BMC Bioinform. **21**(1), 251 (2020)

19. Majaranta, P., Bulling, A.: London

20. Markopoulos, E., Luimula, M., Ravyse, W., Ahtiainen, J., Aro-Heinilä, V.: Human computer interaction opportunities in hand tracking and finger recognition in ship engine room VR training. In: Markopoulos, E., Goonetilleke, R.S., Ho, A.G., Luximon, Y. (eds.) AHFE 2021. LNNS, vol. 276, pp. 343–351. Springer, Cham (2021). https://doi.org/10.1007/978-3-030-80094-9_41

21. Menges, R., Kumar, C., Staab, S.: Improving user experience of eye tracking-based interaction: introspecting and adapting interfaces. ACM Trans. Comput. Hum. Interact. **26**(6), 37:1–37:46 (2019)

22. Murnane, M., Higgins, P., Saraf, M., Ferraro, F., Matuszek, C., Engel, D.: A simulator for human-robot interaction in virtual reality. In: IEEE Conference on Virtual Reality and 3D User Interfaces Abstracts and Workshops, VR Workshops 2021, Lisbon, Portugal, 27 March–1 April 2021, pp. 470–471. IEEE (2021)
23. Petersen, G.B., Petkakis, G., Makransky, G.: A study of how immersion and interactivity drive VR learning. Comput. Educ. **179**, 104429 (2022)
24. Soro, A.: Gestures and cooperation: considering non verbal communication in the design of interactive spaces. Ph.D. thesis, University of Cagliari, Italy (2012)
25. Sprengel, U., et al.: Virtual embolization for treatment support of intracranial AVMs using an interactive desktop and VR application. Int. J. Comput. Assist. Radiol. Surg. **16**(12), 2119–2127 (2021)
26. Vryzas, N., Matsiola, M., Kotsakis, R., Dimoulas, C., Kalliris, G.: Subjective evaluation of a speech emotion recognition interaction framework. In: Cunningham, S., Picking, R. (eds.) Proceedings of the Audio Mostly 2018 on Sound in Immersion and Emotion, Wrexham, United Kingdom, 12–14 September 2018, pp. 34:1–34:7. ACM (2018)
27. Vu, T.H., Misra, A., Roy, Q., Choo, K.T.W., Lee, Y.: Smartwatch-based early gesture detection 8 trajectory tracking for interactive gesture-driven applications. Proc. ACM Interact. Mob. Wearable Ubiquitous Technol. **2**(1), 39:1–39:27 (2018)
28. Wang, L., Wang, H., Dai, D., Leng, J., Han, X.: Bidirectional shadow rendering for interactive mixed 360° videos. In: IEEE Virtual Reality and 3D User Interfaces, VR 2021, Lisbon, Portugal, 27 March–1 April 2021, pp. 170–178. IEEE (2021)
29. Wang, Z., Xie, L., Wei, H., Zhang, K., Zhang, J.: Omnidirectional motion input: the basis of natural interaction in room-scale virtual reality. In: 2020 IEEE Conference on Virtual Reality and 3D User Interfaces Abstracts and Workshops, VR Workshops, Atlanta, GA, USA, 22–26 March 2020, pp. 699–700. IEEE (2020)
30. Wienrich, C., Gross, R., Kretschmer, F., Müller-Plath, G.: Developing and proving a framework for reaction time experiments in VR to objectively measure social interaction with virtual agents. In: Kiyokawa, K., Steinicke, F., Thomas, B.H., Welch, G. (eds.) 2018 IEEE Conference on Virtual Reality and 3D User Interfaces, VR 2018, Tuebingen/Reutlingen, Germany, 18–22 March 2018, pp. 191–198. IEEE Computer Society (2018)

A New Approach to Assist Virtual Image Accessibility for Visually Impaired People

Edwige Pissaloux[1]($^{(\boxtimes)}$) , Lilia Djoussouf[1] , Katerine Romeo[1] ,
Velazquez Ramiro[2] , Simon L. Gay[3] , Ngoc-Tan Truong[1] ,
and Son Duy Dao[1]

[1] LITIS, University of Rouen Normandy, Rouen, France
`edwige.pissaloux@univ-rouen.fr`
[2] Universidad Panamericana, Aguascalientes, Mexico
[3] LCIS, University of Grenoble Alpes, Valence, France

Abstract. Currently, graphical data is becoming increasingly ubiquitous with new technologies. However, today's technologies are still of limited access to such representations (images, graphs, charts...) for Visually Impaired People (VIP). The quantity and quality of presented information are key points of efficient accessibility. Therefore, this paper proposes the presentation of such information via a tactile gist (a tactile representation of essential data). New rules for 2D data representation (e.g. paintings, images, maps) are proposed via the tactile gist, which helps us, especially VIP, to understand them. These rules are deduced from experiments lead with VIP for tactile gist representations on two supports - thermoformed paper and dedicated original force-feedback based device named F2T (Fore Feedback Tablet). These rules take into account the human touch/haptic sense specificities and human cognitive capabilities. Such rules should be included in the design of any assistance to 2D data accessible by the VIP.

Keywords: Tactile gist representations · 2D data accessibility · Force-feedback tablet (F2T) · Virtual images · Perception · Visually Impaired People (VIP)

1 Introduction

Nowadays, culture, education, and many daily life tasks are getting increasingly reliant on 2D data such as pictures, schematics or maps. However, accessing such information is still difficult for Visually Impaired People (VIP). Traditional

This research has been financially supported, via different research projects, by the CCAH (Le Comité National Coordination Action Handicap), Région de Normandie, and European Commission (FEDER) and ANR (Inclusive museum Guide). We thank students and staff of the University of Rouen Normandie, and the VIP, members of our research team or from VIP charities, for their participation in our evaluations.

M. Antona and C. Stephanidis (Eds.): HCII 2022, LNCS 13309, pp. 251–261, 2022.
https://doi.org/10.1007/978-3-031-05039-8_18

screen readers and braille devices are not adapted to convey 2D data efficiently, limiting VIP's inclusion in society and lowering the quality of their life.

The access to the culture, especially to the artworks presented in museums, designed mainly for sighted people, are not accessible to VIP. In traditional approach (provided e.g. by classic museum guides), artworks are oculo-centred representations accessible for the sighted public. The VIP accessibility is considered thanks to a transcription of some visual information into audio descriptions; sometimes, static tactile representations [1] are also available. Figure 1 gives two examples of artworks' presentations, which target the VIP, from the British Museum (Fig. 1a and b), and the Fine Art Museum, Rouen, France (Fig. 1c and d). Both examples use the same technology (namely, thermo-inflation) to fix a 3D scene on a 2D support. Figure 1a presents a scene from the Greek temple in relief with its fronto-parallel and orthographic projections (Fig. 1b). Figure 1c presents Sisley's Seine River painting and its fronto-parallel projection (Fig. 1d). Both representations try to make a "tactile copy" of the observed 3D scenes, which are not relevant for tactile/haptic explorations. Indeed, these representations are overloaded with details, which imply long exploration time and high cognitive load. Moreover, the details' superposition does not allow human fingertips [2] to extract the meaning from the object's contours (edges). Furthermore, the physical nature of the supports does not allow to implement the scaling operations (zooming in and out), as those presentation are unchangeable (frozen). Therefore, such oculo-centric-tactile representations cannot be easily perceived by VIP.

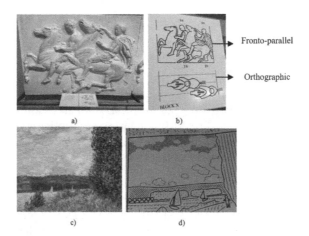

Fig. 1. Static tactile representations a) the moulded friezes of a Greek temple, British Museum; b) fronto-parallel and orthographic projections of relief from a); c) Boats on Seine by Sisley and d) their thermoformed representation.

However, the artworks can be perceived in a de-visualized way [1], i.e. perceived without vision (or only with vision as a secondary sense) in a multimodal way. Such a presentation will create new aesthetic and emotional impressions, deepen our knowledge of the creative gesture and lead to the effective inclusion of all audiences to digital society. Therefore, considering the de-visualization principle a new generation of museum guides will offer new experiences of artworks. We propose its integration via a simulation of natural cognitive processing (i.e. via an artificial intelligence cognitive process) which underpins concepts/percepts emergence from stimulations following sensory-motor theory of visual perception [3].

Therefore, this paper proposes a new approach to design representations of 2D data accessible for VIP, based on the concept of "a tactile gist presentation" (Sect. 2). A set of rules, deduced from experiments lead with VIP, is proposed, allowing the creation of haptic (physical and virtual) representations of images on different supports, such as thermoformed paper or an original force-feedback based haptic device, named F2T (Sect. 3). Some examples of created virtual images, which can be explored by any public via tactile or haptic assistance, are provided in Sect. 4. Section 5 encompasses some future works.

2   Gist Concept

Visual gist is a global minimal information presenting an image where usually only a few objects of important size are perceived [4,5]. The gist representation can be seen as a global and rough "map" of an image as it allows to grasp a minimal meaning of the image in a single glance [6]. Therefore, the role of gist presentation is threefold: (1) representing an image in a synthetic way, (2) allowing the relative localization of objects in an image, and (3) assisting the decision for further behavior (e.g. analyzing the image in more details or changing the image). In function of the support, we speak about the visual or tactile (haptic) gist.

An example of the (visual) gist representation is shown in Fig. 2; its left image (a) is the scene of "Raven and fox" extracted from the Bayeux Tapestry, XI century (France, [7]), while right image (b) represents its associated (tactile) gist where 4 circles delimit four important areas each having a specific cognitive meaning.

a)   b)

Fig. 2. a) Example of Bayeux Tapestry "Raven and fox", its gist representation of a 2D image [7].

3 Rules for Creation of Haptic Representation of Images Accessible to VIP

The rules for creation of haptic gist representation have been established thanks to a series of experiments with end-users [8–11]. To create VIP experience of haptic images, a specific evaluation procedure has been defined (cf. Fig. 3). In our case, the gist representation is implemented based on two supports: thermoformed paper (A path) and the original force-feedback tablet (B path). The (A) path allows the perception, thus the evaluation, of the static elements of tactile gist (e.g. a tree, a cheese). The (B) path, thanks to force-feedback tablet F2T providing haptic and kinesthetic representation, allows the perception (feeling), and the evaluation of static and dynamic elements of an image (e.g. to follow object edges or the speed of the dropped cheese).

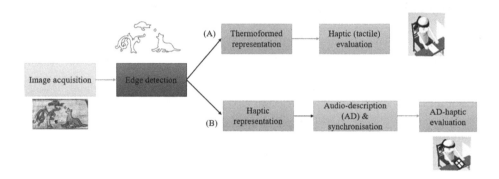

Fig. 3. Procedure for haptic image accessibility evaluation.

Early evaluations, with VIP or blindfolded participants, of different images' gist representations [8–11] allowed establishing the following rules and definitions of tactile/haptic representations of images:

Rule 0. A haptic gist presentation of an image (painting) should be built as this image surjective projection.

Rule 1. The tactile gist consists of a set of regions having an important meaning for considered images.

Rule 2. A gist of an object is defined by its bounding box (simplified and approximated).

Rule 3. An ad hoc, but cognitively useful, simplification and/or approximation of the haptic gist of an image are mandatory.

Rule 4. A bounding box of a gist should be clearly spatially isolated from others to extract its semantic meaning during the manual exploration (spatial separations between boxes should be introduced, if necessary).

Rule 5. The tactile-only representation is relevant for isolated simple objects' representations, close to known geometric figures.

Rule 6. The tactile-only representation is insufficient for complex figure comprehension.

Rule 7. The tactile gist should be completed by an ad hoc audio-description.

Thermoformed and haptic representations of images by tactile gist are shown in more detail in Sects. 3.1 and 3.2, respectively.

3.1 Thermoformed Representation of Tactile Gist

Gist representation using thermoformed papers can be used to help VIP to perceive a static scene or image with their fingers. By applying the above rules, the final tactile gist for Fig. 2a, which has been validated with VIP and blindfolded students, is shown in Fig. 4. It should be observed that the initial relative positions between objects of the scene have been enlarged by adding the additional space for fingertips exploration (cf. Rule 4). This tactile gist representation can be directly printed using a thermoforming printer.

The thermoformed representations allow us to create representations of the scene containing the static elements only; they may help to find the most relevant approximations and simplifications. However, the tuning of their representations is time-consuming and complex, and their effective realization requires a dedicated printer. Being mono-modal, their comprehension may be difficult when manually explored. Moreover, it is impossible to change the thermoformed display because each image requires its thermoformed representation.

a)   b)

Fig. 4. Initial (a) and final (b) tactile gist presentation of the scene "Raven and fox" of Bayeux Tapestry.

A force-feedback tablet can overcome such limits and it allows accompanying the tactile/haptic representations by an audio description lead to a TAD (Tactile-Audio-Described) representation.

3.2 Haptic Effects for Gist Representation

The Force Feedback Tablet (F2T, Fig. 5a) is a new architecture, based on the force-feedback principle, to generate haptic effects associated with visual cues used by painters such as height/depth variations, borders (edges), and textures.

The F2T acquires the user's movement intentions via the thumbstick, independently from the current end-effector movement (Fig. 5b). This specificity allows the implementation of a wide variety of dynamic and interactive haptic effects useful for 2D data representations. Some of them have been already provided by the F2T (edge and relief, flow, rail, attractors, and active guidance); others are still under investigation.

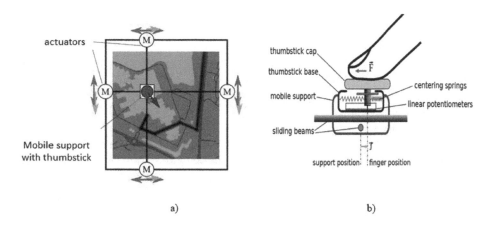

a)   b)

Fig. 5. a) F2T architecture (attached to a screen on which a map is displayed); b) thumbstick architecture which local movement depends on the image content at (x, y) [11].

F2T principle is presented in Fig. 6. The initial intended speed V' is the movement generated by the device to follow the user's finger. The output speed V' is modified by haptic effects that are applied to the mobile support, and $P(x,y)$ is the current position of the mobile support on the available surface (screen attached to F2T). The force-feedback principle allows producing several haptic effects, which add offsets to the control speed V'. These effects can be cumulated by applying them successively. In this case, the output speed V' of an effect is used as the input speed vector V of the next effect. The number and order of applied effects can be changed according to the desired haptic perceptions to induce.

In our first academic prototype (Fig. 7), the following effects were implemented: edges, and reliefs, attractors, flows, railings, and waves (sine waves simulated). The guidance mode of the device is also presented.

Edge and relief effects allow representing objects' edges. When the edge gradient is small (the slope of the object's edge is small), the user's finger will be either slowed down or accelerated depending on the direction of the edge gradient. This effect can be used to explore a base-relief or to guide the users along a trench, maintaining their finger on a path. When the edge gradient is strong enough, the movement will stop. In that case, the user's finger can slide along the object's edge which speeds up the object's shape recognition.

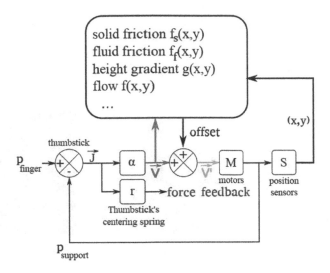

Fig. 6. Principle of different effects generation at (x,y) (frictions, flow, etc.) [11].

Flow effect adds an offset to the finger's movement. The movement offset value and direction can be defined at each point of the surface. It is thus possible to represent dynamic elements with mobile parts (e.g. vehicles or conveyors) or dynamic physic elements (e.g. wind in Fig. 8a).

The rail is an effect with no equivalent in the real world (e.g. Fig. 8b). This effect is based on a predefined a rail curve: movements following the rails will not be affected, while movements crossing the rails will be slowed down (reduction of the component of the movement that is perpendicular to the rails). This effect adds constraints to the user's movements.

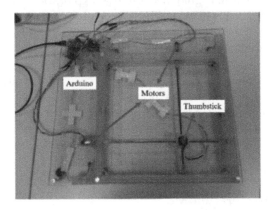

Fig. 7. F2T prototype [11].

Attractors are areas or points generating an attractive or repulsive force on the user's finger (Fig. 8c). The force strength, profile, and range can be predefined for each attractor. This effect can be used to simulate magnetic paths, holes, bumps, or even gravity fields.

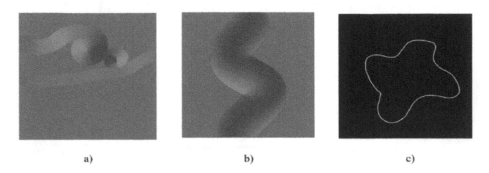

a)   b)   c)

Fig. 8. F2T original haptic effects: a) and b) images encode vector fields that can be used for flow and rail effects, c) attractor image.

After presenting the F2T architecture, Sect. 4 introduces a case study of a real scene using F2T and outlines the principles of the guided mode applying the tactile gist concept.

4   Case Study

For the gist, we can also say that it is minimal information to represent the content of the message of an image. Based on this concept, F2T presents two modes: free exploration and guidance. In free exploration mode, the user can move the thumbstick anywhere on the image. Depending on the thumbstick position, the sound of a corresponding dynamic element will be activated. That helps VIP understanding the general content of the image. Adding more experiences accessing the painting for VIP, F2T proposes the second mode - guidance mode. This mode is powerful; the user does not move the thumbstick. This mode is programmed by a sequence of way points defining the path. This path is built to present the important elements. The thumbstick will be moved automatically following this path. Moreover, the audio-descriptions are also programmed for the corresponding elements (multimodal presentation). Sections 4.1 and 4.2 present the details of the two modes.

4.1   F2T Free Exploration Mode

When creating a gist representation of a considered image displayed by the F2T, the haptic effects introduced above are applied to different parts of the image.

Figure 9a represents scene 24 of Bayeux Tapestry [7]; Figure 9b delimitates four-regions gist where the red region corresponds to the boat and the sea, the yellow region matches the shields placed on the edges of the boat; the dark green region indicates the sail, and the light green region matches the wind (air) which pushes the sail. When the finger is in a specific region, the sounds of the corresponding elements can be activated. The rail effect is applied to the dark green region and will guide accordingly the finger (on the thumbstick) through its shape and with the associated speed (Fig. 9c). The wave of the sea are simulated with a sinusoid function; a sea wave sound is activated when the thumbstick is in the low red region (Fig. 9d). VIP can freely explore this gist representation on F2T.

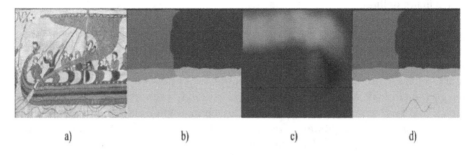

a)   b)   c)   d)

Fig. 9. a) Scene of Bayeux Tapestry [7], b) a gist representation of the image in a); rail effect c) simulates the wind; wave effect d) simulates (via a sinusoid) the wave of the sea. (Color figure online)

4.2 F2T Guided Mode

Besides the free exploration mode (corresponding to VIP natural exploration of tactile representations), F2T provides the guided mode. The guidance assists a detailed exploration of an element of a gist by following its outline. The object's outline is thus represented by a curve (a path) defined by a list of line segments (salient points of the object). Figure 10 gives an example of a path while following the shape of the raven (the pink points). The points of segments are memorized in a text file with attributes of the guidance such as the point coordinates, the exploration speed at this point, the attraction force, etc. Using this file, the F2T control software (Fig. 11) generates a virtual representation of the image that the user can explore in a controlled way.

Fig. 10. The suggested exploration path (pink points) following the raven's shape. (Color figure online)

A simple script language has been developed to load or change images and paths, and to play sound files when predefined conditions are fulfilled (cf. Fig. 11 right). This scripted system makes it possible to define scenarios and synchronize the guidance with audio-descriptions (multimodal presentation), or to change the virtual environment configuration (e.g. change the image or user's profile). Figure 11 presents the guidance mode for "Raven and fox". The paths defined by green points correspond to the four important elements of the scene (tree, raven, cheese, and fox), and constitute a scene overview. An audio-description may accompany the haptic exploration of each element.

Such multimodal guide mode will help VIP to recognize the contours of elements and understand the whole scene.

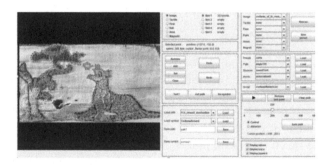

Fig. 11. Guidance mode control panel on F2T interface (green points corresponding to the whole picture guided exploration). (Color figure online)

5   Conclusion

This paper proposes an ICT (Information and Communication Technology) system to assist the de-visualization of artworks. Such accessibility is based on the concept of multimodal presentation of artworks with the gist concept. The gist representation allows building "a map of a scene or image" (the gist of level 1) and can provide a more detailed representation of each element of the "map" (the gist of level 2). Besides the gist representations, new rules for gist implantation on different hardware supports (namely, thermoformed paper and force-feedback tablet) have been established based on experimental evaluation of haptic representations with VIP and blindfolded participants. The thermoformed presentation, although creating faithful representations of the painting, may assist the perception of simple static elements only. The multimodal force-feedback device F2T presented here briefly overcomes this limit as it provides the multimodal tactile-audio-described representations. F2T can generate some haptic effects such as height/depth variations, borders, and textures. This device helps VIP to access 2D data (maps, graph, 2D art...); this paper presented two modes: free exploration and guided mode to access the paintings' different elements. In near future, a new F2T version will be designed as a frame to be clipped on classic screens; the image displayed on a screen will be used by the F2T control system. We will also investigate more haptic and audio effects to generate interactive multimodal representations of images which will be evaluated with VIP.

References

1. Thompson, H.: Blindness Arts (co-ed. V. Warne). Disabil. Stud. Q. **38**(3) (2018)
2. Johnson., K.O.: The roles and functions of cutaneous mechanoreceptors. Curr. Opinion Neurobiol. **11**(4), 455–461 (2001)
3. O'Regan, J.K., Noë, A.: What it is like to see: sensorimotor theory of visual experience. Synthèse **129**, 79–103 (2001)
4. Potter, M.C.: Short-term conceptual memory for pictures. J. Exp. Psychol. Hum. Learn. Memory **2**, 509–522 (1976)
5. Oliva, A.: Gist of the Scene, Neurobiology of Attention, pp. 251–258. Elsevier, Amsterdam (2005)
6. Pissaloux, E., Velazquez, R., Maingreaud, F.: A new framework for cognitive mobility of visually impaired users and associated tactile, device. IEEE Trans. Hum.-Mach. Syst. **47**(6), 2168–2291 (2017)
7. https://www.bayeuxmuseum.com/en/the-bayeux-tapestry/ . Accessed July 2021
8. Romeo, K., Chottin, M., Ancet, P., Pissaloux, E.: Access to artworks and its mediation by and for visually impaired persons. In: Miesenberger, K., Kouroupetroglou, G. (eds.) ICCHP 2018. LNCS, vol. 10897, pp. 233–236. Springer, Cham (2018). https://doi.org/10.1007/978-3-319-94274-2_32
9. Romeo, K., Chottin, M., Ancet, P., Lecomte, C., Pissaloux, E.: Simplification of painting images for tactile perception by visually impaired persons. In: Miesenberger, K., Kouroupetroglou, G. (eds.) ICCHP 2018. LNCS, vol. 10897, pp. 250–257. Springer, Cham (2018). https://doi.org/10.1007/978-3-319-94274-2_35
10. Velázquez, R., et al.: Performance evaluation of active and passive haptic feedback in shape perception (2019)
11. Gay, S., Pissaloux, E., Romeo, K., Truong, N.T.: F2T: a novel force-feedback haptic architecture delivering 2D data to visually impaired people. IEEE Access, 1–11 (2021). Print ISSN2169-3536, Online ISSN 2169-3536. https://doi.org/10.1109/ACCESS.2021.3091441

Elicitation of Requirements for Extended Reality Generation Considering Universal Design for Learning and User-Centered Design for People with Disabilities

Luis Roberto Ramos Aguiar$^{(\boxtimes)}$, Francisco Javier Álvarez Rodríguez ,
Julio César Ponce Gallegos , and César Eduardo Velázquez Amador

Universidad Autónoma de Aguascalientes, Ave. Universidad 940, 22013 Aguascalientes, Mexico
roberto.ramos@edu.uaa.mx

Abstract. Extended Reality (ER) has come to revolutionize how people interact with digital media, this term refers to technologies such as Augmented Reality, Virtual Reality and Mixed Reality. As time progresses, access to these technologies is becoming more accessible to all users, however, when ER is applied to people with disabilities, requirements must be very specific to meet their needs and take advantage of their physical capabilities to improve interaction. Therefore, due to differences that can be encountered from one disability to another, this paper presents preliminary progress of a methodology to build ER applications in users with physical interaction disabilities, in addition, Universal Design for Learning and User-Centered Design are presented as tools to help generating more efficient application for these users. The result of this research shows the first methodological diagram composed by the stages of Analysis, Pre-Production, Production, Post-Production, likewise, activities during analysis stage can be observed to obtain the requirements and products to achieve.

Keywords: Extended Reality · Methodology · Universal Design for Learning · User-Centered Design · Physical interactivity disabilities

1 Introduction

Virtual, augmented and mixed reality (VR, AR, MR) refer to technologies and conceptual approaches studied for spatial interfaces by researchers in engineering, computer science and human-computer interaction (HCI) for several decades [1].

Currently, Extended Reality (ER) has been used as a term for this type of technologies (VR, AR, MR). Through the years, ER has become more accessible to all users and very useful for different areas of knowledge such as medical practice [2], education [3], health [4], physics [5] amount others. However, developing software for such technology is not easy when the user has disability, this is because there may be very specific particularities from user to user according to physical capabilities or means of interaction that these present, therefore, development teams have the need to resort towards tools that help them with graphical interfaces design to ensure greater acceptability, learning and usability as possible.

A model used to improve the teaching of people with disabilities is called Universal Design for Learning (UDL), a model that takes into account the diversity of students and whose objective is to achieve effective inclusion, thus minimizing physical, sensory, cognitive and cultural barriers that may exist in the classroom [6]. Another important approach for people with disabilities is User-Centered Design (UCD), which aims to involve the user in all stages of development by making the user an integral part of the software process, thereby ensuring that all specifications and requirements that the user really wants are met by the software [7].

Consequently, because of the characteristic that can be ER development in users with disabilities, this paper presents a methodological proposal that combines ER, DUA and DCU with the aim of facilitating software development with immersive technology, adhering towards user's needs by applying teaching guidelines to enhance inclusion, likewise, first activities defined for its analysis stage and the artifacts that are intended to be obtained with them are mentioned. This first methodology's general design is composed by Analysis, Production, Pre-Production and Post-Production stages where features to be implemented were defined such as, include users in all development processes, defining requirements, identifying roles within the project, providing DUA guidelines according to the user, designing graphic interfaces according to the type of ER and finally implementing and validating the generated software.

The rest of the paper is organized as follows: Sect. 2 presents background, Sect. 3 refers to development processes analyzed, Sect. 4 methodological proposal, Sect. 5 Basic elements within the software process, Sect. 5.1 analysis, and finally Sect. 6 presents Conclusions and future work.

2   Background

Given this methodological proposal is intended to implement Extended Reality, Universal Design for Learning and User-Centered Design, a description of relevant concepts is given below.

2.1   Extended Reality

Extended Reality has become a term widely used today to encompass all those technologies that provide different means of immersing users. According to Doolani [8] "Extended reality (ER) refers to all real and virtual environments combined, where human-machine interaction occurs through interactions generated by computer technology and hardware. ER technologies consist of virtual reality (VR), mixed reality (MR) and augmented reality (AR)".

In addition, Mattew and Pillai [9] suggest that "Extended Reality refers to technology that provides users with an immersive experience in a simulated world that users can interact with. ER is a term used to collectively refer to technologies such as AR, VR and MR, each of which has some key differences". Finally, Matthews et al. [10] Consider that extended reality is making its way into different application areas such as fitness, telehealth, clinical evaluation, therapy, surgical procedures, education, audio-visual entertainment and gaming.

Augmented Reality. Augmented Reality (AR) is designed to combine the real environment with virtual information. Its interaction is done through virtual objects such as images, text, 3D models, music and more. Its beginnings date back to 1990, when AR applications were used for pilot training [11]. According to the 2011 Horizon Report, AR, with its ability to provide 3D information within the real world, creates new experiences of the world, and suggested that AR should be adopted in the next 2–3 years to provide new opportunities for teaching, learning, research or creative inquiry [12].

AR has been very popular in education, this technology helps to engage students in real-world exploration, increasing their motivation and acquiring better research skills [13, 14]. It was also revealed that it improves laboratory skills in university students and helps them to have a more positive attitude towards physics work [15]. Equally important, AR has also been used with students with disabilities to teach activities related to skills work [16], emotion recognition [17] and mathematical topics [18]. These studies indicate the effectiveness of using AR as an instructional method for people with physical interaction disabilities.

Virtual Reality. Virtual Reality (VR) is one of the fastest growing technologies, consisting in elements that generate representations of reality in real time. Movements of the real world are projected in a virtual world, allowing the user to experience the sensation of being inside the fictitious space experiencing multiple emotions [19]. The concept of VR emerged several years ago, however, for people with little technological knowledge, it is still something fictitious and unknown [20]. Some of VR's elements are three-dimensional images, 360-degree sound, body tracking, interactivity, multi-user systems, tactile feedback and flexibility to build artificial worlds [21].

VR has become necessary to establish therapeutic means that make rehabilitation spaces more flexible for people with disabilities [22, 23], has also been used in the teaching of mathematical subjects [24], cognitive therapies [25] and training in adults and people with disabilities [26]. For this reason, VR is a technology that is not modern but is currently experiencing its golden age thanks to the entertainment sector. Even so, applications are emerging for social, humanitarian, or medical use thanks to the facilities that exist to create their own applications that can help people with physical disabilities to interact with their environment.

Mixed Reality. Another technology referred by ER is Mixed Reality (MR), although most discussions focus on AR and VR, this may be the most interesting for most organizations [27]. MR is an interaction paradigm that aims to seamlessly link physical and (digital) data processing environments. Although mixed reality systems are becoming more and more common, we still do not have a clear understanding of this interaction paradigm [28].

2.2 Universal Design for Learning

When developing learning tools for people with disabilities, it is important to generate applications that consider the particularities that may exist from one disabled user to another. For this reason, it was decided to implement the Universal Design for Learning (UDL), an approach that promotes components for the correct inclusion of all people with disabilities through educational elements. Rogers-Shaw defines UDL [29] as "a framework for teaching-learning operation that conceptualizes knowledge through learner-centered guidelines that emphasize accessibility, collaboration and community". Moreover, Rao and Meo [30] believe that UDL can be used to proactively design lessons that address student variability. Utilizing UDL guidelines, teachers can integrate flexible options and supports that ensure that standards-based lessons are accessible to a range of learners in their classrooms.

UDL presents a set of guidelines for integrating flexible options into curriculum and instruction in three specific domains, representation, action and expression, and engagement. Consisting of nine guidelines and 31 "checkpoints," they provide further definition of how a teacher can build flexible pathways into a lesson.

These guidelines established by UDL can be applied in the construction of computer applications, integrating flexible components to ensure that content can be accessible to a range of people with physical interaction disabilities.

2.3 User-Centered Design

Technology services often have limited reach and suboptimal participation when implemented in the real world. One of the reasons for these failures is that technology-enabled services are not designed for the users and the contexts in which they will be applied [31]. User-Centered Design (UCD) is a philosophy of interface design where the user is permanently considered, which allows finding a visual and functional solution to diverse communicative and functional requirements in computer systems. The UCD consists of knowing some of the user's particularities in order to make the graphic interfaces designed for him more familiar and effective. [32]. Furthermore, Dopp et al. defines it as "A discipline that attempts to base the design of an innovation on information about the people who will ultimately use that innovation" [33]. In fact, it is proposed to establish guidelines for the development of RE focusing on the end user considering their physical limitations to produce a product that meets their needs taking advantage of their physical characteristics, in addition, it is intended that the user is involved in each stage of the methodology, becoming a co-creator. For this reason, it is decided to implement the UCD approach in the proposed model and thereby be close to the person with physical interaction disability to know their perceptions in relation to the RE product to be developed.

3 Methodologies Analyzed

To build this methodological proposal, five research papers were initially analyzed. These papers were selected from a systematic review of more than 600 articles where those with software processes or methodologies applied to ER were identified.

The first paper reviewed was proposed by Hamzah et al. [34] which is called "Development of Augmented Reality Application for Learning Networked Computing Devices" was developed following a methodology composed of stages (phases) such as Envisioning phase (Problem Identification), Planning phase (Planning), Developing phase (Design), Stabilizing phase (Testing), Deploying phase (Implementation), Evaluation phase (System Evaluation), however, there is little emphasis on activities carried out at each stage.

Subsequently, the paper of afnan et al. [35] entitled "School of the Future: A Comprehensive Study on the Effectiveness of Augmented Reality as a Tool for Primary School Children's Education" shows his methodological process to develop software that implements Augmented Reality, in which it is possible to observe stages such as design and development process, showing diagrams to follow when creating your product.

In addition, Krajcovic [36] in his paper entitled "3D Interactive Learning Environment as a Tool for Knowledge Transfer and Retention" presents a methodological diagram that is composed of the stages of Analysis and collection of references, Creation of assets, Virtual environment and creation of the game scenario, testing and use (See Fig. 1). This methodology includes activities such as process specification, requirement of objects to be modeled in 3D, program interaction and correction. According to authors, it can also be used as a basis for the creation of interactive training.

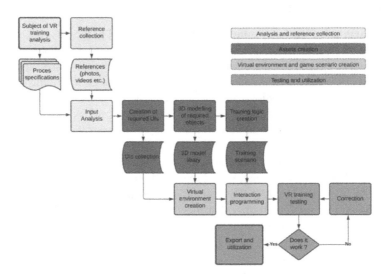

Fig. 1. Development methodology implemented by [36].

Furthermore, Zucci et al. [37] in his paper entitled "Combining immersion and interaction in XR training with 360-degree video and 3D virtual objects" implements a methodology based on human-centered design (HCD) where human needs, capabilities and limitations form the basis for the development of processes that address user objectives in the environment in which a system will be used.

Finally, Van wyk et al. [38] in their paper entitled "An evaluation framework for virtual reality safety training systems in the South African mining industry" implement a methodology composed of different development cycles, within each cycle are the stages of Analysis of the context of the problem, Design of the solution, Development of the solution, Evaluation in practice and Reflection (Stage where the results are observed) (See Fig. 2).

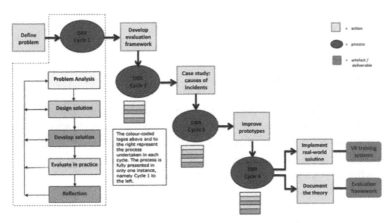

Fig. 2. Process implemented in [38]. Red blocks indicate actions, green blocks indicate artifacts or theoretical products that are the result of each process. (Color figure online)

3.1 Weaknesses Found in Analyzed Processes

A Methodology of ER for people with physical interaction disabilities should consider specific characteristics of targeted users, so elements such as UDL and UCD can be great contributions in the development process. In most of these studies, Methods applied are mentioned in a very general way, without specifying how each stage is applied [34, 35, 37]. However, some of them show in considerable detail how the process is carried out, as well as its stages and activities [36, 38]. It was also found that most of them do not consider UDL and UCD for their implementation, with exception of Zucchi et al. [37], leaving aside important features that could be added within software process if the user was considered as a member of the development team. Another important characteristic that was analyzed was the ER tool they used, although the exposed methods can be implemented with any technology, not defining design guidelines for each one of them can slow down the project.

Given the deficiencies found in processes followed in these research papers, the development of a methodological proposal that implements UDL considering the user with disability as part of development team, may provide new tools for future software products with ER aimed at these specific users. Table 1 show analyzed aspects.

Table 1. Aspects evaluated in methodological processes.

Work analyzed	UCD	AR	VR	MR	UDL
Hamzah et al. [34]	No	Yes	No	No	No
Afnan et al. [35]	No	Yes	No	No	No
Krajčovič [36]	No	No	Yes	No	No
Zucchi et al. [37]	YES	No	Yes	No	No
Van wyk et al. [38]	No	No	Yes	No	No

4   Methodological Proposal

Based on the study of different papers that mentioned methodological processes for conducting their research, a first methodological proposal was made which is divided in four stages (Analysis, Pre-Production, Production, Post-Production). These stages aim to guide development team towards the proper conception of ER based software products for people with physical interaction disabilities (See Fig. 3).

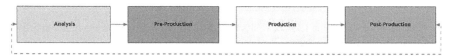

Fig. 3. Main stages of the methodological proposal.

Each stage of this methodology includes different activities to ensure the solution to solve the problem in question. The activities are Definition of requirements, Identification of roles, Universal design for learning, Solution design, Solution implementation, Validation and Use. These activities were results of different works analyzed integrating approaches such as UDL and UCD, in Fig. 4 an extended version of the methodological proposal can be observed.

4.1   Activities Within the Methodology

Below is an overview of how each activity that makes up this methodology for the proper design of RE applications for people with physical interaction disabilities can be achieved.

User with Physical Interaction Disability. According to user-centered design approach, the user with disabilities is part of each stage of the development process, becoming one more element within the methodology. In this way, it is intended to ensure the fulfillment of the needs established in the project and a constant evaluation by the user of all activities carried out.

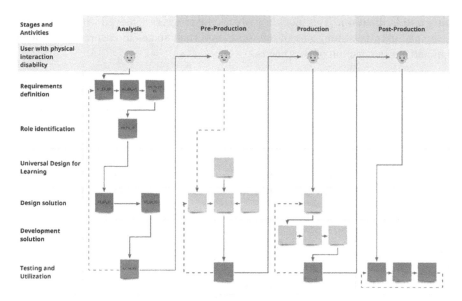

Fig. 4. Methodological proposal in extended version.

Requirement's Definition. In this module the needs of the project are defined by performing activities of extraction, analysis and specification of requirements, each activity must be approved by the end user to ensure the correct identification of requirements of the system to be built.

Role Identification. Building software for people with physical interaction disabilities can become a multidisciplinary project due to the special needs that may arise from one user to another, therefore, this module defines possible roles that will be necessary for the construction of an application with RE. It is important to correctly identify the user's requirements to establish the roles that will be necessary throughout the project, since they will be the ones who will execute the activities that will be presented.

Universal Design for Learning. Considering specific characteristics of people with disabilities to build ER, the Universal Design for Learning module is presented, which shows 9 guidelines and 31 directives that compose it; within each guideline, it is established which type of disability is best supported. Currently, Autism, Hearing, Visual and Dyslexia disabilities are being contemplated.

Solution Design. To design ER, a table is defined with different immersion technologies and the type of disability with which it can be most useful, in addition, graphic interfaces are established to solve the problem identified in the analysis stage, all these interfaces must be approved by the end user.

Solution Development. After defining the ER technology and the graphic interface designs that will provide a solution to the requirements established by the user, in this module the solution is developed using software tools that development team considers most appropriate according to the ER technology selected.

Testing and Utilization. This module analyzes the progress achieved within each stage with the end user, becoming one of the most important stages to ensure user-centered design and the satisfaction of user needs.

5 Basic Elements Within Methodological Process

There are many aspects of software processes that could be modeled, the most common of which are: activities, roles, process steps, structures, artifacts, tools, agents, projects, production support, etc. [39–41]. In this methodological proposal, basic elements of software process are related to the construction of different activities. Figure 5 shows the relationships between basic elements of software process within the methodological proposal.

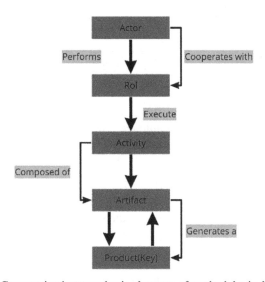

Fig. 5. Cooperation between basic elements of methodological process.

Following a description of each of them as described by Acuña y Ferré [42], Rioseco [41] is given below.

Actor. Is the person responsible for executing the different processes within the methodology, it is characterized by fulfilling one or more roles based on their knowledge or skills. They are grouped into two categories: a) human actors, they are the people who are involved in the software processes and can be organized in teams; b) system actors, they are the hardware or software that make up the processes, they are those who belong to the technological area.

Rol. Due to how multidisciplinary the construction of software projects can be the cooperation of different areas of knowledge becomes feasible. For this reason, a set of responsibilities, rights, and skills necessary to fulfill a software process activity assigned to specific roles are described here.

Activity. It is a stage of process, executed by one or several actors with different roles, who produce changes based on requirements to be fulfilled, these activities will shape the final product following the characteristics of the end user.

Artifac. It is sub product of a process. An artifact can be used by one or more processes to improve the result of development team. There can be as many versions of such an artifact as necessary until the one that satisfies the needs of the software product is achieved.

Product (Key). It is the final version of the artifact which is associated with a key for early identification within development process, this final version must be approved by the user who will use the application.

5.1 Analysis Stage

Currently, this methodological proposal is developing a stage of analysis whose objective is identify requirements of the system to be built, for which purpose it is essential to incorporate the end user in each of its activities, ensuring that product meets the needs of the end user.

This stage is made up of seven activities, each of them designed to be executed sequentially, however, at the end of these seven activities, if necessary, a review of each of them can be carried out, incorporating the user. These activities are based on Chaves' work. [43] entitled "Requirements engineering and its importance in the development of software projects" who presents stages of Extraction, Analysis, Specification and Validation as activities for a correct requirements engineering, in addition, was complemented with UML diagrams and software engineering characteristics obtained from Somerville [44].

Inside this stage you can find activities that belong to areas such as requirements definition, role identification, interface and ER design, software validation and ER application (See Fig. 6).

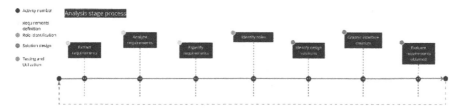

Fig. 6. Process of analysis stage in the methodology proposal.

Table 2 shows general descriptions of each activity included in analysis stage.

Table 2. Description of activities pertaining to analysis stage.

Activity	Description
Extract requirements	In this activity, it is necessary to work together with the end user and experts in the subject to be solved to identify the solution to the problem, the services that should be offered by the system, as well as any restrictions that may arise
Analyze requirements	In this activity, problems with system requirements identified in the Requirements Extraction section must be discovered
Especify requirements	In this activity, specifications of functional and non-functional requirements established for the project are made
Identify roles	Having correctly identified the problem to be solved and the functional and non-functional requirements, it is important to identify the experts who will be part of the system design and implementation
Identify design solution	In this activity, it is necessary to identify the Extended Reality tool that will be implemented to solve the problem, choosing it based on interaction characteristics that are expected by the user who will use the application
Graphic interrface creation	Having identified system requirements (functional and non-functional) and Extended Reality tool to be applied, the first sketches that will help to solve the problem in the Pre-Production stage should be made
Evaluate requirements obtained	In this activity, a synthesis of main characteristics established in this stage must be made, then, they must be evaluated together with the end user to ensure compliance with established requirements in each of the activities, in case of any inconvenience, activities must be analyzed again, and the pertinent modifications must be made

Following development process defined in the methodological proposal, each of its activities has an objective, Role, Artifact, Product and Key. These characteristics can be seen below for each activity (Table 3).

Table 3. Characteristics of activities pertaining to analysis stage.

Activity	Rol	Artifac	Product	Key
Extract requirements	Project leader, End user	Requirements extraction tool	General project requirements	A1_EA_ER
Analyze requirements	Project leader, End user	Tool for requirements analysis	Table with user requirements	A2_EA_AR
Especify requirements	Project leader, End user	Requirements specification tool	Tool for requirements specification	A3_EA_ESPR
Identify roles	Project leader, End user	Software project role instrument	Table of roles	A4_EA_IR
Identify design solution	Project leader, End user, Programmer	ER suggestion instrument according to disability	Extended Reality Toolbox	A5_EA_IH
Graphic interrface creation	Project leader, End user, designer	Any program to create graphical interfaces	Initial graphical interfaces	A6_EA_IG
Evaluate requirements obtained	Project leader, End user	Tool to synthesize the obtained information	Requirements evaluation table	A7_EA_EV

6 Conclusions and Future Work

This paper presented the beginnings of a new methodological proposal developed to produce ER in people with physical interaction disabilities. It also proposes to use Universal Design for Learning and User-Centered Design as tools that can facilitate software design and thereby achieve greater acceptance and use of different physical characteristics that can be presented from user to user.

We analyzed research papers that provided elements that contributed to this methodological proposal, also, these papers can help future researchers who wish to know software processes implemented in the creation of ER tools, in addition, we show activities, artifacts and products of analysis stage to demonstrate characteristics to obtain requirements that we visualize in this first stage methodology, as well as possible roles that can play each of these activities how project leader, end user, designer, and programmer.

As future work, we will continue experimenting with this methodological proposal by defining appropriate activities in requirements definition, role identification, Universal Design for Learning, solution design, solution development, testing and use for Analysis, Pre-Production, Production and Post-Production stages. Finally, once the activities for each of these stages have been defined, we will start with the experimentation of the methodology through case studies in Aguascalientes, Mexico.

The objective will be to produce Extended Reality software for people with physical interaction disabilities and evaluate the performance, usability, and acceptance of applications, as well as to evaluate the performance of methodology with software methodology evaluation tools.

References

1. Çöltekin, A., et al.: Extended reality in spatial sciences: a review of research challenges and future directions. ISPRS Int. J. Geo-Information **9**(7) (2020). https://doi.org/10.3390/ijgi90 70439
2. Andrews, C., Southworth, M.K., Silva, J.N.A., Silva, J.R.: Extended reality in medical practice. Curr. Treat. Options Cardiovasc. Med. **21**(4), 1–12 (2019). https://doi.org/10.1007/s11 936-019-0722-7
3. Xing, Y., Liang, Z., Shell, J., Fahy, C., Guan, K., Liu, B.: Historical data trend analysis in extended reality education field. In: International Conference on Virtual Rehabilitation, ICVR 2021, May 2021. https://doi.org/10.1109/ICVR51878.2021.9483828
4. Logeswaran, A., Munsch, C., Chong, Y.J., Ralph, N., McCrossnan, J.: The role of extended reality technology in healthcare education: towards a learner-centred approach. Futur. Healthc. J. **8**(1) (2021). https://doi.org/10.7861/fhj.2020-0112
5. Yavoruk, O.: The study of observation in physics classes through XR technologies (2020). https://doi.org/10.1145/3429630.3429637
6. CAST. Universal Design for Learning guidelines version 2.0. (2021). https://www.cast.org/impact/universal-design-for-learning-udl
7. Holmlid, S.: Participative, co-operative, emancipatory: from participatory design to service design. In: First Nordic Conference on Service Design and Service Innovation (2009)
8. Doolani, S., et al.: A review of extended reality (XR) technologies for manufacturing training. Technologies **8**(4) (2020). https://doi.org/10.3390/technologies8040077
9. Mathew, P., Pillai, A.: Role of immersive (XR) technologies in improving healthcare competencies: a review. In: Virtual Augmented Reality in Education, Art, Museums, pp. 23–46 (2020)
10. Matthews, B., See, Z.S., Day, J.: Crisis and extended realities: remote presence in the time of COVID-19. Media Int. Aust. **178**(1) (2021). https://doi.org/10.1177/1329878X20967165
11. Caudell, T.P., Mizell, D.W.: Augmented reality: an application of heads-up display technology to manual manufacturing processes (2003). https://doi.org/10.1109/hicss.1992.183317
12. Chen, P., Liu, X., Cheng, W., Huang, R.: A review of using augmented reality in education from 2011 to 2016. In: Innovations in Smart Learning. Lecture Notes in Educational Technology. Springer, Singapore (2017). https://doi.org/10.1007/978-981-10-2419-1_2. 9789811024184
13. Dede, C.: Immersive interfaces for engagement and learning. Science **323**(5910) (2009). https://doi.org/10.1126/science.1167311
14. Sotiriou, S., Bogner, F.X.: Visualizing the invisible: augmented reality as an innovative science education scheme. Adv. Sci. Lett. **1**(1) (2011). https://doi.org/10.1166/asl.2008.012
15. Akçayir, M., Akçayir, G., Pektaş, H.M., Ocak, M.A.: Augmented reality in science laboratories: the effects of augmented reality on university students' laboratory skills and attitudes toward science laboratories. Comput. Hum. Behav. **57** (2016). https://doi.org/10.1016/j.chb. 2015.12.054
16. Chang, Y.J., Kang, Y.S., Huang, P.C.: An augmented reality (AR)-based vocational task prompting system for people with cognitive impairments. Res. Dev. Disabil. **34**(10) (2013). https://doi.org/10.1016/j.ridd.2013.06.026

17. Chen, C.H., Lee, I.J., Lin, L.Y.: Augmented reality-based self-facial modeling to promote the emotional expression and social skills of adolescents with autism spectrum disorders. Res. Dev. Disabil. **36** (2015). https://doi.org/10.1016/j.ridd.2014.10.015

18. Kellems, R.O., Cacciatore, G., Osborne, K.: Using an augmented reality–based teaching strategy to teach mathematics to secondary students with disabilities. Career Dev. Transit. Except. Individ. **42**(4) (2019). https://doi.org/10.1177/2165143418822800

19. Sunrise Medical. Realidad virtual y discapacidad física: la posibilidad de romper cualquier barrera (2018). https://www.sunrisemedical.es/blog/%0Arealidad-virtual-discapacidad/

20. Jiménez, R.: Realidad Virtual, su Presente y Futuro. Univ. Católica Nuestra Señora la Asunción, vol. 1 (2014)

21. Franco, F.G.: Virtual Reality and Disability (1994)

22. Pinzón, I.D., Moreno, J.E.: Realidad virtual como medio facilitador de actividad física en población en situación de discapacidad. Cuerpo Cult. y Mov. **10**(2) (2020). https://doi.org/10.15332/2422474x/6232

23. Sohrabei, S., Atashi, A.: Application of virtual reality in rehabilitation of disabilities: a mini review. J. Pharm. Pharmacol. **9**(5) (2021). https://doi.org/10.17265/2328-2150/2021.05.005

24. Rosli, Z., Shahbodin, F.: Integrating mathematics problem solving process: a virtual reality learning approach. Politek. JAMBI 12 (2018). Indonesia

25. Ahn, S.N.: Combined effects of virtual reality and computer game-based cognitive therapy on the development of visual-motor integration in children with intellectual disabilities: a pilot study. Occup. Ther. Int. **2021** (2021). https://doi.org/10.1155/2021/6696779

26. Chau, P.H., et al.: Feasibility, acceptability, and efficacy of virtual reality training for older adults and people with disabilities: single-arm pre-post study. J. Med. Internet Res. **23**(5) (2021). https://doi.org/10.2196/27640

27. Farshid, M., Paschen, J., Eriksson, T., Kietzmann, J.: Go boldly!: explore augmented reality (AR), virtual reality (VR), and mixed reality (MR) for business. Bus. Horiz. **61**(5) (2018). https://doi.org/10.1016/j.bushor.2018.05.009

28. Coutrix, C., Nigay, L.: Mixed reality: a model of mixed interaction. In: Proceedings of the Workshop on Advanced Visual Interfaces 2006 (2006). https://doi.org/10.1145/1133265.1133274

29. Rogers-Shaw, C., Carr-Chellman, D.J., Choi, J.: Universal design for learning: guidelines for accessible online instruction. Adult Learn. **29**(1) (2018). https://doi.org/10.1177/1045159517735530

30. Rao, K., Meo, G.: Using universal design for learning to design standards-based lessons. SAGE Open **6**(4) (2016). https://doi.org/10.1177/2158244016680688

31. Graham, A.K., Wildes, J.E., Reddy, M., Munson, S.A., Barr Taylor, C., Mohr, D.C.: User-centered design for technology-enabled services for eating disorders. Int. J. Eat. Disord. **52**(10) (2019). https://doi.org/10.1002/eat.23130

32. Galeano, R.: DISEÑO CENTRADO EN EL USUARIO. Rev. Educ. Comun. Tecnol. **2**(4) (2008). http://revistaq.upb.edu.co

33. Dopp, A.R., Parisi, K.E., Munson, S.A., Lyon, A.R.: A glossary of user-centered design strategies for implementation experts. Transl. Behav. Med. **9**(6) (2019). https://doi.org/10.1093/tbm/iby119

34. Hamzah, M.L., Ambiyar, A., Rizal, F., Simatupang, W., Irfan, D., Refdinal, R.: Development of augmented reality application for learning computer network device. Int. J. Interact. Mob. Technol. **15**(12) (2021). https://doi.org/10.3991/ijim.v15i12.21993

35. Afnan, Muhammad, K., Khan, N., Lee, M.Y., Imran, A.S., Sajjad, M.: School of the future: a comprehensive study on the effectiveness of augmented reality as a tool for primary school children's education. Appl. Sci. **11**(11) (2021). https://doi.org/10.3390/app11115277

36. Krajčovič, M., Gabajová, G., Matys, M., Grznár, P., Dulina, Ľ., Kohár, R.: 3D interactive learning environment as a tool for knowledge transfer and retention. Sustainability **13**(14) (2021). https://doi.org/10.3390/su13147916

37. Zucchi, S., Fuchter, S.K., Salazar, G., Alexander, K.: Combining immersion and interaction in XR training with 360-degree video and 3D virtual objects (2020). https://doi.org/10.1109/ISMCR51255.2020.9263732

38. van Wyk, E.A., de Villiers, M.R.: An evaluation framework for virtual reality safety training systems in the South African mining industry. J. South. Afr. Inst. Min. Metall. **119**(5) (2019). https://doi.org/10.17159/2411-9717/53/2019

39. Lonchamp, J.: A structured conceptual and terminological framework for software process engineering (1993). https://doi.org/10.1109/SPCON.1993.236823

40. Conradi, R., Fernström, C., Fuggetta, A.: Concepts for Evolving Software Processes. Res. Stud. Press, pp. 9–31 (1994)

41. Cristián Andrés, R.R.: MODELADO Y MEJORA DE PROCESOS DE SOFTWARE. Pontificia Universidad Católica de Valparaíso (2012)

42. Acuña, S., Ferré, X.: Software process modelling. In: Handbook of Software Engineering and Knowledge Engineering Fundamentals, vol. 1, p. 193 (2001)

43. Chaves, M.: La ingeniería de requerimientos y su importancia en el desarrollo de proyectos de software. InterSedes Rev. las Sedes Reg. **VI**(10), 1–13 (2005). http://www.redalyc.org/articulo.oa?id=66612870011%0ACómo citar

44. Sommerville, I.: Ingeniería de Software (2011)

Hoope Project: User-Centered Design Process Applied in the Implementation of Augmented Reality for Children with ASD

Monica. R. Romero[1]([⊠]) [ID], Ivana Harari[1] [ID], Javier Diaz[1] [ID], and Estela Macas[2] [ID]

[1] Faculty of Computer Science, National University of La Plata, LINTI, Calle 50 y 120, La Plata, Buenos Aires, Argentina
{monica.romerop,iharari,jdiaz}@info.unlp.edu.ar
[2] International Ibero-American University - UNINI Mx, Calle 15 y 36, Campeche, Mexico
estela.macas@doctorado.unini.edu.mx

Abstract. In the present investigation, a little-known disciplinary field that integrates aspects of computer science is delved into: HCI human-computer interaction, usability, accessibility, and on the other hand, children with ASD. The scope of the research includes the analysis, design and implementation of software that uses augmented reality in a playful environment with the aim of reinforcing educational aspects of children diagnosed with ASD, it is in a stage of development and research, currently working on a proof of concept through the implementation of a prototype, the previous studies have been worked for a period of 4 years where aspects related to DCU were considered in a particular way,

Keywords: Accessibility · AR · Autism · User centered design · HCI · Prototype · TIC · ASD

1 Introduction

Autism Spectrum Disorder from now on ASD is a complex neurological disorder [1] which usually lasts a lifetime. Autism is defined as a serious disorder that affects several areas of development [2], defined by other authors as a pervasive developmental disorder [3], is detected, and is externalized through poor communication [4–6]. Difficulty establishing social relationships with their environment [7], and limitation in language, additionally they present problems with the imagination [8] and flexibility of thought [9].

On the other hand, augmented reality, hereinafter RA, is a technology that allows the user to interact with the physical and real world that surrounds him. [10], is the combination of virtual objects, such as 3D graphics or animations, with real environments [11–15].

When we talk about ASD, we glimpse a particular world, complex and difficult to access [16], there are many scientific questions that remain unanswered. In the last 10 years, researchers have carried out studies aimed at improving the living conditions of children diagnosed with ASD [17], through the use of new technologies known as emerging technologies in this particular case we refer to augmented reality [18–21].

AR is used in teaching-learning processes at different levels from preschool to university [22], Gavilanes who considers that AR revolutionizes educational processes at all academic levels due to its high level of motivation and innovation[17]in conjunction with Jaramillo who defines that augmented reality systems enrich real environments with additional information generated by computer [23] due to the unique characteristics that it presents and the motivation that the experience of new learning represents for the students [24, 25].

This study is structured as follows: Sect. 2 explains the project called Esperanza. Section 3 explains the materials and methods that were used in the execution of the investigation. Section 4 presents the results of the study, finally Sect. 5 establishes the conclusions reached from the current execution of the work framed within the doctoral research.

2 Project Hope Motivation

After the studies carried out for this project, there is documentary evidence that AR is a tool that allows improving teaching-learning processes in children with autism. [26–29], of the studies analyzed after a systematic review [30, 31] there are still aspects that have not been addressed in depth, especially focused on experimental work with children with ASD, there is no documented evidence that the construction of software products has implicit at least a minimum percentage of techniques based on user-centered design henceforth HCI [32–34].

On the other hand, the Esperanza Project is developed in the LINTI New Computer Technologies Research Laboratory, of the Computer Science Faculty of the National University of La Plata, Argentina. This project aims to: analyze, investigate, develop, implement and experiment by creating a prototype that makes use of AR to complement educational activities in children diagnosed with ASD, it seeks to know if augmented reality facilitates teaching-learning processes.

The Esperanza project has an approximate development time of 4 years, of which the stated objectives have been successfully completed, such as: The analysis, design and implementation of a software product, through a method to reinforce certain teaching-learning processes of children with TORCH. Figure 1 shows the different phases:

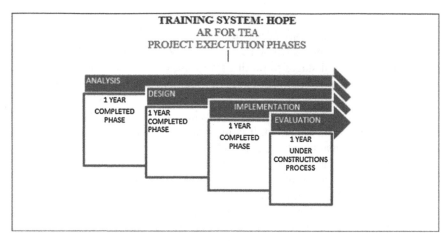

Fig. 1. Design process of the Esperanza project.

3   Methodology

The present work proposes the design of software created from a DCU perspective for children with ASD, the research is presented in the opposite direction to what our knowledge in computer science generally indicates, even though it is a project focused on the construction of a software product - a strongly technological component, we changed this paradigm, and The research began with a study of the end user and their relationship with the environment (children with ASD), for this purpose the particularities of the user were studied, in a broad sense the research was framed in the disorder and in the pedagogical strategies adopted, how and when it is detected, how it is diagnosed, its characteristics, what is important or what are the premises for a child with ASD to learn, how technology affects these children, after this first approach, we understood the child, affections, family, fears.

We begin a new stage, where with the previous information it is sought to estab-lish which technology is better for these children, the use of emerging technology was determined: two of the technologies were analyzed: virtual reality and augmented real-ity, choosing the latter since one of the problems that virtual reality presented is the immersion that it causes in the user, which was an inconvenience detected by the mul-tidisciplinary team that participated as an expert judgment in the investigation, since a reflection was made and it was indicated that one of the problems detected in a child with ASD is the lack of connection with the present with reality, with the professionals that surround him and that virtual reality, far from helping us, could deteriorate this condi-tion, Thus, the use of AR was chosen, which was focused on educational use, including it in certain teaching-learning processes through software with playful characteristics.

The first step was to know how these children learn, unlike other users, a child with ASD is not alone, since he is highly dependent on his family circle (father/mother), and support (teachers, therapists, medical personnel), this made us rethink the original approach since if we wanted the experience to be truly purposeful, our user had to be seen from a new perspective where the needs grow based on the fact that these children are not independent and generally need constant accompaniment.

The investigative process is defined as exploratory, descriptive. and experimental, the project defined several stages to fulfill its purpose where experimental approaches involving users were carried out, from 2017 to February 2021, with the participation of 300 people related to the TEA, some of them providing qualitative information and others qualitative, several studies of various types have been generated that have helped to reinforce the present investigation, it is important to indicate that this process was worked with the accompaniment, support and constant guidance of an academic team from the UNLP -and even more so with a research laboratory focused on new LINTI technologies, together with a multidisciplinary team: parents of children with ASD, accompanying teachers of children with ASD,

The evaluation process of the interaction of a child with ASD consisted of an intrinsic hardware component to bring it closer to the software product, in our case we tested technological devices such as: laptop, smartphone, virtual reality headset, 3D glasses, Kinect) in a progressive process. We show it in Fig. 2 where the four interactions that have been worked on around the project are shown.

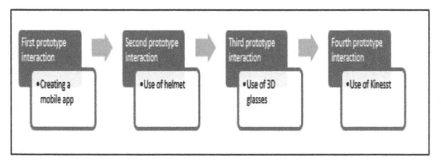

Fig. 2. Prototype designs – Esperanza Project iterations.

3.1 Test of Concept

In this context, concept tests were planned based on different iterations that allowed us to build the prototype of the Esperanza project.

The stages where the original ideas of a product development prototype were defined and conceptualized are defined below, the same ones that have evolved over time, the product has been built from a user-centered approach and in an interactive way, expressed Otherwise, we can indicate that, as we carry out concept tests, the prototype has been fed back, seeking to satisfy the needs of a user that has specific characteristics, in each interaction we verify particular details, so the software design was many times modified, and has been conceived through countless approaches, tests and with the participation of children with ASD supported by a multidisciplinary team.

These meetings were planned to carry out the following stages:

Initial Stage: Call, conditioning, presentation of the prototype.

User research stage: a multidisciplinary team was summoned to carry out the field research.

HCI evaluation stage: in each interaction of the models defined for the prototype, usability testing was carried out observing the interaction between the children with ASD summoned and the multidisciplinary group that participates as an observer, as a guide or as a support and the device (mobile app, helmet, goggles, Kinect). In this project, three of the first prototypes were eliminated for not meeting user expectations.

Reflection and debate stage: after the practical experience, changes were made to the initial prototype, which allowed the project to be assertively consolidated.

Prototype 1: Software and Smart Phone. In the first prototype created in the Esperanza Project, we bet on the review of educational applications created for mobile phones, this proposal supported teaching-learning processes mediated through AR technology, through activities such as imitation, classification, segregation, for this purpose we used cards that allowed the visualization of images of domestic and wild animals in AR through the smartphone, a curricular plan was proposed where some objectives were defined and the evaluation carried out on the child once we carried out the intervention through several sessions It was carried out with the measurement of certain achievements of an indicative, communicational type.

The difficulties that this prototype presented was that it was limited to work at a table and the participation of the teacher, since the child felt fear, that is, he did not want to have the telephone in his hands, so therapies in this sense should necessarily be carried out in the same place, keeping in mind the treating professional who guided and performed the interaction with the hardware and software. However, we were looking for mobility and independence of the child. Figure 3 shows the therapist working with a child with ASD at a table in the children's center and with the use of the smartphone, children with ASD usually tend to stand, move constantly and find it difficult to follow the instructions required. a constant support, for this prototype, in addition to the software, a curricular plan had to be worked on,

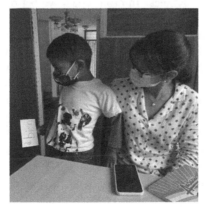

Fig. 3. Designs of software and smartphone prototypes Proyecto Esperanza.

Prototype 2: Software and Use of HDM Helmet. In prototype two, created in the Esperanza Project, we opted for software review, we wanted to use a virtual reality headset (HMD) with the purpose of training social skills in a controlled, repeatable, and safe virtual environment. For this purpose, we used VR-HMD, we specified a curricular plan where some objectives and evaluation through achievements were defined.

The difficulties that this prototype presented was that it carried out an immersion process and the child generated little or nothing feedback with the teacher, followed by the little tolerance of using the helmet, in the planned sessions the time established by the that the work was finished earlier than planned and remained unfinished, even though we achieved the first objective, which consisted of the child's mobility and independence, the learning objectives were not achieved.

In summary, the acceptability to the child was limited, as was the practicality of its use.

Prototype 3: Software and Use of 3d Glasses. In prototype three created in the Esperanza Project, we bet on the use of 3D glasses, our intention was to train teaching-learning processes using software. For this purpose, we used Google -glass, we specified a curricular plan where some objectives and evaluation through achievements were defined.

The difficulties presented by this prototype, was the little tolerance of using the glasses, in the planned sessions the established time was not fulfilled, therefore, the work was finished before the planned and was left unfinished, after the experience with the prototype 2 and prototype 3 we understood that the children with ASD with whom we found ourselves doing the field work felt uncomfortable when trying to put the glasses on them, even when a prior knowledge process was carried out, even the teacher and treating staff used the glasses during the therapies so that it becomes an element in a certain common way, but it was not assertive, despite achieving the mobility and independence of the child, the sessions did not end and therefore the learning objectives were not achieved.

Prototype 4: Software and Kinect. In prototype 4 we bet on the use of natural user interfaces that allow the child to have mobility, freedom, we seek to provide educators with effective strategies that allow them to have greater effectiveness in the teaching-learning processes in children with ASD, so that we develop a playful software to learn certain processes, for this purpose we use a Kinect device and we develop a game called Hoope, we use adaptations to allow the model to meet expectations. For the intervention phase, strategies are proposed to carry out a playful activity mediated through technology using the Hoope system. This system allows the child to interact alone or with the help of the professional who guides the session.

We established and organized the educational process and the environment used for the intervention, this favors learning, understanding of situations, independence from constant reinforcements, and minimization of conflicts caused by confusion or concern. Due to the interest in visual rather than auditory perception, it is essential that each activity is visually structured in a way that promotes understanding and motivation. In Fig. 4 shown below we indicate how the proof of concept of prototype four was carried out, in the first image the staff of the Therapy center, psychologist and psych pedagogue

Fig. 4. Designs of software prototypes and Kinect Esperanza Project.

are shown, in the other photograph we observe a child with ASD who participate in the project by approaching the computer screen.

4 Results

Under the premise of man-computer iteration, the Esperanza project has allowed an approach to the characteristics and particularities of a user (child diagnosed with ASD), the intention was to know and adapt the product to the needs, this process has been carried out through several tests of concept, where as a starting point we carry out the analysis, design and implementation of prototypes that were tested in real environments in educational centers for children with special abilities, perhaps one of the heuristics reached in the investigation is the complexity that the context represents of testing children with ASD.

To date, work has been done on the analysis, design and implementation of four prototypes, the same ones that have been reviewed, used, evaluated not only by the user for whom the product is intended, in our particular case, children with ASD, but additionally other actors involved in the educational process were actively involved, authorities of the educational center who should know the project, its objective, the proposed scope and more than all the possible benefits of having the results first hand, it is imperative to indicate that For almost four years we have collected valuable information that can only be collected through field research, interacting with the study population.

As a starting point, we made a call to the users to participate in the study, the intention is to present the Hope Project, the objectives it pursues, we worked with the parents through informed consent, we also worked with the authorities of the center, and with the treating professionals, to carry out the experimentation, finally this stage ends up teaching the prototype how it works and what it does, how the interventions will be carried out and their duration.

In the second stage, defined as user research, the support of a multidisciplinary team was requested to carry out the field research, the intention is to collect the different points of view of the professionals. For example, in the educational area, a special education teacher establishes a curricular work plan and evaluates whether the learning achievements were achieved, on the other hand, the psychologist carries out the accompaniment for the experimentation with the created product and collects from the first source the behavior of the child, evaluates aspects such as visual contact, non-visual, stress, ICT professionals focus on verifying if the product meets software quality parameters, that is, it is easy to understand for the user, it is adaptable.

Student's t-Test. For the study, we carried out a statistical procedure defined as T Test, or single sample, previously we verified that the values of the sample taken met a normality parameter, (n less than 30), since it was used for the evaluation of the various group prototypes. of independent variables that did not have a specific relationship. We use an alternative hypothesis where we indicate that each of the prototypes put under consideration are different from one another and therefore in the evaluation the participants decided to qualify some variables as numerical data we evaluate the prototypes and as variable data of groups we evaluate: the device, Experimentation with ASD, and Curricular Assessment.

For this as a research team we define a:

- Null Hypothesis: which establishes that there is similarity of the prototypes.
- Alternative or researcher hypothesis: We propose that there are differences in the prototypes to be evaluated despite being measured by the same variables.

We established the level of significance $= 5\% = 0.05$, where, if P in the study would result in a higher level of significance than that established as 0.05, the null hypothesis is discarded and the alternative hypothesis is accepted. Then the most relevant value of the table corresponds to the bilateral SIg, where the estimated value of P is greater than 0.05, so the null hypothesis is discarded and the researcher's hypothesis is accepted, then it can be concluded that the prototypes are different even when have evaluated the same parameters (Table 1).

Table 1. Single sample test.

	TEST-VALUE = 0					
	you	gl	Next (2-sided)	Mean difference	Ninety-five percent confidence interval of the difference	
					Lower	Fig
Prototype I mobile app	2,199	Eleven	0.050	7.8333	−0.009	15,675
Prototype II helmet	2,182	Eleven	0.052	5,5000	−0.049	11,049
Prototype III glasses	2,195	Eleven	0.051	7.1667	−0.021	14,354
Prototype IV Kinect	2,199	Eleven	0.050	8.5000	−0.009	17,009

In the third stage of evaluation of the HCI: considered one of the most important for our project, it was framed in a testing process and user interactions with the product, in this stage usability testing was carried out observing the interaction between the children with ASD summoned and the multidisciplinary group that participates as a direct observer, the teacher or therapist as a guide or support, in the technological field we have two factors: software and hardware, the device (smartphone + mobile app, helmet, glasses, Kinect). In the evaluation process, three dimensions were considered, encompassed in the following aspects: 1) Device or hardware used for the proof of concept, in our case several characteristics are defined to evaluate the use of the device: attractive, functional, aesthetic,

The following were taken into account: 2) Experimentation of the child with ASD, we seek to determine some aspects inherent to the user versus the use, experience with the product and the reaction that is generated, we seek through direct observation to collect the impressions in the experimentation of the software in the sessions planned for this purpose, the visual communication maintained by the child, verbal communication, eye contact and their level of stress of each of the prototypes were evaluated.

Finally, and no less important, we focus on the teaching-learning processes that can be reinforced through the use of AR, 3) Learning process of the child with ASD, we seek to determine some aspects inherent to the user how much he learns, if he is able to specify certain actions, through the software, these previously planned actions are measured through cognitive, procedural or communicational indicators, experience with the product and the assertiveness it generates, for the measurement of the prototypes the Likert scale was used evaluating the device, the experience of the use of the device by a child with ASD, and finally to curricular evaluation the results obtained can be seen in Table 2.

Table 2. Evaluation of built prototypes

User centered design	Characteristic to evaluate	Prototype I: mobile application	Prototype II: helmet	Prototype III: glasses	Prototype IV: kinect
Device	Attractive	4	3	4	5
	Functionality	4	4	3	4
	Esthetic	4	3	4	4
	Information	4	4	4	5
Child experimentation TEA	Verbal communication	4	3	4	4
	Non-verbal communication	5	2	2	5
	Eye contact	4	0	4	5
	stress level	4	3	5	5
Curriculum evaluation	Cognitive indicator	5	4	4	5
	Procedural indicator	4	4	5	4
	Communicative indicator	5	3	4	5
Final weighting		47	33	43	**51**

As a result of all this multidisciplinary and cooperation work, a phase of reflection and debate is concluded, where after the practical experience, changes were made to the initial prototype, which allowed the project to be assertively consolidated.

This is how, according to the results we show in Fig. 3, on the X axis we have entered those characteristics that were evaluated through the proof of concept of each of the prototypes, in terms of the device, the experimentation carried out and finally the curricular evaluation, the scale in terms of the measurement carried out goes from 1 to 5, the first being the lowest of the qualifications and 5 the maximum, the final weighting process can be carried out with a number less than or equal to 55, which represents our 100% for the qualification obtained from each of the prototypes built in the investigative process.

It is important to indicate that prototypes 2 and 3 are the ones that received the least reception, since the child with ASD did not want to use superimposed elements on his body, the fact of using the glasses was not an easy idea, despite the fact that as a team we carried out some strategies teachers and therapists used the same prior to the intervention during regular therapies, exposure sessions were held, trying to find a possible adaptation, but these strategies simply at the time of experimentation did not give a favorable result, in the same way prototype 2 where a virtual reality headset was used, it turned out to be even more invasive, causing the child to increase his stress levels and want to leave the therapy session immediately. Figure 5 shows the scores collected by each prototype evaluated according to the variables defined in each of the characteristics analyzed, each prototype is determined with a color, blue for the prototype that uses a smartphone, in red for the prototype that uses the helmet, in green the prototype that uses 3D glasses, in lilac the prototype referring to the use of Kinect.

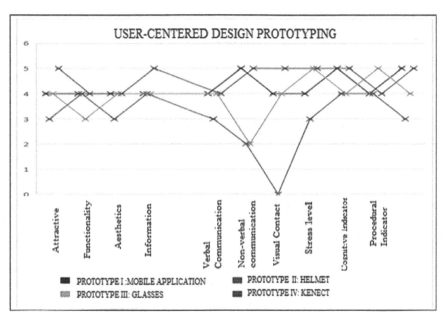

Fig. 5. Weightings achieved by the prototypes made for the Esperanza Project

5   Discussion and Conclusion

In the present investigative work, a study of techniques related to user-centered design DCU in children with ASD has been carried out, a space little studied due to the complexity of planning for the execution of usability tests, additionally exploring usability and accessibility in a software product.

The methodology is a heuristic that created and adapted where a series of phases proposed that allow an adequate DCU to be conducted, certainly these processes are necessary to bring exceptionally reliable products to the market and that have been perceived from a multidisciplinary field trying to have feedback. of the end user, through the analysis, design and subsequent implementation of software tools that seek, from an innovative and simple proposal, to improve the quality of life of children diagnosed with ASD.

So far, four prototypes have created for the Esperanza project. This, far from discouraging us, tells us that we are on the right track, since the product or prototype that obtained the best rating in the evaluation will be accepted and will serve to reinforce some important aspects of the project. teaching learning. The tool, and a plan has been developed for its validation in therapy centers.

The iterations (prototypes) that were carried out in the conception of this research began with the analysis, design and implementation of an app (mobile applications), this prototype was assertive in several aspects, but it avoided the mobility and independence of the child already for to be used he needed to be at a desk accompanied by his teacher, it was observed that the child was afraid to take the smartphone in his hands, so the multidisciplinary team decided to look for a new alternative.

In the second interaction, it was sought that the child will use a helmet where the child would be provided with the mobility that was not obtained with prototype one, however, the helmet turned out to be invasive and moved away from the original conceptualization in terms of augmented reality. the feeling of immersion so this prototype after a proof of concept was discarded.

In the third interaction we decided to bet on the glasses (Google Glass) that allow the deployment of augmented reality and at the same time allow the mobility of the child with ASD, however, when carrying out the experimentation the child could not bear the use of glasses for more than two minutes, which did not allow the established sessions (22 min) to be carried out for the development and intervention of the work plan. After a meeting with the multidisciplinary team, this prototype was discarded.

Finally, the perspectives of the multidisciplinary team are fulfilled in terms of fulfilling characteristics such as mobility that has been provided through prototype four, this is how the use of a Kinect that allows the use of natural user interfaces, and the use of augmented reality was evaluated. Therefore, the system was accepted immediately, currently several tests have been conducted on this prototype that have been satisfactory and it is desired to expand the sample to users with ASD of various conditions to evaluate the result.

We thank the National Secretary of Higher Education Science and Technology SENESCYT-Ecuador for the support provided, as well as the Research Laboratory of New Computer Technologies - LINTI of the Faculty of Computer Science, National University of La Plata.

References

1. Enríquez Pigazo, I.: Trastornos del Espectro Autista: estudio de un caso y propuesta de intervención logopédica (2018)
2. Bleuler, E., Minkowski, E., Manual, S.: El trastorno del espectro autista: aspectos etiológicos, diagnósticos y terapéuticos. Revista Médica del Instituto Mexicano del Seguro Social **55**(2), 214–222 (2017)
3. Contini, L.E., Astorino, F., Manni, D.C.: Estimación de la prevalencia temprana de Trastornos del Espectro Autista. Santa Fe-Argentina. Boletín Técnico **13**, 12–13 (2017)
4. Guzman, G.B., et al.: Introducción a la neurobiolog ' ia y neurofisiolog ' ia del Trastorno del Espectro Autista Introducción a la neurobiología y neurofisiología del Trastorno del Espectro Autista Introduction to the neubiology and neurofisiology of the Autism Spectrum Disord (2016). https://doi.org/10.5839/rcnp.2016.11.02.05
5. Hervás Zúñiga, A., Balmaña, N., Salgado, M.: Los trastornos del espectro autista: aportes convergentes. Pediatr. Aten. Primaria **XXI**(2), 92–108 (2017)

6. Hervás Zúñiga, A.: Un autismo, varios autismos. Variabilidad fenotípica en los trastornos del espectro autista. Rev. Neurol. **62**(S01), 9 (2016). https://doi.org/10.33588/rn.62s01.2016068
7. Rodríguez Medina, J.: Mediacion entre iguales, competencia social y percepcion interpersonal de los ninos con TEA en el entorno escolar (2019). https://doi.org/10.35376/10324/39475
8. Sagarzazu Sacristán, M.: ¿Por qué pinto así? La expresión plástica y artística en adolescentes con Síndrome de Asperger, Autismo de Alto Funcionamiento y/o Trastornos del Espectro Autista, vol. 2017, no. cc, p. 1 (2017)
9. Tsai, L.Y.: Impact of DSM-5 on epidemiology of autism spectrum disorder. Res. Autism Spectr. Disord. **8**(11), 1454–1470 (2014). https://doi.org/10.1016/j.rasd.2014.07.016
10. Aumentada, R., Las, U.N.A.E.D.E.: Aplicaciones de los dispositivos móviles augmented reality, an evolution of theapplication. Rev. medios y Educ. pp. 57 (2012)
11. Sánchez, A.: Evaluación de la tecnología de realidad aumentada móvil en entornos educativos del ámbito de la arquitectura y la edificación. Univ. Politécnica Calalunya, no. Ega Ii, p. 339 (2013)
12. Espinosa, C.P.: Realidad aumentada y educación: análisis de experiencias prácticas augmented reality and education: analysis of practical experiencies. Pixel – Bit. Rev. Medios y Educ. 187–203 (2015). https://doi.org/10.12795/pixelbit.2015.i46.12
13. Fracchia, C., Alonso, A., Martins, A.: Realidad Aumentada aplicada a la enseñanza de Ciencias Naturales. Rev. Iberoam. Educ. en Tecnol. y Tecnol. en Educ. (2015)
14. Rovira, U., Rovira, U., Rovira, U.: El papel de las tecnologías digitales en la intervención educativa de niños con trastorno del espectro autista autism spectrum disorder José-Luis Lázaro-Cantabrana Mercè Gisbert-Cervera, no. 4, pp. 41–54 (2018)
15. Herrera, G., et al.: Pictogram Room: Aplicación de tecnologías de interacción natural para el desarrollo del niño con autismo. Anu. Psicol. clínica y la salud = Annu. Clin. Heal. Psychol. **8**, 41–46 (2012)
16. Medina Rivilla, A., Rodríguez Serna, C.: Potenciar las capacidades de las personas. Modelo para facilitar la comunicación con estudiantes del espectro autista. Rev. Educ. Inclusiva **9**(1), 1–12 (2016)
17. Gavilanes, W., Abásolo Guerrero, M., Cuji, B.: Resumen de revisiones sobre Realidad Aumentada en educación. Rev. Espac. **39** (2018)
18. García Guillén, S., Garrote Rojas, D., Jiménez Fernández, S.: Uso de las TIC en el Trastorno de Espectro Autista: aplicaciones. Edmetic **5**(2), 134 (2016). https://doi.org/10.21071/edmetic.v5i2.5780
19. Basogain, X., Olabe, M., Espinosa, K., Rouèche, C., Olabe, J.C.: Realidad Aumentada en la Educación: una tecnología emergente. Basogain, X., Olabe, M., Espinosa, K., Rouèche, C., & Olabe, J. C. (n.d.). Realidad Aumentada en la Educación: una tecnología emergente. Rev. Mex. Tecnol. 2(3), 14 (2000). http://multimedia.ehu.es
20. Yuen, S.C.-Y., Yaoyuneyong, G., Johnson, E.: Augmented reality: an overview and five directions for AR in education. J. Educ. Technol. Dev. Exch. **4**(1), 119–140 (2011). https://doi.org/10.18785/jetde.0401.10
21. Andrés Roqueta, C., Benedito, I., Soria Izquierdo, E.: Uso de aplicaciones móviles para la evaluación de la comprensión emocional en niños y niñas con dificultades del Desarrollo. Rev. Psicol. y Educ. **12**(1), 7–18 (2017)
22. Lasheras Díaz, C.: La realidad aumentada como recurso educativo en la enseñanza de Español como lengua extranjera. Propuesta de intervención a partir de un manual, p. 63 (2018)
23. Jaramillo Henao, A.M., Silva Bolívar, G.J., Adarve Gómez, C.A., Velásquez Restrepo, S.M., Páramo Velásquez, C.A., Gómez Echeverri, L.L.: Aplicaciones de Realidad Aumentada en educación para mejorar los procesos de enseñanza-aprendizaje: una revisión sistemática Augmented Reality applications in education to improve teaching-learning processes: a systematic review Contenido. Espacios **39**(49), 15 (2018)

24. Gómez, B.D.: La necesidad de nuevas estrategias metodológicas en la educación inclusiva del alumnado autista [The need for new methodological strategies in inclusive education of autistic students]. Ensayos **28**(1), 15–23 (2013). https://doi.org/10.18239/ensayos.v28i0.345

25. Sánchez Bolado, J.: El potencial de la realidad aumentada en la enseñanza de español como lengua extranjera. Edmetic **6**(1), 62 (2016). https://doi.org/10.21071/edmetic.v6i1.5808

26. Romero, M., Harari, I.: Uso de nuevas tecnologías TICS -realidad aumentada para tratamiento de niños TEA un diagnóstico inicial. CienciAmérica **6**(3), 131–137 (2017)

27. Romero, M., Macas, E., Harari, I., Diaz, J.: Eje integrador educativo de las TICS: Caso de Estudio Niños con trastorno del espectro autista. SAEI, Simp. Argentino Educ. en Informática Eje, pp. 171–188 (2019)

28. Romero, M.R., Macas, E., Harari, I., Diaz, J.: Is it possible to improve the learning of children with ASD through augmented reality mobile applications? In: Botto-Tobar, M., Zambrano Vizuete, M., Torres-Carrión, P., Montes León, S., Pizarro Vásquez, G., Durakovic, B. (eds.) ICAT 2019. CCIS, vol. 1194, pp. 560–571. Springer, Cham (2020). https://doi.org/10.1007/978-3-030-42520-3_44

29. Romero, M.R., Diaz, J., Harari, I.: Impact of information and communication technologies on teaching-learning processes in children with special needs autism spectrum disorder, pp. 342–353 (2017)

30. Marín-Díaz, V., Cabero-Almenara, J., Gallego-Pérez, O.M.: Motivación y realidad aumentada: Alumnos como consumidores y productores de objetos de aprendizaje. Motivation and augmented reality: students as consumers and producers of learning objects. Aula Abierta **47**(3), 337 (2018). https://doi.org/10.17811/aula_abierta.47.3.2018.337

31. Láinez, B., Chocarro de Luis, E., Sancirián, J.H.B., López Benito, J.R.: Aportaciones de la Realidad Aumentada en la inclusión en el aula de estudiantes con Trastorno del Espectro Autista contributions of augmented reality in inclusive education with students with autism spectrum disorders. Rev. Educ. Mediática y TIC **7**(2), 120–134 (2018). https://doi.org/10.21071/edmetic.v7i2.10134

32. Almazán Tepliski, F.: Las claves de la usabilidad, los gurúes Nielsen y Krug. Serv. Digit. Bibl. del Congr. Nac. Chile (2005)

33. Macías Morales, M.G., Aguirre Intriago, K.E.: Propuesta tecnológica para el diseño de una página WEB usando los principios de usabilidad de Jakob Nielsen para optimizar el proceso embarque de la empresa TUCHOK S.A. (2017)

34. Sánchez, W.: La usabilidad en Ingeniería de Software: definición y características. Ingnovación. Rep. Investig. **2**, 7–21 (2011)

A User Evaluation Study of Augmented and Virtual Reality Tools for Training and Knowledge Transfer

Evangelia I. Zacharaki[1]([✉])([iD]), Andreas Triantafyllidis[2], Rosa Carretón[3],
Maria Loeck[3], Isidoros Michalellis[1], George Michalakis[1],
Georgios Chantziaras[2], Sofia Segkouli[2], Dimitrios Giakoumis[2],
Konstantinos Moustakas[1], Konstantinos Votis[2], and Dimitrios Tzovaras[2]

[1] VVR Group, Department of Electrical and Computer Engineering,
University of Patras, 26500 Patras, Greece
ezachar@upatras.gr
[2] Information Technologies Institute, Centre for Research and Technology Hellas,
57001 Thessaloniki, Greece
[3] Asociación Nacional de Fabricantes de Áridos, Pl. de las Cortes, 5, 7,
28014 Madrid, Spain
http://www.vvr.ece.upatras.gr

Abstract. Modern augmented and virtual reality (AR/VR) technology open multiple new capabilities in the way people interact, collaborate and deliver or receive information via digital interfaces. Industry workers and operators may especially benefit from such solutions that allow them to get trained, onsite or remotely, using digital copies of the workplace environment. This paper presents the development of AR/VR-based collaborative and telepresence tools, along with a web-based platform for knowledge exchange and interaction, as part of the Ageing@Work project, that enable easy transfer of know-how from experienced (possibly older) to novice workers. The remote collaboration tools facilitate variability in location and working hours, and thus promote age-neutralizing means of participation and cooperation, whereas the knowledge transfer tools support the ageing worker's leadership characteristics within the workplace community, allowing the company or work site to capitalize on her/his experience and expertise gained through the years. The tools were developed in accordance to a user-centred design process and were evaluated by 126 participants in total through online surveys in two pilot sites with regard to core Industry 4.0 processes of mining and machines production, as well as through off-pilot studies. This paper presents analytic outcomes of the assessment of knowledge transfer tools illustrating very positive results on the level of technology acceptance, and the overall potential of the developed solutions to support healthy and productive ageing of workers with enhanced workability.

This work has been supported by the EU Horizon2020 funded project "Smart, Personalized and Adaptive ICT Solutions for Active, Healthy and Productive Aging with enhanced Workability (Ageing@Work)" under Grant Agreement No. 826299.

M. Antona and C. Stephanidis (Eds.): HCII 2022, LNCS 13309, pp. 291–304, 2022.
https://doi.org/10.1007/978-3-031-05039-8_21

Keywords: Augmented reality · Virtual reality · Knowledge transfer ·
Remote collaboration · Technology acceptance · Ageing workers

1   Introduction

Industry appears increasingly dependent on the knowledge, skills and experience of their older workers [1]. This pushes companies to explore ways to keep
older workers employed for a longer period of time and also to support them
to maintain their work ability and increase their employability. There is systematic evidence that sustainable job longevity can be associated with positive
health outcomes. Work can have a positive effect on physical and mental health
and well-being for all workers if working conditions are appropriate [2,3]. For
example, keeping an employee integrated in a social environment such as work,
can provide health benefits [4], as social interaction helps preventing the loss of
cognitive functions [5].

Responding to this need for sustainable job longevity of ageing adult populations, however, is faced with both challenges and opportunities, some of which
arise from the changing workplace conditions. Both the shrinkage and ageing
of the workforce come at a time where Industry 4.0 is booming, resulting to an
ever-increasing impact on the way that contemporary industries, factories as well
as office workplaces, operate based on continuous advances in the fields of artificial intelligence, service and collaborative workspaces, etc. Notably, the tasks of
future companies operating in this context are anticipated to have an increasing
degree of freedom and less structure than before, with the workforce experiencing a change of role. More typical tasks are expected to fall within supervision
of the production line and solving of unexpected problems. Clearly, such positions where the employee acts as a problem solver can find major benefits from
the experience and skills of older workers. Novel work paradigms, such as those
introduced by the gig economy have shown that, once the working arrangements
and conditions are flexible enough and controlled by the worker, the worker may
prefer to remain at work for longer, even if it is sometimes required to learn
how to use a new technology. A core challenge nowadays concerns how this tendency of older workers to remain active at jobs of the gig economy, can as well
be migrated to further workplaces, such as industrial ones, allowing workers to
indulge similar benefits, while at the same time their skills and experience accu-
mulated over time remain valuable assets to the growth of diverse productive
sectors.

Companies have been trying to meet the challenges posed by an ageing workforce by adopting established occupational safety and health practices that promote sustainable working lives. Such practices include life-course approaches
to workplace health, workplace health promotion, introducing return-to-work
measures, adapting work to the individual, and providing structures for lifelong
learning. There are many successful cases that involve at least to a certain extent
the use of digital technologies (e.g. GPS-based personal emergency response systems, basic information technology systems); many of these practices, however,
although efficient, remain predominantly manual/offline.

In this paper we present and evaluate a series of highly adaptive ICT (Information and Communications Technology) tools, including augmented and virtual reality (AR/VR), developed as part of the Ageing@Work project, that envisions to counteract for crucial issues hindering the ageing workers' workability and well-being by facilitating them to remain active and productive for longer [6–8]. Specifically, we address the problem of lifelong learning and knowledge sharing between older and younger workers, as well as remote collaboration. Results and benefits of such solutions are numerous. More efficient and flexible transfer of knowledge by older experienced workers to younger workers allows to boost inter-generational communication and this gathered knowledge remains in the company's knowledge base, while also a worker's network can be created and maintained. In-time solution of problems is facilitated through real-time guidance and with lower risk, while also decreasing the occurrences of machinery downtime due to absence of guidance and mentoring. Surveillance worker duties enhancement increases the personal perceived security, reduces stress and accidents, and supports the decrease of memory of the ageing workforce. All these benefits may lead to increased workability and productivity.

2 Methodology

The Ageing@Work system provides advanced interfaces, in order to support workers' remote collaboration through telepresence, while workability enhancement is further empowered by advanced VR and AR-based lifelong learning tools. The virtual reality tools provide the necessary framework for more experienced workers to create a VR tutorial and load it into the application. On the other hand, less experienced workers can download a tutorial and get trained at home with a VR headset or at the workplace with an AR headset. In addition, the learning tools can provide training sessions for more experienced workers on new machines that they may need to learn to use. The AR platform aims to help workers in distance training, as well as into remote collaboration. The platform consists of two communication applications intended to be used by a remote supervisor (located, for example, at home) and a worker in the workplace, and uses intuitive digital instructions that enrich the physical environment of the workplace, thus facilitating the execution of tasks. Finally, the knowledge exchange platform is a web interface that provides two-way access to the knowledgebase and supports workers in the manufacturing process, allowing them to interact, collect and share relevant knowledge, ideas, and good practice.

2.1 Remote Collaboration Tools

This tool enables ageing workers to collaborate efficiently in a remote setup, to support functionalities like teleconferencing, to receive and offer realistic descriptions of industrial processes [8]. Moreover, the AR tools could also support lifelong learning by providing captured (recorded) sessions of telepresence meetings during unforeseen issues, complex machine maintenance, and support. These materials can be loaded into the Knowledgebase component and used by workers who are willing to learn new tasks and how to operate/service machines.

A basic set of background services is implemented to allow the AR view to work properly, and those include the sensing of the user's location and orientation, the object (machinery) detection in order to let the system know which machines are involved in the scene, and the image segmentation component which allows the 3D virtual object to be rendered in the correct position in relation to the world 3D coordinates (shopfloor coordinates). The AR view is responsible for synthesizing the view of the user through the AR glasses and includes the graphical user interface, the pushed (by the system) notifications, the projection of the element that the distant user may be pointing at, and finally the sound processing (alarms and the speech synchronization between the distant collaborators). To serve the need of educational content provision, the AR component may also offer the possibility to capture telepresence sessions in 2D videos and to upload those materials to the knowledgebase. This functionality is performed by a lightweight session management subcomponent. This architectural element is also responsible for initialing the telepresence session and for annotating the output 2D video recordings (with metadata like machine ids involved in the study, problems solved, timestamps, worker skills, a description of the physical context, etc.).

The physical view of the AR telepresence infrastructure is presented in Fig. 1. The on-site user (young worker) may raise an issue using the AR telepresence tool and podcast the image (through the camera of a head mounted display or an ordinary smartphone camera) to an experienced user (older worker) asking for advice and support. On the other end, the experienced user can interact through the tablet. The Ageing@Work system operates in the meantime to optimize the outcome of the telepresence tool. Specifically, it retrieves the worker having the appropriate experience and skills to support the raised issue and initiates the telepresence meeting, by loading the 3D models and the scenario to run. Figure 2 shows an application example of the AR tool and how it is used for remote worker collaboration.

2.2   VR and AR Based Lifelong Learning Tools

Lifelong learning tools can help the worker adapt to changes in the working environment through corresponding ICT-empowered training processes. These tools consist of components that support the creation and execution of a tutorial process in virtual environments [7,9]. The software implementation was performed in the Unity3D real time development platform, so the tutorial environment can be encoded in Unity Asset Bundles which are archive files that contain platform-specific assets (such as models, textures, audio clips) that can be loaded by Unity at run time. More precisely, the ageing worker can record the steps required to complete one or more tasks and create a tutorial. The tutorial can then be encoded to JSON format as a list of tutorial step objects, containing necessary data (such as the object unique ID, the type of interaction and human readable content), and shared using the knowledgebase API (application programming

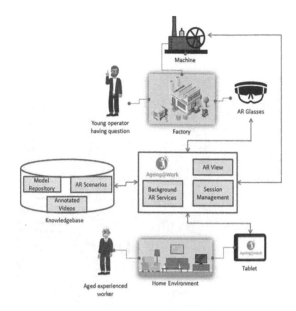

Fig. 1. The physical view of the AR telepresence tool.

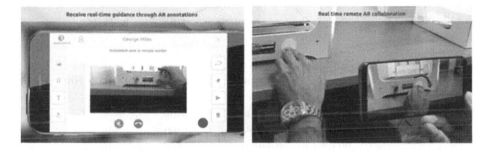

Fig. 2. Application example of AR tool (left) and remote worker collaboration tool (right).

interface). The less experienced worker can connect to the knowledgebase and choose the desired tutorial in order to get trained by following the tutorial steps and the indications recorded by the expert. The system loads from the Asset Bundles files of the 3D environment and sets up the scene in VR (or AR). The tutorial JSON description is decoded and an ordered list of the tutorial steps with the associated voice recordings are created. The user is guided in the training process in the VR environment through indications on the static objects (e.g. buttons) visualized by changing their material properties, or on the dynamic objects (e.g. levers, knobs) by animating ghost objects. A 2D visualization panel is projected in the users' front view in order to guide the trainee through the training process by illustrating the sequence of completed and upcoming steps, along with the performance after each executed task. An example of a user being trained in VR of how to operate a drilling machine is shown in Fig. 3.

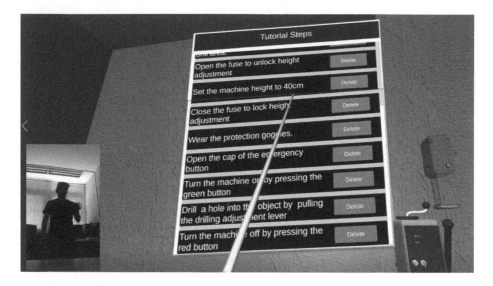

Fig. 3. Illustration of the 2D visualization panel of the VR tutorial creation module.

For the AR version of this tool, the tutorial process can be segmented into discrete steps, automatically or user controlled. Automatic steps' segmentation can be performed by utilizing the background AR services of the AR telepresence tool, such as object detection, location sensing, image segmentation and 3D visual object rendering. At the user-controlled scenario, the tutorials provide visual information to the user about the next steps, but no automatic evaluation is performed, instead the AR telepresence or AR capture is utilized.

2.3   Knowledge Exchange Platform (KEP)

A Knowledge Exchange Platform, in the form of a web-based forum, was implemented to support workers in their interaction and in sharing contextually relevant knowledge and ideas. The KEP enables the creation of user groups to better organize communication and manage the flow of information, workspace and trainings announcements. It communicates through proper routes with the knowledgebase, in order to store and retrieve valuable technical information, training material as well as best practices for both the manufacturing process and workspace procedures. To cater for social aspects, the platform includes social media features, like up/down-voting, options to follow other people and post to other social media. It also aids workers' engagement by rewarding them for contributing. Figure 4 illustrates the main categories and menu items of the KEP, along with a post of a user (question-response) on a job assignment.

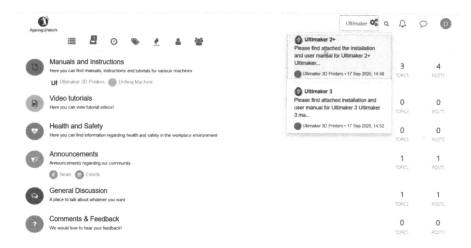

Fig. 4. The main menu of the knowledge exchange platform.

2.4 Evaluation Study

The developed tools were evaluated through online surveys administered through "Google Forms", as it is a simple platform easy to elaborate and complete. Specific sections were included to measure the degree of acceptance regarding the receipt of recommendations by the tool, as well as to measure issues related to privacy and data management. The participants were asked for data on work experience, frequency of use of technology and type of applications used, well-being and satisfaction at work, as well as for the management of personal data. Ethics and privacy issues were considered of high priority. The surveys were translated into local language (one in Spanish and one in German) to be managed by the pilots. In addition, for each of the surveys, videos and images have been included with the demonstration of the tools, to provide to the respondents a greater knowledge of the proposed solution and therefore leading to a more informed response.

To increase the number of respondents and plurality of their profiles, interest groups such as directors or owners of companies, experts in health and safety, lawyers, people dedicated to training or research in mining, etc., have been reached through an additional, *off-pilot*, study. This *off-pilot* study was launched from June to July 2021 and the distributed material had the same content as in the pilot surveys (translated in English).

3 Results

The valuation of the developed tools through online surveys allowed to reach a high number of respondents ($n = 126$) from the *in-pilot* group ($n = 62$), which consisted mainly of extractive industry workers (Asociación Nacional de Empresarios Fabricantes de Áridos – ANEFA) and the *off-pilot* group ($n = 64$)

with workers of diverse profiles and interests. This section presents summarized responses from the workers participating in the surveys. It is important to point out that even though the Ageing@Work solutions are designed for workers between 45 and 65 years old, it was decided to extend the survey to all workers regardless of their age and job, in order to draw conclusions about the future of Ageing@Work solutions and understand if the results obtained can be maintained in the medium and long term.

The profile and responses of each group of participants are presented in the next sections. However, the technology expertise level of the participants (including frequency and type of applications used for everyday life activities) is shown for both groups (pilot and off-pilot) here (in Table 1) in order to provide a better overview of the differences of the two groups and aid in the assessment of responses.

Table 1. Participants experience and use of technology (P: pilot group; OP:Off-pilot group).

Participants experience and frequency in technology use						
Years of experience	0–5	6–10	10–15	15–20	20–25	More than 25
	P: 1.6% OP: 23.4%	P: 3.2% OP: 9.4%	P: 1.6% OP: 21.9%	P: 24.2% OP: 9.4%	P: 27.4% OP: 18.8%	P: 41.9% OP:18.8%
Internet usage	Never	Once a week	More than once a week	Everyday		
	P: 0% OP: 0%	P: 0% OP: 0%	P: 4.8% OP: 0%	P: 95.2% OP: 100%		
Augmented Reality devices or tools	Never	Sometimes	Usually			
	P: 75.8% OP: 84.4%	P: 24.2% OP: 18.8%	P: 4.8% OP: 0%			
Virtual Reality devices or tools	Never	Sometimes	Usually			
	P: 58.1% OP: 71.9 %	P:41.9 % OP: 26.6%	P: 4.8% OP: 0%			

3.1 Pilot Study

Participants' Profile. The majority of the participants who have completed the survey were over the age of 45 years (79%). This is due to the fact that the average age of workers in the extractive industry has increased in recent years, because conditions in mining are harsh and unattractive to young professionals. The percentage of male and female respondents was the same. Most participants have had university education (75.8%). The participants' jobs were mobile machinery operator (8.1%), plant operator (1.6%), office worker (54.8%), remote technical assistant (3.2%), maintenance (6.5%), and other (35.5%), The majority of the workers (93.5%) had more than 15 years of work experience. Aspects of work-related well-being are illustrated in Fig. 5.

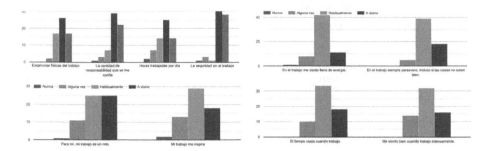

Fig. 5. Statistics on work-related well-being and job satisfaction and job engagement in the pilot group (the corresponding English translation is shown in Fig. 9). Top left: Aspects of the Job position; Top right: Vigor; Bottom left: Dedication; Bottom right: Absorption.

Tools Assessment. Statistics of collected data are presented in the form of percentages of respondents through histograms and bar plots. Results on technology acceptance, including the perceived ease of use and perceived usefulness, as well as on behavioural intention to use and self-efficacy, are shown in Fig. 6 and Fig. 7, respectively. Moreover, responses on data privacy and security are summarized in Fig. 8.

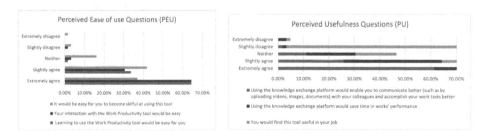

Fig. 6. Statistics on perceived ease of use (left) and on perceived usefulness (right) in the pilot group.

3.2 Off-pilot Study

In addition to Ageing@Work's pilot group, the survey has been circulated to 64 (off-pilot) workers.

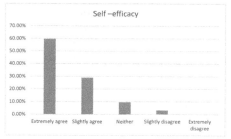

Fig. 7. Statistics on behavioural intention (left) and on self-efficacy (right) in the pilot group.

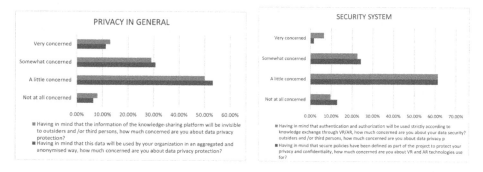

Fig. 8. Results on privacy in general (left) and on the security system (right) in the pilot group.

Participants' Profile. Most of the participants were under the age of 45 years (59.4%) and have a higher education (Masters) degree (50%). The percentage of male and female respondents was quite similar, tilting the balance slightly towards men, with a participation percentage of 54.7%, over 45.3% of female participation. The majority of the participants were office workers (70.3%), but included also remote technical assistants, data or research scientists, public employees, a nurse, and academic positions (faculty members, etc.) with variable years of work experience. Similarly to the pilot group, work-related well-being parameters are shown in Fig. 9.

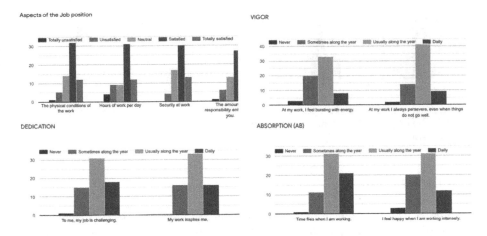

Fig. 9. Statistics on work-related well-being and job satisfaction and job engagement in the off-pilot study. Top left: Aspects of the Job position; Top right: Vigor; Bottom left: Dedication; Bottom right: Absorption

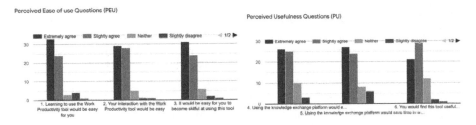

Fig. 10. Statistics on perceived ease of use (left) and usefulness (right) in the off-pilot study.

Fig. 11. Statistics on behavioural intention to use (left) and self-efficacy (right) in the off-pilot study.

Tools Assessment. Questions and statistics of responses on technology acceptance are illustrated in Fig. 10 (showing the perceived ease of use and usefulness) and Fig. 11 (summarizing the data on behavioral intention and self-efficacy), while data privacy and security concerns by the off-pilot group are shown in Fig. 12.

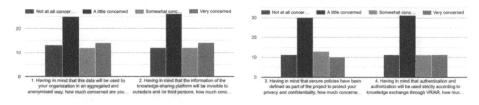

Fig. 12. Results on privacy in general (left) and on the security system (right) in the off-pilot group.

4   Discussion

The aim of this study was to shortly present and evaluate tools that support transferring the long-term experience of older workers to the younger ones. The results on the level of acceptance of the technology are very positive regarding the AR/VR tool and knowledge exchange platform. Regarding the perception of ease of use, the lowest percentage is obtained with respect to the ease of becoming an expert in its use. This reveals a certain reluctance of the users, considering it difficult to use this type of tool. This is expected as, according to the results on frequency of use, most users have never used AR/VR tools. Therefore, it is recommended to keep the tools simple, so that they are easy to be used by the average user, and allow them to focus on the training procedure. Regarding the level of perceived usefulness, the worst result is obtained with regards to considering the tool as a means to save time in carrying out tasks. This may be explained by the fact that some users find it difficult to become an expert in the use of the tools, thus would require more time in the process of familiarization (with the tools) and learning. This highlights again the need to simplify the tools and make them more intuitive. These conclusions are supported by measuring self-efficacy, that shows that about 89% of the respondents in the pilot group extremely or slightly agree that they could use this tool if someone first showed them how to operate it. In addition, when asking the participants of the extractive industry specific questions about the technology, 76–87% consider them attractive and useful in their jobs.

In respect to the off-pilot study, the results on the level of acceptance of the technology are very positive regarding the AR/VR tool and knowledge exchange platform. Regarding the perceived ease of use, 89% of the respondents (extremely or slightly) agree that the tool would be easy to use and that it would be easy to interact with it. In terms of becoming an expert in its use, there are also very positive results, with 86% of the respondents (extremely or slightly) agreeing that it would be easy to become skilled in the use of the tool. These very positive results may be due to a greater knowledge of the group of respondents in how to interact with this type of AR/VR tools. Regarding the perceived usefulness, although the results are less conclusive than the previous ones, the balance continues to be very positive, with the highest number of votes in the category 'Slightly agree' with the statement that the tool would be useful in their job. This may be due to the fact that, since these are questions about the specific effects that the tool can have when used in a daily work context, respondents cannot have a strong opinion when dealing with hypothetical questions. Regarding the intention to use it in the future, 38% of those surveyed extremely agree that they would appreciate adopting the tool, 47% slightly agree and only 15% consider themselves neutral or somewhat in disagreement. We can therefore conclude that the results are positive. Regarding self-efficacy, 84% (extremely or slightly) agree that it is necessary for someone to explain to them in advance how the tool works in order to use it. Regarding the results obtained in the more specific questions about the technology, 84.4% are interested in using these tools, and only 18.7% would prefer to use traditional methods or would not use the tool. We can conclude, therefore, that there is a great acceptance of the technology by the respondents.

About the treatment of private data and security, the majority of the results show little concern by the potential users. While most of the results indicate low concern regarding security and privacy issues, there is a percentage of participants with moderate or high concern about privacy (42%, 41%) and security (26–29%, 34–36%) in the pilot and off-pilot group, respectively. The introduction of guidelines and authentication procedures for data security changed the opinion of the respondents only slightly. Most of them were still concerned about their data, even after introducing such security aspects. It should be mentioned that irrespectively of the participants' perception, security and privacy issues are listed as high priority in the data management process, enforcing strict security measures, and always in compliance with data protection regulations.

5   Conclusions

This paper presented a suite of advanced technological tools that enable workers to interact, gather and share contextually relevant knowledge, ideas and good practices. Through the use of our AR tools, advanced remote collaboration can take place, stimulating good work-related practices, while also facilitating variability in location and working hours, and thus promoting age-neutralizing means of participation and cooperation. The VR-based solution on the other hand, allows to create (or participate in) personal training programs using virtual models of the workplace, avoiding the risks of real working environments. Moreover, the knowledge exchange platform helps workers to easily keep notes of important work aspects, accompanied by images and semantics, and to summarize significant developments that may have taken place upon some absence of the older worker. The former facilitates future easy retrieval of information, regardless working from home or on-site, while the latter serves as a crucial bridge to allow easing the older worker's come-back after some short or long-term absence. Evaluation of the developed tools through online surveys allowed to access diverse professional profiles beyond potential users, such as farm managers, lawyers, engineers, health and safety managers, and has achieved overall a high and representative stakeholders participation. This paper provided an

overview of statistics on data collected about work-related well-being, job satisfaction and job engagement, as well as on technology acceptance, functionalities,
privacy and security, exposing the potential of the developed tools to support
knowledge transfer and workers' engagement in industrial processes.

References

1. Schinner, M., Calero Valdez, A., Noll, E., Schaar, A.K., Letmathe, P., Ziefle, M.:
   'Industrie 4.0' and an aging workforce – a discussion from a psychological and a managerial perspective. In: Zhou, J., Salvendy, G. (eds.) ITAP 2017. LNCS, vol. 10298,
   pp. 537–556. Springer, Cham (2017). https://doi.org/10.1007/978-3-319-58536-9_43
2. Ochoa, P., Lepeley, M.T., Essens, P.: Wellbeing for Sustainability in the Global
   Workplace. Routledge, London (2019)
3. Healthy workplaces for all ages: promoting a sustainable working life - campaign
   guide. https://healthy-workplaces.eu/en/campaign-materials
4. Lövdén, M., Ghisletta, P., Lindenberger, U.: Social participation attenuates decline
   in perceptual speed in old and very old age. Psychol. Aging $\mathbf{20}$(3), 423 (2005)
5. Bassuk, S.S., Glass, T.A., Berkman, L.F.: Social disengagement and incident cognitive decline in community-dwelling elderly persons. Ann. Intern. Med. $\mathbf{131}$(3),
   165–173 (1999)
6. Giakoumis, D., Votis, K., Altsitsiadis, E., Segkouli, S., Paliokas, I., Tzovaras, D.:
   Smart, personalized and adaptive ICT solutions for active, healthy and productive
   ageing with enhanced workability. In: Proceedings of the 12th ACM International
   Conference on PErvasive Technologies Related to Assistive Environments, pp. 442–
   447 (2019)
7. Pavlou, M., Laskos, D., Zacharaki, E.I., Risvas, K., Moustakas, K.: XRSISE: an
   XR training system for interactive simulation and ergonomics assessment. Front.
   Virtual Reality $\mathbf{2}$, 1–15 (2021). https://doi.org/10.3389/frvir.2021.646415. Article
   646415
8. Chantziaras, G., et al.: An augmented reality-based remote collaboration platform
   for worker assistance. In: ICPR 2021. LNCS, vol. 12667, pp. 404–416. Springer,
   Cham (2021). https://doi.org/10.1007/978-3-030-68787-8_30
9. Risvas, K., Pavlou, M., Zacharaki, E.I., Moustakas, K.: Biophysics-based simulation
   of virtual human model interactions in 3D virtual scenes. In: 2020 IEEE Conference
   on Virtual Reality and 3D User Interfaces Abstracts and Workshops (VRW), pp.
   119–124 (2020)

Design for Cognitive and Learning Disabilities

EducationalGames: Web Application for Serious Games for Children with Dyslexia and ADHD

Letizia Angileri[(✉)] and Fabio Paternò

HIIS Laboratory CNR - ISTI, Pisa, Italy
{l.angileri, f.paterno}@isti.cnr.it

Abstract. Epidemiological and etiological studies have shown that, both in the clinical population and in the general population, Dyslexia co-occurs frequently with Attention and Hyperactivity Disorder. For these reasons, this work proposes a solution that aims to stimulate children suffering from both conditions in the relevant cognitive aspects, which are attention, task planning, and language processing. The solution proposed is EducationalGames, a Web application that contains two serious games: "Balloons and Letters Game" and "Robot at School game". It supports tasks which replicate daily living activities, such as preparing the backpack and reading. We present their design, a prototype implementation, and first user feedback.

Keywords: Serious games · Children with dyslexia and ADHD · User-centered design · Web applications

1 Introduction

Cognitive disorders are alterations in cognitive functions that allow the individual to interact with the world. Cognitive functions refer to multiple mental abilities, including learning, thinking, reasoning, remembering, problem solving, decision making and attention [1]. In the infant population, cognitive disorders are common because when one is born, the brain is not fully formed, it is hyperplastic and continues to structure itself from birth onwards. For external or genetic reasons, the child's brain may not function well or may not develop according to a typical line of development, and this can therefore determine atypical development of the brain that gives rise to neurodevelopmental disorders. For example, some neurodevelopmental disorders are Specific Learning Disorders (DSA) or Attention and Hyperactivity Disorder (ADHD).

One of the disorders of the DSA is dyslexia, which affects the evolutionary ability to read, write and speak, affecting the correct learning of a large percentage of the worldwide population. It is most commonly due to a difficulty in phonological processing (the appreciation of the individual sounds of spoken language), which affects the ability of an individual to speak, read, spell and, often, learn language [2].

Around 9% to 12% of the world population is affected by dyslexia [2]. While visual and auditory difficulties might cause troubles in writing and reading, the general intelligence of a person with dyslexia is not affected. Nevertheless, school failures

M. Antona and C. Stephanidis (Eds.): HCII 2022, LNCS 13309, pp. 307–320, 2022.
https://doi.org/10.1007/978-3-031-05039-8_22

and frustration are part of the daily routine for children and parents until dyslexia is diagnosed.

Children with ADHD are hyperactive and impulsive, and exhibit difficulty concentrating, planning, and organizing their (school) work. These characteristics disturb their learning and achievement at school and hinder positive social interactions within the family and with peers.

Children with ADHD represent 3%–5% of the general population of schoolchildren under 16 years. In community samples, ADHD is more frequently diagnosed in boys than in girls (3:1) and in clinical populations even more.

Since these children may be less interested in participating in traditional therapies, serious games aim to support fun activities and therefore can be more attractive for performing interventions [3]. As play approaches help balance motivational and learning elements and integrate play goals and behavioral / cognitive challenges, they have the potential to keep these children more motivated and positively involved in therapeutic processes. In some cases, games are stimulating and give immediate reinforcement to desired behavior [4].

The proposed solution aims to stimulate children with Dyslexia and ADHD in the related cognitive aspects, which are attention, task planning and language processing. The choice is justified by the fact that previous work lack proposals to support children with comorbid ADHD and dyslexia, so we thought it would be interesting to address this aspect in an innovative solution, which should also consider the emotional aspects of the target population. On these assumptions EducationalGames was designed and built: a web application featuring two serious games for children with ADHD and dyslexia comorbidities, designed for children aged 6 to 8 years and which support multiple levels of difficulty; in particular:

- Dyslexia game, foresees three levels of play, aims to stimulate the attention and the visual-spatial channel of reading, so that users can train themselves to discriminate between mirrored or graphically similar letters.
- Game for children with ADHD, has two levels of play, stimulates sustained attention and planning (a component of executive functions).

The implemented application also received a first test with a sample of the target children. The results of the user test were encouraging: the structure of the serious games seems to be suited to their needs for fun and ease of interaction, and their cognitive stimulation, and has provided suggestions for further improvements.

2 Related Work

A recent review of the state of the art [17] found that in recent years a wide variety of technologies have been harnessed to create serious games to cognitively stimulate children. In terms of devices, the tablet is the most used technology in such studies.

Regarding the stimulated cognitive functions, regardless of the characteristics of the various technologies, the most often addressed are those relating to the cognitive aspects that may be lacking in children with ADHD and dyslexia: attention, executive functions (for example, planning skills) and language processing.

Among the solutions adopted by serious games to cognitively stimulate children, one type of approach, which seems to have a certain potential both in terms of usefulness and cognitive stimulation, is to keep motivation high through, for example, the addition of a bonus.

Regarding dyslexia, in 2014 a Spanish team created Dyseggxia a platform consisting of a series of minigames that aims to improve the spelling of children with reading disorders through targeted and playful exercises. According to the method used, the correct words are not proposed but, on the contrary, the solution of the exercises consists in correcting the wrong words [5].

Letterprins is a reading game intended for children who have already started learning to read and requires the intervention of an adult to evaluate the child's performance. It is designed to improve the reading development of children with reading disorders through a variety of reading tasks. The game asks children to pronounce letters or words, while a parent or caregiver must indicate the correctness of the child's answers. The game allows parents to assist children with their homework and record a message to be played at the end of the game.

Regarding ADHD, Fontana et al. [6] suggested Train Brain, a serious game for selective attention training. It is based on storing images in one or more contexts using colored circles. The player must also manually select the difficulty level. In this first approach, the design focuses on a gamification technique of a set of exercises that meet the training objectives. It consists in including some game elements in the exercises to motivate individuals such as: interaction with avatars and feedback. The main objective of these works is to ensure that the training meets the expectations of the experts. Furthermore, the customization does not consider the difficulty of balancing, and the users must control the training without specific guidance on their progression and training needs.

The rationale behind other works is to reuse existing casual games and try to adapt them to meet training goals. The goal is to ensure that the game not only consists of a series of exercises, but also offers users a gaming experience like that offered by classic casual games in order to improve users' motivation and their acceptance of using the game as a training tool. For example, Rijo et al. [7] have developed a game for children with attention deficit and ADHD. The game is designed by matching the learning objectives with certain elements of the game. Specifically, the player is asked to find and collect hidden treasures such as letters, words, faces and objects to achieve training goals. They also added adaptive feedback to encourage children to listen and follow verbal directions.

Research has recently explored the positive effects of videogames on players' wellbeing [11, 12], in term of inducing positive emotions [13], improving mood and decreasing stress, contributing to emotional stability [14], and promoting engaging, self-actualizing experiences such as psychological flow [15, 16], In this perspective, the system we present in this work offers an original contribution considering not only the cognitive impairment, but also the emotional state of the children for example through acoustic and auditory feedback. These tools have been designed to avoid demotivating the children and decreasing their attention (a problematic aspect of children with ADHD), so that they perceive the exercises as a purely playful activity, albeit with the primary objective of rehabilitating the impaired function without neglecting their emotional state (particularly low self-esteem).

3 User Analysis

In order to better understand the target users and their requirements, we have used a number of techniques: interviews with a clinician and a support teacher, empathy maps and personas.

Interviews with stakeholders lasted about 45 min and were conducted online. We interviewed a psychologist with training in neuropsychology who deals with the rehabilitation of children with dyslexia and ADHD, and a support teacher at primary and infant school who every day finds herself instructing children with ADHD and dyslexia.

The questions were designed to understand what children's approach to serious games is and what peculiarities such games should have to be useful to the target children.

After interviewing stakeholders and better delineating the characteristics that serious games should have to be useful to children with ADHD and dyslexia, two empathy maps were created corresponding to two prototypical subjects: Lucia Neri, a girl with dyslexia; Luca Rossi, a child with ADHD.

The empathy map (see example in Fig. 1) was used to represent the emotions, frustrations and needs of the children towards the outside world [9]. For example, Lucia Neri, in addition to having school difficulties, also has emotional, behavioral and relational problems. She thinks it is her fault that she does poorly in school, she judges herself inferior to others in intelligence and ability.

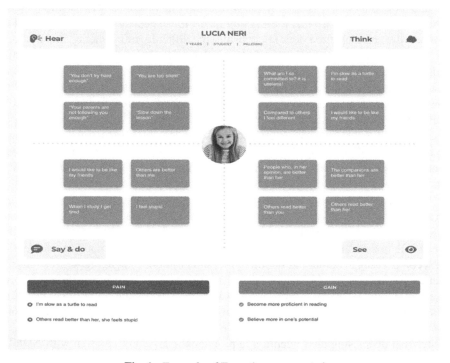

Fig. 1. Example of Empathy map created

Personas (see Fig. 2) can help raise awareness among stakeholders about users' needs [10]. While personas are made-up people, they are based on facts gathered from user research, they were created taking inspiration from films dealing with ADHD and dyslexia themes. We created them to represent the personality, motivation and relationship with technology of the two subjects of the empathy maps (Lucia and Luca). For example, Luca is a child with ADHD (see Fig. 2) and is full of energy, impulsive (he acts without considering the consequence of his actions) and inattentive. In addition, when he behaves well, his parents give him the opportunity to color and draw on the tablet in the "Coloring pages for children!" app. He would like to feel more at ease in various circumstances, and have people around him be proud of him, rather than being continually scolded by teachers or parents.

Luca Rossi

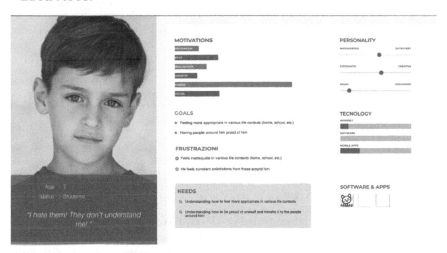

Fig. 2. Example of Personas created

The purpose of the empathy maps and personas was to create an understanding of and emotional identification with users; indeed, the results of these techniques showed that children with dyslexia and ADHD had low self-esteem.

4   Games

Before describing the design of the two serious games in detail, it is essential to emphasize that we have followed a user-centric design method. The review of related work has indicated a lack of games based on the emotional state of the child. In fact, as we have seen in the user analysis, children with ADHD and those with dyslexia have a low level of self-esteem, so the goal of the two serious games is to rehabilitate the deficient area and, at the same time, improve self-esteem while maintaining high motivation through acoustic feedback, increasing scores, level advancement, and gratification at the end of the game, which give the children the feeling that they are helping the character of the game (see Table 1). For example, the first serious game objective is to help the robot (game protagonist) to return to the ground.

In general, in the design of the individual games and the structure of the app, we considered the suggestions of a psychologist regarding the specific difficulties related to the two disorders and how the game should address them. Later, during the game design and interface construction phases, we had further meetings with her to evaluate how specific needs were supported.

Table 1. Mapping between the characteristics of the games and the characteristics of the conditions of children with ADHD and dyslexia

Goals	Ballons and letters game	Robot at school
Stimulate attention	– Collect target elements	– Select the correct letter despite changing the position of the target letter between trials
Improve self-esteem while maintaining high motivation	– Acoustic feedback – Leveling up – Gratification at the end of the game	– Acoustic feedback – Increased scores – Leveling up – Gratification at the end of the game

4.1 Balloons and Letters Game

The "Balloons and letters" game (see Fig. 3) is a Web application developed with HTML5, CSS3, JavaScript and jQuery (JavaScript library). It was designed to stimulate attention and the visual-spatial channel so that the users train themselves to discriminate between mirror or graphically similar letters. The goal is to help a flying robot return safely to the ground by blowing up the balloons one at a time. Each balloon contains a letter or grapheme with two letters. The user task is to explode the one containing the target letter or grapheme indicated at the top left of the screen. The user interacts with the game by clicking on the individual balloons. If the answer is correct, the balloon turns green and the next exercise starts, otherwise it turns red and waits for the next user interaction.

The degree of difficulty is managed both by the level and by the logic of the exercise. Each level presents five exercises, the first level shows: in the first two exercises, one target and two incorrect elements in the balloons, in the last three, the target element, one distractor (element very similar to the target) and one incorrect element. The second level presents six balloons, showing in the first two exercises a target element, a distractor and four incorrect elements, in the last three trials a target element, two distractors and three incorrect. The difficulty of the level is gradually increased as more distractors are presented in the last three exercises. The distractors are generally the mirror images of the letters of the alphabet. In the third level, where there are graphemes with two letters,

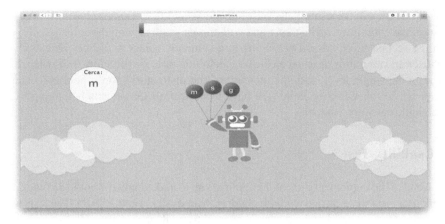

Fig. 3. Ballons and letter game (Color figure online)

the model of the five exercises within a level is applied again, the first two (a target element, a distractor and four incorrect), the last three (a target element, two distractors and three incorrect).

4.2 Robot at School Game

The "Robot at school" (see Fig. 4) was developed with JavaScript (ES6), HTML5 and CSS3. It was designed to stimulate sustained attention and planning skills. As mentioned, one of the difficulties faced by children with ADHD is preparing their backpack, which is a planning task. The goal of this game is to help the robot collect the school items. The user interacts with the game through the keyboard arrows, making the character move along the horizontal axis, while the school elements (target) and the elements of daily life (distractors) fall on the vertical axis. If the robot collects the correct element, it turns green, otherwise red. As for the execution of the game, it is designed on two levels:

Fig. 4. Robot at school game (Color figure online)

- in the first level, the stimuli chosen were everyday life or school objects; among the latter, the child must find a target that will appear randomly on the screen,
- in the second level, stimuli belonging to a semantic category (school objects) were chosen and randomly descend on the screen. In this case, the difficulty is also increased within the single level, with the increase of the distractors (non-school objects also appear). In this case, the child will have to collect all the objects belonging to the semantic category "school".

5   Usability Test

At the end of the implementation of the application, to understand if it could be functional or not, user tests were carried out with children with dyslexia and ADHD. The tests were performed by eight children between the ages of 6 and 8, an average of 7.25 years, three girls and five boys. This is a representative sample of the target audience, as these children have a comorbidity of ADHD and dyslexia.

All participants and the families of the children received information regarding the aims of the research and they provided signed informed consent for participating. There was no financial or other compensation for begin part of the study sample. Participants who agreed to take part in the study were reassured of the voluntary nature of their participation and their right to stop at any time.

After providing informed consent, participants were scheduled for an individual appointment in a week's time. This appointment was used to a) brief the participant about the study procedure; b) to understand the level of use of technological devices d) conduct a supervised session using two serious games and e) finally, the researchers administered the SUS (System Usability Scale) questions to the participants.

The tests were led by the educator and took place via video call. A researcher observed the children at play, taking specific notes in the field diary in relation to technical aspects of the operation and programming of the game. All incidents or problems were documented. The researchers acted merely as observers and did not interfere with the dynamics of the children and the educators.

Firstly, it was very useful to understand the level of use of technological devices, as it affects the perceived complexity in the interaction of the game. For example, Amir is a six-year old boy who often interacts with the tablet and/or smartphone and very little with the PC. He showed difficulties in using the keyboard and mouse, as they are rarely used in his everyday life, but when he got used to them, he could not wait to start playing again. In general, users in the target audience make little use of the PC and a large use of tablets and/or smartphones.

Desktop computers are generally used mainly for web browsing, while the smartphone and/or tablet are used both for web browsing and for interactions with games. For example, Ethan (8 years old) told the clinician that he often plays with both his smartphone and computer, in fact he was one of the few who had little difficulty when interacting with the two serious games.

Later, the children were divided into two subgroups of four, which used two different versions of the games. Both the first and second test groups consisted of one 6-year-old, one 7-year-old and two 8-year-olds.

The first task was to choose the "balloons and letters" game and start it. What emerged during the tests was that younger children take longer to complete the task (see Fig. 5), probably because, apart from the disorder, children of the age of six have difficulty reading and understanding even text in basic language. At the level of scholastic learning, and therefore of writing, the text makes the interaction with the serious game even more complex. Also, during the first task it was noted that all children had difficulty understanding the game instructions, probably because the children were anxious to play immediately. Therefore, it seems useful for the user to have feedback even while playing the game; therefore, the same game was proposed to the second subgroup with a sound feedback to each correct/wrong answer. In this way, the children in the second group asked fewer questions about the instructions and the time to complete the activity decreased (see Fig. 6). In any case, starting from this experience, we can hypothesize that the most appropriate method to remind the children of the instructions may be the addition of a visual stimulus: the system reminds the child of the rule and so he will feel guided during the execution of the task.

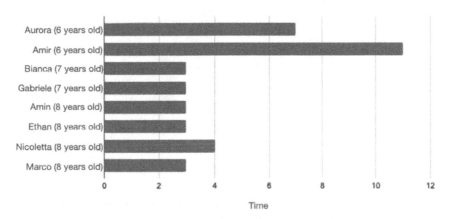

Fig. 5. Time taken for each child

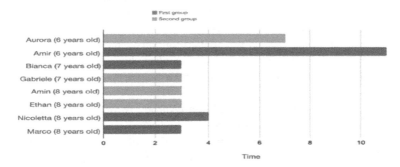

Fig. 6. Time for first and second group

In addition to the difficulty in understanding the instructions, the other complexities encountered were: using the mouse, especially for children who had little experience in using the PC, understanding how to interact with the game (mouse or keyboard).

At the end of the first activity, the educator asked the participant to carry out the second activity: choose the game "robot at school" and play.

Regarding the second activity, the time variable was not relevant because the game has a time set by the system.

The first group was asked to play the game at a higher speed than the serious games tested by the second group. In fact, the first group had difficulty in correctly and quickly identifying the stimulus, while for the second group it was easier, and therefore the performance in terms of errors improved (see Fig. 7).

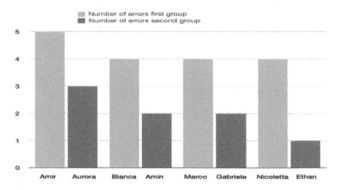

Fig. 7. Number of errors of first and second group

Finally, the SUS questionnaire [8] was used to gauge how usable participants perceived the app to be. This scale is context-specific and does not measure usability in isolation but as a product of the user interface interaction and the specific goals that users expect to accomplish with its use. The SUS questionnaire was completed for both the child and the physician. It was administered during a conversation and showed that children liked the games. When filling out the SUS item "I think I want to use this application frequently" the response was strongly positive, as 50% of the children answered 'more yes than no' and 50% 'absolutely yes'.

Instead, the statement "I found the application very easy to use" prompted more negative than positive feedback (see Fig. 8), as children think that having a person able to help them during the interaction with the game can help them overcome any difficulties encountered (see Fig. 9).

In the end, it was found that four children (Aurora, Amir, Bianca, Gabriele) gave overall modest SUS values (66, 67 and 68, 65).

The highest score was given by Ethan (the result is 90), followed by Nicoletta with 85 and finally Amin and Marco with 77.2. Hence, by improving the usability of the product and the method of explaining the instructions, it appears very likely that these two games can be used by children with ADHD and dyslexia. In any case, the average overall SUS value of the test is equal to 74.4. A positive value that can certainly be improved.

I found the application very easy to use

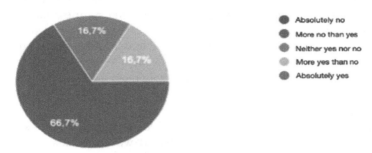

Fig. 8. Answers to one of the SUS questions

I think I would need the support of a person who is already able use the application

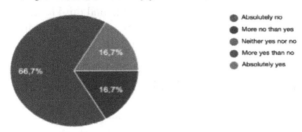

Fig. 9. Answers to one of the SUS questions

As for clinicians' input, we collected data only from one, who was the only operator involved so far, but given his daily experience of working with children with ADHD and dyslexia, his feedback was useful. In fact, according to the speech therapist, if the application were to be more usable from the point of view of explaining the rules of the games, it would be an excellent product to use, as the games in their functionality have achieved the initial purpose: the children exhibited no drops of attention and perceived the exercise as a purely playful activity, even though its primary objective was rehabilitating the impaired function.

However, according to the clinician, a similar digital tool could enrich his work, as serious games could facilitate him in the rehabilitation process, as they allow keeping the young patient's motivation high in order to keep up with therapy, and avoid making the professional exert further efforts, and make the rehabilitation process interesting, interactive and stimulating.

6   Discussion

The present study aimed to evaluate the usability of two serious games for children with dyslexia and ADHD.

From a qualitative point of view, through an observational analysis, the two serious games were appreciated by the young subjects. In fact, they did not show a decrease in attention or motivation, and the application offered easy use even when navigating between the various levels. However, during serious play it was noted that all children had a hard time understanding the game's instructions, possibly because they were eager to play right away. Therefore, it was useful for them to have feedback even while the game is running or to have a button that can help them pause the game and review the instructions.

Furthermore, an attractive design is a key factor in the quality of any activity aimed at children [21] and in order for these games to achieve positive results and impacts it is important to consider how the content is presented, what perceptual and cognitive skills the practice is brought into play and how social and emotional skills are improved [22] and children did better when it was easy for them to understand what they needed to do [17]. For such reasons in this study, after the user test, some improvements have been made, with introduction of support for interaction with touch, new level of difficulty, emotional scale at the end of the execution of the game with five facial icons ranging from sadness to happiness [18, 19], between the second and third level, the transformation of the robot into a 'super robot', a more captivating background, addition of the button that allows you to review the instructions by pausing the game.

7   Conclusions and Future Work

The project presented in this paper consists in the realization of two serious games for children with dyslexia and attention disorder and hyperactivity, which places particular interest and attention to the needs and preferences of young patients. Applying a user-centered design, we have designed and developed a prototype tailored to the child so that it would be easy to use and stimulating for therapeutic purposes.

The design of the prototype posed several challenges: both the design and the implementation, through which we were able to appreciate the complexity of the world of serious games applied to rehabilitation. Serious games must be able to involve the patient so that the level of attention and motivation is maintained during the rehabilitation recovery. For these reasons, the serious games that have been designed and implemented also have the purpose of avoiding discouraging the user during the execution of the task, because demotivation can negatively affect its execution.

Even if it is not possible to do a quantitative clinical analysis of attention, from a qualitative point of view through an observational analysis, the young subjects did not show a decrease in attention or motivation and, apart from some difficulties in understanding the instructions at the beginning, the application was appreciated as it offers easy use even when navigating between the various levels.

The prototype itself has room for improvement. Potential future developments include: the addition of new levels, the ability to provide visual stimuli to the child during play, the doctor's careful monitoring of the course of therapy (including by collecting data from play sessions) and remote customization of game settings for each patient.

The project, while not yet a complete example of a serious gaming platform for the rehabilitation of children with dyslexia and ADHD, thanks to the experience derived from user-centered design and development, the valuable advice of the psychologist and the opinions of the tested children, can evolve towards developing a complete, intuitive and easy-to-use serious game platform for young subjects.

References

1. Cognitive Functioning – an overview | ScienceDirect. https://www.sciencedirect.com/topics/psychology/
2. What is dyslexia. https://eda-info.eu/what-is-dyslexia/
3. Sim, McFarlane, Read: All work and no play: measuring fun, usability, and learning in software for children (2006)
4. Van der Oord, S., Bögels, S.M., Peijnenburg, D.: The effectiveness of mindfulness training for children with ADHD and mindful parenting for their parents. J. Child Family Stud. **21**(1), 139–147 (2012)
5. Rello, L., Bayarri, C., Gorriz, A.: Dyslexia Exercises on my Tablet are more Fun, Spagna 2013
6. Fontana, E., Gregorio, R., Colussi, E.L., De Marchi, A.C.: Trainbrain: a serious game for attention training. Int. J. Comput. Appl. **160**, 4 (2017)
7. Rijo, R., et al.: A new adaptive mysterious bones unearthed: development of an online therapeutic serious game for children with attention deficit-hyperactivity disorder. Procedia Comput. Sci. (2015)
8. Brooke, J.: Sus: a @quick and dirty'usability. Usability Eval. Ind. **189** (1996)
9. Bland, D.: Agile coaching tip – What is an empathy map?, 21 April 2016. https://www.solutionsiq.com/resource/blog-post/what-is-an-empathy-map/
10. Interaction design foundation. https://www.interactiondesign.org/literature/topics/personas
11. Jones, C.M., Scholes, L., Johnson, D., et al.: Gaming well: links between video games and flourishing mental health. Front. Psycol. **5**, 260 (2014)
12. Granic, I., Lobel, A., Engels, R.C.M.E.: The benefits of playing video games. Am. Psycol **69**, 66–78 (2014)
13. Osmanovic, S., Pecchioni, L.: Beyond entertainment: motivations and outcomes of video games playing by older adults and their younger family members. Games Cult. **11**, 1–20 (2015)
14. Russoniello, C.V., O'Brien, K., Parks, J.M.: The effectiveness of casual video games in improving mood and decrising stress. J. Cyber. Ther. Rehabil. **2**, 53–76 (2009)
15. Neri de Souza, F.: Science education with and through ICT: curriculum design and questioning to promote active learning. In: Fonsecs, D., Redondo, E. (eds.) Handbook of Research on Applied E-Learning in Engineering and Architecture Education, vol. 1, pp. 133–158. IGI Global, Hershey (2016)
16. Cowley, B., Charles, D., Black, M., Hickey, R.: Toward an understanding of flow in video games. Comput. Entertain. **6**, 20:1–20:27 (2008)
17. Coma-Roselló, T., Blasco-Serrano, A.C., Laparte, M.A.G., Aguelo Arguis, A.: Mediation criteria for interactive serious games aimed at improving learning in children with attention deficit hyperactivity disorder (ADHD). Res. Pract. Technol. Enhanced Learn. **15**, 25 (2020)
18. Diana et al.: Experience-sampling methodology with a mobile device in fibromyalgia. Int. J. Telemed. Appl. 162673 (2012)
19. Palacios, G., et al.: Ecological momentary assessment for chronic pain in fibromyalgia using a smartphone: a randomized crossover study. Eur J. Pain **18**, 862–872 (2014)

20. Crescenzi, L., Grané, M.: Análisis del diseño interactivo de las mejores apps educativas para niños de cero a ocho años./An analysis of the interaction design of the best educational apps for children aged zero to eight. Comunicar. **46**, 77–85 (2016)
21. Connolly, T.M., Boyle, E.A., MacArthur, E., Hainey, T., Boyle, J.M.: A systematic literature review of empirical evidence on computer games and serious games. Comput. Educ. **59**, 661–686 (2012)
22. Schmidt, J.D.E., De Marchi, A.C.B.: Usability evaluation methods for mobile serious games applied to health: a systematic review. Univ. Access Inf. Soc. **16**(4), 921–928 (2016). https://doi.org/10.1007/s10209-016-0511-y

Tangible Interfaces Applied in the Development of Literacy in Children with Down Syndrome

Mónica A. Carreño-León$^{(\boxtimes)}$ (iD), J. Andrés Sandoval-Bringas (iD), Italia Estrada-Cota, Teresita Alvarez-Robles (iD), Alejandro Leyva-Carrillo, and Rafael Cosío-Castro

Universidad Autónoma de Baja California Sur, La Paz, B.C.S., México
{mcarreno,sandoval,iestrada,tj.alvarez,aleyva,r.cosio}@uabcs.mx

Abstract. Attention to people with disabilities has been a topic of interest for different areas of science and technology. The development of literacy in children with Down syndrome has been a topic of interest given the learning difficulties they present. Thus, different methodological approaches and tools have emerged that are adapted to the special needs of this population. Currently, technology has allowed the introduction of new forms of education and communication with the people who have a disability and, there is interest in the incorporation of these technologies in teaching methods. The main objective of this research is the design of a technological tool that incorporates tangible user interfaces, which can be used by children with Down syndrome to learn to read.

Keywords: Tangible UI · Down's syndrome · Literacy · Human computer interaction

1 Introduction

Reading and writing supposes the opening to the world and with it the feeling of an integral part of it. Por ello, un objetivo prioritario en la educación básica es la adquisición de la lectura. Reading is the main means for the acquisition of new learning, and it does not always happen in the same way [1]. Through literacy, social relationships are enriched, knowing oneself and others and developing skills that prepare them for life: memory, languages, imagination, and the ability to abstract [2].

Down syndrome is a genetic disorder caused when abnormal cell division produces extra genetic material from chromosome 21.

Down syndrome is characterized by a typical physical appearance, intellectual disability, and developmental delays. In addition, it can be associated with heart or thyroid gland diseases. Early intervention programs with a team of therapists and special educators who treat each child's specific situation can be helpful in treating Down syndrome.

Technology has brought great benefits to humanity and is present in practically any area of society. Its evolution has been very rapid, and it has become a fundamental tool for day-to-day use. For many researchers, the development of inclusive technologies to support people with special needs has been a topic of special interest, because through

M. Antona and C. Stephanidis (Eds.): HCII 2022, LNCS 13309, pp. 321–331, 2022.
https://doi.org/10.1007/978-3-031-05039-8_23

these developments their quality of life can be improved and their incorporation into society easier.

For there to really be social integration, it is essential that children and young people with special needs be accepted in regular educational institutions.

1.1 Down Syndrome and Literacy

Down syndrome is a genetic disorder caused when abnormal cell division produces extra genetic material from chromosome 21. Down syndrome is characterized by a typical physical appearance, intellectual disability, and developmental delays. Additional can be related to heart disease or thyroid gland. Intellectual disability can present itself in different ways. Intellectual functioning involves attention problems, memory deficits, slow learning rate, difficulties in the of language and lack of motivation [3].

Children with Down syndrome have certain specific characteristics that must be considered during the teaching process with them. In these children, learning is slow, and it is necessary to go little by little, but if it is related to familiar and significant situations for them, a greater development will be generated [4].

Literacy is one of the types of learning that most favors people's autonomy, but with a very high level of abstraction, which makes this process more complicated for people with intellectual disabilities. Teaching reading skills to children with intellectual disabilities is challenging for teachers because learning abilities vary greatly depending on the intellectual disability. Additionally, differences between children who have the same disability can be enormous [5–8].

Children with Down syndrome typically learn to read the same way as all children. The difference is that they learn at a slower rate and their instruction must match this pace. They also need to develop comprehension and retention skills [5, 9, 10].

1.2 Literacy Method for Children with Down Syndrome

There are different types of reading methods that are better adapted to a specific type of disability or difficulty. Of all the methods, the most used are synthetic (alphabetic, syllabic and phonetic), analytical or global, and mixed [11–14].

The analytic methods (also called global methods) begin with the most complex structures of language, i.e., words and phrases. They are based on global perception and recognition of written words. The second stage is the recognition and learning of syllables [14].

A fundamental aspect for the development of literacy in children with Down syndrome is the educational material used in the process, including teaching support technologies, which should consider the main characteristics in the learning process of this population.

The Troncoso method is a reading and writing teaching system specifically designed to work with people with Down syndrome. This method was developed by María Troncoso, a pedagogue who tried to find a universal way to teach individuals with this developmental disorder. This method focuses on the development of many cognitive skills, including attention and concentration; association of words and symbols with objects;

perception and discrimination; identification of similarity and difference; sort objects to see order or relationship; and develop concepts, such as space, size and shape.

The acquisition of basic skills is quite a challenge for people with Down syndrome. The Troncoso method stands out from other pedagogical alternatives because it is a completely adaptable and individualized system, which can be used in different ways depending on the specific needs of the child. With this method, the initial level of the student or their cognitive abilities does not matter, which makes it a very versatile tool.

The Troncoso method is divided into a series of stages through which the child will acquire all the skills they need to be able to read and write fluently. During them, skills such as drawing lines on paper, syllable recognition or reading speed are worked on in a very progressive and simple way.

By breaking down the learning of each of the skills into its smallest components, the Troncoso method allows even children with very short attention spans or low cognitive levels to acquire all the skills they need to read and write at will. your own pace and with as little difficulty as possible.

1.3 Tangible User Interfaces

In [15] it is mentioned that a tangible user interface (TUI) is an "interface that deals with providing tangible representations to information and digital controls, allowing users to literally grab data with their hands".

They serve as direct and tangible representations of digital information. These augmented physical objects often function as input and output devices that provide users with parallel feedback: passive, haptic feedback that informs users that a given physical manipulation is complete; and digital, visual, or auditory feedback that informs users of the computational interpretation of their action [16]. Therefore, interaction with TUIs is not limited to the visual and auditory senses, but also relies on the sense of touch. Furthermore, TUIs are not limited to two-dimensional images on a screen; Interaction can become three-dimensional.

TUIs are defined as systems that use physical objects to represent and control digital information. Among the advantages of using TUIs, it can be mentioned that they help improve collaboration between children, facilitating learning through digital technology, taking advantage of the human capacity to grasp and manipulate physical objects and materials [17].

Some researchers suggest that through the use of virtual environments, users can practice skills safely, avoiding the consequences of the real world that can become dangerous, mainly for users with special needs. In [18] it is mentioned that Information and Communication Technologies (ICT) can decisively improve the quality of life of people with disabilities, in addition to being one of the few options to access the school curriculum, helping to communication and facilitating social and labor integration. For people with autism, the use of ICT can be considered a powerful tool to enhance and improve communication [19].

Various studies show that tangible interfaces are useful because they promote active participation, which helps in the learning process. These interfaces do not intimidate the inexperienced user and encourage exploratory, expressive and experimental activities.

TUIs have been shown to enhance learning for children by enriching their experience, play and development [20, 21].

The use of tangible interaction in educational settings has been gaining importance, and has been the focus of study through different investigations [22–28].

Some authors address the need for TUIs for people with physical or cognitive disabilities [29, 30], other authors address them as necessary for older adults [31], early childhood [20, 32–34], in other words, these interfaces can have great potential for all people, which is why some authors also consider their use in general, independent of physical, cognitive and age capacities, among others, simply because of their practicality and improvement in the completion of certain tasks [35, 36].

Taking as reference the results of previous investigations, tangible interfaces will be used in this investigation with the purpose of verifying its feasibility. Therefore, the design of a technological tool with an interactive concept with the integration of tangible elements and software applications, which can be used by children with Down syndrome to learn to read, is proposed.

2   Methodology

For the construction of the tool, the life cycle model called evolutionary prototype was adopted. The evolutionary prototype is based on the idea of developing an initial implementation exposing it to user comments and refining it through the different versions until an adequate system is developed, allowing a rapid response to changes that may arise.

During the development of the tool, meetings were held with USAER professors, in order to get them involved from the beginning in the development of the tool. It began by designing a prototype that was refined and expanded until the prototype was complete. Next, each of the stages that were carried out for the development of the tool are described.

2.1   Identification of Requirements

In the meetings that were held, the following requirements could be identified:

- Use of the Troncoso method through a technological environment.
- User care and follow-up.
- Creation of a file for each child who uses the technological environment, in order to have an information repository.
- Automatic generation of progress statistics and results obtained.
- Use of tangible user interfaces.
- Configurable, that is, it adapts to the characteristics of the child with down syndrome, their abilities and needs, their learning and processing pace, their interests, as well as their level of development.
- Friendly interface, that uses visual and auditory elements, in order to motivate its use.

Figure 1 shows the use case diagram of the tool, as well as the actors that interact with it:

- Teacher: Person responsible for the teaching-learning process of the Troncoso method.
- Child: Person with Down syndrome who is learning to read using the Troncoso method.
- Administrator: Person in charge of the correct functioning of the system, with access to all the files and their statistics.

2.2 Design, Development, and Implementation of Prototype

Figure 2 shows the general diagram of the tool where the components and their interaction can be seen:

1) The software that allows the interaction with the RFID reader boards and the tangible user interfaces.
2) Board with 4 RFID readers in a square shape.
3) Tangible user interfaces in the form of cards with representations of images and text.
4) Tangible 3d user interfaces.
5) Board with 5 RFID readers horizontally.
6) Tangible user interfaces in the form of cards with representations of syllables.

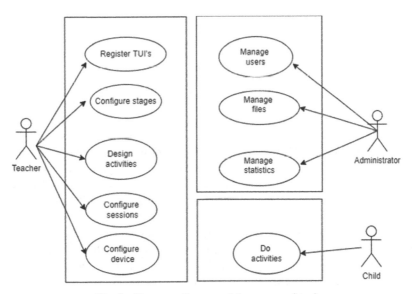

Fig. 1. Use case diagram of the proposed tool.

Tangible User Interface. Historically, children have played with physical objects to learn a variety of skills, a tangible interface (TUI), therefore it would seem like a natural way for them.

For the implementation of the Troncoso method with the use of tangible interfaces, the use of 2d and 3d objects was considered, which can be seen in Fig. 2. An RFID was incorporated into each of these objects, which allows communication with RFID reader boards.

A key component of learning strategies to develop reading skills is interaction [20, 37]. The use of multisensory strategies can help to scaffold literacy learning [16]. Different investigations have shown that the use of tangible interfaces favors the development of reading skills for children with Down syndrome [29, 38, 39].

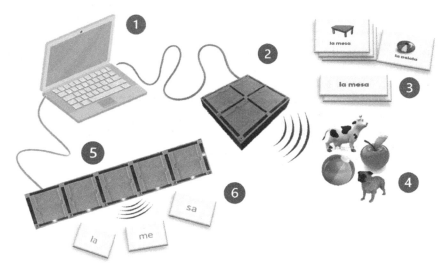

Fig. 2. Main components of the technological tool prototype.

RFID Reader Board. RFID (Radio Frequency Identification) technology allows the use of real objects to interact with the computer, reducing the symbolic load of the interface, simplifying it by making it more natural and improving accessibility. Unlike other tags, RFID tags are immersed in objects without altering their attributes or interfering with user perception.

Figure 3 physically shows the design of the two containers that groups the electronic components used for the operation of the RFID reader board. On the left side, the square-shaped board is shown, with four RFID readers. On the right side, the board is shown in linear form, with five RFID readers. The square board is used in stage 1 of the Troncoso method for global perception and recognition of written words. The linear board is used in stage 2 for syllable recognition and learning.

For the construction of the RFID reader boards, the following basic components were used: Arduino Mega board and RFID-RC522 chip reader [40].

Fig. 3. Physical design of the containers of electronic components of the RFID reader boards.

Software. The software that allows the interaction of the TUI with the RFID reader board. Figure 4 shows the main interface of the technological tool, where the main options are shown: configurations, sessions and do activities.

1. The **Configuration** option allows configuring the different elements involved in the technological tool: tangible user interfaces, RFID reader boards, users, stages of the Troncoso method and the design of activities. The registration of TUI's is done in this section. This can be seen in Fig. 5.
2. The **Sessions** option allow to organize the activities that will be carried out during the interventions with a child with Down syndrome. This section defines the stage of the Troncoso method, as well as the activities that are part of it. Other elements that are considered are the user to whom the planning is directed, the dates of application, among others.
3. The **Do Activities** option allows the child with Down syndrome to start interacting with the technological tool. In this section, the activities previously designed by the teacher are put into practice. Also in this section a record of the performance of each child is kept when carrying out their activities.

Fig. 4. Initial interface of the technological tool prototype.

The special education teacher is the user responsible for configuring the technological tool so that it is part of the activities of the teaching-learning process of a child with Down syndrome.

Fig. 5. Technology tool element settings interface.

3   Results and Conclusions

To explore the feasibility of the developed technological tool, a preliminary evaluation was carried out. The evaluation was carried out in two stages: three teachers from the special education area participated in the first stage. In the second stage a child participated with his teacher.

In the first stage of the study, the technological tool was presented to three teachers in the area of special education, who reviewed each function of the system. Subsequently, they were asked to fill out a questionnaire, which served to quantify the assessment of the technological tool from their perspective. The questions were based on functionality criteria and whose objective was to know if the tool met the initial requirements established by the experts. The results obtained were favorable, the experts agree that the tool meets the requirements and that its use in children with Down syndrome is feasible.

In the second stage of the study, an educational intervention was designed with initial activities of the Troncoso method, to know, from the perspective of the child with Down syndrome, the level of acceptance of the developed technological tool. The tests were carried out in a basic education educational institution, where we worked with a 7-year-old boy diagnosed with Down syndrome, who is in the first phase of learning to read.

During the sessions that were carried out, the child showed considerable interest in using the tangible user interfaces and no problems arose.

The results obtained in the preliminary evaluation of the technological tool with the user are considered favorable. It is important to carry out additional studies to verify the operation with a greater number of users.

The technological tool consists of tasks structured in levels, from low to high complexity, that the teacher can configure to carry out the work sessions.

The results obtained confirm that the incorporation of technological means to the teaching-learning process of reading and writing supposes a support for students with Down syndrome.

References

1. Solé, I.: Estrategias de lectura, Barcelona, España, (1992)
2. Colina, C.: La lectoescritura, un beneficio comunicacional. Procesos de lectura y escritura (2012)
3. King, B.: Intellectual disability: understanding its development, causes, classificaction, evaluation, and treatment. J. Am. Med. Assoc. **299**(10), 1194 (2008)
4. McFadden, A., Tangen, D., Spooner-Lane, R., Mergler, A.: Teaching children with down syndrome in the early years of school. Aust. J. Special Educ. **41**(2), 89–100 (2017)
5. Buckley, S., Bird, G.: Teaching children with down syndrome to read. Down Syndrome Res. Pract. **1**(1), 34–39 (1993)
6. Hsin, C., Li, M., Tsai, C.: The influence of young children's use of technology on their earning: a review. J. Educ. Teechnol. Soc. **17**(4), 85–99 (2014)
7. Sitdhisanguan, K., Chotikakamthorn, N., Dechaboon, A., Out, P.: Using tangible user interfaces in computer-based training systemas for low-functioning autistic children. Pers. Ubiquit. Comput. **16**(2), 143–155 (2012)
8. Neumann, M., Hyde, M., Neumann, D., Hood, M., Ford, R.: Multisensory methods for early learning. In: Beyond the Lab: Applications of Cognitive Research in Memory and Learning, pp. 197–216 (2012)
9. Abbeduto, L., Warren, S., Corners, F.: Language development in down syndrome: from the pre-linguistic period to the acquisition of literacy. Ment. Retard. Dev. Disabil. Res. Rev. **13**, 247–261 (2007)
10. Buckley, S., Beadman, J., Bird, G.: Reading and writing for children with Down syndrome (5–11 years). Down Syndrome Education International (2001)
11. Bentolila, A., Germain, B.: Learning to read: choosing languages and methods. Education for All Global Monitoring Report (2006)
12. Carpio, M.: Eficacia de las estrategias pictofónicas en la enseñanza de la lectura inicial en Costa Rica: un estudio longitudinal. Universidad Autónoma de Madrid, Spain (2012)
13. Norgaard, C., Burleson, W., Sadauskas, J.: Fostering early literacy skills in children's libraries: opportunities for emboided cognition and tangible technologies. In: 11th International Conference on Interaction Design and Children, USA (2012)
14. Troncoso, M., Del Cerro, M.: Síndrome de Down: lectura y escritura. Fundación Iberoamericana Down21, Santander, Spain (2009)
15. Shaer, O., Hornecker, E.: Tangible user interfaces: past, present and future directions. Found. Trends® Hum.–Comput. Interact. **3**(1–2), 23–237 (2009)
16. Shaer, O., Hornecker, E.: Tangible user interfaces: past, present and future directions. Now Publishers Inc. (2010)
17. Ishii, H.: The tangible user interface and its evolution. Commun. ACM **51**, 32–36 (2008)

18. Tortosa, N.: Tecnologías de ayuda en personas con trastornos del espectro autista: guía para docentes. CPR, Murcia, España (2004)
19. Tecno-autismo, Tecno-autismo. https://autismoytecnologia.webnode.es/investigando-/marco-teorico-autismo-y-nuevas-tecnologias/. Accessed 18 Nov 2020
20. Xie, L., Antle, A., Motamedi, N.: Are tangibles more fun?: comparing children's enjoyment and angagement using physical, graphical and tangible user interfaces. In: 2nd International Conference on Tangible and Embedded Interaction, Bonn, Germany (2008)
21. Zaman B., Abeele, V.: How to measure the likeability of tangible interaction with preschoolers. In: CHI Nederland (2007)
22. O'Malley, C.: Literature review in learning with tangible technologies. NESTA Futurelab (2004)
23. Price, S.: A representation approach to conceptualizing tangible learning environments. In: TEI 2008, Bonn, Alemania (2008)
24. Marshall, P.: Do tangible interfaces enhance learning? In: TEI 2007, Baton Rouge, LA, USA (2007)
25. Manches, A., O'Malley, C., Benford, S.: The role of physical representations in solving number problems: a comparison of young children's use of physical and virtual materials. Comput. Educ. **54**, 622–640 (2009)
26. Zufferey, G., Jermann, P.L.A., Dillenbourg, P.: TinkerSheets: Using Paper Forms to Control and Visualize Tangible Simulations, de Third (2009)
27. Guisen, A., Baldasarri, S., Sanz, C., Marco, J., De Giusti, A., Cerezo, E.: Herramienta de apoyo basada en Interacción Tangible para el desarrollo de competencias comunicacionales en usuarios de CAA. In: VI Congreso Iberoamericano de Tecnologías de Apoyo a la Discapacidad (IBERDISCAP 2011), Palma de Mallorca, España (2011)
28. Sanz, C., Baldassarri, S., Guisen, A., Marco, J., Cerezo, E., De Giusti, A.: ACoTI: herramienta de interacción tangible para el desarrollo de competencias comunicacionales en usuarios de comunicación alternativa. In: Primeros resultados de su evaluación, de VII Congreso de Tecnología en Educación y Educación en Tecnología. TE&ET, Buenos Aires, Argentina (2012)
29. Muro Haro, B.P., Santana Mancilla, P.C.G.R.M.A.: Uso de interfaces tangibles en la enseñanza de lectura a niños con síndrome de Down. El hombre y la máquina **39**, 19–25 (2012)
30. Avila-Soto, M., Valderrama-Bahamóndez, E., Schmidt, A.: TanMath: a tangible math application to support children with visual impairment to learn basic arithmetic. In: 10th International Conference on Pervasive Technologies Related to Assistive Environmentes (2017)
31. Galiev, R., Rupprecht, D., Bomsdorf, B.: Towards tangible and distributed UI for cognitively impaired people. In: Antona, M., Stephanidis, C. (eds.) UAHCI 2017. LNCS, vol. 10278, pp. 283–300. Springer, Cham (2017). https://doi.org/10.1007/978-3-319-58703-5_21
32. Gonzalez Gonzalez, C.S.: Revisión de la literatura sobre interfaces naturales para el aprendizaje en la etapa infantil (2017)
33. Devi, S., Deb, S.: Augmenting non-verbal communication using a tangible user interface. In: Satapathy, S.C., Bhateja, V., Das, S. (eds.) Smart Computing and Informatics. SIST, vol. 77, pp. 613–620. Springer, Singapore (2018). https://doi.org/10.1007/978-981-10-5544-7_60
34. Bouabid, A., Lepreux, S., Kolski, C.: Design and evaluation of distributed user interfaces between tangible tabletops. Universal Access in the Information Society, pp. 1–19 (2017)
35. De Raffaele, C., Serengul, S., Orhan, G.: Explaining multi-threaded task scheduling using tangible user interfaces in higher educational contexts. In: Global Engineering Education Conference (2017)
36. Dimitra, A., Ras, E.: A questionnaire-based case study on feedback by a tangible interface. In: Proceedings of the 2017 ACM Workshop on Intelligent Interfaces for Ubiquitous and Smart Learning (2017)

37. Neumann, M., Hyde, M., Neumann, D., Hood, M., Ford, R.: Multisensory Methods for Early Literacy Learning, Beyond the lab: Applications of cognitive research in memory and learning, pp. 197–216 (2012)
38. Jadán-Guerrero, J., Guerrero, L., López, G., Cáliz, D., Bravo, J.: Creating TUIs using RFID sensors—a case study based on. Sensors **15**, 14845–14863 (2015)

Coping with Autism Spectrum Disorder Adolescents' Emotional Suppression with a "One-Bit" Interactive Device

Yu-Chieh Chiu and Wei-Chi Chien[✉]

Department of Industrial Design, Dasyue Road, National Cheng Kung University, No. 1, Dasyue Road, Tainan 701, Taiwan, R.O.C.
p36094098@gs.ncku.edu.tw, chien@xtdesign.org

Abstract. Youth with Autistic Spectrum Disorder (ASD) have unpredictable emotional changes during adolescence. Due to the weakness of understanding other people's emotional cues, ASD adolescents tend to ignore social messages, resulting in an inability to be understood or accepted. Finally, they are labeled with social incompatibility. In this study, we focused on the ASD adolescents' emotional communication with their family members, and the first author conducted an autobiographical design research to explore the interaction pattern and the design potential via a "one-bit" device. In this 128 days' design exploration, we found that even a simple interactive device could motivate youth with ASD to learn and practice their emotional expression under the support and cooperation of the family members.

Keywords: Autistic Spectrum Disorder · Adolescents · Emotions · Family · Autobiographical design

1 Introduction

According to the Diagnostic and Statistical Manual of Mental Disorders (DSM-5, 5th ed.), autism is identified as a spectrum of several mental disorders (autism spectrum disorder: ASD). In 2021 the Centers for Disease Control and Prevention (CDC) reported that every 1 of 44 children is diagnosed with ASD [2]. People with ASD have been diagnosed with rapid growth over the past 20 years. They encounter various challenges throughout their lives, including limited capabilities, repetitive behavior, interest disorders, and barriers in social communication and interaction [3]. The deficits of their reciprocity in social interaction [4] result in difficulties in the development of social relationships [5]. For example, their abnormal social contact patterns cause the inability to engage in two-way communication and dialogue [6], as well as the poverty of mutual emotional exchange [7]. In addition, their language capability, such as reasoning and expression, is often inadequate [8]. They are less likely to make requests or share experiences. Their most apparent linguistic performance is the repetition of the others [9].

Furthermore, almost all patients with ASD experience difficulties in recognizing facial expressions and nonverbal communication [10]. Due to the inability to understand and use the meanings conveyed by gestures, they often show abnormal behavior, such as low eye contact and improper body touch [1]. Furthermore, the incapacity of expressing themselves by using sign gestures makes it severe for them to reason [11, 12].

ASD-related characteristics affect their family participation and pose severe challenges to their family members [13]. According to a survey by Sharpley et al. (1997), parenting stress among ASD's parents stems from the permanent condition that the disorders' patients do not fully recover [14]. The atypical behavioral patterns also contribute to people's resentment of the patients [15]. The social sphere of the entire family may also change significantly due to the "bothering" behaviors of the ASD children. The family may consequently reduce their social activities [16].

Caring for a child with ASD is stressful for parents. A 2010's survey study shows higher stress of ASD's parents than normal ones [17] and even higher than parents of children with Down syndrome and typically developing children [18]. On the one hand, ASD's parents have to deal with the child's emotional, behavioral, and communication problems. On the other hand, they often have to act as therapists, performing tasks, such as developing the children's language skills, monitoring the child's aggressive behavior, and giving the correct instruction [17]. Researchers also identified psychological problems like depression and melancholy of ASD' mothers [18]. Bristol (1987) suggested early recognition of and education about the child's deficits to cope with the stress of parenting ASD children [19]. Communication and consensus are also essential to reduce parents' anxiety.

All in all, it requires the participation of all family members to improve the family's heavy burden with ASD children [19]. However, most current intervention strategies are designed for schools or hospitals. In this study, we aim to improve the family closeness of youth with ASD with the help of interaction design.

Besides, we focused on the intervention strategy to help ASD adolescents to identify their emotions. ASD patients' incapability of identifying emotions or psychological states of others, such as recognizing facial expression, leads to their unconcern about emotional exchange and interpersonal relationships [20–22]. Kanner found that children with ASD face humans in much the same way as dealing with nonliving objects [23]. Hobson's study shows that the patients' intellectual functioning and other indicators were significantly impaired in face-to-face tasks with people but not in the tasks of operating artifacts [22].

The issue of emotion recognition in ASD is worth to be addressed. Dziobek et al.'s Multifaceted Empathy Test showed that people with ASD do have the ability to show emotional empathy [24]. Lacava et al.'s later study shows that ASD patients were able to learn emotional recognition with external aids. In their study, the patients became more aware of their feelings and those of others. They also performed empathic interaction like demonstrating and encouraging others to complete tasks or sharing items needed by others, suggesting that their emotional recognition skills are trainable [20].

In the context of family interaction with ASD family members, while the ASD patients fall back to express their emotions clearly and explicitly, which leads to misunderstandings or tension, this study endeavors to help ASD adolescents to recognize, understand, and verbalize human emotions. It is expected to bring positive effects in the family and enhance the life quality of the family members.

2 Intervention Strategies for ASD

Although some ASD symptoms may diminish with time, the essential difficulties often persist [25]. Besides, they have to cope with the barriers during the transition to adulthood. However, most people with ASD still need help in their daily lives. As an adult, ASD patients' dependency causes a pessimistic idea about their future. Apparently, a healthy social relationship, employment opportunities, and self-determination are still ASD patients' humane needs [26, 27]. Therefore, promoting their functional independence is the goal of ASD intervention to reduce the burden of their life in the long-term.

There is no treatment proven to promise full curation [28]. Some interventions target daily living skills, including behavioral, psychological, and educational development. These treatments are effective in promoting ASD's ability to interact with people under a social norm, positively impacting their families' and personal life satisfaction [29].

The common interventions strategies coping with ASD's behavioral performance include operant conditioning [e.g., 30], applied behavior analysis [e.g., 31], discrete trial training [e.g., 32], and preview transition strategies [e.g., 33]. Operant conditioning applies Skinner's school of conditioning theory to constrain negative actions [34]. The basic principle of applied behavior analysis is to remind ASD patients' reflection on their behavior with the pattern of antecedent-behavior-consequence. Reinforcement is a strategy to motivate positive behavior by associating the patients' good behaviors with good consequences [35]. As a practice of applied behavior analysis, discrete trial training is often used in teaching children with autism by repeating performances and acquiring patterns [36]. In this process, the ASD children's skill training is with the help of physical, verbal, or visual cueing and prompting in this process. If the pattern has been developed, they further repeat the performance to acquire the target behavior. Finally, the transition strategy refers to using verbal or pictorial itineraries to inform the child of upcoming events and prepare their response strategy in advance [33, 37].

As mentioned before, no single strategy is ideal, and the intervention strategy is usually tailored to the patients' needs in practice. The intervention strategies suggest different and potential approaches for our design task. In the following, we present the process and result of our design research.

3 Method

We identified emotional recognition, understanding, and verbalization in a family context as our design goals for adolescents with ASD. To this goal, we conducted an autobiographical design approach, in which the first author designed an artifact for her family interaction with an ASD family member, Tim (pseudonym). Design research about ASD is often difficult due to finding samples. This study should provide close observation and highly reflexive analysis about the research subject.

3.1 Autobiographical Design

Autobiographical research aims to design a system with the self as the target user and evaluate the design through self-use. The core of the autobiographical design is to embody the researcher's or designer's own experience in the system design and exploration, and many systems are used according to the actual needs of the designer or researcher in the design process.

In their 2012 study, Neustaedter & Sengers noted that design research draws on the extensive and authentic use of those who create or construct it, meaning that actual use must be based on the real needs of the researcher rather than pretending to have a target group and anticipating their needs [38]. Also, an autobiographical approach to design can make designers more responsible because it allows them to feel the impact of the device or system on the subject [39]. The first-person experience with close observation could suggest a more accurate and deep understanding of the use situation that is difficult to achieve in other approaches. Besides, the process and result of the design practice could inspire heuretic theory construction with authentic understanding and reflection, especially in complex interpersonal experience research [40]. This personal, experiential understanding can also inspire other new design research.

3.2 Procedure

This autobiographical project lasted 128 days. The first author developed her device and used a diary to collect data from Tim and his family members (including the first author) to document the whole experience. The process included an early survey about Tim's personal preference and behavior, the developing process (70 days), and the usage (58 days). Also, Tim's family members were interviewed about the developed and perceived family interaction. This helps understand their subjective experience and the potential and weaknesses of the design artifact.

As suggested by Anderson's analytical approach of autoethnography [41], the project was under the guidance and supervision of the second author (external insider) to avoid the potential bias from the designer/researcher's attribution bias in the design process and data analysis. Besides, an ASD therapist (the third author) inspected the design and research process to avoid detrimental interventions and provided professional suggestions to infer the result.

3.3 Tim as Subject

To better present our design as an intervention strategy, we briefly describe some of Tim's behavioral characters from our observation as follows.

Tim is a junior high school boy and clinically identified as an ASD patient. He lives together with his parents, and his sister is our first author, who sometimes stays with the family. When Tim was with his family, he often hid his dissatisfaction and showed indifference to peer relationships, making it difficult for the family members to provide appropriate care and concern to him. However, Tim's emotional outbursts are often intense, unpredictable, and sometimes even self-harming. Other family members reported that Tim might have difficulty recognizing his own emotions. As a result, it is challenging for close family members to interpret and understand Tim. His unpredictable and unreasonable emotional changes mainly cause anxiety and stress for the family members to take care of him.

Besides, Tim is frustrated when experiencing any slight change in his life routine. He has fixed interests and prefers physical or electronic artifacts with mechanical and intensive repeating performance. Tim tends to be attached to online videos and sometimes overly preoccupied with crucial social information. If Tim is interested in a specific subject, he likes to phrase his curiosity and repeat to his family members regardless that his mania has become bothering.

3.4 Design Artifact as Intervention Strategy

Our design goal is to help Tim express his emotion properly and understand the family members' emotional status. The artifact to be designed should provide an emotional communication channel for Tim and his family members, which further improves his social skills and the family's well-being. As an intervention strategy, we adopted the discrete trial training method, and a one-bit interactive device (Fig. 1) was designed and prototyped for Tim and the family members to express negative emotion.

The one-bit device is a punching bag with mono input and output. When anyone hits the device, an LED lights on. In our conceptual scenario, Tim, as an oppressive ASD adolescent, is told to punch the device when he feels uneasy, angry, or anxious. Four LEDs on an external circuit board record the usage times (hits). The cumulation of hit times lasts 24 h and starts over at 3 p.m. A secret pushbutton is set up for the parents to reset the counter manually. The appearance of this one-bit device as a doll and a bare electronic board is conceptualized to ingratiate Tim's preference.

By performing the punching, we expect Tim to acquire an alternative strategy to cope with his negative emotion and reduce his emotional suppression. The LEDs are mainly designed for other family members to observe Tim's emotional situation. However, they should also motivate Tim's self-awareness about his own emotions.

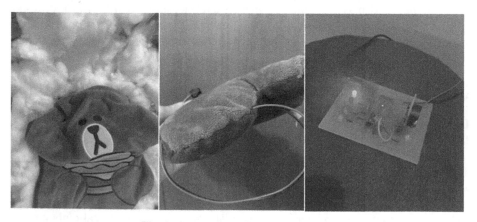

Fig. 1. Prototyping of the one-bit device

A place in the living room of Tim's home is preserved for the installation of the device (see Fig. 2), where Tim can easily approach it, and his parents can always mind the device's status when they are at home.

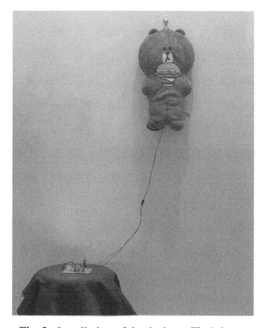

Fig. 2. Installation of the device at Tim's home

4 Results

The first author documented her experience from the first day she started conceptualizing her design. All qualitative data were analyzed, including coding, categorization, and theorizing phases. The result is shown in Fig. 3. Globally, we identified ten different interaction patterns/practices that Tim has performed with his family members. Figure 3 shows the distribution of the ten patterns on the timeline. The ten patterns are grounded in the categories of Tim's behavior and expression, as well as the corresponding reaction of the family members. Describe as follows.

Prototyping phase; 70 days   Test phase; 58 days

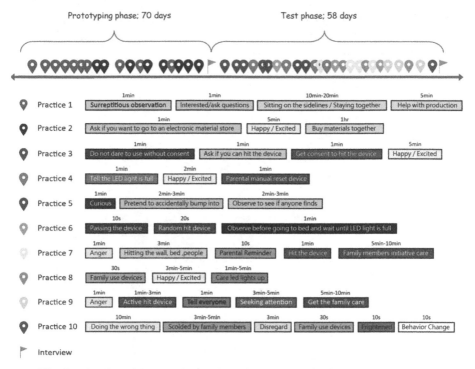

		1min	1min	10min-20min	5min
Practice 1		Surreptitious observation	Interested/ask questions	Sitting on the sidelines / Staying together	Help with production

		1min	5min	1hr	
Practice 2		Ask if you want to go to an electronic material store	Happy / Excited	Buy materials together	

		1min	1min	1min	5min
Practice 3		Do not dare to use without consent	Ask if you can hit the device	Get consent to hit the device	Happy / Excited

		1min	2min	1min	
Practice 4		Tell the LED light is full	Happy / Excited	Parental manual reset device	

		1min	2min-3min	2min-3min	
Practice 5		Curious	Pretend to accidentally bump into	Observe to see if anyone finds	

		10s	20s	1min	
Practice 6		Passing the device	Random hit device	Observe before going to bed and wait until LED light is full	

		1min	3min	10s	1min	5min-10min
Practice 7		Anger	Hitting the wall, bed ,people	Parental Reminder	Hit the device	Family members initiative care

		30s	3min-5min	1min-5min	
Practice 8		Family use devices	Happy / Excited	Care led lights up	

		1min	1min-3min	1min	3min-5min	5min-10min
Practice 9		Anger	Active hit device	Tell everyone	Seeking attention	Get the family care

		10min	3min-5min	3min	30s	10s	10s
Practice 10		Doing the wrong thing	Scolded by family members	Disregard	Family use devices	Frightened	Behavior Change

⚑ Interview

Fig. 3. Timeline of the autobiographic design research and the identified practices

4.1 Prototyping Phase

The prototyping of the device was partially done at the first author's home, in which Tim observed her work, gave some feedback, and learned the usage. This phase lasted 70 days. Although it was only the first author's prototyping phase, her interaction with Tim shows several interesting facts. When the first was finishing the device at home, Tim showed a high interest in using the design device (practice 1 & 2). His early interest lies in the interactive function of the device rather than the symbolic meaning of the usage.

4.2 Early Phase of the Test

In his first experience with the device, Tim triggered the mechanism whenever he passed by and was very excited to see the lighted LEDs. In addition, after "playing" with the device, Tim was excited to show his achievement to his family. He also made repetitive sentences to them, such as, "Look! The lights are on!" or asked his family repeatedly about the correct usage of the device. The family members explicitly guided and informed him of the concept of emotional expression. On the fifth day of the test phase, Tim's mother noticed his unhappy emotion and asked him to hit the device as a proper expression. Tim then made his first attempt and showed the activated device to his mother. His mother returned her pleasure with approval.

Since then, Tim would use the device as a demonstration of his dissatisfaction to the family members, although these are often under the suggestion of others (practice 3).

Moreover, Tim noticed that his family would always respond to him if he activated the device. Therefore, he often presented the activated device to the family as his strategy to mediate his desire to be noticed (practice 4 & 5).

4.3   Later Phase of the Test

After four weeks, we could identify a shift into a more mature usage for Tim and his family. Tim was acquired to link his negative experience to the device and hit the device to display his dissatisfaction (practice 7 & 9). This happened when Tim engaged in some negative experience with his other family members. In this case, he punched and showed the device to demonstrate his dissatisfaction. As a result, the family members reflected on their interaction and tried to reshape it for a better ending.

Besides, although the device became less attractive to Tim, and his initial playful usage had stopped once, he developed an alternative performance to initiate his interaction with other family members. He pretended to fall accidentally onto the device and then observed the family's reaction. The whole family would look at him laughing, and Tim would run away shy (practice 6). Since the situations of having negative emotions are minor, Tim's usage of the device was a mixture of these two patterns.

While we expected the emotional expression to become a fully mature usage pattern, Tim sometimes hit the wall to draw the family's attention when depressed. By his self-harming actions, the whole family stopped their activities in hand and pacified his negative emotions. Our hypotheses suggest that Tim would forget the device's medium in a state of anger, or he had an intense impulse to hit the wall for release, or he could not expect the benefit in coping with the emotion.

4.4   Epilogue

It seemed that the device did provide some change in Tim's behavior. The first author left the device in her family and let Tim and the members use the device. About five months after the start of the project, we were informed about a special event:

It was a common school day. Tim was frustrated by his peer experience at the school and felt excluded. When Tim was back from school, Tim was demotivated to finish his homework. Although his grades and homework have always been a disaster, his mother still expected him to meet the lowest line – do what he can do. On that day, while Tim ignored his mother and continued to watch the video, the mother felt like losing her last hope. She silently moved to the wall and, suddenly, punched the device hardly. She shouted, "I'm so angry!" While the mother thought that Tim would disregard her dissatisfaction as always, surprisingly, Tim got up without saying a word, put away his smartphone playing the video, quickly spread out the homework, and then began to work. All the family members present did not say anything.

We know that Tim was scared by his mother. However, a significant change is that he was aware of the intensity of her anger by the device. It seems that the device has successfully created its symbolic meaning.

5   Discussion and Conclusions

The discussion about the project's outcomes can be divided into two parts, Tim and the whole family. On Tim's part, our goal is his self-awareness of emotions and a better practice of emotional expression. However, we found it highly challenging – although potential – to completely change Tim's behavior by design. By informing him about the usage protocol and reacting to his performance, a new pattern was not really stabilized in a period of two months. Two issues: On the one hand, it could take longer to achieve the transformational goal; on the other hand, family members' reaction to his playful usage was not protocolized. They react to Tim's play with a positive attitude, which might weaken the link between the device and its original goal.

On the family's part, a simple one-bit device motivated new interaction, which generally leads to an experience of relatedness. For Tim's family members, the device helped to recognize Tim's bad emotions, which occurred in the domestic context. Consequently, the family members became more sensitive to the impact of their behavior toward Tim. However, from our observation, they could still not identify Tim's dissatisfaction caused in other contexts, such as his peer relationship or school experience. The reason could be that the emotional articulation via a device needs to be done in a timely manner. However, the device was installed and can only be used at home.

Nevertheless, we unexpectedly identified a couple of new practices of family interaction. First, because of the cute appearance of the device and Tim's playful performance, his self-presentation with the puppy was gracious. The family members were better engaged in the interaction with Tim. Second, although the targeted behavioral transformation was not complete, Tim was able to recognize the device as an emotional channel. Evidence is that he reacted precisely to the mother's performance. This outcome inspired our future work to redesign the device as a bi-directional communication channel.

This study is autobiographical design research with a single-case study. While we should not generalize the result, the outcomes of this study suggest that a simple interactive device could change the family experience with an ASD youth. In conclusion, emotional expression with a one-bit device is too abstract for our ASD subject to acquire in two months and, when the initial attractiveness disappeared, Tim's motivation to use the device in the later stages was sustained by the interaction with the family. The device plays the role of an alternative channel in which specific patterns and interpretations are packaged. Furthermore, despite the limitation of generalization, the autobiographical experience of probing the one-bit device in the first author's domestic life shows different potentials to shape interpersonal experience between ASD children and their families. Finally, we suggest that design as an intervention tool or strategy functions differently in the family context than therapists' intervention treatment in the clinical context. Here, interpretation is situated, and all family members are contributors creating the joint meaning.

References

1. American Psychiatric Association: Diagnostic and statistical manual of mental disorders (DSM-5®). American Psychiatric Pub. (2013)

2. Diament, M.: CDC Says 1 In 44 Kids Have Autism. Disability Scoop (2021). https://www.disabilityscoop.com/2021/12/02/cdc-says-1-in-44-kids-have-autism/29613/. Accesse 5 Feb 2022
3. Fortuna, R.J., et al.: Health conditions and functional status in adults with autism: a cross-sectional evaluation. J. Gen. Intern. Med. **31**(1), 77–84 (2016)
4. Matson, J.L., (ed.): Handbook of Treatments for Autism Spectrum Disorder. Springer, Cham (2017). Doi: https://doi.org/10.1007/978-3-319-61738-1
5. Bhasin, T.K., Schendel, D.: Sociodemographic risk factors for autism in a US metropolitan area. J. Autism Dev. Disord. **37**(4), 667–677 (2007)
6. Shield, A., Wang, X., Bone, D., Narayanan, S., Grossman, R.B.: Conversational correlates of rapid social judgments of children and adolescents with and without ASD. Clin. Linguist. Phon. **35**(2), 172–184 (2021)
7. Evers, K., Steyaert, J., Noens, I., Wagemans, J.: Reduced recognition of dynamic facial emotional expressions and emotion-specific response bias in children with an autism spectrum disorder. J. Autism Dev. Disord. **45**(6), 1774–1784 (2015)
8. Calloway, C.J., Myles, B.S., Earles, T.L.: The development of communicative functions and means in students with autism. Focus Autism Other Dev. Disabilities **14**(3), 140–149 (1999)
9. Hayes, G.R., Hirano, S., Marcu, G., Monibi, M., Nguyen, D.H., Yeganyan, M.: Interactive visual supports for children with autism. Pers. Ubiquit. Comput. **14**(7), 663–680 (2010)
10. Keating, C.T., Cook, J.L.: Facial expression production and recognition in autism spectrum disorders: a shifting landscape. Child Adolescent Psychiatric Clinics **29**(3), 557–571 (2020)
11. Golan, O.: Systemising emotions: teaching emotion recognition to people with autism using interactive multimedia (Doctoral dissertation, University of Cambridge) (2007)
12. Kuusikko, S., et al.: Emotion recognition in children and adolescents with autism spectrum disorders. J. Autism Dev. Disorders **39**(6), 938–945 (2009)
13. Schwartz, J., et al.: Measuring the involvement in family life of children with autism spectrum disorder: a DBPNet study. Res. Dev. Dsabilities **83**, 18–27 (2018)
14. Sharpley, C.F., Bitsika, V., Efremidis, B.: Influence of gender, parental health, and perceived expertise of assistance upon stress, anxiety, and depression among parents of children with autism. J. Intellect. Dev. Disabil. **22**(1), 19–28 (1997)
15. Koegel, R.L., et al.: Consistent stress profiles in mothers of children with autism. J. Autism Dev. Disord. **22**(2), 205–216 (1992)
16. Koegel, L.K.: Interventions to facilitate communication in autism. J. Autism Dev. Disord. **30**(5), 383–391 (2000)
17. Dabrowska, A., Pisula, E.: Parenting stress and coping styles in mothers and fathers of pre-school children with autism and Down syndrome. J. Intellect. Disabil. Res. **54**(3), 266–280 (2010)
18. Dumas, J.E., Wolf, L.C., Fisman, S.N., Culligan, A.: Parenting stress, child behavior problems, and dysphoria in parents of children with autism, Down syndrome, behavior disorders, and normal development. Exceptionality Spec. Educ. J. **2**(2), 97–110. (1991)
19. Bristol, M.M.: Mothers of children with autism or communication disorders: successful adaptation and the double ABCX model. J. Dutism Dev. Disorders **17**(4), 469–486 (1987)
20. Lacava, P.G., Rankin, A., Mahlios, E., Cook, K., Simpson, R.L.: A single case design evaluation of a software and tutor intervention addressing emotion recognition and social interaction in four boys with ASD. Autism **14**(3), 161–178 (2010)
21. Dodge, K.A.: Behavioral antecedents of peer social status. Child Development, 1386–1399 (1983)
22. Hobson, R.P.: The autistic child's recognition of age-and sex-related characteristics of people. J. Autism Dev. Disord. **17**(1), 63–79 (1987)
23. Kanner, L.: Autistic disturbances of affective contact. Nervous Child **2**(3), 217–250 (1943)

24. Dziobek, I., et al.: Dissociation of cognitive and emotional empathy in adults with Asperger syndrome using the Multifaceted Empathy Test (MET). J. Autism Dev. Disord. 38(3), 464–473 (2008)
25. Seltzer, M.M., Krauss, M.W., Shattuck, P.T., Orsmond, G., Swe, A., Lord, C.: The symptoms of autism spectrum disorders in adolescence and adulthood. J. Autism Dev. Disord. 33(6), 565–581 (2003)
26. Rieske, R.D. (ed.): Handbook of Interdisciplinary Treatments for Autism Spectrum Disorder. Springer, Cham (2019)
27. Marsack-Topolewski, C.N., Samuel, P.S., Tarraf, W.: Empirical evaluation of the association between daily living skills of adults with autism and parental caregiver burden. Plos One 16(1), e0244844 (2021)
28. Medavarapu, S., Marella, L.L., Sangem, A., Kairam, R.: Where is the evidence? a narrative literature review of the treatment modalities for autism spectrum disorders. Cureus 11(1) (2019)
29. Emily, G., Grace, I.: Family quality of life and ASD: the role of child adaptive functioning and behavior problems. Autism Res. 8(2), 199–213 (2015)
30. Zhu, V., Dalby-Payne, J.: Feeding difficulties in children with autism spectrum disorder: aetiology, health impacts and psychotherapeutic interventions. J. Paediatr. Child Health 55(11), 1304–1308 (2019)
31. Roane, H.S., Fisher, W.W., Carr, J.E.: Applied behavior analysis as treatment for autism spectrum disorder. J. Pediatr. 175, 27–32 (2016)
32. Lerman, D.C., Valentino, A.L., LeBlanc, L.A.: Discrete trial training. In: Early Intervention for Young Children with Autism Spectrum Disorder (2016)
33. Hume, K.: Transition time: helping individuals on the autism spectrum move successfully from one activity to another. The Reporter 13(2), 6–10 (2008)
34. Skinner, B.F.: The behavior of organisms: An experimental analysis. BF Skinner Foundation (2019)
35. Hernandez, P., Ikkanda, Z.: Applied behavior analysis: behavior management of children with autism spectrum disorders in dental environments. J. Am. Dent. Assoc. 142(3), 281–287 (2011)
36. Smith, T.: Discrete trial training in the treatment of autism. Focus Autism Other Dev. Disabil. 16(2), 86–92 (2001)
37. Banda, D.R., Grimmett, E., Hart, S.L.: Activity schedules: helping students with autism spectrum disorders in general education classrooms manage transition issues. Teach. Except. Child. 41(4), 16–21 (2009)
38. Neustaedter, C., Sengers, P.: Autobiographical design in HCI research: Designing and learning through use-it-yourself. In: Proceedings of the Designing Interactive Systems Conference (2012)
39. Höök, K.: Transferring qualities from horseback riding to design. In: Proceedings of NordiCHI'10 Nordic Conference on Human-Computer Interaction: Extending Boundaries (2010)
40. Chien, W.-C., Hassenzahl, M.: Technology-mediated relationship maintenance in romantic long-distance relationships: an autoethnographical research through design. Human-Comput. Inter. 35(3), 1–48 (2017)
41. Anderson, L.: Analytic autoethnography. J. Contemp. Eethnography 35(4), 373–395 (2006)

Metahumans: Using Facial Action Coding in Games to Develop Social and Communication Skills for People with Autism

Sean Haddick[1]([✉])[iD], David J. Brown[1][iD], Bonnie Connor[2][iD], James Lewis[1][iD], Matthew Bates[1][iD], and Simon Schofield[1][iD]

[1] Nottingham Trent University,
Clifton Campus, Clifton Lane, Nottingham NG11 8NS, UK
sean.haddick@ntu.ac.uk
[2] 1736 Picasso Avenue Suite A, Davis, CA 95618, USA
bonnie@bonnieconnor.com

Abstract. Communication and teamwork are skills underpinned by a person's ability to perceive, interpret and understand another's emotional state, and respond in an appropriate manner. Children, adolescents and young adults with Autism Spectrum Disorder (ASD) struggle with these "emotion recognition skills", often impairing their ability to communicate effectively. A range of interventions have been created and studied, yielding mixed results. Some of these interventions utilise elements of Paul Ekman's research into expression of emotion. This paper reviews and discusses several of these studies, considers the technical problems in each, and proposes a future framework for continued development in this field.

Keywords: Accessible games · Quality of life technologies · Metahuman Creator · Facial Action Coding System · FACS · ASD · Autism

1 Introduction

Autism Spectrum Disorder (ASD) is a life-long neurodevelopmental condition affecting on average one in every 160 children worldwide [1,2]. ASD can impair individuals in a number of ways. The American Psychiatric Association diagnostic criteria include "persistent deficits in social communication and social interaction across multiple contexts" and "restricted, repetitive patterns of behaviour, interests, or activities" [3]. Hallmark features of the condition include deficits in social-emotional reciprocity, nonverbal communicative behaviours used for social interaction, and the ability to develop, maintain, and understand relationships. The behaviour patterns exacerbate inter personal communication when engaged in unplanned or seemingly unplanned social interactions. These deficits can place children with ASD at higher risk of being the victim of bullying and other victimising behaviour [4], which may go unreported in a high number of cases due to lack of ability to perceive bullying behaviour [5].

At this time, many of the ASD treatment and intervention studies focus on intervening during a child's early developmental period prior to entering full-time education. These interventions often involve inclusive engagement and encouraging interaction between children with ASD, resulting in the participating children attaining outcomes approaching par with their Typically Developed (TD) peers [6].

Interventions with older children and adults are less common, and often focus on active training of the participant's understanding of social cues, aiming to improve understanding of social situations and respond appropriately. One study carried out with high functioning autistic adults used six of seven basic emotions (happiness, sadness, anger, disgust, fear, surprise) in an intervention. Results showed the participants displayed a significant increase in the ability to read the face and eyes; however, the effects were limited to the directly trained task, and did not generalise to other outcomes measures [7]. These basic emotions, excluding neutral, form one of the primary components of Ekman's Facial Action Coding System (FACS), a cross-cultural and internationally recognised system for identifying and encoding split-second emotional signals, or micro-expressions universal to humans (Ekman's system includes contempt). FACS, and Ekman's further research, extends far beyond these seven emotions to include other emotional signals within posture, expression, and mannerisms [8]. These nonverbal signals are part of subconscious and non-verbal communication, which people with ASD of all ages have a greater difficulty identifying than TD persons. This struggle with social skills can lead to lower employment outcomes amongst ASD adults; and may restrict them from entering managerial positions [9].

The utilisation of Serious Games-video game design methods and mechanics applied for non-entertainment purposes-in interventions and treatments is becoming increasingly common to many neurodevelopmental disorders, with varying degrees of success in both ADHD [10] and Autism [11]. A Serious Game (JeStiMulE), similar to the one in the above referenced study, included complex emotions and contextualisation. This game showed improved performance when testing participants on a cartoon tasks, and equally promising results on real world character tasks. No evidence was shown regarding how the participants performed when subjected to tasks beyond the range of the intervention game [12]. Whilst some would argue the effectiveness of using computer models or cartoons to perform this training, other studies have shown that TD adults recognise most emotions as effectively on photo-realistic human models in VR when compared to selected images [13].

In this paper we discuss how comprehensive utilisation of FACS within a game environment may aid in the development of generalised social and communication skills and propose a framework for future development and testing of such an environment.

2   Previous Research

2.1   Overview of Studies

Prior studies have shown differing results regarding the benefits of FACS training and testing, particularly regarding whether the skills taught can transfer to more general situations and experiences.

The Bolte et al. study [7] used a repetitive testing and training program. One thousand images were obtained from a variety of sources, which were then shown to a TD control group, either as the complete image or an edited view of the eyes and eyebrows. The TD controls were then asked to identify the emotion. Only images with a 90% or higher rate of agreement were utilised during pre- and post-intervention training. This resulted in a subset of 90 images (50 full face, 40 edited). The training, which utilised a separate range of 500 images, was delivered to 10 adult participants with ASD for 2 h a week over five weeks. During training, the participant was provided with the images and asked to identify the emotion. When the user responded correctly, they were provided with positive visual and audial confirmation. When they responded incorrectly, they were invited to read an explanation as to why, as well as a comic strip of the emotion in context. During pre-and post-intervention testing, the same procedure was performed utilising the two verified image sets separately, albeit with no tutoring provided. The study used a series of behaviour measures pre/post intervention to test its efficacy. The only measure that showed a statistically significant outcome was the face-and-eyes test utilising the 90 image subset (at $p = 0.04$ for the full-face images, and $p = 0.03$ for the eye images). All other measures showed no change "worth mentioning", with the only one mentioned being the rating of stimuli from the International Affective Picture System (IAPS), for which no information was given [7].

In a similar study, Silver and Oakes [14] presented autistic adolescents with a series of more contextualised images and short stories split into 5 sections. In each section, the participant needed to answer 20 problems correctly to advance to the next section. Incorrect responses prompted the user to attempt the same problem again. The training was delivered in 10 half-hour sessions over two weeks, during which the training was completed a mean of 8.4 times per student. Rather than using all of Ekman's basic emotions, this study used two or four multiple choice options for each problem, for example "happy, sad, angry or afraid".

Beyond observing how the participants improved during the training application itself, this study utilised three explicit metrics: a standardised set of 10 expression photographs the participants were asked to identify, 22 cartoons for which they were asked to give and justify an emotion, and Strange Stories- a set of scenarios where the participant must explain something non-literal that is said within. The latter two metrics were assessed by two examiners, whose results agreed with one another. Both Strange Stories ($pp = 0.016$) and the cartoons ($p = 0.041$) showed a significant improvement in performance [14].

In a later study, Serret et al. [12] used a more stylised application. School-age participants with autism spectrum condition (ASC) were taken through two distinct phases. The "Learning Phase" showed participants stylised 3D models out of context using facial expressions, gestures, and sound cues. The "Training Phase" placed these models, voice clips and so on into context, using a variety of tasks in which participants identified emotions and responded to them. Of note, the same action-for example, a fall-was displayed in different contexts and the participant was expected to appreciate the difference to be allowed to advance in the game. This training was delivered in two-hour sessions over four weeks. The effectiveness of the program was measured using a multiple-choice test, similar to ones used in the above referenced studies, in which the participant was shown an image and asked to select an emotion that matched. This test was administered with the in-game models, as well as human photographs that included both face-only and fully posed. The test also included real life images which included context. For most emotions tested, the students showed significant improvement ($p = 0.01$) on both the avatar and the real-life picture tasks. Notable exceptions were avatar facial anger ($p = 0.47$), real-life gestural fear ($p = 0.26$), and mixed results with the contextualised scenes (varying from $p = 0.01$ to $p = 0.85$) [12].

2.2   Issues with Experimental Design in Reviewed Studies

All three of the studies above agree to some extent that the recognition of emotions is a trainable skill; however, especially when it comes to generalisation of this skill, the degree to which the skill can be trained is a point of contention, as well as whether training increases interpersonal communication skills and empathetic reasoning.

Bolte et al.'s study suggests that the skill of emotion recognition can be taught, yet the potential for generalisation to the development of theory of mind is unclear. Despite the overall similarity in the form of the intervention, both Silver and Oakes and Serret et al. suggest that there is some generalisation, albeit to different degrees, through the Strange Stories test and the real-life contextualised images.

Without knowing what measures Bolte used outside of those mentioned in their primary paper, there is only so much conjecture that can be made regarding its outcomes and potential further application. As such, much of the following critique will focus on Serret et al. and Silver and Oakes's studies, which it could be argued, have not truly tested whether the skill that was taught generalised to real-world social communication. In these studies, the experimental design used to evaluate the success of the intervention utilised techniques that bore similarity to the interventions themselves.

The diagnostic tools in these studies used predetermined and standardised stimuli that are designed to provoke a clear and unambiguous response, as opposed to the greater range and ambiguity of human emotion, particularly in context. These stimuli were presented in a controlled environment in which sensory load and extraneous information were reduced. Additionally, participants were allowed to take as much time as needed to formulate a response to each stimulus. Whilst these studies do indeed show that the tasks in question teach skills that generalise well to similar and related tasks, there is insufficient information to determine if the participant's overall communication or emotional processing skills improved in a real life context.

It is plausible that the application in Bolte et al.'s study did not show generalisation because that particular application does not teach the emotion recognition skill in a general manner. This study focused only on the face and facial expressions, with close to half of the images focusing only on the eyes, with no postural training, nor context based scenarios. The only sound provided to the subject were a series of positive or negative feedback sounds. By comparison, the other studies mentioned utilised a range of stimuli that display the face and body, which aids in emotion recognition when the person is at a distance or viewed at an angle, as happens in real life scenarios. Ekman notes that gestural positioning can inform how someone feels during a confrontation, for example the direction one points their feet and places their arms during a conversation such as hands behind the back shows more anxiety and less confidence than hands linked in front.

The training in each study also varied in intensity, length and structure. Silver and Oakes's study progressed through five phases, designed to be performed multiple times. Once a participant trained on one specific aspect of the skill, they progressed to another. A similar structure was used in Serret et al.'s study, with the exception that the program was designed to be completed only once. Conversely, in Bolte et al.'s study, single task was repeated interrupted only by feedback and tutoring, which, as the training task bears much similarity in structure and process to the only measure observed to have significantly improved, could imply that the training in this instance was situation-specific.

2.3   Technological Constraints

What all three training applications have in common is the use of static images to test, and in many cases train, the target skill. Whilst it is a common and sensible technique to assess the target skill on a fundamental level, it is also reasonable to suggest that photographs limit information and context. Emotions do not simply appear on a face and are permanently present. Emotions have a temporal element. In real life the face has visual depth that does not come across in a 2D photograph, nor in a model displayed on a screen.

To address the problem of visual depth, some studies have investigated the feasibility of using high realism virtual-reality avatars for training and evaluation of facial recognition. Of note is one study in which a set of 44 facial avatars were created, selected, and compared to an analogous set of 44 images from the Penn Emotion Recognition Test [15]. These avatars applied Ekman's Facial Action Units, which codes for how individual parts of the face move to produce facial expressions that form a major component of FACS. In this study, only five basic emotions and neutral were utilised - Happiness, Sadness, Fear, Disgust and Anger. The test group was a single cohort of TD adults between the ages of 18 and 65.

This study produced promising results. All six emotions were correctly interpreted approximately as often on the VR avatars as the selected photographs.

The two emotions that varied significantly were disgust and anger. Disgust was correctly identified less frequently (52% of the time on the models, compared to 68% with the photographs), with an increase in misidentification of disgust as fear (16% of all responses to disgust models, compared to 6% of responses to disgust photographs). Anger, on the other hand, was identified more frequently (67% VR compared to 49% photographs) with the greatest change coming from neutral responses (3% compared 17%). Interestingly, there was a notable increase of identification as disgust [13]. Thanks to Serret et al.'s study posting their results in a similar level of detail, we can draw comparisons between the two. In this case, Happiness and Fear were correctly perceived less often in the avatar tasks, and anger was perceived more often. When full gestures were included, anger and disgust were identified less frequently in models compared to photographs prior to training, and slightly more often after. Whilst the overall results show promise, these inconsistencies highlight the difficulty of training the emotion recognition skill in any manner.

These inconsistencies, however, offer insight into the technical challenges of developing an intervention program. Of note, the models in the above referenced studies included a "temporal element" of emotion transitioning from neutral to the target expression. In a questionnaire regarding the experiment, some participants attributed the animations to making the tasks feel "easier". It follows that "neutral" and "none/unknown" would be selected less often, as the viewer can directly see the face moving away from neutral and moving towards an emotion. Interestingly, this experience does not hold universally across the emotions tested. Both sadness and disgust provoked more "neutral" responses. This finding could imply that the transition animation for disgust added unhelpful or misleading information, and the animation for anger specifically added useful information. That fewer participants identified anger as neutral suggests that, in this study, animation made the emotional elements more distinct. The increased rate of identification of anger as disgust provides further support. Similarly, the transition from neutral to disgust may have influence viewers to perceive the stimuli as more fearful and retreating.

A further potential explanation is that these VR models lack posture and context which provide additional information about a person's emotional state. This context is missing in both sets of images, which may explain some errors in both. Returning to the study by Serret et al., before and after training, participants generally scored higher on the contextualised images. Anger was typically associated with aggressive and advancing gestures, proceeding towards the participant, whereas disgust was associated with retreating gestures in which the face and body turn away from the participant [8,16]. This finding aligns with the results found, that the face remaining in the same place was interpreted as an aggressive (not retreating) motion. This finding would be compounded by the perception that the face should be moving in this manner, since the face is otherwise moving.

A third possible explanation is that the faces, while realistic enough to not cause the users any active discomfort, may have been disturbing enough to trigger what is known as the uncanny valley effect [17], a hypothesised relationship between human resemblance of non-human objects, and a human's response to them. According to this hypothesis, a human's emotions about an object become more positive and synchronous as the object takes on more and more of a human appearance, until it reaches a point where it is near, but not truly human in appearance. At this point, human emotions towards the object become more uncomfortable and negative as the "synchronicity" is broken. Eventually, the object becomes realistic enough to feel familiar once again.

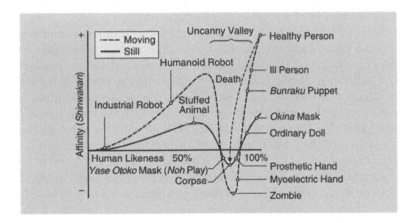

Fig. 1. A graph showing the uncanny valley, a hypothesized relationship between how much an object resembles a human being and how a human will react to that object. "Shinwakan" could be more accurately taken to mean "synchrony". Extracted from [17]

As shown in Fig. 1., the effects are amplified when the object is in motion. It is therefore very possible that people may have found the VR image more uncanny, uncomfortable, and aggressive, thus explaining the slightly higher incidence of anger when presented with disgust. Even a simple chat-bot can fall prey to this effect. In this study, a chat-bot with an avatar displayed was perceived as much more unnerving and incompetent compared to the same algorithm without it, even causing some physiological responses such as increased heart rate [18].

Serret et al.'s study provides further support. The avatars used were distinctly non-human enough to avoid a negative response, yet humanoid enough to retain their usefulness for training. Interestingly, some studies suggest that this effect is absent in ASD children, with participants in tests showing an equal preference across a spectrum of "realism", whereas a TD control group felt the most favour towards explicitly real or explicitly unreal objects [19]. This finding would be at odds with the aforementioned results in Serret et al.'s study, warranting further investigation.

3   Opportunities and Emergent Technologies

3.1   Technological Opportunities

3Lateral's MetaHumans project, now publicly accessible through Metahuman Creator, a cloud-based tool released by Epic Games to work with their Unreal Engine games development platform. These allow for the procedural creation of realistic and easily animated human faces and bodies, within natural human facial constraints. One major demonstration of the technology in 2018 showed the framework's ability to faithfully replicate facial expressions through the motion captured performances of a number of prolific actors.

Metahuman Creator provides a fully rigged and animation-ready asset to use in Unreal Engine, including the full body. This allows for an easier inclusion of context regarding body positioning and gestural indicators, similar to the application utilised in Serret et al.'s study. The rigging provided for the facial structure aligns with the Action Units in the Facial Action Coding System, allowing for straightforward procedural generation of the expressions for any given asset (Table 2). These may be generated manually, or through the use of Motion Capture systems, which may assist in providing a more natural look.

Further, these parameters are finely adjustable, such that facial expressions can be replicated at varying levels of intensity. A potential novel application for this system involves training the participant in a manner similar to how "marked card cheats" train themselves. Some "card cheats" initially practice with clearly "marked" cards, then gradually reduce the intensity of the marked pattern until the pattern is nearly invisible. At this point, someone not trained on the pattern will find it impossible to notice, whereas the trained player will be able to identify the pattern, and thus the card with near perfect accuracy. This approach could be applied to emotion recognition training starting with emotions shown to a high, almost inhuman degree, which may be aided by the aforementioned lack of the uncanny valley. Once the participant is succeeding at a sufficiently high rate, the intensity of the emotion could be reduced until the expression reaches normal or subliminal levels [20] (Table 1). This approach is somewhat analogous to Ekman's own system for training clients to notice micro-expressions described as minor, uncontrollable and brief signals of how a person is feeling (Table 2).

Table 1. A table showing a model generated with Metahuman Creator displaying 4 different intensities of happiness.

Neutral	Low Happiness	Moderate Happiness	High Happiness
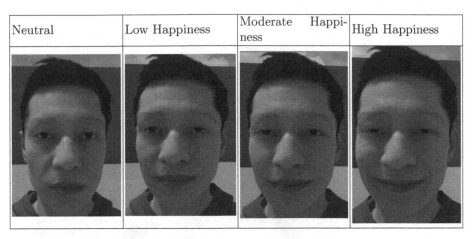			

Metahumans are also sufficiently optimised to work on commercial virtual reality headsets at certain levels of quality. As mentioned prior, this could have benefits and drawbacks. The utilisation of Metahumans in a VR setting may increase immersion with the software, as well as allow the user to approach and view the model from various angles. It could also enhance the context provided by a potential game element, with intractable objects. Further, early studies are promising in showing that VR environments can improve outcomes with interventions regarding ASD [21]. However, it is possible that it could induce subliminal uncanny valley effects, or, if the user is invited to move around the scene, induce many of the classic effects associated with extended VR use, such as motion sickness. There are also multiple accessibility concerns with this approach.

3.2 Development of Improved Experimental Methods

Whereas care must be taken to ensure that the testing of any intervention implemented sufficiently tests the skills required, there are a number of useful aspects of the aforementioned studies that can be utilised here. Of particular note in the implementation phase is ensuring that the facial expressions generated do indeed align with TD people's perception of emotion. Consequently, the methodology that Bolte et al. utilised of testing the image base on a large TD test group, and utilising images, animations and scenarios that have a high agreement rate will be essential in developing an effective intervention. This should also naturally remove any bias arising from the uncanny valley effect. Further, as previously explored, it may also be prudent to ensure that the VR environment not only provides equal or better correct response rates amongst TD persons where possible, but also that the relative error rates for each incorrect response are also as similar to real photographic samples as possible.

352   S. Haddick et al.

Table 2. A table comparing expressions recreated on a model generated with Metahuman Creator against official examples from the Paul Ekman Group [22].

Action Coding	Ekman Group Example	Metahuman Recreation
Happiness - AU 6 (cheeks raised) & 12 (Lip corners pulled back)		
Sadness - AU 1 (Inner brows raised), 4 (whole brow lowered) & 15 (Lip corners depressed)		
Surprise - AU 1, 2 (inner and outer brows raised), 5 (Upper eyelids raised) & 26 (Jaw dropped)		
Fear - AU 1, 2, 4 (inner and outer brows raised, whole brow lowered) 5, 7 (upper eyelids raised, eyelids tightened), 20 (lips stretched) & 26 (jaw dropped)		

(*continued*)

Table 2. (*continued*)

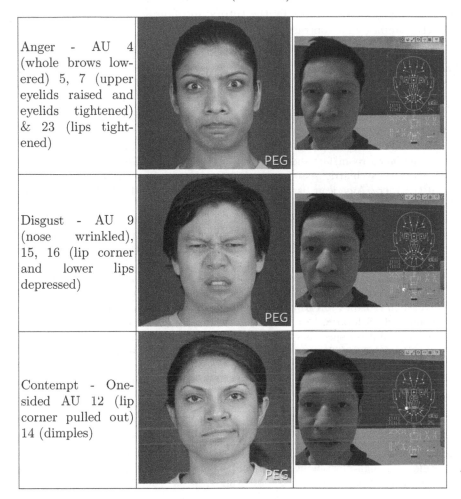

Anger - AU 4 (whole brows lowered) 5, 7 (upper eyelids raised and eyelids tightened) & 23 (lips tightened)		
Disgust - AU 9 (nose wrinkled), 15, 16 (lip corner and lower lips depressed)		
Contempt - One-sided AU 12 (lip corner pulled out) 14 (dimples)		

The two primary objectives of the intervention are to "raise emotion recognition" and "improve communication skills". As well as simply testing the former in a manner similar to the aforementioned studies, Happe's Advanced Theory of Mind Test may also be useful - in this test, similar to the Strange Stories test, the test taker is provided with a scenario in which one character says something factually false. They must then identify the falsehood, and explain the emotional reasoning behind it [23].

As the ASD population is very heterogeneous, it can be a challenge to match subjects for a between-subjects study. As such one alternative approach would be to utilise a within-subject repeated measures design. In such a study, participants alternate between the active intervention session, a control intervention session and testing, thus controlling for differences between what may be a low number of participants [24]. As such, it will be necessary to investigate current training methods utilised by the tutors and families of those with ASD to properly compare and contrast.

References

1. Elsabbagh, M., et al.: Global prevalence of autism and other pervasive developmental disorders. Autism Res. **5**, 160–179 (2012). ISSN 9393792. https://doi.org/10.1002/aur.239
2. World Health Organisation: Autism Spectrum Disorders, June 2021. https://www.who.int/news-room/fact-sheets/detail/autismspectrum-disorders
3. American Psychiatric Association: Diagnostic and Statistical Manual of Mental Disorders. American Psychiatric Association, May 2013. ISBN 0-89042-555-8. https://doi.org/10.1176/appi.books.9780890425596
4. Humphrey, N., Symes, W.: Perceptions of social support and experience of bullying among pupils with autistic spectrum disorders in mainstream secondary schools. Eur. J. Spec. Needs Educ. **25**, 77–91 (2010). ISSN 0885-6257. https://doi.org/10.1080/08856250903450855
5. Hodgins, Z., et al.: Brief report: do you see what I see? The perception of bullying in male adolescents with autism spectrum disorder. J. Autism Dev. Disorders **50**, 1822–1826 (2020). ISSN 0162-3257. https://doi.org/10.1007/s10803-018-3739-y.
6. Strain, P.S., Schwartz, I.S., Barton, E.E.: Providing interventions for young children with autism spectrum disorders. J. Early Interv. **33**, 321–332 (2011). ISSN 1053-8151. https://doi.org/10.1177/1053815111429970. http://journals.sagepub.com/doi/10.1177/1053815111429970
7. Bölte, S., et al.: The development and evaluation of a computer-based program to test and to teach the recognition of facial affect. Int. J. Circumpolar Health **61** (2002). ISSN 1797-237X. https://doi.org/10.3402/ijch.v61i0.17503
8. Ekman, P.: Unmasking the Social Engineer: The Human Element of Security (Ed. by P.F. Kelly). Wiley, New York (2014)
9. Baldwin, S., Costley, D., Warren, A.: Employment activities and experiences of adults with high-functioning autism and asperger's disorder. J. Autism Dev. Disorders **44**, 2440–2449 (2014). ISSN 0162-3257. https://doi.org/10.1007/s10803-014-2112-z
10. Jones, M.R., et al.: Exploring i N/i -back cognitive training for children with ADHD. J. Attention Disorders **24**, 704–719 (2020). ISSN 1087-0547. https://doi.org/10.1177/1087054718779230. http://journals.sagepub.com/doi/10.1177/1087054718779230
11. Zakari, H.M., Ma, M., Simmons, D.: A review of serious games for children with autism spectrum disorders (ASD) (2014). https://doi.org/10.1007/978-3-319-11623-5_9
12. Serret, S., et al.: Facing the challenge of teaching emotions to individuals with low- and high-functioning autism using a new Serious game: a pilot study. Mol. Autism **5**, 37 (2014). ISSN 2040-2392. https://doi.org/10.1186/2040-2392-5-37
13. Gutérrez-Maldonado, J., Rus-Calafell, M., González-Conde, J.: Creation of a new set of dynamic virtual reality faces for the assessment and training of facial emotion recognition ability. Virtual Real. **18**, 61–71 (2014). ISSN 1359-4338-7. https://doi.org/10.1007/s10055-013-0236-7. http://link.springer.com/10.1007/s10055-013-0236-7

14. Silver, M., Oakes, P.: Evaluation of a new computer intervention to teach people with autism or asperger syndrome to recognize and predict emotions in others. Autism **5**, 299–316 (2001). ISSN 1362-3613. https://doi.org/10.1177/1362361301005003007

15. Kohler, C.G., et al.: Facial emotion recognition in schizophrenia: intensity effects and error pattern. Am. J. Psychiatry **160**(10), 1768–1774 (2003)

16. Lopez, L.D., et al.: Postural communication of emotion: perception of distinct poses of five discrete emotions. Front. Psychol. **8** (2017). ISSN 1664-1078. https://doi.org/10.3389/fpsyg.2017.00710

17. Mori, M., MacDorman, K.F., Kageki, N.: The uncanny valley [from the field]. IEEE Robot. Autom. Mag. **19**(2), 98–100 (2012)

18. Ciechanowski, L., et al.: In the shades of the uncanny valley: an experimental study of human–chatbot interaction. Future Gener. Comput. Syst. **92**, 539–548 (2019). ISSN 0167-739X. https://doi.org/10.1016/j.future.2018.01.055

19. Feng, S., et al.: The uncanny valley effect in typically developing children and its absence in children with autism spectrum disorders. PLoS ONE **13**, e0206343 (2018). ISSN 1932-6203. https://doi.org/10.1371/journal.pone.0206343

20. Wilson, P.: Marking Cards for Fun (and Profit). September 2019. https://www.casino.org/blog/marked-cards/

21. Mesa-Gresa, P., et al.: Effectiveness of virtual reality for children and adolescents with autism spectrum disorder: an evidence-based systematic review. Sensors **18**, 2486 (2018). ISSN 1424-8220. https://doi.org/10.3390/s18082486

22. Paul Ekman Group LLC: Universal Emotions - what is emotion? January 2022. https://www.paulekman.com/universal-emotions/

23. Happé, F.G.E.: An advanced test of theory of mind: understanding of story characters' thoughts and feelings by able autistic, mentally handicapped, and normal children and adults. J. Autism Dev. Disorders **24**, 129–154 (1994). ISSN 0162-3257. https://doi.org/10.1007/BF02172093. http://link.springer.com/10.1007/BF02172093

24. Standen, P.J., et al.: An evaluation of an adaptive learning system based on multimodal affect recognition for learners with intellectual disabilities. Bri. J. Educ. Technol. **51**, 1748–1765 (2020). ISSN 0007-1013. https://doi.org/10.1111/bjet.13010

Towards Explainable and Privacy-Preserving Artificial Intelligence for Personalisation in Autism Spectrum Disorder

Mufti Mahmud[1,2]([✉])[iD], M. Shamim Kaiser[3][iD], Muhammad Arifur Rahman[1][iD], Tanu Wadhera[4][iD], David J. Brown[1,2][iD], Nicholas Shopland[1][iD], Andrew Burton[1][iD], Thomas Hughes-Roberts[5][iD], Shamim Al Mamun[3][iD], Cosimo Ieracitano[6][iD], Marzia Hoque Tania[7][iD], Mohammad Ali Moni[8][iD], Mohammed Shariful Islam[9][iD], Kanad Ray[10][iD], and M. Shahadat Hossain[11][iD]

[1] Department of Computer Science, Nottingham Trent University, NG11 8NS Nottingham, UK
[2] CIRC and MTIF, Nottingham Trent University, Nottingham NG11 8NS, UK
muftimahmud@gmail.com, mufti.mahmud@ntu.ac.uk
[3] IIT, Jahangirnagar University, Savar, Dhaka 1342, Bangladesh
[4] Thapar Institute of Engineering and Technology, Patiala 147004, Punjab, India
[5] University of Derby, Kedleston Road, Derby DE22 1GB, UK
[6] University Mediterranea of Reggio Calabria, 89124 Reggio Calabria RC, Italy
[7] Department of Engineering Science, University of Oxford, Oxford OX3 7DQ, UK
[8] The University of Queensland, St Lucia, QLD 4072, Australia
[9] Deakin University, Burwood, VIC 3125, Australia
[10] School of Applied Sciences Physics, Amity University Rajasthan, Jaipur, India
[11] Department of CSE, University of Chittagong, Chittagong, Bangladesh

Abstract. Autism Spectrum Disorder (ASD) is a growing concern worldwide. To date there are no drugs that can treat ASD, hence the treatments that can be administered are mainly supportive in nature and aim to reduce, as much as possible, the symptoms induced by the disorder. However, diagnosis and related treatments in terms of improving communication, social and behavioural skills are very challenging due to the heterogeneity of the disorder and are amongst the largest barriers in supporting people with ASD. Thanks to the recent development in artificial intelligence (AI) and machine learning (ML) techniques, ASD can now be aimed to be detected at an early age. Also, these novel techniques can facilitate administering personalised treatments including cognitive-behavioural therapies and educational interventions. These systems aim to improve the personalised experience for the people with ASD. Acknowledging the existing challenges, this paper summarises the multitudes of ASD, the advancement of AI and ML-based methods in the detection and support of people with ASD, the progress of explainable AI and federated learning to deliver explainable and privacy-preserving systems targeting ASD. Towards the end, some open challenges are identified and listed.

M. Antona and C. Stephanidis (Eds.): HCII 2022, LNCS 13309, pp. 356–370, 2022.
https://doi.org/10.1007/978-3-031-05039-8_26

Keywords: Behavioural data · Education · Federated learning ·
Healthcare data · Multimodal system · Physiological data ·
Rehabilitation · Self-reports · Wearable devices

1   Introduction

1.1   Autism in the Global Context

Autism Spectrum Disorder (ASD), popularly termed as 'Autism', is an umbrella term that encompasses a range of conditions with different abilities and problems. Though a report from the World Health Organisation (WHO) claims that 1 of every 160 people have autism [29], the actual number appears to be very high in the United States of America and Europe. In the United States, it is estimated that about 1 in 54 children of 8 years have ASD, 1 in 77 in Italy while 1 in 160 in Denmark and Sweden and 1 in 86 in the UK. There are no specific data about certain countries, but as shown in Fig. 1 Africa, Europe and Americas are with the highest burden. In children, it can be characterised by difficulties in social communication and in interacting with limited or repetitive behavioural and interest patterns or irregular activities [9]. Diagnosis of ASD is often difficult, especially in the early days, since there are no typical medical tests, such blood tests which are available for other conditions. The diagnosis process starts with the general practitioners or, in some countries, the paediatricians examining subjects to identify any possible signs of autistic traits. In cases where positive signs are noticed, the subjects are potentially referred to specialist psychologists or psychiatrists for further behavioural evaluation [3]. Although the

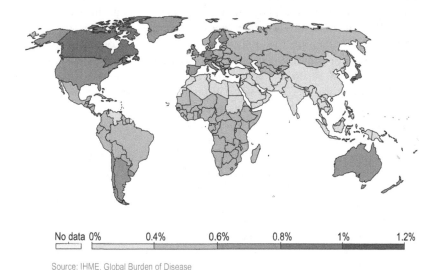

No data 0%   0.4%   0.6%   0.8%   1%   1.2%

Source: IHME, Global Burden of Disease

Fig. 1. Prevalence of autism spectrum disorder worldwide in 2017. Modified from [21].

diagnosis process of autism can start at a very young age, for example, as early as 18 months, the definitive diagnosis usually occurs at an older age due to the complexity in the diagnosis process and the data needed to clearly understand the behavioural traits [2,28].

1.2   Autism and Its Multitudes

ASD is a multifaceted disorder that can affect different people differently. Since the adoption of the Diagnostic and Statistical Manual of Mental Disorders, 5th edition (DSM-5) diagnostic criteria for ASD in 2013 [10], the individuals have been broadly classified to the three levels based on the severity of the disorder: level 1, level 2, and level 3. With growing impairments as the levels go up, people are able to show different extents of social communication skills with restricted and repetitive behaviour. Some of the symptoms belonging to each of the levels are summarised below, however, it should be noted that some of these symptoms might also be manifested by relevant psychiatric comorbidities [11].

(i) **Level 1** *requires some support*
  - *Social communication*: They show social communication deficits which cause significant impairment, have difficulty in initiating social interactions and show atypical or unsuccessful responses to social openings by others. These individuals show a reduced interest in social interactions.
  - *Restricted and repetitive behaviour*: They show inflexibility of behaviour which causes significant interference with functioning in a variety of contexts. Their difficulty in switching from one activity to another leads to problems in organisation and planning that hinder their independence.
(ii) **Level 2** *requires substantial support*
  - *Social communication*: They show substantial deficits in verbal and non-verbal social communication skills with social compromises visible even in the presence of support and show limited initiation of social interactions and reduced or abnormal reactions to social openings by others.
  - *Restricted and repetitive behaviour*: They show behavioural inflexibility and difficulty in coping with changes with restrictive and repetitive behaviours in different contexts. Also they show discomfort and difficulty in changing the object of attention or action.
(iii) **Level 3**: *requires very substantial support*
  - *Social communication*: They show severe deficits in verbal and non-verbal social communication skills that cause severe impairment of functioning with very limited initiation of social interactions, and minimal reactions to social openings by others.
  - *Restricted and repetitive behaviour*: They show severe behavioural inflexibility with extreme difficulty in coping with changes. Restrictive and repetitive behaviours are very frequent and evident in a variety of contexts that interfere with almost all areas of functioning, including great discomfort or difficulty in changing the object of attention or action.

From the functionality perspective, autistic people can be categorised as High-Functioning Autism (HFA) and Low-Functioning Autism (LFA). The differences in terms of abilities and need are very different. While the HFA have average or above average intelligence and may display exceptional skills, the LFA suffer from severe disabilities in nearly all areas of development and require support majorly in educational opportunities, physical and behavioural limitations and functional skills. The severity of the behavioural traits is often used to identify the impairments and understand and diagnose the disorder.

1.3   Autism Diagnosis Process

Typically, the ASD diagnostic process requires professionals to conduct a clinical assessment of developmental age-based activities on various categories, including behavioural excesses, communication, self-care, and social skills. Popular ASD diagnostic tools include the Autism Diagnostic Observation Schedule (ADOS) [17] and the Autism Diagnostic Interview-Revised (ADI-R) [25]. These tools follow the DSM-5 manual, which provides the standard language by which clinicians, researchers, and public health officials communicate about mental disorders [1]. However, due to the lack of concretely identifiable biomarkers and acceptable gold standards in diagnostic criteria, the manual tools heavily rely on behavioural observation data, which are administered and collected by healthcare professionals [28]. This type of data collected from behavioural actions and responses to social situations are often challenging to analyse as they depend on interpretation by the administrator and incompleteness in the data during the collection process [28]. Unlike some other biological data types, such as genetic, wearable and neuroimaging scans which have an optimised and established protocol for collection and analysis, there is no objectified system for capturing constant changes in someone's behavioural data [20].

To mitigate these challenges related to the assessments and accurate detection of ASD, recent years have seen a large number of activities from researchers focusing on using artificial intelligence (AI) and machine learning (ML) based methods to independently and accurately perceive relevant information from diverse sources [12,18,27]. Figure 2 shows a typical AI/ML based data processing pipeline to detect ASD using multimodal data acquired from various sources including self-reports [2], wearable devices [3], neuroimages [20] and behavioural data [23]. The pipeline consists of several steps including preprocessing, feature extraction, selection and fusion, model building and classification. Each of these steps are very important, but some of them may be skipped based on the type of data used.

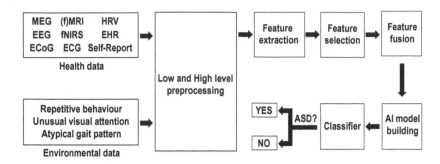

Fig. 2. Diagram of a representative pipeline showing most common steps in an AI-driven multimodal Autism detection system.

2   Artificial Intelligence in Autism Detection

Intelligent data-driven AI/ML based systems have been developed and utilised to detect autism and its severity in people. These systems have been found useful in identifying subjects with ASD and categorising them to different levels based on their social and communication skills and repetitive and unusual behavioural cues. Several sensors have been employed to gather data for accurate model building. Excluding genomics and clinical data, most of the proposed techniques have explored the possibility to be less intrusive in terms of data acquisition. As shown in Fig. 3, the acquired sensor data can be broadly categorised to: (i) *health data* containing recordings from sensors such as accelerometer, gyroscope, magnetometer, temperature sensor, heartbeat sensor, pedometer, brain scans/signals and at the same time electronic health records (EHR) and self-reports; and (ii) *behavioural data* that include global positioning system or GPS, video camera, eye tracker, motion sensors, force plate, Kinect and webcam.

These diverse multimodal data acquired from the body and the environment by means of sensors, electronic health records and self-reports cover two main aspects of the detection process: *the behavioural aspect* and *the affective aspect*. The various data streams related to the health data allow the identification of the affective state of the subject. Though in some cases, the individual data streams (e.g., self-report, heart rate variability, and brain scan/signals) may provide useful inference contributing to the detection of the disorder, when the complementary data streams are fused together, the detection accuracy of the affective state is increased [5]. The same applies in case of the the behavioural data related to the behavioural aspect of the subject. Some individual data streams such as camera, webcam, video camera, and GPS allow the detection of facial expression, body movements and posture, which provide essential information on the current emotional state of the subject as well as any repetitive behaviour including spinning, shaking and obsessive behaviour [16]. These data streams complement other data types, such as eye tracking, Kinect, force plate, which serve as valuable means for identifying attention-related behavioural cues. Once the behavioural cues and the affective states of the subject have been recognised,

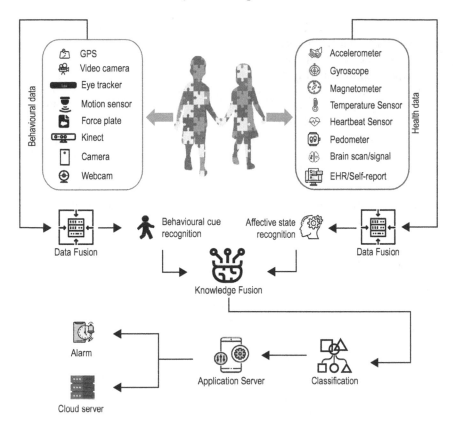

Fig. 3. An example of an Artificial Intelligence-driven multimodal autism detection system from *health data* and *environment data*.

the extracted knowledge is fused and fed to a machine learning based classifier for further classification to ASD and non-ASD. The outcome of the classification is then sent to an application server which runs a decision support system for further action (e.g., alarm, notification, etc.) and model preservation (e.g., contribute to a global model).

2.1 Explainable Artificial Intelligence in Autism Detection

Many of the advanced AI models that are popular today are known as *black box* models as they are difficult to understand, even by the experts who generated them, of their functioning and motivations based on of which these models learn and predict. The problem of inexplicability is intrinsic to the very structure of any system which, even when they are not "opaque", are often extremely complex, especially neural networks, made up of hundreds of hidden layers that transmit millions of signals in ways that are extremely difficult to reconstruct a posteriori. In situations relevant to critical areas of society, including health, care, assistance, independent living, it is essential that the decision making process is transparent and is clearly understood. To achieve this transparency, explainable AI (XAI) can play an essential role [6].

The explainability of AI methods cannot be merely considered as an algorithmic difficulty that demands a combination of best practices in data science and domain expertise, and it has a strong impact in terms of accountability, security and responsibility. XAI aims to allow computational scientists and relevant specialists (as in domain experts) to analyse a solution from end-to-end and to uncover inconsistencies which may lead to a sub-optimal performance in relation to the objectives of the task that the method is aiming to solve. XAI aims to shed light on the three processes of machine learning methods: (i) data analysis, (ii) model assessment and (iii) production monitoring. Figure 4 illustrates the functional block diagram of an XAI system.

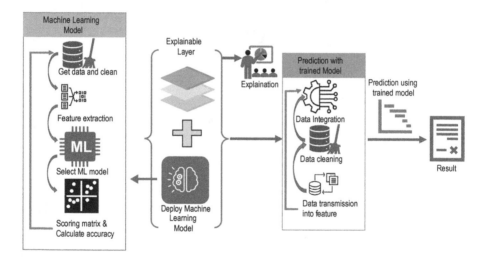

Fig. 4. A representative example of a pipeline with explainable artificial intelligence based approach for autism detection.

AI has been used for ASD care, especially in terms of symptom identification, diagnosis, and support. The detection process of ASD is a very sensitive one, even more sensitive is what strategy will be taken to support the persons with ASD. It is, therefore, necessary to compare predictions with ground truth (e.g., via split test) and evaluate the explainability (reasons) of the decision making (prediction) process [4,19,30].

2.2 Privacy-Preserving Artificial Intelligence in Autism Detection

With the advancement of AI, data privacy has been emphasised. As AI is developing the ability to mimic behaviour patterns, sensitive healthcare data are being shared around the world to help AI/ML algorithms improve people's experience, as well as learn new tasks and techniques across datasets. AI generates better results with more data. The main benefits provided by the FL is that it runs in a centralised server, maintains data security and privacy, forecasts/predicts in real time, it does not require internet and the hardware requirement is also minimum. Due to privacy concerns, we are unable to share very sensitive medical data including patient records across the internet and are still kept within the hospital premises. Federated learning (FL) is a next-generation AI method with better ideas about data privacy where building a model can be trusted to retain data. FL aids in the formation of the AI/ML algorithm and maintains data at the organisational level. As shown in Fig. 5, FL allows each organisation to keep its own private and secured local data and provides flexible models and ML solutions to manage real-time data [14]. Each of the local models is trained on the local data and then the weights of the models are shared with the global model across the internet.

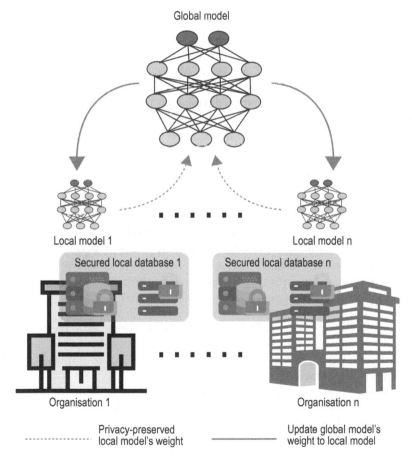

Fig. 5. An example of a *federated learning* based privacy preserving personalised model for autism detection.

Within the context of the current ASD detection framework, there are several sensitive health and behavioural data coming from a vulnerable population. These include electronic health records, self-reports about feelings, brain signals, physiological signals, video clips containing behavioural cues, facial expressions, postures, activities, etc. The FL preserves the data privacy and addresses the concerns related to the use of behavioural and health data. This is done by using the data in offline and online modes for training AI-based data-driven algorithms. The offline training happens through local models and their weights are shared with global models for online training. Depending on the operational context and the type of data, the method will choose a suitable AI technique. The traditional method, such as centralised ML, do not include these benefits and presents high data breach risk and requirs transfer of large files [15].

3   Artificial Intelligence in Autism Support

Recent research results show that people with ASD exhibit high levels of comfort when using digital devices such as computers, mobile phones, and tablets. Individuals identified for specific needs can benefit from a range of AI/ML algorithms. Additionally, a subset of AI/ML models can also serve as an intellectual outlet for those individuals to nurture their creativity. The stakeholders, including doctors, therapists, and educators have begun to explore AI-driven emerging technologies that can aid individuals with ASD in establishing personalised and assistive learning models, tools and social skills.

3.1   Artificial Intelligence in Rehabilitation of People with Autism

Due to the wide range of symptoms and their complexities exhibited in cases of ASD, it is not possible to identify a specific and exclusive treatment for all people with autism. However, there are treatments for ASD that can help them live better. The therapeutic path must be adapted to specific treatment plan, which should be adaptive to evolution and changes of symptoms. This is where AI-based methods can play an important role. Focusing on this, some potential therapies for the people with ASD where AI-driven tools to contribute are specified below:

- AI can facilitate the applied behavioural analysis for the analysis of behaviours, understand their causes and prevent problematic consequences by providing more effective and functional alternatives to improve their cognitive abilities, behaviours and language [24].
- AI-based methods can improve cognitive behavioural therapy delivery focusing on the enhancement of how nutrition, personal hygiene, ability to dress and regulate sleep can be made functional [13].

- Specific behavioural interventions can also be implemented with the help of AI-driven agents, such as robots, in the presence of fairly serious particular behaviours. This can help to decrease their frequency, severity and increase and develop adaptive capacities [26].
- AI-based tools can also support parent training which is an important path to facilitate the active involvement of parents to enable the activation and boost of social interventions to increase communication, facilitate an expansion of interests and promote emotional wellbeing [8].
- AI-based methods can facilitate the development of tools for the TEACCH programme [22] to develop and improve their autonomy to adapting it to their needs (visual cues, reduction of complex social interactions, follow a routine and minimise disturbing sensory stimulations). These intelligent tools can lead to improvements in motor skills, cognitive performance, social functioning and communication with other children [7].
- As an important development in the field of rehabilitation is the robot-assisted therapy which is often regarded as a game changer. People with ASD have benefited greatly from robot-aided therapy in recent years. As a result of advances in AI/ML and advanced robotics, cognitive and mental wellness can now be stimulated [26].

3.2   Artificial Intelligence in Education of Autistic Children

AI-enabled tools help teachers to let autistic students to walk the path of autonomy through exploration of individual skills and talents and adapting teaching strategies to support them. Figure 6 shows a representative AI/ML-based personalised education system which is capable of catering the need of the people with ASD. These kinds of systems are driven by the behavioural agents which serve as the core component of the system. Taking into consideration the behavioural and physiological data, these systems are capable of identifying the affective status of the learner and communicate that to teachers, carers or doctors - if needed. In addition, the communication with supportive agents, such as a robot, can help to detect learning status which can lead to tailor learning materials through an adaptive learning agent considering ontologies from teaching, learner model, task and subject matter. Finally, the adaptive learning material can be fed to the pedagogical agent to deliver to the learner.

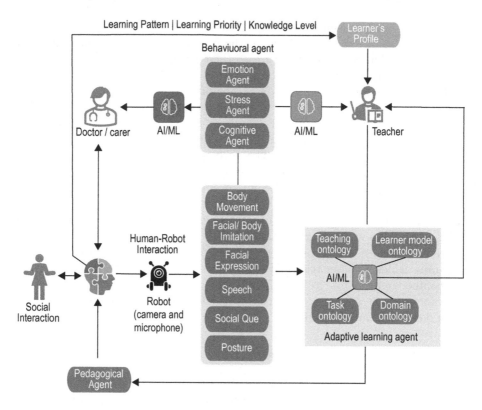

Fig. 6. A representative AI/ML-based personalised education system suitable for people with ASD.

In addition to the intelligent and adaptive learning systems shown in Fig. 6, AI/ML can support didactic strategies such as the ones listed below.

– XAI-driven *task decomposition* tools to allow an initially too complex task to be decomposed into simpler and more accessible sub-objectives. In this process XAI-led techniques can be of great support by creating personalised visual agendas based on individual learning needs. These agendas can visually illustrate different activities of the school day along with their times for the execution of the tasks including breakdown of a topic to be studied and creation of visual and oral cues to facilitate completion.
– XAI-enabled personalised *prompting and fading aid* tools along with relevant instructions can be used to facilitate the acquisition of a skill and consolidate it, even in visual format.
– XAI-driven personalised and *positive reinforcer* tools to create motivational charts and other visual tools to accompany the child as long as the reinforcer is needed.

– Personalised *generalisation and maintenance strategies* driven by XAI to cultivate the ability to extend the learning outside the context in which it was learned, with different people, materials and in different situations.

4   Challenges and Future Research Directions

Despite the ongoing efforts in developing explainable and privacy-preserving artificial intelligence for the personalisation of services to be used by people with ASD, there are several challenges that need to be addressed in the near future for the smooth usage of these tools and their integration in real-life scenarios. As shown in Fig. 7, there are four main areas which require improvement for better detection and support of people with ASD: (i) autism screening, (ii) autism monitoring, (iii) autism assistance and (iv) autism therapy.

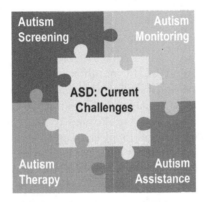

Fig. 7. Major areas of autism research that require attention.

The following list contains some open-challenges in autism detection and support where the multidisciplinary community can contribute.

– **Autism screening**:
  • Due to the heterogeneity in the ASD spectrum, not much data are available for each type of autism. Therefore more data is needed for making more accurate predictions.
  • More light-weight models are needed which are capable of executing in low-resource devices.
  • Novel explainable ML techniques which will be able to outperform the current methods in predicting more accurately the individual ASD cases.
– **Autism monitoring**:
  • Current monitoring devices are quite expensive which is a big barrier for their adoption in low-and-middle income countries.
  • Many of the currently used devices are off-the-shelf and require complete redesigning through co-creation to suit the need of people with ASD.

- Dedicated local communication protocols are needed which will allow faster and prioritised transmission of acquired data.
- **Autism assistance**:
  - Increase trustworthiness and reliability of the current assistive tools and devices so that they are welcome and accepted by the people with ASD.
  - Improve the design of the assistive agents with adaptive behaviour matching the characters of the user's preference.
  - Enhance the data privacy, security and trust issues making the assistive devices and tools to be impenetrable by intruders.
- **Autism therapy**:
  - Develop novel XAI algorithms for real-time processing of acquired data.
  - Develop personalised multi-layer, multi-stage and multimodal federated learning methods for real-time decision rendering.
  - Develop dedicated infrastructure capable of delivering solutions by cutting edge XAI/ML technologies.

5   Conclusion

There is an increasing trend in the number of people with autism spectrum disorder (ASD) worldwide and tackling this has been identified as a matter of priority by many countries now. Due to the extensive range of symptoms, their manifestations in people and the singularities of the conditions, they are challenging to be treated with conventional treatment strategies. To mitigate this, in recent years, growing efforts have been noticed from the artificial intelligence (AI) community to build intelligent systems capable of dealing with ASD and its heterogeneity for personalised and privacy-preserving service delivery. This work summarises the multitude of autism, its diagnosis process, and the role of AI in its detection and support. Focusing on explainable AI and federated learning for autism detection, it also discusses the role of AI in the rehabilitation of people with autism and their education. Towards the end, open challenges and future research directions are listed.

Acknowledgement. This work is supported by the AI-TOP (2020-1-UK01-KA201-079167) and DIVERSASIA (618615-EPP-1-2020-1-UKEPPKA2-CBHEJP) projects funded by the European Commission under the Erasmus+ programme.

References

1. Abbas, H., Garberson, F., Liu, M., Glover, E., Wall, D.: Multi-modular AI approach to streamline autism diagnosis in young children. Sci. Rep. **10**(1), 1–8 (2020)
2. Akter, T., Ali, M.H., Satu, M.S., Khan, M.I., Mahmud, M.: Towards autism subtype detection through identification of discriminatory factors using machine learning. In: Mahmud, M., Kaiser, M.S., Vassanelli, S., Dai, Q., Zhong, N. (eds.) BI 2021. LNCS (LNAI), vol. 12960, pp. 401–410. Springer, Cham (2021). https://doi.org/10.1007/978-3-030-86993-9_36

3. Al Banna, M.H., Ghosh, T., Taher, K.A., Kaiser, M.S., Mahmud, M.: A monitoring system for patients of autism spectrum disorder using artificial intelligence. In: Mahmud, M., Vassanelli, S., Kaiser, M.S., Zhong, N. (eds.) BI 2020. LNCS (LNAI), vol. 12241, pp. 251–262. Springer, Cham (2020). https://doi.org/10.1007/978-3-030-59277-6_23

4. Al Nahian, M.J., Ghosh, T., Al Banna, M.H., Aseeri, M.A., Uddin, M.N., et al.: Towards an accelerometer-based elderly fall detection system using cross-disciplinary time series features. IEEE Access **9**, 39413–39431 (2021)

5. Berman, J., et al.: Multimodal diffusion-MRI and meg assessment of auditory and language system development in autism spectrum disorder. Front. Neuroanat. **10**, 30 (2016)

6. Biswas, M., Kaiser, M., Mahmud, M., Al Mamun, S., Hossain, M., Rahman, M.: An XAI Based Autism Detection: The Context Behind the Detection. In: Mahmud, M., Kaiser, M., Vassanelli, S., Dai, Q., Zhong, N. (eds.) Proceedings Brain Informatics, vol. 12960 LNAI, pp. 448–459. Springer (2021). https://doi.org/10.1007/978-3-030-86993-9_40

7. Boucenna, S., et al.: Interactive technologies for autistic children: a review. Cogn. Comput. **6**(4), 722–740 (2014)

8. Entenberg, G.A., et al.: Using an artificial intelligence based chatbot to provide parent training: results from a feasibility study. Soc. Sci. **10**(11), 426 (2021)

9. Ghosh, T., et al.: Artificial intelligence and internet of things in screening and management of autism spectrum disorder. Sustain. Cities Soc. **74**, 103189 (2021)

10. Grzadzinski, R., Huerta, M., Lord, C.: DSM-5 and autism spectrum disorders (ASDs): an opportunity for identifying ASD subtypes. Mol. Autism **4**(1), 1–6, 103189 (2013)

11. Hendren, R.L., Haft, S.L., Black, J.M., White, N.C., Hoeft, F.: Recognizing psychiatric comorbidity with reading disorders. Front. Psychiatr. **9**, 101, 103189 (2018)

12. Jesmin, S., Kaiser, M., Mahmud, M.: Towards artificial intelligence driven stress monitoring for mental wellbeing tracking during COVID-19. In: He, J., Purohit, H., Huang, G., Gao, X., Deng, K. (eds.) Proceedings of the WI-IAT, pp. 845–851 (2020)

13. Kilburn, T., et al.: Group based cognitive behavioural therapy for anxiety in children with autism spectrum disorder: a randomised controlled trial in a general child psychiatric hospital setting. J. Autism Dev. Disord. 1–14 (2020). https://doi.org/10.1007/s10803-020-04471-x

14. Li, X., Gu, Y., Dvornek, N., Staib, L.H., Ventola, P., Duncan, J.S.: Multi-site fMRI analysis using privacy-preserving federated learning and domain adaptation: abide results. Medical Image Anal. **65**, 101765 (2020)

15. Li, X., Jiang, M., Zhang, X., Kamp, M., Dou, Q.: FedBN: federated learning on Non-IID features via local batch normalization. CoRR abs/2102.07623, pp. 1–27 (2021)

16. Lin, Y.S., Gau, S.S.F., Lee, C.C.: A multimodal interlocutor-modulated attentional BLSTM for classifying autism subgroups during clinical interviews. IEEE J. Sel. Top. Sign. Process. **14**(2), 299–311, 101765 (2020)

17. Molloy, C., Murray, D., Akers, R., et al.: Use of the autism diagnostic observation schedule (ADOS) in a clinical setting. Autism **15**(2), 143–162, 101765 (2011)

18. Nahian, M., Ghosh, T., Uddin, M.N., Islam, M., Mahmud, M., Kaiser, M.S., et al.: Towards artificial intelligence driven emotion aware fall monitoring framework suitable for elderly people with neurological disorder. In: Mahmud, M., Vassanelli, S., Kaiser, M., Zhong, N. (eds.) Proceedings of the Brain Informatics, pp. 275–286 (2020)

19. Nahiduzzaman, M., Tasnim, M., Newaz, N.T., Kaiser, M.S., Mahmud, M.: Machine learning based early fall detection for elderly people with neurological disorder using multimodal data fusion. In: Mahmud, M., Vassanelli, S., Kaiser, M.S., Zhong, N. (eds.) BI 2020. LNCS (LNAI), vol. 12241, pp. 204–214. Springer, Cham (2020). https://doi.org/10.1007/978-3-030-59277-6_19

20. Noor, M.B.T., Zenia, N.Z., Kaiser, M.S., Mamun, S.A., Mahmud, M.: Application of deep learning in detecting neurological disorders from magnetic resonance images: a survey on the detection of Alzheimer's disease. Parkinson's disease and schizophrenia. Brain Inform. **7**(1), 1–21 (2020)

21. Our World in Data: prevalence of autistic spectrum disorder (2017). Online (2022). https://ourworldindata.org/grapher/prevalence-of-autistic-spectrum. Accessed 11 Feb 2022

22. Panerai, S., Ferrante, L., Zingale, M.: Benefits of the treatment and education of autistic and communication handicapped children (TEACCH) programme as compared with a non-specific approach. J. Intellect. Disabil. Res. **46**(4), 318–327, 101765 (2002)

23. Rahman, S., Ahmed, S.F., Shahid, O., Arrafi, M.A., Ahad, M.: Automated detection approaches to autism spectrum disorder based on human activity analysis: a review. Cogn. Comput. 1–28 (2021). https://doi.org/10.1007/s12559-021-09895-w

24. Rehman, I., Sobnath, D., Nasralla, M., Winnett, M., Anwar, A., Asif, W., et al.: Features of mobile apps for people with autism in a post COVID-19 scenario: current status and recommendations for apps using AI. Diagnostics **11**(10), 1923, 101765 (2021)

25. Saemundsen, E., Magnússon, P., Smári, J., Sigurdardóttir, S.: Autism diagnostic interview-revised and the childhood autism rating scale: convergence and discrepancy in diagnosing autism. J. Autism Dev. Disord. **33**(3), 319–328 (2003)

26. Saleh, M.A., Hanapiah, F.A., Hashim, H.: Robot applications for autism: a comprehensive review. Disabil. Rehabil.: Assist. Technol. **16**(6), 580–602 (2021)

27. Sumi, A.I., Zohora, M.F., Mahjabeen, M., Faria, T.J., Mahmud, M., Kaiser, M.S.: fASSERT: a fuzzy assistive system for children with autism using internet of things. In: Wang, S., Yamamoto, V., Su, J., Yang, Y., Jones, E., Iasemidis, L., Mitchell, T. (eds.) BI 2018. LNCS (LNAI), vol. 11309, pp. 403–412. Springer, Cham (2018). https://doi.org/10.1007/978-3-030-05587-5_38

28. Thabtah, F.: Machine learning in autistic spectrum disorder behavioral research: a review and ways forward. Inform. Health Soc. Care **44**(3), 278–297, 101765 (2019)

29. WHO: Autism spectrum disorders. Online (2022). https://www.who.int/news-room/fact-sheets/detail/autism-spectrum-disorders. Accessed 15 Feb 2022

30. Zohora, M.F., Tania, M.H., Kaiser, M.S., Mahmud, M.: Forecasting the risk of type II diabetes using reinforcement learning. In: Proceedings of the ICIEV icIVPR, pp. 1–6 (2020)

Accessibility Criteria for an Inclusive Museum for People with Learning Disabilities: A Review

Linda Münch[1]([✉]) [iD], Tanja Heuer[2] [iD], Ina Schiering[2] [iD], and Sandra Verena Müller[1] [iD]

[1] Faculty of Social Work, Ostfalia University of Applied Sciences, Salzdahlumer Straße 46/48, 38302 Wolfenbüttel, Germany
li.muench@ostfalia.de
[2] Faculty of Computer Science, Ostfalia University of Applied Sciences, Salzdahlumer Straße 46/48, 38302 Wolfenbüttel, Germany

Abstract. This review strives to collect, contrast, and systematize criteria for an inclusive museum for people with learning disabilities in guidelines and scientific publications. The aim is to provide an overview of relevant criteria and information for museums to improve access for people with learning disabilities. In addition, it will be examined to which extent persons with learning disabilities are involved in the development of guidelines or the research of accessibility requirements. A literature review was conducted to identify relevant accessibility criteria for people with learning disabilities. The review highlights that scientific publications focus on exhibits for the inclusion of people with learning disabilities, whereas guidelines propose general actions and measures. In particular, guidelines mention many access preferences for people with learning disabilities, whereas many of these criteria do not appear to be generally accepted yet, because some criteria are considered important by only one guideline. The small number of relevant guidelines and scientific publications identified in this review signifies that people with learning disabilities are only partly considered within the museum context so far. The importance of participatory research approaches is emphasized but commonly not yet been implemented. There is a need for further research that focuses on access preferences and the specific needs of people with learning disabilities in a participatory way. The development of guidelines should be accompanied by scientific studies, and research projects should pursue more participatory research approaches. Furthermore, the benefits of digital assistive technologies as mediation media should be examined in future works even more.

Keywords: Learning disability · Inclusive museum · Museum accessibility · Accessibility criteria

1 Introduction

According to Arinze [2, p. 1] *"the early museums were elitist, uninspiring and aloof as they encouraged only the educated people to visit them. The general public were excluded"*. There is the assumption that the origin of the museum lies in the publication of private collections. The purposes of museums range from attributes of sacred and profane power through a personal demonstration of wealth to the acquisition of knowledge and

M. Antona and C. Stephanidis (Eds.): HCII 2022, LNCS 13309, pp. 371–385, 2022.
https://doi.org/10.1007/978-3-031-05039-8_27

culture [23]. The post-ancient was the beginning of ecclesiastical and royal treasuries. One example is the *"Königliche Schatz-Kammer"* in Dresden, which was established in 1723. Not everyone and only a maximum of three guests at the same time were allowed to visit it [27]. At the end of the 18th century in the context of elucidation and revolution, a location emerges, where objects were permanently stored and exhibited to visit for everyone. Additionally, there was the need of explanations for the exhibits for the wide public [27]. The goal of museum development from then on is the welfare of society as a whole. To make this possible, the museums must be accessible to everyone. Nevertheless, museums define access in different and often competing ways. Bennett [3] described this contradiction in his book "The birth of the museum": On the one hand, there is the demand for more cultural participation and thus for barrier-free access, that museums are accessible to all people and their needs, regardless of their gender, nationality, disability, etc. For this purpose, it is not enough to reproduce information in text form. Visitors should be given the opportunity to experience it via different channels according to their requirements. On the other hand, museums are obliged to restrict the access to collections and public handling, to preserve cultural heritage. Or to put it in Bennett's [3, p. 105] words: *"[...] museum's future as part of the leisure industry, urging that the people should be given what they want, while the latter, retaining the view of museums as instruments of instruction, argues they should remain means for lifting the cultural and intellectual level of the population."*

Thus, today's museums can have an exclusive and inclusive character. Dodd and Sandell [11, p. 15] give an overview about that: *"It will be argued then that museums should have a social purpose - that the functions or activities of collecting, preserving and displaying are not undertaken for their own sake but rather as means to a number of social ends. Those ends may take many forms - museums can inspire, educate, inform; they can promote creativity, broaden horizons and expose people to new ways of looking at the world, all of which have a relevance to discussions about the museum's contribution to social inclusion. They also have the potential to deliver social outcomes less commonly assigned to museums - they can enhance individuals' self-esteem, empower communities to take greater control over their lives, challenge stereotypes and tackle intolerance. Some of them can utilise their social impact to play a direct role in combating some of the problems that disadvantage many diverse communities and individuals described by some as 'socially excluded' - poor health, crime, low educational attainment and unemployment".*

The last decades have prompted museums to rethink their purpose and responsibilities in society. The traditional concept of museums in terms of limiting the reception of their exhibition content and the curation of exhibitions were in contrast to the civic purpose of museums. That is why museums have developed an increasing awareness of the needs of the general public and to think about more participatory conceptions of exhibitions [13]. But there has been also an increasingly professional and academic debate and research around the issues of social inclusion agendas of museums. Dodd and Sandell [11, p. 24] summarize the statements of some critics: *"[...] social inclusion has been responsible for diverting museums from their core purposes and goals, subverting their roles and responsibilities to political and governmental ends, politicising an otherwise 'objective' and 'neutral' organisation, putting collections and their care at risk and transforming curators into social workers".*

Contrary to the critics, specifically in the context of cultural history museum conversation, Graham [17, p. 150] appeals, *"to put forward a model for participation at the museum that rethinks ideas of access, use and participation"*. She argues *"for an understanding of conservation as a participatory practice that prevents the object from not only 'running out' materially, but also running out of people's interest"*. Furthermore, Cachia [6, p. 5] describes curatorial access as a *"creative methodology"*, where she involves artists to make their own artworks accessible to people with disabilities. She uses alternative platforms like a virtual art exhibition as a new possibility of access in contemporary art and *"aims to push against the conventional practices of exhibitions"*. Moreover, French [13, p. 8] advise that museums should consider curating exhibitions in a more collaborative and participatory way. She includes people with learning disabilities as *"inclusive curators"* in the conception of an exhibition.

Because of the extensive socio-political and disability rights policy in recent years also the cultural participation and inclusion of people with disabilities have become a more and more urgent topic and have found their way into the legislation. In Article 30, Paragraph 1 on *"Participation in cultural life, recreation, leisure and sport"*, of the Convention on the Rights of Persons with Disabilities lays down the right of people with disabilities to participate in cultural life. More precisely, it obliges the States Parties to *"take all appropriate measures to ensure that persons with disabilities enjoy access to cultural materials in accessible formats; enjoy access to television programs films, theatre, and other cultural activities, in accessible formats; enjoy access to places for cultural performances or services, such as theatres, museums, cinemas, libraries and tourism services, and, as far as possible, enjoy access to monuments and sites of national cultural importance"* [26, p. 18].

As previously described, the aspect of accessibility is of particular importance in the inclusion agendas of museums. It should be ensured that access to the museum and its mediation content is barrier-free [5]. Access barriers to museums can exist on a spatial, sensory or intellectual level. Examples are uneven paths, unisensory mediation offers, and complex written texts. There is still development potential of accessibility in museums for people with learning disabilities [18, 24]. Nevertheless, some museums already have developed access measures for visitors with learning disabilities (for example: Museum of Modern Art in Manhattan, Victoria and Albert Museum in London and Historical Museum in Frankfurt). There are also some examples of scientific publications and guidelines that have dealt with the access preferences and the design of barrier-free activities of people with various disabilities, including people with learning disabilities, which will be introduced in the following.

This review aims to collect, contrast and systematize criteria for an inclusive museum for people with learning disabilities.

- in guidelines and
- scientific publications.

The aim is to provide an overview of relevant criteria and to provide information for museums to improve access for people with learning disabilities. "Criteria" will be used as a term for the requirements a museum needs to fulfil for barrier-free accessibility for people with learning disabilities. Also, it will be examined to which extent persons with learning disabilities were involved in the development of guidelines or the research of accessibility requirements.

2 Methodology

The review was split into two main steps. As a first step, a general search in the period from January 2021 to February 2021 was conducted to gain knowledge on the subject of museums and people with learning disabilities to identify relevant sources for this field. Sources involve guidelines and scientific publications.

In a second step, a systematic search in the period from March 2021 to April 2021 was performed based on the results of the general overview in the first step. Based on the overview, guidelines and scientific publications were collected depending on the following exclusion and inclusion criteria. Overall, inclusion criteria were that (1) the source is written in German or English and (2) the source refers to people with learning disabilities (all ages) in museums. Depending on the types of sources, different search terms were identified. They will be described in a more detailed way in the following sections. Furthermore, the search and selection strategy for both sources will be summarized.

2.1 Guidelines

Guidelines and handbooks for inclusive museums are classified as grey literature, mostly available as open access, typically provided on the websites of responsible institutions. Searches were conducted using a standard search engine for web search (i.e. Google). The following search terms were used: "guideline", "guide", "handbook", "inclusive", "accessibility", "museum" as well as different terms for "learning disability" which were also used for the search of scientific publications (see Table 1). Thereby, six of the guidelines were found directly using the search terms and one guideline was found through a project, which matches the topic [1]. Two guidelines were excluded because the intended target group was not considered. The following five guidelines were considered for the analysis because of matching inclusion criteria:

- DESIGN FOR ALL – Barrier-free exhibitions in Berlin – Understand checklist [20]
- The inclusive museum – A guideline to accessibility and inclusion [9]
- Towards a participatory museum – A how-to-guide on inclusive activities [14]
- Travel for everyone – Quality criteria: Requirements for people with cognitive impairments [10]
- Come-In! Guidelines [19]

2.2 Scientific Publications

The search is based on databases of academic, primary peer-reviewed scientific publications. The databases PubMed, PsycInfo, Web of Science, ASSIA – ProQuest, ERIC, and Science Direct were chosen, as they cover social sciences, psychological and natural science perspectives. The search was limited to scientific publications that were published from January 2010 to April 2021. Thereby, types of research such as qualitative or quantitative case studies, surveys as well as review studies were included. As Types of documents journal articles, conference proceedings and reports and book chapters were involved. The extraction of the data is exemplary presented in Table 1 for the search strategy.

Table 1. Search strategy (Final search performed on 9th April 2021, plurals were allowed by including wildcards (*). Colum's were combined by the use of the Boolean operator AND.

Learning disability	Museum
(intellectual disab* OR developmental disab* OR intellectual defici* OR mental retard* OR learning disab* OR learning difficult*)	(museum OR exhibition*)

The mixing of keywords ensured that scientific publications, which included the two topics of research focus, were identified. Furthermore, reference lists of retrieved documents were searched for other scientific publications that addressed the inclusion criteria.

A total of 351 research results were retrieved from the database searches (PubMed: n = 43, PsycInfo: n = 38, Web of Science: n = 52, ASSIA – ProQuest: n = 25, ERIC: n = 145, Science Direct: n = 48). Additional 22 scientific publications were gained through citations, reference lists and general hand search. After removing duplicates, the relevance of the remaining 360 results were examined based on the title. According to the title, 63 articles remained and were assessed for eligibility based on the abstracts of which only 23 appeared to be relevant. Of these 23 articles, 9 remaining full-text articles were considered to be relevant, but two were excluded afterwards because of reasons that are explained following. The systematic search process is illustrated in Fig. 1.

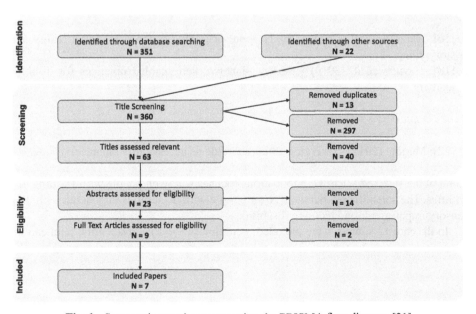

Fig. 1. Systematic search process using the PRISMA flow diagram [21]

Two independent reviewers reviewed the abstracts and the full text screening. Scientific publications were excluded due to lack of relevance when the articles related to other (cultural) facilities, other target groups or focused on technical frameworks and algorithms. When it was obvious through the title that other disabilities (e.g. sensory disabilities) than learning disabilities were meant, there were removed. Was an unspecific wording used, such as "individuals with disabilities" or "visitors with special needs" abstracts and full-texts were screened for the specific meaning or more specifically, whether it includes people with learning disabilities. It was also checked more closely when the word "cognitive disabilities" was used to rule out people with dementia, for example. As well, neurodevelopmental disorders, such as autism spectrum disorder and attention deficit hyperactivity disorders were excluded, when it was not clear if they are accompanied by learning disability. Similarly, when no reference to the museum's context was apparent, for example by general terms like "cultural heritage" or "cultural sites", these studies were also sorted out, during the search. In addition, other types of documents like thesis's were excluded in the full text screening.

At the end, seven relevant scientific publications were selected:

Journal Articles

- [4]: Braden (2016) - Overview of museum offerings for people with disabilities,
- [15]: Garcia Carrizosa et al. (2019b) - Challenges of participatory research with people with disabilities,
- [24]: Reichinger et al. (2018) - Study with interactive gesture-controlled reliefs to explore art,
- [25]: Sheehy et al. (2019) - Review of augmented reality for accessibility.

Conference Proceedings and Reports

- [16]: Garzotto et al. (2018) - Study about accessibility through virtual reality and storytelling,
- [18]: Hayhoe et al. (2019) - Survey of networked enabled practices for disabled learners,

Book Chapters

- [22]: Martins (2012) - Overview of audio guide as accessibility enhancer.

None of the selected scientific publications focuses solely on people with learning disabilities. The scientific publications cover people with disabilities in general, including sensory impairments and learning disabilities.

In the end, 12 sources were included: guidelines (n = 5) and scientific publications (n = 7).

3 Results

The identified types of sources mentioned in the section before, are analyzed in this section. First, the guidelines are considered as basic manual for inclusion-related exhibition design. Based on the foci of the guidelines, categories for criteria are derived. Thereupon, the essential aspects of scientific publications are investigated and contrasted with the defined criteria categories of the guidelines.

3.1 Guidelines

To gain an overview about which criteria are considered as necessary for an accessible museum for people with learning disabilities, the five selected guidelines were investigated. The development of the guidelines is based on findings of research projects in collaboration with associations of people with disabilities [14, 19] as well as on real-world experiences, e.g. made by museums, tourist associations and/or associations of people with disabilities [9, 10, 20]. The guidelines with corresponding criteria are presented in Table 2.

Among the guidelines, there are different emphases. While the guideline designed by LMB & Senatskanzlei Berlin [20] highlight aspects on *Orientation and Guidance*, *Exhibits, Content* and *Access to museums*, the How-to-Guide by Garcia et al. [14] focuses mainly on *Staff, Tours and Workshops*. The guideline from the DMB [9] only underlines the areas of *Exhibits* and *Content* and does not provide any information on the other areas. The DSFT [10] and Interreg CENTRAL EUROPE [19] guidelines concentrate on the areas of *Orientation and Guidance* and *Access to museums*. Based on the foci of the guidelines, the identified criteria are clustered into five categories:

- *Orientation and Guidance*
- *Exhibits*
- *Content*
- *Staff, Tours and Workshops*
- *Access to museums*

The *Orientation and Guidance* category deals with the design and presentation of the exhibition and the need for a guidance system. The category *Exhibits* relate to the presentation and characteristics of the exhibits. The *Content* category is primarily about how the text can be presented to the target group to promote a better understanding. The category *Staff, Tours and Workshops* includes criteria that deal with staff and their visitor-oriented mediation skills. The *Access to museums* category emphasizes that visitors with learning disabilities should get easy-to-read information about accessibility on-site on the Internet before the visit.

Table 2. Criteria guidelines

Criteria \ Guidelines	[20]	[9]	[14]	[10]	[19]
Orientation and Guidance					
3D representation of exhibition rooms	X				X
generous room design	X			X	X
pictorial guidance or thematic route	X			X	X
Exhibits					
multisensory	X	X	X		X
touchable exhibits	X				X
call for action	X	X			
enough space between exhibits	X				X
360° view of some exhibits	X				
economical use of effects	X				
easy to handle	X				
use of different media				X	X
movies in simplified language		X			
quiet-zones and seats	X				
Content					
good structured	X				
central questions for self-discovery	X				
everyday relevance	X				
easy-to-read information	X	X	X	X	X
high-contrast layout	X		X		X
big font	X		X		X
text-to-speech system available	X			X	
visualization with pictorial language	X	X	X	X	
information material should be color-fully illustrated, offered as easy-to-read information	X				
Staff, Tours and Workshops					
trained staff	X				
visitor-oriented mediation offers	X		X		X
repetitions			X		
the transition between activities should be slowly			X		
enough time			X		
simplified language			X		
storyboard style as an additional communication method			X		
Access to museums (Information on the Internet in easy-to-read information about an available illustrated guidance system)					
barrier-free information about the path from the public transport stop to the museum	X			X	X
barrier-free access from the museum entrance to the exhibition	X			X	X
barrier-free access to functional rooms	X			X	X
name and logo of the museum must be recognizable from outside				X	
economical accessibility					X

3.2 Scientific Publications

Garcia Carrizosa et al. [15], Reichinger et al. [24], Sheehy et al. [25] and Hayhoe et al. [18] are releases from the ARCHES (Accessible Resources for Cultural Heritage EcoSystems) project (e.g. literature reviews or evaluation studies). The project units disabled people, technology companies, universities and museums to develop technological solutions in a participatory research process in order to develop new accessibility tools for museums [1]. Braden [4] gives an overview of museum offerings to enhance accessibility for people with disabilities. Garzotto et al. [16] present the concept of Wearable Immersive Social Stories as a new technological tool for museums and describe the design process in cooperation with experts for people with learning disabilities but not with people with learning disabilities themselves. However, the authors added that they want to involve people with learning disabilities in validating the Wearable Immersive Social Stories for future research. Martins [22] refers to a case study about analyzing the offering of audio guides as accessibility enhancers in Portuguese museums and other cultural institutions. They only tested the audio guides with the target group but emphasized the importance also to involve them in the development of audio guides or new exhibitions.

Similar to the guidelines, the mentioned and relevant criteria that could be beneficial for people with learning disabilities within the scientific publications were worked out. As guidelines are more complex and specific than the scientific publications, some categories were merged (Table 3) for a clearer presentation, which summarizes the categories from Table 2.

Table 3. Criteria scientific publications

Scientific Publications / Criteria	[18]	[24]	[15]	[25]	[4]	[16]	[22]
Orientation, Guidance and Access to museums							
planning of the visit					x		
guidance					x		
Exhibits and Content							
multisensory	x	x		x	x	x	
tactile sense					x		
hearing sense		x					x
visual sense		x	x			x	
Staff, Tours and Workshops							
trained staff		x	x				
visitor-oriented mediation offers		x	x		x	x	

The categories *Orientation and Guidance* and *Access to museums* from Table 2 were combined, as well as *Exhibits* and *Content*. As a result, there are three categories for criteria derived from scientific publications:

- *Orientation, Guidance and Access to museums,*
- *Exhibits and Content,*
- *Staff, Tours and Workshops.*

Furthermore, some thematically related criteria were combined into one criterion:

- multisensory = multisensory; call for action
- visual sense = easy-to-read information; high-contrast layout; big font; movies in simplified language; visualization with pictorial language
- trained staff = repetitions; the transition between activities should be slowly; enough time; simplified language
- visitor-orientated mediation offers = mediation offers; storyboard style as an additional communication method

Some criteria of the guidelines were not considered in the further analysis because they were not mentioned in the selected scientific publications. Thereupon, the identified criteria from the scientific publications were assigned to one of the combined categories that fits best. All those criteria that only one guideline mentions as access preferences for people with learning disabilities seem not yet widely approved as such (see Table 2).

Scientific publications and guidelines will be analyzed and contrasted in more detail in the following, based on the respective categories described above.

4   Contrast of Guidelines and Scientific Publications

The guidelines are intended to propose an overview of accessibility-enhancing criteria. They offer an extensive listing of accessibility measures. Whereas scientific publications have the purpose to investigate specific criteria instead of giving an overview of everything. Thereby, the two tables cannot directly be compared. Nevertheless, identified criteria of the scientific publications are contrasted to the ones of the guidelines in the following. By that, the focus was on which criteria are considered in the scientific publications and whether additional criteria and measures, which could be particularly beneficial for people with learning disabilities, were addressed in the scientific publications but not mentioned in the guidelines.

The focal point in the scientific publications is on the category *Exhibits and Content*. The key aspect was on the development of multisensory exhibits and mediation offers to experience the exhibition with different senses. Four scientific publications concentrate on the evaluation of specific mediation offers for people with learning disabilities. They concentrate on existing and new offers for the target group and an evaluation from users' perspective. Therefore, different technologies were investigated, e.g. virtual reality storytelling [16], museum audio guide [22], augmented reality [25] or interactive gesture-controlled reliefs to explore art [24]. The category *Staff, Tours and Workshops* is partly mentioned in the scientific publications. There the focus is on the criteria "visitor-oriented mediation offers". The category *Orientation, Guidance and Access to museums* is the least treated category. The criteria "planning of the visit" and "guidance" are each mentioned by only one scientific publication. Scientific publications do not focus on the accessibility of museums in terms of the necessary accessibility requirements for the directions to and from or within the museum or examine what the mediation skills of the museum staff should be like, but instead investigate specific mediation offers more broadly.

The guidelines propose a wide range of possibilities to ensure an inclusive museum for people with learning disabilities. Many of the mentioned criteria are part of the categories *Orientation and Guidance* and *Access to museums* (see Table 2) which are combined in Table 3, whereas the scientific publications place the least emphasis on this category. Additionally, on guidelines, the need for easy-to-read information is assessed as essential. Easy-to-read information is the only criterion that is appearing in all five guidelines. In the scientific publications, language aspects were maximally mentioned (e.g. *"simplified language"* see [24, p. 36]) but not discussed in detail. It is mainly focused that text should not only be readable but also available as audio and preferably illustrated with pictures or videos. Both in the guidelines and in the scientific publications, the criterion "multisensory" is classified as significant for the accessibility to museums of people with learning disabilities.

5 Discussion

When analyzing the guidelines and scientific publications, it becomes clear that there are different foci between both sources. The guidelines mainly address criteria, which refer to the overall structure and design of the museum and public relations (categories: *Orientation and Guidance, Access to museums*). Scientific publications, in contrast, place most emphasis on the category *Exhibits and Content*, as they are interested in exhibition evaluation towards the target group. The scientific publications do not focus on specific senses but rather on multisensory. Multisensory experience can often be realized using media stations, showing videos using sound and subtitles. In the scientific publications, these media stations are mostly considered useful for the hearing sense giving examples such as audio guides and scanning pens [22]. Next to audio guides, scientific publications also propose more recent technologies such as virtual reality to visualize the exhibits in a more imaginable way [16]. It could be used to provide personal guidance, to make social stories available depending on personal interests, etc. Even though the aspect of "different media stations" were not discussed in the scientific publications, because they only focus on a certain medium, this is important as it makes the exhibition more diversified and going along with that more interesting. Features such as hands-on exhibits and possibly also taste and smell stations help to create a multisensory experience. Eardley et al. [12] also emphasize the importance of the aspect of multisensory in their study. It helps understanding exhibits in their true physical depiction and benefits the learning opportunity of all (disabled) visitors because also our brains deal with information multisensory. Furthermore, multisensory information also enhances autobiographical memory, and therefore the significance of museums at all.

Within the *Content* category, "easy-to-read information" is the only criterion that all five guidelines cite as an essential criterion for the accessibility of people with learning disabilities. Thereby, "easy-to-read" texts are not discussed within the scientific publications. Bearing in mind that people with learning disabilities could have difficulties reading texts [7], it is doubtful that "easy-to-read information" is one of the most important criteria for them. The question arises as to whose reading skills the easy-to-read information is addressing. What is perceived as "easy" or "difficult" depends on the competencies of the individual and cannot be generalized [7]. Beside easy-to-read information, it would be helpful to provide a text-to-speech option on museum websites and audio guides or audible information accessible via QR codes within the exhibition.

The target group is mainly included in the designation of accessibility requirements for guidelines, but the development of these guidelines is not often scientifically investigated. Furthermore, it was not possible to determine the extent, to which people with learning disabilities were involved in the guideline development. Although the scientific publications are scientifically sound, the active involvement of people with learning disabilities in the research process is usually rare. The ARCHES project offers a best practice example. The target group were actively included in the research process, and an interdisciplinary team worked according to scientific standards. Nevertheless, there is a need for further research that focuses on access preferences and the specific needs of people with learning disabilities [18, 24] in a participatory way [25]. Concisely, the development of guidelines should be more scientifically based, and research projects should pursue more participatory research approaches.

This review has some limitations. The first issue is the small number of relevant sources (n = 12) that were included. This may be related to the fact that the focus of the search was on a specific target group and not broadly on disability access as well as on museums instead of general cultural facilities. If during the search no reference to the museum context as well as specifically to the target group was apparent, the sources were sorted out. At the same time, it also reinforces the assumption that people with learning disabilities are still under-examined in the field of cultural participation in museums. In this regard, a closer look at people with learning disabilities and, in particular, their cultural participation in museums would be worth investigating in future research.

Another limitation is that the selection of the databases was more from a social science perspective than from a museum science perspective.

6   Conclusion and Future Directions

Overall, this review has highlighted that research focuses on exhibits for inclusion of people with learning disabilities, whereas guidelines propose a wider range of necessary actions and measures. In particular, guidelines mention many access preferences of people with learning disabilities, whereas many of these criteria do not appear to be generally accepted yet, because some criteria are considered important by only one guideline. This requires further research.

Easy-to-read information is the most commonly used support for people with learning disabilities suggested from the guidelines but should be critically reflected because it depends on the individual what is understood as easy [7]. Both the guidelines and the scientific publications show that multisensory stations within the exhibitions turn out to be relevant for people with learning disabilities. With the implementation of multisensory exhibits, several groups of persons can be addressed and visitors can dedicate on preferred stimulation and benefit of a more interesting visit [12]. In particular, this involves interactive stations with hands-on exhibits to get a feeling of material and structure or allowing explore specific aspects in a playful way.

People with learning disabilities are only partly considered within the museum context so far. Limited mediation offers for people with learning disabilities raise the need for further investigations. In addition, it is recommended that the development of guidelines should consider more scientific standards in the future.

This review addresses museum practitioners so far, because it gives hints on how museums could be created more accessible. To get an idea of what accessibility requirements people with learning disabilities need within museums, it is necessary to involve them in a participatory approach [25]. Rather than museums responding to the needs of people with learning disabilities, further investigations could examine how people with learning disabilities could be supported to actively conduct inclusive projects in museums. One example are the case studies and collaborative projects by French [13], which includes people with learning disabilities as inclusive curators in the conception of a museum exhibition.

In further investigations, we would like to focus on digital assistive technologies as some examples already proved to be useful (e.g. [16]). The advantage of the approach lies in the diversity of the presentation. Not only people with learning disabilities but also others might benefit from that because the needs of people with learning disabilities can also correspond to the needs of people with other disabilities.

Acknowledgments. The research was funded by the Ministry for Science and Culture of Lower Saxony and the Leibniz Association as part of the program "Leibniz-ScienceCampus – Postdigital Participation – Braunschweig".

-NoValue-

References

1. ARCHES. ARCHES helps European museums to become barrier-free with 3D art replicas, mobile phone apps, games and sign language video avatars, (n. d.). https://www.arches-pro ject.eu/
2. Arinze, E.N.: The Role of the Museum in Society. Public lecture at the National Museum, Georgetown, Guyana Monday, May 17 1999. https://pdfcoffee.com/the-role-of-a-museum-pdf-free.html
3. Bennett, T.: The Birth of the Museum: History, Theory, Politics. Routledge, London (1995). https://doi.org/10.4324/9781315002668
4. Braden, C.: Welcoming All Visitors: Museums, Accessibility, and Visitors with Disabilities. Ann Arbor: University of Michigan Working Papers in Museum Studies (2016). http://ummsp. rackham.umich.edu/wp-content/uploads/2016/10/Braden-working-paper-FINAL-pdf.pdf
5. Brinkmeyer, D.: Museum ohne Grenzen – Multimediale Anwendungen und Barrierefreiheit in der Berlinischen Galerie [Museum without borders – multimedia applications and accessibility in the Berlinische Galerie]. In: Hausmann, A., Frenzel, L. (eds.) Kunstvermittlung 2.0: Neue Medien und ihre Potenziale, pp. 105–121. Springer, Wiesbaden (2014). https://link.spr inger.com/chapter/10.1007/978-3-658-02869-5_7

6. Cachia, A.: 'Disabling' the museum: curator as infrastructural activist. Canadian J. Disabil. Stud. **2**(4), 1–39 (2013). https://doi.org/10.15353/cjds.v2i4.110
7. Conners, F.A.: Reading skills and cognitive abilities of individuals with mental retardation. In: Abbeduto, L., (eds.) International Review of Research in Mental Retardation: Language and Communication in Mental Retardation, pp. 191–229. San Diego Academic Press, San Diego, USA (2003). https://doi.org/10.1016/S0074-7750(03)27006-3
8. Deutsch, C.K., Dube, W.V., McIlvane, W.J.: Attention deficits, attention-deficit hyperactivity disorder, and intellectual disabilities. Dev. Disabil. Res. Rev. **14**(4), 285–292 (2008). https://doi.org/10.1002/ddrr.42
9. Deutscher Museumsbund (DMB): Das inklusive Museum – Ein Leitfaden zu Barriere-freiheit und Inklusion [The inclusive museum – A guideline to accessibility and inclusion] (2013). https://www.museumsbund.de/wp-content/uploads/2017/03/dmb-barrierefrei heit-digital-160728.pdf
10. Deutsches Seminar für Tourismus Berlin e.V. (DSFT): Reisen für Alle – Qualität-skriterien: Anforderungen für Menschen mit kognitiven Beeinträchtigungen [Travel for everyone – Quality criteria: Requirements for people with cognitive impair-ments] (2020). https://www.reisen-fuer-alle.de/qualitaetskriterien_fuer_menschen_mit_kog nitiven_beeintraechtigungen_329.html
11. Dodd, J., Sandell, R.: Including museums: perspectives on museums, galleries and social inclusion. Leicester [England: Research Centre for Museums and Galleries, University of Leicester] (2001). https://leicester.figshare.com/articles/report/Including_museums_perspec tives_on_museums_galleries_and_social_inclusion/10076588/1
12. Eardley, A.F., Mineiro, C., Neves, J., Ride, P.: Redefining access: embracing multimodality, memorability and shared experience in museums. Curator: The Museum J. **59** (3), 263–286 (2016). https://doi.org/10.1111/cura.12163. In: 9th International Proceedings on Proceedings, pp. 1–2
13. French, J.: Inclusive curating in contemporary art: a practical guide. ARC Humanities Press. Br. J. Learn. Disabil. **49**(3), 383–384 (2020). https://doi.org/10.1111/bld.12381
14. Carrizosa, H.G., Diaz, J., Krall, R., Faye, A., Skrbic, S., Ganly, F.S.: Towards a participatory museum – A how-to-guide on inclusive activities, Vienna. ARCHES (2019a). https://www.arches-project.eu/wp-content/uploads/2019/07/EnglishGuide_Hyperlinks.pdf
15. Carrizosa, H.G., Diaz, J., Krall, R., Ganly, F.S.: Cultural differences in ARCHES: a European participatory research project—working with mixed access preferences in different cultural heritage sites. Int. J. Inclusive Museum **12**(3), 30–55 (2019b). https://doi.org/10.18848/1835-2014/CGP/v12i03/33-50
16. Garzotto, F., Matarazzo, V., Messina, N., Gelsomini, M., Riva, C.: Improving museum acces-sibility through storytelling in wearable immersive virtual reality. 3rd Digital Heritage Interna-tional Congress (DigitalHERITAGE). In: 24th International Conference on Virtual Systems & Multimedia, pp. 1–8 (2018). https://doi.org/10.1109/DigitalHeritage.2018.8810097
17. Graham, H.C.: Publics and Commons: The Problem of Inclusion for Participation. ARKEN Bulletin, vol. 7, pp. 150–168 (2017). https://www.arken.dk/wp-content/uploads/2017/04/pub lics-and-commons...-by-helen-graham_bulletin-2017-1.pdf
18. Hayhoe, S., Carrizosa, H.G., Rix, J., Sheehy, K., Seale, J.: A survey of networked and Wi-Fi enabled practices to support disabled learners in museums. In: International Conference on Wireless and Mobile Computing, Networking and Communications (WiMob), Barcelona, Spain, 2019, pp. 197–202 (2019). https://doi.org/10.1109/WiMOB.2019.8923129
19. Interreg CENTRAL EUROPE. COME-IN! GUIDELINES (2019). http://www.central2020. eu/Content.Node/COME-IN/COME-IN-Guidelines-FINAL-English-version.pdf

20. Landesverband der Museen zu Berlin e.V. (LMB) & Senatskanzlei Berlin – Kulturelle Angele-genheiten. DESIGN FOR ALL - Barrierefreie Ausstellungen in Berlin – Checkliste Verste-hen [DESIGN FOR ALL – Barrier-free exhibitions in Berlin – Understand checklist] (2011). https://neu.lmb.museum/wp-content/uploads/2021/04/04-checkliste-verstehen.pdf

21. Liberati, A., et al.: The PRISMA statement for reporting systematic reviews and meta-analyses of studies that evaluate health care interventions: explanation and elaboration. J. Clin. Epidemiol. **62**(10), e1–e34 (2009). https://doi.org/10.1016/j.jclinepi.2009.06.006

22. Martins, C.: The museum (audio) guide as an accessibility enhancer. In: Limbach, C., Álvarez de Morales, C., Luque, M.O. (eds.) Accesibilidad en la nueva era de las comunicaciones. Profesionales y universidad: un dialogo imprescindible, Granada: Ediciones Tragacanto, pp. 101–115 (2012). http://hdl.handle.net/10198/8208

23. Pomian, K.: Sammlungen – eine historische Typologie [Collections – a historical typology]. In: Grote, A. (eds.) Macrocosmos in Microcosmo. Berliner Schriften zur Museumskunde, pp. 107–126. Wiesbaden: VS Verlag für Sozialwissenschaften (1994). https://doi.org/10.1007/978-3-663-10698-2_4

24. Reichinger, A., et al.: Pictures in your mind: using interactive gesture-controlled reliefs to explore art. ACM Trans. Access. Comput. **11**(1), 2 (2018). https://doi.org/10.1145/3155286

25. Sheehy, K., Carrizosa, H.G., Rix, J., Seale, J., Hayhoe, S.: Inclusive museums and augmented reality. Affordances, Participation, Ethics and Fun. Int. J. Inclusive Museum, 67–85 (2019). https://doi.org/10.18848/1835-2014/CGP/v12i04/67-85

26. UN General Assembly: Convention on the Rights of Persons with Disabilities (2007). https://www.refworld.org/docid/45f973632.html

27. Walz, M.: Handbuch Museum. Geschichte – Aufgaben – Perspektiven [Manual of Museum. History – Tasks – Prospects]. Stuttgart: J. B. Metzler Verlag GmbH (2016). https://doi.org/10.1007/978-3-476-05184-4

28. World Health Organization: International classification of diseases for mortality and morbidity statistics (11th Revision) (2018). https://icd.who.int/browse11/l-m/en

Explainable Multimodal Machine Learning for Engagement Analysis by Continuous Performance Test

Muhammad Arifur Rahman[1]([⊠])[ID], David J. Brown[1][ID], Nicholas Shopland[1][ID], Andrew Burton[1][ID], and Mufti Mahmud[1,2][ID]

[1] Interactive Systems Research Group, Computer Science and Informatics, Nottingham Trent University, Nottingham, UK
{muhammad.rahman02,david.brown}@ntu.ac.uk
[2] Medical Technologies Innovation Facility, Nottingham Trent University, Nottingham, UK
https://www.ntu.ac.uk/research/groups-and-centres/groups/interactive-systems-research-group/
https://www.mtif.co.uk/

Abstract. The human vision system assiduously looks for exciting regions in the real world, in images and videos, to reduce the search effort for various tasks, such as object detection and recognition. A spatial attention representation can divulge the exciting segments, blocks or regions in such images. The Conners' continuous performance test is a visual assessment technique to evaluate the attention and the response inhibition component of executive control to assess attention deficit hyperactivity disorder (ADHD) and other neurological disorders. Artificial Intelligence and Machine Learning models are advancing ever more complex, going from shallow to deep learning over time. Thus, we can achieve higher accuracy and greater precision. However, this also tends to make these models 'black boxes', reducing the comprehensibility of the logic played out in the various predictions and outcomes. This raises an obvious question - how do we understand the prediction suggested or recommended by these machine learning models so that we can place trust in them? XAI attempts to make a trade-off between precision, accuracy and interpretability to achieve this. This research work presents an Explainable Artificial Intelligence (XAI) model for a continuous performance test, monitoring multisensor data and multimodal machine learning for engagement analysis. The sensor data considered included body pose, Electrocardiograph, eye gaze, interaction data and facial features via accurate labelling of engagement or disengagement for cognitive attention of a Seek-X type task execution. We used decision trees and XAI to visualize the multisensor multimodal data, which will help us assess the model's accuracy intuitively and provide us with the explainability of engagement or disengagement for visual interactions.

Keywords: Multimodal learning · Explainable AI · Decision tree · Engagement analysis

© The Author(s), under exclusive license to Springer Nature Switzerland AG 2022
M. Antona and C. Stephanidis (Eds.): HCII 2022, LNCS 13309, pp. 386–399, 2022.
https://doi.org/10.1007/978-3-031-05039-8_28

1 Introduction

In recent times, inclusive education has been a primary worldwide concern. Researchers across the globe are working towards providing teachers, support staff, and educators with tool-sets to support the assessment and education of children with special educational needs (SEN) as a combined approach towards inclusive education by guiding what pedagogical methodologies are most appropriate for each child depending on their needs. By improving the pedagogical support for these students, they will have an increased chance of inclusion in mainstream classrooms or success in special schools.

Autism spectrum disorder (ASD) is a neurodevelopmental disorder that affects communication and behaviour and can be diagnosed at any stage of life. There is no cure for ASD, but following a diagnosis, early detection of dysregulation events and early intervention may help to diffuse difficult situations in the classroom or at home. With the increasing prevalence of ASD, early detection and possible intervention have become an important challenge [28]. Recently, AI and machine learning (ML) are playing an increasingly dominant role in ASD detection, supporting co-curricular psychology studies. The work of [7,16,25,28] used ML models, performed in silico experiments to simplify and assist the conventional clinical experiments in an optimized way.

Besides the SEN students, recently research across the globe has focused significantly on the ability of children with learning difficulties to recognize [6,33], perceive [31,38] and interpret [22,37] emotional cues. So, research on attention detection or recognition of the emotional state of SEN students are still very open. Though ML is used in many cases to develop supportive tools for educators and SEN students, research in this direction and achieving a higher performance is still a challenge. In recent times, artificial intelligence and Machine Learning models are advancing to be ever more complex, going from shallow to deep learning over time. Precisely in this many ML algorithms has been proposed for attention detection i.e. [4,11,34,36] they are considering unimodal data. Until this date, very few machine learning-based methods which consider multiple modalities have been developed for multimodal fusion tasks.

Identification of attention for an individual is challenging and involves multiple factors [8,48]. Using deep learning models, we can achieve higher accuracy and greater precision. However, this also tends to make these models 'black boxes', reducing the comprehensibility of the logic played out in the various predictions and outcomes. This raises an obvious question - how do we understand the prediction suggested or recommended by these machine learning models so that we can place trust in them? Explainable Artificial Intelligence (XAI) [5] attempts to make a trade-off between precision, accuracy and interpretability to achieve this. Here in this work, we presented an XAI ML approach with multimodal data for attention detection.

2   Literature Review

ML became one of the most integrated part in research domain and playing role in many field from genomics analysis [18,39], image processing [15,17], text processing [14,24], trust management [30], different prediction models [26,41], health care [29,35] and to a growing list of many more. Even a newer research domain well known as Multimodal Machine Learning (MML) is an emerging multidisciplinary research domain that enhances the original goals of ML inspired AI by combining multiple complementary and communicative modalities, including vision, text, image, and many more [32].

MML models deal with heterogeneous types of data which bring added challenges to cope with the different modalities, extract data and develop knowledge from it. The process comprises the separate stages of representation, translation, alignment, fusion and co-learning, which is in itself a complex research area. Representation is the study of how to represent and summarise multimodal data which could be complementary or redundant between multiple modalities. The translation is the stage where acquired data is mapped from one modality to another. Due to the heterogeneity of data, this relationship between the modalities is a significant challenge. Alignment is the identification of the relations between multiple modalities. The next step is fusion, where information is joined from multiple modalities to make a prediction, classification or recommendations. Finally, co-learning is the stage where knowledge is transferred between modalities, their representation, and their predictive models [3].

To support practice in academia and various special needs social settings, the demand of AI embedded in non-autonomous systems is gaining interest for human cognition and enhancing learners, support staff and teachers' capabilities. This differs significantly from approaches that aim to create fully automated AI systems. MML and its analytics aim to create AI through externalisation and replicating human cognition and design artefacts closely linked with humans to increase their cognitive abilities and improve their overall capabilities [9,10,13].

In a research Hilbert at. el. 2017 used machine learning on multimodal biobehavioral data to classify subjects according to the presence of a generalised anxiety disorder (GAD) from mental disorder (MD) from cortisol data, clinical questionnaire data and structural MRI data using MML [21]. In another study [47]

12+2	1+3	5+8	8+4		5+4	8+3	7+3	5+3		2+2	1+3	4+8	8+4
9+2	10+1	11+2	7+5		2-7	7-2	4+6	13-2		9+2	10+1	7+5	6+2
6+5	**13**		3+7		3+7	**9**		6+5		6+5	**11**		3+7
3+9	8+3	14-1	6+7		3+8	1+3	4+8	4+6		3+9	8+3	10-1	7+7
15-2	7+2	4+9	9+2 __		6+2	11-1	7+5	9+2		__ 13-2	7+2	4+6	9+2

Fig. 1. The figure shows a Seek-X quiz. Where for a given cue, we need to find the correct answer out of the wrong one. During an experimental setup, the participants were asked to find or seek the target object from different non-target objects acting as a matrix of noise.

used MML for automated international classification of diseases (ICD) coding, where the ICD coding was adopted widely by physicians and other health care workers. Another study by [45] used MML for automatic behaviour analysis to augment clinical resources in diagnosing and treating patients with mental health disorders. In a more recent study, [46] used a multimodal AI-based framework to monitor individual's working behaviour and stress levels. Identification of this behaviour and stress levels can be achieved with higher precision by fusing multiple modalities obtained from an individual's behavioural patterns. They used a methodology to determine stress due to workload by integrating heterogeneous sensor data streams, including heart rate, posture, facial expressions and computer interaction.

Early identification can notably improve the prognosis of children with ASD. Yet, existing identification models are expensive, time consuming, and mostly depend on the manual judgment of experts [12,43]. A multimodal framework that can fuse data on a child's eye movement and facial expression can help identify children with ASD and improve identification efficiency and explainability. Various ML models, used data types and modalities and their performance for attention detection have been summarized in Table 1.

Table 1. Various ML model, used data type and modality for attention detection.

Ref	Data type	ML model	Accuracy	Modality
[4]	EEG, ECG, HF	DWT, SVM	HF 59.64%, EEG 86.86%	Unimodal
[34]	EEG (3 states)	SVM	71.6% to 84.8%	Unimodal
[36]	EEG	SVM	93.33 ± 8.16	Unimodal
[1]	EEG-based passive BCI	SVM	(Avg.) 91.72%	Unimodal
[11]	Eyeball movement	LR, MLP, SVM, DT	LR 96%	Unimodal
[20]	EEG, GSR, ECG,	GR, RF, SVM	Combined 64%	Multimodal
[27]	Facial expression, Eye gaze			Multimodal
[19]	Text and Image	RNN		Multimodal

3 Methodology and Data Sets

3.1 Data Collection

A child's level of attention can be assessed using mobile devices in a non-intrusive manner. We can observe and record their body posture, facial expression, eye gaze, brain activity (EEG), thermal data, and gesture recognition as forms of data. These data can be collected via different sensors, sometimes wearable and sometimes wirelessly connected. So, a mobile device on which the child is playing a game can be used for a continuous performance test (CPT). The platform tracked students' engagement, performance and attention with a range of sensors. Head tracking and hand tracking from a RealSense camera combined with head tracking data from a Tobii 4C sensor were used. Body positioning was tracked from the combined posture tracking and gesture tracking data from the

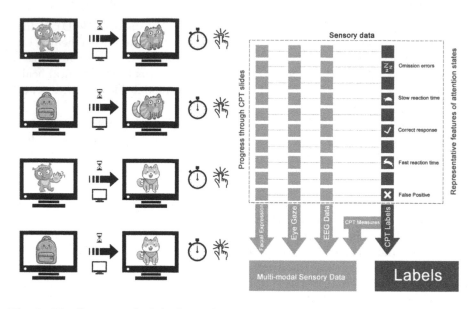

Fig. 2. The figure on the left shows the cartoon of target images that were used in a 'Where's Wally' game. The challenge was to spot Wally in a seek-X type game. The figure on the right shows the multimodal fusion of data obtained from different sensors and their labelling. A detailed explanation is available in [8]

mobile device's motion sensors. The RealSense camera and the Tobii 4C sensor monitored facial features and eye gaze. A Muse headband (in a child-friendly design) was connected wirelessly over Bluetooth and streamed brain activity data. Figure 2 on the left shows the cartoon of target images that have been used to find- 'Where's Wally' game. Where the challenges to spot Wally, a specified character, a seek-X type games. The figure on the right shows the multimodal fusion of multimodal data obtained from different sensors and their labelling. There were 2615 samples obtained from 59 sessions where 4 participants were involved. An in-detail explanation is available in [8]. Figure 3 shows the basic multimodal data flow evaluation technique. Participants were instructed to find Wally in the seek-X type game. As a part of the CPT experiment, different sensors were collecting multimodal data, such as eye-tracking, facial expression and others. After the labelling of data as by [8], we used our XAI model for attention detection. A detailed explanation of the experimental setup is available at [8].

'Engagement is the single best predictor of learning in students with learning disabilities'- [23]. In the Swanson's CPT [44] experiment the participant needs to pay continuous attention to a display screen on an interactive way. Where a game provides them with a pre-defined signal detection challenge. We will say this CPT 'Seek-X type' game as [8] to label multi-sensor data. During the experiment, the participants were asked to find the predefined target object from other non-target objects acting as a matrix of noise like a 'Where's Wally' game. The challenge is to spot Wally, from a grid displayed on the screen. The size

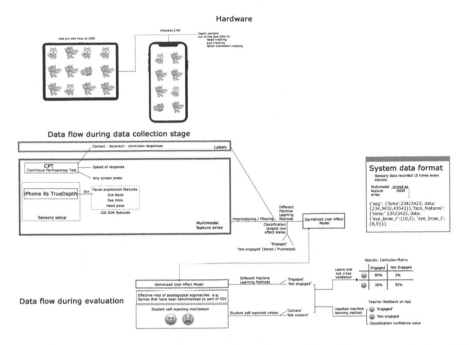

Fig. 3. The figure shows the basic data flow diagram. Participants were instructed to find Wally in the seek-X type game. As part of the CPT experiment, different sensors collected multimodal data like eye tracking, facial expression, and others. After labelling data as by [8], we used our XAI model for attention detection.

of the grids of characters in which to spot Wally in a crowd of characters can be varied. The CPT outcome measures and labels these multimodal data (facial expression, eye gaze, body posture) into high and low attention regions. This provides the labels by which we can assess engagement in the live system.

At the data level, information is highly abstract and the main focus of data fusion is noise reduction and compression. At this level, raw data is processed. Data fusion provides an opportunity for data reduction through data correlations and redundancies. At the feature level, the data has already been processed and the features have been extracted. The fusion is applied to the features themselves rather than the raw data. At the decision level, the data is highly semantic and clear temporal behaviours can be seen in the data. A further detailed explanation of the data prepossessing and fusion is available at [8]. Data frames from these three levels of abstraction with their corresponding CPT attention level labels are used as input into the machine learning layer.

3.2 Decision Tree

The decision tree, a machine learning model, is commonly used in ML, data science and related domains to construct classification tasks based on multiple features or for building prediction algorithms given target variables. If a data

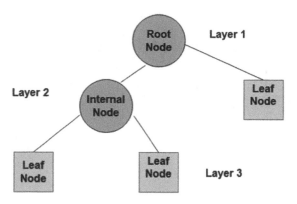

Fig. 4. The figure shows a decision tree where at the root node (layer 1) contains all the instances in a mixed orm. Then it splits into two determinations by predictor variable which is also known as a splitting variable that splits between the left child node and the right child node. For a splitting variable, the split criterion depends on some scoring like the Gini Index or Entropy.

set has a mixture of continuous, categorical, and binary types, we can use a decision tree algorithm for better prediction. The decision tree asks yes/no type-specific questions and take decisions. This model classifies a given population into branch-like segments constructing an upside-down tree having multiple levels or heights with the root node on the top level, internal nodes in between levels, and leaf nodes at the bottom. This ML algorithm is a non-parametric model where no parameter tuning is required at the prior stage and can efficiently deal with a large volume of data. The mathematical formulation is also simple and does not impose a complicated parametric structure. Two branches from a parent node are constructed based on the similarity of the data for a given feature, where impurities are calculated by entropy or Gini index. Figure 4 shows a decision tree. During the development of ML models, the data can be divided into two categories. The first segment is the training set, and the second segment is the testing set. A 75% and 25% or 80% and 20% train and test dataset split is a good choice. Yet, k-fold cross-validation is also widely used in the research community for decision trees. However, to leave one out could be a poor choice if the data size is huge. We use the training data set to construct a decision tree and the test dataset to evaluate its performance to construct the final optimal model [40,42]. We can calculate the accuracy of decision tree algorithm prediction by Eq. 1 where TP indicates the true positive, FP indicates the false positive, TN indicates the true negative, and FN indicates the false negative

$$Accuracy = \frac{TP + TN}{TP + FP + TN + FN}. \tag{1}$$

3.3 Gini Index for Decistion Tree

Impurities in a decision tree are calculated by the Gini Index (GI), which is also known as Gini impurity. When selected randomly, for a specific feature, GI calculates the probability of that classified incorrectly. If in a single class all the elements or samples are linked with or similar type then this class can be termed as pure. GI varies in the range between 0 and 1, where 0 expresses a pure class obtained from a classification, such that all the elements belong to a specific class, whereas a GI score of 1 indicates an absolute impure or distribution of elements came from a random nature. The GI value is somewhat at the middle shows a nearly equal distribution of samples or elements over some classes. During the modelling phase of the decision tree, the feature providing the least GI value is preferred. The GI can be calculated by Eq. 2 which is determined by calculating the sum of squared probabilities of every classes from one. Mathematically-

$$GI = 1 - \sum_{i=1}^{n} (P_i)^2 \tag{2}$$

where P_i represents the probability of a sample being classified for a distinct class.

4   Result Analysis

From the figure we can see that the root node starts with 9639 samples of each of the two classes, with a Gini Index. This is a categorical tree where a lower GI represents a better split. Figure 5 and Fig. 6 shows the full splitting mechanism to spilt the data and to measure the decision taking process of attention detection. However, due to the number of levels of the tree, it might not be readable yet a higher resolution image explains the full scenario. To get a better understanding we pruned the number of layers in Fig. 7 just considering four levels. The figure shown in the root node, eye dwelling is the feature that best split the attention and non-attention classes of the data, using as a threshold a value of 22.859.

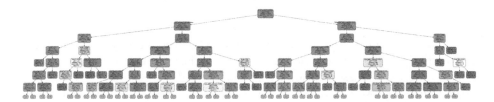

Fig. 5. The figure shows the decision tree for CPT of attention detection from multimodal multi-sensor data up to layer 6. This is an explainable approach and we can easily explain the process of decision making. Due to the size of the tree and the given size of the page, the outcome isn't readable. Yet, a better resolution picture will be easily readable.

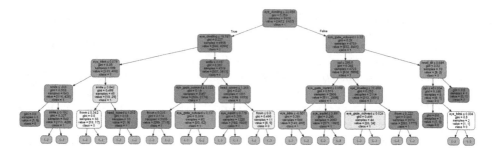

Fig. 6. The figure shows the decision tree for CPT of attention detection from multi-modal multi-sensor data up to layer 4. This is an explainable approach, and we can easily explain the process of decision making.

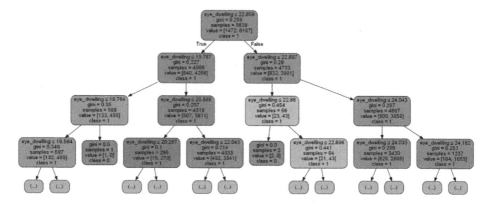

Fig. 7. To get better visualization, we pruned the number of layers in this figure. From the figure we can see that in the root node eye dwelling is the feature that best split the attention and non-attention classes of the data, using as a threshold a value of 22.859. The GI score here is 0.259. From the root node, we get two classes. At level 1, in the left node, we got 4906 samples and in the right node, we got 4733. For the left node of level 1, the threshold value of eye dwelling is 19.767 which splits 4908 samples to further two classes with 640 (left) and 4266 (right) samples with a GI score of 0.227. In the 3rd node of level 2, we can see that the GI score is 0.454, which means both attentive and non-attentive classes are grouped together here.

The GI score here is 0.259 which is not a pure class there are similarities in the chosen class but some impurities are also there. From the root node (let's say level 0) we get two classes. At level 1, in the left node, we got 4906 samples and in the right node, we got 4733. For the left node of level 1, the threshold value of eye dwelling is 19.767 which splits 4908 samples to further two classes with 640 (left) and 4266 (right) samples with a GI score of 0.227. In the 3rd node of level 2, we can see that the GI score is 0.454, which means both attentive and non-attentive classes are grouped together here. In all of these nodes, all the other features of the data (eye blink, squint, eye gaze inward and outward, facial

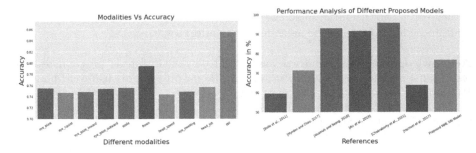

Fig. 8. The figure on the left shows the accuracy for attention detection using an XAI model decision tree for individual modalities. Here we considered eye blink, squint, eye gaze inward and outward, facial feature smile, frown, head tilt and ppi as a unimodal feature. Where the figure on the right shows the comparative performance of our XAI model with different existing ML approaches. The performance of our model is not the best but it did come from an explainable approach. However, as they worked on different dataset the results may also vary as mentioned by [2]

feature smile, frown, head tilt and ppi) were evaluated and had their resulting GI was calculated, however, the decision tree shows that feature that gave us the best results in terms of GI score is eye dwelling.

Figure 8 shows the cooperative performance.In this figure, the left bar graph shows the accuracy for attention detection using our XAI model decision tree for individual modalities. Here the performance for attention detection is shown considering only eye blink, squint, eye gaze inward and outward, facial feature smile, frown, head tilt and ppi as a unimodal feature. Where the right sidebar graph of Fig. 8 shows the comparative performance of our XAI model with different existing ML approaches. The performance of our model is not the best but it did come from an explainable ML algorithm decision tree.

5   Conclusion

In this research work, we presented decision trees from an XAI model for a continuous performance test obtained by monitoring multi-sensor data and multimodal machine learning, for engagement analysis. We considered body pose, eye gaze, interaction data and facial features by objective labelling of engagement or disengagement for cognitive attention of a Seek-X type task execution. We used decision trees, an XAI algorithm, to visualize the decision process of multi-sensor multimodal data, which will help us assess the accuracy of the model intuitively and provide us with the explainability of engagement or disengagement for visual interactions. The accuracy of the model does not give the best possible results, but helps decision making - and it is important that this model is more explainable than the black box-like algorithms of machine learning. As engagement is the single best predictor of learning in students with learning disabilities, we believe, an explainable model for engagement analysis will help to develop a tool useful in inclusive education by assisting teachers, supporting staff and educators with the assessment of children with SEN.

Acknowledgement. This research was co-funded by the Erasmus+ programme of the European Union in the projects Pathway+ (2017-1-UK01-KA201-036761) 'A Mobile Pedagogical Assistant to develop meaningful pathways to personalised learning' and 'AI-TOP' (2020-1-UK01-KA201-079167) 'An AI Tool to Predict Engagement and 'Meltdown' Events in Students with Autism'.

References

1. Aci, C.I., Kaya, M., Mishchenko, Y.: Distinguishing mental attention states of humans via an EEG-based passive BCI using machine learning methods. Expert Syst. Appl. **134**, 153–166 (2019). https://doi.org/10.1016/j.eswa.2019.05.057, https://www.sciencedirect.com/science/article/pii/S0957417419303926
2. Adiba, F.I., Islam, T., Kaiser, M.S., Mahmud, M., Rahman, M.A.: Effect of corpora on classification of fake news using Naive Bayes classifier. Int. J. Autom. Artif. Intell. Mach. Learn. **1**(1), 80–92 (2020). https://researchlakejournals.com/index.php/AAIML/article/view/45
3. Baltrušaitis, T., Ahuja, C., Morency, L.P.: Multimodal machine learning: a survey and taxonomy. IEEE Trans. Patt. Anal. Mach. Intell. **41**(2), 423–443 (2019). https://doi.org/10.1109/TPAMI.2018.2798607
4. Belle, A., Hobson, R., Najarian, K.: A physiological signal processing system for optimal engagement and attention detection. In: 2011 IEEE International Conference on Bioinformatics and Biomedicine Workshops (BIBMW), pp. 555–561 (2011). https://doi.org/10.1109/BIBMW.2011.6112429
5. Biswas, M., Kaiser, M.S., Mahmud, M., Al Mamun, S., Hossain, M.S., Rahman, M.A.: An XAI based autism detection: the context behind the detection. In: Mahmud, M., Kaiser, M.S., Vassanelli, S., Dai, Q., Zhong, N. (eds.) Brain Informatics, pp. 448–459. Lecture Notes in Computer Science. Springer International Publishing, Cham (2021). https://doi.org/10.1007/978-3-030-86993-9_40
6. Bloom, E., Heath, N.: Recognition, expression, and understanding facial expressions of emotion in adolescents with nonverbal and general learning disabilities. J. Learn. Disabil. **43**(2), 180–192 (2010)
7. Bone, D., Goodwin, M.S., Black, M.P., Lee, C.C., Audhkhasi, K., Narayanan, S.: Applying machine learning to facilitate autism diagnostics: pitfalls and promises. J. Autism Dev. Disord. **45**(5), 1121–1136 (2015). https://doi.org/10.1007/s10803-014-2268-6
8. Brown, D., Sherkat, N., Taheri, M.: Modeling engagement with multimodal multisensor data: the continuous performance test as an objective tool to track flow. Int. J. Comput. Inf. Eng. **14**(162), 197–208 (2020)
9. Brown, D.J., Kerr, S., Wilson, J.R.: Virtual environments in special-needs education. Commun. ACM **40**(8), 72–75 (1997). https://doi.org/10.1145/257874.257891
10. Brown, D.J., McHugh, D., Standen, P., Evett, L., Shopland, N., Battersby, S.: Designing location-based learning experiences for people with intellectual disabilities and additional sensory impairments. Comput. Educ. **56**(1), 11–20 (2011). https://doi.org/10.1016/j.compedu.2010.04.014, https://www.sciencedirect.com/science/article/pii/S0360131510001211

11. Chakraborty, P., Yousuf, M.A., Rahman, S.: Predicting level of visual focus of human's attention using machine learning approaches. In: Kaiser, M.S., Bandyopadhyay, A., Mahmud, M., Ray, K. (eds.) Proceedings of International Conference on Trends in Computational and Cognitive Engineering, pp. 683–694. Advances in Intelligent Systems and Computing. Springer, Singapore (2021). https://doi.org/10.1007/978-981-33-4673-4-56

12. Chen, J., Liao, M., Wang, G., Chen, C.: An intelligent multimodal framework for identifying children with autism spectrum disorder. Int. J. Appl. Math. Comput. Sci. (2020). 10.34768/AMCS-2020-0032. https://sciendo.com/article/10.34768/amcs-2020-0032

13. Cukurova, M.: Learning analytics as AI extenders in education: multimodal machine learning versus multimodal learning analytics. In: Proceedings of the Artificial Intelligence and Adaptive Education Conference, pp. 1–3 (2019)

14. Das, S., Yasmin, M.R., Arefin, M., Taher, K.A., Uddin, M.N., Rahman, M.A.: Mixed Bangla-English spoken digit classification using convolutional neural network. In: Mahmud, M., Kaiser, M.S., Kasabov, N., Iftekharuddin, K., Zhong, N. (eds.) Applied Intelligence and Informatics, pp. 371–383. Communications in Computer and Information Science. Springer International Publishing, Cham (2021). https://doi.org/10.1007/978-3-030-82269-9_29

15. Das, T.R., Hasan, S., Sarwar, S.M., Das, J.K., Rahman, M.A.: Facial spoof detection using support vector machine. In: Kaiser, M.S., Bandyopadhyay, A., Mahmud, M., Ray, K. (eds.) Proceedings of International Conference on Trends in Computational and Cognitive Engineering, pp. 615–625. Advances in Intelligent Systems and Computing. Springer, Singapore (2021). https://doi.org/10.1007/978-981-33-4673-4_50

16. Duda, M., Kosmicki, J.A., Wall, D.P.: Testing the accuracy of an observation-based classifier for rapid detection of autism risk. Transl. Psychiat. 4(8), e424 e424 (2014). https://doi.org/10.1038/tp.2014.65, https://www.nature.com/articles/tp201465, number: 8 Publisher: Nature Publishing Group

17. Ferdous, H., Siraj, T., Setu, S.J., Anwar, M.M., Rahman, M.A.: Machine learning approach towards satellite image classification. In: Kaiser, M.S., Bandyopadhyay, A., Mahmud, M., Ray, K. (eds.) Proceedings of International Conference on Trends in Computational and Cognitive Engineering, pp. 627–637. Advances in Intelligent Systems and Computing. Springer, Singapore (2021). https://doi.org/10.1007/978-981-33-4673-4_51

18. Garzon, M., Mainali, S.: Deep structure of DNA for genomic analysis. Human Molecular Genetics (2021)

19. Han, Y., Li, L., Zhang, J.: A coordinated representation learning enhanced multimodal machine translation approach with multi-attention, pp. 571–577. Association for Computing Machinery, New York, NY, USA (2020). https://doi.org/10.1145/3372278.3390717

20. Harrivel, A.R., et al.: Prediction of cognitive states during flight simulation using multimodal psychophysiological sensing–AIAA Information Systems-AIAA Infotech @ Aerospace (2017). https://doi.org/10.2514/6.2017-1135, https://arc.aiaa.org/doi/abs/10.2514/6.2017-1135, archive Location: world

21. Hilbert, K., Lueken, U., Muehlhan, M., Beesdo-Baum, K.: Separating generalized anxiety disorder from major depression using clinical, hormonal, and structural MRI data: a multimodal machine learning study. Brain Behav. 7(3), e00633 (2017). https://doi.org/10.1002/brb3.633, https://onlinelibrary.wiley.com/doi/abs/10.1002/brb3.633

22. Holder, H.B., Kirkpatrick, S.W.: Interpretation of emotion from facial expressions in children with and without learning disabilities. J. Learn. Disabil. **24**(3), 170–177 (1991)

23. Iovannone, R., Dunlap, G., Huber, H., Kincaid, D.: Effective educational practices for students with autism spectrum disorders. Focus Autism Dev. Disabil. **18**(3), 150–165 (2003). https://doi.org/10.1177/10883576030180030301. SAGE Publications Inc Publications Inc Publications Inc

24. Joachims, T.: Learning to classify text using support vector machines, vol. 668. Springer Science and Business Media (2002). https://doi.org/10.1007/978-1-4615-0907-3_2

25. Kosmicki, J., Sochat, V., Duda, M., Wall, D.: Searching for a minimal set of behaviors for autism detection through feature selection-based machine learning. Transl. Psychiatr. **5**(2), e514–e514 (2015)

26. Kourou, K., Exarchos, T.P., Exarchos, K.P., Karamouzis, M.V., Fotiadis, D.I.: Machine learning applications in cancer prognosis and prediction. Comput. Struct. Biotechnol. J. **13**, 8–17 (2015)

27. Li, J., Ngai, G., Leong, H.V., Chan, S.C.F.: Multimodal human attention detection for reading from facial expression, eye gaze, and mouse dynamics. SIGAPP Appl. Comput. Rev. **16**(3), 37–49 (2016). https://doi.org/10.1145/3015297.3015301

28. Liu, W., Zhou, T., Zhang, C., Zou, X., Li, M.: Response to name: a dataset and a multimodal machine learning framework towards autism study. In: 2017 Seventh International Conference on Affective Computing and Intelligent Interaction (ACII), pp. 178–183 (2017). https://doi.org/10.1109/ACII.2017.8273597

29. Mahmud, M., Kaiser, M.S., McGinnity, T.M., Hussain, A.: Deep learning in mining biological data. Cogn. Computat. **13**(1), 1–33 (2021). https://doi.org/10.1007/s12559-020-09773-x

30. Mahmud, M., Kaiser, M.S., Rahman, M.M., Rahman, M.A., Shabut, A., Al-Mamun, S., Hussain, A.: A brain-inspired trust management model to assure security in a cloud based IoT framework for neuroscience applications. Cogn. Comput. **10**(5), 864–873 (2018)

31. Metsala, J.L., Galway, T.M., Ishaik, G., Barton, V.E.: Emotion knowledge, emotion regulation, and psychosocial adjustment in children with nonverbal learning disabilities. Child Neuropsychol. **23**(5), 609–629 (2017)

32. Morency, L.P., Baltrušaitis, T.: Multimodal machine learning: integrating language, vision and speech. In: Proceedings of the 55th Annual Meeting of the Association for Computational Linguistics: Tutorial Abstracts, pp. 3–5 (2017)

33. Most, T., Greenbank, A.: Auditory, visual, and auditory-visual perception of emotions by adolescents with and without learning disabilities, and their relationship to social skills. Learn. Disabil. Res. Pract. **15**(4), 171–178 (2000)

34. Myrden, A., Chau, T.: A passive EEG-BCI for single-trial detection of changes in mental state. IEEE Trans. Neural Syst. Rehabil. Eng. **25**(4), 345–356 (2017). https://doi.org/10.1109/TNSRE.2016.2641956

35. Nasrin, F., Ahmed, N.I., Rahman, M.A.: Auditory attention state decoding for the quiet and hypothetical environment: a comparison between bLSTM and SVM. In: Kaiser, M.S., Bandyopadhyay, A., Mahmud, M., Ray, K. (eds.) Proceedings of International Conference on Trends in Computational and Cognitive Engineering, pp. 291–301. Advances in Intelligent Systems and Computing. Springer, Singapore (2021). https://doi.org/10.1007/978-981-33-4673-4_23

36. Nuamah, J.K., Seong, Y.: Support vector machine (SVM) classification of cognitive tasks based on electroencephalography (EEG) engagement index. Brain-Comput. Interf. **5**(1), 1–12 (2018). https://doi.org/10.1080/2326263X.2017.1338012
37. Ouherrou, N., Elhammoumi, O., Benmarrakchi, F., El Kafi, J.: Comparative study on emotions analysis from facial expressions in children with and without learning disabilities in virtual learning environment. Educ. Inf. Technol. **24**(2), 1777–1792 (2019). https://doi.org/10.1007/s10639-018-09852-5
38. Petti, V.L., Voelker, S.L., Shore, D.L., Hayman-Abello, S.E.: Perception of non-verbal emotion cues by children with nonverbal learning disabilities. J. Dev. Phys. Disabil. **15**(1), 23–36 (2003)
39. Rahman, M.A.: Gaussian Process in Computational Biology: Covariance Functions for Transcriptomics. Phd, University of Sheffield, February 2018. https://etheses.whiterose.ac.uk/19460/
40. Rokach, L., Maimon, O.: Decision trees. In: Maimon, O., Rokach, L. (eds.) Data mining and knowledge discovery handbook, pp. 165–192. Springer, US, Boston, MA (2005). https://doi.org/10.1007/0-387-25465-X-9
41. Sadik, R., Reza, M.L., Al Noman, A., Al Mamun, S., Kaiser, M.S., Rahman, M.A.: COVID-19 pandemic: a comparative prediction using machine learning. Int. J. Autom. Artif. Intell. Mach. Learn. **1**(1), 1–16 (2020)
42. Song, Y.Y., Lu, Y.: Decision tree methods: applications for classification and prediction. Shanghai Arch. Psychiatr. **27**(2), 130–135 (2015). https://doi.org/10.11919/j.issn.1002-0829.215044, https://www.ncbi.nlm.nih.gov/pmc/articles/PMC4466856/
43. Rokach, L., Maimon, O.: Decision trees. In: Maimon, O., Rokach, L. (eds.) Data Mining and Knowledge Discovery Handbook, pp. 165–192. Springer US, Boston, MA (2005). https://doi.org/10.1007/0-387-25465-X-9
44. Swanson, L.: Vigilance deficit in learning disabled children: a signal detection analysis. J. Child Psychol. Psychiatr. **22**(4), 393–399 (1981)
45. Tavabi, L.: Multimodal machine learning for interactive mental health therapy. In: 2019 International Conference on Multimodal Interaction, pp. 453–456. ICMI 2019. Association for Computing Machinery, New York, NY, USA (2019). https://doi.org/10.1145/3340555.3356095
46. Walambe, R., Nayak, P., Bhardwaj, A., Kotecha, K.: Employing multimodal machine learning for stress detection. J. Healthc. Eng. **2021**, e9356452 (2021). https://doi.org/10.1155/2021/9356452, https://www.hindawi.com/journals/jhe/2021/9356452/, publisher: Hindawi
47. Xu, K., et al.: Multimodal machine learning for automated ICD coding. In: Doshi-Velez, F., et al. (eds.) Proceedings of the 4th Machine Learning for Healthcare Conference. Proceedings of Machine Learning Research, vol. 106, pp. 197–215. PMLR, 9–10 Aug 2019. https://proceedings.mlr.press/v106/xu19a.html
48. Zubair, M.S., Brown, D.J., Hughes-Roberts, T., Bates, M.: Designing accessible visual programming tools for children with autism spectrum condition. Universal Access in the Information Society, pp. 1–20 (2021)

Digital Means for Increased Vocational Participation of People with Intellectual Disabilities

Lena Sube[(✉)] [iD] and Christian Bühler [iD]

Department of Rehabilitation Technology, TU Dortmund University, Dortmund, Germany
{lena.sube,christian.buehler}@tu-dortmund.de

Abstract. Due to the COVID-19-pandemic, digital participation has become more important than ever before. Since people with intellectual disabilities (ID) are still facing barriers regarding their vocational and digital participation, the miTAS project aims to improve their participation by providing the miTAS app and the miTAS media box. These offer checklists and instructions based on individual needs. This research aims to find out about the framework conditions for using digital tools in vocational training and vocational rehabilitation of people with ID. Implications for how to manage the digital transformation process in these facilities should be derived as well. Eleven semi-structured group interviews with people with ID and social workers were conducted as videoconferences. The research indicates that the COVID-19-pandemic has influenced daily life in the facilities in different ways. Especially facilities in rural areas are still lacking technical equipment and concepts for providing digital participation. Digital tools offer an added value for the vocational participation of people with intellectual disabilities (ID) such as joint learning, fun, gain of digital competencies, autonomy, and self-efficacy. For the digital transformation process, it takes the support of the management board, human resources, and technical infrastructure. The added value of the new digital tool must be clearly recognizable. Within the facilities, transparency, clarity in internal communication, and an appealing concept are needed. Moreover, the inclusion of people with ID as experts and new ways of peer-to-peer support is highly recommended. Interdisciplinary cooperation can be helpful as well.

Keywords: Digital divide · Vocational training · Digital tools

1 Digital and Vocational Participation of People with ID

Nowadays people with intellectual disabilities (ID) are still facing barriers regarding their vocational and digital participation. This research considers these barriers and presents practical implications of the miTAS project ("multimedia individual training and working assistance system") on how to implement digital tools for an improved digital and vocational participation of people with ID.

The digital change is also called "the 4th industrial revolution" [13] and has been extremely accelerated by the COVID-19 pandemic [3, 4, 24]. The measures to contain the pandemic have led to increased use of remote digital technology [4], Messenger Apps, and increased time of use [8]. In universities, educational and vocational contexts digital alternatives were to be found and various processes went online [24]. The number of active users of social media has been growing worldwide. In the year 2021 4.2 billion people have been using social media and there are 4.95 billion internet users worldwide [31]. But the accelerated digital change also poses challenges, e.g., organizational problems in schools, lack of technical infrastructure, and lack of teachers' media competencies [15]. Inequalities regarding digital participation still exist [4]. Almost 40% of the world's population does not have Internet access [24]. The usage behavior depends on income, gender, and age [8, 24]. Especially senior citizens and people with ID are affected by the "digital divide" [1, 4, 21]. As a result, they do not benefit from the digital transformation the same way most of the population does [21]. So, they do not have the same access and opportunities to use digital media [1, 4, 21]. Furthermore, their access to health and education, economics, and political empowerment is complicated [24].

Due to structural barriers, they are lacking digital access, digital competencies, and digital participation [4, 9, 12, 18, 24]. Structural barriers mean, e.g., lack of time and lack of human resources in social facilities to support people with ID using digital media [4, 10]. Social workers have a key function regarding the digital participation of people with ID [9]. However, many social workers are worried about data protection and liability [10]. In many cases, they do not have the necessary digital competencies either to accompany their clients [9]. Additionally, courses for people with ID are missing in many areas [9]. Rigid regulations in the facilities and the precarious vocational and therefore financial situation of people with ID can be further structural reasons for a lack of digital devices and opportunities to participate digitally [28]. Furthermore, barriers in design and content complicate the use and understanding of people with ID [21, 28, 30]. These various barriers complicate the acquisition of digital and media competencies for these people. During the pandemic, they hindered them from staying in contact. This points out the relevance of digital competencies to step out of isolation and loss of routines [4, 7, 29].

In the vocational context the digital transformation influences work routines and the requirements employees need to fulfill [16]. As a result, digital and media competencies are essential prerequisites for qualification, vocational and social participation [22; 25]. Therefore, media-supported, vocational training can play a key role here. Looking at the employment rate of people with disabilities, it becomes clear that readjustments need to be made. The Convention on the Rights of Persons with Disabilities (CRPD) demands equal rights of people with ID in education, vocational training, and working life. The already difficult process of professional inclusion was further complicated by the impact of the pandemic [5]. In Germany people with disabilities are more likely to be unemployed than people without disabilities. On average, they are less qualified and more affected by long-term unemployment than people without disabilities [3]. More often people with disabilities are employed a-typically [3]. Many employers are unsure about the conditions under which they can hire people with disabilities and about their needs. Especially towards persons with mental disabilities, there are many reservations [3]. In Germany, a huge amount of people with ID works in sheltered workshops for people with disability ("Werkstätten für Menschen mit Behinderung") [28]. These facilities offer vocational rehabilitation but are not part of the first labor market.

Regarding the accelerated digital transformation process due to the COVID-19 pandemic [3], the challenges of digital gaps and inequalities in social facilities need to be focused on more intensively [14]. After all, digital media can offer an added value in terms of vocational participation. The pandemic has highlighted the benefits of digital media and digital applications for education and collaboration. Especially in the vocational context, digital media offer possibilities to increase the participation of people with disabilities. Digital media (e.g., smartphones, tablets) are an adequate medium to structure (work) routines [16, 17]. They can also support users' social interaction [7] and the acquisition of health skills [30]. Digital media offer innovative ways for individualized job training, job coaching, and e-learning of people with ID [11, 16].

A variety of projects aim to increase the vocational participation of people with ID by using digital media. The project LernBAR uses augmented reality to support people with ID in various vocational contexts [16]. Practical approaches as tested in the PIKSL laboratory or the miTAS project enable people with ID to gain basic digital competencies, autonomy, and self-efficiency [20, 21]. Moreover, it opens new professional perspectives for them.

2 Introducing the miTAS Project

The miTAS project aims to improve the vocational and digital participation of people with ID and people on the autism spectrum. For these purposes, the miTAS app, a pedagogical-didactic approach, and the miTAS media box, have been developed. The miTAS app provides options for individual support for tasks and routines in various contexts, where people with ID face problems. It is used in facilities of vocational training and vocational rehabilitation, but also for leisure activities, at home, housekeeping, etc. For example, the miTAS app is used for step-by-step support of cleaning processes in facilities and for preparing meals. It contains individualized multimedia checklists and step-by-step instructions referring to the user's needs and competencies [11]. The miTAS app does not contain predefined content. Every content is created by individuals with ID supported by social workers. The checklists and instructions can contain textual descriptions, videos, photos, and audio instructions. Individual conditions and quizzes can be added. The instructions and checklists can be shared within the facility or with all users of the miTAS app. Shared instructions can be adjusted for individual needs, e.g., further descriptions or multimedia content can be added. Choice of the media is the first option to create accessible content. Then the miTAS app offers various settings to provide accessibility. The contrast, font size, and wallpaper of the app can be adjusted individually. Additionally, the miTAS app offers a read-aloud function, a calendar, and the option to use skype for individual support. Referring to the users' needs different options of access rights can be made.

Based on the results of the first evaluation phase in 2019, the miTAS team has devised the pedagogic didactic approach [11]. This approach maintains five phases according to learning stations at school. Based on these phases the virtual miTAS media box has been developed as blended learning. Especially during the contact ban of the pandemic, the miTAS media box has offered support and orientation for using the miTAS app. There are two versions of the miTAS media box. Both media boxes are created in German. There is a detailed version for social workers which includes a variety of materials. Additionally, there is a version for people with ID that includes less material. The video tutorials and the material in the media box for people with ID are accessible and use easy to read language.

The media box for social workers has been extensively expanded since January 2021. It contains an introduction, basic information about the miTAS project and the miTAS app, information about contact persons for technical and educational concerns, and a list of frequently asked questions. Behind five colorful gears, the five phases with multimedia content can be found. Each phase offers an overview of the content, the purpose of the phase, and implications for the first practical steps in each phase. The phases contain multimedia support such as video tutorials, e.g., for creating accounts and instructions in the miTAS app, textual instructions, and deployment scenarios. Material for evaluating and adopting the use and added value of the miTAS app along with people with ID is available, too. A flyer, a podcast, and material for webinars can also be found. The miTAS media box is freely available and can be used depending on individual needs and interests.

Another approach to support the facilities in getting to know the miTAS app was the miTAS seminar which was also developed based on the results of the first evaluation phase. This seminar was supposed to offer support for the first practical steps with the miTAS app since the participants of the first evaluations phase criticized the lack of support during the first phase [11]. Due to the COVID-19 pandemic, the seminar was adopted as a webinar. The webinar was held as a video conference and presented the theoretical background of the miTAS project, basic information about the project, and led to the use of the miTAS app. The seminar obtained frontal teaching but also interactive group sessions and discussion. At the end of the webinar, the participants were asked to give their anonymous feedback via an online survey. Since January 2021 more than 30 online seminars have been conducted.

3   Methodology and Data Acquisition

Since digital alternatives, such as home-schooling, home-office, and videoconferences, have been provided in many aspects of life [4, 11], it was necessary to find out, how the pandemic has affected the opportunities of people with ID to participate digitally in vocational training and vocational rehabilitation. The intention was to find out about the framework conditions for the use of the miTAS-app or other digital tools in the facilities. The facilities' motivations for the use of old-fashioned and new digital technologies should be surveyed as well. Additionally, implications for how to manage the digital transformation process in facilities for people with ID should be derived.

To find out more about the framework conditions, the guideline contained the questions if and which new digital technologies were used due to the pandemic or will be used in the upcoming years. Additionally, the interviews contained questions about the respondents' needs to use the app or other digital tools more often and about the added value of the miTAS app and miTAS media box. Moreover, the participants were asked how the change process regarding the use of new digital tools should be communicated and managed in the facilities.

Facilities using the miTAS app were asked to participate in the second evaluation phase. The facilities received an information sheet on the process and purpose of the survey. The contact persons of the facilities asked social workers and people with ID to participate in the interviews. Eleven semi-structured interviews with 13 people with ID and 24 social workers of facilities of vocational training and vocational rehabilitation in Germany were conducted in video conferences (2.–9.21). The interviews were transcribed and analyzed according to Mayring & Fenzl [19].

4 Findings

The results of the inductive content analysis show that the COVID-19-pandemic has influenced daily life in the facilities in different ways.

Status quo of Digital Participation. The facilities can be assigned to three groups. The first group of facilities does not yet know how to enable digital participation. The second group developed short-term solutions and the third group was able to build on previous experiences.

Facilities of the first group still don't know yet where to start the digital transformation process in their facility. They want to implement digital tools such as the miTAS app. But they face fundamental barriers, e.g., lack of funding, lack of time, and lack of human resources. Therefore, they face difficulties to accompany their clients in using new digital tools. Another reason, that was frequently mentioned, was the lack of basic technical infrastructure, e.g., Internet access, WIFI, and digital devices. Some of these facilities used old-fashioned ways of bridging the gap, such as exchanging worksheets by mail with the clients who had to stay home. The most common reasons for using old-fashioned ways were lack of knowledge about data protection and liability as well as lack of funding, time, and lack of human resources. Especially facilities in rural areas were using old-fashioned ways because of missing technical infrastructure. People with ID living in rural areas were also lacking internet access and technical devices, e.g., suitable laptops for e-learning and video conferences. As further reasons for using old-fashioned ways, the social workers described a lack of media competencies of the people with ID and were concerned about overwhelming them with the use of new digital tools.

Due to the measures to contain the pandemic, facilities of the second group developed digital alternatives overnight, such as virtual pinboards and video conferences. This group was lacking prior experience and basic competencies with these digital alternatives which made the spontaneous activities more difficult. These facilities would like to evaluate their experiences and develop long-term solutions for digital participation.

Facilities of the third group had already used digital tools before the outbreak of the pandemic and intend to intensify the use. These facilities benefited from previous experience. Technologies that have been intensively used during the pandemic were video conference software. Video conferences provided contact with people with ID, job application training, webinars, and tutoring. Some facilities also offered e-learning, virtual pinboards, digital learning tools, and learning apps.

In general, the facilities use or want to use digital tools not only to offer an alternative during the pandemic but also to increase the autonomy of people with ID. Further reasons for the implementation of new digital tools were that people with ID can experience self-determination and independence through using it. Moreover, self-realization, mobility, and participation can be promoted. Additionally, the social workers want to offer a contemporary tool to increase the vocational participation and to stay up to date. The use of modern technologies is seen as a necessity, which is central to increase inclusion, participation, and accessibility. The miTAS app or other digital tools are supposed to open alternative learning opportunities. The new digital tools should also allow for accessibility and data protection. In addition, technologies could help to reduce stigmas and prejudices and create a hierarchy-free space. Especially the social workers hope for a reduced workload and reduced need for time and human resources through using digital tools.

Referring to the miTAS app the participants described the following aspects as "*potential* added value": "autonomy", "fun", "accessibility", "equality of people with and without disabilities", "increase of digital competencies", "up-to-dateness" and "vividness". As *perceived* added value of the miTAS app most of the participants mentioned "fun" "increase of autonomy" and "fulfills the wish of using a contemporary tool". Further aspects were e.g., "up-to-dateness", "accessibility", "joint learning", "offering a mnemonic" and "increase of digital competencies".

To increase the use of the miTAS app or other digital technologies in vocational training and vocational rehabilitation, most of the participants described a fundamental need for digital infrastructure (e.g., internet access, Wi-Fi, digital devices). Most of them also mentioned the need for human resources. Especially, time resources are needed to get to know the new digital tools and to develop a didactic approach for the implementation. The participants also mentioned app requirements that would improve the accessibility and the usability of the miTAS app, e.g., improving the read-aloud function and adopting the options for offline use. Moreover, the features and the design of the miTAS app should be improved to offer better orientation. Furthermore, the participants mentioned new ideas for features of the miTAS app, e.g., for improving the options of working collaboratively.

Conditions for the Digital Transformation Process. Regarding the digital transformation process, the participants described a need for support from the management board. The management board should improve the technical infrastructure. Its communication should be motivating. The participants recommend transparency during the change process, e.g., they want basic information about the miTAS app, its purpose, and the data protection of new digital tools. The added value of the miTAS app or other digital tools needs to be communicated clearly. Moreover, it's important to present examples of best practices and space to get to know the new digital tools. A communicative exchange and peer-to-peer support should be offered as well. Furthermore, people with ID should be engaged as experts, e.g., they could present their experiences with the miTAS app in the social workers' team meetings. In some cases, the participants recommend that the facilities' leaders oblige the social workers to use digital tools. To communicate the change people with ID and social workers should be approached directly and personally. The facilities want to use the lessons learned from the alternative concepts for interdisciplinary planning processes, in part with IT.

5 Discussion

The chosen methodology was suitable to capture the personal experiences, attitudes, expectations, and needs of the respondents [23, 26]. It allowed for some flexibility as well as adjustments, follow-up questions, and explanations [26]. Due to the pandemic, the interviews were conducted as video conferences which may have made it difficult to perceive nonverbal aspects. Further research should find methods to compensate for this. Although attempts were made to create a trusting and non-judgmental atmosphere influences of social desirability must be considered as well.

These interviews could only be conducted with facilities having the appropriate equipment and which were in contact with the miTAS project. Since the results indicate that there are facilities that are not well equipped technically, further research should investigate how other facilities are equipped that are not participating in the miTAS project. Due to the high value of digital participation in connection with vocational participation, further research should investigate the status quo of digital participation in further facilities of vocational rehabilitation.

The results highlight the perceived and the possible added value of digital tools in vocational training and rehabilitation of people with ID. Digital tools support the acquisition of basic digital competencies and provide experiences of self-efficacy autonomy and joint learning. To achieve these affects, basic requirements need to be fulfilled, e.g., human and time resources. It is relevant for social workers to acquire digital competencies [2, 9, 21, 27]. They should be trained on topics such as liability and data protection. Because of their key function, social workers should be trained didactically to accompany people with ID professionally. Moreover, this research reaffirms the results of studies conducted before the outbreak of the pandemic [1, 2, 4, 10], e.g., regarding the ongoing need for technical infrastructure, Internet access, and technical devices.

To implement digital tools successfully and increase digital participation, it takes a digital transformation process in social facilities. For this process, information about funding should be provided [28]. This also highlights the need for socio-political efforts [4]. Regarding this process within the facilities, it takes new concepts for the digital participation of people with ID. Provision of technical infrastructure (digital devices, Wi-Fi, etc.), a pool of materials, technical support is fundamental to the digital transformation process. Furthermore, the results highlight the need for the management board's commitment and need for clarity and transparency. This research shows that people with ID do have ideas, wishes, needs, and worries regarding the use and usability of digital tools in the vocational context. In the digital transformation process, these aspects should be addressed [24]. Practical approaches to motivate and involve the social workers are incentives, recognizable added value, low-threshold access, division of labor, and peer-to-peer support. Other research projects in this area can also provide practical implications towards the digital transformation process and digital participation such as the inclusive research approach of the Easy Reading Project [6] or the project Lern-BAR [16]. The findings give first implications for the digital transformation process in social facilities. These implications should be evaluated. Moreover, a long-term survey to abbreviate implications for the digital transformation process in these facilities is recommended as well.

6   Conclusion

The results show that the COVID-19-pandemic has boosted the development of visions for digital participation in vocational training and vocational rehabilitation of people with ID. The efforts made so far should be held up to intensify the access to digital participation and therefore to qualification and vocational participation. Nevertheless, there are still facilities that do not offer digital participation. To enable digital and vocational participation a digital transformation process is needed. This also requires the support of the management board, time and human resources, technical infrastructure, and access to digital tools. Information on data protection and liability and a collection of technical recommendations should be provided as well. Within the facilities, it needs transparency and clarity in the internal communication and an appealing concept. Moreover, the inclusion of people with ID as experts and new ways of peer-to-peer support is highly recommended. Interdisciplinary cooperation can be helpful as well. These aspects could help facilities initiate and move the process towards more digital and vocational participation, even in times of pandemics. The miTAS app and the approach to individual adaptation using the pedagogical concept with the media box can contribute to this respect.

Acknowledgements. The miTAS project ("multimedia individual training and working assistance system"), is supported by the Federal Ministry of Education and Research and the European Social Fonds (duration October 2018 – January 2022).

References

1. Alfredsson Ågren, K., Kjellberg, A., Hemmingsson, H.: Digital participation? internet use among adolescents with and without intellectual disabilities: a comparative study. New Media Soc. **22**(12), 2128–2145 (2019). https://doi.org/10.1177/1461444819888398
2. Bosse, I., Zaynel, N., Lampert, C.: MeKoBe. Medienkompetenz in der Behindertenhilfe in Bremen. Bedarfserfassung und Handlungsempfehlung für die Gestaltung von Fortbildungen zur Medienkompetenzförderung (2018). https://www.bremische-landesmedienanstalt.de/upl oads/Texte/Meko/Forschung/MekoBe_Endbericht.pdf . Accessed 07 Feb 2022
3. Bundesministerium für Arbeit und Soziales (BMAS): Dritter Teilhabebericht der Bundesregierung über die Lebenslagen von Menschen mit Beeinträchtigungen. Teilhabe – Beeinträchtigung – Behinderung (2021). https://www.bmas.de/SharedDocs/Downloads/DE/Pub likationen/a125-21-teilhabebericht.pdf;jsessionid=35EE1DB0CF7C17FB3CF1E47ECFE 4EE5D.delivery1-replication?__blob=publicationFile&v=4. Accessed 07 Feb 2022
4. Chadwick, D., et al.: Digital inclusion and participation of people with intellectual disabilities during Covid-19: a rapid review and international bricolage. J. Policy Pract. Intell. Disabil. 1–15 (2022). https://doi.org/10.1111/jppi.12410

5. Department of Work & Pensions: The employment of disabled people 2021. Official Statistics (2021). https://www.gov.uk/government/statistics/the-employment-of-disabled-people-2021/the-employment-of-disabled-people-2021 Accessed 07 Feb 2022
6. Dirks, S.: Empowering instead of hindering – challenges in participatory development of cognitively accessible software. In: Antona, M., Stephanidis, C. (eds.) HCII 2019. LNCS, vol. 11572, pp. 28–38. Springer, Cham (2019). https://doi.org/10.1007/978-3-030-23560-4_3
7. Flynn, S., et al.: The experiences of adults with learning disabilities in the UK during the COVID-19 pandemic: qualitative results from Wave 1 of the Coronavirus and people with learning disabilities study, Tizard Learn. Disabil. Rev. ahead-of-print, No. ahead-of-print. (2021). https://doi.org/10.1108/TLDR-09-2021-0027
8. GlobalWebIndex: Coronavirus Research. March 2020. Release 3: Multi-market research. (2020). https://www.gwi.com/hubfs/1.%20Coronavirus%20Research%20PDFs/GWI%20coronavirus%20findings%20March%202020%20-%20Multi-Market%20data%20(Release%203).pdf. Accessed 07 Feb 2022
9. Heitplatz, V.N.: Fostering digital participation for people with intellectual disabilities and their caregivers: towards a guideline for designing education programs. J. Soc. Incl. **8**(2), 201–212 (2020)
10. Heitplatz, V.N., Sube, L.: Wir haben Internet, wenn das Wetter schön ist!" Internet und digitale Medien in Einrichtungen der Behindertenhilfe. Teilhabe. **59**(1), 26–31 (2020)
11. Heitplatz, V.N., Nellen, C., Sube, L.C., Bühler, C.: Implementing new technological devices in social services: Introducing the miTAS project. In: Petz, A., Miesenberger, K. (eds) Open Access Compendium of the 17th International Conference on Computers Helping People with Special Needs (ICCHP), pp. 109–118 (2020)
12. Heitplatz, V.N., Bühler, C., Hastall, M.R.: Usage of digital media by people with intellectual disabilities: contrasting individuals' and formal caregivers' perspectives. J. Intellect. Disabil. (2021). https://doi.org/10.1177%2F1744629520971375
13. Hess, T.: Digitale Transformation strategisch steuern. Vom Zufallstreffer zum systematischen Vorgehen. Wiesbaden: Springer. (2020)
14. Iivari, N., Sharma, S., Ventä-Olkkonen, L.: Digital transformation of everyday life – how COVID-19 pandemic transformed the basic education of the young generation and why information management research should care?. Int. J. Inf. Manag. **55**, 102183 (2020). https://doi.org/10.1016/j.ijinfomgt.2020.102183
15. Initiative D21: D21 Digital Index 2020/2021. Jährliches Lagebild zur Digitalen Gesellschaft (2021). https://initiatived21.de/app/uploads/2021/02/d21-digital-index-2020_2021.pdf#page=53. Accessed 07 Feb 2022
16. Kunzendorf, M., Materna, D.: Digitalisierung - ein eMotor für berufliche Inklusion? In: Heisler, D., Meier, J. (Eds.) Digitalisierung am Übergang Schule Beruf, pp. 187–210. wbv, Bielefeld (2020)
17. Lancioni, G.E., et al.: People with multiple disabilities use basic reminding technology to engage in daily activities at the appropriate times. J. Dev. Phys. Disabil. **26**(3), 347–355 (2014). https://doi.org/10.1007/s10882-014-9373-5
18. Lussier-Desrochers, et al.: Bridging the digital divide for people with intellectual disability. Cyberpsychol. J. Psychosoc. Res. Cyberspace. **11**(1), Article 1 (2017). https://doi.org/10.5817/CP2017-1-1
19. Mayring, P., Fenzl, T.: Mayring, P., Fenzl, T.: Qualitative inhaltsanalyse. In: Baur, J., Blasius, J. (Eds.) Handbuch Methoden der empirischen Sozialforschung, pp. 633 – 648. Springer, Wiesbaden (2019). https://doi.org/10.1007/978-3-658-21308-4_42
20. miTAS Project: Scientific basis (2022). https://mitas-app.de/navs/englisch/the-pedagogical-didactic-concept/scientific-basis. Accessed 07 Feb 2022

21. Pelka, B.: Digital Participation: Digitale Teilhabe: Aufgaben der Verbände und Einrichtungen der Wohlfahrtspflege. In: Kreidenweis, H. (Eds.). Digitaler Wandel in der Sozialwirtschaft. Grundlagen-Strategien-Praxis, pp. 57–80. Nomos Verlagsgesellschaft, Baden-Baden (2018)
22. Periáñez-Cañadillas, I., Chartina, J., Pando-García, J.: Assessing the relevance of digital competences on business graduates' suitability for a job. Ind. Commer. Train. **51**(3), 139–151 (2019). https://doi.org/10.1108/ICT-09-2018-0076
23. Riesmeyer, C.: Das Leitfadeninterview. Königsweg der qualitativen Journalismusforschung?. In: Jandura, O., Quandt, T., Vogelgesang, J., (Eds.). Methoden der Journalismusforschung, pp. 223–236. VS Verlag für Sozialwissenschaften, Wiesbaden (2011). https://doi.org/10.1007/978-3-531-93131-9_13
24. Seah, K.M.: COVID-19: exposing digital poverty in a pandemic. Int. J. Surg. **79**, 127–128 (2020). https://doi.org/10.1016/j.ijsu.2020.05.057
25. Sonnenberg, K., Arlabosse, A.: Mediale Kompetenz als Voraussetzung gesellschaftlicher Teilhabe - Lebenslange Bildung für erwachsene Menschen mit Behinderungen. Teilhabe **53**(2), 63–68 (2014)
26. Stadtler Elmer, S.: Oral interview (In German). In: Aeplli, J., Gasser, L., Gutzwiller, E. & Tettenborn, A. Empirisches wissenschaftliches Arbeiten. Ein Studienbuch für die Bildungswissenschaften. (4th Ed.), pp. 177–191. Verlag Julius Klinkhardt, Bad Heilbrunn (2016)
27. Sube, L.: Methodische Ansätze zur Einbeziehung pädagogischer Fachkräfte in den Ausbau der digitalen und beruflichen Teilhabe. In: Deutsche Rentenversicherung (Eds.). 30. Rehabilitationswissenschaftliches Kolloquium. Deutscher Kongress für Rehabilitationsforschung - Teilhabe und Arbeitswelt in besonderen Zeiten. Online-Kongress, März 2021, pp. 63–65 (2021a)
28. Sube, L.: Wohnst du noch oder surfst du schon? Wechselwirkungen zwischen kognitiver Beeinträchtigung, besonderen Wohnformen und Möglichkeiten der digitalen Teilhabe. Teilhabe **60**(3), 128–131 (2021)
29. Sube, L.: Die Welt steht Kopf – digitale Tools als Orientierung in stürmischen Zeiten. Zeitschrift des Bundesverbandes Autismus Deutschland e.V. Das besondere Thema Bildung und Beruf. **92**, 23–26 (2021c)
30. Sube, L., Bröhl, J., Kadatz, L., Klose, I., Frings, S., York, J.: Gesundheit – digital und inklusiv: eine Lernsoftware barrierearm gestalten. Prävention und Gesundheitsförderung (2021) https://link.springer.com/article/10.1007%2Fs11553-021-00896-z. Accessed 07 Feb 2022
31. We Are Social & Hootsuite: Digital 2022 Global Overview Report (2022). https://datareportal.com/reports/digital-2022-global-overview-report Accessed 02 Feb 2022

Design of a Virtual Task to Understand the Nature of Collaboration Between Autistic and Neurotypical Adults in Workplace Using Multimodal Data

Mahrukh Tauseef[1]([✉]), Ashwaq Zaini Amat[1], Deeksha Adiani[1], Spencer Hunt[1], Makayla Honaker[2], Amy Swanson[2], Amy Weitlauf[2], and Nilanjan Sarkar[1]

[1] Electrical and Computer Engineering Department, School of Engineering, Vanderbilt University, Nashville, TN, USA
`mahrukh.tauseef@vanderbilt.edu`
[2] Treatment and Research Institute for Autism Spectrum Disorder, Vanderbilt University Medical Center, Nashville, TN, USA

Abstract. Secure employment is an essential milestone of adulthood due to its association with self-sufficiency, personal achievement, and financial stability. Over the years, autistic population has been greatly affected by high unemployment rates, which is often attributed to their social skills deficit. Existing vocational facilities employ long-term intervention programs that rely on qualitative data to assess collaboration and social skills. However, qualitative data might be prone to error and bias. In addition, long-term qualitative analysis requires the presence of an observer throughout the program, which can result in high operational cost of such training facilities. This paper proposes the design of a collaborative virtual environment that includes LEGO building tasks that are mapped to nine dimensions of collaboration, which can be assessed by collecting and analyzing multimodal data captured during the tasks. A feasibility study with 6 participants was conducted to test the system. The results showed that the system was able to correctly capture multimodal data that corresponded to different dimensions of collaboration. Self-reported surveys reflected that the proposed system fostered a collaborative environment for the participants to exercise their social skills.

Keywords: Collaboration assessment · Social skills training · Employment for autistic adults · Autism · Multimodal data · VR-based HCI Systems · Serious games

1 Introduction

Securing employment has become one of the most essential milestones of adulthood due to the self-sufficiency, financial independence, and social acceptance that it has to offer [1]. It is often considered a measure of self-worth, achievement, and societal status [2]. Thus, unemployment can have drastic effects on the

M. Antona and C. Stephanidis (Eds.): HCII 2022, LNCS 13309, pp. 410–426, 2022.
https://doi.org/10.1007/978-3-031-05039-8_30

mental health, development of interpersonal relationships, and financial stability of an individual [3]. In addition, it can increase financial strain on the families of unemployed individuals as well as the government that has to come up with resources to provide support [2].

Autistic individuals are amongst one of the most vulnerable populations who suffer from high unemployment rates. Autism spectrum disorder (ASD) is a complex developmental condition with persistent deficit in social interactions, restrictive interests, and/or repetitive behavior [4]. According to a survey conducted in 2017, about 5.5 million adults had ASD [5]. Despite their cognitive abilities and technical skills, the high unemployment rate amongst autistic adults has been a major concern over the years. A study conducted in 2015 suggested that at least 42% of autistic individuals in their early 20's were unemployed. These findings have been supported by many studies since then [6–8]. In addition, the ever-increasing prevalence of autism amongst children (1 in 44 reported in 2021 [9]) suggests that there will be even more autistic adults seeking employment in the coming years.

Social skills are becoming increasingly important in the current labor market. According to a report led by Microsoft Corporation, the capability to communicate and collaborate with colleagues is among the core skills that they are looking for in future employees [10]. Unfortunately, the high unemployment rate amongst autistic population is often attributed to the challenges many of them face with social interaction and collaboration [2]. Not only does it make it difficult for them to secure employment, but it also becomes challenging for them to maintain it. Wei et al. [6] observed that the average employed autistic adult seems to maintain employment for half the time as compared to an average neurotypical adult. Thus, several government and private vocational intervention programs have been set up to provide autistic individuals necessary support in order to secure employment [2].

Ke et al. [11] conducted a survey and classified existing social skills intervention techniques available for autistic adults and youth into three categories: direct instruction interventions, naturalistic interventions, and technology-based interventions. Direct instruction intervention depends on the presence of a coach or a facilitator who could instruct, role-play or provide feedback [11]. Naturalistic interventions consist of activities designed for autistic individuals and their peers that puts them in a social situation that targets certain skills and provide corrective feedback based on their actions [11]. However, such activities require a well-structured curriculum and constant presence of a facilitator over a series of sessions. Many governmental vocational programs are often underfunded and understaffed to afford a working model whereas private vocational programs that may be able to afford such training can be expensive [2].

Even though direct and naturalistic intervention techniques are more common, technology-based intervention techniques are becoming more popular over the years [12]. This technique supports implementation of conventional methods through video modeling or Virtual Reality (VR) based serious games [11]. They allow the implementation of a variety of easily personalized social scenarios in a controlled environment and reduce added stress by eliminating social scenarios that might induce high anxiety [13]. Since autistic individuals commonly have an affinity for computers, they are more likely to be motivated during technology-based intervention [12,13].

Currently, most intervention techniques, whether they are conventional or technological, rely on surveys and questionnaires filled by facilitators and/or the participants for the assessment of skill training [11]. Such qualitative analysis is prone to bias. In addition, it relies on the constant surveillance of an observer, which can add to the staff's workload as well as the operational cost of a program. Quantitative assessment of collaboration can not only provide unbiased feedback, but it can also reduce the cognitive and financial pressure on these programs. Advancement of human computer interface (HCI) design allows for the development of a VR application that can collect multimodal data that can be used to assess collaboration quantitatively. However, such a system requires mapping of different dimensions of collaboration with measurable data from an HCI system that can be a reliable indicator of collaboration.

In this paper, we propose the design of a naturalistic collaborative virtual environment (CVE) shared by two users that (1) includes two specialized LEGO [14] building tasks that are mapped to nine different collaboration dimensions, and (2) utilizes multimodal data - speech, eye gaze, task progression, and controller input - to determine if the proposed system can capture collaborative interaction between participants.

This paper is structured as follows. Section 2 presents an overview of existing VR-based HCI systems that have been developed for assessing collaboration and social skills. This is followed by the design of our proposed CVE in Sect. 3. Section 4 presents the experimental setup for the feasibility study. The results of the study are shown in Sect. 5 followed by a discussion in Sect. 6 and concluding remarks in Sect. 7.

2   Related Work

Numerous VR-based interventions designed for autistic individuals for social skills training have reported significant improvement in social interaction. Dide-hbani et al. [15] designed a study to investigate the impact of VR-based social skills training on children with ASD. They used a virtual world software called Second Life^{TM} where participants went through different social settings as virtual avatars. Participants interacted with an avatar of a clinician who played different social roles in these scenarios. The results reported significant improvement in the social skills of the children after five weeks of intervention. Another study conducted in Hong Kong reported improvements in social interaction specifically in social reciprocity when a group of children went through real life based social scenarios using a Cave Automatic Virtual Environment [16]. The children were able to interact with one another as well as virtual objects in the system.

Additionally, several VR-based serious games have been designed that specifically focus on collaborative skills training. Silva et al. [17] designed a game for a multitouch table in which young ASD participants worked in pairs to put the uniform on a player together. The game was designed to offer training of four different collaboration patterns: active sharing, passive sharing, joint performance, and unrestricted interaction. The system was evaluated by therapists who observed the participants as they went through different phases of the game. The results showed that the system encouraged the participants to collaborate by showcasing the interactive situations and intentions that corresponded to the four expected patterns of collaboration. Sara et al. [18] designed an intelligent agent that would perform different goal oriented as well as cooperative turn-taking activities with an autistic child. These activities were mapped to different dimensions of collaboration such as reciprocal interaction, sharing intentions, sharing emotions, and other nonverbal cues such as eye gaze. The results of the training reported improvement in collaborative skills.

However, all the aforementioned studies were conducted with autistic children. There are few social and collaborative skills training programs that were designed specifically for autistic adults and even fewer designed for collaborative skill training in a workplace. Kandalaft et al. [12] conducted a version of a study [15] mentioned above with autistic adults and reported improved social skills. One of the most notable VR-based systems for collaborative training focusing on workplace was designed by Microsoft. Their neurodiversity hiring program includes an adaptation of Minecraft that allows candidates to go through different social scenarios that requires team building [19]. However, like all the earlier works mentioned above, the assessment of collaboration relied on the observation of a personnel.

In addition to observations, specialized tests as well as surveys were commonly used to assess and evaluate collaboration. One study utilized multimodal data to assess collaboration skills of autistic population. Alozie et al. [20] presented the design of a real-world collaborative task mapped to different dimensions of collaboration whose assessment relied on the analysis of multimodal data such as verbal communication, head pose, gestures, and eye gaze. However, the collaborative task was designed for autistic children and was mapped to a limited number of dimensions of collaboration.

Motivated by the existing work in the design of VR-based intervention systems that have shown potential for improvement in collaborative skills, we present a novel VR-based collaborative system that addresses some of the current challenges. Our proposed system incorporates a series of LEGO building tasks in a virtual environment to foster natural collaboration between two adult participants over a network. This increases the portability of the system by allowing participants to access it from different locations. The building tasks are mapped to nine different dimensions of collaboration that are important in a workplace. The multimodal data collected during the collaborative game can be used to draw inference about the degree of collaboration between the two participants based on the strategic design of the tasks that relies on collaboration for completion.

3 Design

The design of the CVE-based assessment tasks can be divided into three subsections. Section 3.1 goes through the design of the block-building tasks. Section 3.2 provides an overview of the architecture of the collaborative virtual environment, and Sect. 3.3 presents different dimensions of collaboration and their mapping to the tasks.

3.1 Design of Collaborative Tasks

Unity [21], a commercial game development software, was used to design LEGO-inspired block-building tasks in an environment where two participants sit across from one another with a LEGO mat between them (see Fig. 1). An invisible impenetrable wall was used to divide the LEGO mat such that each participant had access to one-half of the mat. All the LEGO pieces were randomly distributed amongst both participants. They were expected to finish their halves of the structure within a time limit by using the pieces on their side and requesting their partner to share required pieces that they do not have access to.

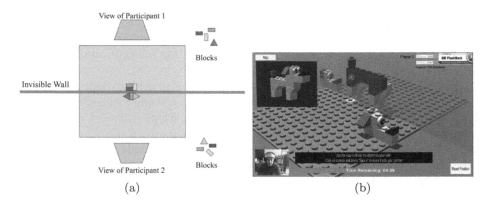

(a)   (b)

Fig. 1. A schematic representation of the top view of the building task layout (b) A snapshot of one of the levels of the game with two participants interacting with one another. The interactive map (top left corner), video of player 2 (bottom left corner), and timer bar (bottom center) can be clearly seen.

The task included two tutorials and two levels. The goal of Tutorial A was to acquaint both players with the controls and features of the task independently whereas Tutorial B was designed for them to practice building a simple object in a shared environment. Both the tutorials included elaborate written instructions for each step. Level 1 required the players to build a piano together whereas Level 2 required them to build a scene from a road intersection together by using an interactive map. The map was provided as an aid to both participants that displayed the object or scene they were building. The map allowed them to go through different layers of an object by pressing the *Page up* and *Page down* keys. (see Fig. 2).

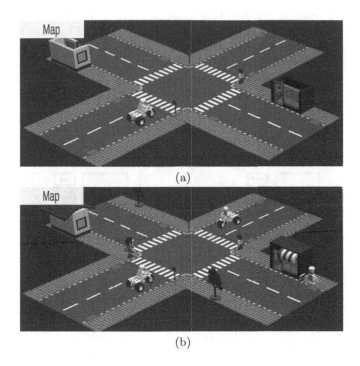

(a)

(b)

Fig. 2. (a) Second layer of the interactive map for level 2 (b) Final layer of the interactive map for level 2

The complexity of the tasks (i.e., number of pieces, shape of pieces, type of task, etc.) was increased from Level 1 to Level 2. The variation in the levels was introduced to encompass all the dimensions of collaboration mentioned in Sect. 3.3. Section 3.2 shows the implementation of a collaboration environment that allows the task to run synchronously over a network for both players while collecting multimodal data.

3.2 System Architecture

The proposed CVE system was implemented to support peer-to-peer communication between two people. Some of the necessary components needed for each participant's setup includes a personal computer with a mouse and keyboard to interact with the task, a webcam and a headset that allows the two players to interact with each other, and an eye gaze tracker that can keep track of where the person is looking. Tobii EyeX Eye trackers [22] were used to collect the eye gaze data and Logitech [23] webcams were used to stream the video of each participant.

Figure 3 illustrates the three main components of the CVE-based system. A Network Communication Layer (NCL) links the participants to a shared virtual environment. This network layer was established using the WebRTC API [24]. WebRTC is an open-source real-time communication API that allows for cross platform multimedia communication between nodes [25]. The built-in AV transmission channel was used to exchange audio-visual data between the two players. WebRTC's data channel was used to update and synchronize participants' interactions with each other and the environment. This includes movements of the block pieces made by either of the participants.

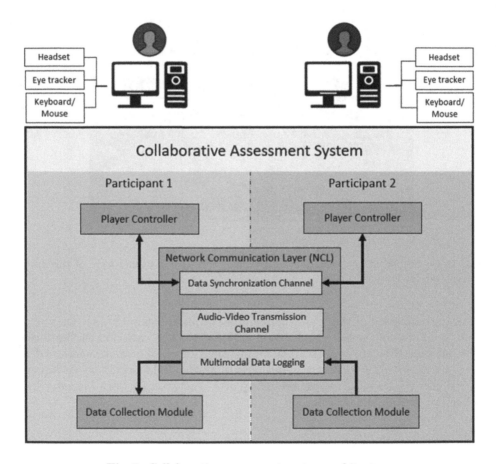

Fig. 3. Collaborative assessment system architecture

Outside of the NCL, there is a Player Controller component and a Data Collection Module for each participant. The Player Controller holds the logic for keyboard buttons presses and mouse clicks when participants manipulate the block pieces. The Data Collection Module stores multimodal input data from participants during the interactions. This includes transcribed speech, gaze points, region of interests (ROIs), keyboard button presses, and time to complete the task. Microsoft Azure's Speech-to-text service [26] was used to transcribe the speech of each participant. The multimodal data collected on each player's side was stored every second with timestamps in a log file on Player 1's PC via WebRTC's data channel. Table 1 defines each entry of the log file.

Table 1. Complete list of multimodal data recorded in the log file from both players

Multimodal data	Description
Timestamp	Instance of time the data was logged
Label	Player 1 or Player 2
Text	Transcribed Speech
Utterance	Number of words uttered
Duration	Duration of the sentence that was uttered
X_Gaze_Point	X-coordinate of where the participant was looking on the screen
Y_Gaze_Point	Y-coordinate of where the participant was looking on the screen
Focused_Object	Name of the Object the participant was looking at
Total_Score	Percentage of pieces latched by both participants
Individual_Score	Percentage of pieces latched by each participant
Piece_Latched	Name of the piece that was just latched
Piece_Shared	Name of the piece that was just shared
Shared_Count	Number of pieces shared by each player
Brick_Selected	Name of the piece that a participant is currently interacting with
Brick_Select_Duration	Amount of time a participant interacted with a certain piece
Active_Effort_Bool	A Boolean that indicates active interaction with the system
Map_Interact_Bool	A Boolean that indicates if a participant is interacting with the map
Time_Remaining	Amount of time remaining once the game ends

3.3   System Measures and Collaboration Matrix Scheme

Although technology-based collaborative intervention has been explored, limited studies looked at the features or dimensions of collaborations that can reflect important communication skills that are essential for workplace collaboration. After extensive research, Meier et al.'s [27] rating scheme for computer-supported collaboration was adapted to design a collaboration matrix that can be mapped to the multimodal data. This matrix was then used to design the levels such that all the collaboration dimensions can be measured by analyzing relevant multimodal data (see Table 2). Designing the levels this way allows for setting varying expectations for collaboration at each level such that participants can get focused on the task at hand without feeling overwhelmed. Setting such expectations also serves as a marker while analyzing the multimodal data of the participant to see if all the expected dimensions of collaboration were exercised.

Table 2. Nine different dimensions of collaboration along with multimodal data that is relevant to each dimension and an example from task design that maps to the dimension

Collaboration dimension	Data relevant to the dimension	Example from the task design that maps to the dimension
Sustaining Mutual Understanding: Do the participants understand each other?	Speech	When an explanation is offered for a question asked by their partner (Tutorial B, Level 1, and Level 2)
Dialogue Management: How are the participants following the etiquette of a conversation?	Speech, eye gaze	When a question is asked and the participant is responding. When the participant is looking at their partner while talking (Tutorial B, Level 1, and 2)
Information Pooling: How often are the participants referring to and/or sharing available information	Speech, Controller Input, Eye gaze	When the participant is talking about or following the instructions. When the participant is looking at or interacting with the map (all levels)
Reaching Consensus How are they coming to a decision together?	Speech	When the participants are discussing if a piece needs to be shared (Tutorial B, Level 1 & 2)
Time Management: How concerned are they about the time constraint?	Speech, Eye Gaze	When the participant looks at the timer and/or mentions if the time is running out (all levels)
Technical Coordination: How are the participants handling technical dependencies?	Speech, Controller Input, Task Progression	When the participants are sharing pieces with each other (Tutorial B, Level 1, and Level 2)
Reciprocal Interaction: Comparable input towards the completion of the task	Controller Input, Task Progression	If the participant is matching the pace and progression of the task on their easily (Tutorial B, Level 1, and Level 2)
Task Division: How was the task divided?	Speech	If the participants came up with a scheme to breakdown, divide and complete their tasks (Tutorial B, Level 1, and Level 2)
Individual Task Orientation: An individual's commitment to complete the task	Speech, Eye Gaze, Task Progression, and Controller Input	How well is a participant doing in finishing the task on their end (all levels)

4   Experimental Setup

A feasibility study was set up to test the designed system. Three autistic adults were paired with 3 typically developed (TD) adults to work on the task together. An ASD-TD pairing was chosen to match real-world circumstances. It is more likely that an autistic individual will end up in a company with a significantly higher number of typically developed individuals. All six participants identified as male within the age range of 18–25 years (mean age = 22.0, SD (Standard Deviation) = 2.16).

The system was set up on two personal computers placed in two different rooms in a lab setting. Both participants were seated in front of their PC's after they signed and handed in a voluntary participation consent form. A screen recording of the participants' display was captured along with the aforementioned multi-modal data. The participants were informed about all the data that was being collected. The study was approved by the Institutional Review Board (IRB) of the authors' university.

Figure 4 shows snapshots of all the levels of the task. Each participant went through Tutorial A to get acquainted with the building tasks independently. Ten minutes were allotted for this level, which was more than the time needed to complete it so that the participants can focus on learning the system without worrying about the time constraint. Support was offered if the participants faced any technical difficulty in this stage. Following Tutorial A, the participants went through Tutorial B, Level 1, and Level 2 in a collaborative environment. Five, 8, and 10 min were allotted for each level, respectively. The task took about 30 min to complete and was followed by a qualitative survey to be filled by each participant.

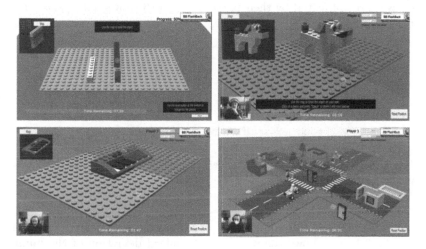

Fig. 4. Snapshot of Tutorial A (top left), Tutorial B (top right), Level 1 (bottom left), and Level 2 (bottom right) from the study

5   Results

All three pairs were able to successfully complete the entire task within the time limits. The log files for all the levels were successfully retrieved. An offline analysis of multimodal data was performed to show that the system can capture different dimensions of collaboration. Some snapshots of the logged data are shown below to demonstrate such mapping.

Sustaining Mutual Understanding: Transcribed speech showed different instances of conversation that presented mutual understanding. Keywords and key phrases like *yes, yeah, no, nope, I agree/do not agree* were used to look for such instances. Figure 5 shows a snapshot of a dialogue exchange between two participants that maps to sustaining mutual understanding.

Timestamp	Label	Text
11:36:34	p2	it looks like all that's left is putting the two keys down.
11:36:36	p1	yeah.

Fig. 5. A snapshot of a dialogue exchange between two participants that displays mutual understanding

Dialogue Management. Dialogue management was tracked by using the transcribed speech as well as the utterance. Bidirectional communication was successfully tracked in the log file i.e., whenever a participant started a conversation, it was always reciprocated by their partner. Figure 6 shows a snapshot of a conversation between a pair of participants when they entered the collaborative environment.

TimeStamp	Label	Text	Utterance	Duration
12:23:43	p2	hey how you doing?	4	00:00.1
12:23:44	p1	hey good.	2	00:01.7
12:23:44	p2	good, let's see if we can figure this one out.	10	00:00.1

Fig. 6. A snapshot of a dialogue exchange between two participants that showcases dialogue management

Utterance recorded the number of words said by each participant in a sentence. Table 3 below shows the mean and standard deviation of the number of words uttered per sentence for two pairs. A t-test was performed to see if there was a significant difference in the number of words uttered per sentence during the task by each participant in a pair. For pair 1, no significant difference was reported ($p > 0.05$) whereas a strong statistically significant difference was reported ($p < 0.0001$) for words uttered by each participant in pair 3. The ASD participant uttered fewer words per sentence as compared to the TD participant. Data from pair 2 was not available for analysis as the utterance was not entirely captured. However, this issue was fixed before the system was tested with pair 3.

Table 3. Mean and standard deviation (STD) of words uttered per sentence by each participant in a pair during the task. P-value of a t-test performed to see if there is a significant difference between the number of words uttered

Pair	Pair 1		Pair 3	
	ASD	TD	ASD	TD
Mean	7.05	5.15	3.99	6.16
STD	5.98	4.11	3.28	5.44
p-value	0.076		<0.0001	

Information Pooling: Exchange and sharing of information were represented by the transcribed speech, gaze data, and the Boolean value set for any interaction with the map using the controller input. Figure 7 shows a snapshot of an instance of information pooling from the speech. Figure 10 shows the *Map_Interact_bool* which is set to 1 whenever a participant interacts with the map.

timestamp	player	utterance
11:35:55	p1	you can go through different layers of the map using page up and page down.
11:35:57	p2	oh, really.
11:35:59	p1	oh yes you can.
11:36:00	p1	yeah.
11:36:00	p2	page up page down.
11:36:02	p1	page up or page down.
11:36:06	p2	oh

Fig. 7. Snapshot of transcribed conversation between two participants in a pair that shows an instance of information pooling

Reaching Consensus: Only a few verbal instances of consensus were noticed among the participants. Keywords including *yes, you're/you are right*, and *I agree* were used to look for any signs of consensus. Figure 8 shows a snapshot of a conversation that reflects agreement.

Time Management: None of the data recorded display any concerns regarding the time limit. No reference to time management was found in any of the conversations nor was any eye gaze data recorded on the time bar.

Technical Coordination. Since the task completion is dependent on participants' ability to share relevant pieces with each other, the expected technical

TimeStamp	Label	Text
12:41:01	p1	i believe you have another cyclist behind this house that's yours.
12:41:02	p2	yep, you're right. let me knock down this house real quick.

Fig. 8. Snapshot of transcribed conversation between two participants in a pair that shows an instance of reaching consensus

coordination was recorded by the system. Keywords and key phrases like *can you send*, *share/pass* or *I need* were used to look for instances in the transcribed speech where a participant is asking their partner to share a relevant piece. Figure 9 shows a snapshot of a conversation between two participants. One participant is asking for a piece which is followed by their partner's verbal affirmation and action of sharing the piece that was recorded as *Piece_Shared* by using controller input.

TimeStamp	Label	Text	Total_Score	Individual_	Piece_Latched	Piece_Shared
12:41:26	p1	i'll need a tree.	65	60		
12:41:27	p2	there you go, ok and this thank you.	65	70		
12:41:27	p1		65	60		
12:41:28	p2		65	70		P010

Fig. 9. A snapshot of multimodal data recorded in the log file that shows an instance of technical coordination

Another measure of technical coordination was time remaining which was logged as soon as a pair was done with the level. Coordination can be assessed by measuring how long did it take a pair to go through different tasks.

Reciprocal Interaction: Reciprocal interaction was measured by comparing the individual score of each participant, number of pieces shared, and record of any active participation on their side. Figure 10 shows snapshot of a log file where *Individual_Score*, *Shared_Count*, and *active_Effort_Bool* can be used as indicators of reciprocal interaction.

TimeStamp	Label	Text	Total_Score	Individual_Score	Shared_Count	active_Effort_Bool	Map_Interact_bool
12:41:36	p1		65	60	5	0	0
12:41:37	p2	then yeah, where's the other cyclist you see? have you seen?	65	70	4	1	0
12:41:37	p1		65	60	5	0	0
12:41:39	p2		65	70	4	0	1
12:41:39	p1		65	60	5	0	0
12:41:40	p2	do you see it?	65	70	4	0	0
12:41:40	p1	do you see it behind the white house? you'll see his helmet.	65	60	5	1	0
12:41:41	p2		65	70	4	0	0
12:41:43	p1		65	60	5	1	0
12:41:44	p2	oh yeah. oh i can't grab him yeah, keep him over.	65	70	4	0	0

Fig. 10. A snapshot of multimodal data recorded in the log file shows an instance of reciprocal interaction

Task Division: No instances of task division were observed through the data analysis.

Individual Task Orientation: Individual task orientation can be easily extracted from the multimodal data. Figure 11 shows all the multimodal data collected from controller input, eye gaze detection, and task progression that can be used to track individual task orientation using the labels *p1* and *p2* for each participant.

TimeStamp	Label	Duration	X_Gaze_Point	Y_Gaze_Point	Focused_Object	Individual_Score	Shared_Count	Brick_Select	Brick_Select_Duration	active_Effort_Bool	Map_Interact_bool
12:41:34	p2	00:00.6	1883.21	105.158	Fixed3	70	4			1	0
12:41:35	p2	00:01.0	1743.97	424.477		70	4			0	0
12:41:36	p2	00:00.7	1743.97	424.477	P012	70	4			0	0
12:41:37	p2	00:00.7	344.291	580.056		70	4	P012	00:02.7	1	0
12:41:38	p2	00:02.4	1106.23	526.198		70	4	P012	00:02.7	1	0
12:41:39	p2	00:02.4	1106.23	526.198		70	4			0	1
12:41:40	p2	00:02.4	1106.23	526.198		70	4			0	0

Fig. 11. A snapshot of multimodal data recorded for 10 s that can be used to assess individual task orientation for participant 2 based on Label = p2

The survey results obtained from each participant can be found in Table 4.

Table 4. Survey results obtained from all participants

Survey question	Scale	Mean	STD
Experience playing the game	1 = Not enjoyable at all, 10 = Very enjoyable	6.7	2.79
Difficulty of the game	1 = Very difficult, 10 = Very easy	6.8	1.62
Communication in the beginning	1 = Not comfortable, 10 = Very comfortable	8.3	1.54
Communication towards the end	1 = Not comfortable, 10 = Very comfortable	9.4	0.85
Allotted time	1 = Not enough, 10 = Too much	6.3	2.10

6 Discussion

The objective of this study was to design a collaborative virtual task and to show that the designed system is capable of recording multimodal data that maps to nine dimensions of collaboration that are essential for collaboration in the workplace. As presented in the previous section, the multimodal data captured by the system can successfully represent mutual understanding, dialogue management, information pooling, consensus, technical coordination, reciprocal interaction, and individual task orientation. However, the system was unable to record any instances of time management or task division.

The amount of time allotted might be one of the reasons why participants were not concerned about time management. This assumption is supported by the results of the survey where participants rated more than enough time when asked for the allotted time. In addition, the system was unable to capture any task division because the existing levels were designed with the block pieces divided between the two players at the beginning of the task shown on the interactive map. Design of an additional *freestyle* level without an interactive map will give the participants more room for decision making and task division as they build something together.

Survey data showed that the participants found the system fairly enjoyable with moderate levels of difficulty (see Table 4). The participant also reported that they were more comfortable communicating with their partners towards the end of the task as compared to the beginning of the task. However, the number of participants is not enough to attribute the increased level of comfort to the design of the system.

A notable observation made from the data analysis was that it could be used to perceive participant's conditions or states. For example, with the multimodal data, we can observe whether a participant was in idle state (i.e., there was no active contribution), struggling (i.e., they were actively participating but making no progress), or in steady state (i.e., they were making progress) over a fixed period of time. This information can be used to design and train an intelligent agent that can offer support catering to the different states (idle or struggling) and upgrade the assessment system to allow for collaborative training.

Only three pairs of participants were enrolled in the study because the objective was to present a proof of concept. Future work includes the design of an intelligent agent that could analyze multimodal data to detect the dimensions of collaboration. The detected dimensions can be compared with the expected collaborative activity for every level to rate collaboration.

7 Conclusion

The motivation behind this work was the unwavering high unemployment rate of autistic population that is often attributed to their social skills deficit. Existing vocational centers are unable to provide cost-effective long-term collaborative skills training because of the added workload on their staff to facilitate and assess collaboration. Existing VR-based systems designed for social skills training mainly focus on autistic children and still depend on personnel for evaluation of collaboration. Our objective was to design a VR-based collaborative virtual task that could assess different dimensions of collaboration using multimodal data. The task was designed to foster a natural collaborative space for an autistic and neurotypical adult to replicate a social interaction that many autistic adults end up having in a workplace. Results of the feasibility study showed that multimodal data can successfully capture different dimensions of collaboration mapped to the task. Future work includes the development of an intelligent agent that can be trained on this multimodal data to automatically detect different dimensions of collaboration.

Acknowledgement. We are grateful for the support provided by NSF grants 1936970 and 2033413 for this research. We would also like to thank the Vanderbilt Treatment and Research Institute for Autism Spectrum Disorders (TRIAD) team; Aislynn Kiser, Katie Wiggins Gregory, and Kelly Luo for their expert advice on interventions for autistic individuals. The authors are solely responsible for the contents and opinions expressed in this manuscript.

References

1. Chen, J.L., Leader, G., Sung, C., Leahy, M.: Trends in employment for individuals with autism spectrum disorder: a review of the research literature. Rev. J. Autism Dev. Disord. **2**(2), 115–127 (2015)
2. Solomon, C.: Autism and employment: implications for employers and adults with ASD. J. Autism Dev. Disord. **50**(11), 4209–4217 (2020)
3. Paul, K.I., Moser, K.: Unemployment impairs mental health: meta-analyses. J. Vocat. Behav. **74**(3), 264–282 (2009)
4. Autism spectrum disorder. https://www.nimh.nih.gov/health/topics/autism-spectrum-disorders-asd
5. Dietz, P.M., Rose, C.E., McArthur, D., Maenner, M.: National and state estimates of adults with autism spectrum disorder. J. Autism Dev. Disord. **50**(12), 4258–4266 (2020)
6. Wei, X., et al.: Job searching, job duration, and job loss among young adults with autism spectrum disorder. J. Vocat. Rehabil. **48**(1), 1–10 (2018)
7. Roux, A.M., Rast, J.E., Shattuck, P.T.: State-level variation in vocational rehabilitation service use and related outcomes among transition-age youth on the autism spectrum. J. Autism Dev. Disord. **50**(7), 2449–2461 (2020)
8. Seagraves, K.: Effective job supports to improve employment outcomes for individuals with autism spectrum disorder. J. Appl. Rehabil. Couns. (2021)
9. Executive summary, December 2021. https://www.cdc.gov/ncbddd/autism/addm-community-report/executive-summary.html
10. 21st century skills and the workplace. https://www.gyli.org/wp-content/uploads/2014/02/21st_century_skills_Gallup.pdf
11. Ke, F., Whalon, K., Yun, J.: Social skill interventions for youth and adults with autism spectrum disorder: a systematic review. Rev. Educ. Res. **88**(1), 3–42 (2018)
12. Kandalaft, M.R., Didehbani, N., Krawczyk, D.C., Allen, T.T., Chapman, S.B.: Virtual reality social cognition training for young adults with high-functioning autism. J. Autism Dev. Disord. **43**(1), 34–44 (2013)
13. Pandey, V., Vaughn, L.: The potential of virtual reality in social skills training for autism: bridging the gap between research and adoption of virtual reality in occupational therapy practice. Open J. Occup. Ther. **9**(3), 1–12 (2021)
14. Official lego®. https://www.lego.com/en-us
15. Didehbani, N., Allen, T., Kandalaft, M., Krawczyk, D., Chapman, S.: Virtual reality social cognition training for children with high functioning autism. Comput. Hum. Behav. **62**, 703–711 (2016)
16. Yuan, S.N.V., Ip, H.H.S.: Using virtual reality to train emotional and social skills in children with autism spectrum disorder. London J. Primary Care **10**(4), 110–112 (2018)
17. Silva, G.F.M., Raposo, A., Suplino, M.: PAR: a collaborative game for multitouch tabletop to support social interaction of users with autism. Proc. Comput. Sci. **27**, 84–93 (2014)
18. Bernardini, S., Porayska-Pomsta, K., Smith, T.J.: Echoes: an intelligent serious game for fostering social communication in children with autism. Inf. Sci. **264**, 41–60 (2014)
19. Neurodiversity hiring: Global diversity and inclusion at microsoft. https://www.microsoft.com/en-us/diversity/inside-microsoft/cross-disability/neurodiversityhiring

20. Alozie, N.M., Dhamija, S.: Automated collaboration assessment using behavioral analytics. International Society of the Learning Sciences (2020)
21. Technologies U. https://unity.com/
22. Celebrating 20 years - global leader in eye tracking, April 2015. https://www.tobii.com/
23. Webcams. https://www.logitech.com/en-us/products/webcams.html
24. https://webrtc.org/
25. Iiyoshi, K., Tauseef, M., Gebremedhin, R., Gokhale, V., Eid, M.: Towards standardization of haptic handshake for tactile internet: a WEBRTC-based implementation. In: 2019 IEEE International Symposium on Haptic, Audio and Visual Environments and Games (HAVE), pp. 1–6 (2019)
26. Speech to text - audio to text translation: Microsoft azure. https://azure.microsoft.com/en-us/services/cognitive-services/speech-to-text/#overview
27. Meier, A., Spada, H., Rummel, N.: A rating scheme for assessing the quality of computer-supported collaboration processes. Int. J. Comput.-Support. Collab. Learn. **2**(1), 63–86 (2007)

Methodology for Co-designing Learning Patterns in Students with Intellectual Disability for Learning and Assessment of Numeracy and Communication Skills

Pratik Vyas(✉)[ID], Romany Thakar[ID], David J. Brown[ID],
and Matthew C. Harris[ID]

Nottingham Trent University, Clifton Campus,
Clifton Lane, Nottingham NG11 8NS, UK
pratik.vyas@ntu.ac.uk
http://www.ntu.ac.uk

Abstract. People with ID tend to need support with most daily tasks, require time for cognition and multiple repetitions during learning of basic skills (APA 2013).Developing their visual learning ability, communication and numeracy skills is important for their daily life but presents challenges. Contextualizing and gamification of communication and numeracy skills into visual formats can help in the learning and assessment processes.Before proceeding to co-design, It is important to explore the existing technological know-how, ability, inclination and acceptance. It is also important to understand accessibility issues and limitations to usage. Teachers, parents and carers are most suited to understand the needs of the students with ID. Semi-structured interviews with such domain experts will help explore the constraints for participant selection, data collection, nature of co-design activities and method of analysis. This knowledge is essential for the success of co-design activities which would include ideation process with the students with ID.

Keywords: Co-design · Intellectual disabilities · Accessible virtual environments · Numeracy education

1 Introduction

1.1 Background

The estimate is that 2.16% of adults in the UK have an intellectual disability (ID) and the variation in presentation of intellectual disabilities can be sub divided based on the level of support required into four levels: mild, moderate, severe and profound. People with mild to moderate intellectual disabilities may be semi-independent in many areas of their lives and possess the ability to learn new skills and information. Studies on education have shown that students with

© The Author(s), under exclusive license to Springer Nature Switzerland AG 2022
M. Antona and C. Stephanidis (Eds.): HCII 2022, LNCS 13309, pp. 427–441, 2022.
https://doi.org/10.1007/978-3-031-05039-8_31

mild ID showed a similar, but delayed (Brankaer 2011) development of abilities as compared to neuro-typical students of the same age. Various tools and techniques for numeracy and communication skills learning and evaluation for neuro-typical students are being currently applied with student with ID along with some special tools created just for students with ID. Many of these learning tools utilise visualization as a means to aid the learning and evaluation but it is unclear if these have been effective and popular with the students with ID. Since so many tools apply data visualization, it is assumed that they could be helpful to supplement the learning and assessment of the numeracy and communication skills for students with ID. It is hypothesised that there is a need for intervention because the current tools and techniques are designed 'FOR' the students with ID. Research method such as co-design integrate user's ideas into solution thus creating a better understanding of the problem faced, and co-ownership of the solution being designed and may have a better chance of being accepted by the community of users. Therefore, co-design method needs to be applied to develop a data visualization based intervention 'WITH' the intended users, which are the students with ID.

1.2   Research Problem

Co-designing with students with ID as a research method has not been applied frequently. Existing methods of co-design need to be tailored to the participants based on their inclinations, severity of ID and support available (Standen Brown 2014). However, how the tailored method should be and what are resources required to conduct co-design is not entirely clear. Thus, there is a need to identify the process of co-design when researching with students with ID. This paper deals with methodological review for building such co-design method within the context of using data visualization based intervention to aid in the learning and assessment of numeracy and communication skills.

1.3   Aim and Objectives

Aim: To investigate how co-design could help in building data visualization (DV) based intervention that can be used to aid numeracy and communication skills learning and evaluation for students with ID.

Objectives: To achieve the aim, the following objectives have been recognised:

Objective 1. To construct a working understanding of key relevant concepts, which include; numeracy and communication skills training tools and techniques for students with ID, co-design with the intellectual disabled.

The objective is to understand the critical issues in numeracy and communication skills training for the intellectually disabled as recognised by different authors and the need for intervention. Then, the literature review demonstrates how the key concepts are relate to each other. It is important to explore prior research in co-designing with the intellectually disabled and review the methods used by such studies. This objective is briefly described in this paper.

Objective 2. To devise a methodology to appropriately apply data collection method and thematic qualitative analysis method for field review.

Field review includes semi-structured interviews with domain experts such as teachers, carers and established researchers working with people with ID. The interviews will explore the constraints for participant selection, nature of co-design activities, useful interventions and the method of evaluation (qualitative and quantitative) that will need to be applied to understand the effect of intervention to the numeracy and communication skills tools and techniques currently being used. The method and its rationale are core of this paper which is part of a series of publications. This paper however, does not provide the data, analysis and findings and focuses solely on developing a theoretical method for field work.

Objective 3. Identifying platforms for development of intervention and the co-design strategy.

A feature driven development method with experts, including the students with ID, their teachers and carers for rolling working versions of platform for applying intervention to the numeracy and communication skills tools and techniques that are currently being used. Further, co-design strategy to apply and study the developed platform needs to be proposed from the data. This is not within the focus of this paper and will be part of future publications.

1.4 Section Summary

The problem recognized is that, though co-designing WITH the students with ID could be useful method for developing data visualization based intervention for learning and evaluation of numeracy and communication skills, it is not well established research method within the context. Therefore, the co-design process needs to be tailored to the specific inclinations and needs of the students with ID. For this reason, the paper explores literature to develop a field study which will be conducted with domain experts such as teachers, carers and researchers with experience of working with students with ID. The paper provides method to analyse the data and proposes a strategy for co-designing WITH the students with ID.

2 Literature Review

2.1 What Is Intellectually Disabled?

The term intellectual disabilities (ID) is used synonymously with "developmental disabilities" and "learning disabilities". The Diagnostic and Statistical Manual of Mental Disorders (DSM-5), defines intellectual disabilities for diagnostic purposes (American Psychiatric Association 2013) as:

- An intellectual impairment that can be formally diagnosed with deficits such as planning, reasoning, problem-solving, judgement and learning from experience to name a few;

430   P. Vyas et al.

- Significant difficulty with daily living skills including looking after themselves, communicating and taking part in activities with others;
- Onset of the intellectual and adaptive deficits during the developmental period

According to Public Health England (2016), only 23% of people with intellectual disabilities are formally diagnosed and recognised by the authorities in the UK. It is hard to determine the accuracy of this estimate because, in practice, not everybody receives a formal testing and nowadays some services that were traditionally designed for people with disabilities originating during developmental periods, now cater for people with acquired brain injury. This already gives some indication of the variation in presentation of intellectual disabilities which can also be sub divided based on the level of support required into four levels: mild, moderate, severe and profound. So, for example, people with profound intellectual disabilities tend to need significant support with most daily tasks and will do for the whole of their lives and they often have additional physical or mobility problems. Comparatively, people with mild to moderate intellectual disabilities may show ability to learn new skills and information and achieve some amount of independence in certain areas of their lives. But many schools often have to group students with varied diagnosis together and sometimes also encourage attending classes with typically developing students to promote peer support (Darling-Hammond et al. 2020). Studies on the level of education of such cohort have shown that students with mild ID showed a similar, but delayed (Brankaer 2011) development of number magnitude processing and symbolic and a non-symbolic representation tasks. Thus, students with same age but with and without ID would perform differently (Brankaer 2013). Many students with mild to moderate ID are capable of acquiring level 1 of the Krajewski model.

Level/topics	Subskills
Level I: basic numerical skills	Quantity discrimination: differentiating between discrete quantities, comparing quantities and using the words "more," "less," or "the same amount," reciting number words, exact number-word sequences.
Level II: quantity-number concept	Imprecise quantity-number linkage: differentiating between "little," "much," and "very much." Precise quantity-number linkage: Counting objects, distinguishing number words. Relations between quantities without reference to number words, number invariance/conservation.
Level III: number relationships	Composition and decomposition of numbers, number relationships (4 is one more than 3).

Fig. 1. A version of Krajewski model adapted from Aunio and Räsänen, 2016

2.2 Understanding Education Tools for Numeracy and Communication Skills Development

It is very important for people with ID to be able to understand basic numeracy and cope with communication to successfully live independently in their day-to-day activities. There are already a few tools & techniques in place to improve their way of education for numeracy & communication. Importance of counting skills and the linkage of numbers and quantities has been explored by many different authors (Sarama and Clements 2009; Krajewski and Schneider 2009; Aunio and Räasänen 2016). These different models explore a common theme called task analysis.

Task Analysis: As per (Moyer and Dardig 1978) task analysis is basically a sequenced list of the subtasks or steps that make up a task is widely used by the special educators. It is counted as one of the critical components for the behavioural approach which is used by the educators to understand and analyse the need of students with ID. For example, Krajewski's model for numerical development (Krajewski and Schneider 2009), has been found to be applicable when describing the numerical development of students with ID (Moser Opitz et al. 2015; Garrote et al. 2015). This model is shown in Fig. 1 and has three levels. Level 1 consists of basic numerical skills where students recite number sequences, recognize number words, discern quantities and develop ability to compare them in terms of more, less, and the same. Level 2 is the acquisition of the quantity-number concept moving from imprecise descriptors such as- a bit, much, or very much, to the precise quantity-number. At level 3, students can compose and decompose numbers including addition and subtraction and understanding equations. It is important to note that the model was developed with focus on neuro-typical children of a certain age range, but has been useful during research with students with intellectual disability at different ages. Aunio and Räsänen (2016) build on Krajewski's model to provide specific Core numerical skills for learning mathematics model as shown in Fig. 2. Their diagrammatic representation include working model for the tasks that could be applied for each levels of Krajewski's model. These two models can be helpful to identify categories of numeracy learning and assessment. Using these to understand current tools and techniques would be helpful in understanding potential data visualization based intervention to be developed WITH students with ID. Thus, these models could be an important scaffolding to build and categorise activities during this research.

Manipulatives: As per Bouck et al. (2014) manipulatives are a common technique in mathematics classrooms that help students understand mathematical concepts and range from physical or 'concrete' to virtual or 'abstract' manipulatives. The physical is mainly about the actual object and these can be analogous or digital objects. For example, Battocchi et al. (2010) used collaborative puzzle games to enhance social interaction in youth with Autistic Spectrum Disorder (ASD) compared to control group of neuro-typical youth. They showed that such collaborative objects improved the interactions and helped with communication for the participants. Thus, there is value in using probes to enhance communication and interaction during co-design sessions. There is a growing set of virtual manipulatives which includes abstract techniques (songs, vibrations etc.), as well as computing environments. For example, Brown, McHugh, et al. (2011) developed an android based location tracking app that could help people with intellectual disabilities to repeatedly plan and practice new routes and then to apply them safely and independently in the real world. Clearly, this should be explored with domain experts and made a part of the co-design activities working WITH students with ID.

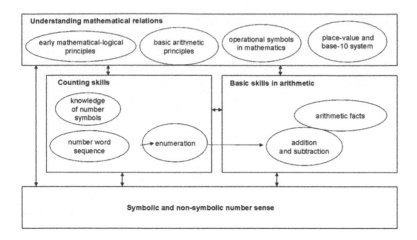

Fig. 2. Core numerical skills for learning mathematics (Aunio and Räsänen, 2016)

Multi-modal and Multi-sensory Approach: Obaid (2013) states that using multi-modal approach for the visual, auditory, and kinaesthetic modalities, sometimes at the same time is useful. They are considered useful because they assist students make sense of material in a variety of different ways. Further, their research noted that multi-sensory techniques have also been used frequently. These are activities that make use of the 5 different senses and are especially useful for teachers dealing with dyslexic students and students with ID. The modalities and senses often go together. Visual medium can be categorised based on immersiveness, e.g. 2d, 3d and head mounted display based (also called Ar/VR). They further enhance spatial awareness aspect through visual media. Perceiving through touch and awareness of body motions is referred to as kinaesthetic perception. Sometimes this includes other senses like smells, textures or tastes to further embed knowledge. Auditory approach ranges from use in instructions, motivators and tools for embedding knowledge e.g. through songs (sometimes associated with dance). When using such multi-modal and multi-sensory technique, there are other aspects that should be considered.

Body Language/In Person: It gets easier for them to understand it better when they see the way a talk is being delivered

In Writing: The best way for them to understand would be using bigger Fonts and bullets point

On Phone: By using clear and concise words and at a slow pace. Using sign languages, gestures, pointing towards picture are the best physical ways of communication. Apart from that a lot for text to speech software and other speak to talk apps like Proloquo2Go,Lamp words for life and ABCmouse are used.

Online Tools and Virtual Presence: During recent years, the virtual meetings with audio-video and online tools and environments have been used in education. However, using these for students with ID remains relatively unexplored area.

Assistive Technology: Use of assistive technologies especially in case of mathematics (Akpan and Beard 2014) where it can be in a form of piece of equipment or a product created by a teacher that is intended to increase a student's functional capacity or assist a student in accessing the general education curriculum. In order to achieve an inclusive classroom, students with impairments have employed tools such as pencil grips and text-to-speech systems. Similarly, Math Simulator games such as Tech tracker, Math Workshop, Virtual Ruler and so many Videos and Songs relating or including maths are also being used (Akpan and Beard 2014). The assistive technology also has practice environments and assessment features. However, there is clearly a gap between use of assistive technology in classroom and use of the learnt concept in real world. For example, Routemate tool helps people with ID to plan and reherse new paths which is real application of the concept of distance. By making the taught concept and its application in real life apparent could make the learning process more engaging and motivating.

Gamification. Paper and pencil versions or card games that exercise and thus develop memory have a long history in education and brain training games for hand held devices are commercially available for the wide variety of contexts. For example, Standen et al. (2009) used a switch-controlled computer game with time limit measurement to assess choice reaction times and found that card based intervention improved the reaction times for people with ID. Similarly, Prins et al. (2011) also verified benefits of adding game elements are associated to enhanced motivation and training performance of children with ADHD. In yet another study, Brown et al. (2008) randomly assigned school aged students with intellectual disabilities to playing a series of observational games that did not rely on memory skills and found that such games could still improve memory performance. Van der Molen et al. (2010) conducted similar research on a larger scale, with mild to borderline intellectual disabilities playing computerised version of the "odd one out" puzzle. The game could be played at any one of seven speeds in one of three versions based on fractions, percentages and decimals. These games designed show that gamification enhances the learning experience, that gamification introduces the hierarchy of difficulty to introduce challenge which can improve engagement, and that gamification needs to reflect a sense of progress and tracking of such progress.

2.3 Section Summary

The intellectually disabled community is growing, and they require assistance for different day to day activities. Learning numeracy and communication and assessment of such skills is important skill. However, the tools and techniques used for this purpose need to be fit for purpose. They need to provide different parts of numeracy knowledge, provide this through manipulatives which are physical or abstract props. To reach different types of learners, the tools could also provide multi-modal as well as multi-sensory approach and utilise assistive technical solutions. Further, gamification can vastly improve learning process for the students with ID. With so many requirements, it is important to explore how students with ID could engage with these aspects through interviews with the domain experts such as teachers, carers and parents. It is also important to understand how would these aspects be applied as a part of data visualization based intervention and used for assessing the measure of success. Thus, This section explored relevant theoretical aspects and the next section should explores practical methodology that could be employed to involve students with ID into the process of understanding the problem and designing the solution WITH them, rather than FOR them.

3   Review of Methods

3.1   What Is Co-design?

Co-design has gained importance in a variety of fields such as; educational institutions (e.g. ISTEAD, Stanford etc.), government organizations (e.g. the US Social Innovation Fund, Social Innovation within the European Horizon 2020 Flagship Initiative, "The Innovation Union"), third sector non-profits (e.g. the Young Foundation, the Centre for Social Innovation Toronto, and the Centre for Social Innovation Vienna etc.) and more recently a growing section of the private sector. Co-designing happens when facilitator goes beyond own creative practice to draw out problem understanding and creative solutions WITH a community who is facing the problem and will benefit from a solution. The researcher in co-design process is a facilitator to help with design thinking being applied by such community as well as any multi-disciplinary experts associated with them. Any project is truly successful only when the community affected by the change are comfortable with the methods applied to bring the change. This is why co-design ensures participants have "contribution to a shared knowledge-base", and contributing members are invested in the success of the solution generated. During co-design the knowledge is generated through interactions (Platts 2013) and application of design thinking through various activities. Thus, if co-design is important, it is also important to understand what the design thinking process means during this research.

3.2   Design Thinking

Design thinking usually applies convergent and divergent activities to find a creative solution to the problem. Divergent activities include ideation of new ideas by asking generative design questions. Usually the goal is to 'brainstorm'

(Osborn 1963) as many new and unique ideas as possible, and build a plethora of choices. On the other hand, convergent activities focus on analysing the ideas generated and filtering useful ideas so that a decision can be made of which ideas should proceed for testing and development. Crucial part of the design thinking process includes framing the problem and co-evolving the understanding of the problem with the solutions (Dorst 2017). Design thinking is the ability to solve problems which are considered wicked because it challenges the problem itself to build an understanding on the inherent paradoxes that make the problem wicked. The idea is to go beyond the regular logical questions and create different perspective or 'frames' of references on the purpose or value being created through the solving of the problem. A common example of wicked problem solved with design thinking can be seen with transportation department where the customer's enquiry about bus while waiting at the bus-stop became point of enquiry. Simple logical problem solving, or what Dorst (2017) calls closed problem solving, they accept the premise of the problem which is that 'the product solves a particular need of the customer'. Thus, the 'What' product we are dealing with and 'How' it will be used remain the focus of such logical problem solving process. Closed problem solving calls attention to investigating additions to the product features, improving packaging, improving aesthetics etc. Essentially, these solutions are perfectly acceptable and add to the value offering of the organization and their brand. However, with the example of transportation department, timetables were used on bus stops as a value offering to satisfy the customers' enquiry and the solution was considered unsuccessful. This is because the perspective always leads to enquiry into what other needs could be satisfied through that product. However, design thinking calls for challenging the premise

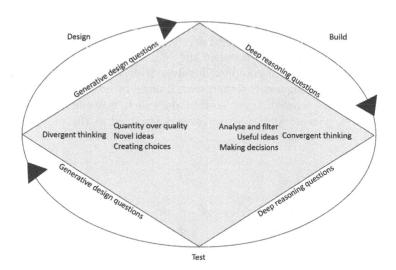

Fig. 3. Convergent Divergent design thinking, a visualization adapted from Lawson 2006

Fig. 4. Wicked problem with open and closed reasoning adapted from Dorst 2011

of the problem; that the product is able to fulfill the needs of the customer may have been true at one time but, is that the case now? This means re-investigating into understanding the needs of the customer to 're-frame' the problem. Such 'framing' is a small but significant part of the design thinking process and it is significant because it provides grounds for co-evolving the problem space and the solution space through divergent and convergent activities (Cockton 2020). Usually, all that is known is the aspired value that needs to be generated and such problems require, what Dorst (2017) calls, 'open forms of reasoning'. Such process is called as design driven innovation. For the transportation department it meant understanding why customers were unhappy and reaching the root of problem which was not knowing at the bus-stop 'when' the bus was arriving next. Such design driven innovation process is not a simple linear process and poses problems as explained below.

3.3   Design Driven Innovation and Fuzzy Front End of Design:

The process of design driven innovation applies design thinking (Lawson 2006) and deals with wicked problems (Dorst 2017) so that understanding of problem 'frames' and solutions can co-evolve (Cockton 2020). Such co-evolving activities during co-design form a part of, what Sanders and Stappers (2008) refer to as the fuzzy front end of the design driven innovation process. The representation of the fuzzy front end shown in the Fig. 5 can be interpreted to define the path to be random and complex, involves wide range of activities, has to be performed by co-designers together, with limited or no knowledge of the process. The co-designers are different stakeholders such as students with ID, their teachers, carers, parents and even researchers involved in the process. As seen

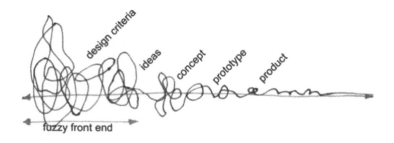

Fig. 5. Design driven innovation and the fuzzy front end Sanders and Stappers, 2008

in section on intellectual disability, there are different severity of condition and sometimes, they are associated with different physical disabilities. These combination of conditions can limit the participation and insights provided during this research. Thus, the researcher of study needs to have good insight into the co-designers before they can create and facilitate co-design activities. For this reason, a preliminary study with domain experts is required before creating activities for co-design.

3.4 Section Summary

During co-design, the researcher of the study has the responsibility to create activities which will enable the stakeholders to apply the design driven innovation process. Thus, the researcher of the study is not designing the solution or understanding the problems, but simply facilitating the discussion where co-designers co-evolve the understanding of the problem and the solution. This is challenging work, and it is even more challenging when working with students with ID. Thus, there is need to conduct preliminary study with domain experts such as teachers, carers and parents of students with ID.

4 Conclusions

4.1 Field Review and Interviews with Experts

Before any co-design activities can be planned, a field review will be needed. This is because, students with ID have their individual requirements and field review will help the researcher to understand them. For example, which activities do a certain group of students respond to, how do they engage, and what instructions they would require are some of the details that the field review should explore. Thus, field review will need to be conducted with experts on ID such as teachers, carers, parents and other researchers with experience of working with students with ID. The method of qualitative interview is considered appropriate because interviews could provide information that the researcher of this study may not have thought about. Semi-structured interviews will help explore and understand common themes, but exploring information not known will remain very important part of the method. Intellectual disability is often associated with physical disability. These could bring additional complexity to the co-design process. The field review can help explore what constraints on selection of participants are required, so that appropriate participants could be selected. This will then help the researcher decide on the co-design activities appropriate for the selected participants. There are many different tools that can be used for data collection during co-design. The field review can also help explore which tools would suit the particular study. For example, using role play for a group of students with ID could be selected as method for data collection during co-design sessions based on the findings from interviews during field review.

4.2   Co-design Session with ID Group

The sessions for co-design would require the students with ID to work with their teachers, carers and parents to engage in activities which aid in understanding how they learn numeracy and communication skills. These sessions would explore where such knowledge is applied and provide context to the knowledge gained. The co-design sessions will then focus on techniques which are popular for learning and assessment of numeracy and communication skills. Many assistive technologies are currently available and understanding pros and cons of each would provide an understanding of potential co-designed system. These could then also help in creating manipulative props which are either physical (real objects), abstract (songs etc.) or virtual objects. The co-design could also explore how the material can be accessed through multi-sensory approaches and integrate gamification into the assistive technologies.

4.3   Cross-validation with Other Researchers

The outcomes of the co-design sessions will need to be cross-validated. This is to deal with Hawthorne effect, inter-research bias and correct interpretation of qualitative data. During this process, it is not just important to involve other researchers, but also experts such as teachers, carers and parents could be involved to help understand what the participants are trying to co-design. This can be done either through post-co-design interviews to verify the findings with the participants. Or a separate group of experts not involved in co-design can help to interpret the findings.

4.4   Limitations and Future Work

There is limited literature on designing 'With' students with ID. The literature that exists, highlights that teachers, carers and parents are important to the process of understanding, involving and interpreting co-design sessions with students with ID. However, no clear plan is shared as a method during such studies and the focus seems to be on findings of such sessions. This paper identifies this as important gap in knowledge and builds on this methodological aspect. Another limitation of the study is that it focuses on researcher of the study being completely new to working with students with ID. However, many studies are conducted by researchers with lot of expertise in the domain of ID. The study is designed for a specific case of learning and assessment of numeracy and communication skills. However, there are many more studies where co-design could be useful.

4.5   Section Summary

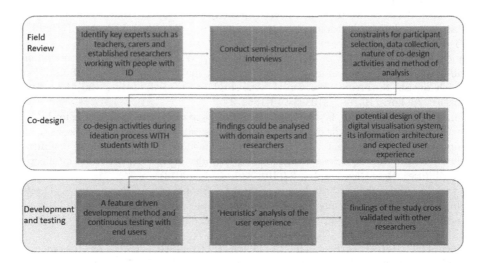

Fig. 6. Author's view of method of data collection

As seen in the figure, the paper reviews different aspects of methodological approaches, and presents a three stage method. The field work will explore through interviews with experts, key criteria for participant selection, ways in which students with ID selected can be engaged in co-design and how data can be collected during co-design process. The next section deals with creating co-design activities and facilitating them so that students with ID, their teachers, carers and parents can help in co-designing an understanding of the problems they face with regard to learning and assessment of numeracy and communication skills. The activities could further help in designing solution which could be appropriate for the problem and explore how existing tools could be used for this and what features could be involved. Finally, the findings from co-design sessions need to be verified with other researchers and experts to ensure the correct interpretation is understood. This could further be used as requirements for a system to be developed and such system could be tested with the participants as intervention to improve the tools and techniques for learning and assessment of numeracy and communication techniques.

References

Akpan, J.P., Beard, L.A.: Assistive technology and mathematics education. Univ. J. Educ. Res. **2**(3), 219–222 (2014)

American Psychiatric Association: Diagnostic and Statistical Manual of Mental Disorders (DSM-5®). American Psychiatric Publishing (2013). http://ebookcentral. proquest.com/lib/ntuuk/detail.action?docID=1811753

Aunio, P., Räsänen, P.: Core numerical skills for learning mathematics in children aged five to eight years-a working model for educators. Eur. Early Childhood Educ. Res. J. **24**(5), 684–704 (2016)

Battocchi, A., et al.: Collaborative puzzle game: a tabletop interface for fostering collaborative skills in children with autism spectrum disorders. J. Assist. Technol. **4**, 4–13 (2010)

Bouck, E.C., Satsangi, R., Doughty, T.T., Courtney, W.T.: Virtual and concrete manipulatives: a comparison of approaches for solving mathematics problems for students with autism spectrum disorder. J. Autism Dev. Disord. **44**(1), 180–193 (2013). https://doi.org/10.1007/s10803-013-1863-2

Brankaer, C., Ghesquière, P., de Smedt, B.: Numerical magnitude processing in children with mild intellectual disabilities. Res. Dev. Disabil. **32**(6), 2853–2859 (2011)

Brankaer, C., Ghesquière, P., de Smedt, B.: The development of numerical magnitude processing and its association with working memory in children with mild intellectual disabilities. Res. Dev. Disabil. **34**(10), 3361–3371 (2013)

Brown, D., McHugh, D., Standen, P., Evett, L., Shopland, N., Battersby, S.: Designing location-based learning experiences for people with intellectual disabilities and additional sensory impairments. Comput. Educ. (2011). https://doi.org/10.1016/j.compedu.2010.04.014

Brown, D.J., McIver, E., Standen, P.J., Dixon, P.: Can serious games improve memory skills in people with ID? J. Intellect. Disabil. Res. **52**(89), 678 (2008). http://irep.ntu.ac.uk/id/eprint/17156/

Cockton, G.: Worth-Focused Design, Book 1: Balance, Integration, and Generosity. Synthesis Lectures on Human-Centered Informatics, vol. 13, no. 2, p. i-143 (2020)

Darling-Hammond, L., Flook, L., Cook-Harvey, C., Barron, B., Osher, D.: Implications for educational practice of the science of learning and development. Appl. Dev. Sci. **24**(2), 97–140 (2020). https://doi.org/10.1080/10888691.2018.1537791

Dorst, K.: The core of 'design thinking' and its application. Des. Stud. **32**(6), 521–532 (2011)

Dorst, K.: Notes on Design How Creative Practice Works. BIS Publishers, Amsterdam (2017)

Garrote, A., Moser Opitz, E., Ratz, C.: Mathematische Kompetenzen von Schülerinnen und Schülern mit dem Förderschwerpunkt geistige Entwicklung: Eine Querschnittstudie. Empirische Sonderpädagogik **7**(1), 24–40 (2015)

Krajewski, K., Schneider, W.: Early development of quantity to numberword linkage as a precursor of mathematical school achievement and mathematical difficulties: findings from a four-year longitudinal study. Learn. Instr. **19**(6), 513–526 (2009)

Lawson, B.: How Designers Think: The Design Process Demystified. Architectural Press, Oxford (2006)

Moser Opitz, E., Schnepel, S., Ratz, C., Iff, R.: Diagnostik und Förderung mathematischer Kompetenzen. In: Kuhl, J., Euker, N. (eds.) Evidenzbasierte Diagnostik und Förderung von Kindern und Jugendlichen mit intellektueller Beeinträchtigung, pp. 123–151. Hogrefe, Bern (2015)

Moyer, J.R., Dardig, J.C.: Practical task analysis for special educators. TEACH. Except. Child. **11**(1), 16–18 (1978). https://doi.org/10.1177/004005997801100105

Obaid, M.A.S.: The impact of using multi-sensory approach for teaching students with learning disabilities. J. Int. Educ. Res. (JIER) **9**(1), 75–82 (2013)

Osborn, A.F.: Applied Imagination: Principles and Procedures of Creative Problem Solving, 3rd edn. Charles Scribner's Sons, New York (1963)

Platts, J.: The fault line in Chinese reflective thinking. Philos. Study **3**(10), 945 (2013)

Prins, P.J.M., Dovis, S., Ponsioen, A., ten Brink, E., van der Oord, S.: Does computerized working memory training with game elements enhance motivation and training efficacy in children with ADHD? Cyberpsychol. Behav. Soc. Netw. **14**(3), 115–122 (2011). https://doi.org/10.1089/cyber.2009.0206

Public Health England: Learning Disabilities Observatory People with learning disabilities in England 2015: Main report About Public Health England (2016). www.facebook.com/PublicHealthEngland

Sanders, E.B.N., Stappers, P.J.: Co-creation and the new landscapes of design. Codesign **4**(1), 5–18 (2008)

Sarama, J., Clements, D.H.: Early childhood mathematics education research. Routledge (2009)

Standen, P.J., Brown, D.J.: Mobile learning and games in special education. In: The SAGE Handbook of Special Education: Two Volume Set, Second Edition, pp. 719–730. SAGE Publications Inc (2014). https://doi.org/10.4135/9781446282236.n44

Standen, P.J., Anderton, N., Karsandas, R., Battersby, S., Brown, D.: An evaluation of the use of a computer game in improving the choice reaction time of adults with intellectual disabilities. J. Assist. Technol. **3**(4), 4–11 (2009). https://doi.org/10.1108/17549450200900029

Van der Molen, M.J., Van Luit, J.E.H., Van der Molen, M.W., Klugkist, I., Jongmans, M.J.: Effectiveness of a computerised working memory training in adolescents with mild to borderline intellectual disabilities. J. Intellect. Disabil. Res. **54**(5), 433–447 (2010). https://doi.org/10.1111/j.1365-2788.2010.01285.x

Design with Caregivers: Enhancing Social Interaction for Children with Down Syndrome

Han Zhang[1] , Xu Sun[1,2(✉)] , Cheng Yao[3], Yanhui Zhang[1], Qingfeng Wang[1], and Ning Lei[1]

[1] University of Nottingham Ningbo, China, 199 Taikang East Road, Ningbo 315100, China
{hvxhz2,xu.sun,yanhui.zhang,qingfeng.wang,
biynl3}@nottingham.edu.cn
[2] Nottingham Ningbo China Beacons of Excellence Research and Innovation Institute, 211 Xingguang Road, Ningbo 315100, China
[3] Zhejiang University, 866 Yuhangtang Road, Hangzhou 310058, China
yaoch@zju.edu.cn

Abstract. Children with Down Syndrome face major challenges in maintaining active social interaction. HCI research has well explored the design of computer-aided systems to support education for teachers and therapists, but comparatively less work has been considered in the case of social behavior learning for Down Syndrome children and their caregivers. Many challenging behaviors originate from misunderstanding DS children's emotions, body language, and verbal expressions. To better investigate the barriers to maintaining active social interaction for DS children and their caregivers, we conducted a social activity with an organization providing therapeutic treatment for DS children. Situated in a co-designed drama rehearsal activity for acting, storytelling, and socializing, our field observations and semi-structured interviews with family caregivers, therapists, and volunteers have illustrated certain behavior characteristics of DS children that may hinder communication and understanding with their caregivers. Based on this field study, we are contributing a nuanced understanding of the behavior issues of DS children during social interactions. Furthermore, we are proposing a collaborative partnership model to engage both non-professional and professional caregivers in developing a safe, effective, flexible, caring mode to allow DS children to be more self-independent in broader social contexts. Finally, we have brought forward the suggestion that the visual analytics technique can be used as a novel mediated form of assistive technology to support social behavior learning and personalized intervention.

Keywords: Down syndrome children · Social behavior learning · Design with caregivers · Visual analytics

1 Introduction

The Birth Defects Prevention and Treatment Report [18] states that Down Syndrome (DS) is a common chromosomal anomaly that occurs in 14.7 of every 10,000 live births

M. Antona and C. Stephanidis (Eds.): HCII 2022, LNCS 13309, pp. 442–452, 2022.
https://doi.org/10.1007/978-3-031-05039-8_32

in China, resulting in the birth of approximately 23,000 to 25,000 DS Chinese children each year [18]. These high rates are troubling, and are triggering an increased level of attention to the quality of life for DS children and their caregivers. Research has shown that children with DS are characterized by active social development and high visual ability, which provides opportunities for self-independence and engagement in normal society [4]. However, they frequently face significant challenges in maintaining effective social interaction owing to language disorders, low self-control in their emotions, motor problems, and cognitive impairment [3], calling for an urgent comprehension of each child's behaviors to enable the design of personalized interventions and therapy.

Individuals' performance characteristics during social interaction are highly personalized, and this is especially the case for children with DS, where sometimes their exaggerated emotions and body language can only be understood by specific caregivers with whom they have established long-term, high-intimacy relationships. Current strategies for understanding behaviors and evaluating learning abilities are still designed by therapists through daily observation, tests, interviews, and language sample analysis [20]. This process can be very time-consuming and a heavy burden for professional caregivers. In addition, most social interactions happen outside the school or clinic environment, where non-professional caregivers (i.e., peers, volunteers) have little prior knowledge of DS children's behaviors, resulting in low efficiency in communication, learning activities, and social interactions. Especially for parents, the experience of having a child with DS is both unexpected and stressful. Nevertheless, it is parents who play the decisive role in tapping their children's potential capabilities and applying effective interventions. Prior research showed that when daily experiences discuss the child's developmental delay or challenging behaviors, parents efficiently run into emotional strain as they discuss their hopes and fears, developmental concerns, uncertainty, and feelings of distress [19]. Hence, a novel way of mediated support technology, designed to help multiple types of caregivers improve their communication with DS children and thereby to better manage their behavior, should be explicitly considered.

Prior work on such a multi-phase, complex development disorder suggests that self-tracking and feedback systems are essential in assessing treatment effectiveness [14]. DS children spend most of their time at home, where they can experience various types of therapy treatment. To date, information communication technology and assistive devices (i.e., multi-sensory stimulation, virtual reality environments, language transcript software) have been well explored by HCI research [7], presenting promising evidence that these applications can enable children with DS to be more social and independent. Additionally, previous studies have shown that technological solutions can be helpful when leveraging the social aspect with multiple caregivers to improve the socialization of children with DS. Nevertheless, the adoption of high-tech tools remains limited for a number of reasons, including (1) insufficient contextual information [2]; (2) high costs [4]; (3) single behavior assistance or single conversation assistance [14]; (4) the need for a high level of professionalism; and (5) the level of acceptance varying from one child to another, one school to another, and even by country [4].

To better understand the common problems faced by DS children and their caregivers, we conducted a qualitative field study focused on three caregiver groups, including family caregivers, therapists, and volunteers. Our findings have allowed us to distill goals for

DS children and their caregivers that can be addressed through design. In this paper, therefore, we:

(1) Characterize the primary challenges associated with caregivers' understanding of DS children's behavior during social interaction.
(2) Examine the applicability of HCI research supporting communication and social interaction to this group and identify opportunities to create a collaborative partnership model.
(3) Discuss how advanced mediated technology can support DS children by providing integrated, visualized feedback of their behavioral indicators to improve understanding between DS children and their caregivers.

2   Related Work

Social Behaviors of DS Children and Observation of Daily Living. Children with DS are often seen as cheerful, affectionate, and sociable, but they may struggle with understanding, managing, and identifying emotions as a consequence of cognitive and language delays. Most DS children will be associated with lifelong Sensory Processing Disorder (SPD), a neurological disorder in which the brain is unable to integrate certain sensory information received from the body, invariably resulting in poorer nonverbal requesting and language expression [23]. Thus, the social behavior of DS children is always characterized by a lack of social-emotional communication, an inability to share their interests and respond to other's communication initiation, the avoidance of eye contact [5], failure to carry out normal social interaction adjust with contexts, and difficulties in maintaining collaborative work or playing games [21], among other factors. These challenging behavioral features cause serious understandable problems and ineffective communication between DS children and caregivers. However, research on improving social interactions, including DS children's social-emotional learning and social communication skills, is much scarcer. Previous designs and methods applied in the healthcare domain suggested that the patient-generated health data in daily life can help caregivers understand and manage patients' habits and behaviors more effectively [17]. To generate detailed health data, Hong et al. [11] introduced a concept named Observations of Daily Living (ODL), designed to visually depict daily behavior indicators, status indicators (i.e., mood, energy level, appetite), and the socio-environmental context by using the storyboard technique. This study provides evidence that visual OLDs can serve as a powerful toolkit with which to support patients' emotional journeys and life experiences, and ultimately support both parent-children interaction and data-driven medical conversations. Thus, we have identified a need to explore how to visually present DS children's social interactions that enable multiple types of caregivers to recognize their behavioral indicators and expressive language, which will facilitate learning DS children's behavioral characteristics, and thereby create personalized treatment strategies.

Assistive Technology for Caregivers-Children Interaction Support. Supporting children with physical and mental disabilities with regard to some of their physical functions and altering behaviors in the context of daily life has already been studied in some depth in the field of HCI, constituting a significant body of literature under the heading of assistive technology [2–4]. In addition, real-time automatic social behavior recognition has been proven useful to behavior reflection and change [13]. To date, notable advances have been made in supporting parent-children interaction therapy, especially for children diagnosed with Autism Spectrum Disorder [10], Attention Deficit Hyperactivity Disorder [13], dyslexia [12], developmental language disorder [1], to name a few. Guiding by assistive technology, current research can be categorized or monitoring conversation for developmental interventions and non-verbal expressive behavior for behavioral change [14].

The motivation for monitoring conversation in behavioral therapy is that it aims primarily to allow caregivers to determine their role and think back to their talking or parenting strategy during interactions. Huber et al. [13] developed SpacialTime, which is a conversation monitoring system that provides automatic feedback on parents' spoken dialogue to improve parent-child interaction. Song et al. [22] proposed TalkLIME, which is a mobile system that provides real-time feedback about how much time parents and children speak during a conversation, to improve parent-children interaction and reinforce parent-training intervention. Chan et al. [6] produced WAKEY, a technology-based system including the WAKEY app used by parents, a stuffed animal toy used by children, and RFID tags, used by both parties. This design aimed to use the toy and event tags to guide children to better prepare their morning routine, and the use of the application gives parents a number of recommended phrases to suit their goals based on tracking and analysis of their experience. Meanwhile, non-verbal behavioral change study focuses on real-time feedback for caregivers through the automatic analysis of behaviors, including acoustic sensing and motion-sensing. MAMAS, which is designed by Eunkyung et al. [14], provides mealtime assistance that integrates multimodal sensor data to improve parents' self-awareness of their words and behaviors during mealtimes.

Nevertheless, previous work has been proven that diverse sensory data generated from different intelligent systems will leave a heavy cognitive load on non-expert users. To avoid causing unnecessary distractions during social activities, integrating multimodal sensory data becomes a growing topic in the HCI area [14]. Several studies have evaluated that interactive visualization can serve as great promise in aiding users to gain insight into complex, multi-modal data [15]. More specifically, many behavioral visualization tools have been designed to support caregivers in healthcare-related contexts. To assist healthcare professionals in clinical analysis, for example, BEDA used data analysis and visualization techniques to make pattern analyses across conditions with different sensory inputs [15]. TipoVis allows users to compare two social and communicative behaviors during a screening session [9]. Furthermore, work from Kosara and Mackinlay [16] asserted that visualization for storytelling could also lead to deeper analysis and effective communication among users.

Through this way, we are completing the study by evaluating key features and future directions from caregivers' perspectives for using technology-mediated tools to enhance social interactions for DS children. We discuss both the opportunities and the necessity of integrating non-verbal behavior indicators and verbal expression elements into overall behavioral pattern analyses and personalized intervention design. We also hypothesize that a new approach, using visual analytics technology, can be a powerful tool with which to accelerate multi-aspect, collaborative therapy treatment for both DS children and their caregivers.

3 Methodology

The research is guided by three research questions: (1) What challenges do DS children encounter when maintaining conversation and socializing within a small group during social activity? (2) What barriers and enablers have worked to either limit or support caregivers' understanding of DS children's social behaviors? (3) What assistive mediated technology can effectively support caregivers' understanding of DS children and promote personalized therapy treatment in daily life? To answer these questions, we conducted an experimental study with LemonTree House, an education training school in China that provides therapy and specific education training for children with DS.

3.1 Procedures

The research consists of three parts: first, **we conducted preliminary semi-structured interviews with primary family caregivers (i.e., parents) and therapists at school**. These interviews helped us to ascertain which barriers caregivers commonly encounter in their daily interactions with these children, and how they handle any challenging behaviors. Meanwhile, the results of the preliminary interviews both helped our volunteers to better understand DS children's preferences and characteristics, and give us insights into which features we should track and observe during social interactions.

As Geller and Porges stated, "effective social communication can only occur during states when we experience safety" [8], so for this study, we chose a naturalistic social environment rather than a clinical context to conduct the experiment. To understand the children's behavioral changes and any learning progress during social interactions, **we then co-designed a drama performance activity with therapists, family caregivers, and volunteers** from the Drama Club in the University of Nottingham Ningbo, China, where the children's behaviors and performances (i.e., emotions, eye tracking, gestures) were recorded using cameras. This study included 11 DS children (4 girls and 7 boys) aged from 5 to 19 years, with mild-to-moderate cognitive and motor impairments. Children attended drama rehearsals every Saturday during one term, along with therapists, parents, and volunteers. The therapists first aligned drama roles based on each child's cognitive level and learning ability. Each practice group consisted of one volunteer and one child, where the volunteer helped the child understand, memorize, and play their part through storytelling, video, and games. Meanwhile, we observed and recorded how the children's behaviors and learning progress (i.e., receptive and expressive language, narrative contents) were changing. The pace and content adjusted according to the learning progress.

After each rehearsal, we conducted **semi-structured interviews** with the caregivers, including the therapists, parents, and volunteers. To augment their memories with additional detail, we applied a stimulated recall methodology to review the recorded rehearsal videos with the family caregivers and the therapists, to focus on the children's verbal and nonverbal cues to indicate their preferences and challenges when socializing with the volunteers. We kept the interview topics consistent across the therapists, the family caregivers, and the volunteers while adapting the specific question phrasing for each group. Topics addressed included (1) awareness of the verbal and non-verbal behavioral data, (2) experiences and challenges that occurred during the activities, and which interventions had positive impacts, (3) the DS children's preferences related to the use of information technologies in their daily life, and (4) whether and how non-expert caregivers appropriated commonly available technologies to support their communication and behavior management tasks. For the therapists, the topics also addressed family caregivers' participation in consultations and other care-related communication (e.g., electronic forms of communication with children and their caregivers). We also probed their experiences of communicating behavioral performances with both volunteers and family caregivers, to learn their perspectives on the impact of computing systems on behavioral tracking and feedback visualizing reports.

3.2 Data Collection and Analysis

The interviews and observations were run concurrently from October to December 2021. We conducted four preliminary interviews individually with therapists (T1 and T2) and family caregivers (F1 and F2). The co-design session included five therapists and two volunteers. Therapists in this session included one speech and language therapist (T1), one sensor processing therapist (T2), and three special education teachers (T3, T4, and T5). The after-rehearsal interview session included two family caregivers (F1 and F2), three therapists (T1, T2, and T3), and five volunteers (V1, V2, V3, V4, and V5).

We conducted a thematic analysis [7] of the interview transcript and observational notes with NVivo 12 and performed inductive open coding throughout the interviews and observations, which aimed to determine the inner connections and patterns between the codes as they emerged. After revising the results, we explained the generated themes with examples and quotations from this study.

4 Findings

When discussing the themes resulting from our analysis, we present combined data from the interview and observations. In reporting on findings, we refer to family caregivers with the label "F", therapist caregivers with the title "T" and volunteers with the title "V", while the DS children are labeled "C" (e.g., F1, T1, V2, and C2).

Three main themes emerged from our analysis. The first investigates the challenges of maintaining effective social interactions between caregivers and DS children, and which strategies caregivers use to overcome, or fail to handle, any understandable problems, and the reasons for the same. The second finding explores how the collaborative partnership model can enhance social interactions for DS children. Finally, we discussed assistive technology, including "multimodal behavioral indicator integration", "visual display observation" and "personal-centered performance reports" which may speak to effective intervention and treatments.

A Nuanced Investigation of DS Children's Social Behavioral Issues. DS children usually have a wide range of constraints in their social lives related to cognition, mobility, health, and expressive language skills. Therapists and family caregivers described how it was both beneficial and essential for DS children to maintain active social interactions to allow them to be more self-independent in broader social contexts, and to relieve the burden placed on caregivers to manage their daily routines. For example, F1 and C3 explained how *"understandable problems, especially communication problems"* can make school time difficult for these children, further affecting their motivation for attending school. During the rehearsal session, V1 and V3 stated that *"...if they don't know how to use language to express themselves, we can only guess from their facial expressions or body language what they might be thinking at the time."*

Meanwhile, non-verbal expressions can also be challenging for unfamiliar caregivers to understand. In this case, V1 stated that *"... their emotional feelings can be too intense or forceful for normal people. I remembered one child kissed the volunteer on his face when they first met, and then the volunteer seemed to have difficulty accepting this behavior."* Sometimes for the more complex situations, such as reluctant or resistant behavior, it is even more difficult for volunteers to use reinforcement to continue communication, or to allow children to focus on tasks at the beginning, because unfamiliar caregivers always fail to understand children's feelings and the reasons for the same. T3 said, *"their unique way to communicate feelings places a heavy burden on unfamiliar caregivers"*, thereby asking them to *"pay attention to the child's emotions at all times, and to reassure the child if he or she becomes afraid or cries during the teaching process."* Consequently, in this study, we paid attention to which particular behavioral characteristics hinder DS children from regular social interactions.

Following the observation and recall session, we summarized the social behavior descriptions of our participants in two respects: low-verbal expressions and confusing nonverbal behaviors. Among these features, low-verbal indications include slurring, repetition of words, lack of logic, lack of narrative content. In contrast, non-verbal behavioral indicators include exaggerated facial expressions and body language, sudden emotional outbursts, changes in volume or tone of voice, and fluttering eye lids during communication.

By applying stimulated recall methodology to review the rehearsal video, the therapists illustrated: (1) how to allow unfamiliar caregivers to have a direct overview of a specific DS child's behavior performance characteristics, and (2) how to accelerate collaborative communication between a primary caregiver and an unfamiliar caregiver, which could be a solution to breaking any interaction barriers for DS children.

A Collaborative Partnership Model to Create Safe, Normalized, and Friendly Social Environments. Caregivers described the importance of DS children being integrated into broader social contexts, with the prerequisite of joining in a safe, friendly social environment where people treat them equally, understand their feelings, and adequately reflect their behaviors. T2 gave details of how a collaborative partnership can be used to create a platform on which both primary and professional caregivers may share their experiences, and label DS children's social behavior characteristics to support understanding and improve interaction quality. In addition, such collaborative partnerships may also benefit the parent-children relationship by relieving parents' level of stress and uncertainty. F2 explained that "*Sometimes, children can behave well at school, but when they are at home, they often refuse to do things they can perform well, like planning their routines, doing their homework. We don't know if we are choosing an inappropriate way of talking with them. We try to seek help from teachers, but it's impossible to talk to teachers very often*". Similarly, both teachers and therapists are of the opinion that home therapy can provide the most effective intervention with regard to DS children's behavior, because they spend most of their time at home. "*We always pay attention to changing children's challenging behavior, but if parents can learn their emotions, and expressions, and adopt proper intervention, and even the progress of children's social behavior performances, they can be more confident in the parent-children interactions.*"

According to the requirements, we have proposed a collaborative partnership model (shown in Fig. 1.) to: (1) meet the requirements of multiple types of caregivers; (2) work together to enhance social behavior learning; and (3) better coach DS children to suit broader social contexts.

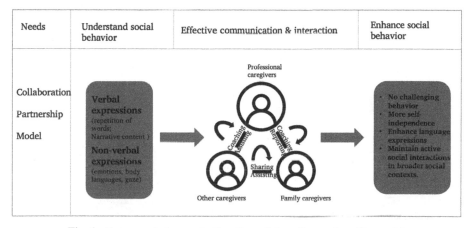

Fig. 1. Framework demonstrating the collaboration partnership model

Assistive Technology to Support Social Behavior Learning. As described above, a collaborative partnership model can be used to ensure caregivers are aware that continuous tracking of DS children's social, and behavioral indicators is both recommended and beneficial. However, it is very challenging for parents to regularly keep a record of their children's developmental milestones, because they are often occupied with other responsibilities [14]. As T1 explained, "*…, we tried to use diaries to allow parents to record their experiences in parent-children interaction and children's challenging behavior, but this method did not last for more than a few days because they did not know how to describe accurately any behavior characteristics*". In addition, non-professional caregivers often lack the knowledge with which to identify and document developmental milestones [14]. This is especially true for new parents, who have not yet achieved a tacit understanding with their children, so they will easily feel nervous, uncertain, and under stress. F2 stated that he always suffered from being unable to distinguish between his child's emotions when he was in early childhood. A similar situation also occurs in respect of understanding children's body language and verbal expressions. In this case, T3 expressed her concern about how assistive technology could help family caregivers to establish an automatic tracking and feedback system which allows non-professional caregivers to have a direct overview of children's behavior performances. Specifically, integrating verbal and non-verbal cues can improve the accuracy of analyzing overall behavior performances.

Under this concern, we have proposed a visual analytics toolkit framework (shown in Fig. 2) which can integrate multi-modal sensor data while leveraging domain knowledge and computing strength. The interactive visualization technique has demonstrated significant promise in aiding people to gain insights into complex, multi-modal data. Thus, the visualization technique, as a novel example of mediated assistive technology in this field, can be adopted as a powerful method for facilitating communication and understanding between family members and their children, as well as enhancing effective collaboration among caregivers.

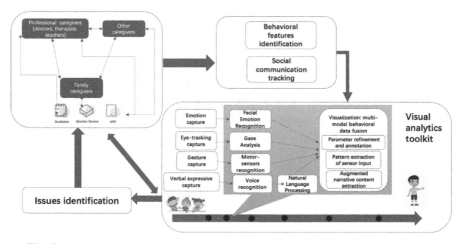

Fig. 2. Framework demonstrating the design procedure of the visual analytics toolkit

5   Conclusion

In conclusion, we have investigated issues relating to keeping DS children socially active, and the identified technological and personalized intervention opportunities to promote the ability to understand their social behaviors. Based on the requirements of multiple caregivers, we have proposed a collaborative partnership model which can gather caregivers together to support social behavior learning and thereby achieve effective intervention. This model may also act as a guide for the future design of assistive social technology, which may be suitable for broader audiences in a variety of social contexts (i.e., in clinics, at home, and beyond). We have shed light on how the visual analytics technique can be a powerful tool with which to synthesize children's multiple behaviors and learning progress, leading to the design of improved education materials and the arrangement of personalized learning tasks.

References

1. Adamson, L.B., Kaiser, A.P., Tamis-LaMonda, C.S., Owen, M.T., Dimitrova, N.: The developmental landscape of early parent-focused language intervention. Early Childh. Res. Q. **50**, 59–67 (2020)
2. Alammary, J., Al-Haiki, F., Al-Muqahwi, K.: The impact of assistive technology on down syndrome students in Kingdom of Bahrain. Turk. Online J. Educ. Technol.-TOJET **16**(4), 103–119 (2017)
3. AlBeeshi, A., Almahmoud, E., Almahmoud, E., Alosaimi, N., Alshammari, H.: Designing a writing grip for children with down syndrome that can enhance learning process, reduce writing exhaustion and improve quality of life. In: Stephanidis, C., Antona, M., Ntoa, S. (eds.) HCII 2020. CCIS, vol. 1294, pp. 3–9. Springer, Cham (2020). https://doi.org/10.1007/978-3-030-60703-6_1
4. Al-Moghyrah H.: Assistive technology use for students with Down syndrome at mainstream schools in Riyadh, Saudi Arabia: teachers' perspectives. J. Educ. Pract. **8**(33) (2017)
5. Berger, J., Cunningham, C.C.: The development of eye contact between mothers and normal versus down's syndrome infants. Dev. Psychol. **17**(5), 678–689 (1981)
6. Chan, M.Y., et al.: WAKEY: Assisting parent-child communication for better morning routines. In: Proceedings of the 2017 ACM Conference on Computer Supported Cooperative Work and Social Computing, pp. 2287–2299. ACM, Oregon (2017)
7. Dai, J., Moffatt, K.: Making space for social sharing: insights from a community-based social group for people with dementia. In: Proceedings of the 2020 CHI conference on Human Factors in Computing Systems, pp. 1–13. ACM SIGCHI, Honolulu (2020)
8. Geller, S.M., Porges, S.W.: Therapeutic presence: neurophysiological mechanisms mediating feeling safe in therapeutic relationships. J. Psychother. Integr. **24**(3), 178 (2014)
9. Han, Y., Rozga, A., Dimitrova, N., Abowd, G.D., Stasko, J.: Visual analysis of proximal temporal relationships of social and communicative behaviors. Comput. Graph. Forum **34**(3), 51–60 (2015)
10. Hassanabadi, H.: The effectiveness of parent-child interaction therapy for children with high functioning autism. Procedia Soc. Behav. Sci. **5**, 994–997 (2010)
11. Hong, M.K., Lakshmi, U., Olson, T.A., Wilcox, L.: Visual ODLs: Co-designing patient-generated observations of daily living to support data-driven conversations in pediatric care. In: Proceedings of the 2018 CHI Conference on Human Factors in Computing Systems, pp. 1–13. ACM SIGCHI, Montreal (2018)
12. Huang, Y., He, M., Li, A., Lin, Y., Zhang, X., Wu, K.: Personality, behavior characteristics, and life quality impact of children with dyslexia. Int. J. Environ. Res. Public Health **17**(4), 1415 (2020)
13. Huber, B., et al.: SpecialTime: automatically detecting dialogue acts from speech to support parent-child interaction therapy. In: Proceedings of the 13th EAI International Conference on Pervasive Computing Technologies for Healthcare, pp. 139–148. ACM Digital Library, Trento (2019)
14. Jo, E., Bang, H., Ryu, M., Sung, E.J., Leem, S., Hong, H.: MAMAS: supporting parent-child mealtime interactions using automated tracking and speech recognition. Proc. ACM on Hum.-Comput. Interact. **4**(CSCW1), 1–32 (2020)

15. Kong, H.K., Karahalios, K.: Addressing cognitive and emotional barriers in parent-clinician communication through behavioral visualization webtools. In: Proceedings of the 2020 CHI Conference on Human Factors in Computing Systems, pp. 1–12. ACM SIGCHI, Honolulu (2020)

16. Kosara, R., Mackinlay, J.: Storytelling: the next step for visualization. Computer **46**(5), 44–50 (2013)

17. Loke, L., Blishen, A., Gray, C., Ahmadpour, N.: Safety, connection and reflection: designing with therapists for children with serious emotional behaviour Issues. In Proceedings of the 2021 CHI Conference on Human Factors in Computing Systems, pp. 1–17 (2021)

18. Ministry of Health of People's Republic of China. Report on birth defects prevention and treatment of PRC (2012). Beijing: Ministry of Health of People's Republic of China (2012). [Chinese]

19. Ogundele, M.O.: Behavioural and emotional disorders in childhood: a brief overview for paediatricians. World J. Clin. Pediatr. **7**(1), 9–26 (2018)

20. Price, L.H., Hendricks, S., Cook, C.: Incorporating computer-aided language sample analysis into clinical practice (2010)

21. Regaieg, G., Kermarrec, G., Sahli, S.: Designed game situations enhance fundamental movement skills in children with down syndrome. J. Intellect. Disabil. Res. **64**(4), 271–279 (2020)

22. Song, S., Kim, S., Kim, J., Park, W., Yim, D.: TalkLIME: mobile system intervention to improve parent-child interaction for children with language delay. In: Proceedings of the 2016 ACM International Joint Conference on Pervasive and Ubiquitous Computing, pp. 304–315. Association for Computing Machinery, Heidelberg (2016)

23. Tavassoli, T., Miller, L.J., Schoen, S.A., Brout, J.J., Sullivan, J., Baron-Cohen, S.: Sensory reactivity, empathizing and systemizing in autism spectrum conditions and sensory processing disorder. Dev. Cogn. Neurosci. **29**, 72–77 (2018)

Design for Visual Disabilities

D-Braille: A Digital Learning Application for People with Low Vision

Abdalah Amadou Gueye and Swati Chandna$^{(\boxtimes)}$

SRH University Heidelberg, Heidelberg, Germany
AbdalahAmadou.Gueye@stud.hochschule-heidelberg.de, swati.chandna@srh.de

Abstract. Visually impaired people have trouble getting visual information, affecting their learning progress and day-to-day life. The Braille system was introduced to teach blind and low vision people to read and write. However, teaching them how to use and understand Braille is also essential. Low visioned people usually use Braille, but due to lack of resources and more time consumption, it becomes difficult for them to learn Braille, affecting their learning growth. Therefore, this paper presents a mobile application interface called "D-Braille" for people with low vision. This application has been designed specifically for people new to Braille who want to learn Braille from the beginning. This application helps them to learn and feel simultaneously. They will gain access to tutorials to verify the spelling of terms and practice letters on the Braille display. The application's main features are learning to read and practicing reading letters and words. Such a user-friendly application will enable users with low vision to learn to read letters and words with the braille dots on their fingertips connected by the Braille keyboard.

Keywords: Braille · Visually impaired · Mobile application · User interface design

1 Introduction

Globally there are 2.2 billion people who have near or distant vision impairment. Of those 2.2 billion, half of the people are not even aware of vision impairment [1]. Different kinds of visual impairment that vary between individuals can impact several developmental zones, notably personality, intellect, language, and cognitive development. In addition, the social development of children is influenced negatively as they cannot understand the nonverbal cues and cannot make eye contact [2].

Low visioned people usually use Braille, but due to lack of resources and more time consumption, it becomes difficult for them to learn Braille, which affects their learning growth. Also, the resources available can become costly for some people as their costs can vary from 500–2000 dollars. The Braille system was introduced in 1824 for low vision and blind people and was adopted from the military-based "Night Reading" system. It is a system that consists of touch reading and writing for blind and low vision people. Braille consists of 6 dots, two horizontal and three vertical dots. It's read from left to right, and both hands are used in the process. It also contains punctuation equivalents and provides symbols to indicate the grouping of characters. The reading, on average, is 125 words per minute and can go up to 200 words per minute in some cases. Therefore, all the printed words can be read and enjoyed by the blind and visually impaired people just like everyone else [4]. Over the years, many other methods have been introduced to support blind or visually impaired reading. Several of them, though, were elevated copies of printed letters.

From a basic typewriter created in the nineteenth century to assist blind people in writing intelligible letters to a mobile phone app that lets blind people "see" and comprehend their environment, technology has advanced tremendously over the years. By increasing freedom and safety, assistive technology can improve the quality of life for visually impaired people. Additionally, these technologies can alleviate their anxiety of social isolation by encouraging them to take a trip outside their usual location and interact socially [5]. Braille reading and writing are the two essential needs for visually impaired or blind people. But, as we see, it is difficult for a child or an adult who just started learning the Braille system to read and write simultaneously. Therefore, they need to be trained to do both jobs together.

Touch-based applications are in trend as everyone uses a smartphone in their day-to-day life. Both android and IOS phones come with voice-over technology developed to help blind and visually impaired people to access the phone's main features and give them access to use smartphones just like other ordinary people. Braille touch mobile and mBraille are the applications developed for smartphones and provide the user with the ability to learn Braille using their mobile phones. mBraille allows the user to learn to write letters or characters, practice writing the letters in the application, and play some learning games. It was developed in Bangladesh and allowed the users to learn to write English and Bangla letters [6].

Such applications have been implemented for many years, but most of the applications only train writing Braille letters and words. And hence, there is a need to create a generic platform where visually impaired people can learn how to read Braille letters and words. A user-friendly application that will enable the users to learn reading letters and words with the feel of the braille dots on their fingertips.

Therefore, in this paper, we present the first, to our knowledge, a mobile application interface called "D-Braille" for people with low vision. This application has been designed specifically to teach read and write letters, numbers, and words and practice them to learn better. The main objective of this application is to provide a user-friendly interface where the user will be able to use the application without facing any problem interacting and understanding how it works, and learn how to use braille in the easiest way possible. We have conducted two assessments to measure the task solving abilities of low vision people carefully.

Our results show that our was more engaging to interact with and promoted the low vision people more feature to use compared to existing applications.

2   Related Work

In recent years, the concept of developing solutions to teach Braille has gained popularity. VinithaIt et al. [3] developed a software solution for teaching braille letter recognition to young blind people. It lets users engage with the computer by interacting with the integrated NFC-tag blocks with Braille characters fetched on both sides. Young people interact with the system through a tangible interface to provide information and receive audio feedback through a voice-based interface. The virtual interface consists of a block with Braille characters embossed on the sides, and an NFC (Near Field Communication) tag is attached to the bottom. The blocks are small enough to be operated with small hands and sturdy materials such as wood and plastic to allow children to survive rough handling. The groove-based surface enables multiple blocks to be placed simultaneously and hides the NFC tag reader linked to the PC. When the young child puts the block on the surface, the Software detects the letters and provides proper auditory feedback.

Mobile braille touchscreen [2] was to help users, significantly visually impaired students, to learn Braille. The braille touch mobile app has voice narration to enable users, especially the visually impaired, to use the app. The narrator's voice uses Google's text-to-speech technology. The braille touchscreen application on a mobile phone has six main functions: learning, practice, writing, translation, configuration, help. There is also an additional feature called Speed Writing Compute. The virtual braille keyboard layout in the Braille Touch Mobile app has six buttons and a 3×2 binary matrix layout (Fig. 1).

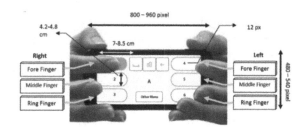

Fig. 1. Virtual braille keyboard [2]

mBraille application mobile app was designed for VIS-focused elementary education as shown in Fig. 2. Besides auditory and vibration responses for elementary school students or trainees, this app includes all characters and words in Bengali and English Braille. Student users will gain access to tutorials to verify the spelling of terms and practice letters in Braille. The application is operable on Android phones. The screen contains six dots, which the user can press. Some features of the application are [7]. It includes letters to learn, which offer users to learn letters. This sub-function will explain which points must be pressed to write a particular letter. Practice letter provides the necessary tools to practice the letters learned in the "Learn Letters" sub-function. However, this application works only on low-cost Android phones. However, these Android phones might not be available in the future, and therefore, more alternatives need to be explored.

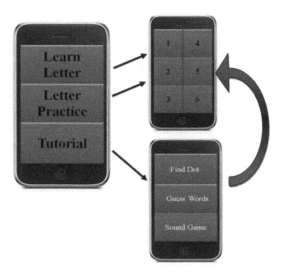

Fig. 2. mBraille user interface [7]

From the research mentioned above, it is clear that many educational applications have been introduced in recent years. However, no generic educational mobile application exists for people with visual impairment to learn and practice letters, words, and sentences at a low cost. Therefore, we first design and implement a generic mobile application to learn and practice braille in this paper. Also, we evaluate this application with eight low-sighted people to check the usability.

3   Research Methodology

To develop an effective design for the digital braille application, we first interviewed two teachers at the University of Education in Germany. They are teaching Braille and the five low-vision people from a non-government organization. Through this interview, basic needs were identified. The students were using the Braille display to learn Braille. But, because of COVID-19, they could not go to the schools and learn Braille in person with teachers. They also added that these Braille displays were expensive and not affordable because of the high cost. The needs were collected, and initial designs were created and evaluated.

3.1 Software Architecture

The system is made up of several components. The primary application has three user-facing features. The first feature, "learn and practice reading Letters," enables users to read and practice letters while receiving audio feedback. The second feature, named "learn and practice reading words," allows users to learn and practice reading letters. The third and most essential lesson is "Learn and practice reading numbers," which enables users to learn and practice reading numbers. The application uses the database to store and retrieve data for the users. The system employs a Braille keyboard to provide input and receive output. The application uses device Bluetooth and voice-over features to connect to the Braille keyboard. It is required to enable the voice-over function in the IOS device to use the app since this allows the app to provide audio feedback. The application's initial feature teaches the user to read letters from "A" to "Z" one by one. Upon completion of each letter, it announces which letter it was. The microservice architecture of the application is shown in Fig. 3. Furthermore, users can go back and go to the main menu.

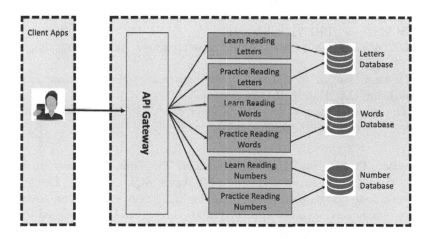

Fig. 3. Microservice architecture

Application Flow. The main features of the application are designed in English and German language. When users launch the application, they have six alternatives to choose from. On the screen, there are six buttons:

1. Learn Reading Letters
2. Practice Reading Letters
3. Learn Reading Words
4. Practice Reading Words
5. Learn Reading Numbers
6. Practice Reading Numbers

Since the application is for visually impaired people while navigating through the options, the voice feedback will help the users know which button they are on; an animation will indicate where they are navigating. To navigate, they have to use the Braille keyboard. Once they know which mode they want to learn, they must press okay from the Braille keyboard.

Learn Reading Letters, Words and Numbers

– In these mode, the user navigates through the numbers 1 to 6 using mobile application, while the application's audio feedback tells them which digits are dotted as well as what is clicked on the screen. Every letter or dot touched will be felt on the braille.
– To check which letter is dotted, the user presses the "NEXT" button.
– In the new screen, voice feedback pops out, displaying which letter, word or number it was.
– The user now has three alternatives to select from:
  • Either they can go back and recheck the numbers if they are confused by clicking the "PREVIOUS" button.
  • Or they can go to learn the following letter by pressing the button "NEXT".
  • Or they can go to the main menu to change their learning mode by pressing the "HOME ICON" button.
    The same process is done when they choose to learn reading words or learn to read numbers.

Application Design and Implementation. The application is implemented with react native framework and Microsoft Azure SQL database. The application's home page design, seen in Fig. 4, is the first screen visually impaired users encounter when they open the app. The home screen has been designed to make it more noticeable to them. The colors blue and yellow were chosen for the design because they are more visible to visually impaired individuals. The animation on the middle of the screenplays by indicating which button the user has clicked, with the assistance of voice feedback. On the main screen, users have four options to choose from and two others on the next page: learn Reading letters, practice reading letters, learn reading words, practice reading words, and learn reading numbers practice reading numbers.

Figure 5 displays a standard screen which is the first screen of all the three learning modes of the application. It consists of seven buttons, of which the first six are numbers from 1 to 6. Some of them are colored in blue to show that the

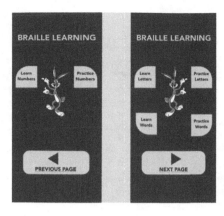

Fig. 4. Home screen of the application (Color figure online)

button is clicked. For example, it is dot 1 and the button "NEXT" to see the result on the second screen. For example, in here the result is "Dot 1 is shown and represents letter a". On the other hand, voice feedback will always mention what is on the screen and what is clicked in order to guide the user. Then the user can click "NEXT" for the following letter or "PREVIOUS" to repeat the letter, Or click the "HOME ICON" to go to the main screen.

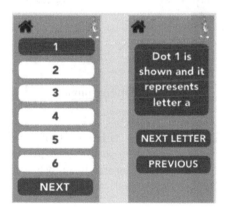

Fig. 5. Letter 'a' dots (Color figure online)

Figure 6 displays a screen which is the second part of the application, and it is learning words. It consists of learning short-form words by starting with the words beginning with the letter A. Firstly simple words like "About," "Above," "After" will be shown to the users. Then, according to what he will select, "About" in this scenario, he will feel dot 1 and 2 on the braille representing the short form of "About." Then that explanation will be given at the final screen when he clicks "NEXT."

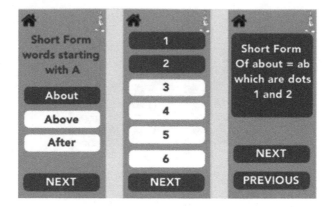

Fig. 6. Learn word starting with A

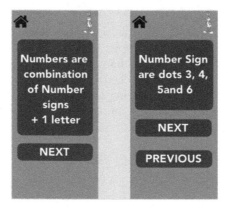

Fig. 7. Learning number

Figure 7 displays the screen of the third part of the application, and it is learning numbers. It consists of learning numbers where first an explanation of how number works is given. It is different from other learning concepts here since it is a combination. Users must first know to read the letter before learning numbers.

Figure 8 shows the result user has clicked dot 1, which is letter a, and is asked to add a number sign which he was thought in Fig. 7. Then after adding the number sign on the second screen, the third screen shows the result and explains how the process was done.

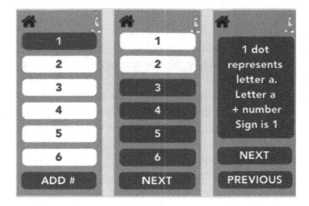

Fig. 8. Learn reading number one

4 Usability Testing and Verification

- *Participants:* The application is evaluated with the five low-vision people interviewed earlier and two teachers who are expert users of Braille display. Here, we conducted a study to understand the application from the user's perspective.
- *Apparatus:* The usability testing was performed in the presence with the D-Braille application running on iPhone.
- *Procedure:* At first, we introduced the application and explained the concepts in detail. After that, we gave them approximately 15 min to get comfortable with the application. Some of the participants already started to give the feedback as follows:
  - The error messages should also come via a voice and haptic feedback
  - Color of the button can be darker
  - Size of the animations and button can be increased more

  We gave a few tasks to the participants to check the users' efficiency, effectiveness, and satisfaction. The tasks given to the participants are listed below:
  1. Could you please go to the learn reading letters and read out letter "S"?
  2. Could you please go to the learn reading number and read out numbers "2"?
  3. Could you please go to the learn reading number and read out numbers "1" and "5"?
  4. Could you please go to the learn reading number and read out words "Ant" and "Cat"?
- *Results*
  1. The animation is not visible.
  2. The numbers and letters are visible. The users mentioned it would be nice if they could increase the size of the buttons by themselves.
  3. Users suggested adding the guide for connecting the Braille display with the smartphone
  4. Users suggested adding dark mode in the application to adapt it easily.

5   Discussions

- **Target Audience:** Visually impaired and blind people are the primary audience for the application. Although, the application can be used for learning Braille by ordinary people as well.
- **Opportunities:** The application is unique such that all the features of the application are merging to provide a stage for visually impaired people to learn how to read in a faster way at their own pace. The most astonishing thing about the application is that it is integrated with a Braille keyboard that helps users learn and feel simultaneously.
- **Future Scope:** The current application helps the users to learn how to read Braille letters. They can even feel the dots by their fingertips using the Braille display. The application consists of three functionalities, of which the first functionality has been developed. The scope for the future of this project consists of the wrest two functionalities: "Practice Reading Letters" and "Practice Reading Words." The use cases for these functionalities are already being created. The requirements for these functionalities are React Native Developer, Braille Keyboard, Microsoft Azure SQL database. An AI function that can assist users in talking to the app to get to a specific letter they wish to study is another feature that may be introduced to the app. Users will have greater freedom due to this functionality, and the application will be more feasible. This functionality can be implemented using "speech to text" AI technology.

6   Conclusion

To conclude, the developed application has provided a platform for visually impaired and blind people to read the letters from 'a to z' and feel the braille dots in the braille keyboard. The application helps them to grow their knowledge and allows them to learn at their own pace. As discussed in the long term, the application will develop further and have more advanced features. It will stand out from other applications as it is integrated with the Braille keyboard, unique. The application is built with React Native, an open-source framework that is entirely free to use. Microsoft Azure SQL cloud data storage is being utilized for the initial data storage, which may be expanded in the future to hold more complex data when the application is developed further. Since the Braille Focus 40 keyboard integrates the application and can be only connected to IOS devices, therefore, for now, the application can only be installed on IOS devices such as iPhones and ipads.

References

1. History of braille. https://brailleworks.com/braille-resources/history-of-braille/. Accessed 2 Oct 2021

2. Cahya, R.A.D., Handayani, A.N., Wibawa, A.P.: Mobile braille touch application for visually impaired people using double diamond approach. In: MATEC Web of Conferences, vol. 197, p. 15007. EDP Sciences (2018)
3. Gadiraju, V., Muehlbradt, A., Kane, S.K.: Brailleblocks: computational braille toys for collaborative learning. In: Proceedings of the 2020 CHI Conference on Human Factors in Computing Systems, pp. 1–12 (2020)
4. Hakobyan, L., Lumsden, J., O'Sullivan, D., Bartlett, H.: Mobile assistive technologies for the visually impaired. Surv. Ophthalmol. **58**(6), 513–528 (2013)
5. Jafri, R.: Electronic braille blocks: a tangible interface-based application for teaching braille letter recognition to very young blind children. In: Miesenberger, K., Fels, D., Archambault, D., Peňáz, P., Zagler, W. (eds.) ICCHP 2014. LNCS, vol. 8548, pp. 551–558. Springer, Cham (2014). https://doi.org/10.1007/978-3-319-08599-9_81
6. Nahar, L., Jaafar, A., Ahamed, E., Kaish, A.: Design of a braille learning application for visually impaired students in Bangladesh. Assist. Technol. **27**(3), 172–182 (2015)
7. Nahar, L., Jaafar, A., Sulaiman, R.: Usability evaluation of a mobile phone based braille learning application "mbraille". Malays. J. Comput. Sci. 108–117 (2019)

The Role of Technology for the Inclusion of People with Visual Impairments in the Workforce

Till Halbach[1]([⊠]) [iD], Kristin Skeide Fuglerud[1] [iD], Tonje Fyhn[2], Kristin Kjæret[3], and Terje André Olsen[3]

[1] Norwegian Computing Center, Oslo, Norway
till.halbach@nr.no
[2] NORCE Norwegian Research Centre, Bergen, Norway
[3] The Norwegian Association of the Blind and Partially Sighted, Oslo, Norway

Abstract. In this study, we have acquired the experiences of five individuals with visual impairments as job seekers and employees. Our focus has been on technology, but we have also shed light upon topics such as training, technical support, aid schemes, attitudes, and the employer-employee relationship. The interviews with our informants show that being able to use ICT is vital for participation in the workforce. At the same time, technologies introduce a number of technical and related challenges. One of the most important measures to remedy these challenges and achieve a higher degree of digital inclusion in the working life, would be to amend the Norwegian legislation, such that it no longer exempts the labor market from the requirement on universal design of ICT.

Keywords: Digital inclusion · Universal design · Accessibility · IT · ICT · Technology · Assistive tech · Work · Working life · Workforce · Workplace · Facilitation · Impairment · Disability · Low vision · Blind

1 Introduction

For a great share of jobs in today's societies, there is a high demand for technical skills, in particular with regard to information and communication technology (ICT) (Bjønness et al. 2021). This coherence has increased further with the Covid-19 pandemic. At the same time, it is known that the share of people with impairments who are unemployed, but want to work, has changed little in Norway since 2006, which marks the beginning of the statistics (Statistisk sentralbyrå 2020). Several recent studies, described below, have shown that employees with vision impairment are particularly affected by the proliferation of ICT.

In this work, we have focused on people with visual impairments and gathered knowledge about in which circumstances technology acts as an enabler, and when it is a disabler or barrier for their participation in the workforce. Our work is divided into two parts: In the first, we have surveyed recent related research and other work in the intersection of the following fields: work, vision impairment, and technology. The work

M. Antona and C. Stephanidis (Eds.): HCII 2022, LNCS 13309, pp. 466–478, 2022.
https://doi.org/10.1007/978-3-031-05039-8_34

has been published as a technical report in Norwegian (Fuglerud, Fyhn, et al. 2021). In the second part, we present five case studies of employees with vision impairment and their experiences with technology throughout their work career. This work has also been published in Norwegian as a technical report (Halbach et al. 2022).

1.1 Abbreviations

- AT: assistive technology
- CRM: customer relationship management
- HR: Human Resources (Department)
- ICT: information and communication technology
- IT: information technology
- NABP: (The) Norwegian Association of the Blind and Partially Sighted
- NAV: (The) Norwegian Labor and Welfare Administration
- NGO: non-governmental organization
- OS: operating system
- UD: universal design

2   Related Work

An overview over related work has been published in Norwegian as a technical report by the authors (Fuglerud et al. 2021). The interviews in the current study are partly based on these findings and were carried out after the completion of the literature review.

The barriers and possibilities of ICT and AT for people with disabilities in the working life is a research area with several different theoretical starting points and perspectives. It spans academic disciplines such as technology, design, working life, rehabilitation, economics, law, human rights, social work and sociology. The overview in (Fuglerud, Fyhn, et al. 2021) covers 56 publications and is mainly related to the labor market in Norway. It includes peer reviewed publications and gray literature, such as surveys, reports, and master theses. The reviewed publications vary with regard to data quality and methodology. Most of the publications are not peer-reviewed. Also, most of the studies are qualitative, and few quantitative studies have been carried out. Nevertheless, the results seem to point in more or less the same direction, which strengthens the overall conclusions. In the following, we highlight some of the most important findings.

In many of the reviewed publications, "vision impairment" is only accounted for as part of the greater topic "human impairment". The literature were thematically categorized and structured according to the following six broader topics: Research, universal design and human impairment, information- and communication technology (ICT) and assistive technology (AT), public administration and training, employer perspective, and society.

One important finding regarding the topic "research" is that while we found a number of publications documenting ICT barriers, there is a lack of peer-reviewed literature that investigates how the ongoing digitalisation within the working life affects inclusion or exclusion of people with disabilities. Moreover, there are research gaps when it comes to which strategies and measures are most effective for inclusion of people with impairments in the workforce, and especially regarding digital barriers and universal design (Bufdir 2020; Gulliksen et al. 2021; LDO 2015; Proba 2019).

Research on inclusion of people with disabilities in the labor market has documented a wide range of barriers (Chhabra 2021), including technological barriers and lack of universal design of ICT (Fuglerud et al. 2021; Gulliksen et al. 2021; Halbach et al. 2020; Halbach and Tunold 2020; Proba 2020). Universal design (UD) comprises the design of products, applications, and environments in such a way that it is accessible and usable by all people without the need for adaptation or specialization (Miljøverndepartementet 2007). Thus, the goal of UD of ICT is to increase the usability and accessibility of mainstream ICT products and services. The principles of universal design have been solidified in both international and national legislation (European Telecommunications Standards Institute (ETSI) 2021; Kulturdepartementet 2017; United Nations (UN) 2006), but does not yet cover domain specific ICT systems used in working life.

One of the most important findings of the literature study is that many administrative systems and domain-specific software systems, such as economy, CRM or electronic patient record systems are not universally designed. The degree of universal design can impact whether employees with disabilities can use a software system independently (Fuglerud et al. 2021; Halbach et al. 2020; Halbach and Tunold 2020). In particular we find that digital barriers arise due to lack of compatibility with AT. Compatibility with AT is one of the requirements of universal design of ICT (Fuglerud et al. 2014). Also, the development of AT seems to receive less attention than mainstream technology, which results in less-than-optimum quality and delays for people that are dependent on AT.

The lack of regulation with regard to universal design of technology used in working life is likely one important reason why there is little consciousness of universal design and human diversity among developers, testers, and designers of administrative or domain specific software systems. People with impairments are typically not sufficiently involved during the development of such systems (Gulliksen et al. 2021; Walday et al. 2016). While cost-benefit analysis of ICT solutions in general is a well researched field, very few attempts have been made when it comes to analyzing the effects of UD of ICT solutions in the work life (Fuglerud et al. 2015; Halbach and Fuglerud 2016a, b; Proba 2019).

The literature suggests further that both competence and attitudes of public administrations seem to limit exploitation of the possibilities provided by technology with regard to increased work inclusion for people with visual impairments. Moreover, better coordination of efforts is necessary across all the different parts of the administration to give a more holistic service to both employers and employees. The literature states that the training offered by public actors varies widely, and in many instances it is not universally designed, which renders it useless to people with impairments (Fuglerud et al. 2020; Fuglerud et al. 2021; Fuglerud and Solheim 2008; Mordal et al. 2020). For example, it is assumed that students can follow instructions visually.

People with weak digital skills have a lower degree of employment than those with strong digital skills (Bjønness et al. 2021). But good digital skills are not enough if the systems in the workplace do not have good enough accessibility for the employee. 21% of those outside the Norwegian labor force experience a lack of universal design as an obstacle to becoming better at using digital tools (Bjønness et al. 2021). In one survey, which was conducted among 300 members of the Norwegian Association of Blind and Partially Sighted (NABP), 84% answered that they experienced barriers when using a computer, and 75% answered that they needed help because of this (Halbach et al. 2020).

Important findings with regard to the employer perspective is that the majority have little or no experience with employees with impairments, and that there are attitudinal barriers (Fyhn et al. 2019; Spooner 2017). Studies have shown that job seekers with visual impairments were assessed least positively compared with job seekers with other types of disabilities, minority backgrounds, or various health problems (Chhabra 2020; Fyhn et al. 2019). Another barrier is that technical personnel at the workplace are not sufficiently trained with technical accessibility in mind. Often, this results in a lack of or non-optimum facilitation of the (digital) workplace (Halbach et al. 2020).

The literature regarding society shows that there are potentially huge benefits from the inclusion of a greater share of individuals with impairments in the workforce. Statistics Norway (SSB) estimates that 27% of all unemployed persons with disabilities in Norway wish to join the workforce. Only 43% of Norwegian people with disabilities are employed, compared to 74% in the general population (Bufdir 2015). According to the European Commission's Disability rights strategy (EC 2021) it is essential to implement the UNCRPD principle of mainstreaming the universal design approach for better accessibility and provision of reasonable accommodation for persons with disabilities into the society.

While there are legislation and public support schemes in place to facilitate work life participation for persons with disabilities, the legislation and its enforcement are scattered over multiple laws and public institutions. In many cases this leads to unclear responsibilities, and lack of awareness and knowledge about the rights and possibilities. This calls for a clearer division of responsibilities and perhaps also simplifications.

3 Interviews

The case studies comprise conversations with 11 individuals, hereof five employees with visual impairments, five management staff, and one HR representative. The informants were recruited from professional contacts within the project group. The conversations were conducted as semi-structured in-depth interviews on the phone or as a video meeting. We had prepared two interview guides, one for employees and one for employer representatives, with a series of questions we wanted to get answered, but depending on the dynamic of each conversation we also touched upon related topics. The employees' interviews were carried out prior to the employers' interviews. Speech from the conversations was recorded, transcribed, anonymized and then went through a thematic analysis (Nowell et al. 2017).

The employee population consisted of two females and three males between 30 and 60, all of Norwegian ethnicity. Three employees worked reduced (50–60%) due to various reasons, ranging from "nice with spare time" to following the physician's advice with regard to health, rehabilitation, and physical training. While one employee had highschool as the highest educational degree, the others had up to four years of college or university on their CV. Two of the informants gave their own IT skills a "medium" and three a "strong" rating. The one low-vision individual made use of various magnification technologies, both of technical and non-technical nature. For the four who were entirely blind, the use of screen readers was common, both on PC and phone. Two of the employers can be classified as public and three as private sector, and there was geographical variation in the population.

3.1 Topics

The analysis of transcripts identified the following topics of interest. Where different informants contribute to the themes, this is specified accordingly.

Personality, Skills, and Educational Training. The employees' self-assessment varied somewhat, but they all had in common that they described themself as being proactive, forward-leaning, independent, and self-securing. The population's mainly good technical skills (self-assessed), and the fact that they all rated themselves as experts for their AT, must be seen in the light of these adjectives as a direct effect. This is exemplified by the story of one informant who was supposed to teach a co-worker a tool she did not know herself yet. She thus first taught herself how to handle the tool properly and then showed her co-worker.

The informants were critical in a number of ways regarding educational training on AT and IT systems in general. There were voices that the training is too hard to get, i.e. taking too much time before the first class is held, that classes are not offered frequently enough, and that five-hour sessions implies too much information. In fact, what is often needed is training/help on demand, and this cannot be provided by training courses. Moreover, much of the training comes in a format which is not universally designed, leaving it useless for low-vision recipients.

Jobseeker Experiences. For some of the informants, the Norwegian Labor and Welfare Administration (NAV) partly played a role during job seeking in terms of giving advice and organizing interim positions. However, they all have in common that they eventually landed their first job on their own. In fact, three of the informants had negative experiences with NAV in regard to job seeking. One was advised to seek jobs she was not qualified for, at workplaces with other low-vision employees. Another was told that the best option would be to apply for social-security income, even though this person was newly educated and eager to work. Yet another received the advice to become a painter/decorator, even though that person could not see colors.

Job Interview and Hiring Process. There was great variation in the individual experiences with job interviews and hiring process, ranging from "alright" and "agile" to meeting prejudices. For some, it was beneficial to ask a third party to join the job interview, not only in terms of getting help in an unknown environment, but also because these helpers could inform the employer about appropriate public support schemes.

The picture regarding applying for these schemes is not clear, though. Some employers said "it is OK after you have done it a couple of times", while others stated that the process is cumbersome and time consuming. Several informants and employers mentioned internal mentoring schemes as an upside for both employee and employer in the beginning. And even though some employers expressed to have implemented facilitation of the physical workplace, the tone was that employees with impairments need as much or as little time during startup as compared to others.

Superior, Work Environment, and Co-workers. While one superior had experience with an impaired employee, having someone with no or low vision was new for all of them. As a consequence, the superiors had little knowledge about the employees' technical and non-technical needs. The culprit for this situation are partly the employees themselves, as they in certain situations abstain from communicating some of their needs and problems with the management.

The following list of aspects summarizes the traits of a leader as expected by the employee informants: Taking responsibility, being a problem solver, flexible, and clear, having the ability to see others, having good knowledge about a particular human resource, share relevant information, being open regarding challenges, and being assuring. One informant denoted the superior's knowledge about functional impairment and its effects as a "to be or not to be".

The influence of the work environment and co-workers was also emphasized by the employees. The co-workers' knowledge regarding what it means to have an impairment is according to the informants essential for the coordination of tasks and a general understanding of an employee's abilities and disabilities. When it comes to getting help, though, co-workers are mentioned as being third in line, after help by self-help and help by personal assistant or secretary assistant, but before help by a superior.

Neither HR nor customers were mentioned as important factors in this respect.

Assistive Technology, Facilitation, and Inclusion Strategies. The blind informants employed screen readers on PC and phone. The informant with low vision used magnifier applications, both separate and built-in into the OS. Other AT includes braille reader, letter reader, dictaphone, and color reader. The general preference among informants was to have their own devices for proper installation of applications and the right settings.

Some employers had implemented facilitation of the physical workplace, such as braille labels for signs and tactile guiding elements. In one case, however, a more costly investment, to enhance the poor acoustics of an open-space office was not made. This resulted in trouble for the informant to hear their screen reader. The technical customization was often done by the informants themselves and sometimes by Technical Support. The integration of AT with the existing IT systems, often domain-specific software but also generic office solutions, was often said to be problematic or in the worst case impossible. As one informant put it: "There is always something" (talking about technical problems) and applies not only to the initial installation but also to later upgrades. This is exemplified by the story of one informant who said that, after a technical upgrade, she was unable to do her most important task for nine months. IT Support were not able to fix it, and eventually she was assigned other tasks.

Public Supporting Institutions and Schemes. The informants' opinions about public supporting institutions and schemes is dominated by negative sentiments. More than once we heard about "bureaucratic" and "rigid" institutions and cumbersome application processes. The story of a financial aiding scheme, which first was granted, then withdrawn, then granted again, indicates that a certain amount of randomness is part of the experience. The informants' experiences are, however, not solely black and white. Some commented that their contact person in NAV had been very helpful and proactive, and they were quite satisfied with the help they got.

The interviews revealed a number of various institutions and schemes which are relevant for employers and employees with impairments. As this list is specific to the Norwegian context, it is not repeated here, and the interested reader is referred to the original technical report (Halbach et al. 2022).

It appears that the high number of relevant institutions makes it difficult for people with visual impairments to navigate in the jungle of responsibilities, in particular when it comes to the organization of educational training on AT, complicating information flow and implying many referrals to the right recipient for a request and unnecessary delays. There also is a high number of supporting schemes, and our conversations revealed that some are little known to (and used by) employees and employers alike.

Attitudes and Discrimination. Employees' attitudes are naturally quite varied. When encountering difficulties, some try to hold a low profile: "I think it is embarrassing to be so exposed". Yet others are the opposite and stand up for themselves: "I would not want to work for somebody who does not accept my impairment". This corresponds to the above description of informants as self-confident and forward-leaning individuals. All employers displayed politically correct attitudes and expressed that one has to "see each single human and ask how they could contribute", that it is about seeing "possibilities rather than limitations", and that organizations as part of the society also have an obligation for inclusion. There were, however, subtle statements which revealed different positions. One superior expressed that a lot of facilitation is needed for low vision, and another stated that it is crucial that the employee with an impairment is motivated to do most of the facilitation themselves: "We as an employer do not have the time to deal with all that", referring to technical facilitation, application for public support schemes, and so on. This also signals employers' perception that additional work is expected to be carried out by employees with a disability, possibly at the cost of their productivity.

We also heard a story of discrimination, where one particular employee had experienced to be rejected access to the office due to a co-worker's alleged allergy against fur. However, it is entirely legal for owners of guide dogs in Norway to take them wherever needed.

Covid-19 Pandemic. The effects of the Covid-19 pandemic were mixed. While some did not have any customized equipment at home and therefore got a special permit to attend the office during home office times, others stated that their equipment at home was much better suited to their needs.

Efficiency and Costs. The employers were satisfied or very satisfied with how their employees with low vision solved tasks and stated that their efficiency was satisfactory or highly satisfactory and comparable to their co-workers. As one superior put it: "[The management] is very impressed by the way she works and how efficient she is". Here, one of the employees gave us a possible explanation by mentioning that he often tries to meet higher (perceived) requirements towards himself than the others. He also confirmed that over-performing and stamina are strategies to compensate for an impairment and to prevent discriminating attitudes. Some of the employees admitted that they needed more time for particular tasks, for instance to acquire new knowledge or manage new tools. This was then compensated for by over-performing in other areas. One informant explained her high working efficiency by the fact that she knew the PC keyboard shortcuts so well.

Other Aspects. Multiple informants reported that being unemployed has affected their mental state in a negative way, which once again illustrates the importance of employment. Technological barriers and other challenges, however, apparently lead to a lot of frustration and may thus counteract the positive effects of being employed.

When it comes to what are good technical solutions for communicating and interaction, the picture is not coherent. Solutions which are presented as good by some are pointed out as poor by others. This may indicate that personal liking and preference play major roles besides universal design.

Civil society organizations like the NABP were seldom mentioned in the interviews. One had received help from this organization to set up their equipment at home, and one had enrolled in a class on how to use a particular screen reader. Both narratives show that an NGO can fill the gaps which are left blank by an employer or the authorities.

3.2   Categories

The findings from the aforementioned topics were structured further and generalized in the below four main categories.

Technology:

- The use of technological means, especially AT, is crucial for the participation of individuals with impairments in today's working life.
- The technology partly eases the work day of impaired employees but also introduces a number of challenges, in particular when IT systems, including domain-specific systems, are combined with individual AT. This may be due to the lack of universally designed solutions, insufficient testing with AT, and low-quality AT.

Inclusion strategies and barriers:

- Each individual's personality, technical competency and skills, as well as personal effort, may be a resource to counteract the challenges experienced with technology.
- The low-vision and blind employees in this study get their job description and tasks customized.
- The (Norwegian) public support schemes "Reading and Secretary Assistant" and "Personal Assistant" may compensate for most of the technological difficulties experienced by the informants in this study.
- The majority of IT support staff has insufficient knowledge about the combination of domain-specific systems and AT.
- A great share of educational training is not universally designed, such that it is not beneficial for individuals with impairments.

Employer and work environment:

- Superiors of impaired employees are in a key position with regard to the organization of tasks, facilitation of the workplace, influence on work environment and attitude, and inclusion in general.
- Few superiors and employees in general have sufficient knowledge about the needs of co-workers with low vision.
- Some employees have experienced discriminating practice and attitudes by their employers due to their visual impairment.
- Typically, employers view the physical facilitation of the workplace as manageable and implement the necessary steps, but simultaneously neglect technical measures.

Public support institutions and schemes:

- Some public support schemes in Norway have a good effect but are not well known and/or used.
- There is potential for improvement when it comes to the coordination of schemes among public support institutions in Norway.
- The informants in this study have had poor experiences with low competency and negative and prejudiced attitudes of public institutions with regard to the assessment of their ability to work.

4   Discussion

The experience by one particular informant about the re-assignment of tasks after technical barriers points at three crucial aspects which are paralleled in the other narratives: 1) Many existing IT systems are not universally designed, with the result that they do not work together with AT. 2) Many technical-support departments lack the proper knowledge regarding AT. 3) The assignment of other tasks is an often used strategy when technical problems are encountered and also illustrates the high dependence of low-vision employees on their AT. We need to add, though, that often it is possible to distribute the workload over several employees according to personal abilities, and in many cases both superiors and employees are satisfied with how the task assignment is solved.

Two more aspects can be derived by the story of another informant regarding the role of AT suppliers in Norway. One particular supplier was unable to set up the AT on her system properly and failed to do so several times, with the consequence that she could not do her work for more than half a year. She suggested strengthening the requirement for the suppliers to successfully install the AT by linking that requirement to financial sanctions. Her personal strategy to cope with the situation was to make extensive use of the secretary assistant, which of course is quite costly. The aspects are thus: 4) There are insufficient requirements towards the suppliers of AT for the successful installation of their software. And 5), public supporting schemes can solve and are often used to solve situations with technical shortcomings.

The results from the thematic analysis of interviews confirms many of the findings from the literature review. In addition, some new aspects complete the picture further, including: 1) A high level of technical skills can be the consequence of a high number of technical problems an employee with vision impairment typically has to solve. 2) Many vision-impaired employees are given suboptimal job tasks due to technical problems. 3) Physical facilitation typically receives more attention than technical facilitation. 4) Human assistance and adaptation of tasks as a strategy in case of technical problems may stand in the way for the development of more universally designed solutions.

The findings in the literature overview, together with the interview findings, lead to the following list of recommendations.

- Amending the Norwegian legislation, such that it no longer exempts the labor market from the requirement on universal design of ICT, is likely an important measure to achieve a higher degree of digital inclusion in the working life.
- Informational campaigns among organizations' managements and other employees regarding diversity may be effective in increasing knowledge and improving attitudes towards employees with visual impairments.
- Additionally, informational campaigns on assistive technologies and diversity may be effective. The campaigns should be targeted at work and career consultants, as well as caseworkers at the Norwegian Labor and Welfare Administration.
- The Norwegian Labor and Welfare Administration should consider strengthening some of their support schemes (for instance, "Guidance for Work").
- It should be considered to strengthen the programs for reading / writing assistants and personal assistants as backup in case of technology failure and organize them on an hourly basis.
- Digital accessibility and facilitation should get the same attention as physical facilitation and universal design of buildings and environments by the authorities and public and private organizations.

4.1 Limitations

The validity of this work is limited by the following considerations.

The population cannot be said to be representative for employees with low vision due to the low number of participants (N = 5) and a recruitment based on convenience sampling. Also, the assessment of education and technical skills shows that the employee informants likely are among the more resourceful ones in the workforce. The limited project budget has further resulted in only one researcher carrying out the thematic analysis. The credibility of the analysis would have been enhanced by additional researchers. Finally, it is stressed that verification of the individual narrative has been outside the scope of this work. As the employees' interviews were prior to the employers' interviews, it has however been possible to verify some of the employee claims by comparing them with what had been said by the employer.

5 Conclusion

In this work, we have studied various aspects related to the role of technology in the working life for employees with visual impairments. Our study shows that this is an interdisciplinary and complex area.

We first surveyed relevant literature on the Norwegian labor market. Although there is a lack of peer-reviewed literature, we found many reports and studies that document profound barriers related to ICT systems used in working life for people with visual impairments. This includes lack of universal design, compatibility with assistive technology, as well as ICT-related training and technical support. Nevertheless, there is little research on the effects of universal design of ICT and other ICT-related measures on the inclusion of people with disabilities in the labor market.

We then conducted a series of in-depth interviews with both employees and employers. We have not found any area of conflicting results, meaning that our findings underline the results from previous research. However, our conversations also revealed a few new insights.

The main message is that a labor market with equal opportunities for all will not be accomplished by tomorrow. Nevertheless, we believe to have increased our understanding of all relevant areas, and we have identified a number of aspects that can be improved. Our recommendations target both developers and suppliers of ICT systems, employers, administrative authorities, as well as law makers. A thorough analysis of the effects of each countermeasure has, however, been outside the scope of this work and remains for future research.

Even though all measures will contribute in some way, we are convinced that amending the Norwegian legislation, such that it no longer exempts the labor market from the requirement on universal design of ICT, may be the most important measure to achieve a higher degree of digital inclusion in the working life for persons with visual impairments. Work participation depends to a large degree on the accessibility of the ICT solutions for employees with visual impairment. As of today, many ICT solutions are not universally designed, resulting in inclusion barriers. This conclusion is likely applicable to other forms of impairment and other countries as well.

We round off by citing one particular informant who formulated: "Incredible what one can accomplish with just a little facilitation"!

Funding and Acknowledgments. This work received funding from the Norwegian Directorate for Children, Youth and Family Affairs. The project was a collaboration between two research institutes and Norwegian Association of Blind and Partially Sighted (NABP). The authors wish to thank all informants for sharing invaluable insight in their working life.

References

Bjønness, A.M., Midtbø, T., Størset, H., Ulven, C.H.: Befolkningens digitale kompetanse og deltakelse: Med et ekstra blikk på seniorer og ikke-sysselsatte. Kompetanse Norge (2021). https://www.kompetansenorge.no/statistikk-og-analyse/publikasjoner/befolkningens-digitale-kompetanse-og-deltakelse/
Bufdir. Arbeid og aktivitet. Barne-, Ungdoms- Og Familiedirektoratet. Statistikk Og Analyse. Levekårsstatus for Personer Med Nedsatt Funksjonsevne. Arbeid Og Aktivitet (2015). http://www.bufdir.no/Statistikk_og_analyse/Nedsatt_funksjonsevne/Arbeid/
Bufdir. Universell utforming - tilstandsanalyse og kunnskapsstatus. Barne-, ungdoms- og familiedirektoratet (Bufdir) (2020). https://bufdir.no/Bibliotek/Bufdirs_publikasjoner/Dokumentside/?docId=BUF00005140

Chhabra, G.: Turning a blind eye to employers' discrimination? Attitudinal barrier perceptions of vision impaired youth from Oslo and Delhi. Disabil. Soc. 1–24 (2020)

Chhabra, G.: Social resilience in the labour market: learning from young adults with visual impairments in Oslo and Delhi. Young Child. **29**(5), 508–528 (2021)

EC. Union of Equality: Strategy for the Rights of Persons with Disabilities 2021–2030 (COM(2021) 101 final) (2021). European Commision

European Telecommunications Standards Institute (ETSI). EN 301 549 v3.2.1 (2021–03): Accessibility requirements for ICT products and services (2021). https://www.etsi.org/deliver/etsi_en/301500_301599/301549v/03.02.01_60/en_301549v030201p.pdf

Fuglerud, K.S., Fyhn, T., Halbach, T., Kjæret, K., Olsen, T.A.: Teknologi og inkludering av personer med nedsatt syn i arbeidslivet: Kunnskapsoppsummering. Norsk Regnesentral (2021)

Fuglerud, K.S., Halbach, T., Skotkjerra, S.E.: Challenges with assistive technology compatibility in universal design. Assist. Technol. Res. Ser. **35**, 55–59 (2014)

Fuglerud, K.S., Halbach, T., Tjøstheim, I.: Cost-benefit analysis of universal design (p. 37). Norsk Regnesentral (2015). http://publications.nr.no/1422438427/Cost-benefit-anayses-universal-design-fuglerud.pdf

Fuglerud, K.S., Kjæret, K., Tunold, S.: iStøtet – IT-støtte for synshemmede eldre: Inkludering i informasjonssamfunnet – motivasjon, opplæring og oppfølging (No. 1048). Norsk Regnesentral og Norges Blindeforbund (2020). https://www.nr.no/directdownload/1585640846/Fuglerud-et-al_2020_iStoetet-prosjektrapport.pdf

Fuglerud, K.S., Solheim, I.: Synshemmedes IKT - barrierer: Resultater fra undersøkelse om IKT-bruk blant synshemmede (No. 1016). Norsk Regnesentral (2008)

Fuglerud, K.S., Tonje, F., Halbach, T., Kjæret, K., Olsen, T.A.: Teknologi og inkludering av personer med nedsatt syn i arbeidslivet: Kunnskapsoppsummering (No. 1054). Norsk Regnesentral (2021)

Fuglerud, K.S., Tunold, S., Kjæret, K.: Social contact for older people with visual impairment through mastery of smartphones: barriers and suggested solutions. In: Verma, I., (Ed.), Universal Design 2021: From Special to Mainstream Solutions, vol. 282, pp. 415–428. IOS Press (2021)

Fyhn, T., Johnsen, T.L., Øyeflaten, I., Jordbru, A., Tveito, T.H.: Resultatrapport for kompetanseprosjektet Mangfold på arbeidsplassen. Norce (2019). https://norceresearch.brage.unit.no/norceresearch-xmlui/bitstream/handle/11250/2624405/Resultatrapport%20Mangfold%20p%C3%A5%20arbeidsplassen.pdf?sequence=1&isAllowed=y

Gulliksen, J., Johansson, S., Larsdotter, M.: Ny teknik och digitala lösningar för ökad inkludering i arbetslivet. Nordens välfärdscenter (2021). https://nordicwelfare.org/publikationer/ny-teknik-och-digitala-losningar-for-okad-inkludering-i-arbetslivet/

Halbach, T., Fuglerud, K.S.: On assessing the costs and benefits of universal design of ICT. Stud. Health Technol. Inform. **229**, 662–672 (2016)

Halbach, T., Fuglerud, K.S.: Reflections on cost-benefit analyses concerning universal design of ICT solutions. In: Blashki, K., Xiao, Y., (Eds.), Proceedings of 10th International Conference on Interfaces and Human Computer Interaction. IADIS (2016b). http://ihci-conf.org/

Halbach, T., Fuglerud, K.S., Kjæret, K., Fyhn, T., Olsen, T.A.: Kanskje du kunne bli maler? - Fem personer med nedsatt syn forteller om sine erfaringer som arbeidssøkere og arbeidstakere (No. DART/01/22). Norsk Regnesentral (2022)

Halbach, T., Tunold, S.: Ambivalens av IKT i synshemmedes arbeidsliv (2020)

Halbach, T., Tunold, S., Tjøstheim, I.: Teknologiens ambivalens for arbeidstakere med nedsatt syn (No. 1049). Norsk Regnesentral (2020)

Kulturdepartementet. Lov om likestilling og forbud mot diskriminering (likestillings- og diskrimineringsloven, LOV-2017–06–16–51) June 2017. https://lovdata.no/dokument/NL/lov/2017-06-16-51

478   T. Halbach et al.

LDO. CRPD 2015r Ombudets rapport til FNs komité for rettighetene til mennesker med nedsatt funksjonsevne - et supplement til Norges første periodiske rapport. Likestillings- og diskrimineringsombudet (2015r). https://www.ldo.no/globalassets/_ldo_2019/03_ombudet-og-sam funnet/konvensjoner/fns-konvensjon-for-personer-med-nedsatt-funksjonsevne/crpd2015rapp ort.pdf

Miljøverndepartementet. T-1468 B/E Universell utforming. In: Regjeringen. no. regjeringen.no. (2007) https://www.regjeringen.no/no/dokumenter/t-1468-universell-utforming/id493083/

Mordal, S., Buland, T., Wendelborg, M.T., Wik, S.E., Tøssebro, J.: Betydningen av hjelpemidler og tilrettelegging for funksjonshemmede barn og unges mestring og deltakelse i skolen (No. 2020:00647). Sintef Digital og NTNU (2020). https://www.nav.no/no/nav-og-samfunn/kun nskap/forskningsrapporter-og-evalueringer-finansiert-av-nav/rapporter-navs-tiltak-og-virkem idler/betydningen-av-hjelpemidler-og-tilrettelegging-for-funksjonshemmede-barn-og-unges-mestring-og-deltakelse-i-skolen

Nowell, L.S., Norris, J.M., White, D.E., Moules, N.J.: Thematic analysis: striving to meet the trustworthiness criteria. Int. J. Qual. Meth. **16**(1), 1609406917733847 (2017)

Proba. Kunnskapssammenstilling og evaluering av regjeringens handlingsplaner for universell utforming (No. 16). Proba samfunnsanalyse (2019). https://bufdir.no/globalassets/global/nbbf/ universell_utforming/kunnskapssammenstilling_og_evaluering_av_regjeringens_handlings planer_for_universell_utforming.pdf

Proba. Erfaringer med bruk av IKT-løsninger blant personer med funksjonsnedsettelser (No. 4). Proba samfunnsanalyse (2020). https://proba.no/wp-content/uploads/Rapport-2020-4-Erf aringer-med-IKT-l%C3%B8sninger-blant-personer-med-nedsatt-funksjonsevne.pdf

Spooner, C.: Visual impairment and work: experiences of visually impaired people. Disabil. Soc. **33**(3), 499–501 (2017). Routledge. https://doi.org/10.1080/09687599.2017.1414346

Statistisk sentralbyrå. 09338: Sysselsatte i alt 15–66 år og sysselsatte med nedsatt funksjonsevne (prosent), etter kjønn, alder, statistikkvariabel og kvartal. Statistikkbanken. SSB 3 September 2020. https://www.ssb.no/statbank/table/09338/tableViewLayout1/

United Nations (UN). Convention on the Rights of Persons with Disabilities (CRPD) (2006). https://www.un.org/development/desa/disabilities/convention-on-the-rights-of-persons-with-disabilities.html

Walday, M., Solhaug, T.H., Laurin, S.: Digitale hindre for økt sysselsetting (p. 109). Funka og Implement Group (2016).

LiDAR-Based Obstacle Detection and Distance Estimation in Navigation Assistance for Visually Impaired

Bineeth Kuriakose$^{(\boxtimes)}$ ⓘ, Raju Shrestha ⓘ, and Frode Eika Sandnes ⓘ

Department of Computer Science, Oslo Metropolitan University, Oslo, Norway
bineethk@oslomet.no

Abstract. People with visual impairments can face challenges with independent navigation and therefore may use traditional aids such as guide dogs, white canes, or a travel companion for navigation assistance. In recent years, researchers have been working on AI-based navigation assistance systems. Obstacle detection and distance estimation are two of the key challenges in such systems. In this paper, we describe a LiDAR-based obstacle detection and distance estimation technique. A lightweight deep learning-based model called EfficientDet-LiteV4 is used for obstacle detection, and a depth map from the LiDAR is used to estimate the distance to the obstacles. We have implemented and tested the approach with the LiDAR integrated into a Raspberry Pi4 board. The results show good accuracy in detecting the obstacles and in estimating distance.

Keywords: Navigation · Visually impaired · LiDAR · Deep learning · Assistive technology · Obstacle detection · Distance estimation

1 Introduction

Navigation or wayfinding for people with visual impairments is a prevailing challenge in the scientific community. Independent navigation could increase the level of independence [1]. However, travelling alone in unfamiliar environments can be challenging.

People with visual impairments typically use aids such as guide dogs, white canes, or depend on a travel companion. In addition to those conventional aids, diverse assistance systems and solutions have been proposed in the literature to address issues involved in the navigation of people with visual impairments [2]. Some of the main problems related to such systems are linked to portability and providing real-time environmental information in the immediate vicinity during navigation to avoid obstacles and prevent accidents [3].

In recent years, researchers have been actively exploiting artificial intelligence and machine learning to develop universally accessible navigation solutions [4]. In addition, different technologies and hardware are explored in the development

© The Author(s), under exclusive license to Springer Nature Switzerland AG 2022
M. Antona and C. Stephanidis (Eds.): HCII 2022, LNCS 13309, pp. 479–491, 2022.
https://doi.org/10.1007/978-3-031-05039-8_35

of navigation assistance systems. It might be inspired by the miniaturization of electronics and the advancement in processing power and sensing capabilities of various devices [1]. Among those, one prominent technology is LiDAR (Light Detection and Ranging) cameras.

LiDAR is a remote sensing technology that uses one or multiple laser beams to estimate distance measurements. LiDAR system sends a pulse of light and estimate distance based on the time it takes for the emitted pulse to return back. Some advantages of LiDAR sensors include high resolution and accuracy in measurements, easy conversion to 3D maps to interpret the environment, performance in low light conditions, and speed as it offers indirect distance measurements that do not need to be decoded or interpreted[1]. Because of these reasons, LiDAR technology has become a useful device for obstacle detection, avoidance, and safe navigation through various environments. LiDAR is commonly used in robotics and autonomous vehicles [5,6].

In this paper, we propose using a miniature LiDAR that can acquire visual image and depth information for accurate obstacle detection and distance estimation in a navigation assistance system for the visually impaired. A lightweight deep learning-based model called EfficientDet-LiteV4 is used for obstacle detection, and a depth map from the LiDAR is used to estimate the distance to the obstacles. We have assessed the performance and compared the results with our previous works, which use smartphone-based object detection and distance estimation methods for navigation assistance.

This paper is organized as follows. Section 2 discusses related works, and Sect. 3 describes our proposed LiDAR-based obstacle detection and depth estimation methods and their implementation. Section 4 describes the experiment involved. Results and discussions are presented in Sect. 5. The paper concludes in Sect. 6.

2   Related Works

Obstacle avoidance is vital during navigation for visually impaired users. Obstacle or object detection involves identifying and locating obstacles in the environment, enabling a safe navigation. This section discusses related literature and notable developments in three areas: obstacle detection, distance estimation, and some literature reported on miniature hardware-based navigation systems and RGBD-based obstacle detection systems.

2.1   Obstacle Detection

Typically, there are two machine learning-based approaches used for obstacle detection in a navigation assistance system. In traditional machine learning (ML) based methods, computer vision techniques are used to look at various features of visual input data (typically image or video), such as the color histogram or edges,

---

[1] www.leddartech.com/why-lidar/.

to detect and identify objects. On the other hand, modern deep learning-based methods employ convolutional neural networks (CNNs) to perform end-to-end object detection, in which features do not need to be defined explicitly but rather extracted automatically [7]. Because of this and the availability of ever-increasing computational capabilities required by deep learning models, researchers most recently tend to use deep learning models over traditional ML models.

A deep learning-based object detection model typically has three major components: a *backbone network* that extracts features from a given image; a *feature network* that has the backbone as the input and a list of fused features that denotes salient characteristics of the image as the output; and the *final class/box network* that uses the fused features to predict the object class and location of each object in the image.

Most of the popular object detection models belong to the Region-Based Convolutional Neural Network (R-CNN) family. This includes the models R-CNN, Fast R-CNN, Faster-RCNN, Mask R-CNN, etc. Over the years, they have become both more accurate and more computationally efficient [8]. One of the limitations of such models is their larger size and need of high computational power which limit their use in edge devices. Hence models belonging to the single-shot family are being started to be explored by researchers. Examples includes MobileNet+SSD [9], You Only Look Once (YOLO) [10] in several variants, SqueezeDet [11], etc. SSDs make great choices for models destined for mobile or embedded devices [4,12]. In this work, we use a relatively new, lightweight, and efficient object detection model, called EfficientDet-LiteV4 model [13]. Section 3.1 describes the model in more details.

2.2   Distance Estimation

In earlier times, most navigation assistance prototypes that provide distance information used ultrasonic sensors such as SR04 [1]. Ultrasonic sensors measure the distance of a target object by emitting ultrasonic sound waves and converting the reflected sound into an electrical signal. Typical disadvantages of conventional ultrasonic sensors include limited range, inaccurate readings, and inflexible scanning methods [14]. RGB-D cameras have started to be used in navigation systems to acquire depth information along with the color image. Major limitation in the RGBD depth-sensing technology is that it fails to capture depth information in four critical contexts: (1) distant surfaces (>5 m), (2) dark surfaces, (3) brightly lighted indoor scenes, and (4) outdoor scenes with sunlight [15]. Furthermore, another limitation of currently existing RGB-D cameras is their size factor, which is comparatively more extensive, making it inconvenient to use in a portable navigation system. Still, researchers explored the option of RGB-D cameras for depth estimation in their navigation assistant prototypes [16,17]. Various smartphone-based distance estimation methods applied in navigation systems for visual impairments can be found in the literature [18]. In this work, we use an RGB-D camera that utilizes LiDAR technology to estimate the distance to the obstacles.

2.3   Miniature Hardware-Based Navigation Systems

There are several navigation assistance systems reported in the literature which use various modes to process information about the obstacles, their type and/or distance. These systems use hardware such as Raspberry Pi, Arduino, Jetson, smartphones, or even a laptop connected with necessary components such as a camera for data processing and computation.

Rahman and Sadi [19] proposed a Single Shot Detector (SSD) model with MobileNet to recognize indoor and outdoor objects. The system consisted of a laser sensor that helps the user to identify directions. The system sends information collected to a remote server for processing. However, the authors did not explicitly mention the usage of such an arrangement and how they deal with privacy issues since the data might contain private and personal information such as images of people. Moreover, the model used for the obstacle detection was comparatively heavy-weighted, which could take a long execution time. Hence, it would not work as a practical solution in a real-time navigation environment. In a similar attempt, Joshi et al. [20] explored a Jetson nano-based system using MobileNet-SSD. The system provides only an overview of identified obstacles to the user without providing other relevant details such as distance to obstacles that are helpful during navigation.

Afif et al. [21] used the RetinaNet model for object detection in their proposed navigation system. Even though the model is claimed to provide high accuracy, the experimental evaluation showed high inference time, rendering it unsuitable for real-time operation. In another work [22], the authors used camera and time-of-flight sensors as its primary system components. The system's accuracy was low, and it was not intended for outdoors.

The system reported in [23] consisted of an ATmega328 microcontroller embedded with an Arduino Uno. An HC-SR04 ultrasonic sensor was used to identify obstacles. The primary limitations associated with the system were its inability to recognize types of obstacles and the use of ultrasonic sensors, which were not accurate compared to other modern distance estimation sensors.

Anandan et al. [24] described an outdoor and indoor navigation system for the visually impaired using Raspberry Pi. The system used SURF (Speeded Up Robust Features) algorithm for obstacle identification and ultrasonic sensors for distance estimation. The main limitation of the system was in the accuracy in detecting the obstacles.

2.4   RGBD-Based Obstacle Detection Systems

Researchers also explored the potential of RGB-D-based cameras in navigation assistant systems for people with visual impairments. The Navigation assistance for visually impaired (NAVI) system proposed by Aladren et al. [16] used a consumer RGB-D camera to acquire both depth and visual information. The system uses RGB-D system to fuse range information and color information to detect obstacle-free paths. But it does not give much information such as the type of obstacle.

The authors in [25] put forwarded an indoor navigation system that uses a wearable RGBD camera mounted on head to construct a 2D map for the surrounding environment. An optimal path is generated fro the 2D map. The system also used an ultrasonic sensor to detect obstacles along the path. A Raspberry Pi 3 B+ board was used as the central processing unit. Even though the work mentioned path planning in detail, it did not explain how the RGB images captured from the camera were used for obstacle identification.

Lee and Medioni [17] also investigated the potential of an RGB-D camera in a navigation system. The RGB-D camera was placed in the user's eye position to capture scenes. A laptop was used for data processing. The major limitation of the system is the portability and inconvenience associated with the system due to the carriage weight of all the hardware [1]. The system creates indoor maps which guide the users to navigate. Like in [16], the system was also incapable of giving information about obstacles such as its type.

3   LiDAR-Based Obstacle Detection and Distance Estimation

With the development of technologies, more and more miniature LiDAR cameras that can acquire both high-resolution color image and depth information simultaneously are available in the market. In this work, we use such a high-resolution miniature Intel RealSense LiDAR Camera L515[2] (see Fig. 1) for accurate obstacle detection and distance estimation. The camera can detect obstacles up to 9 m and weighs only 100 g. The low weight and small form factor make it suitable for specific applications such as navigation.

The Intel RealSense SDK 2.0[3] and other tools such as Intel RealSense API enable configuration, control, and access to the streaming data. It's extensive language support including Python makes it easy to implement the proposed solution.

The RGB image acquired with the LiDAR camera is sent to an object detection model to detect objects there in and their bounding boxes. The model and the methods we used for obstacle detection and distance estimation is described in the following subsections. After that, the preceding subsection describes the implementation done for testing and evaluation of the proposed methods.

3.1   Obstacle Detection

Our previous works explored the pre-trained MobileNet+SSD [12] and YOLOv5m [4] as obstacle detectors. Even though these models provided reasonably good accuracy, we look for a better alternative as new models are introduced to the scientific community to achieve more accurate detection results at the same time with minimum inference time.

---

[2] www.intelrealsense.com/lidar-camera-l515/.

[3] www.intelrealsense.com/sdk-2/.

In this work, we used an EfficientDet object detection model [13], which proved to be efficient and it can produce a reasonably good accuracy for detecting objects from an image/video. EfficientDet uses EfficientNet [26] as its backbone network for improved efficiency. EfficientNet is based on a CNN architecture and scaling method that uniformly scales all depth/width/resolution dimensions using a compound coefficient. Combining the new backbone and BiFPN (Bidirectional feature pyramid network), the small-sized EfficientDet-D0 base-line was developed, and then a compound scaling was applied to obtain EfficientDet-D1 to D7. Each consecutive model has a higher compute cost but provides higher accuracy.

EfficientDet-Lite is a derivative of EfficientDet trained on the MS COCO dataset [27], optimized for TensorFlow Lite and designed for mobile CPU, GPU, and EdgeTPU. The accuracy of *lite* models is comparatively less than conventional object detection models, which require high-end GPUs and processors. However, as a tradeoff, the computation time of conventional models is significantly higher than *lite* models. Moreover, while designing a real-time navigation solution, factors such as low inference time, small model size to deploy in a portable device, comparatively good accuracy should be considered [28]. Considering these, we have used the most recent version of the EfficientDet-Lite model, EfficientDet-LiteV4, to transfer learn and train with our custom dataset. The reason for choosing this version is the model's accuracy and size compared to other lightweight object detection models without compromising inference time[4].

Dataset: We have created a custom dataset for testing and evaluating the proposed obstacle detection model. The dataset consists of 15 object classes relevant to indoor and outdoor navigation scenarios, namely, *bed, bench, billboard, cabinetry, chair, door, fire hydrant, kitchen appliance, person, stairs, table, traffic light, tree, vehicle,* and *waste container.* Each of these classes has around 5000 images. The images were collected from various sources, which are publicly available such as Google Open Images [29], ImageNet [30], and images acquired by ourselves. After examining the extracted images, we found that many images require some preprocessing, such as labeling. Those images were labeled using the LabelImg[5] annotation tool. We used the PASCAL VOC data format to save the annotations from the images.

3.2   Distance Estimation

The bounding boxes of the objects on an RGB image detected by the object detection model are projected onto its corresponding depth image acquired by the LiDAR camera. The estimated distance of an obstacle from the camera/user is then calculated by median averaging the depth data within its bounding box.

---

[4] www.github.com/google/automl/tree/master/efficientdet.
[5] www.github.com/tzutalin/labelImg.

3.3   Implementation

TensorFlow Lite Model Maker[6] library was used to train the proposed object detection model using the custom dataset. The Model Maker uses transfer learning to reduce the amount of training data required and shorten the training time.

A Raspberry Pi4 board is used for implementing and testing the proposed methods. Intel RealSense LiDAR Camera is connected to the Raspberry Pi4, and power is supplied from a portable power bank, as shown in Fig. 1. Since a Raspberry Pi4 board is smaller and easier to carry than a heavier hardware device such as a laptop, we considered it a portable and practicable solution for navigation assistance. Only essential components such as the LiDAR camera, which is essentially needed for our application, are included in the experiments.

Fig. 1. A photo illustrating intel realsense LiDAR L515 depth camera connected to a Raspberry Pi4 board along with a portable power bank.

4   Experiments

This section elucidates how the experiments were conducted for obstacle detection and distance estimation.

4.1   Obstacle Detection

The object detection model was trained on an HP G4 Workstation with an Intel Xeon processor with 32 GB RAM and NVIDIA GeForce GTX 1070 GPU. The platform settings of the experiment are TensorFlow-GPU 2.4, NVIDIA CUDA toolkit 11.0, and CUDNN 8.1. The model was trained, validated, and tested by randomly shuffling and splitting the dataset in the ratio of 80:10:10, respectively.

---

[6] www.tensorflow.org/lite/guide/model_maker.

486   B. Kuriakose et al.

The default epochs in the Model Maker library[6] were 50. However, we run 100 epochs. The number was found to achieve better accuracy as determined through hyperparameter optimization using the validation dataset. The default batch size 64 was used. The training model was exported to *tflite* format. The Model Maker library applies a default post-training quantization technique when exporting the model to *tflite* format. This technique can help reduce the model size and inference latency while improving the CPU and hardware accelerator inference speed[7].

4.2 Distance Estimation

To evaluate the performance of the distance estimation, we tested distance measurements on five different types of obstacles, *billboard, chair, waste container, door,* and *table.* The obstacles were placed at different distances, and the actual distance of an obstacle from the camera/user was measured using a measuring tape. The measurement was done to the nearest edge point of the objects. The obstacles with varied sizes were chosen intentionally to check whether the size of the obstacles affects distance estimation. The *waste container* obstacle we considered in this experiment was smaller. We also tried to check if the sunlight affects the distance estimation by placing a *chair* outdoor under direct sunlight.

5 Results and Discussions

Figure 2 illustrated object detection and depth estimation results where RGB images and depth map images are given with the bounding boxes around the detected objects are marked. The elaborated results from obstacle detection and distance estimation methods are given and discussed in the following subsections.

5.1 Obstacle Detection

Table 1 shows the results from the object detection model in terms of prediction accuracy of the 15 object classes in the custom dataset. The prediction results were reasonably good, with an average accuracy of around 88%. The results show that *cabinetry* and *stairs* are the only two object classes where accuracy is below 80%. The quality of images and annotations could be reasons for the low accuracy in those two classes. We observed that in some cases, the model failed to detect objects correctly because of similarities in some object classes. For example, there were false detections between white *doors*, walls, and long *billboard.* This was probably because of the pattern similarity in those objects.

Even though the class categories in the dataset for obstacle detection are limited (15), we tried to include object classes relevant to the navigation scenario. Since this is a proof-of-concept, it is possible to extend this with more classes

---

[7] www.tensorflow.org/lite/performance/post_training_quantization.

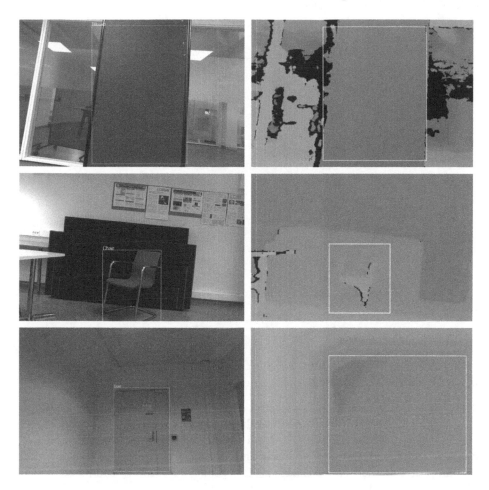

Fig. 2. (a) (Left column) Three different obstacles/objects (*billboard, chair,* and *door*) on the RGB images as detected and marked with bounding boxes by the object detection model. (b) (Right column) Depth map images with the marked bounding boxes around the obstacles after mapping with corresponding RGB images.

in the future. The average accuracy of around 88% is not the best compared to other heavy-weight object detection models, and it is anticipated from the lightweight model used. Nevertheless, considering the various aspects required for a real-time navigation application (see Sect. 3.1), the proposed obstacle detection model's performance could be considered reasonably good, as low computation time enables real-time environmental information without much delay than conventional models. The results from the model also show it has fewer parameters (29 M) and model size (49 MB), which makes it possible to deploy in a less-powerful portable device such as Raspberry Pi.

Table 1. Performance of the proposed obstacle/object detection model in terms of percentage accuracy.

Obstacle	Accuracy(%)
Bed	95.4
Bench	93.7
Billboard	84.6
Cabinetry	78.4
Chair	94.7
Door	83.2
Fire hydrant	88.9
Kitchen appliance	92.7
Person	84.7
Stairs	79.5
Table	90.9
Traffic light	83.7
Tree	81.5
Vehicle	94.1
Waste container	94.6
Average	87.6

5.2 Distance Estimation

Table 2 shows the actual and estimated distance of the four obstacles from our experiment from the proposed method. It also provides estimated distance from the best method, the *Rule of 57*, from among the various smartphone-based distance estimation methods from our previous work [18]. The results show that the proposed method can estimate distance more accurately compared to the *Rule of 57* method.

Another advantage of using LiDAR cameras for distance estimation compared to smartphones is that LiDARs can detect obstacles at longer distances (900 cm in the case of the LiDAR camera used in this work). The smartphone-

Table 2. Observations of distance estimation from various obstacles (all in centimeters).

Obstacle	Actual distance	Estimated distance (Proposed method)	Estimated distance *(Rule of 57* [17])
Billboard	100	100.0	74.8
Chair	200	200.0	209.6
Waste Container	300	299.5	312.4
Door	500	500.1	485.0
Table	900	898.9	Unable to estimate

based method had a distance limit of 500 cm. Moreover, the results were not consistent at a 500 cm distance. Therefore, the estimated distance in the case of *door* at 500 cm from the smartphone-based method was recorded by averaging five readings due to its fluctuating nature. Smartphone-based also failed to report any result when the obstacle was placed at less than 100 cm. One disadvantage with the LiDAR camera-based method is that it needs to be connected to a computer (e.g., Raspberry Pi). This could raise portability concerns and cause inconvenience to the user. On the other hand, the portability factor is positive for the smartphone-based method. Therefore, one could note this tradeoff while designing a navigation assistant system while making a design choice.

When the smallest obstacle from the test set, the *waste container*, was placed at 50 cm, the smartphone-based method could not detect any result. However, the proposed solution using LiDAR gave the result as 49.5 cm. When we experimented with the *chair* obstacle placed outdoor under the sunlight, the obstacle detection model was able to detect the obstacle as a *chair*. However, the distance estimation method failed to estimate the distance well. It estimated a distance of 281.7 cm against the actual distance of 300 cm. Surprisingly, the smartphone-based method also showed similar results, with an estimated distance of 280.4 cm. The performance degradation with the LiDAR method could be because of interference to its depth estimation system from the infrared light from the sun. This issue is cross-checked with the manufacturer's website and found that this LiDAR camera is recommended for indoor environments[2]. However, in other applications such as autonomous vehicles, LiDARs are used together with other devices such as laser reflectors, radars, and stereo cameras to address the influence of sunlight[8]. 3D LiDARs, which are very expensive compared to 2D LIDARs, can also solve the issue to a certain extent[8]. Nevertheless, in application scenarios such as navigation assistance, where portability is also a significant concern, installing additional reflectors or devices only to use outdoors may not be a preferred design choice.

6   Conclusion

The proposed LiDAR-based method, which used an EfficientDet-LiteV4 model, shows reasonably good performance in terms of obstacle detection and distance estimation indicating its potential to be used in a navigation assistance system for individuals with visual impairments. Using a LiDAR camera connected with a Raspberry Pi and a power bank asks for proper camera placement and needs for carrying the hardware, which might raise portability concerns. And the performance degradation of the LiDAR cameras when it is used under bright sunlight could limit their use in outdoor navigation. We believe this research could bring valuable insights to the use of LiDARs in portable navigation assistance solutions for the visually impaired.

---

[8] www.sevensense.ai/blog/localization.

References

1. Kuriakose, B., Shrestha, R., Sandnes, F.E.: Tools and technologies for blind and visually impaired navigation support: a review. IETE Tech. Rev. 1–16 (2020)
2. SSMR, U.o.S.: Understanding the Needs of Blind and Partially Sighted People: their experiences, perspectives, and expectations (May 2009). https://www.rnib.org.uk/knowledge-and-research-hub/research-reports/general-research/understanding-needs
3. Kuriakose, B., Shrestha, R., Sandnes, F.E.: Multimodal navigation systems for users with visual impairments-a review and analysis. Multimodal Technol. Interact. **4**(4), 73 (2020)
4. Kuriakose, B., Shrestha, R., Eika Sandnes, F.: Towards independent navigation with visual impairment: a prototype of a deep learning and smartphone-based assistant. In: The 14th PErvasive Technologies Related to Assistive Environments Conference, pp. 113–114 (2021)
5. Han, J., Kim, D., Lee, M., Sunwoo, M.: Enhanced road boundary and obstacle detection using a downward-looking LIDAR sensor. IEEE Trans. Veh. Technol. **61**(3), 971–985 (2012)
6. Peng, Y., Qu, D., Zhong, Y., Xie, S., Luo, J., Gu, J.: The obstacle detection and obstacle avoidance algorithm based on 2-D Lidar. In: 2015 IEEE International Conference on Information and Automation, pp. 1648–1653. IEEE (2015)
7. Zou, Z., Shi, Z., Guo, Y., Ye, J.: Object Detection in 20 years: A Survey. arXiv preprint arXiv:1905.05055 (2019)
8. Zhao, Z.Q., Zheng, P., Xu, S.t., Wu, X.: Object detection with deep learning: a review. IEEE Trans. Neural Netw. Learn. Syst. **30**(11), 3212–3232 (2019)
9. Liu, W., et al.: SSD: single shot multibox detector. In: Leibe, B., Matas, J., Sebe, N., Welling, M. (eds.) ECCV 2016. LNCS, vol. 9905, pp. 21–37. Springer, Cham (2016). https://doi.org/10.1007/978-3-319-46448-0_2
10. Redmon, J., Divvala, S., Girshick, R., Farhadi, A.: You only look once: unified, real-time object detection. In: Proceedings of the IEEE Conference on Computer Vision and Pattern Recognition, pp. 779–788 (2016)
11. Wu, B., Iandola, F., Jin, P.H., Keutzer, K.: Squeezedet: unified, small, low power fully convolutional neural networks for real-time object detection for autonomous driving. In: Proceedings of the IEEE Conference on Computer Vision and Pattern Recognition Workshops, pp. 129–137 (2017)
12. Kuriakose, B., Shrestha, R., Sandnes, F.E.: Smartphone navigation support for blind and visually impaired people - a comprehensive analysis of potentials and opportunities. In: Antona, M., Stephanidis, C. (eds.) HCII 2020. LNCS, vol. 12189, pp. 568–583. Springer, Cham (2020). https://doi.org/10.1007/978-3-030-49108-6_41
13. Tan, M., Pang, R., Le, Q.V.: EfficientDet: scalable and efficient object detection. In: Proceedings of the IEEE/CVF Conference on Computer Vision and Pattern Recognition, pp. 10781–10790 (2020)
14. Borenstein, J., Koren, Y.: Obstacle avoidance with ultrasonic sensors. IEEE J. Robot. Autom. **4**(2), 213–218 (1988)
15. Litomisky, K.: Consumer RGB-D Cameras and their Applications. Rapport Technique, University of California, vol. 20, p. 28 (2012)
16. Aladren, A., López-Nicolás, G., Puig, L., Guerrero, J.J.: Navigation assistance for the visually impaired using RGB-D sensor with range expansion. IEEE Syst. J. **10**(3), 922–932 (2014)

17. Lee, Y.H., Medioni, G.: RGB-D camera based wearable navigation system for the visually impaired. Comput. Vis. Image Understand. **149**, 3–20 (2016)

18. Kuriakose, B., Shrestha, R., Sandnes, F.E.: Distance estimation methods for smartphone-based navigation support systems. In: Arai, K. (ed.) IntelliSys 2021. LNNS, vol. 295, pp. 658–673. Springer, Cham (2022). https://doi.org/10.1007/978-3-030-82196-8_49

19. Rahman, M.A., Sadi, M.S.: IoT enabled automated object recognition for the visually impaired. Comput. Meth. Programs Biomed. Update **1**, 100015 (2021)

20. Joshi, R., Tripathi, M., Kumar, A., Gaur, M.S.: Object recognition and classification system for visually impaired. In: 2020 International Conference on Communication and Signal Processing (ICCSP), pp. 1568–1572. IEEE (2020)

21. Afif, M., Ayachi, R., Said, Y., Pissaloux, E., Atri, M.: An evaluation of RetinaNet on indoor object detection for blind and visually impaired persons assistance navigation. Neural Process. Lett. **51**(3), 2265–2279 (2020)

22. Noman, M., Stankovic, V., Tawfik, A.: Portable offline indoor object recognition system for the visually impaired. Cogent Eng. **7**(1), 1823158 (2020)

23. Ramadhan, A.J.: Wearable smart system for visually impaired people. Sensors **18**(3), 843 (2018)

24. Anandan, M., Manikandan, M., Karthick, T.: Advanced indoor and outdoor navigation system for blind people using Raspberry-Pi. J. Internet Technol. **21**(1), 183–195 (2020)

25. Hakim, H., Fadhil, A.: Indoor wearable navigation system using 2D SLAM based on RGB-D camera for visually impaired people. In: Peng, S.-L., Hao, R.-X., Pal, S. (eds.) Proceedings of First International Conference on Mathematical Modeling and Computational Science. AISC, vol. 1292, pp. 661–672. Springer, Singapore (2021). https://doi.org/10.1007/978-981-33-4389-4_60

26. Tan, M., Le, Q.: EfficientNet: rethinking model scaling for convolutional neural networks. In: International Conference on Machine Learning, pp. 6105–6114. PMLR (2019)

27. Lin, T.-Y., et al.: Microsoft COCO: common objects in context. In: Fleet, D., Pajdla, T., Schiele, B., Tuytelaars, T., (eds.) ECCV 2014. LNCS, vol. 8693, pp. 740–755. Springer, Cham (2014). https://doi.org/10.1007/978-3-319-10602-1_48

28. Kuriakose, B., Shrestha, R., Sandnes, F.E.: SceneRecog: a deep learning scene recognition model for assisting blind and visually impaired navigate using smartphones. In: 2021 IEEE International Conference on Systems, Man, and Cybernetics (SMC), pp. 2464–2470. IEEE (2021)

29. Krasin, I., et al.: OpenImages: a public dataset for large-scale multi-label and multi-class image classification. Dataset **2**(3), 18 (2017) https://github.com/openimages https://github.com/openimages

30. Deng, J., Dong, W., Socher, R., Li, L.J., Li, K., Fei-Fei, L.: ImageNet: a large-scale hierarchical image database. In: 2009 IEEE Conference on Computer Vision and Pattern Recognition, pp. 248–255. IEEE (2009)

An Exploratory Study on the Low Adoption Rate of Smart Canes

Rezylle Milallos$^{(\boxtimes)}$, Vinita Tibdewal, Yiwen Wang, Andre Udegbe, and Tae Oh

Rochester Institute of Technology, Rochester, NY 14623, USA
{rm7312,vt2173,yw7615,ao3353,thoics}@rit.edu

Abstract. People who are blind and visually impaired (BVI) primarily rely on white canes for everyday mobility. Smart canes were introduced to address the limitations of traditional white canes and to inform users of their surroundings more efficiently. While the smart cane's advantages are evident, these devices are not used often in the BVI community. To gain a better understanding of the low adoption rate, we spoke with orientation and mobility specialists for some background on BVI mobility, conducted a survey to gauge user awareness and initial perceptions of the smart cane, and interviewed 16 participants for an in-depth view regarding their smart cane experiences. While most of the participants' apprehension was based on initial product cost, we found that other factors like user personality, durability, battery life, experience bias, as well as the lack of awareness from the users all contribute to the low adoption rate of smart canes. As such, our findings are structured based on four main themes: (1) Impact of Participant Characteristics on Adoption, (2) Perceived Advantages and Disadvantages, (3) Product-Related Concerns, and (4) Building Trust. We contribute a user-centered investigation on the merits of the smart cane and suggestions for future design considerations based on user feedback.

Keywords: Human-centered computing · Accessibility · Individuals with disabilities and assistive technologies · Internet of Things

1 Introduction and Related Work

Navigation safety is key for BVI individuals. They utilize several mobility aids to ensure they are able to efficiently navigate in a safe manner and reduce the risk of bodily injury [20]. Individuals with visual impairment typically rely on a white cane, guide dog, sighted guides, and/or mobile applications (e.g., GPS apps, AIRA), among others [1,3]. The use of the standard white cane dates back to the 1940s [17,34] and has become not just a popular mobility aid but also a symbol for blindness [34]. Despite being widely used, the white cane has several limitations that can make it ineffective. For example, the white cane has a short detection range because it is limited to the length of the cane. This reduces

© The Author(s), under exclusive license to Springer Nature Switzerland AG 2022
M. Antona and C. Stephanidis (Eds.): HCII 2022, LNCS 13309, pp. 492–508, 2022.
https://doi.org/10.1007/978-3-031-05039-8_36

the reaction time before bumping into an obstacle which could result in bodily injury. As such, extra care has to be taken while using the cane, leading to a reduced speed in movement [17] and consequently reducing self-confidence when navigating [20]. Another key disadvantage of the white cane is the inability to detect objects that are elevated from the ground such as low-hanging branches; these objects will be missed by the sweeping motion of the user. This might result in some serious injuries that may be detrimental to the individual. In their survey about the nature and causes of head-level and fall accidents, Manduchi et al. reported that about 92% of participants had experienced some form of the head level incident and over 45% of blind participants experience this form of an accident once a month or less [20].

The advancement in technology and computing has led to the push for modern ubiquitous devices. This opens up the enhancement of devices, such as the white cane, for better functionality [16]. Smart canes currently exist either as research prototypes in the lab or as commercially available products for purchase. Available products include, but are not limited to, UltraCane (2010) [5], Smart-Cane ™(2014) [4], WeWalk (2017) [6], and BAWA Cane (2018) [2]—with prices ranging from $100 to over $1000 plus shipping. Researchers share design suggestions that focus on detecting obstacles and providing voice or audio [19,30,35], haptic [8,11,27,31], a combination of both sound and touch [13,22], vibrotactile biofeedback [29] and thermal feedback [26]. Previous research also looked at using more affordable materials and ergonomic-conscious design [7] as well as directly supporting users through a force feedback mechanism built inside a ball attached to the tip of the cane [9]. Although the smart cane has undergone significant development and have previously evaluated better than traditional white canes in terms of obstacle detection and avoidance, it is still beset by the low adoption rate of BVI individuals [17].

As with every technology, increasing penetration among the target population is necessary. Lindley et al. discussed that investigation on the implications of technology adoption is essential to HCI research to assess the viability of a product and to determine how it will be used by its intended users as part of their daily lives [18]. Our study was guided by the following research question: *What are the potential reasons for the low adoption rate of smart canes?*

We first conducted informal discussions with two orientation and mobility (O&M) specialists about BVI mobility and their thoughts on the smart cane. Based on these discussions and our initial research, we designed a survey that was sent out through different channels and received 57 valid responses where only 19.15% of users have tried a smart cane before. We then followed up on 16 participants who agreed to share more of their thoughts in one-on-one interview sessions and analyzed the data resulting in four main themes: (1) *Impact of Participant Characteristics on Adoption* (i.e., different user personalities and how these may affect their decision to use a smart cane), (2) *Perceived Advantages and Disadvantages* (i.e., user impressions and understanding of the smart cane), (3) *Product-Related Concerns* (i.e., concerns and needs related to the cost and technical aspects of the product), and (4) *Building Trust* (i.e., confidence in the product and other external influences). We found that a large percentage of users have only heard of the smart cane but never tried it. This research provides an in-depth look on the personalities and expectations of BVI users regarding smart cane technology as well as potential ways to promote adoption of the smart canes.

2   Methods

The study began by engaging in an in-person discussion with O&M specialists from the Association for Blind and Visually Impaired (ABVI) in Rochester, NY. We referred to them as subject matter experts to gain more background their thoughts about the smart cane and about the user's mobility experience. They were asked questions related to the process of getting clients, their teaching methodology, and their awareness of smart cane technology. Based on the responses from the O&M specialists and background research, an exploratory survey was designed and distributed through various channels (e.g., Twitter, Reddit). The participants were asked to complete the survey first; a phone interview was then scheduled if they expressed interest in further study. The purpose of the interview was to gather in-depth data and additional context around the survey responses. We received 57 complete survey responses and conducted 16 semi-structured interviews.

2.1   Survey

Survey Design. A survey was conducted to help gauge the users' awareness, understanding, and impression of the smart cane. It consisted of 86 questions exploring the navigation and mobility assistance options used by the BVI community, the mobility challenges they face, resources used to stay updated on new technology, barriers for using a smart cane, and their experience in using a smart cane (if any). The survey was hosted on the Qualtrics XMP Platform and both qualitative and quantitative data were collected. It was tested for accessibility with commonly used screen readers on both desktop and smartphones (Android and iOS). Based on the results from the accessibility tests, the matrix table questions were changed to separate multiple-choice questions as the matrix table was not accessible through the screen readers. The O&M specialists also provided suggestions for appropriate wordings and framing of the sentences to increase understandability. After accommodating their feedback, a pilot study was conducted with 4 people (3 people with vision, 1 person who was blind) and modified the flow of the survey accordingly before sending it out. The survey was posted on Reddit, Twitter, and was sent to more than 30 BVI organizations across the US.

Survey Participants. A total of 97 people responded to the survey. Out of those, 63 people completed the survey and 57 participants (blind: 40, low vision:

14, legally blind: 2, severe low vision: 1) were selected for analysis through purposeful criterion sampling. The sampling criteria for the participants were: (1) must identify as blind or low vision; (2) uses assistance for mobility; (3) equal to or more than 18 years old; (4) has been living in the United States for most of their life as our focus was on the US population. Among the 57 selected participants, 54 used white canes, 39 used smartphone applications, 13 used guide dogs, 6 used smart devices, and 9 used other options (sighted guides and a subset of smart devices). Thus, an overlap was observed in the usage of different navigation options.

Survey Analysis. In the survey, a separate set of questions for people who have heard about smart canes, used a smart cane, and owns a smart cane were added. Out of 57 responses, 41 participants have heard about smart canes but not used it. As such, Likert type questions centered around the reasons for not trying or using a smart cane garnered more neutral (i.e., "Neither Agree nor Disagree") answers than was expected as shown in Table 1. Because of this, data was not analyzed for significance. The large number of neutral responses, however, suggests that users are not familiar enough with the smart cane to make final judgments about the product.

Table 1. Likert scale data from the survey for potential reasons for not trying/using a smart cane

Likert scale question	Strongly Agree	Agree	Neither Agree nor Disagree	Disagree	Strongly Disagree
I don't know where to get a smart cane	11	16	8	2	4
I don't want to deal with technology	1	6	6	9	19
The smart cane was not available at that time	13	7	14	2	5
I felt that the smart cane was seeking unwanted attention	2	5	14	5	15
No technical assistance was available	4	7	22	3	5
I felt that the smart cane was not safe to use	2	7	19	9	4
I was not confident about using the smart cane	7	5	13	4	12
I felt that the smart cane was not easy to use	2	7	21	4	7

2.2 Interview

Interview Design. In the 45-min semi-structured interview sessions, participants were asked questions related, but not limited to, their experience with mobility and navigation technologies, barriers to adoption, and options to improve smart cane adoption. A few questions were modified based on the participant's survey responses. We also followed up on their smart cane impressions and experiences. The questionnaire was pilot tested 5 times (1 blind person) and modified to get the correct flow and to address any leading questions.

Interview Participants. From the survey given earlier, participants were asked if they were willing to join us for an in-depth interview about their experiences. 16 BVI participants were recruited, ranging between 22–80 years old with an average age of 56.38 years and average cane experience of 27.81 years. Most of the participants used multiple mobility devices such as white canes, guide dogs, smartphone apps, and other smart devices. They were also located in 6 different states in the US which represented diversity in their environment—some lived in bigger cities while others are located in more suburban areas. The participants were chosen because they have some level of smart cane awareness (i.e., have heard of it before).

Interview Data Collection and Analysis. The participants were based at various locations in the United States; all the interviews were conducted using a Zoom conference call. One researcher lead all the interviews; all the other researchers participated in the data analysis. A thematic analysis was completed on Miro by first open coding the data in different post it notes and grouping them together until four main themes were achieved—all of which are highlighted in Table 2.

Table 2. Themes, sub-themes, and the explanation behind each.

Impact of Participant Characteristics on Adoption
Participant Characteristics - who they are, what their abilities are, and how these affect their choice of navigation
Social Acceptability - how others influence their navigation option
Perceived Advantages and Disadvantages
User Impressions - what they know about smart canes
Potential Applications - how they think this can help them that other devices already cannot do
"Smart Cane is Not Needed" - why they think this does not help them
Product-Related Concerns
Financial Constraints - are the added benefits worth the cost
Durability and Portability - is the product reliable and will it withstand daily wear and tear
Cognitive Load - are the additional feedback options too much
Building Trust
Trial and Training - what will encourage them to buy it
Awareness and Influence - how do they gather information and what affects decision-making

3   Findings

The themes informed by our thematic analysis (Table 2) will help guide this section. Because our survey and interview findings support one another, we present the results of both methods in this section so as to prevent repetition. Data from survey participants are labeled S[x], while interview participants are coded as P[x].

3.1   Impact of Participant Characteristics on Adoption

Among the 16 participants we interviewed, many of them described their personalities, abilities, and hobbies in detail by sharing their backgrounds and stories. The data showed a relationship between participant characteristics and their decision to choose specific mobility aid options. This section also discussion participant attitudes regarding the use of smart canes in public in terms of social acceptability.

Participant Characteristics. This section introduces three main personality factors that could affect the utilization of advanced mobility aid tools like smart canes. Although there might be intersections between an individual's independence, curiosity, and self-confidence, those characteristics were separated to make their attitudes clearer.

Independence. Some participants who identified as independent or those who pursued to be more independent under the assistance of mobility devices showed more unwillingness to rely on a sighted guide. P11 was inclined to use a smart cane because *"it would be a huge tool to use to be able to be more independent."* Several participants mentioned that they liked socializing, enjoyed outside activities, and preferred to go out in public without the help of others. For example, P6 stated that:

> *"I'm very independent. So sometimes, it's hard to let other people guide me if I'm out in public and I'm using my cane because I try to really rely on my cane to find any obstacles in everything. So I will rely on people at certain times but I try to be as independent as I can."*

Curiosity. Most of the participants were inquisitive about travelling to new places and experiencing new technologies. Some participants shared that they were frequent travellers. P9 mentioned having friends who travel and *"use their smartphones to get around airports, get around cities, strange cities."* P2 has also travelled all over the country using a white cane.

Tech enthusiasts were also categorized as curious. For example, P1 was *"big into computers and my hobby is home automation and anything smart"*. This can also be seen in the survey responses where 68.29% of responses said that they were comfortable dealing with technology. However, it should be noted that there were some participants who mentioned they were not a very *"techy person [P10]"* or that they did not *"rely on technology for navigation because things like poor internet and unupdated maps occur [P16]."* Curious participants were more inclined to try out smart canes and evaluate if it works for their lifestyle.

Self-confidence. It was observed that participants who felt less confident while navigating used multiple mobility options when they went out. For example, P3 used both cane and sighted guide for safety because they did not *"feel confident enough anymore"* because of deteriorating vision. S48 also said, *"I would like to feel more confident using a white cane and to be able to navigate places that I am not familiar with."* On the flip side, participants who were very confident in their daily routines did not see the benefit of the smart canes for their current situation.

Of the 30 survey participants that said they were *strongly interested* in learning about smart canes, more than half of them explained in the reasoning part that they were curious about the technology and were striving to be more independent and confident in their daily lives. However, it should be noted that the aforementioned personality types are only reflective of the interview participants. This research does not assume that these personalities represent the entire population and understand that there is a large variety of user characteristics within the BVI community.

Social Acceptability. There were some discussion about the social stigma of using the white cane. The results not only provide more evidence to support prior research but also add some mutual concerns (i.e., those concerning both visually impaired and sighted persons) regarding BVI individuals interacting with others in the social context. These social acceptability concerns could vary depending on the situation (i.e., people travelling alone in crowded places may have different experiences from those walking their daily route). This section presents the feelings and perspectives of participants towards using mobility devices in social settings.

Neutral and Negative Feelings. Participants had mixed feelings on social acceptance with the assistive tools they used in public—some participants had neutral attitudes, some were concerned about social stigma and first impressions, and almost half of the participants did not mention anything about social acceptability. The participants with neutral attitudes, like P2, mentioned that another person's *"assumption is [not] going to change how I use (the cane)."* Meanwhile, other participants reported that they sometimes get uncomfortable navigating new places, especially crowded areas, with their white canes. P5 shared, *"I'm on parade, everybody, here comes this blind [person]. Let's look at [them] with [their] cane."* To add, P12 specifically mentioned avoiding the use of white canes in public because it made them feel different from others. Furthermore, it took them a long time to adapt to the cane technically and accept it emotionally. As P12 shared, *"I didn't want to look different and I didn't want to really admit that I was losing more of my sight."*

These negative feelings elicited by the social stigma against the white cane discouraged the participants from trying out the smart cane. Both commercially available canes and known research prototypes are usually bulky in design and may attract more attention than a white cane would.

Mutual Influence. Some participants expressed their thoughts on how they tried their best to stay conscious of the surroundings when using their preferred mobility tool. For example, canes may be too bothersome in crowded places, while guide dogs may not be allowed in certain public places. P12 relied on the guide dog most of the time but avoided bringing the dog in places with fireworks or other places that *"wouldn't be good for [the guide dog]."* To add, P7 noted that BVI users needed to be more alert in places like train stations because inadequate information from the white cane could be a safety risk to other people (i.e., accidentally pushing someone off the platform). On the other hand, participants also noted that other people sometimes acted as barriers in their mobility: too much noise from other people hindered their hearing ability, strangers who tried to help ended up being ineffective, and other people suddenly coming up in the participants' central vision promoted feelings of anxiety.

3.2 Perceived Advantages and Disadvantages

This section highlights participants' impressions and the potential applications of smart canes based on their understanding. In some cases, participants thought that smart canes did not provide them with any unique navigation feature.

User Impressions. Most participants have not used a smart cane before. They have only heard of them through conferences, word-of-mouth, social media, or blog posts. Some participants, like P11, thought *"it's a device, for my understanding, that hooks up to your white cane that you already have."* while other participants, including P14, highlighted the obstacle detection capabilities of smart canes (e.g., overhead or waist high, drop offs like in construction):

> *"My understanding is it will give you some information that a dumb cane, just a regular cane won't, won't give you like, for instance, finding obstacles that are like maybe, waist high, something the cane wouldn't find or even maybe lower, like for a barrier, like some kind of construction barrier."*

It is good to note that while smart canes were mostly developed for their obstacle detection capabilities, the notification *"could tell you where the obstacle is but it can't tell you what the obstacle is that you're going to figure out anyway when you touch it with your cane. So there's an obstacle and anyways you touch it with your cane.",* P1 says. This suggests that the information provided by the obstacle detection system of smart canes may not be sufficient.

A lot of participants focused on the feedback notifications like vibration and audio as those were the smart cane features that stood out to them the most. One participant, on the other hand, highlighted the GPS navigational assistance provided by some smart canes. While some of these impressions were true, it should be noted that most participants were unsure of their answer thereby showing a lack of understanding on actual smart cane features.

Potential Applications. Less than half of the participants shared their excitement with the smart cane technology. P7 pointed out that it may *"just become part of an every day thing."* P16 said that the *"smart cane would be of advantage"* and shared specific scenarios where smart canes would be of most use:

> *"If you're going [to] places that you're not familiar with or if you're going in to busy places where there's lots of people or if you have a community with kids in it, with things are left out on the sidewalks."*

P16 said that receiving an earlier warning through the smart cane would help increase the reaction speed in avoiding obstacles.

"Smart Cane Is Not Needed." While there are certainly advantages to the smart cane, a few participants directly mentioned that they will not be purchasing the smart canes as the benefits do not outweigh the cost. Additionally, participants noted that they had already found alternatives solutions (i.e., other mobility devices, apps, or AI-based technologies) that help them combat the limitation of traditional white canes. This sentiment was also echoed in some of the survey responses. According to S37,

> *"The smart cane a luxury product that will make blind people not use their skills and instead rely on something that can glitch and die."*

3.3   Product-Related Concerns

This section details multiple concerns related to the product design that prompted concerns and apprehensions about the smart cane, which contributed to users feeling like the smart canes were not a worthy investment. These included cost, durability, portability, battery constraints, and cognitive load. Some participants were more likely to try the smart cane if these issues were resolved.

Financial Constraints. One resounding concern expressed by all participants involved the costs associated with the purchase of a smart cane (i.e., they were worried about the financial implications of owning a smart cane). 66.67% of survey answers noted that the biggest barrier they had in adopting smart canes is its high cost. Assistive tools are always pricey and as such, the participants were forced to prioritize which ones they need the most and what fits their budget. S64 said,

> *"It all comes down to cost. 99% of the time I don't have a piece of equipment I'm interested in because it's too expensive. I'm trying to complete my masters degree and have no job, not for lack of trying. So if somethings too pricey, no dice".*

Durability and Portability. The participants were concerned about the durability of smart canes and gave examples of various situations to describe their considerations. They talked about water resistance under inclement weather, in particular, such as pouring rain and snow. Participants also pointed out the weight of the smart cane because some of them suffer from other health issues related to lack of mobility. Also, few participants mentioned that they were concerned if smart canes could hurt them or other people around by quickly unfolding and popping it back up. P4 explains,

"I would like to suggest the durability of the cane and then also how compact it is. One of the challenges with the regular cane is folding it up and then trying to keep it together and making it pop too quickly now that you might get hurt."

They were also concerned about battery life and charging issues while using a smart cane, especially since canes are meant to be used most of the day.

Cognitive Load. Based on their previous experiences, almost all participants mentioned that one prominent feature of the smart cane is obstacle notification through haptic and audio feedback. Participants emphasized the importance of contextual and timely feedback—smart canes should not only randomly vibrate but provide an idea on what type of obstacle is coming up. Additionally, participants noted the balance of different feedback options because it can have an impact on the cognitive load of the user. P10 mentioned that the vibration could cause them to *"lose my focus on my cane technique itself, or I would slow down a lot."* and that users should not *"worry about focusing on some vibration or some other type of sensory input"* while they are walking. Some participants did note that haptic feedback will be useful in noisy environments but were worried they would miss out on the notification if the vibration is too subtle or is uninformative. P5 states, *"I wonder if it's just haptic, Will that tell me? How will that tell you that there's an obstacle in front of you?"*

While some participants thought that accompanying audio can provide more context (e.g., street names and signs), they were worried that multiple feedback methods might disrupt their focus on different environmental cues which may increase the likelihood of accidents and collisions. Several participants mentioned that *"there are other ways of doing it [detecting obstacles] that I think might be as reliable or more reliable than smart canes, namely, that's echolocation [P7]."* With other feedback methods increasing the cognitive load of the user, participants are worried that they may not be able to fully utilize their native navigational skills and in turn, fail to recognize surrounding activities such as the traffic flow.

3.4   Building Trust

This section discusses the importance of access, training, and external influences in the adoption of smart canes. While most interview participants were interested in smart canes and 84.21% of survey participants were trusting of new technologies, access to the product was a large barrier. Survey responses showed 65.85% of the participants did not know where to get a smart cane.

Trial and Training. Some participants mentioned that they were able to try out smart canes through conventions or research studies. Unfortunately, not all

BVI users have the opportunity to join those venues. P7 shares that *"we don't really get a chance to demonstrate it [or] to try this smart cane outside for any length of time."* All the participants want assurance that the smart canes would provide them additional benefits and will work better than their traditional white canes—they believe that trials can promote their confidence in a new product.

Furthermore, participants get confused on what features to expect from a smart cane because of the wide variety of products, both commercially-available ones and those that are still research prototypes. P6 shares that after attending a research study, they were surprised to find that *"it didn't have all of the technology that I've read about in smart canes."* Those who have once been let down by previous iterations have a lesser likelihood of trying out newer versions of the cane. Most participants also emphasized that accompanying training can make a difference in learning new technologies. P15 expands on this in the statement below:

> *"What would really be helpful is when the designers hand something, hand a piece of assistive technology, they should also find a way to arrange for some kind of training. Maybe not just provide a manual, but also provide a human being that you can call and ask questions. That would be helpful."*

Awareness and Influence. While trial and training are crucial, the participants first wanted to be informed about the progress with smart cane technology. According to both the survey and interview participants, the information can be delivered through social media advertising (e.g., blind groups, Facebook, chat rooms), TV ads, or from their friends and family. While others mentioned public places as good places to advertise and try out smart canes (i.e., similar to the availability of electric scooters and bikes as rentals), some participants, including P10, said that those places may not be the best avenue *"because most people wouldn't know how to use them"* unless there was an accompanying lesson or module in the area.

Participants mentioned that the adoption of any new kind of mobility or navigation technique or technologies can be heavily influenced by O&M instructors. These specialists and trusted in their field and as such, participants are more likely to be confident in the product if it is endorsed by the O&M instructor. However, some specialists prioritize mastery of native mobility and navigation skills instead of with the aid of technology, as explained by P2 below:

> *"There's kind of different philosophies of training and I think a lot of them (O&M specialists) would say that it's important for people to like, get the fundamental skills of using a cane, like understanding their environment, without technology [because] technology can always fail."*

Trust in the product can also be improved through word-of-mouth. Some participants mentioned that they follow blind forums or newsletters and only try out new technologies after some of their peers endorse it.

4   Discussion

The work from this research sought to emphasize possible reasons for the low adoption rate of smart canes within the BVI community even after being in development for over 50 years. This study indicates that the participants' concerns with other mobility options, such as the white cane, contributed to the low awareness of the smart cane and directly affected the interest level of potential users. Hence, we critically analyzed the impressions and expectations from the participants' perspectives which we believe would inform the future product and service design process from the manufacturer and designer point of view.

4.1   Impressions Based on White Canes

While HCI researchers think that smart canes are a good way to transition white cane users into smarter technology because of their similar cognitive model [28], we found that the participants' negative experiences with the white cane affected their first impressions of smart canes. For example, white canes need to be replaced often and as such, participants believed that smart canes would also suffer from the same flaw. Issues regarding social stigma against assistive devices like the traditional white cane also get carried over to the smart cane, confirming and extending on previous work from Shinohara *et al.* on social acceptability [33]. This is exacerbated by the fact that smart canes contain additional systems that make them bulkier and more noticeable than the white cane. While social acceptability may be less of a concern as participants get older [25], HCI researchers should consider user's feelings of self-consciousness, vulnerability, or embarrassment [14]. Future studies may consider providing methods to make mobility aids more inconspicuous in terms of aesthetics factors [32]. Additionally, novel features such as built-in OCR readers and indoor navigation should be considered to increase the benefits of the smart cane and make it more appealing to BVI users [24].

4.2   Addressing Concerns and Increasing Awareness

While the smart canes are rich with new features, users still have a lot of reservations regarding their reliability and consistency, especially against other mobility and navigation options [24]. These product-related concerns should be addressed before beginning any trial or training for new smart canes. Previous research have proposed some solutions to smart cane concerns about battery life such as providing Navigation mode, Eco mode and Offline mode [23].

Additionally, the result of our analysis suggested that there was not enough information available about the smart cane to BVI individuals. Leveraging O&M specialists' direct access to individuals within the community would get the word out faster [24]. However, it was also identified that the limited availability of O&M specialists, expensiveness and unavailability of devices, and inadequate technology training provided to the O&M specialists might lead to reduced exposure of the latest technology to the community [12]. Virtual sessions may be provided to multiple clients at a time; this might be more efficient because it reduces travel time, increases user attendance per session, and speeds up the information relay process. Additionally, up-to-date data on current smart cane developments may be shared through BVI gatherings, conferences, organizations, and other media outlets to help build confidence in newer options.

4.3   User Inclusion into Product and Service Design

As HCI researchers, we need to consider users' needs to get a deeper understanding of the viability of the product from its prototype phase all the way to its adoption. While previous research work in this field tried to address usability issues [15,17,27], our research identified the user's ultimate goals and other combinations of navigation options that BVI users currently take advantage of to help them with mobility and navigation. For example, based on the the the characteristics of the participants, the goal is to provide users with better assistive options that will support the independent, curious, and less confident personalities. Although these personal factors are hard to easily reach and define, we propose several guidelines to help stakeholders of smart cane to achieve a better design.

Inclusive Design. BVI users want the smart cane to be able to accommodate all essential environments such as public transportation, sidewalks, crossroads, and noisy places. The feedback method was important across several participants, with most preferring a combination of vibro-tactile and auditory feedback present in a smart cane; this, in their opinion, would aid them in effective commuting. However, this also comes with a possible fallback as there might be an increased cognitive load to the user trying to process both feedback at the same time [15,21]. Also, there are possible situations where the auditory feedback would not be optimal as mentioned in the mutual effect of social acceptance in Sect. 3.1. For example, participants would feel uncomfortable receiving auditory input in places where making noise could easily catch another's attention (e.g., concerts, restaurants). On the contrary, having a lot of background noise might reduce the effectiveness of this feedback method [15]. There was also concern among the participants about the steep learning curve associated with using both feedback methods in a dynamic environment. Adding an easy-to-reach customization option for different feedback mechanisms (e.g., tactile switch, button) may help improve usability.

With the above stated recommendations, it is therefore imperative that future development should dive deeper into designing more ergonomic smart canes that fit well into different scenarios by providing multiple feedback depending on the environment and making the product portable and easy to store [7]. It should also consider the body constraints of users, including, but not limited to, the length of human arms and the weight a person's muscles can handle; we can make smart canes more lightweight and adjustable, for example. In addition, adapting the smart cane design and components to fit people of various skill levels would make the adoption rate easier as it would require less initial training [31]. As guided by the results stated in Sect. 3.3 and the work by Pariti *et.al.* [27], the cane must be lightweight, compact, portable, and easy to swing to increase the mobility of users and therefore, the usability of the product. The physical constraints BVI users might face such as an occupied hand for the smartphone and muscle fatigue when holding the cane for too long should be considered in the design. We may consider adding built-in features to the smart cane that would otherwise be present in smartphones (e.g., indoor GPS navigation). Additionally, some participants in our study had limited depth perception and a poor sense of direction, which limits self-reliance during a commute. Hence, the content of formal training should be customized based on the ability of the user and any additional limitations caused by different usage scenarios.

Service Design. As mentioned in Sect. 3.4, providing a trial-based service system for the smart cane could lead to an increased interest rate among the community as the end-users would be able to get a first-hand glimpse into the true workings of the smart cane and ways they could benefit from it. To provide availability for trial, smart canes could be placed at some public places—airports, museums, and lending libraries, for example [24]. The participants had some concerns regarding initial training for the smart canes but most of the participants were excited about this idea. While previous research studies allowed users to try out the smart cane, they only typically spend about an hour or less for the whole evaluation which consists of introduction, training, testing, and pre/post interviews or questionnaire, with the training section lasting [10,27]. HCI researchers may choose to provide longer training times or lend their smart cane prototypes to their participants for a longer diary study. We need to actively find ways to integrate and adopt these new technologies into the user's daily lives and not stop in short evaluations or comparisons [18,36]. Conducting training sessions for interested individuals could be one resource for the users to try out the smart cane in an appropriate way. If done right, there would be a cascade of information sharing within the community which would result in an increased interest in the adoption level. This route also opens the smart cane to critique and feedback on its performance in the real world which can be advantageous to manufacturers as the information can be used to make continuous iteration to their product so it meets the standards of the community.

5 Conclusion

Commercial smart canes are available in the market which provide haptic, audio, and other forms of feedback to inform users about upcoming obstacles. Although these smart canes target the limitations of the traditional white canes, it has not been widely adopted by the BVI community for daily use. This research highlights the implications for adoption that HCI researchers should consider in future smart cane studies. While its high price is the biggest deterrent for most users, product-related concerns, low awareness, limited resources for trial, and limited interest from OM specialists also greatly affected user trust and confidence and therefore, their purchasing decisions. The lack of standardization in the smart cane technology also makes it more difficult for people to judge and manage their expectations on commercially available smart canes. Future smart cane developments should consider user inclusion into product and service design such that participants have a chance to get more acquainted with the smart cane and be able to provide suggestions for improvement.

References

1. 10 fascinating facts about the white cane. https://www.perkins.org/stories/10-fascinating-facts-about-the-white-cane. Accessed 26 Mar 2021
2. Bawa cane. https://www.bawa.tech. Accessed 26 Mar 2021
3. Guiding eyes FAQ. https://www.guidingeyes.org/about/faqs/. Accessed 26 Mar 2021
4. Smartcane overview. http://smartcane.saksham.org/overview/. Accessed 26 Mar 2021
5. Ultracane. https://www.ultracane.com/ultracane. Accessed 26 Mar 2021
6. Wewalk smart cane for visually impaired and blind people. https://wewalk.io/en/. Accessed 26 Mar 2021
7. Akash, S., Rahman, M.: QFD-based smart cane design: a technology to assist visually impaired. Int. J. Bus. Anal. Intell. **6**(1), 25 (2018)
8. Asad, S., Mooney, B., Ahmad, I., Huber, M., Clark, A.: Object detection and sensory feedback techniques in building smart cane for the visually impaired: an overview. In: Proceedings of the 13th ACM International Conference on Pervasive Technologies Related to Assistive Environments, pp. 1–7 (2020)
9. Branig, M., Engel, C.: Smartcane: an active cane to support blind people through virtual mobility training. In: Proceedings of the 12th ACM International Conference on PErvasive Technologies Related to Assistive Environments, pp. 327–328 (2019)
10. Buchs, G., Simon, N., Maidenbaum, S., Amedi, A.: Waist-up protection for blind individuals using the eyecane as a primary and secondary mobility aid. Restorative Neurol. Neurosci. **35**(2), 225–235 (2017)
11. Chen, Q., Khan, M., Tsangouri, C., Yang, C., Li, B., Xiao, J., Zhu, Z.: CCNY smart cane. In: 2017 IEEE 7th Annual International Conference on CYBER Technology in Automation, Control, and Intelligent Systems (CYBER), pp. 1246–1251. IEEE (2017)
12. Deverell, L., et al.: Use of technology by orientation and mobility professionals in Australia and Malaysia before covid-19. Disability Rehabil. Assistive Technol. 1–8 (2020)
13. Guerrero, J.C., Quezada-V, C., Chacon-Troya, D.: Design and implementation of an intelligent cane, with proximity sensors, GPS localization and GSM feedback. In: 2018 IEEE Canadian Conference on Electrical & Computer Engineering (CCECE), pp. 1–4. IEEE (2018)
14. Hogan, C.L.: Stigma, embarrassment and the use of mobility aids. Int. J. Orientation Mob. **5**(1), 49–52 (2012). https://doi.org/10.21307/ijom-2012-009
15. Hollyfield, R.L., Foulke, E.: The spatial cognition of blind pedestrians. J. Vis. Impairment Blindness **77**(5), 204–210 (1983)
16. Khan, I., Khusro, S., Ullah, I.: Technology-assisted white cane: evaluation and future directions. Peer J. **6**, e6058 (2018)

17. Kim, S.Y., Cho, K.: Usability and design guidelines of smart canes for users with visual impairments. Int. J. Des. **7**(1) (2013)
18. Lindley, J., Coulton, P., Sturdee, M.: Implications for adoption. In: Proceedings of the 2017 CHI Conference on Human Factors in Computing Systems, pp. 265–277. CHI 2017, Association for Computing Machinery, New York, NY, USA (2017). https://doi.org/10.1145/3025453.3025742, https://doi-org.ezproxy.rit.edu/10.1145/3025453.3025742
19. Maidenbaum, S., et al.: The 'eyecane', a new electronic travel aid for the blind: technology, behavior & swift learning. Restorative Neurol. Neurosci. **32**(6), 813–824 (2014). https://doi.org/10.3233/RNN-130351
20. Manduchi, R., Kurniawan, S.: Watch your head, mind your step: mobility-related accidents experienced by people with visual impairment. Dept. Comp. Eng., Univ. California, Santa Cruz, Tech. Rep (2010)
21. Martinez, M., Constantinescu, A., Schauerte, B., Koester, D., Stiefelhagen, R.: Cognitive evaluation of haptic and audio feedback in short range navigation tasks. In: Miesenberger, K., Fels, D., Archambault, D., Peňáz, P., Zagler, W. (eds.) ICCHP 2014. LNCS, vol. 8548, pp. 128–135. Springer, Cham (2014). https://doi.org/10.1007/978-3-319-08599-9_20
22. Megalingam, R.K., Nambissan, A., Thambi, A., Gopinath, A., Nandakumar, M.: Sound and touch based smart cane: better walking experience for visually challenged. In: 2014 IEEE Canada International Humanitarian Technology Conference-(IHTC), pp. 1–4. IEEE (2014)
23. Messaoudi, M.D., Menelas, B.A.J., Mcheick, H.: Autonomous smart white cane navigation system for indoor usage. Technologies **8**(3), 37 (2020)
24. Milallos, R., Tibdewal, V., Wang, Y., Ogueh Udegbe, A., Oh, T.: " would the smart cane benefit me?": perceptions of the visually impaired towards smart canes. In: The 23rd International ACM SIGACCESS Conference on Computers and Accessibility, pp. 1–3 (2021)
25. MP Hoogsteen, K., A. Osinga, S., LPA Steenbekkers, B., FA Szpiro, S.: Functionality versus inconspicuousness: attitudes of people with low vision towards OST smart glasses. In: The 22nd International ACM SIGACCESS Conference on Computers and Accessibility. ASSETS 2020, Association for Computing Machinery, New York, NY, USA (2020). https://doi.org/10.1145/3373625.3418012, https://doi-org.ezproxy.rit.edu/10.1145/3373625.3418012
26. Nasser, A., Keng, K.N., Zhu, K.: Thermalcane: exploring thermotactile directional cues on cane-grip for non-visual navigation. In: The 22nd International ACM SIGACCESS Conference on Computers and Accessibility. ASSETS 2020, Association for Computing Machinery, New York, NY, USA (2020). https://doi.org/10.1145/3373625.3417004, https://doi-org.ezproxy.rit.edu/10.1145/3373625.3417004
27. Pariti, J., Oh, T.: Understanding the hand and wrist strains caused by smart cane handles with haptic notification. In: The 22nd International ACM SIGACCESS Conference on Computers and Accessibility. ASSETS 2020, Association for Computing Machinery, New York, NY, USA (2020). https://doi.org/10.1145/3373625.3418028,https://doi-org.ezproxy.rit.edu/10.1145/3373625.3418028
28. Roentgen, U.R., Gelderblom, G.J., Soede, M., De Witte, L.P.: Inventory of electronic mobility aids for persons with visual impairments: a literature review. J. Vis. Impairment Blindness **102**(11), 702–724 (2008)
29. Routson, R.L., Bailey, M., Pumford, I., Czerniecki, J.M., Aubin, P.M.: A smart cane with vibrotactile biofeedback improves cane loading for people with knee osteoarthritis. In: 2016 38th Annual International Conference of the IEEE Engineering in Medicine and Biology Society (EMBC), pp. 3370–3373. IEEE (2016)

30. Saaid, M.F., Mohammad, A., Ali, M.M.: Smart cane with range notification for blind people. In: 2016 IEEE International Conference on Automatic Control and Intelligent Systems (I2CACIS), pp. 225–229. IEEE (2016)
31. Sakhardande, J., Pattanayak, P., Bhowmick, M.: Smart cane assisted mobility for the visually impaired. Int. J. Electr. Comput. Eng. **6**(10), 1262–1265 (2012)
32. dos Santos, A.D.P., Ferrari, A.L.M., Medola, F.O., Sandnes, F.E.: Aesthetics and the perceived stigma of assistive technology for visual impairment. Disability Rehabil. Assistive Technol. 1–7 (2020). https://doi.org/10.1080/17483107.2020.1768308
33. Shinohara, K., Wobbrock, J.O.: In the shadow of misperception: assistive technology use and social interactions. In: Proceedings of the SIGCHI Conference on Human Factors in Computing Systems, pp. 705–714. CHI 2011, Association for Computing Machinery, New York, NY, USA (2011). https://doi.org/10.1145/1978942.1979044
34. Strong, P.: The history of the white cane (2009)
35. Wahab, M.H.A., et al.: Smart cane: assistive cane for visually-impaired people. arXiv preprint arXiv:1110.5156 (2011)
36. Yoo, D., Ernest, A., Serholt, S., Eriksson, E., Dalsgaard, P.: Service design in HCI research: the extended value co-creation model. In: Proceedings of the Halfway to the Future Symposium 2019, pp. 1–8 (2019)

A Software Architecture for a Personalized and Context-Aware Indoor Navigation System

Maria Teresa Paratore[(✉)] and Barbara Leporini

Institute of Information Science and Technologies "Alessandro Faedo" – ISTI Italian Research Council, Pisa, Italy
{mariateresa.paratore,barbara.leporini}@isti.cnr.it

Abstract. This paper proposes a context-aware model for a mobile indoor navigation system in which users' needs play a key role. We will present an overview of the underlying architecture, describe the main data involved, and show how they are used; we will especially focus on the role of the users' preferences and accessibility needs, since they are the key elements that allow to build a personalized and inclusive user experience. Thanks to a service-oriented architecture, a mobile application will be able to retrieve the most adequate information for its user about a specific point of interest in the environment, and issue a personalized notification. Examples of interaction with the system from the perspective of back-end operators will also be provided, in which we will show how the model entities are translated into practice during the configuration phase of the system. We will pay particular attention to the case of visually impaired users, for whom accessible navigation apps have proven to be effective assistive solutions to achieve better social inclusion and autonomy. We will assume to be using BLE beacons and an Android mobile app for our simulations, anyway we will show that our model is generalizable. Finally, future possible enhancements of the system will be discussed.

Keywords: Internet of Things · Personalization · User interfaces · Accessibility · Bluetooth low-energy beacons · User centered design

1 Introduction

The pervasiveness of mobile devices and the constant evolution of the sensors shipped within them has led to a constantly increasing number of mobile applications for navigation and positioning during the latest years. The Global Positioning System (GPS) technology is extensively used when it comes to outdoor environments. GPS-based navigation apps such as Google Maps [7] have become extremely popular and are now considered essential utilities on every smartphone, moreover, mapping and localization platforms such as those provided by Google offer services than can be easily integrated by developers in any mobile application. From food delivery to real estate services, many popular mobile apps include georeferenced maps as part of their functionalities or simply to provide better user experience.

© The Author(s), under exclusive license to Springer Nature Switzerland AG 2022
M. Antona and C. Stephanidis (Eds.): HCII 2022, LNCS 13309, pp. 509–520, 2022.
https://doi.org/10.1007/978-3-031-05039-8_37

Indoor localization systems cannot rely on GPS, and require ad hoc hardware infrastructures and positioning techniques tailored on the physical characteristics of the target environment (such as thickness and geometry of the walls). Thanks to the constant evolution of such technologies, mobile applications for indoor localization are growing more and more popular [19, 21]. Wi-Fi, Radio-frequency identification (RFID), Bluetooth Low Energy (BLE) and Ultra Wide Band (UWB) [3, 15, 24], possibly combined in hybrid systems [13], are among the most popular infrastructures adopted.

Context-aware mobile apps for indoor navigation have their main application fields in the Internet of Things (IoT) and Smart Cities projects, and have proven to be effective assistive solutions for persons with visual impairments [2, 8, 15, 20], as means of increasing social inclusion and autonomy. While visiting an indoor or outdoor environment, visually impaired users should be able to rely upon a navigation app in order to get information about their actual position, route planning, and accessibility warnings. This would enable them to get to a specific place in the safest and more effective way.

Navigation apps, anyway, are also an effective means to help visually impaired users build a mental representation (aka "cognitive map") of a specific environment. This is particularly important in a training phase, i.e. before physically accessing an unknown or rarely visited place [12].

Many studies exist that describe indoor positioning and tracking solutions based on different technologies, mainly focused on how to develop effective wayfinding strategies and build robust infrastructures that minimize localization errors [14, 22, 26] scarce attention, anyway, is dedicated to issues related to the design of an effective user experience, and to the aspects of presentation and personalization of the information. Studies focused on technologies that support mobility for users with visual impairments outline the strategies adopted to improve user interactions without providing detailed description of the design [2, 20].

Guerreiro et Al. [8] conducted a survey with two focus groups of visually impaired users to assess common interaction issues encountered with an indoor navigation app; their findings show that, besides ad hoc strategies to convey information such as the haptic and audio channel, each user has their own peculiar needs (e.g., interaction ways vary whether they use a white-cane or a guide-dog). Finally, Wang et Al. [25] investigated the ways users cope with indoor wayfinding, and found out it is affected by their age and gender.

In this paper, we will focus our attention on the concept of personalization applied to the user experience as well as to the quality of the delivered information. We will describe a context-aware model for a mobile indoor positioning system, which leverages user's needs and preferences to build a personalized conceptual view of the physical space, while at the same time providing information tailored upon the user's interests and specific needs.

2 Two User Scenarios

In order to clarify the concept of personalization introduced in the previous section, we describe two user scenarios for an app to guide visitors through a museum.

2.1 User Scenario 1: Senior Experienced User

Anna, a 75-year-old retired teacher, loves art and regularly visits exhibitions and muse-ums. Anna is used to deepen the knowledge of the works of art that most strike her, but she has some vision problems, and sometimes it is tiring for her to read captions and booklets provided by cultural institutions. She would be glad to have a mobile appli-cation to get the most from her visits; she would in particular appreciate an app that provided her with extra contents in a downloadable format, in order to learn more about the artworks when she gets home. Moreover, she would find it very handy if the app provided a functionality to render real-time captions in an accessible format for persons with vision problems. Such a functionality may show a caption as every piece of art is approached; captions should be rendered on the device's screen in large, high contrast fonts.

2.2 User Scenario 2: Young Non-experienced User with Visual Impairment

Ben is a 20-year-old student. He is visually impaired and a white cane user. Ben rarely visits museums; he is not an art enthusiast, but he is a curious person and likes to explore new places. On such occasions, one of his main concerns is to find suitable routes for visually impaired visitors. He would appreciate a mobile application that helped him with this task by signaling areas that pose accessibility issues. He is not interested in having a deep insight of the pieces of art exposed, anyway, he would like if the app provided, for each artwork, an audio file containing its title and a short description.

These user scenarios highlight that the level of interest/experience of a user in a given environment (e.g. their attitude towards museum visits) shapes the amount and quality of information that the app provides them. On the other hand, possible special needs could hinder not only the physical exploration of the space (as in the case of mobility issues), but also the user experience with the app itself (as in the case of visual impairments). Disability issues must be hence kept into account by developers both when designing the user interfaces and when deciding which kind of information should be conveyed to users.

In our architecture, the problem of tailoring the information content is delegated to a backend service, that is responsible for recognizing the proper piece of information, associating it to the correct format, and returning it to the app for presentation. The mobile app will hence be responsible for issuing notifications related to the presence of POIs and rendering the information obtained by the backend service; potential users' disabilities, such as visual impairments, must be taken into account in the design of the user interfaces and, more broadly, of the user experience.

3 Architecture Overview

The first requirement for an indoor positioning system is to make users aware of rele-vant places or objects in the surrounding space, known as Points of Interest (POIs). Our architecture is meant to be generalizable with respect to the hardware adopted for the positioning, anyway, in order to develop our model, we assumed to rely on an infras-tructure based on BLE transmitters (AKA beacons), in which each POI is signaled by

512   M. T. Paratore and B. Leporini

a beacon via its unique identifier (UID), that is broadcast to every Bluetooth-enabled device. BLE beacons benefit of ease of installation, low power consumption and fair localization accuracy [8, 9]. This has led to a wide diffusion of such transmitters in public urban areas and buildings, which makes it also possible to rely on pre-existing BLE infrastructures to develop positioning applications for different purposes.

Figure 1 shows an overview of our architecture, which is based on a service-oriented approach [11]. The navigation system's front-end for the user is provided by a mobile application; as soon as the app receives the UID from a beacon, it will issue a request to a RESTful web service, notify the user and present the retrieved information. Data exposed by the REST are created and modified via a web application which enables operators to translate the physical environment into logical entities; it in fact enables operators, among other functionalities, to search through the installed beacons, associate a beacon to a POI and define its information content. A dedicated server is also present, which will be queried by the app to fetch maps of the surrounding environment, or of parts of it.

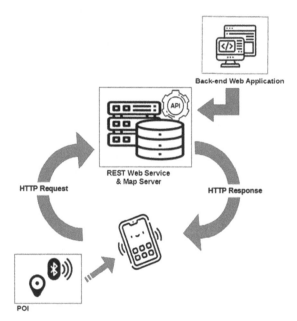

Fig. 1. An overview of the architecture.

4 Mapping Physical Entities to a Logical Model

Indoor localization systems are typically adopted to guide users through complex indoor environments (such as hospitals or airports, museums), as well as restricted outdoor areas such as university campuses; parks or cultural sites. Information related to POIs may be of varying degrees of complexity, depending on the context and the purpose for which the system is conceived. For instance, a mobile app that guides visitors through museums and exhibitions will not only provide navigation hints, but also detailed information about specific objects in the environment recognized as artworks. A POI must be hence associated to a type, which identifies its function; a typical POI may be an ATM, an artwork or a physical barrier which is relevant from an accessibility point of view [6]. Figure 2 shows the class diagram of our model, which is directly related to the well-known concept of Building Information Management (BIM) modelling [16]. A BIM model provides a thorough description of a building in terms of its structural elements (via CAD mappings) and allows to describe functional properties and relationships between those elements, as if they were database records. An example of an open-source BIM modelling tool is the indoor map editor provided by the OpenStreetMap (OSM) project, in which basic entities that may be given a meaning by means of attributes named "tags" [17, 18]. The figure shows how the objects in our model are related each other and categorized.

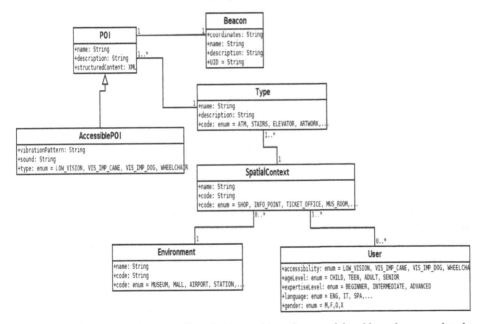

Fig. 2. A class diagram that describes the key entities of our model and how they are related.

The Beacon class contains the coordinates of the transmitting device and its unique identifier; a POI is related to just one beacon via the UID, while a Type object describes the purpose of the POI itself. Furthermore, a POI is related to the surrounding environment via the Context class, which assigns a specific purpose to a portion of environment (a shop, a ticket office, a museum's room, etc.). Finally, the Environment class describes the highest hierarchical entity in the model; it semantically identifies the indoor environment according to its wider function, which may be a railway station, a museum, a shopping mall, etc.

Figure 3 shows how POIs are related to other entities in our model according to our database schema. It highlights the relationship between a particular spatial context and the types of POIs it can contain. It also shows that additional complex information can be associated with a POI via an XML document, namely the *info_content* field.

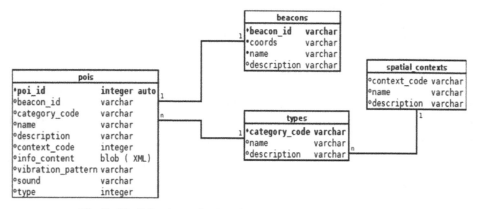

Fig. 3. The DB schema for the tables related to POIs in our model.

4.1 Accessibility and Personalization

Every user has their own preferences, related to factors such as age, gender, and personal experiences and needs; moreover, possible impairments may hinder the accessibility of the mobile app for navigation and compromise the whole user experience [4]. Figure 4 shows how the User class translates into the Preferences section of an Android application developed as a front-end prototype for two different environments: a museum and a railway station. User interfaces (UIs) in the figure were designed in order to avoid accessibility issues (e.g. default Android preferences widgets were avoided since they were based on pop-ups). In order to guarantee a thorough accessible user experience, anyway, not only the mobile app must be properly designed, but also the backing services must assure to deliver the proper content [11].

In our model, we designed the *AccessiblePOI* class, a specialization of the POI class whose purpose is to identify a POI as accessible to a particular category of users with special needs and define special audio and haptic feedbacks to be issued by the mobile app contextually with the POI notification. *AccessiblePOIs* are the key entities upon which an accessible user experience of navigation can be built, since they make it possible to define routes in the surrounding space in which every accessible object or place is properly highlighted and notified. A flight of stairs or an elevator, for instance, should be considered as *AccessiblePOIs*, and consequently the mobile app should signal them much more clearly to visually impaired users than to others. Moreover, contents associated to these POIs may be adapted according to specific rendering needs, e.g. if a screen reader or a magnifier is used.

Fig. 4. The Preferences section of the mobile app as it appears in different environments: a museum and a railway station.

Figure 5 shows the layout of a form to create a new POI via the back-end application; one of the beacons installed in the environment can be associated to the POI via a drop-down menu or by choosing one item on a map that shows also its coordinates. A section of the form is related to accessibility; it provides functionalities by which operators can define haptic or audio feedbacks associated to the POI and choose the categories of users with special needs which can benefit from this POI. For every POI object, structured content may be associated, that accounts for detailed information and additional content to be provided to users; this information is modelled via the *structuredContent* field of the POI class, associated to an XML document.

4.2 Structuring the Information Content

One of our main concerns was to provide each user with information tailored on their profile. In order to do so, each POI object was associated to an XML document containing exhaustive information about the point of interest, structured upon users' features, such as language, age, expertise and special needs. A detailed description of the XML Schema designed for our model is beyond the scope of this paper and will be omitted for simplicity's sake.

Fig. 5. Editing GUI for a new POI.

Figure 6 shows a portion of an XML document associated to a POI; the root, i.e. the *structuredContent* element, is related to the POI type via an attribute (e.g. "artwork") and contains a variable number of *complexDescription* children elements, each characterized by attributes related to customization, namely "language", "age", "expertise" and "accessibility". Each *complexDescription* node contains a short descriptive text element (which will be used as. a caption for notifications issued by the navigation app), HTML content to be shown as a detailed description within the app, and a variable number of *file* elements, which refer to additional multimedia contents such as mp3 tracks of an audio-guide or pictures of a building's entrances, and the relative descriptive metadata. XML is the data format of choice when it comes to working with structured data that can be presented differently. Depending on the request issued by the mobile app to the web service, it will respond with the proper information content extracted (and possibly transformed) from the whole document.

Back-end operators can add a new piece of structured content directly when creating a new POI (see Fig. 5). A wireframe of the user interface for creating and editing this kind of complex, structured information is shown in Fig. 7.

```
<structuredContent type="artwork">
<complexDescription language="en" age="teen" expertise="beginner">
    <caption>Did you know? This is the most famous painting by Leonardo da Vinci!</caption>
    <description>
            <![CDATA[ <h1>Sample HTML</h1> Lorem ipsum... ]]>
    </description>
    <file mime-type="image/jpeg" size="66415">
        <url>http://myserver.org/MyMedia/repository/images/11-12-2021/4fc380.JPG</url>
        <title>Mona Lisa</title>
        <copyright/>
    </file>
    <file mime-type="audio/mpeg" size="2647200">
        <url>http://myserver.org/MyMedia/repository/audioguides/amgfd285.mp3</url>
        <title>Leonardo for Kids - Mona Lisa </title>
        <copyright/>
    </file>
</complexDescription>

<complexDescription language="it" age="elderly" expertise="advanced">
    .....
</complexDescription>

    .....
</structuredContent>
```

Fig. 6. Part of an XML file containing the structured description of a POI.

Sample notifications issued by the mobile app are shown in Fig. 8; samples refer to different users for the same POI. The POI object of the model is responsible for the title of the notification and the vibration or audio hints (if any), via the description, sound (audio-hint) and vibration-pattern fields (see Fig. 2). The first refers to a young visually impaired user with a "beginner" level of expertise; the notification contains a short and clear text message (that will be read by the smartphone's screen reader) and contains a play button that fires the playback of a descriptive audio file meant for a compatible target audience. The second notification, on the other hand, is addressed to a young experienced user with no disabilities; the caption shown in the system's window is a long text. Tapping on the window will open a section of the app where detailed html formatted information will be displayed, together with additional multimedia contents, if any.

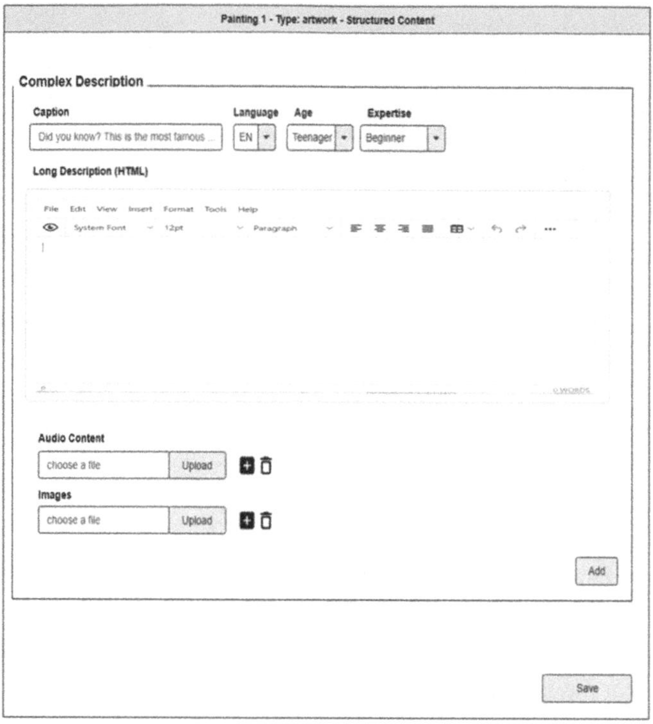

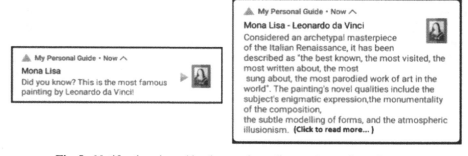

Fig. 7. The GUI for creating and updating structured content associated to a POI.

Fig. 8. Notifications issued by the app depending on the user's preferences.

5   Conclusions and Future Work

We have presented the software architecture of a versatile system for indoor positioning and navigation, with samples of implementation. Our aim was to provide a software back-end which was reusable and highly configurable according to the physical structure of the environment, the context of use and the users' needs and preferences, with particular attention to special features related to accessibility.

The data model and UIs designed for the system operators were conceived to make its configuration as intuitive as possible. Our architecture is generalizable, provided that each electronic device associated to a POI broadcasts a unique identifier; anyway, depending on the associated transmitter, a POI may broadcast richer information, such as data collected by sensors, or even a URL [23, 24] We are planning to provide the POI object with more optional fields as a consequence. We will also investigate more aspects related to accessibility for users with visual impairments; to this extent, we are planning to expand our architecture to include wearable technologies, such as haptic bracelets [5]. This would imply to enhance our backend model with more accessibility options, as such devices allow for more complex and semantically significant haptic hints.

Acknowledgements. This work was funded by the Italian Ministry of University and Scientific Research through the TIGHT PRIN Project - Tactile InteGration for Humans and arTificial systems.

References

1. Accessible Maps - Project homepage: https://accessiblemaps.de/?page_id=215&lang=en
2. Ahmetovic, D., Gleason, C., Ruan, C., Kitani, K., Takagi, H., Asakawa, C.: NavCog: a navigational cognitive assistant for the blind. In: Proceedings of the 18th International Conference on Human-Computer Interaction with Mobile Devices and Services (MobileHCI 2016). Association for Computing Machinery, New York, NY, USA, pp. 90–99 (2016)
3. Alarifi, A., et al.: Ultra wideband indoor positioning technologies: analysis and recent advances. Sensors, **16**(5), 707 (2016)
4. Ballantyne, M., Jha, A., Jacobsen, A., Hawker, J.S., El-Glaly, Y.N.: Study of accessibility guidelines of mobile applications. In: Proceedings of the 17th International Conference on Mobile and Ubiquitous Multimedia (MUM). Association for Computing Machinery, New York, NY, USA, pp. 305–315 (2018)
5. Barontini, F., Catalano, M.G., Pallottino, L., Leporini, B., Bianchi, M.: Integrating wearable Haptics and obstacle avoidance for the visually impaired in indoor navigation: a user-centered approach. IEEE Trans. Haptics, **14**(1), 109-122 (2021)
6. Ghiani, G., Leporini, B., Paternò, F.: Supporting orientation for blind people using museum guides. In: CHI 2008 Extended Abstracts on Human Factors in Computing Systems. Association for Computing Machinery, New York, NY, USA, pp. 3417–3422 (2008)
7. Google Maps website: https://developers.google.com/maps?hl=en
8. Guerreiro, J., Ahmetovic, D., Sato, D., Kitani, K., Asakawa, C.: Airport accessibility and navigation assistance for people with visual impairments. In: Proceedings of the 2019 CHI Conference on Human Factors in Computing Systems. Association for Computing Machinery, New York, NY, USA, vol. 16, pp. 1–14 (2019)
9. He, Z., Cui, B., Zhou, W., Yokoi, S.: A proposal of interaction system between visitor and collection in museum hall by iBeacon. In: 10th International Conference on Computer Science & Education (ICCSE), pp. 427–430 (2015)
10. Ivanov., R.: RSNAVI: an RFID-based context-aware indoor navigation system for the blind. CompSysTech 2012 (2012)
11. Jørstad, I., Van Thanh, D., Dustdar, S.: Personalisation of Future Mobile Services (2004)
12. Khan, A., Khusro, S.: An insight into smartphone-based assistive solutions for visually impaired and blind people: issues, challenges and opportunities. Univ. Access Inf. Soc. **20**(2), 265–298 (2020). https://doi.org/10.1007/s10209-020-00733-8

13. Kanaris, L., Kokkinis, A., Liotta,A., Stavrou, S.: Fusing Bluetooth beacon data with Wi-Fi Radiomaps for improved indoor localization. Sensors, **17**(4), 812 (2017)
14. Karam, S., Vosselman, G., Peter, M., Hosseinyalamdary, S., Lehtola, V.: Design, calibration, and evaluation of a backpack indoor mobile mapping system. Remote. Sens. **11**(8), 905 (2019)
15. Martínez-Sala, A., Losilla, F., Sánchez-Aarnoutse, J., García-Haro, J.: Design, implementation and evaluation of an indoor navigation system for visually impaired people. Sensors, **15**(12), 32168-32187 (2015)
16. McArthur, J.J.: A Building Information Management (BIM) framework and supporting case study for existing building operations. Maint. Sustain. Procedia Eng. **118**, 1104–1111 (2015)
17. OpenStreetMap Tags reference: https://wiki.openstreetmap.org/wiki/Simple_Indoor_Tagging
18. OpenStreetMap website: https://wiki.openstreetmap.org/
19. Otero, R., Lagüela, S., Garrido, I., Arias, P.: Mobile indoor mapping technologies: a review. Autom. Constr. **120**, 103399 (2020)
20. Plikynas, D., Žvironas, A., Budrionis, A., Gudauskis, M.: Indoor navigation systems for visually impaired persons: mapping the features of existing technologies to user needs. Sensors, **20**(3), 636 (2020)
21. Schadler, T.: Mapping Trends, Part Two: Indoor Positioning and Mapping Standards, 20 Nov 2019 https://www.forbes.com/sites/forrester/2019/11/20/mapping-trends-part-two-indoor-positioning-and-mapping-standards/?sh=418fa33eba57
22. Subedi, S., Pyun, J.: A survey of smartphone-based indoor positioning system using RF-based wireless technologies. Sensors, **20**(24), 7230 (2020)
23. The official Eddystone protocol specification: https://github.com/google/eddystone/blob/master/protocol-specification.md
24. The official iBeacon documentation: https://developer.apple.com/ibeacon/
25. Wang, C., Chen, Y., Zheng, S., Liao, H.: Gender and age differences in using indoor maps for wayfinding in real environments. ISPRS Int. J. Geo Inf. **8**(1), 11 (2019)
26. Lu, C.X., Rosa, P., Zhao, S., Wang, B., et al.: See through smoke: robust indoor mapping with low-cost mmWave radar. In: Proceedings of the 18th International Conference on Mobile Systems, Applications, and Services (2020)

Enhancing the Blind and Partially Sighted Visitors' Experience in Museums Through Integrating Assistive Technologies, Multisensory and Interactive Approaches

Roberto Vaz[1]([✉]) [iD], Diamantino Freitas[1] [iD], and António Coelho[1,2] [iD]

[1] Faculty of Engineering, University of Porto, 4200 465 Porto, Portugal
`{robertovaz,dfreitas,acoelho}@fe.up.pt`
[2] INESC TEC, 4200-465 Porto, Portugal

Abstract. Despite the growing concern and several efforts to make museums accessible to visually impaired publics, their participation in these institutions is still limited, frustrating their desired inclusion. These visitors often experience multiple barriers in museological environments, and there is a lack of assistive technologies to promote access to exhibits, allow contextual information, and support mobility and orientation inside museum spaces.

This paper presents the accessible, interactive, and multisensory exhibition "Mysteries of the Art of Healing", which is organized in ten moments of an on-site visit to a history and science museum in Portugal, mediated by a set of technological solutions: an interactive 3D layout plan of the museum, seven high-fidelity prototypes of accessible interactives with thirteen 3D replicas, and one mobile application that acts as an assistive navigation guide during the entire visit. For its development, several principles proposed by a group of 72 blind and partially sighted persons to improve their autonomy during visits to museums were taken into account, namely: to provide sensory, intellectual, and physical access throughout the entire museum experience.

Evaluation results with 25 visually impaired participants revealed the applicability of the developed solutions within this museum visit context, and global satisfaction results showed to be very positive and correlated to four variables: pleasantness of interacting with digitally fabricated objects, entertainment provided by the ten experiences, interaction with the developed accessible interactives, and pleasantness regarding the handling of manually fabricated replicas.

Keywords: Visual impairments · Museums · Accessibility · Technology · Visitor experience · Multimodal · Multisensorial

1 Introduction

Museums undertake the hard mission of preserving humanity's heritage while exhibiting and communicating this heritage to provide society with insights and opportunities to experience art, culture, history, and sciences, among other subjects. This complexity

M. Antona and C. Stephanidis (Eds.): HCII 2022, LNCS 13309, pp. 521–540, 2022.
https://doi.org/10.1007/978-3-031-05039-8_38

increases when dealing with publics with impairments since an equal access to those places and exhibitions that include all members of society is expected.

Being aware that an important part of the world population lives with different types of disabilities, museums are, more than ever, conscious of the importance of including these individuals and welcoming them in their spaces, exhibitions, and programs [1]. In fact, the World Health Organization [2] estimates that 2.2 billion people globally have a vision impairment, of whom about 36 million are blind, 217 million have moderate to severe vision impairment, 188.5 live with mild visual impairment, and 1.8 billion have near vision impairments.

Despite the social functions of museums being at the very core of their existence, a recent report from the European Union [3] stressed the inaccessibility of cultural premises, venues, and contents as barriers to visually impaired citizens' participation in culture. Regarding their visits to museums, it is estimated that only 5.5% of these persons visit museums in Europe [4], which exposes a significant potential market.

Several authors [5, 6] relate barriers to the blind and partially sighted visitors' participation with the fact that museums remain mostly visually oriented. The situation is worsened by a frequent lack of physical, intellectual, and sensory access to exhibits or replicas, increased by the inaccessibility to use information and communication technology-based alternatives or augmentative communication resources that may allow different interactions to sighted visitors [7–9].

Even though visually impaired visitors are considered one of the most difficult groups to address in museums, information and communication technology can contribute to a beneficial impact on serving these publics by diminishing the barriers to accessibility [8, 9], although being rarely used. Moreover, positive economic effects are expected with the implementation of inclusive digital technologies to promote access to exhibitions [10], since they offer new possibilities to interact with museums and their themes, which can also bring non-disabled visitors closer to museum collections, broadening their sensory experiences [11].

This paper aims to contribute to the fields of human-computer interaction and accessibility in museums by presenting the accessible exhibition "Mysteries of the Art of Healing: A multisensory experience over 5000 years of history", developed for the Pharmacy Museum of Porto (Portugal) as a result of the doctoral research of the first author [12]. This exhibition – mediated by technological solutions to promote interactive and multisensory experiences during the on-site visit – was conceptualized and implemented by taking into account an integrative framework previously co-created with 72 visually impaired persons [13] to improve their autonomy during visits to museums: to provide sensory, intellectual, and physical access throughout the entire museum experience.

The article begins with the discussion of assistive technologies to enhance visually impaired visitors' experiences in museums. It proceeds with the process of designing, prototyping, and implementing the accessible exhibition, followed by the evaluation results by 25 visually impaired participants concerning: hedonic and pragmatic aspects of the interaction with eight high-fidelity prototypes, their perceptions of the visiting experience and global satisfaction. The article ends with some conclusions and future work directions.

2   Contributions of Accessible Digital Interactives for Visually Impaired Visitors in Museums

By using digital media solutions as mediators to increase the accessibility of exhibitions and spaces, some museums are allowing visually impaired patrons to have more enthusiastic and inclusive experiences [9].

Haptic interfaces, can benefit from the dynamic nature of the kinesthetic sense and generate forces, allowing for the exploration of virtual copies of museum and gallery collections, solving, as well, the issue that some institutions face regarding the storage for a duplicate collection of physical replicas. They can mainly contribute to enhancing the sensory access of those virtual replicas. However, when multimodal approaches are used, the intellectual access can be increased, as well, by audio description and other complementary sounds [10, 14].

Other museums are using 3D-scanning and printing technologies to provide digitally augmented touch replicas, offering multisensory experiences (tactile and auditive) that help blind and partially sighted visitors formulate mental images of the objects [15, 16]. With Near Field Communication (NFC) tags, touch-sensitive sensors, and others embedded inside the objects, these solutions can enhance visually impaired patrons' sensory and intellectual accessibility. Despite enabling visitors to interactively obtain contextual information about the exhibits, they also offer the advantages of reconstructing their original form.

In turn, gesture-based interactive tactile reliefs tracked users' interactions by computer-vision systems, which facilitates the exploration of specific parts in more detail, enriched by contextual audio description [15, 17]. They are particularly useful to provide access to bas-reliefs of 2D original artworks, like paintings and photos. In this case, sensory and intellectual accessibility can be improved through multimodality.

Other projects [18–20] relate to the use of assistive technologies to promote better physical access, autonomous indoor navigation, and wayfinding in museums. These solutions are based on hyper-directional guidance systems [18], and mobile applications with sound instructions, connected to Bluetooth low energy (BLE) beacons to update users' current location [19], and computer vision to identify tags placed throughout the visiting path floor [20].

Different from the explored solutions, the project of Anagnostakis et al. [21] allows these visitors to use a hybrid solution that supports their orientation and mobility, together with the possibility of touching exhibits and knowing more about them by listening to contextual audio descriptions. Approaches like this one seem to be the more suitable for the in-museum experience, taking into account a previous research conducted with 72 blind and partially sighted individuals that allowed to co-create an integrative and multisensory framework to enhance future experiences in museums for these publics, based on their expectations and necessities [13]. Furthermore, most of the reviewed projects only propose multisensory strategies combining touch and audio, but none of them explored olfactory or tasting opportunities.

The following section explores the steps involved in designing, prototyping, and implementing an accessible, interactive, and multisensory exhibition, based on several dimensions of the co-created framework. This project aims to be an example of how visually impaired visitors' limited experiences in museums can be surpassed and their visits enhanced by moving beyond accessibility: by embracing inclusion and focusing on the creation of multimodal and multisensory human-computer technological approaches to foster engaging and exciting visiting opportunities, while encouraging their spontaneous and autonomous participation.

3   Design, Prototyping and Implementing the Accessible Interactive Exhibition "Mysteries of the Art of Healing"

The "Mysteries of the Art of Healing: A multisensory experience over 5000 years of history" was laid out across the entire floor of the Pharmacy Museum of Porto's permanent exhibition to allow visually impaired visitors the same experience of moving through the entire museum space and stimulate a genuine sense of inclusion.

The exhibition unfolds in ten accessible stops – highlighted in Fig. 1 in distinct colors and with a brief description – each exploring a specific museological theme, mediated by ubiquitous technologies that allow visitors to have autonomous and non-conventional interactions with replicas of exhibits (points #1 to #7) and exhibition spaces of the museum (points #0, #8 and #9).

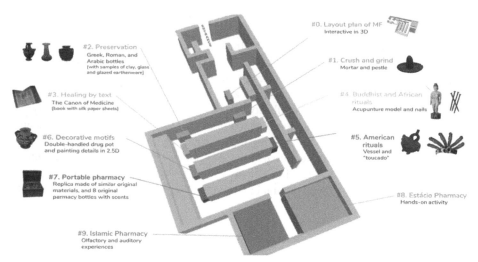

Fig. 1. Overview of the exhibition "Mysteries of the Art of Healing" conceptualized for the Pharmacy Museum of Porto.

After the #0 interactive, the following accessible point communicates the importance of crushing and grinding substances for prehistoric humans. Next, ancient civilizations started to store and preserve their prepared pharmacological substances. The third stop explores the theme of healing by text and its importance. The following accessible point conveys the theme of rituals for healing in four world locations. The storytelling proceeds with the exploration of middle-aged pharmaceutical ceramics and their decorative motifs, followed by the theme of the portable pharmacies. The visit ends in actual Estácio (old corporate) and Islamic (example of style) pharmacies, where visitors can explore them while learning their history.

During the visit, individuals can therefore experience the museum in multisensory ways, by independently interacting with eight high-fidelity prototypes that automatically detect the user's actions and promote sensory and intellectual access:

- A 3D-printed layout plan of the museum (point #0, in Fig. 1), with eleven interactive areas that render contextual audio-described contents when pressed. The tactile exploration of this 3D-layout plan introduces information to visitors about: the exhibition and the physical space where it happens; the locations of the eight accessible interactives and the 3D-replicas of artifacts from the museum collection that each one contains; the location of two real pharmacies existing at the museum; and the related museological themes which will be explored in each interactive point.
- Seven high-fidelity prototypes of accessible interactives, exhibiting a total of twelve 3D-replicas of museum objects and one bas-relief, available to be handled during the visit. Whenever visitors use these objects (by handling them or opening them), the user interfaces' corresponding systems automatically present voice-overs with museological and audio-described information related to the corresponding exhibit. One case also incorporates olfactive user experiences (point #7, in Fig. 1), in which visitors have access to eight original pharmacy bottles of the collection containing pharmacological substances with typical odors to smell.

Concerning the visitors' physical access, one mobile application based on augmented reality conveys contextual text-to-speech audio information regarding their location and orientation inside the museum. This application acts as an assistive navigation guide throughout the entire visit, also presenting audio-described and museological information about the two real pharmacies existing at the museum (point #8 and #9, in Fig. 1). When entering these pharmacies, visitors can have tactile and audio experiences in both cases, added by an olfactive experience when entering the Islamic one (#9) – where two hidden bowls containing spices and incenses let them smell typical Islamic scents, as it seemed to be in the original environment.

Details about the development of the exhibition will be presented next.

3.1 Developing the Digitally and Manually Fabricated Objects

The eight digitally fabricated artifacts were produced through photogrammetry. First, the shapes and texture of the original artifacts were collected into digital images, allowing to obtain an average of 199 photographs for each object. The second phase of producing the digitally fabricated artifacts regarded the individual image processing in a photogrammetric software – Agisoft Metashape [22], to generate each 3D virtual model. A post-processing step followed, aiming to fill some holes resulting from 3D reconstruction errors, flatten the models' base, smooth their surfaces, and create specific holes to accommodate a real acupuncture needle (for the acupuncture model of the point #4, in Fig. 1).

Besides the eight 3D models, one bas-relief of the painting on the back of the double-handed drug pot was also developed (see the object of point #6, in Fig. 1), given that it represents an essential museological aspect of this artifact and was intended to provide visitors tactile access to this visual information.

The last phase of developing the digitally fabricated replicas was printing them, as illustrated in the left images of Fig. 2. The Ultimaker Cura software [23] was used to prepare the files, and a BQ Witbox 3D printer with 1.75 mm PLA – Polylactic Acid, white filament, was used to print the objects. All 3D-objects were printed on a real scale, excepting the acupuncture model, which was reduced by a scale factor of 1:5.

A general view of the nine digitally fabricated artifacts is presented in the image on the right of Fig. 2, allowing comparing the various objects' dimensions with a 1€ coin.

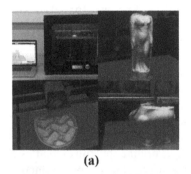

(a)

(b)

Fig. 2. From left to right: a) Illustrative photos of the 3D printing process; b) The nine digitally fabricated replicas and a 1€ coin placed next to them.

In addition to the digitally fabricated artifacts, four additional objects were manually fabricated using materials similar in texture and colors to the originals since their handling could enhance the haptic perception, and visitors with low vision who still can enjoy seeing colors could have an improved visual perception. Also, the museological aspects to convey with these exhibits had more to do with their function and materiality than with their shapes. Figure 3 presents these four fabricated objects.

Fig. 3. The four manually fabricated objects using materials similar to the originals.

3.2 Developing the 3D Interior Layout Plan of the Museum

Aiming to provide visitors with a hands-on interactive activity while introducing them to the Pharmacy Museum of Porto and its exhibition space, a 3D-layout plan of the museum's interior was developed and made available on the accessible interactive #0.

A bi-dimensional floor plan of the entire space was used as a reference to design a 3D virtual model from scratch, using the Blender software [24]. The 3D-model includes the museum entry, reception, walls, corridors, physical obstacles, the display cases containing the exhibits, and the rooms with both Estácio and Islamic pharmacies. The accessible interactives were also included on their respective locations in the museum space, so visitors could also get to know in advance where they would find them during the visit. After this, holes were designed in the virtual model for the correct fit of the eleven moveable pieces, corresponding to the eight accessible interactives, the two pharmacies, and the museum reception.

The layout plan was then 3D-printed in three stages, as illustrated in the image on the left of Fig. 4. The final result of the digitally fabricated layout plan of the museum with all parts assembled is shown on the right of Fig. 4, next to a 1€ coin. Its maximum dimensions are 343 mm in length, 197 mm in width, and 22.5 mm in height.

(a)   (b)

Fig. 4. From left to right: a) Illustrative photos of the 3D printing process; b) The 3D interior layout plan of the museum.

3.3 Conceptualizing Interaction and Development of High-Fidelity Prototypes

The next step of the exhibition development involved designing the conceptual model of interaction, creating physical constraints to accommodate the objects and the electronic systems, and implementing the conceptualized interaction model into high-fidelity prototypes.

Designing the Conceptual Model of Interaction. The conceptual model of interaction aimed to integrate the 3D objects on the tangible interfaces and establish how visitors' interaction with the systems would occur, by encouraging them to focus their attention on the voice-overs while having both hands free to explore the objects, one at a time. The design considered the inputs provided by the individuals who participated in the development of the co-created framework, and one blind collaborator validated the final conceptual model.

It was conceptualized that the act of picking up an object would identify an interest in finding out more about it (a click is provided as audio feedback, and the respective voice-over starts), while putting it back down indicates a loss of interest or lack of intention to continue accessing associated content (the respective voice-over stops gradually with a two-second fade-out audio effect). Moreover, for the cases of the replica of the book "The Canon of Medicine" (#3) and the portable pharmacy (#7), the interaction with both objects focuses on the analogy of their use in everyday-life contexts [25], respectively: opening a book to read it and closing it when finishing the reading, and opening a box to access its stored contents and closing it after.

It is worth mentioning for the cases of the three accessible interactives which have two or three replicas (i.e., #2, #4 and #5), that if a visitor is already handling one replica and picks up another one (or two when applied), an audio warning message is presented, informing users about the systems' correct operation.

For the case of the 3D layout plan, when a visitor presses a button, both haptic and audio feedback are provided, and the respective voice-over starts. The voice-over playing stops when pressing another moveable part, and a new one starts.

Implementing the Conceptual Model of Interaction into High-fidelity Prototypes. The development of the eight high-fidelity prototypes included: designing the electronic hardware system architecture for each system and conducting a technical viability study with various sensors; programming the software to support the desired interaction model; developing eight physical constraints to accommodate the exhibits and the 3D layout plan; and building everything together. A generic system architecture for the accessible interactives is presented in Fig. 5.

There are two types of user interfaces: seven accessible interactives are based on the use of one, two, or three objects (type A), while the other interface is based on push buttons connected to the moveable pieces of the 3D layout plan (type B).

For the case of the interfaces with objects (type A), LDRs – Light Dependent Resistors were placed on specific points of the physical constraints to detect light intensity variations whenever objects are picked up, opened, closed, or put back in their respective places. It was also necessary to create independent electric circuits for each user interface

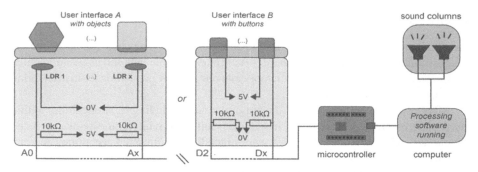

Fig. 5. A generic system architecture overview of the eight accessible interactives.

and connect it to Arduino Leonardo microcontrollers' analog input ports (indicated as A0 and Ax in the figure).

Regarding the type B user interface, visitors can interact with eleven moveable pieces, each one connected to a push-button. When pressed, these switches connect two points in an electric circuit and are connected to an Arduino Leonardo's digital input ports (indicated as D2 and Dx in the figure).

The software running on the microcontrollers interprets the signals received from the LDRs and the push-buttons every 100 ms. Based on these inputs, it is decided what information must be presented to users (feedback, voice-overs, or warning messages). This decision is then interpreted by the open-source Processing software [26] running on the associated computer, connected to the Arduino microcontroller via serial communication. Finally, the corresponding information defined in the conceptual model of interaction is presented by loudspeakers.

Figure 6 aims to illustrate the process of assembling the high-fidelity prototypes, where it is possible to observe: the eight physical constraints developed to accommodate the replicas, the connections made on the bottom of these structures and inside objects, and the physical structure developed to accommodate the 3D layout plan.

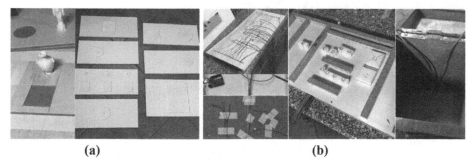

(a)   (b)

Fig. 6. From left to right: a) Photos of the developing process of the physical constraints; b) Photos of the implementation of the high-fidelity prototypes.

3.4   An Assistive Guide with Location-Based Information

The NaviLens mobile app [27] was used to enhance visitors' physical access inside the museum, allowing adding contextual information to printable tags and using augmented reality to guide users in outdoor and indoor environments by presenting them orientation information through audio.

After testing this solution inside the museum and concluding its applicability within this project, several tags were placed in specific points to provide visitors with an assisted orientation and wayfinding. The tags were placed at the museum reception, on each exhibit case, and at the Estácio and Islamic pharmacies' entrance. Then, contextual information was added for each tag, accordingly, to inform visitors about which area they were approaching. The tags were also included to sign the beginning of the exhibition and inform visitors that they should keep walking along corridors to arrive at the next accessible interactives and pharmacies.

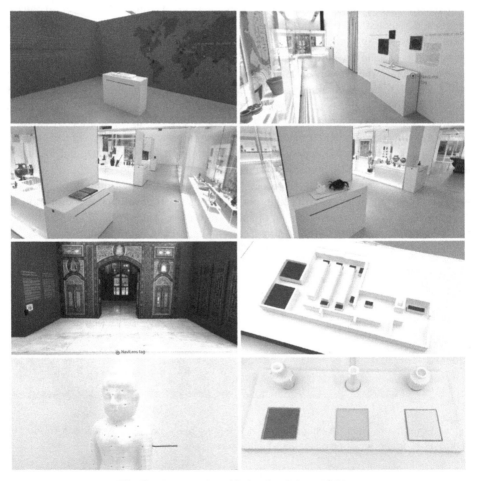

Fig. 7. Photographs with details of the exhibition.

3.5 The "Mysteries of the Art of Healing" Exhibition

The exhibition "Mysteries of the Art of Healing: A multisensory experience over 5000 years of history" was installed in March 2021 at the Pharmacy Museum of Porto. Some illustrative photographs of the exhibition are presented in Fig. 7, where it is possible to observe: the eight accessible interactives with their respective exhibits displayed on their tops; some of the NaviLens tags placed on the accessible interactives and at the entrance of the Islamic pharmacy; the 3D layout plan of the museum finished, with red velvet covering the eleven interactive pieces; the acupuncture model with a real needle stuck; and the samples of clay, glass, and glazed earthenware corresponding to the original materials of the replicas of Greek, Roman, and Arabic bottles.

4 Evaluation

4.1 Sampling Process, Research Instrument and Tools for Data Analysis

Aiming to randomly sample participants for the evaluation phase, the information about the exhibition was spread to 12 associations, 3 schools, and 5 other institutions working with visually impaired people, mainly located in the North and Center Regions of continental Portugal; in 4 private groups of visually impaired persons on Facebook; and on social media to the general public.

The research instrument was used in three different moments of the visits for gathering quantitative and qualitative data related to the user experience and the visiting experience:

- An initial questionnaire with 16 questions (pre-visit): to understand the profile of the participants, their habits regarding visits to museums before the COVID-19 pandemics, their previous knowledge about the museum, and usage of technology.
- Observations (during the visit): about the participants' interaction with the 3D layout plan and the other seven accessible interactives. It was also used the think-aloud technique with 4 participants during their visits to gather data about their verbal reactions, comments, and expressed thoughts in real-time.
- Semi-structured interviews with 20 questions (after the visit): to gather data about the participants' perception of the interaction with the accessible interactives and exhibits; their perceptions of multisensory experiences, the acquired knowledge, and the integrated access; and their perception of the visiting experience.

The evaluation phase occurred between the 5th and the 17th of April of 2021 *in situ*, during which 25 visually impaired persons visited the exhibition and accepted to participate in the study. The visits lasted on average for 59 min and 10 s (SD = 12 min and 47 s), ranging from a maximum of 1 h and 28 min and a minimum of 44 min.

The quantitative data gathered was processed to produce descriptive statistics and exploratory data analysis about the research topic, and inferential statistics for testing the correlation between the global satisfaction and the assessed aspects of the experience. The interviews and data gathered from the think-aloud were transcribed manually, and a qualitative analysis based on thematic analysis [28] was performed.

4.2 Evaluation Results

Participants' Profile. The 25 participants had different degrees of visual impairment: 52% reported to be blind and 48% partially sighted. Regarding the blind individuals, 28% were early blind, and 24% were late blind, with an average age of vision loss of 32 years old (M = 32; SD = 12.5). Considering the visual degrees of low vision visitors', 20% had severe, 16% moderate, and 12% mild visual impairments.

The sample was composed of 52% females and 48% male participants, with ages ranging from 11 to 88 years old (M = 43.5; SD = 23.9). Their predominant age group was between 42–49 (24%), followed by 13 or younger (16%), and 74 or older (16%). The age groups of 14–17 and 50–57 relate to 12% of the sample in both cases, while the ages between 26–33 and 34–41 represent 8% and 4%, respectively.

Regarding the visitors' education level, the basic school represents the highest education level completed by 52% of the participants, the secondary school by 16%, and 32% mentioned they had completed higher education: 16% hold a bachelor's degree, 12% a master's degree, and one participant holds a doctoral degree. Their occupation was also diversified: 32% were retired, 8% were unemployed but actively searching for a job, 28% were students, and the remaining eight participants (32%) mentioned distinct occupations: researcher, Braille specialist, archive conservator, economist, programmer, translator, businesswoman and assistant operator.

Visitors came from diverse places of continental Portugal to attend the exhibition: 76% lived in the District of Porto, 12% in the District of Aveiro, and the remaining three individuals came from Lisbon (4%), Braga (4%), and Bragança (4%).

Technology Use. All participants stated they use ICT in their daily lives, mentioning it is very common to use their mobile phones or smartphones and computers almost every day for work or leisure purposes. When asked to indicate the level of difficulty or facility regarding its use (measured in a 5-point Likert scale), the average of the answers was 3.88 (SD = 1.27), meaning participants considered ICT use close to easy.

Museums Visiting Habits and Awareness of the Pharmacy Museum. Concerning the visiting habits before the COVID-19 pandemic, the participants indicated they seldom visited museums (44%), visited once or twice in a year (16%), visited three or four times in a year (16%), and that they had never visited museums before (12%). On the other hand, 12% mentioned they used to go to museums at least five times a year.

When asked if they knew about the existence of the Pharmacy Museum of Porto, 92% of the participants informed they did never hear about the museum before the visit, and 8% mentioned they did know about it. However, none of the participants had ever visited the museum, meaning that this was their first visit this institution.

Regarding how they got to know about the exhibition, 44% stated friends as the primary source of information, followed by social media (32%), schools (28%), associations (20%), a Braille periodic publication (12%), by family members (8%), and in the news on the Internet (8%).

Results of the Participants' Interaction with the Accessible Interactives. The results concerning the participants' interaction with the eight accessible interactives are presented in Fig. 8, organized by the interaction aspects under analysis for each case.

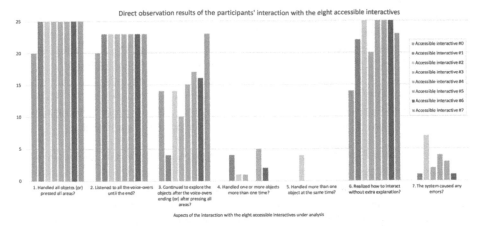

Fig. 8. Results concerning the participants' interaction with the eight accessible interactives.

Objects Handling and Pressed Areas of the 3D Layout Plan. Concerning the interactive 3D layout plan (#0), it is concluded that 80% of the participants pressed all the moveable areas while exploring it, while 20% did not. For the case of the other seven accessible interactives (#1 to #7), it was verified that the totality of participants handled all replicas of objects in exhibition.

Listening to the Voice-overs. Only the five individuals who did not press all the interactive areas of the 3D layout plan did not listen to all the voice-overs until the end (despite having listened to the voice-overs of the areas they interacted with until the end), while the remaining 80% did. Regarding the accessible interactives #1 to #7, 92% of the sample listened to all the replicas-related voice-overs until the end.

Exploration After the Voice-Overs Ending. It was verified that 56% of the participants continued to interact with the 3D layout plan after listening to all voice-overs: to tactile exploring some areas of the museum in more detail, making sense of the exhibition path to follow next, and how to exit the exhibition after the end of the visit. The portable pharmacy (#7) was the most used after the voice-overs ended, by 92% of visitors, who kept discovering and smelling the different pharmacological substances of the eight original bottles. For the accessible interactive #5, with the pre-Columbian vessel and the indigenous "toucado", 68% of individuals continued handling the objects after the end of their explanations. In the accessible interactive #6, 64% of participants dedicated extra time exploring the bas-relief of the painting. It was registered that 60% of visitors kept exploring the acupuncture model (#4) to figure out the diverse acupuncture points. The Greek, Roman, and Arabic bottles (#2) were examined by 56% of participants after hearing the respective voice-overs while sensing the material samples similar to the originals (i.e., glass, glazed earthenware, and clay). Ten visitors (40%) continued to explore the sheets of the replica of the book (#3) after listening to its audio contents. The less explored object after the audio-described information ended was the mortar and pestle (#1), in which only 16% of participants continued to sense the different irregularities mentioned in the voice-over.

Objects Handling More than One Time. 20% of visitors handled objects more than one time in the case of the accessible interactive #5, the mortar and pestle (#1) was handled more than one time by 16% of participants, the double-handled drug pot (#6) by 8%, and the Greek bottle (#2) and the book (#3) by one individual (4%), each one.

Handling More than One Object at the Same Time. This scenario was verified only for the accessible interactive #2 and happened because 16% of participants and their com-panions picked up two or the three replicas of the bottles simultaneously.

Interaction Without Extra Explanation. The 3D layout plan (#0) was the one that caused more confusion regarding its interaction: 56% of visitors understood how to interact with it without extra explanation, while 44% did not figure it out by themselves. Several participants informed they did not realize there were buttons to press, since this information was only provided by the mobile app. Concerning the cases where visitors had to pick up the exhibits, 88% realized by themselves the system's operation of the accessible interactive #1, and all participants realized how to use the others following the same interaction model (#2, #4, #5, and #6) without additional clarification. Regarding the case of having to open the book (#3), 80% figured it out by themselves, and for the case of the accessible interactive containing the portable pharmacy (#7), 92% of indi-viduals understood how to interact with it by themselves.

System Errors. 28% of the errors were verified during the participants' interaction with the accessible interactive #2, 16% with the #4, 12% with the "toucado" (#5), and 8% while using the accessible interactive #3. One error (4%) was observed for #1 and #6, respectively. For the accessible interactives #0 and #7 no errors caused by the system were registered.

Results of the Participants' Perception About the Visit. The following subsections present the results of the participants' perception about: the interaction with the accessible interactives, the multisensory experiences, learning assessment, integrated access for mobility and orientation, and the visiting experience assessment.

Perceptions About the Interaction with the Accessible Interactives. Participants evaluated both the easiness and pleasantness of interacting with the eight accessible interactives, measured in two 5-point Likert scales. The results showed a very easy interaction with the accessible interactives containing the replicas (M = 4.72; SD = 0.54) and an easy interaction with the 3D layout plan (M = 4.08; SD = 1.04). By analyzing the data related to the pleasantness of interaction, it is concluded that participants perceived it as very pleasant for all the accessible interactives, i.e., the 3D layout plan (M = 4.6; SD = 0.58) and the other seven interactives (M = 4.8; SD = 0.41).

Perceptions About the Multisensory Experiences. Visitors revealed they had very pleasant interactions while handling the digitally fabricated objects (M = 4.76; SD = 0.52) and the manually fabricated ones (M = 4.88; SD = 0.33). Regarding their perceptions about the voice-over's duration, they considered it very near the ideal (M = 2.83; SD = 0.38): the vast majority of participants highlighted the audio described contents as being out-standing, with a perfect balance between the museological themes and the objects' description. The results of the perception of entertainment provided by the eight accessible interactives revealed that the visually impaired visitors found the experiences very entertaining (M = 4.58; SD = 0.5). Their five favorite experiences were the portable pharmacy (84%), the indigenous "toucado" (48%), the Estácio pharmacy (44%), the 3D layout plan of the museum (40%) and the replica of the book (40%). When questioned about the experiences they liked the least, all participants stated all the experiences were unique and that it was unimaginable to point out one they did not like.

Perceptions of Learning. Participants perceived they had learned a lot during their visits to the exhibition (M = 3.8; SD = 0.41). When asked to provide a brief verbal resume of what they have learned, all participants mentioned at least one thing they did not know before the visit, with 46 answers registered in the total. From the thematic analysis performed, for main themes emerged: the history and evolution of the pharmacy (48%); how different civilizations deal with health and what pharmacological objects they used (44%); how some civilizations practice religious rituals to ask for health (36%); and general curiosities related to pharmacy themes (20%). Regarding what they considered that better helped their learning, all visitors mentioned it was the simultaneous combination of the handling of the objects with the voice-overs. Two representative quotations follow: "This interaction is what stimulates the interest in the piece itself", and "Given the touch and audio at the same time, I felt transported to a new world in each object". One visitor also mentioned that the sense of smell contributed to her/his learning about the pharmacological substances available at the portable pharmacy. Another participant stressed the samples of the materials provided on the accessible interactive #2 as a "genial idea because I got the whole image of the bottles from their handling, the voice-overs, and the touch of the materials".

Perceptions About the Integrated Access for Mobility and Orientation. The evaluation results revealed that visitors perceived the quality of their mental image of the museum space as good, based on exploring the interactive layout plan (M = 4.12; SD = 0.83). Concerning the use of the app for mobility and orientation – utilized only by sixteen participants (64%) – and its contribution to supporting their navigation, the evaluation results showed they perceived it as easy to use (M = 3.69; SD = 1.01). However, the app was perceived as contributing only moderately to supporting visitors' navigation throughout the museum (M = 2.75; SD = 1). These results are in line with the direct observations made during the visits: it was frequent people did not use the smartphone vertically, as initially instructed, or covered the camera lenses with their fingers, or the companions or other visitors at the museum covered the tags, so the app could not detect the tags and participants kept walking without knowing the supposed direction.

General Perceptions About the Visiting Experience. Regarding the general perceptions about the visiting experience, participants were asked to assess their autonomy and global satisfaction. Their autonomy during the visits was perceived as partially (M = 3.32; SD = 1.03), and some visitors explained that "The museum's configuration itself does not help an autonomous visit", and that "It was my first time visiting this museum, so it is normal that I'm not as autonomous as desired because I did not know the space". Concerning the assessment of global satisfaction, it was concluded that participants perceived the visiting experience as very satisfying (M = 4.56; SD = 0.58).

Results of the Correlation Analysis Between the Global Satisfaction and the Accessed Aspects of the Experience. The Spearman's rank correlation coefficient was used to test the degree of association between variables given the reduced sample of the study (n = 25), the data did not follow a normal distribution, and the use of Likert scales to assess the various aspects. A significance level of 5% was considered for the analysis of the inferential statistics, and the correlation strength was interpreted according to the classification of Evans [29].

Table 1 reports the results of the correlation between the global satisfaction expressed by participants with the various assessed aspects of their experiences of using the systems and visiting the exhibition. Its analysis allows concluding that four variables present statistical significance and are correlated to the participants' global satisfaction (presented in bold font).

Table 1. Spearman correlation between the global satisfaction of the participants' visiting experience with the assessed aspects.

	Assessed aspects of the experience	n	p-value	r
Perception about the interaction	[1.1] Perception of easiness regarding the interaction with the 3D layout plan	25	0.221	0.288
	[1.2] Perception of pleasantness regarding the interaction with the 3D layout plan	25	0.265	0.232
	[2.1] Perception of easiness regarding the interaction with the other accessible interactives	25	0.065	0.375
	[2.2] Perception of pleasantness regarding the interaction with the other accessible interactives	25	**0.023**	**0.452**
Perception about the multisensory experiences	[3] Perception of pleasantness regarding the interaction with the digitally fabricated objects	25	**<0.001**	**0.656**
	[4] Perception of pleasantness regarding the interaction with the manually fabricated objects	25	**0.038**	**0.417**
	[5] Perception of the duration of the voice-overs	24	0.591	−0.115
	[6] Perception of entertainment about the experiences provided	24	**0.004**	**0.567**
Perceptions of learning	[9] Perception of learning during the visit	25	0.396	0.178

(continued)

Table 1. (*continued*)

	Assessed aspects of the experience	n	p-value	r
Perception of the integrated access	[12] Perception of quality of the mental image of the museum space	25	0.09	0.346
	[13] Perception of difficulty of using the app for mobility and orientation	16	0.912	0.03
	[14] Perception of the app's contribution to supporting navigation	16	0.198	–0.339
	[15] Perception of autonomy during the visit	25	0.209	0.26

The first correlated variable was the *Perception of pleasantness regarding the interaction with the digitally fabricated objects*, with a strong positive correlation (r = 0.656), which was supported by several commentaries that individuals made during their interviews, like, "Touching the objects was the best part of the visit".

The variable *Perception of entertainment about the experiences provided* was the second most related factor, presenting a moderate positive correlation (r = 0.567) with the global satisfaction expressed. This entertainment was provided during the ten accessible experiences, enabling the combination of touching and handling activities with the voice-overs' contents and smelling experiences in two cases. Two representative statements follow: "I'm extremely satisfied, the exhibition is very well organized. It seems that time has flown, and I didn't notice!", and "I completely forgot the world outside".

The third variable, *Perception of pleasantness regarding the interaction with the other accessible interactives*, presented a moderate positive correlation (r = 0.452). For this case, the vast majority of participants mentioned during their interviews that they enjoyed simply picking up the objects to start hearing their contents and putting them back down when finishing, having both hands free to interact with them all the time. One participant commented, "The visit was amazing! I've visited many museums in my life, but I've never seen anything like this! This new technology is amazing!".

The fourth factor correlated with the global satisfaction expressed by the participants was the *Perception of pleasantness regarding the interaction with the manually fabricated objects*, with a moderate positive correlation (r = 0.417). This result is not completely unexpected since the assessment of the favorite accessible interactives included three objects in the four highest rank: the portable pharmacy, the "toucado", and the replica of the book. Furthermore, the observed visitors' reactions when interacting with them for the first time showed they were enjoying these experiences.

5   Conclusions and Future Research

The overall visiting experience of the "Mysteries of the Art of Healing" exhibition can be concluded as being very positive. Although about 68% of individuals were not regular museum attendees, they informed leaving the visit very satisfied and reported feeling curiosity, enthusiasm, engagement, happiness, surprise, and interest, which was possible to observe during their visits.

The interaction with the accessible interactives displaying the objects proved to be easier than with the one with the 3D-layout plan of the museum, but the interaction with all of them proved to be very pleasant. The direct observation of the users' interaction with the eight accessible interactives allowed concluding that the vast majority of visitors handled all replicas and pressed all the areas of the layout plan, listened to all the voice-overs and, in some cases, continued to explore the objects after the ending of their audio contents. This last aspect can inform that the physical characteristics of the objects in the exhibition and the different experiences provided by each one captivated the visitors' attention. These factors, added to the near-ideal voice clips' durations and the highlighted perfect balance between its audio description contents, seemed to be the key for the individuals' perception of learning a lot during the visit.

Some interaction errors caused by the systems were verified, which need to be addressed in the future. However, most errors were observed during the use of the app for orientation and wayfinding, concluded by participants as only moderately support-ing their navigation inside the museum and not contributing to their sense of autonomy. Several visitors suggested complementing it with physical information, as tactile floor pavings augmented with sound, and future research should study how other auditory and vibro-tactile technologies can contribute to assist their mobility and orientation. Never-theless, this aspect was not correlated with the global satisfaction, which concluded as principal factors: the handling of the digitally and manually fabricated objects, the level of entertainment experienced during the visits, and the perception of pleasantness while interacting with the accessible interactives #1 to #7.

Despite the objectives of the evaluation stage contemplated only the 25 visitors with visual impairments, some curious behaviors of the spontaneous public (including children, teenagers, adults, and seniors), were observed while using the accessible inter-actives, like handling the 3D objects and searching for the originals on the permanent exhibition while listening to their contents. Those observations allowed concluding that the potential of this project was not only for the visually impaired visitors but also for the sighted ones. It is an example that the effort for accessibility ended benefiting other persons during their visits to the museum, allowing them to explore replicas of the collection through touch, sound, and smell, apart from vision.

Acknowledgments. This work is a result of the project Operation NORTE-08–5369-FSE-000049 supported by Norte Portugal Regional Operational Programme (NORTE 2020), under the POR-TUGAL 2020 Partnership Agreement, through the European Social Fund (ESF). The authors also acknowledge Agisoft LLC for supporting this research, Neosistec for making available NaviLens tags, Dr. Marisa Silva, Dr. António Silva, and all participants and individuals who contributed to this research.

References

1. ICOM: The theme 2020 – Museums for equality, diversity and inclusion, http://imd.icom. museum/international-museum-day-2019/museums-as-cultural-hubs-the-future-of-tradit ion/. Accessed 03 Feb 2022
2. World Health Organization: World report on vision. World Health Organization, Geneva (2019)
3. Pasikowska-Schnass, M.: Access to Cultural Life for People with Disabilities. European Union, Brussels (2019)
4. Dash, K., Grohall, G.: Economic Impact of Creating and Exhibiting 3d Objects for Blind and Visually Impaired People in Museums. Economica Institute of Economic Research, Vienna (2016)
5. Devile, E., Kastenholz, E.: Accessible tourism experiences: the voice of people with visual disabilities. J. Policy Res. Tourism, Leisure Events **10**(3), 265–285 (2018). https://doi.org/10. 1080/19407963.2018.1470183
6. Hayhoe, S.: Blind Visitor Experiences at Art Museums. Rowman & Littlefield, London (2017)
7. Vaz, R., Freitas, D., Coelho, A.: Visiting museums from the perspective of visually impaired visitors: experiences and accessibility resources in Portuguese museums. Int. J. Inclusive Museum **14**(1), 71–93 (2021). https://doi.org/10.18848/1835-2014/CGP/v14i01/71-93
8. Carrizosa, H., Sheehy, K., Rix, J., Seale, J., Hayhoe, S.: Designing technologies for museums: accessibility and participation issues. J. Enabling Technol. **14**(1), 31–39 (2020). https://doi. org/10.1108/JET-08-2019-0038
9. Vaz, R., Freitas, D., Coelho, A.: Blind and visually impaired visitors' experiences in museums: increasing accessibility through assistive technologies. Int. J. Inclusive Museum **13**(2), 57–80 (2020). https://doi.org/10.18848/1835-2014/CGP/v13i02/57-80
10. Andrade, E., et al.: Inclusive Technologies in Museums: For a Better Access to Culture for Blind and Visually Impaired People. Economica Institute of Economic Research, Vienna (2015)
11. Eardley, A., Mineiro, C., Neves, J., Ride, P.: Redefining access: embracing multimodality, memorability and shared experience in museums. Curator Museum J. **59**(3), 263–286 (2016). https://doi.org/10.1111/cura.12163
12. Vaz, R.: Blind or Partially Sighted Visitors in Museums: Enhancing the Visitors' Experience through Assistive Technologies. University of Porto, Porto (2021)
13. Vaz, R., Freitas, D., Coelho, A.: Perspectives of visually impaired visitors on museums: towards an integrative and multisensory framework to enhance the museum experience. In: 9th International Conference on Software Development and Technologies for Enhancing Accessibility and Fighting Info-exclusion, pp. 17–21. ACM, New York (2020). https://doi. org/10.1145/3439231.3439272
14. Romeo, K., Chottin, M., Ancet, P., Pissaloux, E.: Access to artworks and its mediation by and for visually impaired persons. In: Miesenberger, K., Kouroupetroglou, G. (eds.) ICCHP 2018. LNCS, vol. 10897, pp. 233–236. Springer, Cham (2018). https://doi.org/10.1007/978-3-319-94274-2_32
15. Reichinger, A., Schröder, S., Löw, C., Sportun, S., Reichl, P., Purgathofer, W.: Spaghetti, sink and sarcophagus: design explorations of tactile artworks for visually impaired people. In: Proceedings of the 9th Nordic Conference on Human-Computer Interaction, pp. 82:1–82:6. ACM, New York (2016). https://doi.org/10.1145/2971485.2996471
16. Quero, L., Bartolomé, J., Cho, J.: Accessible visual artworks for blind and visually impaired people: comparing a multimodal approach with tactile graphics. Electronics **10**(3), 297 (2021). https://doi.org/10.3390/electronics10030297

17. Reichinger, A., Carrizosa, H.G., Travnicek, C.: Designing an interactive tactile relief of the meissen table fountain. In: Miesenberger, K., Kouroupetroglou, G. (eds.) ICCHP 2018. LNCS, vol. 10897, pp. 209–216. Springer, Cham (2018). https://doi.org/10.1007/978-3-319-94274-2_28
18. Hishida, Y., Hirayama, M.: A route guiding system for visually impaired persons using a hyper-directional speaker. In: 2018 International Workshop on Advanced Image Technology (IWAIT), pp. 1–4. IEEE, New York (2018). https://doi.org/10.1109/IWAIT.2018.8369668
19. Meliones, A., Sampson, D.: Blind MuseumTourer: a system for self-guided tours in museums and blind indoor navigation. Technologies **6**(1), 4 (2018). https://doi.org/10.3390/technolog ies6010004
20. Croce, D., et al.: Supporting autonomous navigation of visually impaired people for experiencing cultural heritage. In: Seychell, D., Dingli, A. (eds.) Rediscovering Heritage Through Technology. SCI, vol. 859, pp. 25–46. Springer, Cham (2020). https://doi.org/10.1007/978-3-030-36107-5_2
21. Anagnostakis, G., et al.: Accessible museum collections for the visually impaired: combining tactile exploration, audio descriptions and mobile gestures. In: Proceedings of the 18th International Conference on Human-Computer Interaction with Mobile Devices and Services Adjunct, pp. 1021–1025. ACM, New York (2016). https://doi.org/10.1145/2957265.2963118
22. Agisoft Metashape Homepage, https://www.agisoft.com. Accessed 03 Feb 2022
23. Ultimaker Cura Homepage, https://ultimaker.com/software/ultimaker-cura. Accessed 03 Feb 2022
24. Blender Homepage, https://www.blender.org. Accessed 03 Feb 2022
25. Preece, J., Rogers, Y., Sharp, H.: Interaction Design: Beyond Human-Computer Interaction. John Wiley & Sons, West Sussex (2015)
26. Processing Homepage, https://processing.org. Accessed 03 Feb 2022
27. NaviLens Homepage, https://www.navilens.com/en/. Accessed 03 Feb 2022
28. Braun, V., Clarke, V.: Using thematic analysis in psychology. Qual. Res. Psychol. **3**(2), 77–101 (2006). https://doi.org/10.1191/1478088706qp063oa
29. Evans, J.: Straightforward Statistics for the Behavioral Sciences. Thomson Brooks/Cole Publishing Co., Pacific Grive (1996)

Geometric Thinking and Learning Through Educational Video Gaming in Learners with Visual Disabilities

Natalia Vidal[✉] and Jaime Sánchez

University of Chile, Santiago, Chile
nataliamelissavv@gmail.com, jsanchez@dcc.uchile.cl

Abstract. Much of the educational software that supports geometry learning is intended for sighted children, since its main stimulus is based on images, which do not provide enough information to children with vision problems. Consequently, software has been developed to support geometry learning in blind students, however, the understanding of the subject by these students remains complicated.

This work consists of the development of a video game to support children who are blind attending 5th to 8th year of primary school in the construction of concepts and geometric thinking in everyday contexts. The game was implemented for mobile phones with touch screen, allowing an interaction based mainly on vibration and sound.

In the game, called GeoHouse, the player must help with a house move, placing objects in a new house. The geometric exercises include the search for tiles in the Cartesian plane and their isometric transformations, concepts that are studied in primary school.

Subsequently, usability evaluations were carried out with both children who are blind and their math teachers. The level of acceptance of the video game by the students was quite varied, while teachers considered it a useful tool applicable to their classes. Impact evaluations were also carried out, resulting that the video game helped students learn after interacting with the software for a longer time.

Keywords: Children with visual disabilities impaired · Video game · Geometry learning

1 Introduction

Diverse educational computing platforms are used to support the teaching of geometry in schools. However, much of this software is intended for sighted children, since their main stimulus is based on images of figures, numbers, and theorems, shown on a computer screen, which provide little or no information to children with visual disabilities.

Currently, children with visual disabilities are instructed in a special way to learn geometry, using different materials with relief and well-defined shapes. However, it is not an easy task since the mental maps that these students construct are different from those of a sighted person.

M. Antona and C. Stephanidis (Eds.): HCII 2022, LNCS 13309, pp. 541–555, 2022.
https://doi.org/10.1007/978-3-031-05039-8_39

Consequently, some software has been developed to respond to this issue for learners with visual disabilities, whose stimuli are mainly based on audio and tactile sensations. However, the understanding of geometry and its application in everyday life remains complex for these children.

This work presents the design, implementation, and evaluation of GeoHouse, a videogame created to support children with total and partial blindness in the construction of geometric concepts and thinking in an everyday context. In this way, students who are blind will better understand the correspondence between a 3-dimensional place (everyday environment) and its representation on a 2-dimensional map (Cartesian plane).

Main users are children with total or partial blindness from 5th to 8th year of primary school and, also, differential math teachers, who can provide and configure the game.

The software was developed for Android mobile phones with touch screen, using Unity3D and C#. The interaction occurs through touches on the screen, vibration and sound, also considering the use of contrasting colors for children with partial blindness.

In the game's story, the player has to help a friend called Lucy to move objects inside a house. The player has to use a 2D map to find out where each object should go as a result of a geometry exercise on a Cartesian plane.

The geometric exercises consist of searching for specific tiles on the floor (equivalent to squares on a Cartesian plane) or their isometric transformations (translations, rotations, and reflections). The game has three levels of difficulty for each type of exercise and a tutorial level.

2 Related Work

Most of the technological tools aimed at people with visual disabilities help develop their orientation and mobility (O&M) skills. Some of them are the following:

- Legend of Iris [1]: Video game for children inspired by The Legend of Zelda that includes puzzles with 3D audio. It is played with a computer, headphones and a joystick control. Players can also use Oculus Rift headphones, allowing them to orient themselves in the game, moving their heads. The game has additional interfaces so teachers can see the children progress.
- AudioPolis [2]: Video game where thieves are searched in a city. The player walks the streets, while receiving sounds and haptic information from a 3D cursor (Novint Falcon).
- Audio Haptic Maze [3]: Video game to escape from a maze in the shortest possible time. It is played with headphones and a 3D cursor.
- mAbES (Mobile Audio-based Environment Simulator) [4]: This video game allows the user to walk a museum based on a real one. It requires a mobile phone with touch screen and headphones.
- AudioDoom [5]: Video game with 3D sound where the player must navigate the corridors of a spaceship, while interacting with different objects and shooting monsters. The game was designed for children and requires a wireless joystick.
- AudioSIM [6]: Video game based on The Sims that deals with the daily life of an athlete, who has to learn to orient himself in a Sport Campus. The game includes

3D audio feedback and requires an Xbox 360 joystick, allowing the player to receive vibrations when colliding with objects.

- Virtual Cane System [7]: System that allows the user to explore virtually places before visiting them in real life. It requires a desktop computer and a Nintendo Wii controller, which works like a stick, helping to explore the surroundings and receiving auditory and haptic feedback.
- Terraformers [8]: Galactic video game with 3D sound and contrasting 3D graphics that are generated in real time. It requires a numeric keyboard of a computer as an input interface.
- MOVA3D [9]: 3D video game based on audio feedback that requires a haptic device called Digital Clock Carpet. The player must explore a closed place to find pocket watches, while fleeing from enemies. The Digital Clock Carpet is a circular carpet on which the player must be placed and it is divided into 12 parts like an analog clock.

Some computational tools that support the teaching of geometry in blind learners are:

- Math Melodies [10]: Software available for iPad devices to learn basic mathematics. It allows finding treasures through audio, images and math exercises for sighted and blind children.
- Audio Wizard [11]: Video game for geometric learning of isometric transformations and the Cartesian plane. The player represents a magician who goes through various mazes and meets several riddles related to translations, rotations and reflections of a magic cube. The main source of information consists of sound and vibration from an Xbox 360 joystick. It also includes graphical interfaces for partially blind children.
- AudioGeometry [6]: Video game developed for Android tablet. The player survives a shipwreck and reaches the Geometric Island from which he must escape, while deciphering geometric puzzles. Sound and vibrations on a touch screen inform the user about the status of the game and his actions.
- From Dots to Shapes [12]: Auditory video game that helps in the teaching of geometry and reinforces orientation and mobility skills. It is intended as a complement to classic geometric teaching methods, allowing the shape recognition by two-dimensional sound with frequency changes in a graphic tablet. It includes 3 classic mini-games:

  - Simon: Helps to find points on the plane, receiving different sounds in sequence, whose notes will determine a location in the plane, that the player has to repeat, touching the correct points on the screen.
  - Points Connecting: Helps to recognize lines, listening to sounds of 2 points in the plane (as in the previous game), which should be joined in the screen. It also allows the player to recognize a line shape by two-dimensional sound to identify the points of the plane that form it.
  - Concentration: Helps to recognize pairs of equal figures, using a classic game called Concentration (also known as Memorize).

- Clicks [13]: Digital device for children that mixes manipulation of physical structures with auditory feedback from a tablet. The physical structures correspond to 3D prints that represent lines, shapes and angles, which when placed on the tablet are detected by an app. For example, the application asks for an isosceles triangle, the learner constructs the triangle with 3D prints on the tablet and, finally, the app detects if the shape made is correct.

- Lugram for the blind [14]: Based on a game called Lugram, a puzzle for building geometric figures. Exercises are performed on a 3 × 3 matrix where each cell is a basic unit corresponding to a complete square or its different halves (rectangle on the right, rectangle on the left, rectangle above, rectangle below, lower left triangle, upper left triangle, lower right triangle and upper right triangle). The game requires a keyboard, whose numeric keys are associated with cells of the matrix, generating different sounds.
- GEOVIB [15]: Software for use in inclusive geometry classes. Geometric shapes can be explored, using sound and vibration from a tablet. For example, touching each vertex of a figure will generate a distinctive sound and touching the edges will generate a vibration. Sounds also change depending on how close the user is to a vertex.

3   General Procedure

For the development of this work, the following steps were carried out:

1. Previous research: Bibliographic reviews were carried out on geometry video games for blind people. Also, visits were made to the Colegio de Ciegos Santa Lucía, located in Santiago, Chile, to observe how children with blindness used this kind of applications.
2. Prototypes: The plot of the video game was designed and software prototypes were implemented, receiving feedback from differential teachers. Icon and sound tests were also carried out on teachers and students to choose the right resources for the game. For the software development, Unity 3D was used with C# programming language (C Sharp) and a development methodology based on Rapid Prototyping [16], which allows generating incremental prototypes, while receiving feedback from the users.
3. Usability tests: The usability of the prototypes was evaluated with children and teachers from the Colegio de Ciegos Santa Lucía. As tests were carried out, adjustments were made to the software, based on discoveries made. The participants correspond to 12 children between 5th and 6th year of primary school (see Table 1) and 2 mathematic teachers (see Table 2), to whom a questionnaire was applied to record their opinions about the video game.
4. Impact evaluation: Game sessions were held with different children from those who participated in the usability tests. The geometric knowledge of these children was previously evaluated by a special education teacher and was evaluated again at the end of the game sessions to measure the new knowledge acquired. The participants were 9 children between 5th and 8th year of primary school from the same educational establishment (see Table 3), who interacted with the game at different levels of difficulty and performed geometry exercises with physical material to check their understanding of the contents.

Table 1. Sample of users corresponding to children with total or partial visual impairment who course between 5th and 8th year of elementary school.

User	Age	Year of elementary school	Blindness
1	12	7th	Partial
2	12	7th	Partial
3	11	6th	Total
4	10	5th	Total
5	12	7th	Partial
6	14	8th	Partial
7	14	8th	Partial
8	12	7th	Total
9	11	6th	Partial
10	13	7th	Partial
11	12	6th	Partial
12	12	7th	Partial

Table 2. Sample of users corresponding to teachers of blind children between 5th and 8th year of elementary school.

User	Years of elementary school teacher	Educator type
p1	5th and 6th	Differential educator
p2	7th and 8th	Mathematics teacher

Table 3. Sample of users participating in the impact assessment.

User	Age	Year of elementary school	Blindness
i1	13	6th	Partial
i2	11	5th	Partial
i3	12	6th	Partial
i4	11	5th	Partial
i5	11	5th	Partial
i6	11	5th	Partial
i7	15	8th	Total
i8	11	6th	Total
i9	11	6th	Partial

4 Video Game Description

The solution of this work is an educational software built as a video game to motivate learning in children.

The stage and story script were developed to link concepts of geometry with everyday life. The Cartesian plane can be quite abstract for children during a class (even sighted children). For this reason, the video game has a context that helps them better understand how to apply these geometric concepts. In particular, the game makes users switch from a 3D to 2D view and vice versa continuously so the children can understand how the Cartesian plane represents any real space.

4.1 Story

The player arrives with his friend Lucy to a new house to which they will move. Lucy mentions that she has already left some furniture inside the new house, but at that moment she must go to work and needs the player to continue ordering. She introduces Jimmy, the driver of the moving truck, who will give the objects one by one to the player so he can place them where they belong in the house.

During the game, the player receives each object from Jimmy and talks on the phone with Lucy, who tells him where the object should go in the house, in geometric terms, since the floor of the house is divided into tiles that represent squares of the Cartesian plane. The objects to be moved can be chairs, tables, lamps, pictures and plants.

Upon completing the game, Lucy arrives at the house and congratulates the player for his efforts in helping with the move.

4.2 User Interaction

When you touch any element of the interface, that element changes its color and causes a short vibration. In this way, users can feel each component of the game.

At the moment the user plays, there are two interaction views: 3D view and 2D view (map).

3D View. Figure 1 shows an example of 3D view. The main character is controlled with 90° degree turns and forward steps. The user must slide their finger on the screen horizontally to rotate and down to take a step. This is with the aim of going to find a new object or bring an object to its correct place.

2D View. Figure 2 shows an example of 2D view. The floor is divided into 6 × 13 tiles, which represent squares in the first Cartesian plane quadrant. Every time a tile is touched, there is a piano key sound. If the user drags their finger across the screen and changes the row of tiles, the sound will change in height. In this way, the upper rows of the Cartesian plane will have higher sounds than the lower ones and users will know when they change rows by moving their finger across the map. Also, if users use earphones, they can perceive the squares on the left and right side, while navigating through the columns of the grid.

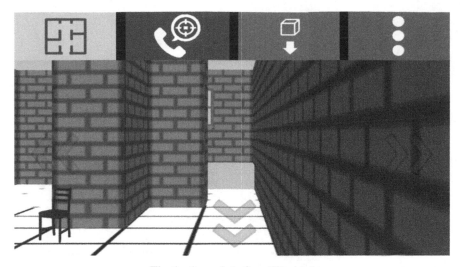

Fig. 1. Game interface (3D view)

When touching any tile twice in a row, a voice is heard, saying which square has been touched. For example, the voice can say "2 point 5", alluding to the square (2,5) of the Cartesian plane.

If the tile contains an object, is part of a wall, or is the current location of the player-controlled character, a distinctive sound is heard when dragging the finger over each of those elements on the touch screen. When you touch this kind of tile twice in a row, a voice is heard, indicating what the element is and its location.

To select a tile on the 2D map, you must double-tap the chosen square and activate the button "select square".

The 2D map mechanism is essential in this video game. Distinctive sounds are a great help for the visually impaired as they are the reference when searching for other elements in an interface.

Buttons. Figures 1 and 2 show the buttons available to the user while playing in both views (on top of the screen).

By touching a button once, a voice is heard, indicating which button is being touched and, by touching it twice in a row, the corresponding function is activated. For example, if the user taps the button once to switch to the map view, a voice is heard saying "Go to map", and double tapping brings up the map interface.

This kind of button is very important in software aimed at people with visual disabilities. When touching a button, they cannot know which button it is and it would not be convenient to activate its function to find out, since errors and actions that the user does not intend to carry out could occur.

In "more options" (button on the right with 3 dots in a vertical line) are all the options not seen in the immediate interface. When activating the button, a new interface appears with each new option, occupying the entire screen, in such a way that the user can scroll one option at a time, sliding his finger horizontally (see Fig. 3). The mechanism is the

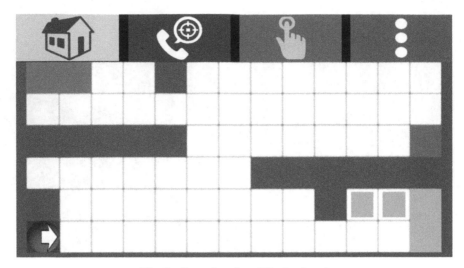

Fig. 2. Game interface (2D view/map)

same for the main menu options and its sensitivity works the same as the small buttons on the game interface.

Fig. 3. Options during the game. The user must navigate through 3 screens, sliding his finger horizontally across it. The buttons, in this case, are: "Return to game" (exit options), "help" and "Go to main menu" (discard current game).

4.3 Game Modes

There are 5 game modes in GeoHouse:

- Tutorial or practice
- Simple mode
- Translations game
- Rotations game
- Reflections game

The tutorial has only 1 level of practice in the backyard of the house. The player doesn't move any objects, since the objective is to practice using the map, the controls, etc. Here the simplest exercise of the Cartesian plane is performed, which consists of finding a square *(x, y)*. Voice instructions are available each time an interface is visited for the first time. These instructions tell the user how to interact with the device screen, such as swiping horizontally to navigate through the options.

The rest of the modes have 3 levels, which correspond to the first, second and third floors of the house (see Fig. 4). In the simple mode the user plays with the same exercises as the tutorial, while in the rest the user plays with isometric transformations. Each level is made up of 4 exercises, that is, 4 objects to be moved around a house floor. The geometry exercises that the user must perform to pass the levels are:

- Square exercises: The player must go to the square/tile *(x, y)*.
- Translation exercises: The player must go to the square resulting from the translation of the square *(x0, y0)* in the translation vector *(x', y')*, that is, he must go to the square *(x0 + x', y0 + y')*.
- Rotation exercises: The player must go to the square resulting from the rotation in D degrees of the square *(x0, y0)*, in relation to the axis *(x', y')*, where $D = \{90, 180, 270\}$.
- Reflection exercises: The player must go to the square resulting from the reflection of the square *(x0, y0)*, in relation to a value of *X* or *Y* (vertical or horizontal axis respectively).

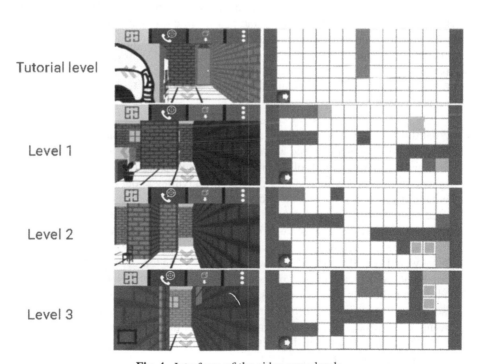

Fig. 4. Interfaces of the video game levels

An exercise editor is included for the video game. This means that a sighted person can modify the arguments of translations, rotations and reflections to control the difficulty of the game for a course or a particular student.

A registry system is also included that stores a file inside the device where the video game is installed. The file contains data from the different exercises that are performed, such as the date, the game mode, the level, the arguments and the time it took the player to find the solution. With this data, a teacher can check the student's performance with the video game.

5   Results

5.1   End User Questionnaire for Students

The results of an End User Questionnaire for students are presented below. This questionnaire was applied to 12 children, however, one of them did not complete all the answers. Table 4 shows the average marks of the statements corresponding to a section of questions with scale (marks from 1 to 7).

The marks given by the students, in general, were varied. Some looked quite excited playing the video game, while others got bored very quickly, which was reflected in the results. Because of that, the average marks are intermediate, with a final average of 5, 5.

Statements regarding difficulty and learning (such as number 4 and 8) have higher marks, which suggest that the video game has a difficulty that allows a user to stay focused, which would help them learn with a longer use of the application.

On the other hand, the results of statements such as 1 or 2 show that the video game needs more motivating characteristics for children, either in graphic or auditory form.

Below is a summary of the results of open questions of the End User Questionnaire for students.

- "What did you like about the video game?": The fact of being able to move freely inside the house was a repeated answer in this question. Others noted they liked the opening scene. As the results of the previous part of the questionnaire, there were also negative responses, saying that they did not like anything about the video game.
- "What did you not like about the video game?": Three users did not like the game sound the repetitive voice of instructions. On the other hand, there was a user who did not like the game because he didn't understand the numbers (coordinates) and, therefore, the instructions.
- "What would you add or change to the video game?": In this case, the responses were varied, but the decrease of the voices and the improvement of the images stand out and swipe indications (these changes were done in next prototypes). There was also a suggestion about adding instructions that say where to move in the house (which was not considered, since the children should orient themselves with the information of the coordinates and cardinal points and not with indications such as "now turn to the right ",", go forward 1 step ", etc.).
- "What do you think the video game can serve you for?": Seven people referred to mathematical learning and orientation. Two other users found no use for the video game.

Table 4. Average marks for each statement in the End User Questionnaire for students.

Statement	Average mark (1–7)
1. I like the videogame	5.2
2. The game is fun	5.5
3. The game is challenging	5.8
4. The game make me stay focus	6.3
5. I would play the game again	5.6
6. I would recommend this game to other children	6.2
7. The game let me know about new things	6.0
8. The game has easy and difficult parts	6.5
9. I felt controlling the situations in the game	5.0
10. The game reacts to my actions	6.4
11. The game is easy to use	4.6
12. The game is motivating	4.9
13. The game adapts to my rhythm	4.5
14. I like the sounds of the game	5.3
15. The sounds of the game are clearly identifiable	5.4
16. The sounds of the game give me information	5.1
17. I like the images of the game (only children with partial blindness)	5.0
18. The images of the game are clearly identifiable (only children with partial blindness)	4.9
19. The images of the game give me information (only children with partial blindness)	5.3

5.2 End User Questionnaire for Teachers

The results of the questionnaire applied to 2 teachers who teach mathematics to children with visual impairments are described below. Figures 5 and 6 show the marks set by them in the "Questions with scale" section (marks from 1 to 7):

Both teachers liked the video game in general, although they mentioned that the software lacks more playful features to be more entertaining for children, such as more "alive" music and sounds. They agreed that the video game is very challenging and has an adequate level of difficulty for their students.

In general, they believed that the contents treated in the software are relevant, except for the rotation exercises, which are even more complex for the students.

As sighted people, teachers had difficulty orienting themselves as they relied heavily on images, even though the voices indicated where the user was looking. For this reason, they did not perfectly control the game situations and concluded that it was not very easy to use.

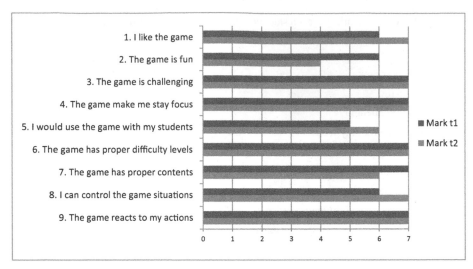

Fig. 5. Results of "Questions with scale" section in the End User Questionnaire for teachers t1 and t2. Contains statements from 1 to 9.

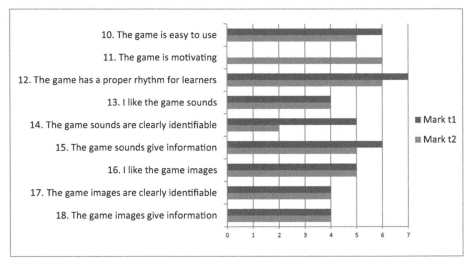

Fig. 6. Results of "Questions with scale" section in the End User Questionnaire for teachers t1 and t2. Contains statements 10 to 18.

One of the teachers gave a "2" mark to the way the sounds are identified, saying that they were similar and did not sound loud enough. However, it was not an opinion made by a special education teacher in this case, but by a math teacher. According to a special education teacher who supported this work, a blind user has a better ability to differentiate sounds than sighted people.

Regarding the images, the teachers suggested marking more the edges of walls and tiles, along with improving the color contrast between the different elements of the screen, which was done in next prototypes.

5.3 Impact Evaluation

The results of the evaluation of geometric knowledge and mental representation applied to the students before and after the game sessions are presented below.

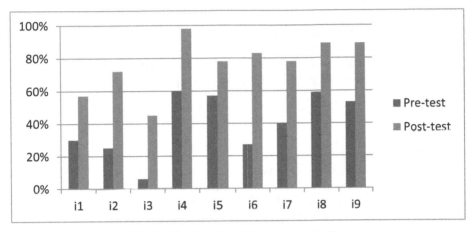

Fig. 7. Final results of the impact evaluation

Figure 7 shows that there is a notable improvement in the geometric knowledge of the students. In the case of 5th grade students, the results may be affected by the geometry unit taught by teachers during the game session period. This means that the learning obtained by these children is influenced by both the video game and the math classes. However, the rest of the participating students showed a very similar improvement without having taught that content in the classroom.

5.4 General Observations

Most students are used to using mobile devices. This would allow them to use the game on their own (not necessarily in the classroom).

Totally blind children must hold the device with their hands when using the video game. This helps them to control the direction of their maneuvers on the screen and to better feel the vibrations.

When exploring the interface, students have a habit of short tapping the screen, instead of dragging their finger across it, to find out which buttons can be pressed. This is a problem for totally blind children as it prevents them from exploring the screen so that they have an idea of which places have already been explored and which have not.

When touching a button twice, some partially blind students did so very slowly. Two completely blind children used to deflect their finger down once they found it and ended up double-tapping outside the button.

Partially blind children rely heavily on their eyesight (like sighted people) when using the device and find it difficult to pay real attention to the instructions. Some users scanned the screen with their fingers before hearing all the explanatory voices. For example, a student skipped those instructions when performing maneuvers on the screen, which did not allow him to hear all the information.

They all learned by themselves to move around the house and to identify the different elements of the map (obstacles and the correct square).

In general, it did not take long for the students to find the correct tile on the map, but in 3D game, users took more time. Some kept coming back to the map and getting to the right position on their own, but others had to get a little help. It was also observed that some were guided by a green square (correct tile) that can be seen on the floor and they did not apply coordinates to reach it.

At first, some did not know what a coordinate *(x, y)* of the Cartesian plane meant, so a little explanation had to be given, using the game map as a tool.

6 Conclusion

This work consisted of the development of a video game to support children who are blind, coursing between 5th and 8th year of elementary school, in the construction of concepts and geometric thinking in everyday contexts. The software was implemented for mobile phones with touch screen and Android operating system, allowing an interaction based mainly on touches, vibration and sound.

The game called Geohouse applies geometric concepts related to the Cartesian plane in the context of a house move. The video game is intended for students who should have at least a general idea of what the Cartesian plane is, based on their curriculum. Also, a house move is a daily situation because it allows the player to go through the floors of a house, using a map.

Showing the different versions of the game to teachers of a school for the blind not only allows them to see progress in the project and give feedback, but also gives them an idea of what other things are possible to implement in future computational tools that they would like propose.

To validate the usefulness of the video game, usability evaluations were carried out with both children who are blind and their math teachers. Impact evaluations were also carried out to measure the learning gained by students with blindness after interacting with the software for a longer time.

The results of the usability evaluations showed varied opinions by the students. Some of them said the video game was fun and others, something boring. Clearly, every child has different tastes and, above all, high expectations when playing a new video game.

On the other hand, the results of the impact evaluations indicate that there was a significant improvement in student learning after using the video game. In the case of 6 of 9 students evaluated, part of the learning obtained could also be due to the beginning of the geometry unit at school during the period of these evaluations, which subtracts some reliability from these results. However, there was also a major improvement in the other 3 children.

This work can serve as a basis for the implementation of other similar educational video games that include important usability aspects such as tactile sensitivity of different interface elements.

Acknowledgements. This work was funded by FONDECYT1150898 and by CONICYT's Basal Funds for Centers of Excellence, Project FB0003.

References

1. Allain, K., et al.: An audio game for training navigation skills of blind children. In: IEEE 2nd VR Workshop on Sonic Interactions for Virtual Environments (SIVE) Conference: The 14th Web for All Conference (2015)
2. Sánchez, J., Espinoza, M., de Borba Campos, M., Merabet, L.: Enhancing orientation and mobility skills in learners who are blind through video gaming. In: 9th ACM Conference on Creativity and Cognition (2013)
3. Sánchez, J., de Borba Campos, M.: Development of navigation skills through audio haptic videogaming in learners who are blind. In: Procedia Computer Science, vol. 14, pp. 102–110 (2012)
4. de Borba Campos, M., Sánchez, J., Martins, A.C., Santana, R.S., Espinoza, M.: Mobile navigation through a science museum for users who are blind. In: Lecture Notes in Computer Science, vol. 8515 (2014). https://doi.org/10.1007/978-3-319-07446-7_68
5. Lumbreras, M., Sánchez, J.: Interactive 3D Sound Hyperstories for Blind Children. In: CHI 1999 Proceedings of the SIGCHI conference on Human Factors in Computting Systems, pp 318–325 (1999)
6. Sánchez, J., Viana, W., de Castro Andrade, R.M.: Multimodal interfaces for improving the intellect of the blind. In: XX Congresso de Informática Educativa – TISE 2015, vol. 1, pp 404–414 (2015)
7. Lahav, O., Gedalevitz, H., Battersby, S., Brown, D., Evett, L., Merritt, P.: Virtual environment navigation with look-around mode to explore new real spaces by people who are blind. In: Disability and Rehabilitation, vol. 40, pp. 1072–1084 (2018)
8. Westin, T.: Game Accessibility Case Study: Terraformers – a Real-Time 3d Graphic Game (2004)
9. Sánchez, J., Rodríguez, J.P.: Videogame for Improving Orientation and Mobility in Blind Children (2010)
10. Ahmetovic, D., Bernareggi, C., Mascetti, S., Alampi, V., Gerino, A.: Math melodies, supporting visually impaired primary school students in learning math. In: Conference: The 14th Web for All Conference, p. 26 (2017)
11. Pardo, G.M.: Videojuego Educativo para el Aprendizaje de Geometría en niños no videntes, University of Chile (2016)
12. Roth, P., Petrucci, L.S., Assimacopoulos, A., Pun, T.: From dots to shapes, an auditory haptic game platform for teaching geometry to blind pupils. In: ICCHP 2000, International Conference on Computers Helping People with Special Needs, pp. 603–610 (2000)
13. Adusei, M.: Geometry Appcessory for Visually Impaired Children (2017)
14. Lucic, B., Sedlar, N.V., Delic, V.: Computer Game Lugram - Version for Blind Children. Telfor J. 3(1), 54–59 (2011)
15. Schmidt, J.: GEOVIB – An Application to Support Visually Impaired and Blind Children in Following Geometry Lectures (2017)
16. Jain, A.: A Beginner's Guide to Rapid Prototyping. https://medium.freecodecamp.org/a-beg inners-guide-to-rapid-prototyping71e8722c17df. Accessed 2019

Author Index